Spon's
House Price
Data Book

Spon's House Price Data Book

M. C. FLEMING
Professor of Economics,
Department of Economics,
Loughborough University of Technology

J. G. NELLIS
Senior Lecturer in Economics,
Cranfield School of Management,
Cranfield Institute of Technology

With the assistance of
HELEN LITT

London
E. & F. N. SPON

First published in 1987 by
E. & F. N. Spon Ltd
11 New Fetter Lane, London EC4P 4EE
© *1987 M. C. Fleming and J. G. Nellis*

Printed in Great Britain at the
University Press, Cambridge

ISBN 0 419 14230 4

British Library Cataloguing in Publication Data

Fleming, M. C.
  Spon's house price data book.
  1. Dwellings—Prices—Great Britain
  I. Title II. Nellis, J. G. III. Litt, Helen
  333.33′8 HD7333.A3

ISBN 0-419-14230-4

Contents

		Page
Preface		vii
Acknowledgements		viii
List of Abbreviations		ix
1	Measurement, Interpretation and Evidence	1

PART I GOVERNMENT DATA SOURCES

2	DOE/BSA BS4 Survey	23
3	DOE Five Per Cent Sample Survey	33
4	Bank of England Survey of Banks' Mortgages	58
5	DOE/ABI Survey of Insurance Companies	61
6	Inland Revenue: Survey of Conveyances	64
7	Inland Revenue: Valuation Office Property Market Report	69
8	Northern Ireland Department of Finance and Personnel (PPRU)	156

PART II INSTITUTIONAL DATA SOURCES

9	Abbey National Building Society	169
10	Anglia Building Society	216
11	Halifax Building Society	229
12	Incorporated Society of Valuers and Auctioneers	271
13	Leeds Permanent Building Society	276
14	National House-Building Council	286
15	Nationwide Building Society	296
16	Northern Rock Building Society	347
17	Principality Building Society	352
18	Ryden Residential Ltd	356
19	Woolwich Equitable Building Society	360

Appendix A	Other Sources of Data	374
Appendix B	Definitions of Official Standard Regions	380
Appendix C	List of Names and Addresses	384

Index A	Data Sources	389
Index B	Countries, Regions and Counties	391
Index C	Towns and Localities	394
Index D	Subject	396

To Ruth and
Helen and Gareth

Preface

This book provides the first comprehensive collection and analysis of information about house prices in the United Kingdom. There is a very keen interest in both the level of house prices and house price movements and there is a very large number of sources which attempt to satisfy this interest. However, the large number of sources means that the information they provide is scattered over a wide range of publications, many of which, such as press releases, are relatively inaccessible. It seemed worthwhile, therefore, to try to bring all this information together in one place. Further, while the large number of sources that exist serve to increase the range of data available, unfortunately, they also serve to generate confusion, for the information they provide is sometimes in conflict. As a consequence, there is an important need for a guide to the nature of the various sources to help the user in the use and interpretation of the available data. This book serves that need.

The interest in house-price information arises for a number of reasons all of which demand accurate and reliable data. At a practical level, the information is of use to surveyors, valuers, town planners, local authorities, estate agents and other professionals involved in the housing market. House-price figures form the basis of expectations which influence private buying and selling decisions in both boom and slump periods. The information is useful to businessmen concerned with location decisions and regional deployment of staff. Reliable measurement is essential for research on the determinants of house prices and the causes of inflation. Beyond the direct practical use of reliable information, there remains its intrinsic interest because of the growth of home ownership and the fact that for many people housing represents the most valuable asset they will obtain. Thus, for all these reasons, it is essential that the nature and limitations of the available information on house prices should be understood.

This book, therefore, serves two purposes. First, it provides a comprehensive survey of sources of house-price information, a full account of the methodology and other technical details for each source and a complete set of the data available. These data cover various periods of time back to 1946. The main current source of information excluded is that obtained in qualitative surveys of trends in house prices conducted by the RICS. These surveys are meant to provide quick impressions of contemporary trends and there seems no advantage in reproducing the full historical series here. Full details of this source are given in Appendix A. Other sources excluded are those which have now been discontinued and *ad hoc* surveys, particularly those carried out from time to time by the Planning Departments of local authorities. Details of all these sources are also given in Appendix A.

The second main purpose is to provide an appraisal of the problems involved in measuring house prices and the way these problems have been met, if at all, in the available series. This provides the essential framework for considering the problems of interpretation associated with the available series and their usefulness for different purposes.

The first chapter provides a general discussion of the main problems of measurement and interpretation, classifies the available sources (eighteen altogether) in the light of this discussion and briefly examines some of the evidence they provide about price levels and long-term price movements. The remaining chapters take each source in turn, providing full technical details and a complete set of the data available.

Acknowledgements

We are grateful to the holders of the copyright of the material included in this volume for giving permission for it to be reproduced. The statistical data in Chapters 2 to 5, Chapter 8 and the material in Appendix B are reproduced by permission of the Controller of Her Majesty's Stationery Office. Thanks are also due to:

Inland Revenue Valuation Office, Abbey National Building Society, Anglia Building Society, Halifax Building Society, Incorporated Society of Valuers and Auctioneers, Leeds Permanent Building Society, National House-Building Council, Nationwide Building Society, Northern Rock Building Society, Principality Building Society, Ryden Residential Ltd, Woolwich Equitable Building Society.

We should also like to express our appreciation of the work carried out by Helen Litt, who has been responsible for compiling all of the data contained in this volume and for preparing Appendix A. Finally a special word of thanks is due to Stephen Fleming for his work in proof-reading the data tables.

List of Abbreviations

ABI	Association of British Insurers
BIA	British Insurance Association
BS	Building society
BSA	Building Societies Association
CB	County Borough
DOE	Department of the Environment
E&W	England and Wales
FOO	Former owner-occupier
FTB	First-time buyer
GB	Great Britain
HMSO	Her Majesty's Stationery Office
ISVA	Incorporated Society of Valuers and Auctioneers
LA	Local authority
LCES	London and Cambridge Economic Service
NHBC	National House-Building Council
NI	Northern Ireland
PD	Particulars of Deposit
PPRU	Policy Planning and Research Unit (Northern Ireland Department of Finance and Personnel)
RICS	Royal Institution of Chartered Surveyors
RPI	Retail Prices Index
UK	United Kingdom
VOPMR	*Valuation Office Property Market Report*

1. Measurement, Interpretation and Evidence

The measurement of average house prices raises a number of problems depending on the use to which the information is to be put. An appreciation of these problems and of the methods used to deal with them is important for understanding the available data and avoiding pitfalls in their use and interpretation. The purpose of this chapter, therefore, is to consider these problems, the methods of measurement used and related matters which are important for purposes of interpretation. It is thus meant to provide an essential background against which all of the data included in this volume may be assessed. This is particularly important in view of the large number of sources that exist and the confusion that surrounds the conflicting evidence they sometimes provide. Currently, there are eighteen main sources of information covering various periods of time back to 1946.

The discussion here is in general terms. Full technical details for each source of data (following a standard form of arrangement in which the matters discussed here are treated systematically) are given at the beginning of each chapter dealing with that source. But we take the opportunity here to provide a summary classification of the available sources in order to highlight their points of similarity and difference. A commentary is also included on the most useful sources for different purposes and a summary review of the evidence they provide is given. The chapter is arranged as follows:

1.1 Purposes of measurement
1.2 Problems of measurement
1.3 Solutions to measurement problems
1.4 Other problems of comparison
1.5 The analysis of data sources
1.6 Comparative classification of data sources
1.7 The choice of appropriate series
1.8 The evidence on price trends, 1946-1986 and price levels in 1986

1.1 PURPOSES OF MEASUREMENT

The users of house-price data require the information for three main purposes:

(a) to measure price movements over time,
(b) to measure average price levels at a particular point of time, and
(c) to make comparisons of price levels between one area of the country and another

Broadly speaking, users may be divided into two groups. On the one hand there are those who are directly involved in the housing market either as buyers and sellers or in providing professional services of one kind or another to buyers and sellers. On the other hand, there are those who are not so involved but who are interested in the measurement and analysis of trends and in research on the housing market.

The second group of users are generally more interested in the measurement of price movements over time (information often presented in the form of index numbers) rather than the actual level of prices as such. An index of house prices is, of course, used officially as a constituent in measuring changes in the cost of housing services incorporated in the Retail Prices Index (RPI). An index of prices is also of use to those, such as valuers, property insurers and owners contemplating sales who wish to make an estimate of the likely current market value of a property on the basis of information about the price for which it had been sold at some time in the past. This is particularly useful in cases where information on actual current transactions in the same area (which could be used for comparative "benchmark" purposes) is lacking, either because of the specific characteristics of the property it is desired to revalue, or because of the more general absence of local market information.

Data on average prices, as opposed to price movements, are naturally of primary interest to potential house-buyers. In this case there is also a special need for more detailed information because the interest of a buyer focuses less on a single average than on the dispersion of prices for different categories of property in different locations. Such information is also of interest to those who provide advice and other services to both buyers and sellers.

Information on differences in price levels between one area of the country and another naturally concerns those who are thinking of moving from one area to another, but it is also of interest to town planners and to firms contemplating location decisions and the relocation of key employees.

It is also important to distinguish the measurement of price movements from the measurement of price levels as such because the primary data needed to provide the basis of such measurements are not necessarily the same in each case and the measurement problems differ. The measurement of price levels requires representative coverage of all sectors of the market, whereas the measurement of price movements does not require such coverage, provided that the price movements in different sectors are similar. In this case, data drawn from one sector may be adequately representative of the market as a whole.

1.2 PROBLEMS OF MEASUREMENT

The main problem of measurement, and one which affects both the measurement of price levels and price movements, is that few houses are identical: they may differ according to a wide variety of physical characteristics such as size, type, garden, garage, quality of fixtures and fittings, etc. Even where similar houses are built, they are unique in having a fixed location, the regional and other localized attributes of which (for example, convenience of access to schools, transport facilities, shops etc. and the general environmental quality of the neighbourhood) also influence price. Until recently little or no attention was paid to the influence of these factors in measuring house prices: most sources merely took a *simple* average of the prices of all houses sold in a particular time period. But simple averages of house prices cannot be compared unless the houses traded retain the same mix of characteristics over time and this mix does not differ between different sources. But this is not the case. The mix of properties built and sold from one period to another has changed markedly and the coverage of different sources varies. For example, over the period from 1970 the proportions of different types of dwelling on which building societies have granted mortgage loans have varied considerably (Table 1.1). The proportions of terraced houses and flats and maisonettes have increased considerably at the expense of detached and semi-detached houses and bungalows. For new dwellings, however, it is notable that the proportion of detached houses has increased. Likewise, the age distribution of dwellings mortgaged has also varied considerably over the period since 1970 (Table 1.2). The proportion of new dwellings has more than halved while among the non-new dwellings those built before 1919 have increased their share of transactions very considerably. As a consequence of changes in the mix of these and other characteristics, simple average prices do not compare like with like*.

The problem is not unique to housing. It also has to be faced in attempts to measure price movements generally, as in the RPI. The latter is based on a standard of comparison, namely a standard "basket" of goods that people typically purchase, which is then repriced in successive time periods. To adopt the same principle for housing would require the existence of standard houses, both new and non-new, which are regularly sold and re-sold. Unfortunately, the problem is not so readily solved in this context since there is no such thing as a "standard" house and because locational factors play such a crucial role in determining prices. Further, there is a keen interest in the average *level* of prices (as opposed to measuring rates of change) in the case of houses but not in the case of other goods. Unlike housing, no attempt is made to measure the average price of, for example, cars or food.

---

* For further discussion of the evidence on house prices in this context see Fleming and Nellis (1981 and 1985a)

Table 1.1   Distribution of dwellings by type mortgaged by building societies

Per cent

Year	Bungalow	Detached house	Semi-detached house	Terraced house	Flat or maisonette	Total
New dwellings						
1970	24	24	35	13	4	100
1975	15	35	30	14	6	100
1980	14	41	24	15	5	100
1985	13	31	24	20	12	100
1986	14	37	21	17	11	100
Non-new dwellings						
1970	14	19	40	24	4	100
1975	12	21	36	24	7	100
1980	9	16	33	33	10	100
1985	7	14	31	35	13	100
1986	7	14	31	34	14	100
All dwellings						
1970	17	20	39	21	4	100
1975	12	24	35	22	7	100
1980	9	20	32	30	9	100
1985	8	15	30	34	13	100
1986	8	17	30	32	13	100

Totals may not equal 100 due to rounding

Source: *Housing and Construction Statistics* and *BSA Bulletin* (DOE Five Per Cent Sample Survey of building society mortgages)

Table 1.2   Distribution of dwellings by age mortgaged by building societies

Per cent

Year	New dwellings	Built before 1919	Built from 1919 to 1939	Built after 1939	Total
1970	27	17	22	34	100
1975	19	19	19	43	100
1980	15	28	18	39	100
1985	11	28	17	43	100
1986	10	28	17	45	100

Totals may not equal 100 due to rounding

Source: as for Table 1.1

1.3   SOLUTIONS TO MEASUREMENT PROBLEMS

There are three possible solutions to the problem of measuring house prices and house-price inflation rates on a like-for-like basis. One is to calculate average prices for more homogeneous groups of houses (for example, by type, by size, by age, etc.) and then to combine these in fixed proportions into a grand or *weighted* average. This average is useful for measuring *changes* over time because it relates to a standard set of houses and thus is not influenced by change in the mix. Sources which have adopted this method are:

Department of the Environment (price index - not average prices) - see Chapter 3
Abbey National Building Society - see Chapter 9
Leeds Permanent Building Society - see Chapter 13
Nationwide Building Society - see Chapter 15

The major limitation of this method is that it is only possible to allow for a small number of house characteristics. The existing measures only adjust for up to four house characteristics (namely, house type, size, age and region) in arriving at an overall weighted average price or index. Consequently, the degree of adjustment is limited and there may remain, therefore, an important element of non-comparability.

A second method of solving the problem of non-comparability is to employ statistical techniques to estimate the influence that each individual house characteristic, for which information is available, has on price - for example, the price difference made by an extra bedroom, the existence of a garage or garage space etc. These measurements may be referred to as "characteristics-prices". It is then possible to remove the influence of a varying mix of characteristics (and so to measure price changes for a standardized set of houses) by adding up these characteristics-prices in *fixed* proportions according to the mix of characteristics possessed by houses traded in some base period (the base period can, of course, be changed from time to time in the light of any significant changes in the mix). This method has been employed by the authors to compile national and regional standardized indices for the Halifax Building Society.* These cover the period from January 1983 and are now compiled by the Society on regular monthly and quarterly bases (see Chapter 11). The analogy with the standard basket of goods in the RPI will be obvious, although in our case we are dealing with a standard bundle of house characteristics rather than a basket of goods as such. It will be appreciated that this method requires the collection of a large amount of data on house characteristics at both national and regional levels in order to obtain accurate estimates of the characteristics-prices.

A third solution to the problem is to obtain the opinions of experts working in the housing market as surveyors and valuers etc. about "typical" prices and price changes. This method is based, therefore, on subjective estimates but it has the virtue of attempting to deal with the problem of mix variability. The Royal Institution of Chartered Surveyors (RICS) and the Incorporated Society of Valuers and Auctioneers (ISVA) publish data on this basis and some building societies publish similar assessments.

1.4 OTHER PROBLEMS OF COMPARISON

Apart from differences, if any, which arise because of the method employed to try to take account of differences in the mix of transactions from one time period to the next as outlined above, differences which may affect the comparability of one series with another also arise for four other sorts of reason. These are:

(a) Coverage of the market
(b) Measurement timing
(c) Transactions at market and non-market prices
(d) Geographical coverage

1.4.1 Coverage of the market

An important matter is how well any one source covers all house-sale transactions and thus how representative it is of the total market. Most of the data available are derived from building society sources. The first issue, therefore, concerns the representativeness of building society transactions in the context of the total housing market.

Building societies are the major source of loans for house purchase in the United Kingdom, but they are not the only source: finance is also provided by insurance companies, banks and local authorities as well as by ready money and loans from other sources. Comprehensive statistics of the relative importance of these sources are not available, but

---

* For a full account of the methodology see Fleming and Nellis (1984 and 1985b)

estimates drawn from the National Movers Survey carried out by the Department of the Environment (DOE) in 1973 suggest that at that time building societies were responsible for financing only two-thirds of house purchases (DOE, 1977, p.83). From the point of view of measuring house prices this would be of no consequence if there were no differences between the building society sector of the market and those served by the other sources of finance. There is evidence, however, to suggest that this is not the case. The survey referred to above (DOE, 1977) showed that house transactions financed by insurance companies and banks were at higher average price levels than building society transactions, and those financed from other sources were generally lower priced. Subsequent data from a 20 per cent sample of sales of dwellings in 1975, particulars of which were returned to the Inland Revenue, indicate that both mean and median prices drawn from the official building society surveys were generally higher than for all transactions (see Table 1.3 below). It will be seen that this was particularly the case with secondhand dwellings, a major explanation being that building societies financed a relatively small proportion of such dwellings at the lower end of the price range. There would appear to be no reason to believe that these surveys refer to atypical years. If this is the case the official statistics based on surveys of building societies should be regarded as tending to overstate the true average price level.

Table 1.3 Comparison of house prices for building societies and total market*, 1975

	Mean	Median
	£	£
New dwellings		
Building societies - DOE/BSA survey	12234	-
Building societies - DOE 5% sample	12013	10300
Total market (all sales)*	11860	10350
Non-new dwellings		
Building societies - DOE/BSA survey	11880	-
Building societies - DOE 5% survey	11734	10460
Total market (all sales)*	10949	10000

* The data on "all sales" refer to England and Wales whereas for building societies they refer to the UK. Adjustment of the latter to exclude Scotland and Northern Ireland (where average prices at this time were lower) would tend to increase the differential still further over those for all sales.

Sources: Department of the Environment, *Housing Policy Technical Volume Part II*, Chapter 6, Appendix E (HMSO, London 1977) and *Housing and Construction Statistics*, **24**, Table 38 (HMSO, London 1978).

It should also be noted with regard to the *institutional* sources of finance that the share of the market served by building societies and other institutions has varied considerably at different times. In the period since 1970, the annual share of building societies has varied widely from 56 per cent to 96 per cent of the market. Other bodies have also taken widely varying shares ranging from 2 to 36 per cent for banks, 0 to 24 per cent for local authorities and 0 to 5 per cent for insurance companies (see Table 1.4). In addition, banks and insurance companies tend to concentrate their lending *up-market* while local authorities traditionally lend *down-market*. Consequently, divergent movements in the relative importance of these institutions have had an important influence in distorting the house-price figures based *solely* on building society sources - first in one direction and then in another as these institutions enter and leave the housing market at different points in time. In recent years it is likely that the major increase in bank mortgage lending in 1981 and 1982 had an important influence in tending to bias the building society figures downwards whilst their partial withdrawal in 1983-84 tended to exaggerate the size of the price increases suggested by building society data during 1983-84. The bias may have been reversed again in 1985 when banks almost regained their 1983 market share. In 1985, the average price of houses financed by banks' mortgages was some £14,000 higher than that financed by building societies - a difference of more than 40 per cent (Table 1.5). Houses purchased with insurance company finance were also more highly priced on average - a difference of £10,000 (over 30 per cent) compared with building societies.

Table 1.4   Distribution of net mortgage advances by institutional source
United Kingdom, 1970-85

Per cent

Year	Building societies	Banks	Local authorities*	Insurance companies	Other sources
1970	87	3	6	3	1
1971	88	5	6	1	1
1972	80	12	7	-	1
1973	71	11	12	4	2
1974	63	4	24	5	4
1975	76	2	17	2	4
1976	95	2	2	-	2
1977	96	3	-	1	-
1978	94	5	-1	1	-
1979	82	8	5	4	1
1980	79	8	6	4	3
1981	66	25	3	2	4
1982	56	36	4	1	2
1983	75	24	-2	1	2
1984	86	12	-1	2	2
1985	78	22	-3	1	1

Totals do not always equal 100 due to rounding

* Negative signs in this column indicate an excess of repayments over gross advances, i.e. decrease in mortgage balances outstanding during the period.

Source: *Housing and Construction Statistics*, HMSO, London

With regard to data from *individual* building societies, it is likely that they differ because of differences in their representativeness arising from differences in their regional coverage and in their lending policies, as well as differences in the methods of analysis described above. With regard to lending policies, differential mortgage rates offered by some societies at different times mean that they attract relatively more business at the upper or lower ends of the housing market from time to time and thus bias their average price figures accordingly.

Table 1.5   Average prices by institutional source of mortgage funds
             All dwellings   UK 1985

| Source | Prices recorded at: | |
	Mortgage approval stage	Mortgage completion stage
	£	£
Building Societies		
DOE/BSA BS4 Survey (Chapter 2)	33,188	31,876
DOE Five Per Cent Sample Survey (Chapter 3)	–	31,103
Banks (Chapter 4)	47,100	–
Insurance Companies (Chapter 5)	–	41,300

Source: see relevant chapters for details

1.4.2 Measurement timing

The main distinction with regard to timing is between the recording of price information at the mortgage approval stage or the mortgage completion stage. The gap between these two stages may be around 2 to 3 months, thus data at the approval stage provide an earlier indication of price movements than completions data. It also records information on a more precisely defined point of time because completions data, by contrast, necessarily refer to prices which will have been agreed at various *earlier* periods of time. On the other hand, mortgage approvals do not necessarily proceed to completion and others may proceed at amended prices. But it is thought that the proportion of mortgage approvals that are cancelled or amended in this way is fairly small. Only one source (the Anglia Building Society) records information at the valuation stage. This may precede approvals by around 2 to 3 weeks and thus provide an even earlier indication of price trends. But again it will be appreciated that some of these potential transactions may not proceed or may proceed only at amended prices.

1.4.3 Market and non-market prices

Another measurement problem results from the fact that some house-transactions take place at non-market prices. They are, therefore, not representative and ought to be excluded to remove the bias they introduce. The most important category of non-market price sales over recent years has been the sale of council houses to their tenants at heavily discounted prices (see Tables 3.7 and 3.8 in Chapter 3). Other examples would be sales to other sitting tenants and sales between relatives. Some sources exclude some or all of these categories, others exclude none.

1.4.4 Geographical coverage

The final general matter worthy of note is that the geographical coverage of different sources varies. The main explicit distinction is between the United Kingdom, Great Britain or England and Wales. But some sources may be restricted to a smaller area (for example, Wales, Scotland or Northern Ireland, or even local areas). Some individual building societies, of course, may have uneven geographical coverage but this is not defined in the published data. Some societies, however, attempt to compensate for this factor by employing national weighting factors drawn from official statistics.

1.5 THE ANALYSIS OF DATA SOURCES

As explained earlier, each of the following chapters presents a complete set of data available from each of the main sources. In each case this is preceded by full information about the particular data source. This is presented in a standard format as follows:

1. Technical details. This covers all the matters, discussed in this chapter, which are important for purposes of interpretation. It also provides a summary guide which indicates at a glance the kinds of data available from that source. It is arranged under the following headings:

    (a)   Source of data and timing
    (b)   Types of data and periods covered
    (c)   Frequency
    (d)   Geographical coverage
    (e)   Method of analysis

2. List of tables. This gives details of the contents of each table and the time periods covered.

3. Cross-classifications of data. This gives a summary guide to the various cross-classifications of data (eg. by type, age, size of house, etc.) which may be found in the tables.

4. Publications. This gives details of publications under three headings:

    (a)   Data
    (b)   Descriptions of methodology
    (c)   Supplementary studies.

Altogether data from eighteen different sources are presented in this volume: seven from government sources (i.e. collected by government departments) in Part I and eleven published by individual institutional sources in Part II. A summary classification of these sources is presented below. Appendix A contains a summary of discontinued and other miscellaneous sources, data from which are not included in this volume. Appendix B defines the official standard regions as they applied before 1965, from 1965 to March 31st 1974 and from 1st April 1974. Appendix C lists the addresses of all the sources covered in this volume.

1.6 COMPARATIVE CLASSIFICATION OF DATA SOURCES

A summary classification of the available sources of data is presented in Table 1.6. The purpose of the table is to show at a glance how all the sources compare in terms of the nature of the data they provide. It will be seen that of the seven government sources only two - both provided by the Inland Revenue - give comprehensive coverage of the housing market but, unfortunately, they are limited in other ways. One of them is based not on statistical surveys but on reports of *typical* prices provided by official valuers working in the field. The other is directly based on statistical information obtained as part of a survey of conveyances. This survey is not intended to provide information about house prices as such, but information about the number of transactions and their total value enables average values to be calculated. Unfortunately, the survey is confined to England and Wales and to transactions in one week only each year, and there is a considerable time lag before publication. Also, by virtue of covering all transactions, it includes some properties which will have been sold at non-market prices. Of the other five government sources, one is confined to Northern Ireland and the other four are confined to particular sources of mortgage finance: two surveys of building societies, a survey of insurance companies and a survey of banks (the last two surveys providing price range data only from which estimated average prices are derived).

Among the eleven individual institutional sources, covered in Part II, all but two emanate from building societies. One of the two exceptions is the Incorporated Society of Valuers and Auctioneers (ISVA) which provides data based on valuations of *typical* houses by its members. This source differs from all others in that it is not based on actual transactions. The other exception is the National House-Building Council (NHBC) which

Table 1.6 Summary comparison of data sources*

SOURCE		THE DATA BASE				MIX-ADJUSTMENT	
Chapter ref	Name	Geographic coverage	Mortgage timing	Source of mortgage	Exclusion of non-market prices	Average prices	Index numbers
2	DOE/BSA BS4	UK	A & C	Building Socs	Yes	No	No
3	DOE 5% Sample	UK	C	Building Socs	No	No	Yes
4	Banks Survey	UK	A	Banks	No	No	No
5	DOE/ABI Survey	UK	C	Insurance Cos	No	No	No
6	Inland Revenue: Conveyances	E&W	C	All	No	No	No
7	Inland Revenue: *VOPMR*	GB	T	All	Yes	No	No
8	PPRU (Northern Ireland)	NI	C	All	Yes	No	No
9	Abbey National BS	UK	A	Abbey National BS	No	Yes	No
10	Anglia BS	UK	V	Anglia BS	Yes	No	No
11	Halifax BS	UK	A	Halifax BS	Yes	No	Yes
12	ISVA	E	T	All	Yes	No	No
13	Leeds Permanent BS	UK	A	Leeds Perm BS	Yes	Yes	No
14	NHBC	E&W/GB	C	All	Yes	No	No
15	Nationwide BS	UK	A	Nationwide BS	Yes	Yes	Yes
16	Northern Rock BS	N Eng	A	Northern Rock BS	Yes	No	No
17	Principality BS	W	C	Principality BS	Yes	No	No
18	Ryden Residential Ltd	S Cit	A	Halifax BS	Yes	No	No
19	Woolwich Equitable BS	UK	T	Woolwich Eq BS	Yes	No	No

* The analysis in this table refers to the nature of the data as currently compiled. Changes that have occurred over time are set out in the technical details given at the beginning of each chapter.

Abbreviations: A = mortgage approval stage   C = mortgage completion stage   E & W = England and Wales
GB = Great Britain   N Eng = North of England   NI = Northern Ireland   S = Scotland
S Cit = Scottish Cities   T = *typical* prices (estimated by surveyors and valuers, not based on mortgage data)
V = valuation stage

provides information about the prices of houses built, or to be built, by housebuilders registered with the Council. It relates solely, therefore, to new houses.

The data compiled by individual building societies are published mainly for publicity purposes. Their main value in comparison with the official DOE surveys of building societies is that they provide data which pre-date or supplement the official government statistics either in providing more timely data or breakdowns not available elsewhere. They are also important in providing alternative mix-adjusted series which are needed for the measurement of price movements. A list of the available sources arranged in chronological order according to starting date is given below. It will be seen that only one source predates 1950, and only four sources predate 1970. The rest were developed during the 1970s and 1980s. The choice of series for long-term analysis is therefore very restricted.

Starting date of series	Source	Chapter reference
1946	Nationwide Building Society	15
1956	DOE/BSA BS4 Survey of Building Societies	2
1965	DOE Five Per Cent Sample Survey of Building Societies	3
1968	DOE/ABI Survey of Insurance Companies	5
1973	Inland Revenue Survey of Conveyances	6
1974	Anglia Building Society	10
1975	Halifax Building Society	11
1976	Abbey National Building Society	9
1978	ISVA	12
	Leeds Permanent Building Society	13
	PPRU (Northern Ireland)	8
1979	Woolwich Equitable Building Society	19
1981	NHBC	14
1982	Bank of England Survey of Banks' Mortgages	4
1983	Inland Revenue *VOPMR*	7
	Principality Building Society	17
	Ryden Residential Ltd	18
1984	Northern Rock Building Society	16

With regard to the breakdowns published by each source, Table 1.7 below provides a summary analysis of the current breakdowns available and notes limitations in coverage to particular geographical areas.

With regard to mix-adjusted series, there are only five sources which provide such data (as noted earlier): the DOE Five Per Cent Sample Survey of building societies (Chapter 3), the Abbey National Building Society (Chapter 9), the Halifax Building Society (Chapter 11), the Leeds Permanent Building Society (Chapter 13) and the Nationwide Building Society (Chapter 15).

In the next section we comment on the most important series for the measurement of price levels and price movements and then turn to examine the evidence they provide.

1.7 THE CHOICE OF APPROPRIATE SERIES

The choice of appropriate series depends on the kind of information required. The primary distinction is between information on price levels and information on price movements. With regard to price levels, the most important question relating to any source is its representativeness of all house-purchase transactions, whilst in the context of measuring price movements, a more important question is that of mix-adjustment. A second distinction is between regional or other more localized data, as opposed to national statistics, and sub-classification of the data according to house or buyer characteristics. Naturally, a further consideration influencing choice is any restriction in the time period covered by each source and any restriction to a particular geographical area. Information on those matters is summarized in Section 1.6 above.

1.7.1 Measuring price levels

National data. With regard to the measurement of price levels, the most comprehensive source (covering *all* house-purchase transactions) is the Inland Revenue Survey of Conveyances. But, as indicated above, this is severely limited in other ways. Of the other sources, the most comprehensive *regular* coverage of transactions is that based on the DOE/BSA BS4 Survey. The survey is restricted to building societies but covers all transactions of the largest 16 societies (currently) and, since 1981, has excluded sales to sitting tenants. The survey, however, does not provide breakdowns by type of house, by type of buyer or by region. For these the choice rests between information drawn from the DOE Five Per Cent Sample Survey of building societies or from one of the big individual societies. The DOE five per cent sample is more representative than individual societies, but the latter prepare more timely data and use larger data bases. With regard to the individual societies, however, it needs to be appreciated that some publish simple average prices while others publish weighted averages (see Table 1.6). They are not, therefore, directly comparable.

House characteristics. The most detailed breakdowns of data on price levels according to house characteristics (summarized in Table 1.7) are those provided by the Inland Revenue *VOPMR* (Chapter 7) and the Halifax and Nationwide Building Societies (Chapters 11 and 15, respectively). Most sources provide analyses of house price levels according to type of house and several according to age but only two provide breakdowns by size of house (a third source -Ryden Residential Ltd - has recently been discontinued and, in any case, was confined to Scotland). Information is collected in the DOE Five Per Cent Sample Survey of building societies which would enable analyses of average prices according to these characteristics to be made but they are not currently published. Only one source (Inland Revenue Survey of Conveyances) provides data on freehold and leasehold property.

Local data. With regard to local data on price levels, most sources provide regional breakdowns, but only four sources provide sub-regional analyses of price levels (all but one - Anglia Building Society - being restricted to a part of the UK only) - see Table 1.7. Four sources provide data at the level of particular towns but only two of these cover the whole country (GB or UK) - Inland Revenue *VOPMR* and the Woolwich Equitable Building Society.

Buyer type. With regard to breakdowns of prices according to buyer type (first-time buyers and former owner-occupiers) it will be seen (Table 1.7) that currently only three sources now provide such analyses (DOE Five Per Cent Sample Survey and the Halifax and Nationwide building societies).

Regional comparisons. The inter-regional comparison of absolute price levels is beset by the same problem of mix-variability as the measurement of price movements over time. The only source which publishes actual average prices on a mix-adjusted basis is the Nationwide Building Society (Chapter 15). Otherwise, comparisons are probably best made using one of the sources that provide detailed breakdowns according to house characteristics, sub-classified by region - see Table 1.7 and the discussion above.

It will be clear, therefore, that despite the wide range of sources of house-price data that currently exist, there is not quite the embarrassment of choice that this might suggest, once the interest of the user moves away from national aggregates to more localized data and breakdowns by house and buyer characteristics. Interest in historical, rather than current, data also restricts the range of choice, especially for periods before 1970.

1.7.2 Measuring price movements

For the purpose of measuring price movements the choice must rest on one of the mix-adjusted series. The main choice is between that provided by the DOE (Chapter 3) or those provided by the Halifax Building Society (Chapter 11) or the Nationwide Building Society (Chapter 15).

The Halifax Building Society series has the advantage that the data base employed is larger than that used by other sources, has good national coverage (see Fleming and Nellis, 1985b) and takes account of more house characteristics in the mix-adjustment procedure than the DOE or other societies. It also uses the most sophisticated methodology for mix-adjustment. However, the series only extend back to 1983. For periods before 1983, the choice rests between the Nationwide Building Society and the DOE weighted indices. The

Table 1.7 Current data breakdowns available from each source

SOURCE		HOUSE DATA						
Chapter ref	Name	All	New	Non-new	Type	Size	Age	Freehold/ Leasehold
2	DOE/BSA BS4	*	*	*				
3	DOE 5% Sample	*	*	*	*	+	+	
4	Banks Survey	*						
5	DOE/ABI Survey	*	*	*				
6	Inland Revenue - Conveyances	*						*
7	Inland Revenue - *VOPMR*		*	*	*	*	*	
8	PPRU (Northern Ireland)		*	*	*			
9	Abbey National BS	*						
10	Anglia BS	*	*	*			*	
11	Halifax BS	*	*	*	*		*	
12	ISVA	*			*			
13	Leeds Permanent BS	*			*			
14	NHBC		*		*			
15	Nationwide BS	*	*	*	*		*	
16	Northern Rock BS	*			*		*	
17	Principality BS	*	*	*				
18	Ryden Residential Ltd++				*	*	*	
19	Woolwich Equitable BS				*	*	*	

+   Data available but not published
++ Discontinued in 1986

LOCAL DATA			BUYER DATA	CROSS-CLASSIFICATIONS		AREA
Regions	Sub-regions	Towns	FTB/FOO	2-way	3-way	
						UK
*			*	*	+	UK
						UK
						UK
*				*		E&W
		*			*	GB
	*			*	*	NI
*						UK
*	*			*		UK
*			*	*	*	UK
*						England
*				*		UK
*				*	*	E&W/GB
*			*	*	*	UK
	*			*	*	N England
	*	*		*		Wales
		*		*		Scottish cities
		*			*	UK

former has an advantage over the DOE in having a larger data base, a better house-size variable and a longer historical series, but the limitation to one society introduces a potential source of bias depending on its representativeness (although, as noted earlier, a system of weights drawn from official statistics, rather than the Society's own transactions, is employed to try to overcome any bias that might arise for this reason). Although the mix-adjusted sources are confined to building societies and are thus potentially open to bias because of the influence of other institutions taking a varying share of the market at the upper or lower ends from time to time, the mix-adjustment process takes account of this factor. Therefore, the series are not subject to the bias that may affect the series based on simple average prices.

1.8 THE EVIDENCE ON PRICE TRENDS, 1946-1986 AND PRICE LEVELS IN 1986

Finally, we turn to highlight some of the evidence provided by the major sources on price trends and price levels, before presenting all of the detailed data available from each source.

1.8.1 Price trends, 1946-1986

Figure 1.1 below shows the inflation of *new* house prices over the forty years since 1946, based on Nationwide Building Society information, this being the only source which can be traced continuously over this time period (but for new houses only - data for non-new houses are only available from 1952). It will be seen that from 1946 up to the early 1970s the rate of increase of prices was at a much lower level than for the subsequent period. In fact, from 1946 to 1971, the average compound inflation rate was 5.8 per cent per year, whereas from 1971 to 1986 the rate of increase doubled to 14.9 per cent per year. Over the whole period from 1946 to 1986, the average price of new houses increased by more than thirty three times. Year by year rates of increase are shown in Figure 1.2. It will be seen that the fluctuations are considerable, with particularly dramatic surges between 1971/72 (47 per cent) and 1978/79 (29 per cent). Throughout virtually the entire period from 1971, annual changes have exceeded those for the earlier period. The period as a whole is characterised by a generally rising trend. Over the four decades from 1946 to 1986, the average rate of increase was 9.2 per cent per year. This conceals average rates which have risen in each decade from 4.5 per cent to 13.8 per cent (Table 1.8). It will be seen that these rates themselves conceal much more volatile rates of change from year to year, ranging from 1 per cent to 47 per cent (Table 1.8 and Figure 1.2). The preceding analysis has focused on new dwellings but it is clear that the picture for non-new dwellings is very similar (see Table 1.9 below).

Table 1.8   Average annual rates of inflation in new house prices
             1946-1986

| | | | Per cent |
	Average	High	Low
Whole period			
1946-1986	9.2	47	1
Decade by decade			
1946-1956	4.5	5	1
1956-1966	5.8	8	1
1966-1976	12.8	47	4
1976-1986	13.8	28	6

Source: Nationwide Building Society

Figure 1.1   Inflation of new house prices

United Kingdom 1946 – 1986

Index 1946 Q4 = 100*

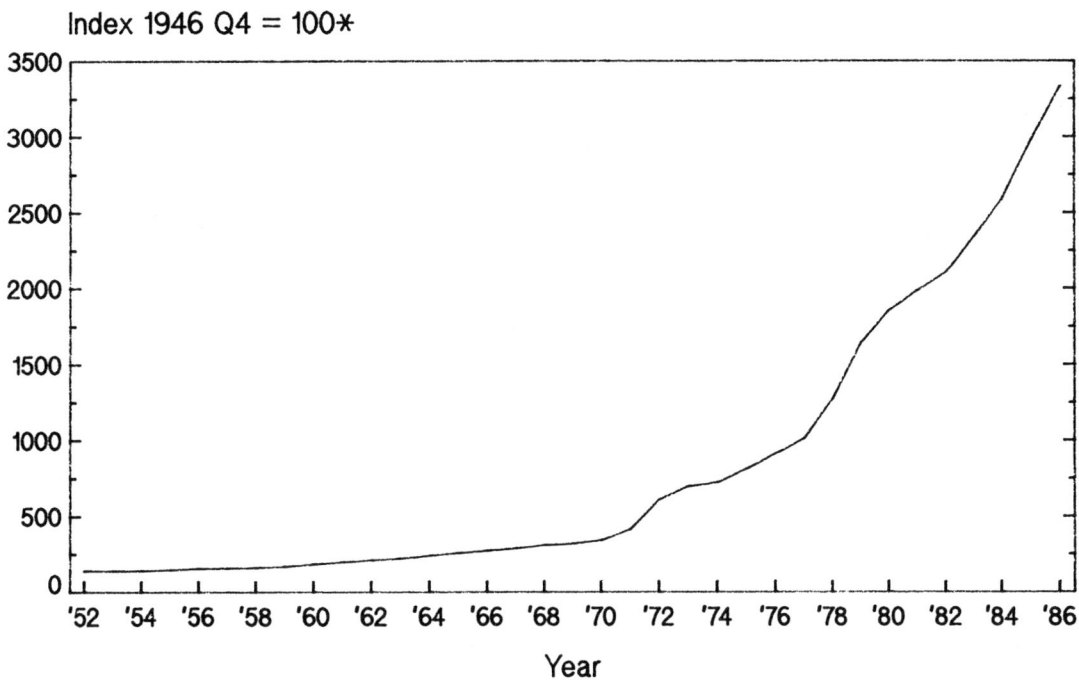

* Series for the years 1947–1951 inclusive are not available

Source: Nationwide Building Society

Figure 1.2   Annual percentage changes in new house prices

United Kingdom 1952–1986

Per cent

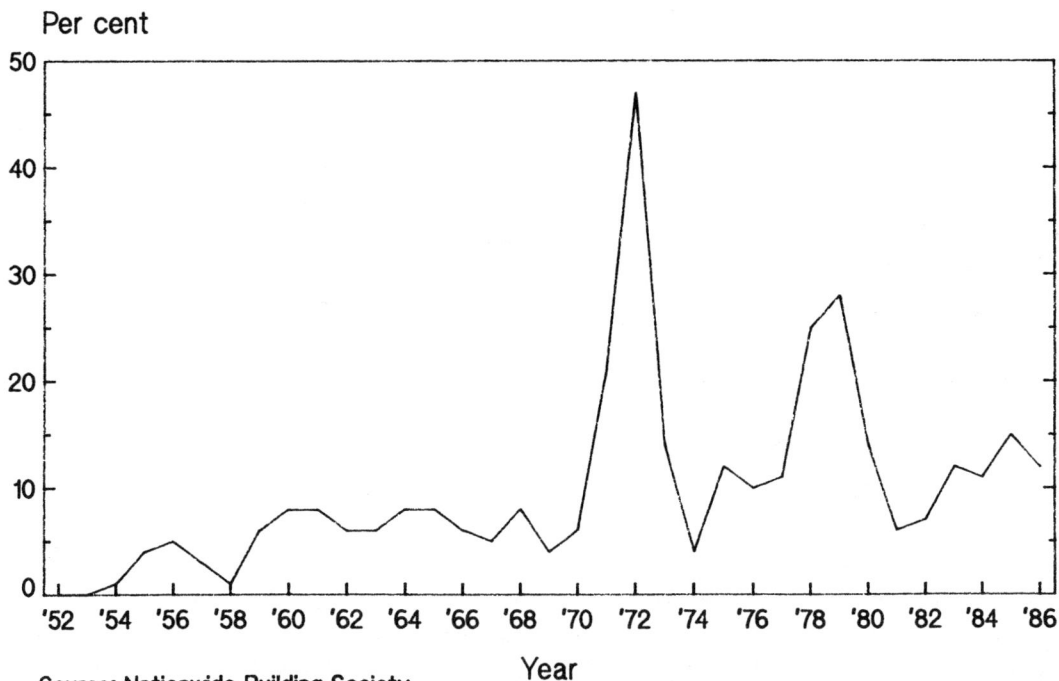

Source: Nationwide Building Society   Year

15

MEASUREMENT, INTERPRETATION AND EVIDENCE

Restriction of the analysis above to the information available from one building society naturally involves the potential deficiency that it may not be representative of all transactions. We turn briefly, therefore, to consider this question. For more recent periods it is possible to compare the information with that available for *all* building societies. The price changes for new dwellings can be compared over the three decades from 1956 while the price changes for non-new and all dwellings can be compared over the two decades from 1966. The comparison is shown in Table 1.9.

It should be appreciated that the comparison is subject to two reservations. The most important reservation is that the Nationwide Building Society series is a mix-adjusted series, while that for all societies is based on simple average prices until the last decade, for which an official weighted (mix-adjusted) series is also available (shown in parentheses in Table 1.9). The other reservation is that the series for all building societies are based on mortgages *completed*, while those for the Nationwide Building Society are based on mortgages *approved*. The latter series may be expected to run ahead of a completions series in times of inflation. Bearing these reservations in mind, it will be seen that there is a fairly close correspondence between the series for comparable groups of dwellings and time periods. It would seem safe to conclude, therefore, that the Nationwide Building Society series do provide a reasonably reliable indication of long-run trends, particularly given the fact that it is a mix-adjusted series.

Table 1.9   Comparative rates of change in house prices: all building societies and
Nationwide Building Society series
(Average annual compound rates)

Per cent

Period	New dwellings		Non-new dwellings			All dwellings	
	All societies	NWBS	All societies	NWBS		All societies	NWBS
				Modern	Older		
Fourth qtr							
1946–1956	–	4.5	–	3.6	4.3	–	–
1956–1966	5.7	5.8	–	5.9	6.1	–	6.0*
1966–1976	13.0	12.8	11.3	11.9	12.7	12.6	12.2*
1976–1986	12.8 (12.6)	13.8	11.5 (12.6)	12.8	13.1	11.6 (12.6)	12.9

Sources and notes:

All societies: Based on DOE/BSA BS4 survey of building societies (completions series - see Chapter 2) except for the figures in parentheses which are based on the DOE weighted index (see Chapter 3)

NWBS: Nationwide Building Society series (see Chapter 15) - approvals data, mix-adjusted except for the period 1946-1956 (* indicates figures derived from data given in Appendix Table to Chapter 15).

1.8.2   National price levels in 1986

We now turn to the evidence on average price levels in the UK as a whole in 1986. As we explained earlier, it is unfortunately not possible to quote an average price covering all transactions because of the limited coverage of the data available from either government or institutional sources. For the purpose of the commentary here, we use the official sample survey of *all* building societies (see Chapter 3) because it covers the most important source of finance and provides the most detailed data. It should be remembered, however, that houses bought with mortgage loans from other institutions are generally more highly priced than those financed by building societies: in 1985, for example, those properties financed by banks and insurance companies were around 40 per cent and 30 per cent more expensive, respectively (see Table 1.5). On the other hand, those bought without loans or with loans from other sources tended to be lower priced (Table 1.3).*

Turning to the houses mortgaged by building societies, we focus attention on the price differences for new and non-new houses, type of house and type of buyer (FTB and FOO).

Table 1.10   Average prices by house type, 1986
              Building Societies - United Kingdom

House type	New houses	Non-new houses*	All houses*	
			Average prices	Index (All = 100)
	£	£	£	
Bungalows	41,744	42,044	41,911	116
Detached	57,051	57,897	57,707	159
Semi-detached	31,220	33,480	33,321	92
Terraced	35,218	27,621	28,016	77
Flats & maisonettes	36,772	32,647	33,043	91
All	43,562	35,464	36,276	100

* The figures quoted *include* sales to local authority sitting tenants

Source: *Housing and Construction Statistics* and *BSA Bulletin* (DOE Five Per Cent Sample Survey of building society mortgages)

Table 1.11   Average prices by buyer type, 1986
              Building Societies - United Kingdom

Buyer type	New houses	Non-new houses	All houses
	£	£	£
Former owner-occupiers	50,729	44,429	45,200
First-time buyers:			
Former LA sitting tenants	-	14,060	14,060
Other first-time buyers	32,481	28,644	28,979
All first-time buyers	32,481	27,016	27,444
All buyers (excluding LA sitting tenants)	43,562	36,769	37,488

LA = local authority

Source: *Housing and Construction Statistics* and *BSA Bulletin* (DOE Five Per Cent Sample Survey of building society mortgages)

* Compare also the data in Table 3.1 (Chapter 3) and Table 6.1 (Chapter 6)

MEASUREMENT, INTERPRETATION AND EVIDENCE

The average price for all houses in 1986 was £36,276. This concealed a price differential between new and non-new properties of over £8,000 - £43,562 as against £35,464 (see Table 1.10). The variation by type of house is considerable, ranging from nearly 60 per cent above the overall average for detached houses (£57,707) to over 28 per cent below for terraced houses (£28,016). There is very little difference between the prices of new and non-new properties when analysed by type, except in the case of terraced houses (for which the difference exceeds £7,000) and for flats and maisonettes (for which there is a difference of £4,000) - new houses being the more expensive in both cases on average.

Marked differences also exist between prices paid by different types of buyers. For example, in 1986, former owner-occupiers bought properties which, on average, were some £18,000 more expensive than those bought by all first-time buyers: £45,200, as against £27,444 (see Table 1.11). Even after excluding those properties sold to local authority sitting tenants (at heavily discounted prices) the difference is still over £16,000 (in 1986 the average price paid by local authority sitting tenants was £14,060). Corresponding differences can be seen for both new and non-new properties.

1.8.3 Regional price levels in 1986

We turn finally to an analysis of house price differences in 1986 across the regions of the United Kingdom, again using data drawn from the official sample survey of building societies (see Chapter 3). The regional definitions are given in Appendix B. Figure 1.3 illustrates the proportional variations in average prices for *all* houses in each region, taking the UK average as equal to 100. The most expensive region is Greater London, with prices 50 per cent *above* the UK average and the cheapest region is the Northern with prices more than 30 per cent *below*. It follows that average prices in the Northern region are less than half those prevailing in Greater London (£25,509 as against £56,242, respectively - Table 3.2, Chapter 3 refers). They are also little more than half those prevailing in the South East generally.

Figure 1.3   Regional variations in average house prices, 1986

All dwellings

UK = 100 (£37488)

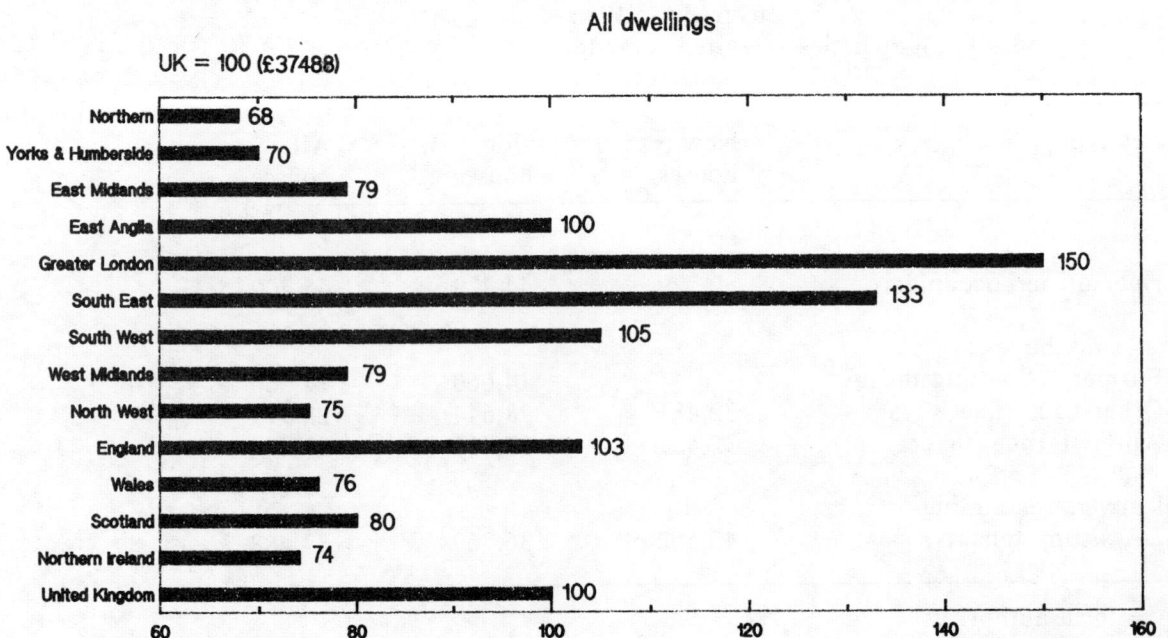

Northern	68
Yorks & Humberside	70
East Midlands	79
East Anglia	100
Greater London	150
South East	133
South West	105
West Midlands	79
North West	75
England	103
Wales	76
Scotland	80
Northern Ireland	74
United Kingdom	100

Source: DOE Five Per Cent Sample Survey

18

THE EVIDENCE ON PRICE TRENDS, 1946-1986 AND PRICE LEVELS IN 1986

The figure reveals the "North-South divide" very clearly: the regions with average prices above or equal to the national average are all concentrated in the south - East Anglia, Greater London, South East and South West. All other regions in England as well as Wales, Scotland and Northern Ireland have prices around 20 to 30 per cent below the national average.

Regional analyses of the data according to new and non-new houses and buyer type (FTB and FOO) are shown in Table 1.12. The most notable point is that the regional differences are very much more pronounced for non-new houses than for new houses. It is also notable that for new houses the Northern region no longer remains the cheapest (Northern Ireland, Scotland, Wales and Yorkshire and Humberside all had lower average prices in 1986). Analysis by buyer type shows a very similar regional pattern to that for all dwellings.

Table 1.12   Regional variations in average house prices: new, non-new and buyer type, 1986*

Region	New houses	Non-new houses	Buyer type	
			FOO	FTB
Northern	83	67	70	67
Yorks & Humberside	80	69	71	69
East Midlands	88	77	79	78
East Anglia	99	99	96	103
Greater London	129	153	153	162
South East	127	134	129	130
South West	100	105	101	105
West Midlands	94	76	81	76
North West	86	74	77	73
England	104	103	103	103
Wales	80	75	76	77
Scotland	82	80	83	84
Northern Ireland	72	71	75	82
United Kingdom	100	100	100	100

*   Data *exclude* local authority sitting tenants

Source: *Housing and Construction Statistics* and *BSA Bulletin* (DOE Five Per Cent Sample Survey of building society mortgages)

These marked regional differences in average house prices are the result of many factors. As discussed earlier, the mix of properties sold in any time period has an important effect on average prices - and it is known that this varies from region to region (Fleming and Nellis, 1981). It should also be borne in mind that *within* the regions there are considerable variations in prices.

Finally, it will be appreciated that house prices in general are determined by supply and demand factors, including buyers' purchasing power, changes in the number and size of households, the availability of mortgage finance and rates of new housebuilding, to name but a few. It is not our aim here to provide an economic interpretation of such factors; suffice it to say that any such discussion of the causes of house price inflation or regional disparity of prices must begin with a clear understanding of the underlying nature of the house price data available from the various sources. Satisfying this need is the central aim of this volume.

MEASUREMENT, INTERPRETATION AND EVIDENCE

REFERENCES

DOE (1977) *Housing Policy Technical Volume Part II*, HMSO, London.

Fleming, M.C. and Nellis, J.G. (1981) "The interpretation of house price statistics for the United Kingdom", *Environment and Planning A,* **13**, 1109-1124

Fleming, M.C. and Nellis, J G. (1984) *The Halifax House Price Index: Technical Details.* Halifax Building Society, Halifax. (Available free from the Society).

Fleming, M.C. and Nellis, J.G. (1985a) "Research policy and review 2. House price statistics for the United Kingdom: a survey and critical review of recent developments", *Environment and Planning A*, **17**, 297-318.

Fleming, M.C. and Nellis, J.G. (1985b) "The application of hedonic indexing methods: a study of house prices in the United Kingdom", *Statistical Journal of the United Nations Economic Commission for Europe*, **3**, 249-70

PART I　Government Data Sources

2. DOE/BSA BS4 Survey

2.1 TECHNICAL DETAILS

(a) Source of data and timing

Building societies' lending records at mortgage approval and completion stages (mixed until 1975, then separate series thereafter).

(b) Types of data and periods covered

Average prices: 1956 to date.
An index of average prices (new houses) was also published until the 1970s; it was then discontinued and is not reproduced in this volume.

Available data

DATA BREAKDOWNS	DATA TYPE
	AVERAGE PRICES
HOUSE DATA	
All houses	*
New/Non-new	*
Type	
Size	
Age	
LOCAL DATA	
Regions	
Sub-regions	
Towns	
BUYER DATA	
First-time buyer	
Former owner-occupier	

(c) Frequency

Monthly and quarterly (only quarterly before 1975)

(d) Geographical coverage

United Kingdom from 1975 (previously Great Britain)

(e) Method of analysis

Data are obtained from a panel of building societies showing the total number of advances made for house purchase and the total value of the houses purchased for new and non-new houses at both the approval and completion stages. These data are used to calculate average prices and, at one time, an index of average prices. The data collected and the coverage of the survey have changed on a number of occasions. An historical account of its development based on one provided by the Building Societies Association (BSA) is given below.

From 1956 to 1974 quarterly returns were obtained from a panel of 80 building societies accounting for some 75 per cent of building society lending. All *new* houses mortgaged to these building societies were covered and the sampling error was therefore thought to be small. In 1972 it was discovered that some societies had been reporting prices at the completion stage and others prices at the approval stage. Societies were asked what practice they had adopted and this enabled two sub-series - for the approval and completion stages - to be calculated.

A new monthly return (designated BS4) was introduced in early 1974. This return provides information on the number and value of mortgage advances and house prices for new and non-new houses at both approval and completion stages. Some 50 societies comprising 90 per cent of the total assets of the building society movement completed the return and this large sample meant that much more reliability could be placed on the resultant figures.

In 1981 the details of the BS4 return were revised and the sample reduced to the largest 17 (16 by the end of 1986) societies, comprising over 80 per cent of the total assets of the building society industry. The revised return enables the average price of houses for which there is a free market value to be calculated. The previous return made no distinction between such houses and, for example, council houses purchased at a discount. The reduced sample and the changed definition mean that there is a discontinuity in the series between the end of 1980 and the beginning of 1981.

Reliable figures from the BS4 return are available only from the beginning of 1975 but it is obviously helpful to use existing data to provide a consistent back-run of figures. The Department of the Environment has therefore adjusted past figures to make them compatible with the BS4 series. For existing dwellings the DOE Five Per Cent Sample Survey has been used to calculate figures at the completion stage back to 1966 (see Chapter 3). Because the sample survey results are only based on a five per cent sample they should be treated with caution and they are not a reliable indicator of short-term trends. For new houses an index based on the DOE/BSA BS4 Survey has been used. The figures for the period since 1967 are reasonably reliable but those between 1963 and 1966 are based on a smaller sample and are therefore subject to a greater margin of error. It is not possible to break down the new house-price series into approval and completion stage figures before 1963. However, by chance, in that year the approval and completion stage average prices were the same and, for the purposes of any long-term comparison, it has been assumed by the DOE that this applied throughout the period between 1956 and 1962.

2.2   LIST OF TABLES

Average prices

2.1   United Kingdom: all, new and existing dwellings. 1956- annual and quarterly
2.2   United Kingdom: all, new and existing dwellings. 1956- monthly

2.3   CROSS-CLASSIFICATIONS OF DATA

None

2.4   PUBLICATIONS

(a)   **Data**

Housing and Construction Statistics. HMSO, London. Quarterly and annual volumes
BSA Bulletin. Building Societies Association, London. Quarterly
A Compendium of Building Society Statistics. Building Societies Association, London. Annual
BSA Press Release. Building Societies' Monthly Figures. Building Societies Association, London. Monthly

(b) Description of methodology

A Compendium of Building Society Statistics. 6th edition, Building Societies Association, London. 1985

(c) Supplementary studies

None

DOE/BSA BS4 SURVEY

AVERAGE PRICES (at approval and completion stages) 1956 –

2.1 UNITED KINGDOM: ALL, NEW AND EXISTING DWELLINGS
Annual and Quarterly

£

Year	AT MORTGAGE APPROVAL STAGE			AT MORTGAGE COMPLETION STAGE		
	All	New*	Existing	All	New*	Existing
1956		2280			2280	
1957		2330			2330	
1958		2390			2390	
1959		2410			2410	
1960		2530			2530	
1961		2770			2770	
1962		2950			2950	
1963		3160			3160	
1964		3460			3360	
1965		3820			3660	
1966		4100		3850	3910	3820
1967		4340		4080	4150	4050
1968		4640		4340	4330	4340
1969		4880		4660	4690	4650
1970		5180		5000	4990	5010
1971		5970		5650	5510	5710
1972		7850		7420	6920	7610
1973		10690		10020	9630	10170
1974		11340		11100	11140	11090
1975	12119	12406	12057	11945	12234	11880
1976	12999	13442	12906	12759	13132	12679
1977	13922	14768	13764	13712	14343	13589
1978	16297	17685	16026	15674	16792	15447
1979	21047	22728	20739	20143	21455	19886
1980	24307	27244	23854	23514	26131	23085
1981	24810	28028	24374	24503	27910	24040
1982	25553	28508	25167	24577	27914	24149
1983	28593	31678	28146	27192	30943	26662
1984	30811	34160	30342	29648	33416	29112
1985	33187	37308	32673	31876	36295	31299
1986	38121	43646	37499	36869	42319	36238
1956 1		2240			2240	
2		2280			2280	
3		2300			2300	
4		2280			2280	
1957 1		2290			2290	
2		2290			2290	
3		2340			2340	
4		2380			2380	
1958 1		2360			2360	
2		2400			2400	
3		2410			2410	
4		2390			2390	
1959 1		2390			2390	
2		2400			2400	
3		2410			2310	
4		2420			2420	
1960 1		2430			2430	
2		2480			2480	
3		2560			2560	
4		2640			2640	
1961 1		2690			2690	
2		2740			2740	
3		2790			2790	
4		2850			2850	

* It is not possible before 1963 to break down the new house-price series into approval and completion stage. It has been assumed by the DOE that they were the same for the period 1956-1962 - see Section 2.1 (e).

Year	AT MORTGAGE APPROVAL STAGE			AT MORTGAGE COMPLETION STAGE		
	All	New	Existing	All	New	Existing
1962 1		2910			2910	
2		2930			2930	
3		2950			2950	
4		3010			3010	
1963 1		3080			3110	
2		3130			3120	
3		3160			3190	
4		3280			3190	
1964 1		3370			3340	
2		3420			3340	
3		3520			3390	
4		3600			3420	
1965 1		3700			3560	
2		3800			3600	
3		3850			3680	
4		3920			3790	
1966 1		4010		3660	3800	3580
2		4080		3800	3910	3750
3		4210		3950	3930	3950
4		4150		3980	3980	3970
1967 1		4270		3950	4020	3920
2		4310		4070	4160	4020
3		4360		4170	4170	4180
4		4420		4100	4230	4040
1968 1		4510		4190	4200	4190
2		4700		4300	4320	4280
3		4690		4460	4350	4510
4		4710		4440	4470	4420
1969 1		4720		4500	4550	4480
2		4840		4610	4660	4580
3		4940		4770	4740	4780
4		5040		4750	4790	4370
1970 1		5000		4810	4870	4780
2		5180		4850	4890	4840
3		5300		5110	5060	5120
4		5230		5150	5100	5170
1971 1		5600		5240	5190	5270
2		5770		5450	5390	5470
3		6190		5790	5570	5870
4		6350		6000	5760	6090
1972 1		6650		6340	6080	6440
2		7380		6850	6430	7010
3		8680		7960	7240	8220
4		9440		8520	7930	8750
1973 1		10150		9240	8810	9400
2		10640		9780	9460	9910
3		10960		10420	9970	10590
4		11240		10760	10340	10920
1974 1		11230		10960	10850	11010
2		11160		10840	10960	10800
3		11450		11170	11200	11170
4		11490		11270	11420	11220
1975 1	11492	11818	11411	11399	11852	11288
2	12117	12401	12053	11695	12052	11609
3	12403	12664	12351	12275	12404	12247
4	12367	12746	12291	12255	12566	12189

AVERAGE PRICES (at approval and completion stages) 1956 –

2.1 UNITED KINGDOM: ALL, NEW AND EXISTING DWELLINGS
  Annual and Quarterly (continued)

£

Year		AT MORTGAGE APPROVAL STAGE			AT MORTGAGE COMPLETION STAGE		
		All	New	Existing	All	New	Existing
1976	1	12432	12942	12321	12286	12738	12191
	2	12956	13385	12864	12538	12948	12448
	3	13350	13682	13282	13070	13274	13026
	4	13280	13831	13170	13091	13522	12996
1977	1	13312	13986	13171	13159	13813	13023
	2	13672	14463	13522	13376	13931	13260
	3	14102	14951	13955	13926	14523	13818
	4	14353	15442	14153	14115	14900	13970
1978	1	14711	16185	14414	14443	15556	14236
	2	15655	17115	15358	14951	16157	14689
	3	17147	18389	16917	16233	17219	16036
	4	18049	19550	17765	17270	18343	17046
1979	1	18804	20612	18445	18270	19579	18025
	2	20435	22118	20120	19242	20696	18940
	3	22069	23650	21795	20939	21895	20753
	4	23065	25036	22724	22047	23588	21746
1980	1	23385	26191	22888	22349	24524	21956
	2	24429	27208	23965	23051	25710	22566
	3	24633	27715	24191	24100	26763	23688
	4	24664	27952	24223	24267	27466	23804 **
1981	1	24796	28512	24286	24383	27847	23902
	2	25537	28612	25122	24780	28232	24329
	3	24952	27990	24561	24984	28135	24575
	4	23790	26794	23360	23756	27392	23229
1982	1	23804	27123	23353	23188	27122	22674
	2	25362	28391	24974	24042	27389	23619
	3	25955	28594	25621	25115	28040	24764
	4	26688	29605	26301	25360	28678	24908
1983	1	26904	30570	26403	25706	29791	25234
	2	28612	31825	28126	26547	30562	25989
	3	29756	32245	29398	28213	31486	27724
	4	29251	32096	28830	28383	31665	27846
1984	1	29400	33086	28874	28034	32054	27481
	2	31021	34345	30543	29146	32858	28626
	3	31706	34906	31289	30728	34272	30248
	4	31095	34337	30635	30360	34172	29764
1985	1	31630	35657	31083	30502	34842	29951
	2	32859	36555	32384	31473	35584	30899
	3	33560	37624	33081	32226	36316	31714
	4	34554	39477	33969	33338	38070	32719
1986	1	35317	40469	34716	33716	39265	33099
	2	38097	43442	37484	35660	40908	35044
	3	39494	45063	38910	38134	43267	37579
	4	39409	45748	38680	39222	44969	38490
1987	1	40672	47460	39869	38840	45996	38012

** Indicates discontinuity in the series between 1980 and 1981 caused by revision of the sample
of building societies in the survey.

DOE/BSA BS4 SURVEY

AVERAGE PRICES (at approval and completion stages) 1975 –

2.2 UNITED KINGDOM: ALL, NEW AND EXISTING DWELLINGS
Monthly

£

Year		AT MORTGAGE APPROVAL STAGE			AT MORTGAGE COMPLETION STAGE		
		All	New	Existing	All	New	Existing
1975	Jan	11452	11804	11369	11300	11893	11157
	Feb	11350	11754	11248	11354	11833	11236
	Mar	11668	11893	11611	11530	11833	11455
	Apr	11927	12273	11848	11536	11970	11431
	May	12091	12280	12047	11680	12006	11599
	Jun	12337	12667	12266	11865	12185	11791
	Jul	12437	12663	12392	12134	12367	12082
	Aug	12475	12721	12426	12353	12498	12324
	Sep	12304	12613	12243	12350	12356	12349
	Oct	12471	12726	12421	12259	12455	12216
	Nov	12318	12734	12237	12269	12483	12224
	Dec	12292	12783	12189	12236	12766	12125
1976	Jan	12420	12920	12312	12342	12702	12271
	Feb	12359	12793	12264	12198	12676	12096
	Mar	12502	13082	12375	12310	12817	12199
	Apr	12771	13309	12654	12457	12868	12373
	May	12951	13297	12875	12484	12981	12373
	Jun	13141	13552	13055	12667	12988	12594
	Jul	13401	13610	13358	12871	13192	12800
	Aug	13339	13710	13264	13177	13323	13148
	Sep	13309	13726	13224	13183	13321	13153
	Oct	13219	13806	13101	13109	13457	13033
	Nov	13329	13725	13251	13047	13457	12958
	Dec	13297	14003	13156	13119	13658	12998
1977	Jan	13450	14006	13332	13189	13848	13059
	Feb	13296	13918	13166	13192	13849	13054
	Mar	13294	14062	13079	13136	13819	12989
	Apr	13564	14313	13417	13299	13885	13175
	May	13643	14435	13489	13306	13879	13186
	Jun	13882	14718	13731	13521	14135	13394
	Jul	14069	14850	13934	13730	14207	13641
	Aug	14166	15009	14021	13946	14656	13822
	Sep	14145	15042	13988	14045	14738	13917
	Oct	14306	15295	14127	14114	14791	13994
	Nov	14442	15453	14257	14055	14825	13915
	Dec	14425	15688	14189	14143	15105	13957
1978	Jan	14557	15940	14291	14398	15189	14261
	Feb	14518	16024	14215	14330	15533	14107
	Mar	15050	16556	14734	14570	15848	14319
	Apr	15241	16847	14898	14770	15973	14525
	May	15608	16983	15329	14898	16178	14621
	Jun	16127	17556	15852	15196	16310	14939
	Jul	16688	17952	16458	15819	16787	15618
	Aug	17191	18448	16958	16309	17358	16107
	Sep	17566	18758	17342	16594	17540	16403
	Oct	17725	19186	17453	16964	17899	16773
	Nov	18101	19526	17833	17318	18220	17130
	Dec	18378	20000	18063	17560	18964	17259
1979	Jan	18486	20128	18157	18076	18994	17915
	Feb	18721	20720	18327	18254	19495	18023
	Mar	19152	20943	18798	18457	20118	18127
	Apr	19751	21569	19400	18802	20307	18502
	May	20464	22252	20130	19219	20760	18893
	Jun	21043	22517	20776	19676	20977	19401
	Jul	21739	23120	21499	20464	21230	20309
	Aug	22123	23904	21824	21125	22229	20919
	Sep	22391	23985	22107	21296	22348	21093
	Oct	22876	24700	22560	21870	22868	21603
	Nov	23138	25130	22800	22149	23593	21870
	Dec	23226	25362	22849	22228	24459	21779

AVERAGE PRICES (at approval and completion stages) 1975 –

2.2 UNITED KINGDOM: ALL, NEW AND EXISTING DWELLINGS
Monthly (continued)

£

Year		AT MORTGAGE APPROVAL STAGE			AT MORTGAGE COMPLETION STAGE		
		All	New	Existing	All	New	Existing
1980	Jan	23275	25842	22843	22496	24331	22172
	Feb	23196	25939	22703	22178	24604	21732
	Mar	23633	26679	23086	22373	24617	21956
	Apr	24168	27008	23676	22837	25472	22556
	May	24439	27448	23926	22882	25669	22387
	Jun	24663	27159	24268	23420	26032	22941
	Jul	24743	27571	24323	23726	26554	23255
	Aug	24605	27674	24167	24318	27279	23877
	Sep	24551	27903	24086	24285	27492	23958
	Oct	24671	27880	24241	24355	27464	23908
	Nov	24746	27909	24316	24165	27283	23719
	Dec	24564	27986	24099	24276	27636	23780 **
1981	Jan	24305	28017	23804	24430	27945	23983
	Feb	24433	28424	23903	24035	27507	23549
	Mar	25096	28729	24595	24381	28053	23863
	Apr	25503	28827	25049	24602	28354	24139
	May	25575	28678	25157	24738	28010	24316
	Jun	25536	28357	25161	25000	28302	24537
	Jul	25504	28574	25114	25118	28232	24721
	Aug	24935	27972	24544	25185	28163	24804
	Sep	24412	27433	24018	24600	27993	24141
	Oct	24121	27064	23723	24243	28554	23643
	Nov	23649	26583	23224	23636	26486	23239
	Dec	23525	26717	23042	23356	27142	22760
1982	Jan	23561	26973	23099	23440	27994	22922
	Feb	23552	26706	23115	22937	26564	22464
	Mar	24097	27497	23640	23188	27016	22655
	Apr	24859	27941	24469	23858	27513	23396
	May	25552	28452	25174	24158	27318	23775
	Jun	25690	28789	25294	24097	27346	23672
	Jul	25779	28457	25459	24899	28122	24517
	Aug	26060	28571	25733	25336	28030	25027
	Sep	26019	28726	25667	25120	27965	24758
	Oct	26502	29621	26091	24997	28054	24600
	Nov	26702	29590	26329	25277	28975	24802
	Dec	26871	29604	26495	25781	28917	25310
1983	Jan	26802	30367	26341	25700	29324	25325
	Feb	26788	30252	26305	25419	30217	24862
	Mar	27083	30989	26536	25929	29788	25449
	Apr	27998	31495	27492	26470	30756	25929
	May	28717	32046	28209	26441	30601	25882
	Jun	29113	31912	28676	26728	30375	26158
	Jul	29769	32417	29391	27817	31364	27304
	Aug	29889	32311	29533	28490	31350	28061
	Sep	29620	32020	29279	28338	31754	27814
	Oct	29361	32246	28947	28178	31605	27666
	Nov	29430	32303	29005	28343	31627	27832
	Dec	28921	31704	28495	28614	31744	28031
1984	Jan	29060	32934	28497	27904	31623	27446
	Feb	29205	32886	28683	28055	32228	27466
	Mar	29786	33350	29279	28121	32210	27523
	Apr	30540	34065	30049	29086	32583	28621
	May	31082	34492	30575	28877	32838	28340
	Jun	31406	34448	30970	29461	33094	28911
	Jul	31843	34979	31428	30279	33925	29786
	Aug	31913	35417	31471	31080	34528	30638
	Sep	31309	34274	30917	30849	34394	30335
	Oct	31152	33961	30763	30431	34511	29854
	Nov	30961	34305	30484	30127	33847	29582
	Dec	31194	34840	30659	30548	34168	29873

** Indicates discontinuity in the series between 1980 and 1981 caused by revision of the sample
  of building societies in the survey.

Year	AT MORTGAGE APPROVAL STAGE			AT MORTGAGE COMPLETION STAGE		
	All	New	Existing	All	New	Existing
1985 Jan	31289	35465	30722	29986	34864	29430
Feb	31391	35775	30798	30190	34938	29586
Mar	32105	35700	31617	30456	34755	29867
Apr	32810	36870	32273	31276	35816	30683
May	32834	36240	32391	31388	35545	30811
Jun	32938	36577	32489	31754	35426	31205
Jul	32884	36401	32475	32119	35815	31647
Aug	33541	38124	33001	32262	36282	31793
Sep	34236	38335	33745	32312	36925	31706
Oct	34680	39164	34150	33070	37249	32545
Nov	34384	39472	33773	33141	37769	32581
Dec	34602	39831	33981	33664	39066	32873
1986 Jan	34552	40087	33901	33316	39268	32741
Feb	35299	40066	34739	33591	38920	32968
Mar	35936	41179	35331	34184	39551	33541
Apr	37414	42639	36791	34947	39987	34374
May	38070	43135	37491	35714	41042	35113
Jun	38804	44597	38160	36218	41514	35555
Jul	39483	44848	38947	37353	42841	36753
Aug	39637	45098	39062	38378	43481	37852
Sep	39364	45277	38711	38777	43537	38245
Oct	39512	45472	38840	40175	44528	39664
Nov	39303	45654	38577	38510	44326	37792
Dec	39397	46218	38587	38789	46024	37748
1987 Jan	39691	46548	38875	38335	45580	37633
Feb	40355	47385	39513	38784	46054	37933
Mar	41561	48127	40796	39291	46210	38391

3. DOE Five Per Cent Sample Survey

3.1 TECHNICAL DETAILS

(a) Source of data and timing

Building societies' lending records at mortgage completion stage

(b) Types of data and periods covered

Average prices: 1965 to date. Survey commenced in 1965 but most of the present analyses run only from 1968 Q2.
Weighted index of average prices: 1969 to date

Available data (regularly published)

DATA BREAKDOWNS	DATA TYPES	
	AVERAGE PRICES	INDEX NUMBERS
HOUSE DATA		
All houses	*	*
New/Non-new	*	*
Type	*	
Size		
Age		
LOCAL DATA		
Regions	*	*
Sub-regions		
Towns		
BUYER DATA		
First-time buyer	*	
Former owner-occupier	*	

(c) Frequency

Quarterly (certain breakdowns of data only *published* annually)

(d) Geographical coverage

United Kingdom and official standard regions (defined in Appendix B)

The data for the standard regions are based on the former Economic Planning Regions as defined from 1 April 1974. Approximate figures have been produced for the period from 1968 Q2 to 1974 Q1 for the North, Yorkshire & Humberside, East Midlands, South East (excluding Greater London), South West, and North West regions which were altered; precise figures for the new regions cannot be recalculated because they are not exact combinations of the old counties and county boroughs by which the old data are coded.

DOE FIVE PER CENT SAMPLE SURVEY

(e) Method of analysis

Data are obtained from a regular survey by the DOE. Larger building societies complete questionnaires on a sample of five per cent of new mortgage advances; smaller societies provide a slightly larger sample.

Average prices: simple averages for all house sales, including sales at discounted prices.

Index numbers: until 1982 index numbers were based on simple averages of house prices, no allowance being made for the influence of changes in the mix of houses traded in terms of type, size, etc. In 1982 a mix-adjusted index was introduced and carried back to 1968 Q2. A description is given in *Economic Trends*, October 1982 (see Section 3.4(b) for details).

The mix-adjusted index is based on weighted average prices. These allow for the influences of changes in the mix of three house characteristics (type, size and age, where age represents a distinction between new and non-new dwellings) and changes in the regional distribution of house-purchase transactions. The procedure involves the generation of a matrix consisting of 156 cells, each representing a cross-classification of these characteristics. For each cell a mean price is calculated in each successive time period. An overall weighted average is then calculated, the weights being the number of transactions in each cell over the period mid-1968 to mid-1974 up to 1982 and since then an annually updated set of weights based on mortgages in the previous three years.

3.2   LIST OF TABLES

Average prices

3.1   United Kingdom: all, new, existing dwellings; type of buyer. 1965-
3.2   Regions: all dwellings. 1968-
3.3   Regions: new and existing dwellings. 1969-
3.4   Regions: type of buyer. 1969-
3.5   United Kingdom and regions: type of dwelling. 1979-
3.6   United Kingdom: type of dwelling -all, new, non-new. 1969-
3.7   First-time buyers: United Kingdom and regions. 1983-
3.8   First-time buyers: United Kingdom - type and age of dwelling. 1983-

Weighted index

3.9   United Kingdom: all, new, non-new dwellings. 1968 Q2-
       Regions: all dwellings. 1969-

3.3   CROSS-CLASSIFICATIONS OF DATA

(a) Two-way classifications

Numbers in the grid below refer to the corresponding tables compiled for this data source

Average prices and weighted index(*)

34

(b) Three-way classifications

None

3.4 PUBLICATIONS

(a) Data

Housing and Construction Statistics. HMSO, London. Quarterly and annual volumes.
BSA Bulletin. Building Societies Association, London. Quarterly.
A Compendium of Building Society Statistics. Building Societies Association, London. Annual.

(b) Description of methodology

Evans, A.W., *Studies in Official Statistics 26: The Five Per Cent Sample Survey of Building Society Mortgages.* HMSO, London, 1975.
Department of the Environment, "A New Index of Average House Prices", *Economic Trends*, 348, October 1982, pp.134-8.

(c) Supplementary studies

Distribution of dwelling prices regularly published in *Housing and Construction Statistics* and in *BSA Bulletin*.

Unpublished analyses may be supplied by the Department of the Environment on request or on payment of a fee.

DOE FIVE PER CENT SAMPLE SURVEY

AVERAGE PRICES (at completion stage) 1965 –

3.1 UNITED KINGDOM:
ALL, NEW AND EXISTING DWELLINGS; TYPE OF BUYER

£

Year		All	New	Existing	TYPE OF BUYER	
					First-time Buyer	Former Owner-occupier
1966		3840	3953	3776		
1967		4050	4154	4001		
1968		4344	4447	4290		
1969		4640	4736	4598	4097	5418
1970		4975	5051	4946	4330	5838
1971		5632	5609	5640	4838	6666
1972		7374	6988	7519	6085	8965
1973		9942	9683	10043	7908	11900
1974		10990	11114	10950	9037	13049
1975		11787	12013	11734	9549	13813
1976		12704	13084	12618	10181	15160
1977		13650	14324	13513	10857	16246
1978		15594	16923	15312	12023	18792
1979		19925	21124	19675	14918	24074
1980		23596	26245	23145	17533	28959
1981		24188	28119	23642	18166	30110
1982		23644	28205	23083	17762	30634
1983		26471	30817	25901	19513	34260
1984		29106	33080	28557	22174	36717
1985		31103	36103	30476	23742	39390
1986		36276	43562	35464	27444	45200
1965	Nov/Dec	3637	3806	3548		
1966	1	3661	3887	3534		
	2	3772	3910	3702		
	3	3917	3938	3904		
	4	3981	4060	3926		
1967	1	3911	3988	3873		
	2	4030	4148	3971		
	3	4147	4198	4125		
	4	4070	4234	3993		
1968	1	4184	4286	4137		
	2	4290	4402	4229	3782	4997
	3	4474	4502	4459	3984	5112
	4	4450	4606	4363	3988	5072
1969	1	4478	4598	4421	3987	5173
	2	4572	4663	4529	4059	5346
	3	4730	4740	4726	4141	5552
	4	4754	4946	4676	4181	5566
1970	1	4785	4950	4723	4169	5669
	2	4816	4913	4778	4207	5672
	3	5108	5122	5103	4428	5969
	4	5127	5188	5104	4464	5957
1971	1	5238	5329	5201	4566	6198
	2	5393	5373	5400	4649	6424
	3	5772	5699	5800	4945	6814
	4	5995	5936	6014	5143	7029
1972	1	6326	6235	6361	5393	7549
	2	6832	6583	6927	5773	8290
	3	7878	7191	8119	6366	9634
	4	8451	7960	8639	6813	10288
1973	1	9222	9062	9283	7446	11083
	2	9639	9276	9790	7652	11544
	3	10337	10015	10461	8140	12285
	4	10709	10515	10785	8579	12733

Year		All	New	Existing	TYPE OF BUYER	
					First-time Buyer	Former Owner-occupier
1974	1	10871	10872	10871	8921	13136
	2	10778	11030	10677	8865	12997
	3	11073	11204	11030	9154	13108
	4	11135	11309	11087	9141	12979
1975	1	11180	11585	11081	9214	12976
	2	11632	11607	11639	9459	13507
	3	12144	12273	12115	9669	14230
	4	12024	12500	11917	9748	14309
1976	1	12188	12495	12119	9852	14533
	2	12454	12976	12331	10015	15010
	3	13006	13310	12935	10327	15452
	4	13114	13498	13029	10522	15538
1977	1	13101	13795	12949	10570	15550
	2	13322	13881	13219	10788	15884
	3	13773	14375	13653	10832	16386
	4	14139	15004	13968	11135	16819
1978	1	14252	15621	13982	11178	17096
	2	14878	16237	14580	11561	17840
	3	16067	17084	15853	12189	19481
	4	17208	18638	16890	13200	20751
1979	1	17901	19059	17675	13701	21806
	2	19131	20372	18870	14204	23249
	3	20835	21557	20682	15607	24733
	4	21807	23355	21474	16278	26344
1980	1	22326	24667	21868	16817	27327
	2	23065	25528	22618	17246	28201
	3	24254	27056	23785	17618	29811
	4	24497	27832	24015	18284	30148
1981	1	24227	27971	23678	18234	29776
	2	24670	28564	24129	18551	30366
	3	24566	28562	24033	18295	30677
	4	23183	27289	22616	17558	29462
1982	1	22029	27169	21352	17087	28622
	2	23121	28066	22523	17575	30008
	3	24295	28141	23843	18114	31382
	4	24579	29121	24013	18094	31605
1983	1	24992	29573	24485	18467	32689
	2	25805	30466	25194	19365	33410
	3	27509	31178	27004	19829	35523
	4	27594	31813	26981	20471	35298
1984	1	27233	31541	26682	20821	35174
	2	28644	32053	28161	21990	35901
	3	30281	34325	29738	22945	37624
	4	29759	33870	29151	22677	37630
1985	1	29013	34774	28341	22228	37421
	2	30952	34744	30451	23849	38978
	3	31435	36247	30837	23795	39616
	4	32518	37763	31826	24807	40978
1986	1	33497	40316	32799	25677	42378
	2	34964	43158	34050	26965	43345
	3	37993	43946	37346	28305	46739
	4	37887	45781	36924	28525	47315

DOE FIVE PER CENT SAMPLE SURVEY

AVERAGE PRICES (at completion stage) 1968 –

3.2 REGIONS: ALL DWELLINGS

Year	North	Yorks & Humberside	North West	East Midlands	West Midlands	East Anglia
1969	3714	3436	3922	3791	4348	4298
1970	3942	3634	4184	3966	4490	4515
1971	4389	4023	4949	4390	4926	4968
1972	5413	4880	5724	5621	6232	7031
1973	7414	7059	7836	8191	8775	9849
1974	8444	8289	8890	9191	10252	10996
1975	9601	9058	9771	9989	10866	11528
1976	10453	9995	10500	10646	11621	11850
1977	11773	10722	11523	11367	12528	12176
1978	13044	12099	13410	12810	14342	13968
1979	15443	15003	16902	15836	18493	18461
1980	17710	17689	20092	18928	21663	22808
1981	18602	19202	20554	19465	21755	23060
1982	18071	18180	20744	19487	20992	23358
1983	20032	20863	22832	22026	23131	25830
1984	22604	22356	24410	24377	24989	28296
1985	22786	23338	25125	25539	25855	31661
1986	24333	25607	27503	28483	28437	36061
1968 2	3247	3292	3562	3627	4032	4015
3	3481	3384	3769	3873	4190	4008
4	3660	3430	3791	3648	4046	3985
1969 1	3526	3321	3758	3757	4303	4033
2	3693	3436	3934	3767	4351	4165
3	3776	3487	3964	3815	4303	4470
4	3833	3481	4017	3828	4434	4489
1970 1	3679	3476	4138	3724	4447	4113
2	3952	3575	4119	3695	4236	4351
3	4012	3837	4232	4165	4631	4668
4	4033	3590	4230	4154	4618	4795
1971 1	4165	3719	4265	4074	4679	4547
2	4154	3919	4358	4231	4590	4732
3	4433	4189	4554	4505	5112	5065
4	4709	4184	4726	4648	5224	5366
1972 1	4810	4296	5082	4728	5291	5598
2	4955	4514	5395	5190	5643	6359
3	5782	5100	5832	6064	6566	7391
4	6045	5543	6505	6480	7435	8566
1973 1	6588	6011	7106	7396	7854	8782
2	7056	6874	7470	8049	8442	9398
3	7874	7526	8542	8432	9292	10538
4	8241	7887	8461	9135	9658	10868
1974 1	8190	8044	8760	8818	10183	10798
2	8340	8154	8382	9276	9738	10252
3	8353	8226	8949	9718	10285	11375
4	8728	8344	9238	8979	10171	11266
1975 1	8786	8710	9019	9647	10173	10974
2	9537	8627	9622	9926	10596	12235
3	9775	9349	10258	10121	10843	12326
4	10139	9279	9991	10181	10806	11890
1976 1	9812	9255	10305	10076	11384	11189
2	10323	9755	10035	10557	11491	11649
3	10724	10539	10840	11230	11651	11927
4	10859	10307	10825	10659	11924	12563
1977 1	11357	10144	10334	10963	11906	11559
2	11538	10240	11271	11645	12419	11867
3	11721	10782	11700	11633	12525	11994
4	12294	11439	12321	11194	13029	13057

South East	Greater London	South West	Wales	Scotland	Northern Ireland
5792	6195	4496	4168	4609	3941
6223	6882	4879	4434	5002	4387
7284	7397	5564	4803	5407	4650
9914	11113	7771	5935	6233	4934
13164	14447	10868	8382	8595	6181
13946	14857	11606	9401	9775	8710
14664	14918	12096	10083	11139	10023
15548	15566	13003	11129	12974	12860
16466	16745	13555	11673	14236	15722
18915	19160	15503	13373	16147	18395
24675	25793	20494	17061	19371	21824
29832	30968	25293	19363	21754	23656
29975	30757	25365	20155	23014	19890
29676	30712	25514	19662	22522	20177
33764	34640	28000	22533	23822	20859
37334	39346	30612	23665	25865	21455
40487	44301	32948	25005	26941	23012
48544	54863	38536	27354	28242	25743
5339	5990	4212	3791	4189	4290
5506	6137	4334	4059	4631	4474
5643	6084	4389	4004	4372	4450
5564	6271	4322	4105	4492	4478
5640	6026	4546	3970	4595	4572
5941	6224	4550	4267	4625	4730
5963	6254	4541	4282	4688	4754
5937	6798	4631	4201	4644	4785
6015	6569	4732	4407	5099	4816
6404	6923	4942	4624	5056	5108
6441	7177	5104	4462	5153	5127
6730	7189	5201	4415	4984	5238
6908	7860	5307	4732	5042	5393
7438	8070	5687	5017	6010	5772
7857	8445	5967	4948	5376	5995
8199	9392	6297	5391	5570	6326
9046	10552	7096	5382	6183	6832
10782	11878	8383	6120	6724	7878
11902	13109	9114	6822	6542	8451
12434	14133	10303	7709	7714	9222
12965	14051	10626	7742	7953	9639
13582	14774	11252	9047	9289	10337
13841	14912	11397	9618	9366	10709
13923	15214	11477	9166	9731	10871
13743	14722	11297	8600	9838	10778
13863	14546	11838	9420	9897	11073
14147	14890	11504	10082	9665	11135
14041	14473	11779	9223	9958	11180
14574	15087	11674	9843	10924	11632
15065	15264	12189	10735	11638	12144
14794	14774	12027	10305	11788	12024
15041	14824	12323	10963	12200	12301
15267	13361	13138	10422	12793	11905
15908	15649	12980	11444	13258	13964
15922	16359	12507	11710	13569	13169
16134	16581	13081	11101	13263	16169
13124	16318	13166	11787	13773	14587
16535	16930	13589	11875	14627	15503
16855	17019	14105	11780	14932	16345

DOE FIVE PER CENT SAMPLE SURVEY

AVERAGE PRICES (at completion stage) 1968 –

3.2 REGIONS: ALL DWELLINGS (continued)

Year		North	Yorks & Humberside	North West	East Midlands	West Midlands	East Anglia
1978	1	12155	11069	12102	11519	13096	12656
	2	12971	11728	12920	12403	13623	13641
	3	13340	12551	14300	13529	14502	14116
	4	13751	13049	14432	13820	16293	15543
1979	1	13452	13304	15108	14022	16520	17235
	2	14680	14290	15932	15716	17761	16663
	3	16859	15527	17480	16834	19031	17459
	4	16778	16845	18984	16677	20531	20304
1980	1	16792	17074	19202	17859	21186	21361
	2	17192	17395	19491	18269	21336	23308
	3	18929	17967	20680	19747	22335	23759
	4	17804	18209	20810	19701	21810	22635
1981	1	19064	19092	20489	19473	22075	22984
	2	19041	19650	20220	19429	22594	23601
	3	18640	19610	21250	19745	21849	22742
	4	17690	18370	20235	19202	20472	22943
1982	1	17628	17351	19627	19072	20284	20965
	2	17605	17666	19543	19226	21376	22748
	3	18166	18294	21618	20089	21103	24170
	4	18759	19107	21815	19405	20987	24823
1983	1	18680	19593	21551	20942	21623	25333
	2	19974	20819	21769	21596	21982	25606
	3	20125	21912	24135	22944	24527	25385
	4	21662	21153	23838	22680	24459	27043
1984	1	20126	21210	22939	23120	23529	26109
	2	22334	21749	23669	24526	24888	27685
	3	23615	23690	25738	25000	25847	29352
	4	23790	22420	24779	24602	25339	29364
1985	1	22736	21832	23748	24460	24140	29159
	2	22969	23401	24806	24252	26257	30641
	3	22848	23452	25785	26245	26694	32124
	4	22607	24315	25831	26769	25919	33669
1986	1	22591	23856	26195	26185	26675	33760
	2	24331	25395	26627	27956	27461	34370
	3	26653	25989	28763	29316	29511	36967
	4	23724	26751	28079	29834	29563	38502

£

South East	Greater London	South West	Wales	Scotland	Northern Ireland
17230	17526	14239	12642	14728	16362
17645	18374	14821	12570	15615	17835
19570	19886	15949	13613	16506	19752
21304	20881	17007	14651	17506	19510
22229	23037	17922	14516	18529	18471
23548	24682	20100	16296	18568	20606
25689	26957	20901	18015	20569	23590
27403	29059	23062	19016	19793	24629
28468	29005	23190	18240	20820	23326
29268	30868	24547	18749	20604	23759
30314	31954	26507	19065	23161	25399
30892	31703	26525	21129	22202	22412
30250	30017	24468	19642	22520	20425
29990	31564	26354	20411	23384	19635
30335	30941	26059	21837	23623	20185
29216	30363	24442	18109	22400	19430
26584	28398	23858	19150	21298	18885
29150	30037	24769	18752	22060	19811
30987	30784	25954	19925	22902	20868
30922	32934	26752	20676	23399	20831
31857	32808	25887	21019	22709	20561
32484	33959	27729	21035	23948	20203
35497	35370	28660	23648	24130	21885
35276	36447	29772	24590	24022	20921
34928	36459	28135	23620	24203	21872
36601	39304	30381	22955	26144	20686
38350	39779	31697	24400	26770	22085
38257	41081	31706	23563	25914	21249
37880	39753	29509	24272	25531	20990
39771	43689	33389	24205	27562	22385
41126	44995	33948	25386	26959	24565
42602	47593	34207	25942	27438	23735
44508	49289	35500	25580	27424	23349
46561	53254	37443	26902	27535	25691
50696	57816	40316	28667	29065	26871
51049	57728	40156	27668	28778	26568

DOE FIVE PER CENT SAMPLE SURVEY

AVERAGE PRICES (at completion stage) 1969 –

3.3 REGIONS: NEW AND EXISTING DWELLINGS

Year	North	Yorks & Humberside	North West	East Midlands	West Midlands	East Anglia
NEW DWELLINGS						
1969	4022	3841	4252	4101	4422	4326
1970	4356	4023	4402	4257	4624	4507
1971	4806	4407	4823	4678	5182	4950
1972	5890	5516	5854	5729	6269	6871
1973	8098	7749	8061	8376	9205	9539
1974	8916	8982	9726	9414	10545	10975
1975	10301	9811	10738	10319	11533	11371
1976	11474	10750	11858	11412	12122	12146
1977	13000	12035	13498	12231	13685	12562
1978	15288	14064	15664	14463	16937	14542
1979	17951	18426	19595	17920	20724	18883
1980	21929	21855	25426	22186	25740	25122
1981	24817	25340	27145	25056	26223	26201
1982	27575	24689	27676	25216	25895	25992
1983	28040	26227	28547	27935	28543	28136
1984	29448	28814	29380	29930	30608	31365
1985	33283	30858	31189	32069	32416	34774
1986	36103	35041	37478	38281	41069	43134
EXISTING DWELLINGS						
1969	3598	3266	3765	3606	4313	4276
1970	3797	3495	4098	3830	4436	4521
1971	4220	3875	4362	4244	4820	4979
1972	5206	4593	5670	5568	6217	7139
1973	7078	6738	7743	8094	8620	10028
1974	8266	8007	8632	9085	10166	11008
1975	9397	8842	9550	9888	10715	11592
1976	10156	9759	10245	10444	11504	11743
1977	11502	10424	11168	11149	12307	12042
1978	12552	11665	12971	12418	13817	13793
1979	14934	14301	16435	15335	18037	18333
1980	16900	17035	19332	18266	20885	22197
1981	17966	18443	19828	18538	21030	22321
1982	17352	17458	20092	18658	20257	22905
1983	19160	20249	22232	21155	22343	25379
1984	21827	21638	23883	23610	24144	27684
1985	21847	22691	24539	24620	24989	31112
1986	23369	24771	26692	27234	27071	34887

£

South East	Greater London	South West	Wales	Scotland	Northern Ireland
5908	7588	4567	4250	4919	4089
6327	7694	4954	4533	5438	4792
7242	8738	5538	4946	5673	5005
9726	11653	7440	5983	6597	5080
13696	15885	10708	7969	8387	6262
14808	17148	11584	9427	10539	8559
15429	18676	11852	10393	11871	11020
16031	19551	12727	12023	13929	14295
17038	18697	13516	12290	16326	17591
20136	23588	15805	14858	16982	20707
25800	27913	20504	18316	20186	23484
31670	37006	27082	23023	24196	27057
32819	35792	27498	25764	27028	25925
33184	33611	27222	26297	27739	25603
36889	35612	30789	31432	30873	25187
40301	41572	32051	32048	31007	25819
44609	45486	35596	33171	33594	27291
55478	56136	43763	34700	35871	31529
5742	6059	4456	4115	4493	3820
6185	6793	4848	4378	4853	4116
7298	7842	5575	4717	5297	4344
9966	11066	7913	5909	6071	4851
12997	14333	10934	8674	8692	6121
13703	14705	11615	9388	9498	8792
14511	14735	12162	9977	10933	9675
15444	15432	13076	10854	12692	12353
16343	16676	13564	11510	13941	15215
18642	18976	15425	13035	15889	17581
24437	25710	20492	16760	19082	21254
29513	30777	24907	18800	21225	22640
29552	30583	25025	19330	22288	18354
29214	30575	25241	18904	21808	18830
33333	34578	27583	21672	22685	19377
36898	39193	30370	22915	24754	19734
39906	44227	32535	24281	25799	21242
47709	54792	37806	26556	27410	23522

DOE FIVE PER CENT SAMPLE SURVEY

AVERAGE PRICES (at completion stage) 1969 –

3.4 REGIONS: TYPE OF BUYER

Year	North	Yorks & Humberside	North West	East Midlands	West Midlands	East Anglia
FIRST-TIME BUYERS						
1969	3376	2970	3461	3347	3771	3779
1970	3456	3138	3687	3536	3925	4020
1971	3843	3411	3977	3769	4226	4336
1972	4694	4084	4818	4724	5399	6034
1973	6098	5635	6408	6556	7270	8213
1974	6984	6846	7407	7728	8219	8980
1975	7743	7387	7885	8069	8584	9508
1976	8333	7996	8228	8442	9124	9726
1977	9144	8319	9002	9113	9622	9970
1978	10423	8899	9926	9769	10754	11296
1979	12017	11170	12602	11496	13321	13852
1980	13565	12820	14641	13915	15746	17366
1981	13972	13889	15554	14111	16659	17548
1982	13224	13353	15340	14518	15658	18045
1983	14743	15647	16744	15978	16582	19765
1984	17001	17253	18387	18135	18429	21753
1985	17295	17604	18984	19044	19188	24449
1986	18187	19253	20447	21367	20744	28076
FORMER OWNER-OCCUPIERS						
1969	4188	4018	4552	4460	5160	4997
1970	4554	4353	4876	4773	5340	5252
1971	4969	4897	5209	5246	5995	5852
1972	6454	6136	6844	6851	7467	8525
1973	8986	8513	9415	9827	10418	11468
1974	9954	9880	10725	11084	12091	12996
1975	11258	10513	11475	11784	13011	13247
1976	12557	11937	12641	12751	13965	13842
1977	14116	12812	13851	13687	15011	14330
1978	15786	15088	16414	15635	17455	16436
1979	19178	18433	20367	19567	22664	21978
1980	22374	22200	25211	23553	26596	26778
1981	23836	24197	26014	25036	27216	28169
1982	25231	24443	26972	25732	27541	28055
1983	27208	26707	29555	28766	30800	31629
1984	28926	27631	30998	30806	32382	35029
1985	28949	29555	32093	32900	33658	38393
1986	31448	32059	34775	35685	36650	43283

South East	Greater London	South West	Wales	Scotland	Northern Ireland
5055	5640	3944	3595	4010	3521
5333	6119	4292	3903	4262	3896
6092	7137	4808	4146	4646	4115
7770	9779	6463	5057	5392	4360
10259	12233	8919	6785	6917	5304
11377	12979	9617	7939	8121	7620
11594	13065	9977	8450	9140	8523
12055	13498	10456	8836	10539	10165
12756	14081	10945	9681	11576	12500
14137	15719	12198	10734	12970	14711
17800	20936	15545	12847	15273	16508
21479	24925	19133	14627	16643	18867
21811	25288	19546	14760	17398	15381
22061	25043	19321	15248	17020	15856
24197	27825	20856	16660	17560	16821
27347	32635	23633	18809	19697	17618
29855	36829	25313	19635	20572	18863
35835	45221	29052	21126	22085	21223
6726	7186	5186	4963	5248	4813
7156	8061	5547	5095	5821	5349
8547	9215	6448	5751	6287	5510
11935	12933	9115	7264	7375	5936
15253	17060	12376	10147	10312	7840
16022	17671	13501	11294	11744	10379
16805	17431	13957	12054	13234	11720
18393	19343	15244	13641	15362	15562
19436	20777	15816	13956	16765	18323
22491	24345	18101	15763	19120	20990
29256	32085	23866	20548	23323	26009
35705	39092	29657	24113	26904	29276
36130	38552	30157	25793	28538	28907
36668	40408	31460	26651	29918	29621
41801	45856	34414	30154	32858	29777
45608	51569	37082	30084	34109	30821
50128	56972	39849	32599	35443	31192
58496	68981	45666	34565	37322	33734

DOE FIVE PER CENT SAMPLE SURVEY

AVERAGE PRICES (at completion stage) 1979 –

3.5 UNITED KINGDOM AND REGIONS: TYPE OF DWELLING

Year	United Kingdom	North	Yorks & Humberside	North West	East Midlands	West Midlands	East Anglia
BUNGALOW							
1979	21803	19109	17556	21547	18035	21618	17774
1980	25811	22959	21119	24899	22384	26160	22375
1981	27999	25018	23799	27500	24733	26778	24408
1982	28456	25102	25384	26021	24258	26769	24201
1983	31435	29736	27540	29403	26660	29918	28014
1984	34701	31755	28769	32582	31611	33161	29863
1985	37696	32199	31560	34902	33118	34952	33367
1986	41991	34637	33757	37512	35911	36342	37826
DETACHED HOUSE							
1979	30108	26257	24544	27574	23681	27854	25400
1980	37041	30457	30463	35520	29258	33089	32424
1981	38099	31934	32685	36115	30371	34169	32826
1982	39008	36390	32711	38864	31188	34658	34772
1983	43615	37283	36124	41563	34992	39591	38238
1984	46829	39415	38653	43882	37544	40430	42040
1985	50903	40187	41648	45631	41125	42050	46770
1986	57707	42399	44867	49851	44760	46002	53291
SEMI-DETACHED HOUSE							
1979	17890	16238	13851	16085	12929	15906	15995
1980	21648	19073	17055	19388	16203	18832	19787
1981	22662	19368	18479	20425	16880	20001	19954
1982	22103	17992	16705	21039	16932	18932	20010
1983	24244	19802	19483	22615	18543	20346	21534
1984	26989	23584	21956	23656	21109	21921	24475
1985	28832	23650	22752	24642	21990	23129	26863
1986	33321	25570	24549	26982	23342	24670	31136
TERRACED HOUSE							
1979	14879	11085	9256	10124	9690	11407	12518
1980	17337	12522	11539	12474	11686	13590	15964
1981	18236	13321	12676	13387	12238	14245	17163
1982	17774	13096	12777	13906	12978	14400	17058
1983	19346	14652	14157	14407	14201	15114	18120
1984	22018	16671	15231	15977	15861	16159	20524
1985	23849	17148	16570	16615	17026	17090	23170
1986	28016	18321	17936	17648	19222	18693	26574
PURPOSE-BUILT FLAT							
1979	16010	9152	14701	14519	11202	14303	11775
1980	19073	12298	15409	15655	13008	15706	15280
1981	20235	13033	17839	16987	14136	15519	18293
1982	19535	12734	12950	14730	12311	14468	17413
1983	21617	13199	16548	16867	11994	14535	17491
1984	24137	13991	17430	19094		17431	18777
1985	26230	14818	18401	20126		17418	21777
1986	31157	16787	18483	21671	18922	18472	26442
CONVERTED FLAT							
1979	17531						
1980	21643						
1981	21232						
1982	21704						
1983	24795	13973	17490	21075	15400	16142	15867
1984	27147	16427					24375
1985	30059	19234					
1986	36701	16286					

Note: gaps indicate small samples

South East	Greater London	South West	Wales	Scotland	Northern Ireland
27339	29647	23719	18066	22769	23039
32651	40102	28536	21454	24436	25703
33910	43155	29634	23460	28575	25744
35465	45467	31011	22785	28547	25160
39238	47331	34526	27328	30949	27406
45937		36851	28746	34770	27401
49385		41637	32427	36793	28790
58730	70824	46016	37754	37120	31066
37899	49994	29736	25334	26434	30363
46615	60433	37851	29627	33124	34479
47084	60793	38441	32136	33200	33279
48029	59082	38608	33671	35864	34430
55000	71363	43279	37637	38246	36109
60842	77488	46921	38619	40225	34725
67119	93875	52018	43209	42544	39854
78882	108365	60643	42422	45846	41734
22342	29509	18215	15373	19183	16587
27367	35420	23161	18221	21425	19485
28321	36777	23498	18718	23039	17563
28152	36754	23695	18335	22834	18551
30490	41531	25541	20921	23289	18647
34754	47753	28454	22486	25188	20291
38760	52528	30607	23059	26567	21597
46351	65805	35459	25462	29492	23389
18305	24243	15001	11471	16404	14439
21811	29814	18442	13522	19205	13504
22849	29455	19262	14530	18292	10041
22518	29012	19545	14587	17458	10779
25032	32307	20990	16034	17031	11611
28643	38850	22967	17870	19067	11240
31509	43607	25386	18401	21211	13362
38090	53257	29002	19766	22419	15011
16769	19764	15750		13106	
20702	24903	17666		14714	
21715	24742	18366		16424	
21104	24741	18342	13082	17357	
23922	27636	19530	16925	18535	21956
26531	31971	21719	19423	20104	
29235	36019	24895	20154	20731	23212
34626	44897	27318	25168	22353	21436
15401	20622	14051		15890	
18339	26015	19262		16606	
19035	24616	19484		18276	
19567	24941	20491		19827	
22234	28934	20270	24127	22114	18500
	32424	23294	23236		
27956	37299	25382		23207	
32508	48001	28670		25442	

DOE FIVE PER CENT SAMPLE SURVEY

AVERAGE PRICES (at completion stage) 1969 –

3.6 UNITED KINGDOM: TYPE OF DWELLING – ALL, NEW, NON-NEW

Year	BUNGALOW			DETACHED HOUSE			SEMI-DETACHED HOUSE		
	All	New	Non-new	All	New	Non-new	All	New	Non-new
1969	4619	4396	4819	6722	6315	6952	4217	4034	4288
1970	4917	4603	5119	7166	6684	7406	4480	4212	4569
1971	5472	5052	5743	8171	7439	8568	4988	4644	5113
1972	7093	6127	7763	10768	9131	11824	6547	5694	6851
1973	9728	8427	10515	14457	12654	15811	8918	7688	9345
1974	10949	10388	11206	15978	14623	16746	9715	8763	9994
1975	11969	11529	12102	16885	15660	17364	10257	9155	10474
1976	13406	12855	13586	18587	17171	19121	11259	10310	11445
1977	14405	14077	14497	20323	18728	20892	12158	11402	12281
1978	16917	16493	17040	23422	21911	24079	13848	13220	13952
1979	21802	19515	22627	30108	26976	31550	17889	16567	18095
1980	25811	24319	26235	37041	33330	38670	21647	20046	21848
1981	27999	27389	28164	38010	36008	38733	22665	21961	22733
1982	28456	27753	28616	39010	37988	39307	22107	22963	22029
1983	31435	30723	31600	43615	41741	44137	24244	24653	24206
1984	34701	33509	34990	46829	46084	47033	26989	25976	27100
1985	37696	35984	38092	50903	49311	51353	28832	28250	28888
1986	41991	41744	42044	57707	57051	57897	33321	31220	33480

£

TERRACED HOUSE			FLAT OR MAISONETTE		
All	New	Non-new	All	New	Non-new
3605	4568	3390	4479	4994	4304
3867	4974	3645	4733	5350	4493
4346	5339	4161	5519	5796	5438
5864	6798	5729	7347	7332	7351
7889	9324	7634	8929	9489	8787
8557	10040	8292	9164	9100	9178
9175	10291	9013	9990	10388	9914
9573	10753	9408	10624	10847	10586
10273	11705	10081	11211	11414	11180
11676	13408	11463	13030	13100	13020
14877	17014	14656	16414	16521	16401
17338	20796	17067	19769	20316	19718
18234	21816	17992	20533	22585	20331
17776	22279	17482	20108	21579	19924
19346	24326	18976	22514	23207	22415
22018	27333	21604	25077	25398	25028
23849	29671	23432	27550	29291	27343
28016	35218	27621	33043	36772	32647

DOE FIVE PER CENT SAMPLE SURVEY

AVERAGE PRICES (at completion stage) 1983 –

3.7 FIRST-TIME BUYERS: UNITED KINGDOM AND REGIONS

Year	United Kingdom	North	Yorks & Humberside	North West	East Midlands	West Midlands	East Anglia
ALL FIRST-TIME BUYERS							
1983	19513	14743	15647	16744	15978	16582	19765
1984	22174	17001	17253	18387	18135	18429	21753
1985	23742	17295	17604	18984	19044	19188	24449
1986	27444	18187	19253	20447	21367	20744	28076
FORMER LOCAL AUTHORITY SITTING TENANTS							
1983	11351	8996	9385	9382	8529	9985	11912
1984	11959	10332	9260	9775	9856	9820	11518
1985	12698	10220	9525	9506	10141	10266	12307
1986	14060	10415	10143	10377	10816	10050	14206
OTHER FIRST-TIME BUYERS							
1983	21397	17318	16962	17965	17352	18319	21390
1984	23566	18187	17941	19024	18946	19674	23235
1985	25154	18483	18490	19738	20003	20139	26105
1986	28979	19507	20137	21208	22583	21949	29866

£

South East	Greater London	South West	Great Britain	England	Wales	Scotland	Northern Ireland
27825	24197	20856	19591	19950	16660	17560	16821
27347	32635	23633	22321	22784	18809	19697	17618
29855	36829	25313	23886	24440	19635	20572	18863
35835	45221	29052	27616	28485	21126	22086	21223
18378	15139	12268	11477	11739	9695	10575	8287
15556	18703	13309	12249	12734	10492	10518	7891
17199	20081	13096	12946	13415	10224	11264	8616
20397	23486	14863	14287	14564	10719	12309	9009
29036	26123	22529	21437	21671	18514	20303	19859
29122	33683	25038	23637	23963	19900	22053	20935
31601	38316	26662	25238	25693	21058	22520	21873
37532	46879	30354	29070	29883	22326	24238	23636

DOE FIVE PER CENT SAMPLE SURVEY

AVERAGE PRICES (at completion stage) 1983 –

3.8 FIRST-TIME BUYERS: UNITED KINGDOM – TYPE AND AGE OF DWELLING

£

Year	TYPE OF DWELLING					AGE OF DWELLING		
	Bungalow	Detached House	Semi-detached House	Terraced House	Flat/ Maisonette	Pre-1919	1919-39	Post-1939
ALL FIRST-TIME BUYERS								
1983	24171	32307	19302	17109	21071	19067	19921	19648
1984	26320	35526	22070	19461	23737	21100	22962	21703
1985	28840	38657	23060	20989	26069	22799	24552	23225
1986	31486	44026	26258	24259	30735	26428	29344	27563
FORMER LOCAL AUTHORITY SITTING TENANTS								
1983	14239	19072	11015	11154	12598	15592	10636	11185
1984	11482	20006	11684	11898	12696	15932	11570	11864
1985	14010	21033	11911	12881	14099	15397	12272	12663
1986	14481	19077	13226	14335	16180	18676	13230	14022
OTHER FIRST-TIME BUYERS								
1983	24743	33052	22051	18725	21810	19196	22221	22801
1984	26953	36027	24178	20726	24128	21169	24825	24728
1985	29564	39321	25392	22156	26509	22890	26507	26224
1986	32177	44504	28675	25557	31291	26524	31744	30094

DOE FIVE PER CENT SAMPLE SURVEY

WEIGHTED INDEX (at completion stage) 1969 –

3.9 UNITED KINGDOM: ALL, NEW AND NON-NEW DWELLINGS
    REGIONS: ALL DWELLINGS

Year		North	Yorks & Humberside	North West	East Midlands	West Midlands	East Anglia	South East
1969		19.5	18.9	18.6	19.1	20.3	19.0	18.7
1970		20.5	19.8	19.4	20.0	20.8	20.0	20.1
1971		22.7	21.7	21.1	22.0	22.4	21.7	23.3
1972		28.2	26.5	26.7	28.2	28.7	30.8	32.7
1973		38.4	38.0	37.0	41.4	40.7	43.0	43.4
1974		43.6	44.0	42.4	45.6	45.7	46.7	44.8
1975		48.7	48.4	45.2	49.0	48.5	48.4	46.7
1976		54.4	53.8	49.7	53.0	52.6	51.4	49.8
1977		61.9	57.9	54.5	56.6	57.1	53.4	53.0
1978		69.2	65.1	63.2	64.0	65.9	61.5	62.1
1979		84.6	81.6	81.6	80.9	84.3	79.2	82.6
1980		100.0	100.0	100.0	100.0	100.0	100.0	100.0
1981		106.9	112.2	106.1	107.9	104.4	105.4	104.5
1982		111.5	112.8	108.9	111.3	106.1	109.1	106.1
1983		124.1	126.7	120.2	122.5	115.2	119.0	120.3
1984		134.3	135.5	127.0	135.0	123.5	130.9	136.0
1985		134.9	143.4	132.8	145.3	128.5	146.5	149.9
1986		146.0	156.0	146.0	161.0	141.0	171.0	176.0
1968	2							
	3							
	4							
1969	1	18.6	18.4	18.2	18.9	20.5	17.7	18.2
	2	20.3	18.9	18.6	18.9	20.2	18.9	18.5
	3	20.0	19.5	18.7	19.2	19.7	19.7	18.9
	4	19.5	18.9	18.8	19.3	21.0	19.4	19.2
1970	1	19.4	19.2	19.0	19.2	20.6	18.4	19.1
	2	20.3	19.6	19.1	19.0	20.0	19.4	19.8
	3	21.0	20.4	19.9	20.5	21.2	20.2	20.5
	4	20.9	19.8	19.6	20.9	21.0	21.2	20.5
1971	1	24.2	20.2	20.1	20.8	21.4	19.8	21.4
	2	21.7	21.0	20.6	21.4	21.4	20.6	22.2
	3	22.9	22.2	21.3	22.3	22.7	22.0	23.7
	4	24.1	22.7	21.9	23.1	23.6	23.6	25.2
1972	1	25.0	23.3	23.6	24.0	24.5	24.1	26.8
	2	26.2	24.9	24.9	26.1	25.9	27.6	30.0
	3	29.9	27.2	27.5	29.9	30.2	33.2	35.4
	4	31.8	30.2	30.6	32.7	34.0	38.2	39.2
1973	1	33.7	32.7	33.5	37.7	36.8	39.9	41.9
	2	37.3	36.7	35.9	40.1	39.5	42.3	43.1
	3	41.2	40.3	40.0	43.6	42.8	44.6	44.2
	4	42.6	42.2	39.8	45.6	44.3	45.7	44.7
1974	1	41.6	42.8	41.4	43.8	44.6	46.9	44.9
	2	42.3	44.3	41.3	45.7	44.3	45.2	45.4
	3	43.4	43.8	42.6	47.7	46.3	46.8	44.3
	4	45.5	44.7	44.0	45.2	46.7	47.1	45.0
1975	1	45.0	45.7	43.3	48.3	46.7	46.4	45.2
	2	49.1	46.8	44.2	48.1	47.9	47.9	46.4
	3	48.9	49.4	45.9	49.3	48.7	48.7	47.3
	4	48.7	50.8	46.8	50.7	50.3	50.6	47.4
1976	1	52.4	51.2	48.2	51.4	51.3	48.6	48.3
	2	53.0	52.5	49.3	51.7	51.5	51.0	49.5
	3	55.4	55.8	50.4	54.5	53.2	51.6	50.1
	4	56.5	55.2	51.2	54.1	54.0	53.8	51.2
1977	1	59.6	55.7	50.7	54.4	54.4	50.8	51.7
	2	60.5	55.5	52.6	56.7	56.6	51.9	52.2
	3	61.9	58.3	55.6	58.0	57.7	52.6	52.7
	4	65.4	60.8	56.8	57.2	58.7	57.2	54.7

54

Greater London	South West	Wales	Scotland	Northern Ireland	United Kingdom		
					All	New	Non-new
18.2	17.6	20.2	20.7	17.7	18.9	19.9	18.7
20.1	18.7	21.6	22.1	19.1	20.1	20.9	19.6
23.2	21.2	23.3	24.0	20.4	22.5	22.7	22.4
33.0	30.3	29.4	28.3	22.1	30.1	28.9	30.4
42.8	42.2	40.6	38.4	25.8	41.0	39.3	41.6
43.8	45.1	45.1	43.7	34.4	44.4	44.5	44.4
44.8	46.4	48.9	49.5	42.1	47.0	47.4	46.7
48.1	49.5	54.0	59.2	53.3	51.2	52.1	50.9
51.5	52.7	56.8	64.7	65.1	55.1	56.4	54.7
61.3	60.8	65.7	72.9	75.1	63.8	65.4	63.1
82.0	80.1	83.8	87.2	90.0	82.5	81.0	82.7
100.0	100.0	100.0	100.0	100.0	100.0	100.0	100.0
103.1	103.2	108.5	109.4	97.2	105.5	107.0	104.7
104.6	106.9	114.5	116.7	101.2	108.1	112.0	107.0
117.6	118.4	126.0	131.0	108.9	120.6	122.0	121.0
136.5	127.4	131.0	139.0	112.7	132.3	133.0	132.0
156.0	139.8	141.0	147.0	120.5	143.6	143.0	144.0
190.0	161.0	150.0	155.0	129.0	164.0	165.0	163.0
					17.4		
					17.8		
					17.8		
18.2	17.3	19.7	20.7	17.5	18.5		
17.8	17.8	19.2	20.9	18.5	18.8		
18.4	17.7	19.8	20.7	17.2	19.0		
18.3	17.8	21.4	20.5	17.6	19.2		
19.6	17.6	20.6	21.2	19.0	19.3		
19.2	18.4	21.4	22.5	18.8	19.6		
20.6	19.1	22.4	22.1	19.5	20.5		
20.8	19.5	22.0	22.9	18.9	20.5		
21.3	20.2	21.6	22.5	20.4	21.0		
22.6	20.2	23.0	22.9	20.4	21.6		
23.6	21.5	24.1	25.4	21.3	22.9		
25.0	22.7	24.0	24.3	19.6	23.9		
27.9	24.3	26.1	25.5	21.2	25.4		
31.2	27.4	27.1	28.1	21.5	27.8		
35.4	32.5	30.2	29.8	25.0	32.0		
39.8	35.9	33.9	30.0	22.5	35.3		
41.7	39.6	36.6	34.6	23.3	38.2		
42.3	41.2	38.5	35.9	24.3	40.1		
44.4	44.4	42.9	41.8	25.7	42.8		
43.1	43.9	44.9	41.3	30.2	43.3		
44.6	45.3	43.1	42.6	33.0	43.9		
43.0	44.1	43.7	43.7	35.6	44.0		
42.8	45.7	45.3	44.1	36.0	44.4		
44.5	45.1	47.8	44.0	34.8	45.0		
42.6	46.1	46.7	45.7	38.3	45.2		
45.2	45.6	47.8	47.7	39.0	46.4		
46.4	46.7	50.8	51.4	43.7	47.8		
44.8	47.1	49.8	52.3	44.7	48.3		
46.3	49.7	52.5	55.3	49.9	49.3		
48.1	49.8	52.7	58.6	50.0	50.6		
47.9	49.6	54.2	60.7	58.6	51.8		
49.4	50.6	55.5	60.8	54.7	52.6		
50.9	50.1	54.3	61.6	61.1	53.0		
49.1	51.1	56.6	62.7	64.1	53.8		
52.2	52.6	56.9	65.7	65.0	55.4		
52.8	55.5	58.6	67.3	67.0	57.1		

DOE FIVE PER CENT SAMPLE SURVEY

WEIGHTED INDEX (at completion stage) 1969 –

3.9 UNITED KINGDOM: ALL, NEW AND NON-NEW DWELLINGS
   REGIONS: ALL DWELLINGS (continued)

Year		North	Yorks & Humberside	North West	East Midlands	West Midlands	East Anglia	South East
1978	1	64.4	60.1	57.1	58.6	60.2	54.9	57.1
	2	68.6	63.2	60.9	62.9	62.6	60.9	58.1
	3	69.6	67.4	66.2	65.7	66.4	63.6	64.0
	4	74.8	69.8	68.5	69.1	75.1	66.4	69.5
1979	1	74.1	72.1	73.2	73.1	74.5	72.8	73.7
	2	80.7	80.2	77.7	79.2	81.9	73.5	79.3
	3	89.1	85.3	84.2	84.3	87.1	82.0	85.5
	4	93.2	88.3	91.2	87.4	93.4	87.6	92.6
1980	1	93.5	93.1	94.4	94.1	96.3	94.0	95.8
	2	97.8	99.4	98.5	98.8	98.0	101.5	99.3
	3	105.3	103.4	103.0	105.6	102.7	102.7	101.3
	4	102.0	104.0	103.6	102.0	103.3	100.7	102.6
1981	1	104.5	108.4	103.8	103.5	103.4	103.0	104.0
	2	107.6	113.2	106.6	108.2	105.0	104.8	103.8
	3	109.2	114.9	108.5	110.8	105.9	105.4	105.4
	4	105.8	113.2	105.2	108.6	101.2	107.4	105.4
1982	1	108.3	108.6	104.3	109.6	102.2	103.0	99.8
	2	108.7	111.0	106.1	113.0	106.7	107.2	105.4
	3	110.7	113.8	111.8	114.8	106.8	112.1	109.0
	4	117.6	117.2	113.6	108.5	108.2	112.7	109.5
1983	1	117.0	119.0	116.1	117.3	111.6	114.3	114.4
	2	121.3	124.8	114.9	120.3	113.2	117.1	116.5
	3	124.8	130.2	122.1	123.4	118.3	118.8	124.3
	4	125.9	130.9	121.8	127.8	115.9	119.2	125.4
1984	1	125.0	130.1	123.5	130.7	118.6	125.0	128.2
	2	127.8	132.3	123.8	134.8	121.4	127.7	132.9
	3	135.2	139.8	128.7	136.7	124.7	133.0	138.9
	4	135.3	135.9	129.2	136.6	125.4	136.6	142.7
1985	1	134.2	139.6	129.5	140.8	122.1	139.2	141.4
	2	133.5	142.1	130.4	137.9	127.6	141.2	148.0
	3	137.5	141.8	133.7	148.7	132.0	146.5	151.9
	4	133.2	149.7	137.2	152.1	130.8	155.3	156.3
1986	1	140.0	147.4	141.5	150.2	134.5	163.5	161.9
	2	145.1	154.7	141.7	161.6	136.4	167.0	169.0
	3	152.0	156.0	149.0	161.0	145.0	171.0	180.0
	4	142.0	162.0	149.0	168.0	147.0	178.0	188.0

Greater London	South West	Wales	Scotland	Northern Ireland	United Kingdom		
					All	New	Non-new
55.5	55.8	62.4	66.7	69.0	58.4		
60.7	58.3	63.1	70.2	71.9	61.2		
63.3	61.7	67.1	75.0	76.2	65.5		
66.5	67.4	70.6	78.7	81.1	70.1		
74.8	71.0	73.1	80.7	79.4	73.8		
79.7	77.3	80.7	84.1	85.6	79.5		
84.4	82.6	87.5	91.7	95.0	85.6		
90.0	90.0	93.1	91.5	101.6	91.3		
95.2	93.7	93.9	95.9	95.0	94.9		
100.1	95.9	98.8	96.7	99.3	98.7		
100.8	105.4	101.6	103.6	106.3	102.7		
102.7	103.7	106.6	102.0	99.7	102.9		
98.5	99.3	102.9	104.9	96.5	103.1		
105.0	104.3	108.3	110.2	95.0	105.9		
104.0	107.6	117.5	111.3	97.9	107.6		
104.6	100.8	105.3	111.8	99.3	105.5		
97.3	103.1	105.9	111.3	96.8	102.9		
104.6	106.2	115.0	116.3	102.4	107.4		
106.5	107.1	117.6	117.3	100.5	110.1		
110.0	111.3	118.1	121.1	105.1	111.7		
112.0	110.0	117.8	121.7	97.4	115.0	116.0	115.0
115.8	116.7	125.6	126.6	105.7	119.0	122.0	118.0
120.6	118.6	134.1	124.8	113.3	124.0	122.0	124.0
123.1	122.2	134.8	129.5	112.9	125.0	127.0	125.0
124.8	120.9	131.0	128.4	115.2	125.8	129.0	125.0
136.5	126.0	133.8	134.0	110.9	130.3	130.0	130.0
139.5	129.7	135.9	138.6	113.0	134.9	136.0	135.0
143.2	131.7	137.8	139.1	113.3	136.7	136.0	137.0
142.3	129.6	141.4	137.9	116.4	136.4	140.0	136.0
153.9	139.1	144.1	142.9	114.0	141.6	140.0	142.0
157.0	141.3	147.6	141.9	124.1	145.1	143.0	146.0
165.8	146.8	146.0	145.2	125.3	149.3	149.0	150.0
171.8	151.5	141.5	149.4	125.5	153.2	154.0	153.0
185.7	157.8	144.1	152.5	131.8	159.6	163.0	159.0
194.0	164.0	157.0	155.0	131.0	167.0	165.0	167.0
208.0	169.0	155.0	158.0	133.0	172.0	174.0	172.0

4. Bank of England Survey of Banks' Mortgages

4.1 TECHNICAL DETAILS

(a) Source of data and timing

Based on returns for mortgages recorded at the approval stage from a sample of banks accounting at the end of 1986 for about 82% of total monetary sector (that is, the UK offices of institutions either recognized as banks or licensed to take deposits under the Banking Act 1979, including the Trustee Savings Banks) loans for house purchase.

(b) Types of data and periods covered

Estimated average prices: 1983 to date

Available data

DATA BREAKDOWNS	DATA TYPE AVERAGE PRICES
HOUSE DATA All houses New/Non-new Type Size Age	*
LOCAL DATA Regions Sub-regions Towns	
BUYER DATA First-time buyer Former owner-occupier	

(c) Frequency

Annual

(d) Geographical coverage

United Kingdom

(e) Method of analysis

The published average prices are *estimates* derived from the distribution of purchase prices provided by the responding banks - see (a) above. All properties, including any sold at non-market prices, are covered.

4.2 LIST OF TABLES

Estimated average prices

4.1   United Kingdom: all dwellings. 1983-

4.3 CROSS-CLASSIFICATIONS OF DATA

None

4.4 PUBLICATIONS

(a) Data

Housing and Construction Statistics, HMSO, London. Annual

(b) Description of methodology

None

(c) Supplementary studies

None

BANK OF ENGLAND SURVEY OF BANKS' MORTGAGES

ESTIMATED AVERAGE PRICES (at approval stage) 1983-

4.1 UNITED KINGDOM: ALL DWELLINGS

		£
Year	All	
1983	35100	
1984	45300	
1985	47100	
1986	49100	

5. DOE/ABI Survey of Insurance Companies

5.1 TECHNICAL DETAILS

(a) Source of data and timing

Based on returns made to the DOE at the mortgage completion stage by a sample of insurance companies, which generally account for about 50% of insurance company mortgage advances. These show the number of primary loans made for house purchase broken down according to the price band of the house.

(b) Types of data and periods covered

Estimated average prices: 1968 to date

Available data

DATA BREAKDOWNS	DATA TYPE
	AVERAGE PRICES
HOUSE DATA	
All houses	*
New/Non-new	*
Type	
Size	
Age	
LOCAL DATA	
Regions	
Sub-regions	
Towns	
BUYER DATA	
First-time buyer	
Former owner-occupier	

(c) Frequency

Quarterly

(d) Geographical coverage

United Kingdom

(e) Method of analysis

The published average prices are *estimates* derived from the distribution of purchase prices returned by the responding insurance companies - see (a) above. All properties, including any sold at non-market prices, are covered.

DOE/ABI SURVEY OF INSURANCE COMPANIES

5.2 LIST OF TABLES

Estimated average prices

5.1 United Kingdom: all, new and existing dwellings. 1968–

5.3 CROSS-CLASSIFICATIONS OF DATA

None

5.4 PUBLICATIONS

(a) Data

Housing and Construction Statistics. HMSO, London. Quarterly

(b) Description of methodology

None

(c) Supplementary studies

None

DOE/ABI SURVEY OF INSURANCE COMPANIES

ESTIMATED AVERAGE PRICES (at completion stage) 1968 –

5.1 UNITED KINGDOM: ALL, NEW AND EXISTING DWELLINGS

£

Year	All	New	Existing	Year	All	New	Existing
1968	5574	5302	5705	1978 1	19440	19830	19360
1969	6340	5850	6570	2	19970	20470	19850
1970	6850	6410	7010	3	21770	20810	21930
1971	7160	6850	7270	4	22970	21200	23310
1972	9280	8360	9540				
1973	14600	12860	15060	1979 1	24170	24990	24060
1974	15390	14830	15540	2	26780	24520	27210
1975	15790	15880	15780	3	30030	28430	30300
1976	16550	16850	16480	4	30250	30810	30170
1977	17930	18140	17900				
1978	21140	20590	21240	1980 1	29470	31730	29150
1979	27980	27230	28090	2	29410	31660	29020
1980	30570	32510	30280	3	32090	32950	31960
1981	32230	35050	31860	4	31400	34350	30980
1982	32770	37210	32210				
1983	37000	41400	36500	1981 1	31390	34660	30940
1984	39600	46600	38800	2	31790	33010	31630
1985	41300	47100	40600	3	32770	35820	32370
1986	46200	51400	45700	4	32830	36490	32340
1968 1	5199	5028	5293	1982 1	30780	36730	30080
2	5454	5142	5606	2	33140	36640	32680
3	5675	5435	5783	3	33490	36950	33050
4	5830	5504	5987	4	33350	38360	32680
1969 1	5928	5462	6153	1983 1	34600	38100	34100
2	6393	5866	6637	2	35600	41000	34900
3	6544	6062	6755	3	39100	43200	38600
4	6515	6021	6732	4	37700	42100	37100
1970 1	6702	6120	6932	1984 1	39700	44900	39100
2	6557	6289	6660	2	39300	46900	38300
3	6948	6483	7118	3	39500	45500	38900
4	7120	6718	7262	4	40000	49100	38800
1971 1	7085	6582	7281	1985 1	38700	44500	38100
2	6826	6637	6900	2	39900	45200	39900
3	7235	6888	7357	3	43200	49900	42400
4	7447	7255	7520	4	42500	47400	41800
1972 1	7571	7334	7665	1986 1	44100	49300	43500
2	8170	7930	8260	2	45800	48300	45600
3	10130	8770	10490	3	47000	54100	46200
4	11590	9830	11950	4	47200	52600	46600
1973 1	12500	10940	12950	1987 1	46900	55200	46100
2	14210	12790	14560				
3	15280	13360	15730				
4	16180	14230	16750				
1974 1	15670	14280	16100				
2	14830	14570	14900				
3	15390	14970	15480				
4	15670	15490	15700				
1975 1	15110	15490	15000				
2	15410	15870	15300				
3	16110	15800	16190				
4	16500	16360	16530				
1976 1	16180	16560	16090				
2	15850	16530	15690				
3	16960	16690	17010				
4	17160	17680	17050				
1977 1	16990	17860	16830				
2	17400	17180	17440				
3	18460	18350	18480				
4	18720	19100	18650				

6. Inland Revenue: Survey of Conveyances

6.1 TECHNICAL DETAILS

(a) Source of data and timing

Based on the "particulars deposited" on the transfer of interest in real property (land and buildings), covering all transactions in one week only, either in October or November, each year.

(b) Types of data and periods covered

Average prices: 1973 to date (latest data available at the time of writing (April 1987) relate to 1984 owing to time lag in publication)

Available data

DATA BREAKDOWNS	DATA TYPE AVERAGE PRICES
HOUSE DATA	
All houses	*
New/Non-new	
Type	
Size	
Age	
Freehold/leasehold	*
LOCAL DATA	
Regions	*
Sub-regions	
Towns	
BUYER DATA	
First-time buyer	
Former owner-occupier	

(c) Frequency

Annual

(d) Geographical coverage

England and Wales, subdivided into official standard regions (defined in Appendix B)

(e) Method of analysis

These surveys are not intended to provide information about house prices as such, but information about the number of transactions and their total market value in one week of each year enables average values to be calculated. It is these figures that are presented in the tables below. The surveys cover *all* transactions, including those carried out at non-market prices.

6.2   LIST OF TABLES

Average prices

6.1   England & Wales and regions: freehold, leasehold and all dwellings. 1973 - 1984

6.3   CROSS-CLASSIFICATIONS OF DATA

(a)   Two-way classifications

See Section 6.2 above for details

(b)   Three-way classifications

None

6.4   PUBLICATIONS

(a)   Data

Inland Revenue Statistics. HMSO, London. Annual

(b)   Description of methodology

Economic Trends. HMSO, London.

Articles published irregularly in *Economic Trends* are as follows:

Dunn, A.T. and Astin, J.A. "Surveys of Conveyancing". May 1974

Dunn, A.T. "Conveyancing Since 1973". September 1976

Dunn, A.T. and Ganguly, A. "Recent Trends in Sales of Land and Buildings".
February 1978

Dunn, A.T. and White, G.C. "Trends in Sales of Land and Buildings, 1973-79".
March 1979

Dunn, A.T. and White, G.C. "Trends in Sales of Land and Buildings, 1973-79".
March 1980

Dunn, A.T. and Rizki, U.M. "Trends in Sales of Land and Buildings, 1977-81".
May 1983

(c)   Supplementary studies

See references in (b) above.

INLAND REVENUE: SURVEY OF CONVEYANCES

AVERAGE PRICES (at completion stage) 1973 –

6.1 ENGLAND & WALES AND REGIONS:
   FREEHOLD, LEASEHOLD AND ALL DWELLINGS

Survey Month	Northern	Yorks & Humberside	North West	East Midlands	West Midlands	East Anglia	South East
FREEHOLD DWELLINGS							
1973 Oct	5540	5117	5769	6801	6960	9119	12818
1974 Oct	6038	6404	6271	7878	8012	9752	13759
1975 Nov	6697	7392	7587	8603	9068	9739	13777
1976 Nov	8300	8587	8166	8663	8996	10101	14262
1977 Nov	9226	8972	9046	9768	10197	11603	16162
1978 Nov	10204	10303	11769	11353	12132	13656	19486
1979 Nov	12374	12996	14627	14370	16076	18171	26882
1980 Nov	15081	14799	15452	16836	18295	21133	28537
1981 Nov	13525	15318	16792	18133	18523	21823	28008
1982 Nov	13289	15289	18318	17006	16885	21667	30442
1983 Nov	17966	17759	20566	20833	20536	25625	33775
1984 Nov	19388	21250	21889	23243	22936	26977	42374
LEASEHOLD DWELLINGS							
1973 Oct	5525	4682	4597	2907	4800	4902	7353
1974 Oct	7429	4800	4804	5495	6573	10000	11840
1975 Nov	6849	6116	5732	4831	6515	7519	7791
1976 Nov	8186	6385	7008	7916	7084	11236	9244
1977 Nov	10811	7064	6734	4464	5316	7353	11157
1978 Nov	9101	7874	7215	6469	7850	11628	11788
1979 Nov	12972	9136	10656	6734	11826	9950	17664
1980 Nov	13812	11680	12401	11885	11668	11673	14859
1981 Nov	14723	13740	14782	10727	13973	8418	16703
1982 Nov	13636	14000	14000	12000	12800	12500	17818
1983 Nov	17000	14706	15769	12500	12143	25000	20000
1984 Nov	18182	16000	17174	20000	16296	20000	23077
ALL DWELLINGS							
1973 Oct	5538	5062	5343	6595	6426	8847	12175
1974 Oct	6239	6142	5684	7803	7626	9762	13547
1975 Nov	6722	7219	6893	8487	8350	9641	13058
1976 Nov	8282	8290	7770	8627	8520	10167	13698
1977 Nov	9462	8733	8130	9487	8763	11434	15670
1978 Nov	10021	9965	9899	11163	11106	13553	18540
1979 Nov	12471	12469	13163	14083	15022	17721	25825
1980 Nov	14861	14408	14325	16307	16512	20153	26722
1981 Nov	13659	15131	16148	17306	17626	19934	26524
1982 Nov	13333	15147	17039	16852	16190	21143	28680
1983 Nov	17826	17368	18987	20500	18857	25600	31818
1984 Nov	19167	20667	20294	23117	21618	26522	38360

			£
Greater London	South West	Wales	England & Wales
10191	11033	5801	8584
13648	11479	7386	9975
12595	11784	7533	10356
13312	12359	9009	10938
15614	13742	10356	12448
20350	16558	11812	14975
28665	22851	13788	19727
30437	23334	15297	21851
28995	26221	14635	21757
31341	25591	15897	22297
36087	28125	17794	26047
53333	30556	19028	29646
11866	7958	5591	6530
9534	8368	6020	7243
9606	6221	6855	7160
10058	9544	7897	8289
13946	10690	9590	8923
14118	12548	10886	10364
24908	17241	10043	15286
22986	15251	11494	15456
23745	17735	12484	17103
23884	21667	13125	18086
28553	20000	12941	19815
38382	20769	13158	23598
10626	10631	5752	8184
12447	11226	6967	9411
11610	11248	7351	9714
12182	12073	8703	10419
15089	13451	10184	11758
17818	16166	11606	14001
27293	22355	12891	18848
27646	22478	14390	20477
26900	25556	14200	20861
28464	25252	15426	21562
33089	27273	16824	24859
46370	29320	17802	28311

7. Inland Revenue: Valuation Office Property Market Report

7.1 TECHNICAL DETAILS

(a) Source of data and timing

Based on reports made by Inland Revenue District Valuers using information derived from the "particulars of deposit" of house sales, coupled with knowledge and experience of local property markets.

(b) Types of data and periods covered

Price ranges: 1983 to date

Available data

DATA BREAKDOWNS	DATA TYPE
	AVERAGE PRICES
HOUSE DATA	
All houses	
New/Non-new	*
Type	*
Size	*
Age	*
LOCAL DATA	
Regions	
Sub-regions	
Towns	*
BUYER DATA	
First-time buyer	
Former owner-occupier	

(c) Frequency

Biannual (information published at end-March and end-October each year)

(d) Geographical coverage

A large number of representative towns in Great Britain located in the following regions: Northern, Yorkshire and Humberside, North West, East Midlands, West Midlands, East Anglia, South East, Inner London, Outer London, South West, Wales, Scotland (included since Spring 1984 only).

(e) Method of analysis

District Valuers throughout Great Britain provide information about *typical* properties, based on all house sales (but excluding those sold at non-market prices). Detailed descriptions of the "typical" properties are given in an Appendix to these technical details. The information is extracted from particulars of deposit (PD) which are approximately three months out of date when received. The Valuers therefore may allow for subsequent market trends when reporting, using such other evidence and impressions as they have, rather than simply adhering to PD data. Data are rounded to nearest £500.

Percentage price changes for individual regions are also published (though these are not reproduced here). The percentage figures for each region are based on a simple average of the mid-points of price ranges for principal towns (no weighting is applied).

7.2 LIST OF TABLES

Price ranges - new dwellings

7.1 -7.7	Great Britain - towns:	Yorkshire and Humberside, North West, Northern by house type/size. Autumn 1983-
7.8 -7.14	Great Britain - towns:	East Midlands, West Midlands, East Anglia by house type/size. Autumn 1983-
7.15-7.21	Great Britain - towns:	Inner London, Outer London by house type/size. Autumn 1983-
7.22-7.28	Great Britain - towns:	South East by house type/size. Autumn 1983-
7.29-7.35	Great Britain - towns:	South West, Wales by house type/size. Autumn 1983-
7.36-7.41	Great Britain - towns:	Scotland by house type/size. Spring 1984-

Price ranges - secondhand dwellings

7.42-7.48	Great Britain - towns:	Yorkshire and Humberside, North West, Northern by house type and age. Autumn 1983-
7.49-7.55	Great Britain - towns:	East Midlands, West Midlands, East Anglia by house type and age. Autumn 1983-
7.56-7.62	Great Britain - towns:	Inner London, Outer London by house type and age. Autumn 1983-
7.63-7.69	Great Britain - towns:	South East by house type and age. Autumn 1983-
7.70-7.76	Great Britain - towns:	South West, Wales by house type and age. Autumn 1983-
7.77-7.82	Great Britain - towns:	Scotland by house type/size and age. Spring 1984-

7.3 CROSS-CLASSIFICATIONS OF DATA

(a) Two-way classifications

None

(b) Three-way classifications

New dwellings by town by house type/size - Tables 7.1-7.41
Secondhand dwellings by town by house type and age - Tables 7.42-7.82

7.4 PUBLICATIONS

(a) Data

Valuation Office Property Market Report. Biannual (Surveyors Publications, London)

(b) Description of methodology

None

(c) Supplementary studies

Valuaton Office Property Market Reports include commentaries provided by District Valuers on developments in their districts.

APPENDIX: PROPERTY TYPE DESCRIPTIONS

New dwellings: England and Wales (current)

1 bed starter house, estate type

> Starter home usually built in blocks of four, back to back on an estate; central heating; very small front and rear gardens; car parking space in communal area.
> Ground Floor - living room, kitchen
> 1st Floor - 1 bedroom, bathroom/wc
> Floor area 50 m sq

2 bed terraced house, estate type

> Terraced house on an estate; single fronted; full central heating; small front and rear gardens; car parking space in communal area.
> Ground Floor - living room, kitchen
> 1st Floor - 2 bedrooms, bathroom/wc
> Floor area 70 m sq

3 bed semi-detached house, estate type

> Semi-detached house on an estate; single fronted; full central heating; front and rear gardens; single car garage.
> Ground Floor - living room/dining room, kitchen
> 1st Floor 3 bedrooms, bathroom/wc
> Floor area 80 m sq

4 bed detached house, estate type

> Detached house on an estate; full central heating; front and rear gardens; double garage.
> Ground Floor - 2/3 living rooms, kitchen, wc
> 1st Floor - 4 bedrooms, bathroom/wc, en suite shower/wc
> Floor area 135 m sq

2 bed flat in 2/3 storey block

> First floor self contained flat in a two or three-storey block; full central heating; car parking space in communal area.
> 1st Floor - living room, 2 bedrooms, kitchen, bathroom/wc
> Floor area 40 m sq

Note: Floor areas

> For all the types of house described above, the floor area shown is the reduced covered area, which is the area of the Ground and First floors based on external measurements. For the flat described above the floor area shown is the effective floor area, which is the area of the living room, bedrooms, kitchen and bathroom/wc and excludes the hallway area.

New dwellings: Scotland (current)

3 bed semi-detached house, estate type

> Typical 2 storey semi-detached 3 bedroom house built by private developers; front and rear garden; full central heating. Overwalls area around 95 m sq. Single garage.

3/4 bed detached house, estate type

> Detached house, similar to semi-detached house described above, but larger. Overwalls area around 110 m sq.

Better quality estate detached house

> Better quality estate detached house, generally on good plot; full central heating; may have 2 bathrooms, cloakroom and wc. Overwalls area around 160 m sq. Double garage.

2 bed flat in 3 (or more) storey block

> First floor 2 bedroom flat in purpose built 3 or more storey blocks or terraces; full central heating. Single garage/parking.

Secondhand dwellings: England and Wales (current)

Pre-1919 terraced house (modernized)

> Terraced house with two-storey wing at rear; built about 1875; small forecourt and rear garden; rear access. Modernisation includes rewiring, new roof, and modern fittings in the kitchen and bathroom/wc.
> Ground Floor - 2 living rooms, kitchen
> 1st Floor - 3 bedrooms, bathroom/wc
> Floor area 100 m sq

Inter-war semi-detached house (modernized)

> Semi-detached house, single fronted with 2 bay windows; built mid-1930s; front and rear gardens; single garage. Modernisation includes rewiring, full central heating and modern fittings in the kitchen and bathroom/wc.
> Ground Floor - 2 living rooms, kitchen
> 1st Floor - 3 bedrooms, bathroom/wc
> Floor area 95 m sq

Post-1960 semi-detached house

> Semi-detached house, single fronted; built early 1960s; full central heating; front and rear gardens; single garage.
> Ground Floor - living room/dining room, kitchen, wc
> 1st Floor - 3 bedrooms, bathroom/wc
> Floor area 95 m sq

Post-1960 detached house

> Detached house on a good estate; built in 1960s; full central heating; good sized front and rear gardens; double garage.
> Ground Floor - 2/3 living rooms, kitchen, wc
> 1st Floor - 4 bedrooms, bathroom/wc
> Floor area 160 m sq

Post-1960 flat in 3 (or more) storey block

> First floor flat in 3 or more storey block; built early 1960s; lift; full central heating; car parking space in communal area.
> 1st Floor - living room, 2 bedrooms, kitchen, bathroom/wc
> Floor area 50 m sq

Note: Floor areas

> For all the types of house described above, the floor area shown is the reduced covered area, which is the area of the Ground and First floors based on external measurements. For the flat described above the floor area shown is the effective floor area, which is the area of the living room, bedrooms, kitchen and bathroom/wc and excludes the hallway area.

Secondhand dwellings: Scotland (current)

2 bed tenement flat, c1900

Typical 2 bedroom first floor tenement flat built around 1900.

3/4 bed semi-detached or terrace house, c1900

Typical 3/4 bedroom semi-detached or terrace house built around 1900.

Mid-1960s 3 bed semi-detached house, estate type

Typical 2 storey semi-detached 3 bedroom house built by private developers; front and rear garden; full central heating. Overwalls area around 95 m sq. Single garage.

Mid-1960s 3/4 bed detached house, estate type

Detached house, similar to semi-detached house described above, but larger. Overwalls area around 110 m sq.

Mid-1960s better quality estate detached house

Better quality estate detached house, generally on good plot; full central heating; may have 2 bathrooms, cloakroom and wc. Overwalls area around 160 m sq. Double garage.

Mid-1960s 2 bed flat

First floor 2 bedroom flat in purpose built 3 or more storey blocks or terraces; full central heating. Single garage/parking.

PRICE RANGES: AUTUMN 1983

7.1 GREAT BRITAIN: TOWNS BY HOUSE TYPE - NEW DWELLINGS

£

	Semi-detached house estate type		Detached house estate type		Detached house individually designed		Flat in 3 (or more) storey block	
	From	To	From	To	From	To	From	To
YORKSHIRE AND HUMBERSIDE								
Harrogate	25000	33000	34000	43000	53000	65000	27000	36500
York	22500	27500	32500	37500	45000	65000		
Bradford	18500	25000	23750	30000	39000	50000	16000	22500
Calderdale	18000	24000	31000	37500	42500	55000	22000	30000
Kirklees	20000	25000	28000	34000	43000	53000		
Leeds	23000	31000	31000	38000	50000	65000	20000	35000
Wakefield	21000	26000	27000	35000	43000	55000		
Barnsley	18500	21500	24000	26000	41000	45000	12500	14500
Doncaster	21000	24000	25000	30000	50000	65000		
Grimsby	17450	20000	22000	27500	45000	55000		
Hull	23000	25000	29500	31500	45000	47500	15000	22500
Humberside	18000	29500	25000	36000	37500	57000	15000	25750
Rotherham	26500	28500	32000	40000	46000	55000	24000	30000
Sheffield	23000	27000	29000	36000	48000	53000	18000	25000
NORTH WEST								
Bolton	28000	32500	34850	44500	67000	74250	17500	21000
Manchester	22500	26250	25000	29500	45500	55000	19000	25000
Oldham	25000	30000	31000	36000	50000	55000	23000	28000
Rochdale	25000	30000	40000	45000	55000	60000		
Salford	26000	28000	31000	40000	53000	60000	19000	32000
Stockport	28000	32500	35000	46000	51500	65000	20000	28500
Wigan	21500	25500	28500	31500	45000	55000		
Blackburn	20500	24500	25750	31000	46500	60000		
Burnley	20000	27500	23000	36000	37500	60000	11000	14750
Lancaster	20750	25750	28000	39000	46000	62000	23500	36000
Preston	21000	25000	29500	34000	45000	52000	17500	20000
Chester	24250	25250	30000	40000	46000	55000	22250	24250
East Cheshire	22500	31000	30000	42000	42000	63000		31000
Liverpool	23000	27000	27000	32000	46000	57000	18500	22000
St Helens	23000	28000						
Sefton	28000	33000	35000	45000	65000	70000	20000	31000
Warrington	26000	28000	36000	38000	55000	57000	20500	23500
Wirral	21500	25000	29500	36000	49000	62500	20000	26000
NORTHERN								
Newcastle	25000	30000	30000	35000	40000	50000	25000	35000
Northumberland	22500	30000	28000	34000	45000	65000	23500	28000
Sunderland	26000	32500	30000	40000	45000	60000	18000	22000
Tyneside			32000	37000	47000	55000		
North Cleveland	25000	30000	30000	35000	45000	54000	14250	19000
South Cleveland	19500	20500	27000	28000	40000	41000	13500	14000
Darlington	25000	28500	30000	38000	50000	60000	23000	28000
Durham	21000	25500	25000	35500	40000	64500		
Carlisle	21000	26000	30000	37000	38000	48000		
South Lakeland	22000	26000	28000	35000				

7.2 GREAT BRITAIN: TOWNS BY HOUSE TYPE - NEW DWELLINGS

£

	Semi-detached house estate type		Detached house estate type		Detached house individually designed		Flat in 3 (or more) storey block	
	From	To	From	To	From	To	From	To
YORKSHIRE AND HUMBERSIDE								
Harrogate	26000	34000	35000	44000	54000	66000	27000	36500
York	22500	27500	32500	37500	45000	65000		
Bradford	18500	25000	24000	30000	39000	50000	16000	22500
Calderdare			31000	37500	50000	60000	22000	30000
Kirklees	20500	25000	28500	34500	44000	54000		
Leeds	23000	32000	32000	42000	50000	60000	20000	35000
Wakefield	21500	26000	27500	38000	44000	56000		
Barnsley	19500	22500	24000	27500	42000	46000	13000	15000
Doncaster	22000	25000	26000	31250				
Grimsby	18000	24500	22000	29500	45000	55000	25000	27000
Hull	23000	25000	29500	31500	45000	47500	15000	22500
Humberside	25000	30000	37500	43000	70000	85000	22000	27500
Rotheram			32000	38000				
Sheffield	23000	27500	30000	37000	48000	54000	18000	25000
NORTH WEST								
Bolton	29750	32500	34850	44500	67000	74250	17500	21000
Manchester	23000	27000	25500	30000	45500	55000	19000	25000
Oldham	25000	30000	31000	36000	50000	55000	23000	28000
Rochdale	27000	31000	42000	46000	57000	60000		
Salford	26000	28000	31000	40000	53000	60000	19000	32000
Stockport	31000	34000	43500	48500	62500	67500	25000	28500
Wigan	21500	25500	28500	31500	45000	55000		
Blackburn	20500	26000	25750	31000	46500	63000		
Burnley	21000	28000	25000	37500	40000	60000		
Lancaster	23000	27000	30000	35000	45000	65000	27500	35000
Preston	25000	28000	34000	40000	50000	55000	20000	22000
Chester	24250	25250	30000	40000	50000	60000	22250	24250
East Cheshire	22500	25000	35000	40000	47500	52500		
Liverpool	24000	28000	23000	33000	46000	57000	19000	22500
St Helens	25000	30000	40000	45000				
Sefton	28000	33000	35000	45000	65000	70000	25000	32000
Warrington	27250	29500	37000	39000	55000	57000	20500	23500
Wirral	22000	25500	30000	36000	49500	63000	20000	26000
NORTHERN								
Newcastle	25000	30000	35000	40000	50000	70000	25000	35000
Northumberland	31000	32500	34000	37000	43000	70000		
Sunderland	27000	36000	34000	41000	48500	66000		
Tyneside	25000	30000	33000	38000	50000	58000		
North Cleveland	25000	27750	30000	32000	45000	52000	14250	19000
South Cleveland	19500	21000	27000	28500	40000	42000	13500	14000
Darlington	25000	30000	30000	38000	52000	64000	24000	29000
Durham	25000	26000	33000	36000	65000	67000		
Carlisle	23000	25000	27000	33000	38000	42000		
South Lakeland	22000	26000	28000	36000				

PRICE RANGES: AUTUMN 1984

7.3 GREAT BRITAIN: TOWNS BY HOUSE TYPE – NEW DWELLINGS

£

	Semi-detached house estate type		Detached house estate type		Detached house individually designed		Flat in 3 (or more) storey block	
	From	To	From	To	From	To	From	To
YORKSHIRE AND HUMBERSIDE								
Harrogate	27000	35000	36000	44500	55000	67000	27500	36500
York	24000	28000	32500	37500	50000	65000		
Bradford	19250	26000	25000	31500	40000	51500	16500	23000
Halifax			32000	39000	50000	65000		
Huddersfield	21000	25500	29000	35000	46000	56000		
Leeds	23500	33000	33000	43000	50000	61000	21000	36000
Wakefield	22000	26000	28000	39000	44000	56000		
Barnsley	19500	22500	24000	27500	42000	46000	13000	15000
Doncaster	23000	26000	27000	32500				
Grimsby	19000	25000	25000	34000	45000	55000	27000	28000
Hull	23500	26000	29500	34500	45000	47500	15500	23000
Beverley	25000	32500	37500	45000	70000	85000	22000	30000
Rotheram			31000	38000				
Sheffield	24000	28250	32500	39000	48000	55000		
NORTH WEST								
Bolton	30000	32750	35000	45000	69000	78000	17750	21250
Manchester	23500	28000	26000	30750	47000	56750	18000	24000
Oldham	25500	31000	32000	39000	50000	55000	23000	28000
Bury	29000	33000	44000	47500	60000	70000		
Salford/Trafford	26500	28500	31500	40000	55000	65000	19000	32000
Stockport	32250	35250	46500	51500	70000	75000	25000	28500
Wigan	22500	27000	29500	33000	50000	57500		
Blackburn	21500	27000	26500	32000	48000	65000		
Burnley	21000	28000	25000	37500	40000	60000		
Lancaster	23000	27000	30000	35000	45000	65000	27500	35000
Preston	25000	28000	34000	40000	50000	55000	20000	22000
Chester	25250	25400	35000	43000	57000	65000	22250	24250
Crewe	22500	25000	35000	40000	48500	53500		
Liverpool	24500	29000	26000	35000	46000	57000	19000	25000
St Helens	30000	35000	40000	45000				
Southport	29000	33000	36000	45000	65000	70000	26500	34000
Warrington	27000	29000	38000	41000	56000	58000	21500	24500
Wirral	22000	26000	30000	36500	50000	64000	20000	26000
NORTHERN								
Newcastle	25000	30000	35000	42000	50000	70000	30500	40000
Morpeth	31000	33500	34000	38000	43000	72000		
Sunderland	28000	36500	35000	42750	48500	69750		
Whitley Bay	25500	31000	34000	39000	50000	60000		
Stockton	27000	30000	31000	33000	45000	52000	14250	19000
Middlesbrough	20000	21500	27500	29000	42000	44000	13500	14500
Darlington	25000	32000	30000	38000	55000	67000	24000	29000
Durham	25000	27000	33000	37000	65000	67000		
Carlisle	23500	25500	27500	33500	38000	42000		
Barrow	24000	28000	30000	38000				

PRICE RANGES: SPRING 1985

7.4 GREAT BRITAIN: TOWNS BY HOUSE TYPE - NEW DWELLINGS

£

	Semi-detached house estate type		Detached house estate type		Detached house individually designed		Flat in 3 (or more) storey block	
	From	To	From	To	From	To	From	To
YORKSHIRE AND HUMBERSIDE								
Harrogate	27500	36000	36000	44500	57000	72000	28000	37000
York	26000	28000	33000	37500	52500	65000		
Bradford	19750	27000	25750	32500	41000	52750	16750	23000
Halifax			32000	39000	50000	65000		
Huddersfield	22000	26500	30000	36000	47000	57000		
Leeds	23500	34000	33000	44000	51000	62000	22000	36000
Wakefield	22500	26500	28000	39000	44000	56000		
Barnsley	19500	23000	24000	28000	42000	46000	13500	15000
Doncaster	24000	27000	32000	35000				
Grimsby	19000	27000	27000	40000	45000	60000	27000	30000
Hull	24000	26500	31000	36000	46000	48500	15500	23000
Beverley	25000	35000	37500	47500	70000	85000	22000	32500
Rotherham			32000	39000				
Sheffield	25000	30000	32500	39000	48000	55000		
NORTH WEST								
Bolton	30000	32750	35000	45000	69000	78000	17750	21250
Manchester	23750	28500	26250	31250	47000	56750	18000	24000
Oldham	25500	32000	32000	43000	50000	56000	23000	28000
Bury	30000	35000	44000	50000	65000	75000		
Salford/Trafford	26500	30000	33000	41000	55000	70000	19000	33250
Stockport	33250	36250	47750	53000	70000	75000	25500	29500
Wigan	23000	27500	30000	33500	50000	58000		
Blackburn	23000	27000	27000	33000	48000	65000	23500	34000
Burnley	22000	30000	27000	39000	40000	60000		
Lancaster	25000	30000	32000	37000	45000	65000	19000	26000
Preston	26000	29000	35000	42000	52000	58000	20000	22000
Chester	25500	28000	35000	43000	57000	68000	22250	24250
Crewe	23000	25500	36000	41000	49500	54500		
Liverpool	24500	30000	26000	35000	47500	58000	19000	25000
St Helens	30000	35000						
Southport	29000	33000	36000	45000	65000	70000	27500	35000
Warrington	27000	29000	38000	41000	56000	58000	21500	24500
Birkenhead	22500	27500	30000	37500	50000	64000	20000	26000
NORTHERN								
Newcastle	25000	30000	32500	42000	50000	75000	30500	42000
Morpeth	31500	34000	34500	38500	44000	73000		
Sunderland	28500	36500	35500	43000	49500	72000		
Whitley Bay	25500	31000	34000	39000	50000	60000		
Stockton	27000	30000	31000	33000	45000	52000	14250	19000
Middlesbrough	20000	22000	28000	30000	42500	44500	13500	15000
Darlington	25000	32000	31000	38000	55000	67000	24000	29000
Durham	25500	27500	35000	39000	67000	69000		
Carlisle	25000	27500	24000	35000	38500	42500		
Barrow	25000	29000	30000	38000				

7.5 GREAT BRITAIN: TOWNS BY HOUSE TYPE/SIZE - NEW DWELLINGS

£

	1 Bed Starter house estate type		2 Bed Terraced house estate type		3 Bed Semi-detached house estate type		4 Bed Detached house estate type		2 Bed Flat in 2/3 storey block	
	From	To	From	To	From	To	From	To	From	To
YORKSHIRE AND HUMBERSIDE										
Harrogate	20500	23500	23500	28000	28000	33000	57000	65000	21000	24000
York	16500	19750	21250	24500	26250	32250	48500	54000	33000	40000
Bradford	15000	16000	18000	21000	18500	25500	42500	54000	17000	24000
Halifax	17000	20000	18000	24000	22500	25000	55000	60000		
Huddersfield			16000	20000	20250	25500	44500	50000		
Leeds	19500	23000	22000	28000	25500	35500	50000	66000	21000	32000
Wakefield	16500	17500	18500	20500	22500	26000	42500	58000	18000	23000
Barnsley	16000	18000	20250	22250	23500	25500	47000	49000	16500	18500
Doncaster	17350	21000	21500	24000	23500	27500	38500	60000	18000	22000
Grimsby	14000	15000	18500	20500	20000	22000	34000	38000	26000	30000
Hull	16000	17000	20000	21000	25000	28000	42000	47000	25000	28000
Beverley	14000	15000	20000	22000	27000	33000	50000	55000	27000	30000
Rotherham	16500	18000	20000	22500	25500	28500	42000	44000	18500	19500
Sheffield	15500	19000	17000	22000	25000	30000	44000	52000	17500	23000
NORTH WEST										
Bolton	13500	17250	17000	20000	17000	22500	46750	60500	11500	13250
Manchester	20850	24000	25000	32950	25500	33500	40500	44500	17000	23600
Oldham			21000	23000	27000	31500	60000	65000		
Bury	14500	18500	20500	24250	26500	29000	55000	65000	21000	23500
Salford/Trafford	20000	21000	23000	28000	27000	30500	50000	70000	17000	28000
Stockport	20200	23500	26000	28000	30500	32000	62500	67500	21000	28000
Wigan	13500	17000	20000	25000	25000	30000	47500	55000	32500	32500
Blackburn			17950	18995	18500	23500	40000	52000	15000	23200
Burnley	18000	20000	21000	25000	23000	30000	42000	54000	17000	19500
Lancaster	17000	19000	21000	23000	25000	27000	43500	48500	17500	24500
Preston	17500	18500	22750	23250	27000	29995	64500	66000	23000	25000
Chester	18500	22500	25500	27500	24000	29500	46000	52000	19500	22500
Crewe	18000	18000	19000	19850	19950	23995	50300	50300	18300	18300
Liverpool	14500	15500	17000	23000	24000	29500	44500	60000	16500	21500
St Helens	18750	19500	21000	25000	27000	28500	47000	50000		
Southport	18250	19000	23000	25500	27000	29950	52500	56500	24000	28000
Warrington	14500	15000	23000	25000	25000	27000	50000	55000	15000	16000
Birkenhead	18500	22000	23000	25500	27500	29500	49500	57250	24500	25500
NORTHERN										
Newcastle	19000	23000	21000	25000	27000	32250	55000	80000	30500	43000
Morpeth	17500	19000			31500	34000	44000	73000		
Whitley Bay	17000	22500	25500	28000	26000	32000	55000	62500	21000	29000
Stockton			21000	24500	26500	27500	41000	49750	14000	14500
Middlesbrough	16000	18000	20000	22000	27000	28000	50000	55000	12500	15000
Darlington	16500	18750	19000	20000	23000	26000	42000	46000	16500	22000
Durham					30000	30000	60000	65000		
Carlisle			22000	24000	23000	25000	49000	51000	21000	23000
Barrow	15000	16250	19500	20500	26000	30000	45000	52000		

INLAND REVENUE: VALUATION OFFICE PROPERTY MARKET REPORTS

PRICE RANGES: SPRING 1986

7.6 GREAT BRITAIN: TOWNS BY HOUSE TYPE/SIZE - NEW DWELLINGS

£

	1 Bed Starter house estate type		2 Bed Terraced house estate type		3 Bed Semi-detached house estate type		4 Bed Detached house estate type		2 Bed Flat in 2/3 storey block	
	From	To	From	To	From	To	From	To	From	To
YORKSHIRE AND HUMBERSIDE										
Harrogate	21000	25000	23500	28000	27000	33000	52500	60000	20000	30000
York	16500	19750	21500	25500	26250	32250	48500	58000		
Bradford	15750	17000	18000	22500	19500	28000	45000	57000	17000	24000
Halifax	17000	21500	19000	24000	23000	26500	56000	62000		
Huddersfield			16500	20500	24000	27250	47000	52500		
Leeds	16500	23000	22000	28000	27000	35500	50000	66000	21500	32000
Wakefield	17000	17500	19000	21000	24000	27000	45000	60000	18000	23000
Barnsley	16000	18000	20250	22250	24500	26500	48000	52000	17500	19000
Doncaster	16250	19500	19500	22750	25500	29000	38500	60000	17750	26750
Grimsby	14000	15000	18500	21000	20000	22000	34000	40000	25000	30000
Hull	16500	17500	21000	22500	25000	28500	42000	47000	25000	28000
Beverley	14000	15000	20000	22000	27000	33000	50000	55000	27000	30000
Rotheram	16500	18000	20000	22500	25500	28500	42500	48000	19250	20000
Sheffield	16000	19000	19000	25000	26000	32000	44000	52000	17500	23000
NORTH WEST										
Bolton	14000	17250	17000	20750	18000	23500	47500	61000	12000	14500
Manchester	16000	22000	20000	34500	25500	33500	40500	44500	17000	23600
Oldham			21000	23000	27000	31500	60000	65000		
Bury	14500	18500	21000	25000	26500	29500	55000	67500	21000	24000
Salford/Trafford	19000	25000	21000	28000	29500	40000	52500	75000	17000	28000
Stockport	20500	24250	26250	28750	31500	33500	62500	68250	23000	30000
Wigan	15000	17000	13500	18250	24000	27000	60000	64000		
Blackburn	16500	18000	18250	19500	18950	24500	42000	55000	15250	25000
Burnley	18000	20000	21000	25000	23000	30000	42000	55000	17000	20000
Lancaster	17500	19500	21500	23500	26000	28000	47000	53000	18000	25000
Preston	17500	18500	23000	23500	27000	30000	64500	67000	23000	25000
Chester	18500	22500	25500	28500	25000	30000	50000	62500	19500	25000
Crewe	18000	18000	18500	21000	20500	24000	50000	53000	18000	18500
Liverpool	15000	17000	18000	24000	23500	30000	44500	64000	16500	25000
St Helens	18750	19500	23000	25000	27000	29000	47000	50000		
Southport	18500	19250	23500	25500	27250	30250	52500	56500	24000	28000
Warrington	14500	15000	23000	25000	25000	28000	50000	60000	16000	17500
Birkenhead	18500	22000	23000	25500	27500	29500	49500	57250	24500	25500
NORTHERN										
Newcastle	19000	23000	21250	26950	27000	32500	55000	80000	30500	46500
Morpeth	17500	19500			32500	35000	45000	75000		
Sunderland			20000	24550	27500	28500	44250	58000		
Whitley Bay	17000	23500	25500	28000	26000	32000	55000	63000	22000	30000
Stockton			21000	25000	27000	29000	45000	56000	14000	15000
Middlesbrough	16000	18000	20000	22000	27000	28500	50000	55000	12500	15000
Darlington	16500	18750	19250	20750	24000	27500	42500	47500	16500	22000
Durham	18000	20000	21000	23000	29500	31000	60000	65000	16000	18000
Carlisle			22000	24000	24000	27500	50000	55000	22000	25000
Barrow	15750	17000	20500	23000	28000	31000	48000	55000	20000	21000

PRICE RANGES: AUTUMN 1986

7.7 GREAT BRITAIN: TOWNS BY HOUSE TYPE/SIZE - NEW DWELLINGS

£

	1 Bed Starter house estate type		2 Bed Terraced house estate type		3 Bed Semi-detached house estate type		4 Bed Detached house estate type		2 Bed Flat in 2/3 storey block	
	From	To	From	To	From	To	From	To	From	To
YORKSHIRE AND HUMBERSIDE										
Harrogate	21000	25000	24000	28000	28000	34000	55000	60000	22000	32000
York	16750	19750	22750	26250	30000	34000	52500	63500		
Bradford	16500	18000	18000	24000	20500	29000	47500	60000	17000	24000
Halifax	18000	22500	20000	24000	24250	27500	57500	64500		
Huddersfield			18000	22000	25500	28000	47500	55000		
Leeds	17000	23000	22000	28000	28000	36000	52500	67500	21000	35000
Wakefield	17000	17500	20000	22000	25000	29000	45000	62500	18000	23000
Barnsley	16500	18500	20250	22500	24500	27000	49000	55000	18000	20000
Doncaster	17000	20000	19500	23000	25500	29000	40000	65000	17750	26750
Grimsby	15500	16500	18500	21000	21000	24000	34000	41000	27500	31000
Hull	16500	17500	21500	23000	25500	31500	43500	48500	25000	28000
Beverley	14000	16000	21000	23500	27000	33000	50000	55000	27000	30000
Rotheram	16500	18000	20500	23000	26000	29000	45000	52000	19250	20000
Sheffield	16000	19000	20000	26500	27000	33000	45000	53000	17500	23000
NORTH WEST										
Bolton	14000	17250	18000	21500	19000	24750	48500	60500	12000	14500
Manchester	16000	22000	17500	36500	22500	37500	45000	60000	17000	25000
Oldham			21000	23000	27000	31500	60000	65000		
Bury	14500	18000	21500	26500	27000	30000	55000	67500	21000	24000
Salford/Trafford	19000	25000	21000	28000	32000	37000	52500	76000	17000	28000
Stockport	20950	25000	26500	29500	32500	34250	64000	72250	23500	31000
Wigan	15000	17500	13750	18500	25000	27500	60000	64000		
Blackburn	16500	18500	18750	20000	19500	25000	42000	56000	15750	25500
Burnley	18500	20500	21500	25500	24000	31000	46000	60000	17000	20000
Lancaster	18000	20000	22000	24000	26500	28500	48000	56000	18500	25000
Preston	18000	20000	23500	24000	28000	31500	65000	67500	23000	25000
Chester	18500	22500	26000	30000	25000	32000	60000	70000	22000	26000
Crewe			19750	21500	22500	25500	50000	58000	20000	20500
Liverpool	15000	17000	18500	25000	23500	30000	44500	64000	16500	25500
St Helens	18750	19500	23000	25000	27000	29000	47000	50000		
Southport	19250	20000	25000	28000	28000	32000	48500	57500	25000	29000
Warrington	14500	15000	23000	25000	27500	30000	57500	67500	17500	20000
Birkenhead	18500	22000	23000	25500	27500	29500	49500	66500	22500	25500
NORTHERN										
Newcastle	19500	23500	22000	30000	37500	45000	50000	75000	25000	35000
Morpeth	17900	21000			32500	36000	47500	80000		
Sunderland	17600	18000	20500	25000	27500	30000	46000	60000		
North Tyneside	17000	23500	25500	28000	26000	32000	55000	63000	22000	30000
Stockton			21000	25000	27000	29500	46000	56000	14000	15000
Middlesbrough	16000	18000	20000	22000	27000	28500	50000	55000	12500	15000
Darlington	16500	18750	19250	25750	24000	27500	42500	47500	16500	22000
Durham	18500	20500	21500	23500	31000	31000	61500	67000	16400	18500
Carlisle			26000	28000	27000	30000	52000	57000	24000	27000
Barrow			20500	24000	28500	31500	51000	58000		

80

PRICE RANGES: AUTUMN 1983

7.8 GREAT BRITAIN: TOWNS BY HOUSE TYPE - NEW DWELLINGS

£

	Semi-detached house estate type		Detached house estate type		Detached house individually designed		Flat in 3 (or more) storey block	
	From	To	From	To	From	To	From	To
EAST MIDLANDS								
Boston	20000	25000	23500	32500	37500	52500		
Lincoln	21000	25000	26000	32500	40000	55000		
Mansfield	19500	23500	24000	27500	45000	54000		
South Notts C	19000	28000	26500	38000	55000	85000	14000	20500
Chesterfield	21500	27500	31000	38000	46000	57000		
Derby	19500	24000	21500	35000	35000	65000	13000	17000
Kettering	20000	24000	30000	35000	48000	60000		
Leicester	23000	25000	28000	37000	35000	50000		
Northampton	21000	28000	28000	32000	49000	57000		
N Leicestershire	22500	24000	29000	34000	46500	65000		
S Leicestershire	23000	28000	33000	38000	42000	55000		
W Derbyshire	20500	28500	24500	35000	40000	50000	16500	27500
WEST MIDLANDS								
Birmingham	28500	32000	34000	37000	62000	75000	20000	23000
Coventry	21000	32500	25000	39000	39000	61000	13500	32500
Dudley	24000	28000	28000	38000	50000	75000	16500	27500
Sandwell							13000	16000
Walsall	22000	26500	27000	33000	41500	48500	13500	18500
Wolverhampton	21500	25000	27500	35000	50000	65000		
Lichfield	21500	27000	25500	37000	47500	72500	20000	37500
N Warwickshire	19500	24000	25000	34000	33000	55000	12000	13000
Shropshire	20000	25500	23000	29500	47500	63000		
Stafford	21000	25000	30000	35000	50000	65000		
Stoke-on-Trent	19500	24000	25500	31500	43500	56000		
Warwick			36500	42000	57500	65000		
H'ford & W Worcs	24000	29000	35000	40000	55000	60000	22000	25000
E Worcester	20000	25000	25000	42500	45000	73500	16000	27500
EAST ANGLIA								
Cambridge	23000	35000	29500	40000	48000	69000	24500	40000
Peterborough	18000	25000	22000	35000	38000	64000	15000	25000
Ipswich	23500	28000	29000	35500	50000	60000		
Bury St Edmunds	22500	30000	27500	37500	40000	55000	17500	22500
N Norfolk	19500	26000	25000	35000	42500	60000		
W Norfolk	21000	25000	28000	30000	41000	44000	25000	36000
Norwich	25000	29000	29950	40000	47500	60000		

PRICE RANGES: SPRING 1984

7.9 GREAT BRITAIN: TOWNS BY HOUSE TYPE - NEW DWELLINGS

£

	Semi-detached house estate type		Detached house estate type		Detached house individually designed		Flat in 3 (or more) storey block	
	From	To	From	To	From	To	From	To
EAST MIDLANDS								
Boston	20500	23500	22500	28500	40000	52500		
Lincoln	22000	25000	28000	33000	45000	55000		
Mansfield	20000	24500	25000	29000	46500	56250		
Nottingham	23000	25000	36000	38500	52500	85000		
S Nottinghamshire	24000	28000	32000	38000	55000	75000	16000	19500
Chesterfield	26350	29000	37500	40000	48500	56000		
Derby	20000	25000	23000	35000	38000	65000	13000	17000
Kettering	21000	25000	32000	38000	48000	62000		
Leicester	24000	26000	29000	38000	47000	50000		
Northampton	22000	30000	30000	40000	50000	62500		
N Leicestershire	25000	27500	32000	36000	55000	70000		
S Leicestershire	23500	28500	33500	38000	45000	60000		
W Derbyshire	27500	29500	30000	35000	50000	53500	25000	27500
WEST MIDLANDS								
Birmingham	28500	32000	34000	37000	62000	75000	20000	23000
Coventry	20000	32500	27000	39000	40000	65000	14500	32500
Dudley	24500	30000	28500	39000	55000	80000	17000	27000
Sandwell	22000	25000	25000	30000	32500	35000	13000	18000
Walsall	22000	26500	27000	33000	41500	52000	13500	18500
Wolverhampton	22000	25500	27500	35500	50000	65000		
Lichfield	26000	28000	35000	40000	50000	60000	25000	28000
N Warwickshire	20000	25000	25000	34000	35000	55000		
Shropshire	22000	26000	25500	29500	52000	63000		
Stafford	24000	28000	33000	38000	50000	65000		
Stoke-on-Trent	20000	25000	26000	32000	44000	56500		
Warwick			37250	43000	60000	67500		
H'ford & W Worcs	24000	27000	30500	36000	55000	75000	22000	25000
E Worcester	20000	25000	25000	40000	47500	60000	18000	27500
EAST ANGLIA								
Cambridge							32000	38000
Peterborough	20000	30000	25000	44500	45000	65000	15000	25000
Ipswich	25000	30000	30500	38000	52500	65000	18500	27500
Bury St Edmunds	22500	31500	27500	39000	40000	57500	18500	23500
N Norfolk	20500	28000	26500	37000	47500	69000	28000	32000
W Norfolk	24500	26000	30000	33000	44000	49000	25000	36000
Norwich	27500	30000	35000	42500	50000	60000	25000	30000

7.10 GREAT BRITAIN: TOWNS BY HOUSE TYPE - NEW DWELLINGS

£

	Semi-detached house estate type		Detached house estate type		Detached house individually designed		Flat in 3 (or more) storey block	
	From	To	From	To	From	To	From	To
EAST MIDLANDS								
Boston	20500	24000	22500	28500	40000	52500		
Lincoln	23000	25000	29000	34000	45000	55000		
Mansfield	20000	25000	25000	36500	46500	60000		
Nottingham	24000	26000	35000	45000	55000	95500		
Carlton (Notts)	25000	28000	33000	39000	60000	80000	17500	21000
Chesterfield	26750	29750	28500	33500	50000	59500		
Derby	21000	25500	26000	35000	40000	65000	13000	17000
Kettering	23000	28000	33000	39000	50000	65000		
Leicester	25000	27000	30000	39000	45000	55000		
Northampton	24000	31000	32000	45000	52500	65000		
Loughborough			32000	36000	55000	70000		
Hinckley	25000	30000	35000	39500	46500	61500		
Buxton	28250	30000	32500	35000	51000	55000	25000	27500
WEST MIDLANDS								
Birmingham	29000	32500	34500	37500	62000	75000	20000	23000
Coventry	20000	34000	27000	39000	40000	65000	15000	34000
Dudley	25000	31000	30000	40000	57000	80000	17500	28000
Sandwell	22000	25000	25000	30000	32500	35000	13000	18000
Walsall	22000	26500	27000	33000	41500	52000	13500	18500
Wolverhampton	22250	25750	27500	36500	50000	67500		
Lichfield	27250	28750	36750	42500	52500	61500	26000	29000
Nuneaton	20000	27500	28000	35000	35000	55000		
Shrewsbury	23000	27000	26000	31000	54000	65000		
Stafford	24500	29000	34000	38000	50000	65000		
Stoke-on-Trent	20000	25000	26000	32000	42000	56500		
Leamington Spa			38500	44500	62000	70000		
Worcester	25000	28000	31000	38000	55000	75000	22000	25000
Kidderminster	20000	25000	27500	40000	50000	60000	19000	27500
EAST ANGLIA								
Cambridge	35000	45000	45000	55000	80000	95000	35000	55000
Peterborough	20000	30000	30000	45000	50000	65000	18500	25000
Ipswich	26000	31500	32000	40500	56000	70000	20000	29000
Bury St Edmunds	23500	32000	28000	39000	40000	58000	19000	24000
King's Lynn	25000	31000	37500	39500	49000	51000		
Norwich	29000	31000	37500	45000	50000	60000	26000	30000

PRICE RANGES: SPRING 1985

7.11 GREAT BRITAIN: TOWNS BY HOUSE TYPE - NEW DWELLINGS

£

	Semi-detached house estate type		Detached house estate type		Detached house individually designed		Flat in 3 (or more) storey block	
	From	To	From	To	From	To	From	To
EAST MIDLANDS								
Boston	22000	25000	25000	30000	45000	55000		
Lincoln	23000	25000	29000	35000	45000	55000		
Mansfield	22500	26000	25000	36500	46500	60000		
Nottingham	24000	26000	35000	45000	55000	96500	24500	26500
Carlton (Notts)	26000	29000	34000	40000	60000	80000	18000	22000
Chesterfield	27250	29750	29250	34000	50000	52000	17000	25000
Derby	22000	25500	26000	35000	45000	67500	14000	17500
Kettering	23000	28000	33000	39000	50000	65000		
Leicester	25500	27500	30600	39750	46000	56500		
Northampton	25000	32000	35000	47500	55000	70000		
Loughborough			32000	36000	55000	77000		
Wigston	26500	31500	41500	43000	49000	61500		
Buxton	28000	30000	32500	35000	51000	57500	25000	28000
WEST MIDLANDS								
Birmingham	29000	35000	35000	42500	60000	80000	21000	27500
Coventry	22000	34000	30000	44000	44000	67000	15000	34000
Dudley	25000	31000	30000	40000	57000	80000	17500	28000
Sandwell	25000	30000	30000	37000	40000	45000	13000	18000
Walsall	22750	27500	28000	34000	42000	52000	13500	18500
Wolverhampton	22250	26000	27500	36500	50000	67500		
Lichfield	27250	29000	36750	43000	52500	62500	26000	29500
Nuneaton	20000	28000	28000	36000	38000	60000	15000	18000
Shrewsbury	24000	27000	28000	33000	55000	65000		
Stafford	24500	29000	34000	39000	50000	65000		
Stoke-on-Trent	20000	25000	26000	32000	45000	60000		
Leamington Spa			39500	46000	64000	72000		
Worcester	26000	30000	31000	40000	56000	75000	22000	25000
Kidderminster	20000	25000	25000	42500	50000	65000	19000	30000
EAST ANGLIA								
Cambridge	37000	48000	47500	59000	83000	90000	36500	57000
Peterborough	23000	31000	26000	47000	40000	77000		
Ipswich	28000	33000	33000	41500	58000	75000	22000	30000
Bury St Edmunds	29000	33000	31500	40000	40000	60000	20000	25000
King's Lynn	25000	29000	33000	39000	48000	60000		
Norwich	29500	31500	37500	45000	52500	67500	26000	32500

7.12 GREAT BRITAIN: TOWNS BY HOUSE TYPE/SIZE - NEW DWELLINGS

£

	1 Bed Starter house estate type		2 Bed Terraced house estate type		3 Bed Semi-detached house estate type		4 Bed Detached house estate type		2 Bed Flat in 2/3 storey block	
	From	To	From	To	From	To	From	To	From	To
EAST MIDLANDS										
Boston	16000	17000	18000	19000	19000	21000	37500	40000	15000	16500
Lincoln	16000	16500	19000	19500	23000	24000	47000	48000		
Mansfield	16500	17250	23500	24250	24000	26000	47500	60000		
Nottingham	16250	17000	20250	21250	32250	33250	70000	77500	16500	17000
Carlton (Notts)	20000	21000	22000	24000	27000	30000	47500	67500	19500	23000
Chesterfield	17000	20000	19750	23750	26500	29750	43000	60000	17000	25000
Derby	13750	15250	18000	22000	22000	25500	45000	72500	15000	18500
Kettering			21000	22000	25000	28000	55000	67000	33000	35000
Leicester	18000	19000	22000	24750	27000	29000	55000	60000	17000	18000
Northampton	16000	21000	18500	22500	24000	34000	50000	65000	17500	20500
Loughborough	16950	18950	20000	23000	24000	27500	54000	59000		
Buxton	15750	17750	19000	22000	29000	31000	52500	58000	26000	30000
WEST MIDLANDS										
Birmingham	17750	22000	22500	27750	25000	34500	42500	62500	15000	25000
Coventry	15750	17750	21500	23500	28000	33500	60000	65000	25000	26000
Dudley	16500	20000	20000	23000	25500	29500	47500	57500	15000	25000
Sandwell	15500	17000	23000	24500	27000	30000	45000	50000	15000	18000
Walsall	18250	19750	19750	21250	23500	30000	44000	54000	14000	19500
Wolverhampton	15000	16250	17500	21000	20000	25000			17500	20500
Lichfield	17250	19500	19750	23750	26500	30000	51000	61000	16350	19000
Nuneaton	16000	18500	18000	22000	23500	30000	44000	55000	16000	20000
Shrewsbury	13500	16000	19500	21000	22500	27000	40000	46000	18500	21000
Stafford	16000	18000	18000	20000	21000	24000	45000	55000	15000	17000
Stoke-on-Trent	15000	17500	17500	19000	21000	25000	39000	55000	15000	17500
Leamington Spa			22500	25000			63000	68000		
Worcester	19500	21000	22000	24250	25750	28000	52500	65000	22000	24000
Kidderminster	16000	18000	18000	21250	19000	24000	40000	60000	15500	17000
EAST ANGLIA										
Cambridge	22500	32500	31000	34500	38500	40000			34500	48500
Peterborough	15000	22000	20000	25000	25000	28000	46000	60000	22000	42000
Ipswich	20750	21500	22000	27500	27500	34500	48500	65000	23000	27500
Bury St Edmunds	20000	23000	26500	29000	29500	32500	43000	50000	28500	32500
King's Lynn	18500	21000	19000	25000	27000	33000	50000	60000	24000	28000
Norwich	20000	22000	25500	28000	30000	32500	52500	67500	26500	31000

PRICE RANGES: SPRING 1986

7.13 GREAT BRITAIN: TOWNS BY HOUSE TYPE/SIZE - NEW DWELLINGS

£

	1 Bed Starter house estate type		2 Bed Terraced house estate type		3 Bed Semi-detached house estate type		4 Bed Detached house estate type		2 Bed Flat in 2/3 storey block	
	From	To	From	To	From	To	From	To	From	To
EAST MIDLANDS										
Boston	16000	17000	18500	19500	19500	21500	37500	40000	16000	17500
Lincoln	16000	16500	19500	20000	23500	24500	48000	50000	20000	35000
Mansfield	16750	18000	24300	26300	25500	29000	45500	67000		
Nottingham	16500	17500	20750	21750	33500	37000	71500	79000	17000	18000
Carlton (Notts)	20000	21000	23000	24500	28000	31000	55000	70000	20500	23500
Chesterfield	17500	20500	20750	24750	26750	30000	43000	60000	17250	25000
Derby	14000	15500	18000	22000	22500	26000	45000	75000	15000	18500
Kettering			21000	21950	24000	29000	50000	65000	23500	35000
Leicester	19000	21500	22750	25000	27250	30000	62500	67500	18000	21000
Northampton	16500	21500	19000	23000	25000	35000	52500	67500	18000	21000
Loughborough	17500	19500	20000	23000	25000	29000	55000	65000	15000	17000
Buxton	15750	17750	19500	23000	29000	31000	53500	59500	26000	30000
WEST MIDLANDS										
Birmingham	17750	22000	22500	29000	25000	30000	57500	62500	16000	25000
Coventry	16000	18000	22000	24000	28000	33500	55000	70000	21000	26000
Dudley	17000	20500	21000	24000	26000	30000	47500	60000	15000	25000
Sandwell	15500	17000	23000	24500	27000	30000	45000	50000	15000	18000
Walsall	18250	19750	20000	21750	24200	31000	45300	55600	14000	19500
Wolverhampton	15250	16500	17750	21750	21000	26500			17500	22000
Lichfield	17500	19750	20500	24500	27000	30500	52000	62500	16500	19250
Nuneaton	16000	18500	18000	22000	23500	31000	47000	58000	16000	20000
Shrewsbury	14000	16500	19500	21500	22500	27000	41000	47500	18500	22000
Stafford	17000	19000	19000	21000	22000	25000	47500	57500	18000	20000
Stoke-on-Trent	15250	17750	17500	19000	21500	25500	39000	55000	15000	17500
Leamington Spa			23500	26500	28500	32000	66000	72000		
Worcester	20000	21500	22000	25000	27500	31000	54750	70000	22000	24000
Kidderminster	16000	18000	18000	22500	20000	26000	40000	62500	16000	19000
EAST ANGLIA										
Cambridge	31000	35000	36000	42000	45000	50000	75000	100000	38000	70000
Peterborough	17750	22950	21000	25500	25000	28500	47000	66000	23000	42000
Ipswich	21000	22250	23000	28000	29000	36000	51000	67500	23500	28000
Bury St Edmunds	21750	24750	27000	30000	31000	35000	48500	56500	29500	34000
King's Lynn	17300	21000	22000	26000	26500	33500	52750	60000	24000	28000
Norwich	22000	24000	26950	29250	33000	35000	52000	70000	27000	32000

7.14 GREAT BRITAIN: TOWNS BY HOUSE TYPE/SIZE - NEW DWELLINGS

£

	1 Bed Starter house estate type		2 Bed Terraced house estate type		3 Bed Semi-detached house estate type		4 Bed Detached house estate type		2 Bed Flat in 2/3 storey block	
	From	To	From	To	From	To	From	To	From	To
EAST MIDLANDS										
Boston	16500	17500	19000	20000	21000	23500	38000	41000	16500	18000
Lincoln	17000	17500	22500	23000	25500	26500	49000	51000	22500	37500
Mansfield	16750	18000	24300	26300	26000	29000	45500	69000		
Nottingham	16750	17750	21000	22000	33500	37000	71500	79000	18000	19000
Carlton (Notts)	20000	21000	23000	24000	29000	32500	57500	72500	20500	23500
Chesterfield	17500	20500	20750	24750	26000	31000	43500	61000	17250	25000
Derby	14500	16000	18500	22500	23500	27500	47500	80000	15000	18500
Kettering			23500	25000	30000	32500	55000	75000	25000	37000
Leicester	20000	21500	26000	28500	31000	34500	65000	70000	19000	22000
Northampton	17000	22000	20000	25000	26000	38000	52500	70000	18000	23000
Loughborough	17500	19500	21000	24000	26000	30000	57500	67500	16000	18000
Buxton	16250	18250	21500	26000	30000	33000	55000	62000	27500	32000
WEST MIDLANDS										
Birmingham	18100	23000	22950	29500	29600	38950	58500	67500	17000	27500
Coventry	16500	18500	22500	25000	28500	34000	55000	70000	21000	26000
Dudley	18000	21500	22000	25000	28000	33000	50000	65000	15000	25000
Sandwell	15000	17500	23500	25500	27500	31000	46000	52000	15000	18000
Walsall	18500	20000	20500	23000	24750	32500	46000	58000	14500	21000
Wolverhampton	15250	16500	18000	22000	22000	27500			17500	22000
Lichfield	18500	21000	21500	25500	28500	31500	56000	67000	17750	20500
Nuneaton	17500	20000	20000	24250	23500	31000	47000	58000	17000	21000
Shrewsbury	16000	18500	20000	24000	25000	28000	47500	57500	18500	25000
Stafford	18000	20000	20000	22000	24000	27000	50000	60000	18500	21000
Stoke-on-Trent	15250	17750	17500	19000	21500	25500	39000	55000	15000	17500
Leamington Spa			26000	29500	31500	35000	72000	78000		
Worcester	20000	21500	22500	26000	30000	34000	57500	70000	22500	24500
Kidderminster	17250	19500	19500	24000	22000	28000	45000	65000	17500	20500
EAST ANGLIA										
Cambridge	36000	41000	39000	49000	47500	55000	80000	105000	42000	75000
Peterborough	17750	25750	20000	30000	28000	35000	50000	80000	18250	42500
Ipswich	22500	24750	24750	29500	31250	38000	53500	70000	24750	30000
Bury St Edmunds	23000	26000	29000	31500	35000	39500	55000	63500	29500	34000
King's Lynn	19000	22000	23000	30000	27500	35000	54000	65000	25000	30000
Norwich	24500	26500	28000	31500	35000	37500	57000	75000	30000	37000

PRICE RANGES: AUTUMN 1983

7.15 GREAT BRITAIN: TOWNS BY HOUSE TYPE - NEW DWELLINGS

£

	Semi-detached house estate type		Detached house estate type		Detached house individually designed		Flat in 3 (or more) storey block	
	From	To	From	To	From	To	From	To
INNER LONDON								
Hackney	44000	49000					29750	34000
Camden							44000	54500
Islington							40000	50000
Bexley/Greenwich	40000	47500	47000	52000	60000	115000	30000	39000
Lewisham	43250	48500	48500	54000	59250	80000	29000	40000
Southwark	37500	45000	45000	60000			30000	37500
H'smith & Fulham							35000	50000
Kens'ton/Chelsea	90000	165000					40000	95000
Wandsworth	46000	67000			110000	130000	33000	70000
Westminster	70000	130000					37000	68000
OUTER LONDON								
Barking & N'ham	30000	36000					27000	30000
Enfield	46500	50000	52000	56000	75000	80000	40000	42000
Haringey							26000	28500
Havering	34000	45000	50000	60000	75000	95000	25000	40000
Redbridge	39000	52000	44000	61000			34000	45000
Barnet	38000	50000	45000	60000	70000	95000	40000	55000
Ealing	35000	48000	44000	56000	70000	140000	30000	46000
Harrow	48000	51000	62000	65000	80000	83000	38000	42000
Hillingdon	40000	47000	52000	60000	82500	95000		
Hounslow	44000	46000		60000			34000	37500
Bromley	43000	49500	50000	60000	75000	90000	32500	43000
Croydon	41500	50000	53500	59500	74000	82500	31500	39000
Kingston	53000	58000	60000	70000	110000	120000	38000	48000
Merton					90000	155000	32000	60000
Richmond	48000	60000	63000	90000	90000	125000	40000	50000

PRICE RANGES: SPRING 1984

7.16 GREAT BRITAIN: TOWNS BY HOUSE TYPE - NEW DWELLINGS

£

	Semi-detached house estate type		Detached house estate type		Detached house individually designed		Flat in 3 (or more) storey block	
	From	To	From	To	From	To	From	To
INNER LONDON								
Hackney	45000	50000					30000	34500
Camden							46200	57250
Bexley/Greenwich	42000	49500	49000	54500	60000	115000	31000	40000
Lewisham	45500	51000	51000	57000	62000	83000	30500	42000
Southwark	42500	50000	45000	60000			35000	40000
H'smith & Fulham							50000	60000
Kens'ton/Chelsea	75000	175000					42500	100000
Westminster	73000	130000					37000	68000
OUTER LONDON								
Barking & N'ham	34000	41000					30000	33000
Enfield	46500	50000	60000	65000	77500	82500	42000	47500
Haringey							27000	29000
Havering	35000	45000	50000	60000	83000	100000	26000	40000
Redbridge	40000	53500	45500	63000			35000	46500
Waltham Forest	40000	50000	55000	60000			30000	42500
Barnet	40000	52500	46500	62500	75000	105000	42000	56500
Ealing	36000	54000	45000	58000			30000	46000
Harrow	52000	54000	65000	68000	85000	88000	40000	43000
Hillingdon	45000	50000	60000	67500	85000	100000		
Hounslow	44000	46000					35000	42000
Bromley	45000	53000	53000	62500	77500	90000	35000	43000
Croydon	42750	51500	55000	61250	76250	85000	32500	40000
Kingston	54000	60000	61500	72000	110000	125000	38500	50000
Merton	42500				110000	160000	35000	70000
Richmond	60000	65000	85000	95000	125000	150000	55000	65000

PRICE RANGES: AUTUMN 1984

7.17 GREAT BRITAIN: TOWNS BY HOUSE TYPE - NEW DWELLINGS

£

	Semi-detached house estate type		Detached house estate type		Detached house individually designed		Flat in 3 (or more) storey block	
	From	To	From	To	From	To	From	To
INNER LONDON								
Tower Hamlets	40000	42000	47000	49000			30750	34000
Camden							48500	60000
Hackney	45000	50000					30000	35000
Bexley	44000	51500	51000	56500	63000	120000	32500	42000
Lambeth							32000	52000
Lewisham	47750	53500	53500	59750	64500	86500	32000	44000
Southwark	45000	52500	47500	62500			36500	42500
Fulham							50000	65000
Kens'ton/Chelsea	80000	185000					50000	120000
N Westminster	76000	136000					39000	71000
OUTER LONDON								
Romford	42000	47000	53000	47000	100000	139500	30000	45000
Enfield	47500	51000	61500	67000	79000	84000	43000	49000
Haringey							34000	42000
Redbridge	42000	55000	46000	65000	65450	74750	35000	47500
Barnet	50000	55000	57500	67500	85000	115000	42000	56500
Ealing							30000	75000
Harrow	58000	60000	70000	72500	93500	97500	44000	47500
Hillingdon	48000	58000	65000	72500	90000	115000		
Hounslow	46000	48000					36000	43000
Bromley	47500	57500	55000	65000	90000	105000	40000	50000
Croydon & Sutton	45000	55000	57500	65000	80000	90000	35000	45000
Merton/Wandsworth	45500	80000			120000	170000	38000	75000
Kingston	56500	63000	64500	75500	115000	131000	40500	52500

INLAND REVENUE: VALUATION OFFICE PROPERTY MARKET REPORTS

PRICE RANGES: SPRING 1985

7.18 GREAT BRITAIN: TOWNS BY HOUSE TYPE - NEW DWELLINGS

£

	Semi-detached house estate type		Detached house estate type		Detached house individually designed		Flat in 3 (or more) storey block	
	From	To	From	To	From	To	From	To
INNER LONDON								
Tower Hamlets	40000	44000	48000	52000				
Camden							51500	62000
Hackney	50000	65000					32000	40000
Bexley	45000	54000	53000	59000	65000	125000	33500	43500
Lambeth							35000	52000
Lewisham	52000	60000					35000	45000
Southwark	45000	55000	47500	65000			37500	45000
Fulham							55000	80000
Kens'ton/Chelsea	90000	195000					52500	127000
N Westminster	80000	145000					54000	90000
OUTER LONDON								
Romford	43000	55000	53000	65000	100000	140000	35000	60000
Enfield	47500	54000	61500	70000	90000	92500	43000	52000
Redbridge	47500	57500	74000	76500	75500	90000	37500	50000
Barnet	55000	65000	60000	70000	95000	125000	45000	57500
Harrow	62000	64000	75000	75500	97500	100000	47500	50000
Hillingdon	51000	60000	67500	75000	95000	120000	30000	45000
Hounslow	47000	50000					37500	45000
Bromley	55000	60000	65000	85000	110000	130000	50000	55000
Croydon & Sutton	47500	57500	60000	75000	80000	92500	36000	53000
Merton/Wandsworth	50000	85000			125000	180000	42000	80000
Kingston	62000	68000	69500	82000	123500	140000	44500	57000

PRICE RANGES: AUTUMN 1985

7.19 GREAT BRITAIN: TOWNS BY HOUSE TYPE/SIZE - NEW DWELLINGS

£

	1 Bed Starter house estate type		2 Bed Terraced house estate type		3 Bed Semi-detached house estate type		4 Bed Detached house estate type		2 Bed Flat in 2/3 storey block	
	From	To	From	To	From	To	From	To	From	To
INNER LONDON										
Beckton/Newham	33000	35000	38000	43000	46000	56000	65000	83000	40000	69000
Camden									48000	75000
Hackney			45000	60000	50000	75000			33500	45000
Bexley	30000	37500	42000	50000	55000	65000	70000	130000	40000	50000
Lambeth	37750	42000	47950	62000					38500	42000
Lewisham			38500	41500					34500	39500
Southwark	32500	37500	35000	50000	37500	60000	75000	150000	35000	42500
Fulham									50000	78000
Kens'ton/Chelsea									57000	135000
N Westminster			58000	58000						
OUTER LONDON										
Romford	32500	35000	43000	46000	45500	58000	100000	150000	37000	62500
Enfield	35500	37000	45000	57500	55000	60000	95000	97000	45000	53000
Redbridge	33000	38000	40000	49000	40000	52500	80000	100000	38000	46000
Barnet	39000	42000	48000	52000	60000	65000	85000	120000	44000	46000
Greenf'd/Northolt	35000	40000	45500	51000					35000	39500
Harrow	37500	39000	46000	47500	60000	62000	105000	110000	42500	44000
Hillingdon	37000	52000	43000	55000	49000	70000	100000	135000	34000	52000
Hounslow	34000	39000	44000	49000	68000	80000	100000	132500	37000	43000
Bromley	34150	37000	38500	47000	52000	63000	125000	150000	54000	62000
Croydon & Sutton	32000	38000	38000	47500	49000	59000	80000	107000	38000	56000
Merton/Wandsworth	35000	39000	43000	50000	55000	70000	140000	200000	44000	88000
Kingston	35000	37500	52500	60000	60000	70000	120000	130000	45000	65000

PRICE RANGES: SPRING 1986

7.20 GREAT BRITAIN: TOWNS BY HOUSE TYPE/SIZE - NEW DWELLINGS

£

	1 Bed Starter house estate type		2 Bed Terraced house estate type		3 Bed Semi-detached house estate type		4 Bed Detached house estate type		2 Bed Flat in 2/3 storey block	
	From	To	From	To	From	To	From	To	From	To
INNER LONDON										
Beckton/Newham	36000	37500	39000	44000	46000	56000	65000	87000	42000	72500
Camden									50000	78000
Hackney			50000	65000	60000	80000			33500	45000
Bexley/Greenwich	30000	40000	42000	55000	57500	67500	75000	130000	40000	50000
Lambeth	39000	44000	51500	66500					42500	46000
Lewisham			40000	44000					35500	42000
Southwark	35000	42500	37500	60000	40000	70000	75000	160000	37500	47500
Fulham									60000	100000
Kens'ton/Chelsea									60000	137500
N Westminster			65000	66000						
OUTER LONDON										
Romford	35000	39000	43500	47000	47000	65000	105000	160000	38000	65000
Enfield	38000	40000	45000	62000	60000	65000	97500	105000	47000	55000
Redbridge	33000	38000	41000	50000	42000	55000	85000	110000	38000	47000
Barnet	40500	44000	50000	54000	62000	67000	90000	130000	44000	48000
Greenf'd/Northolt	37500	45000	47500	55000					40000	45000
Harrow	38500	40000	47000	49500	61000	63000	112000	115000	43000	44500
Hillingdon	38000	45000	44500	56000	55000	70000	85000	150000	40000	65000
Hounslow	36000	42000	47500	52000	68000	85000	105000	150000	39000	47000
Bromley	34500	37500	39000	48000	52000	60000	100000	135000	45000	55000
Croydon & Sutton	35000	40000	43000	53000	55000	65000	87500	110000	44000	64000
Merton/Wandsworth	35000	40000	45000	52000	58000	75000	145000	290000	55000	105000
Kingston	38500	41500	58000	65000	75000	80000	135000	155000	50000	70000

PRICE RANGES: AUTUMN 1986

7.21 GREAT BRITAIN: TOWNS BY HOUSE TYPE/SIZE - NEW DWELLINGS

£

	1 Bed Starter house estate type		2 Bed Terraced house estate type		3 Bed Semi-detached house estate type		4 Bed Detached house estate type		2 Bed Flat in 2/3 storey block	
	From	To	From	To	From	To	From	To	From	To
INNER LONDON										
Beckton/Newham	38000	42000	40000	45000	50000	60000	75000	90000	34000	38000
Camden									70000	100000
Hackney			55000	75000	65000	86000			37000	52500
Bexley/Greenwich	35000	40000	42500	60000	60000	70000	80000	135000	42000	50000
Lambeth	41500	46000	54500	70000					47000	51000
Lewisham			42000	46000					40000	48000
Southwark	40000	50000	42500	65000	47500	80000	90000	190000	42500	80000
Fulham									75000	120000
Kens'ton/Chelsea									65000	145000
OUTER LONDON										
Romford	39000	41000	46000	54000	59000	67000	105000	135000	42000	50000
Enfield	45000	47000	46000	62000	62500	67500	110000	130000	49000	60000
Redbridge	36000	42000	44000	57000	47000	60000	100000	135000	40000	54000
Barnet	45000	54000	57000	67000	69000	74000	100000	145000	46000	54000
Ealing									50000	65000
Harrow	42000	44000	55000	60000	65000	70000	120000	125000	43000	44500
Hillingdon	42000	50000	50000	62000	62000	78000	100000	175000	45000	75000
Hounslow/Feltham	40000	46000	51000	57000	75000	96000	115000	165000	43000	52000
Bromley	38000	42000	48000	55000	60000	67000	105000	135000	48000	58000
Croydon & Sutton	40000	48000	50000	65000	63000	75000	100000	185000	48000	66000
Merton/Wandsworth	37000	46000	47000	55000	70000	90000	180000	300000	60000	105000
Kingston	41000	45000	62000	66000	75000	85000	140000	170000	55000	75000

7.22 GREAT BRITAIN: TOWNS BY HOUSE TYPE - NEW DWELLINGS

£

	Semi-detached house estate type		Detached house estate type		Detached house individually designed		Flat in 3 (or more) storey block	
	From	To	From	To	From	To	From	To
SOUTH EAST								
Bedford	25500	29000	32500	39000	50000	65000		
N Hertfordshire	35000	42000	38000	45000	75000	85000	22000	26000
Luton	35000	40000	42500	51500	70000	80000	27000	30000
St Albans	40000	45000	47500	55000	82500	92500	27500	40000
Watford	42000	48000	45000	55000	73000	98000	32000	45000
Basildon	30000	38000	40000	50000	65000	80000	19000	24000
Chelmsford	28500	39000	35000	50000	58000	95000	20000	30500
Colchester	27000	30000	36000	40000	54000	59000	22500	24000
Harlow	30000	60000	40000	75000	50000	150000	28000	75000
Southend on Sea	29000	38500	36500	45000	69000	75000		
Brighton	30000	34000	37000	42000	60000	70000	25000	30000
Canterbury	27000	40000	34500	47500	50000	65000	26500	40000
Eastbourne	30000	37500	33000	41500	52500	67500	27500	33000
East Kent	27000	35250	31000	41250	46000	59500	20500	30750
Maidstone	36000	40000	45000	51000	60000	72500	21500	24500
Medway	30000	37500	35000	40000	50000	60000		
Tunbridge Wells	35000	40000	40000	47500	67500	75000	27500	32500
Chichester	30000	40000	43000	58000	55000	85000	30000	36000
Guildford	35000	46000	53000	60000	71000	90000	29250	40000
North Surrey	39000	60000	46000	78000	71000	130000	28000	41000
Reigate	33500	40000	37500	47500	55000	85000	30000	36000
Worthing	32000	37500	40000	47500	64000	78000	26000	32000
East Berkshire	39000	42000	48000	56500	72000	80000	29500	34000
N Bucks	34000	36000	43000	46000	68000	70000		
Oxford	34500	72500	38500	55000	45000	79500	25000	42500
W Oxfordshire	25000	37000	30000	45000	42000	65000	20000	29000
Reading	32000	37000	44000	54000	65000	75000	26000	29000
S Bucks	34000	41000	48000	58000	70000	90000	26000	45000
Basingstoke	29500	40000	38000	45000	63000	82500	23500	35000
Portsmouth	32500	35000	42000	46000	52500	57500		
Solent	27500	33500	34000	40000	50000	60000	22000	24000
Winchester	30000	37000	36000	44000	55000	70000	29500	35500
Solent (IOW)	22000	26000	26000	31000	42500	48000		
Southampton	27000	32000	33000	43000	50000	80000	30000	45000

PRICE RANGES: SPRING 1984

7.23 GREAT BRITAIN: TOWNS BY HOUSE TYPE - NEW DWELLINGS

£

	Semi-detached house estate type		Detached house estate type		Detached house individually designed		Flat in 3 (or more) storey block	
	From	To	From	To	From	To	From	To
SOUTH EAST								
Bedford	29500	33000	37000	42000	60000	75000		
N Hertfordshire	41000	46000	42000	48000	78000	85000	24000	28000
Luton	35000	42500	45000	55000				
St Albans	42500	47500	50000	60000	85000	95000	35000	42500
Watford	43000	50000	46000	60000	75000	100000	33000	46000
Basildon	32000	40000	42000	50000	65000	80000	20000	25000
Chelmsford	30000	40000	40000	45000	70000	90000	24000	28000
Colchester	28000	32000	36750	43000	55000	65000	23500	25000
Harlow	40000	60000	50000	75000	100000	150000	45000	75000
Southend on Sea	31000	40000	40000	48000	72000	78000	25000	60000
Brighton	32500	37500	40000	45000			27500	32500
Canterbury	30000	42000	37000	50000	50000	68250	30000	42000
Eastbourne	31000	38000	35000	42500	60000	80000	27500	35000
East Kent	32000	37500	35000	45000	46500	63000	22000	35000
Maidstone	36000	43000	46000	53000	64000	75000	22500	25500
Medway	30000	35000	35000	40000	55000	65000		
Tunbridge Wells	38000	43000	44000	52000	74000	83000	30000	35000
Chichester	40000	42000	50000	58000	75000	92500	32500	40000
Guildford	42000	47650	55000	60000	69000	91000	47500	57500
North Surrey	40000	60000	46000	78000	72000	130000	30000	41000
Reigate	38000	48000	49000	60000	70000	100000	32000	40000
Worthing	33000	39000	42000	50000	67500	75000	27000	33000
East Berkshire	43000	49000	54000	60000	80000	90000	33000	38000
N Bucks	36000	38000	44000	47500	77500	82500		
Oxford							27500	42500
W Oxfordshire	27500	35000	35000	42000	47500	60000	20000	22000
Reading	34000	39000	48000	59000	70000	80000	28000	32000
S Bucks	35000	42000	50000	58000	74000	88000	30000	42000
Basingstoke	33000	39000	40000	47500	68000	72000		
Portsmouth	35000	37500	42000	47500	55000	61000		
Solent	29500	35500	36000	42000	54000	64000	24000	28000
Winchester	35000	43000	45000	55000	65000	75000	38000	42000
Solent (IOW)	25000	27500	28000	32000	45000	50000		
Southampton	29000	38000	33000	47000	50000	80000	30000	48000

INLAND REVENUE: VALUATION OFFICE PROPERTY MARKET REPORTS

PRICE RANGES: AUTUMN 1984

7.24 GREAT BRITAIN: TOWNS BY HOUSE TYPE - NEW DWELLINGS

£

	Semi-detached house estate type		Detached house estate type		Detached house individually designed		Flat in 3 (or more) storey block	
	From	To	From	To	From	To	From	To
SOUTH EAST								
Bedford	32000	35000	38500	44000	62500	75000	35000	38500
Hertford	44000	48000	47500	49000	85000	105000	25000	30000
Luton	42500	45000	56000	60000				
St Albans	45000	50000	57500	67500	95000	105000	40000	47000
Watford	45000	52000	49000	64000	80000	110000	35000	48000
Basildon	34000	42500	42500	55000	70000	90000	21000	27000
Chelmsford	31500	42000	42000	47250	73500	94500	25250	29500
Colchester	30000	34000	38000	44000	55000	69000	24500	26000
Loughton	40000	60000	50000	75000	100000	150000	45000	75000
Southend-on-Sea	34000	42500	44000	52000	75000	81000	27000	62000
Brighton	33000	38000	42000	48000	90000	130000	30000	35000
Canterbury	32000	44000	39000	52500	50000	71500	32000	45000
Eastbourne	33500	40000	37500	45000	65000	90000	29000	36000
Folkestone	30000	37500	35000	50000	50000	65000	23000	35000
Maidstone	38000	44000	47000	54000	67500	76500	23000	26500
Gill'ham/Chatham	35000	40000	40000	45000	57500	67500		
Tunbridge Wells	33000	42000	45000	55000	75000	85000	30000	35000
Horsham	40000	43000	50000	59000	75000	95000	32500	42000
Guildford	45000	49000	62000	70000	72000	94000	55000	65000
Walton-on-Thames	50000	70000	60000	80000	80000	140000	45000	60000
Reigate	44000	55000	50000	70000	75000	115000	34000	45000
Worthing	34000	40000	44000	52000	70000	80000	28000	35000
Maidenhead	46000	52000	56000	63000	84000	97500	35000	42000
Aylesbury	39000	41000	48500	52500	75000	85000	28000	32000
Oxford							30000	58000
Banbury	29000	37000	37000	45000	50000	62000	22000	24000
Reading	36000	41000	50000	62000	73000	84000	29000	34000
High Wycombe	40000	47500	55000	62500	80000	95000	34000	43000
Basingstoke	34000	45500	43500	54000	70000	75000		
Havant	35000	41000	42000	47500	55000	61000		
Fareham	32500	39000	40000	46000	60000	80000	25000	32000
Winchester	37500	46000	48250	58750	70750	81750	40750	45000
Newport(IOW)	25500	28000	28500	32500	50000	55000		
Southampton	30000	40000	35000	48000	52000	80000	33000	50000

INLAND REVENUE: VALUATION OFFICE PROPERTY MARKET REPORTS

PRICE RANGES: SPRING 1985

7.25 GREAT BRITAIN: TOWNS BY HOUSE TYPE - NEW DWELLINGS

£

	Semi-detached house estate type		Detached house estate type		Detached house individually designed		Flat in 3 (or more) storey block	
	From	To	From	To	From	To	From	To
SOUTH EAST								
Bedford	35000	37000	40000	45000	62500	75000	29000	38500
Hertford	45000	50000	48000	52000	90000	115000	30000	40000
Luton	38500	45000	58000	61000				
St Albans	46000	51000	58500	68500	100000	115000	41000	48000
Watford	47250	55500	51500	67000	90000	110000	36750	50000
Grays	35000	44000	44000	58000	70000	95000	22000	29000
Chelmsford	33000	43000	43000	49500	75000	90000	25500	30000
Colchester	32000	36000	40000	48000	58000	73000	25000	28000
Loughton	60000	65000	70000	75000	130000	140000	40000	70000
Southend-on-Sea	36500	45000	46000	55000	78000	85000	28000	64000
Brighton	35000	40000	45000	50000	90000	130000	30000	35000
Canterbury	33500	44500	41000	55000	55000	75000	33500	46500
Eastbourne	34000	42000	38000	46000	70000	95000	29500	37000
Folkestone	30000	37500	37000	50000	53000	65000	23000	35000
Maidstone	40000	45000	48000	55000	69500	77500	24000	27000
Gill'ham/Chatham	35000	46000	41000	48000	59000	74000		
Tunbridge Wells	35000	44000	47000	57000	75000	85000	30000	35000
Horsham	41000	45000	56000	59000	90000	100000	36000	43000
Guildford	47500	50000	65000	75000	77000	95000	57500	67500
Walton-on-Thames	51000	71500	61000	81500	85000	150000	46000	61000
Reigate	45000	60000	52000	75000	80000	125000	35000	48500
Worthing	38000	45000	48000	56000	75000	85000	29000	36000
Maidenhead	50000	58000	62000	70000	90000	110000	40000	45000
Aylesbury	43000	48000	50000	65000	80000	100000	28000	32000
Oxford							32000	58000
Banbury	30000	38000	38000	46500	51500	64000	22000	24500
Reading	37000	42000	52000	65000	75000	86000	30000	35000
High Wycombe	42500	50000	58500	67000	85000	105000	36000	45000
Basingstoke	35000	45500	47000	58000	73000	78000		
Portsmouth/Havant	36500	38500	44000	48500	58000	65000		
Fareham	35000	42500	44000	50000	60000	80000	25000	32000
Winchester	40500	49500	53000	64000	74000	85250	42500	47000
Newport(IOW)	27000	30000	35000	40000	50000	55000		
Southampton	30000	40000	35000	48000	55000	80000	33000	50000

PRICE RANGES: AUTUMN 1985

7.26 GREAT BRITAIN: TOWNS BY HOUSE TYPE/SIZE - NEW DWELLINGS

£

	1 Bed Starter house estate type		2 Bed Terraced house estate type		3 Bed Semi-detached house estate type		4 Bed Detached house estate type		2 Bed Flat in 2/3 storey block	
	From	To	From	To	From	To	From	To	From	To
SOUTH EAST										
Bedford	21500	26000	28000	33000	34000	40000	64000	66000	34000	38500
Hertford	35000	38000	38000	45000	45000	50000	80000	85000	33000	36000
Luton	28000	30000	34000	38000	41500	46500	72000	79000	30000	35000
St Albans	31000	36500	38000	45000	47000	52000	85000	110000	40000	45000
Watford	33000	34000	44000	45000	49000	58000	100000	125000	38500	52500
Basildon	23000	25500	30000	33000	36000	40000	68000	76000	28000	31000
Chelmsford	21000	26000	27000	32000	32000	40000	68000	80000	25000	30000
Colchester	25000	27000	29000	31000	34000	38000	63000	66000	25000	27000
Loughton/Chigwell	33600	34400	41500	43000	65750	72800	89600	112000	34200	37500
Southend-on-Sea	27000	30000	30000	33000	36000	39000	70000	77000	25000	57500
Brighton			32000	34500	38000	42000	100000	140000	32000	36000
Canterbury	25000	27500	28000	31000	33500	43000	53500	76000	32000	45000
Eastbourne	26500	28000	30250	33000	34000	38000	65000	82500	28500	37000
Folkestone	19000	25000	21000	34500	30250	38250	54000	66000	22500	34750
Maidstone	24000	26000	30000	34000	39000	45000	72000	85000	24000	28000
Gillingham	21500	25000	26000	30000	33000	44000	59000	65000	21000	23000
Tunbridge Wells	31000	35000	38000	40000	42000	46000	80000	100000	32500	38500
Horsham	35500	36000	37500	38500	50000	52000	97000	110000	39000	43000
Guildford	36500	40000	44000	47500	50000	56000	90000	95000	37500	43000
Walton-on-Thames	37000	39750	44000	46000	55750	78000	90000	155750	50000	66750
Reigate	32500	37000	38500	48000	47500	64000	85000	130000	37000	43000
Worthing	28000	32000	36000	40000	42000	48000	82000	90000	33000	37000
Maidenhead	38500	39500	48000	51000	51000	56000	95000	115000	38500	44000
Aylesbury	30000	32000	35000	38000	37500	39500	67000	72000	28000	31000
Oxford	34000	35000	43000	46000	49500	51000			36000	57000
Banbury	24500	25000	25500	26500	32000	38000	51000	56000	24000	26000
Reading	32000	34000	38000	40000	46000	48000	71000	75000	36000	37000
High Wycombe	31000	38000	42000	48000	41000	49000	90000	120000	36000	43000
Basingstoke	27000	29000	31500	34250	37000	42000	70000	75000	28500	30000
Portsmouth/Havant	26000	29000	30500	36000	36500	39500	70000	80000	30000	33000
Fareham	25500	27500	30000	34000	37500	42000	65000	75000	27500	30000
Winchester	31500	31500	35000	37500	37500	42500	67000	85000	30000	40000
Newport(IOW)	19000	21000	22000	24000	28000	32000	50000	55000	22000	26000
Southampton	20000	25000	27000	29500	32000	36000	50000	80000	23000	27000

PRICE RANGES: SPRING 1986

7.27 GREAT BRITAIN: TOWNS BY HOUSE TYPE/SIZE - NEW DWELLINGS

£

	1 Bed Starter house estate type		2 Bed Terraced house estate type		3 Bed Semi-detached house estate type		4 Bed Detached house estate type		2 Bed Flat in 2/3 storey block	
	From	To	From	To	From	To	From	To	From	To
SOUTH EAST										
Bedford	25000	27500	31500	35000	40000	45000	70000	75000	35000	40000
Hertford	32000	35000	40000	47500	45000	50000	100000	125000	35000	40000
Luton	30000	32000	39500	42000	44000	49000	75000	82000	32000	37500
St Albans	35000	42500	42500	50000	50000	57500	95000	120000	42500	50000
Watford	34000	36000	46000	48000	52000	61000	105000	130000	40500	55000
Basildon	24500	28000	32000	37000	38000	44000	72000	80000	30000	35000
Chelmsford	22750	28500	29500	34500	34000	42500	73500	87500	28000	32000
Colchester	26000	28000	30000	32000	35000	40000	64000	69000	26000	29000
Loughton/Chigwell	37000	46200	53000	55250	66500	77250	97500	130000	36750	41000
Southend-on-Sea	29000	32000	33000	37500	39000	42500	74000	80000	27500	60000
Brighton	27000	30000	33000	36000	39000	43000	110000	140000	35000	40000
Canterbury	26000	29000	29500	32500	35000	45000	56000	87000	33500	47000
Eastbourne	27750	29250	31000	34000	37000	41000	72500	90000	30000	39000
Folkestone	21000	26600	25000	34500	32000	40000	57500	70000	25000	37500
Maidstone	26000	29000	32500	36500	42000	48000	75000	88000	26000	31000
Gillingham	23000	28000	29000	33000	39000	47000	62000	72000	23000	27000
Tunbridge Wells	33000	38000	40000	43000	45000	50000	85000	115000	33000	40000
Horsham	37650	38650	39750	40250	51000	60000	100000	120000	43000	46000
Guildford	38500	41500	44000	48500	52000	58000	92000	98000	37500	43000
Walton-on-Thames	39000	41500	46000	57500	60000	78000	92000	167000	51000	68000
Reigate	35000	40000	40000	50000	55000	75000	95000	145000	40000	60000
Worthing	32000	34000	37000	39000	44000	47000	87000	92000	34000	37000
Maidenhead	40500	42500	50000	55000	54000	60000	99000	120000	40000	46000
Aylesbury	31500	33000	36500	39000	39000	44000	70000	75000	30000	33000
Oxford	38000	41500	44000	51000	56000	63500			36500	57000
Banbury	25500	26500	27000	28500	34250	40500	54000	60000	24000	26500
Reading	34000	36000	40000	43000	47500	52500	75000	90000	37500	40000
High Wycombe	34000	40000	42000	48000	44000	50000	90000	120000	36000	44000
Basingstoke	30000	34000	35000	40000	44000	51000	72000	79000	32000	37000
Portsmouth/Havant	27000	30000	33500	36000	38000	41000	77500	87500	30000	33000
Fareham	27750	29000	32000	35000	37500	42000	70000	80000	26000	30000
Winchester	28950	33800	37000	39500	39500	44500	70000	90000	32000	42000
Newport(IOW)	20000	22000	24000	26000	29000	34000	53000	60000	22000	26000
Southampton	27500	30000	29000	32500	33000	39500	50000	85000	26000	30000

INLAND REVENUE: VALUATION OFFICE PROPERTY MARKET REPORTS

PRICE RANGES: AUTUMN 1986

7.28 GREAT BRITAIN: TOWNS BY HOUSE TYPE/SIZE - NEW DWELLINGS

£

	1 Bed Starter house estate type		2 Bed Terraced house estate type		3 Bed Semi-detached house estate type		4 Bed Detached house estate type		2 Bed Flat in 2/3 storey block	
	From	To	From	To	From	To	From	To	From	To
SOUTH EAST										
Bedford	28500	31500	36500	40000	45000	50000	76000	81000	38500	44000
Hertford	37500	40000	45000	50000	47500	55000	105000	125000	37500	42500
Luton	33000	36500	42000	46000	46000	52000	80000	90000	35000	41500
St Albans	38500	46000	47500	56000	54000	63000	105000	130000	47500	56000
Watford	37000	39000	48750	51000	55000	65000	112500	137500	43000	57500
Basildon	26000	30000	34000	40000	40000	48000	75000	88000	31000	38000
Chelmsford	24250	30000	31500	36500	36000	45000	78000	92000	29500	33500
Colchester	29000	32500	32000	36000	42000	47000	65000	75000	30000	36500
Loughton/Chigwell	40000	49250	57250	59500	72000	83500	105000	145000	40000	45000
Southend-on-Sea	32000	35000	36000	40000	42500	47500	82500	90000	32000	65000
Brighton					40000	45000	115000	150000	37500	42500
Canterbury	28000	31000	31500	35000	38000	48000	60000	93500	35000	49000
Eastbourne	29000	31000	33000	36000	40000	44000	80000	100000	31500	40000
Folkestone	22000	28000	26000	36000	33500	42000	60000	75000	26000	39000
Maidstone	30000	34000	36000	40000	48000	60000	80000	100000	30000	35000
Gillingham	27000	32000	30000	36000	44000	55000	66000	79000	25000	30000
Tunbridge Wells	35000	40000	40000	45000	47000	55000	90000	120000	34000	45000
Horsham	39000	42000	45000	47500	55000	62500	110000	150000	44000	48000
Guildford	39500	44000	47000	52500	55000	63000	96000	104000	39000	45000
Walton-on-Thames	45000	50000	55000	65000	70000	85000	100000	175000	55000	75000
Reigate	45000	52000	50000	70000	62500	80000	120000	175000	47000	65000
Worthing			38000	42000	48000	52000	90000	95000	37000	42000
Maidenhead	43500	46000	54000	60000	60000	66000	108000	130000	44000	50000
Aylesbury	36000	37500	39000	41000	45000	49500	95000	110000	33000	35000
Oxford	42000	45000	46000	52500	57500	65000	110000	130000	40000	58500
Abingdon	35500	37500	39500	43000	48000	52000	75000	90000	39000	41000
Reading	38000	41000	42000	45000	52000	56000	85000	92000	40000	44000
High Wycombe	38000	45000	45000	52000	48000	57000	98000	130000	40000	49000
Basingstoke	37000	41500	44000	47000	56000	60000	85000	90000	41000	43000
Portsmouth/Havant	27000	30000	34500	39000	42000	45000	82000	94000	32000	35000
Fareham	29000	30250	33500	36500	39500	44000	75000	90000	27000	31500
Winchester	32500	37500	38000	41000	45000	50000	80000	100000	36000	44000
Newport(IOW)			26000	28000	30000	35000	63000	70000		
Southampton	27500	34000	32000	34000	35000	40000	60000	90000	27500	33000

7.29 GREAT BRITAIN: TOWNS BY HOUSE TYPE - NEW DWELLINGS

£

	Semi-detached house estate type		Detached house estate type		Detached house individually designed		Flat in 3 (or more) storey block	
	From	To	From	To	From	To	From	To
SOUTH WEST								
Bournemouth	26450	32500	42500	48950	65000	90000	30000	36000
West Dorset	26000	32000	31750	34750	47500	60000	28000	31000
Carrick	22500	25750	26750	32000	40000	48000	23000	28750
Exeter	27500	31000	30000	35000	51000	57500	21000	25000
North Devon	23000	26000	30000	36000	55000	65000	16000	25000
Plymouth	28000	33000	37500	42000	55000	65000	18500	28000
Restormel	18000	28500	24000	36000	34000	50000		
Somerset	24000	28500	30000	35000	45000	55000	18500	22500
Torbay	26000	29500	32750	35750	55000		29500	36500
Bath	27000	39500	32500	50000	55000	90000	20000	40000
Bristol	26000	30000	37000	42000	65000	75000	25000	27000
Cheltenham	25000	34000	32000	40000	50000	75000	25000	34000
Gloucester	23000	27500	27500	35000	45000	60000	27500	32500
North West Avon	24500	27500	32000	42000	55000	75000		
North Wiltshire	21000	26000	29000	35000	55000	65000	19000	21000
South Wiltshire	29000	36500	36000	44000	54500	68000		
WALES								
Afan	16000	24000	20500	29500	26250	46250		
Cardiff	32000	37000	35000	40000	52000	64000	26000	29000
West Dyfed	22000	26000	24000	30000	39000	50000		
East Dyfed	18000	25000	25000	32000	40000	50000		
Merthyr Tydfil	20000	25000	30000	37000	40000	50000		
Pontypridd	18750	27750	18000	34000	33500	51500		
Swansea	19000	27500	22000	34000	38000	60000	20000	30000
Abergavenny	27000	29000	30000	38000	45000	50000		
Bangor	16500	21000	18500	27500	33500	42000		
Colwyn Bay	18000	25000	26000	35000	35000	48000	15000	40000
Newport	24750	29250	28000	36500	46000	52500		
Welshpool	22000	26000	24000	28000	38000	42000		
Wrexham	16500	22000	22000	30000	35000	50000	15000	25000

PRICE RANGES: SPRING 1984

7.30 GREAT BRITAIN: TOWNS BY HOUSE TYPE - NEW DWELLINGS

£

	Semi-detached house estate type		Detached house estate type		Detached house individually designed		Flat in 3 (or more) storey block	
	From	To	From	To	From	To	From	To
SOUTH WEST								
Bournemouth	26450	32500	42500	48950	67500	92500	30000	36000
West Dorset	28500	32500	32500	37500	47500	60000	30000	32500
Carrick	26000	31000	32000	37500	46000	55000	25000	30000
Exeter	30000	35000	32500	50000	60000	75000	21000	26500
North Devon	24000	27000	30000	33000	55000	65000	22000	25000
Plymouth	30000	34500	40000	45000	57000	66000	20000	29000
Restormel	21500	31500	25000	37500	40000	60000		
Somerset	26500	29000	32500	36500	52000	57500	21000	23500
Torbay	28000	30000	38500	40000	60000	80000	30000	42500
Bath	33000	42500	45000	52500	65000	92500	30000	42500
Bristol	26000	30000	37000	42000	70000	80000	25000	27000
Cheltenham	26000	35000	33000	41000	50000	75000	25000	35000
Gloucester	23000	29000	32500	40000	50000	70000	22500	32500
North West Avon	25500	29000	33500	45000	60000	80000		
North Wiltshire	22000	27000	30000	36000	55000	65000	19500	21500
South Wiltshire	34750	38000	41750	45750	64500	70750		
WALES								
Afan	22500	26000	27500	31000	40000	50000		
Cardiff	32500	38000	36000	41000	55000	65000	26500	29500
West Dyfed	22000	26000	24000	30000	39000	50000		
East Dyfed	18500	26000	25750	33000	42000	52000		
Merthyr Tydfil	23000	27000	30000	35000	40000	50000		
Pontypridd	16400	26000	18000	34000	29000	46850		18850
Swansea	20000	29000	23500	36500	40000	65000	21500	32500
Abergavenny	27000	29000	30000	33000	45000	50000		
Bangor	20000	22000	27000	28500	38000	42000		
Colwyn Bay	25000	30000	32500	40000	40000	50000	25000	40000
Newport	25250	29850	28550	27250	48500	56500		
Welshpool	24000	28500	26500	32000	40000	46000		
Wrexham	17300	23000	22000	30000	36500	50000	18000	30000

PRICE RANGES: AUTUMN 1984

7.31 GREAT BRITAIN: TOWNS BY HOUSE TYPE - NEW DWELLINGS

£

	Semi-detached house estate type		Detached house estate type		Detached house individually designed		Flat in 3 (or more) storey block	
	From	To	From	To	From	To	From	To
SOUTH WEST								
Poole	27250	33500	43500	50000	67500	92500	30500	37000
Weymouth	30000	35000	35000	40000	50000	60000	30000	33000
Truro	28000	34000	35000	41000	50000	60000	27500	33000
Exeter	32000	37500	35000	50000	60000	80000	22000	28000
Barnstaple	25000	28000	30000	36000	50000	65000	20000	25000
Plymouth	33000	38000	42000	47000	61000	71000	23000	30000
St Austell	22500	31500	30000	47500	40000	67500		
Taunton	28000	32500	35000	39000	54000	59000	28000	35000
Torquay/Paignton	29500	31500	40000	45000	62500	85000	30000	42500
Bath	34000	43500	46000	53500	67500	92500	32500	42500
Bristol	26500	31000	37500	42500	72000	82000	25000	27000
Cheltenham	29000	39000	36500	45000	55000	80000	26000	36000
Gloucester	23000	32500	32500	42500	50000	75000	22500	32500
Weston-s-Mare	26500	31000	34500	47000	65000	82000		
Swindon	22500	28000	31000	37500	57000	67000	19750	21750
Salisbury	37000	40500	44500	48750	68000	74750		
WALES								
Bridgend	23500	28000	29000	32500	40000	52000		
Cardiff	32750	38000	36500	41500	56000	66500	27000	30000
Haverfordwest	22000	26500	25000	30000	40000	53000		
Llanelli	19500	27000	26500	34000	44000	54000		
Merthyr Tydfil	23000	27000	30000	35000	40000	50000		
Pontypridd	16750	26000	18250	34500	29500	47000		
Swansea	21000	30000	24000	37500	45000	67500	21500	33500
Abergavenny	27000	30000	30000	34000	45000	52000		
Bangor	21000	23000	27000	29000	39500	44000		
Llandudno	25000	30000	32500	40000	40000	50000	25000	40000
Newport(Gwent)	26000	31000	29500	38500	50000	58000		
Newtown	25500	28500	27500	34000	43500	48500		
Wrexham	17750	23500	22500	33500	37500	52500	18000	30000

7.32 GREAT BRITAIN: TOWNS BY HOUSE TYPE - NEW DWELLINGS

£

	Semi-detached house estate type		Detached house estate type		Detached house individually designed		Flat in 3 (or more) storey block	
	From	To	From	To	From	To	From	To
SOUTH WEST								
Poole	30500	34950	35950	48000	75000	87750	36000	51750
Weymouth	30500	35750	36000	42000	50000	60000	30000	35000
Truro	29000	36000	37000	43000	55000	65000	27500	33000
Exeter	33000	39750	42000	48000	60000	80000	23000	33000
Barnstaple	27000	30000	34000	38000	60000	65000	25000	30000
Plymouth	34000	38000	43500	48000	63000	74000	23000	30000
St Austell	23000	31500	30000	47500	42500	70000		
Taunton	28500	33500	37000	43000	58000	78000	28500	36000
Torquay/Paignton			42000	47500	65000	90000	30000	42500
Bath	37000	44500	46000	55000	75000	95000	33500	45000
Bristol	26500	32000	38000	44000	75000	85000	25000	28000
Cheltenham	29000	39000	36500	50000	56000	87000	26000	40000
Gloucester	23250	33000	32500	43000	50000	78000	22500	32500
Weston-s-Mare	27000	32000	35500	50000	67500	85000		
Swindon	29000	33000	35000	42000	65000	75000	21000	23000
Salisbury	38000	41750	46000	50000	70500	77500		
WALES								
Bridgend	24000	28000	29000	33500	40000	55000		
Cardiff	33000	38500	36500	42000	56500	67000	27250	30500
Haverfordwest	23000	26500	26000	31000	41000	54000		
Llanelli	19750	27500	27000	35000	45000	55000		
Merthyr Tydfil	23000	27000	30000	35000	42500	52500		
Pontypridd	16750	26000	18250	34500	29500	47500	18000	20000
Swansea	22000	32000	26000	40000	45000	70000	21500	45000
Abergavenny	31000	35000	34000	38000	51000	58500		
Bangor	21000	23000	27000	29000	39500	44000		
Llandudno	25000	30000	32500	40000	40000	55000	25000	40000
Newport(Gwent)	26000	31000	29500	38500	50000	59000	25000	29000
Newtown	25500	28500	27500	35000	43500	48500		
Wrexham	18000	23500	24500	33500	40000	55000	20000	30000

PRICE RANGES: AUTUMN 1985

7.33 GREAT BRITAIN: TOWNS BY HOUSE TYPE/SIZE - NEW DWELLINGS

£

	1 Bed Starter house estate type		2 Bed Terraced house estate type		3 Bed Semi-detached house estate type		4 Bed Detached house estate type		2 Bed Flat in 2/3 storey block	
	From	To	From	To	From	To	From	To	From	To
SOUTH WEST										
Poole	24500	28000	32995	33250	36750	39950	55000	60850	25000	30000
Weymouth	23000	27000	27000	30000	30000	34500	47500	55000	28000	31000
Truro	21000	25000	24200	29000	29000	37000	60000	78000	28000	34500
Exeter	24000	25000	25000	30000	35000	37500	75000	80000	22500	27000
Barnstaple			20000	22000	26500	28500	52500	57500	18000	26500
Plymouth	25000	28000	25000	32500	32000	40000	50000	72000	23000	30000
St Austell			19000	21000	24000	27500	37500	55000		
Taunton	19500	21500	25000	26500	33000	35000	53000	60000	23000	27000
Torquay/Paignton		22000	27500	29000	33000	35000	63500	77500	27500	35000
Bath	22000	24000	28500	31500	37500	43500	58500	85000	32500	38500
Bristol	21000	22250	24500	28500	28750	34250	48000	62500	25500	27250
Cheltenham	23500	26000	25000	31000	26000	35000	58000	90000	28500	35000
Gloucester	19000	22000	21000	24000	31000	36000	44250	76500	24000	32500
Weston-s-Mare	20000	22000	22500	25000	27500	31000	52500	65000	22000	47000
Swindon	19000	23000	25000	27500	32000	38000	60000	68000		
Salisbury	26250	28250	33000	35750	38000	42000	67500	74000	25000	27500
WALES										
Bridgend	15500	18000	17750	21500	24500	28500	42000	55000		
Cardiff	21000	22500	30000	32000	35250	38000	64000	70000	22500	24750
Haverfordwest	16000	16000	19000	19000	25500	25500	60000	62000		
Llanelli	17000	18500	20500	22000	22000	26000	45000	57000		
Merthyr Tydfil			19500	20500	23000	24000				
Pontypridd	17500	18250	18000	22500	19500	27500	31000	52500	16000	20000
Swansea	18000	24000	21000	30000	24000	34000	42000	60000	24000	50000
Abergavenny	21000	24000	26500	28500	32500	36000	57000	61500	26000	32000
Bangor	14000	15000	21000	23000	23000	25000	38000	42000	12000	13000
Colwyn Bay	15750	18000	18500	24000	24000	27500	42500	50000	17500	19500
Newport(Gwent)	15500	18500	16000	17500	26500	31000	48000	54000	15500	17000
Newtown	17500	20000	20000	22500	24000	28500	37500	46000	17500	20000
Wrexham	14250	14500	16950	17850	18500	22950	45000	55000	20500	23500

PRICE RANGES: SPRING 1986

7.34 GREAT BRITAIN: TOWNS BY HOUSE TYPE/SIZE - NEW DWELLINGS

£

	1 Bed Starter house estate type		2 Bed Terraced house estate type		3 Bed Semi-detached house estate type		4 Bed Detached house estate type		2 Bed Flat in 2/3 storey block	
	From	To	From	To	From	To	From	To	From	To
SOUTH WEST										
Poole/Bournem'th	28000	30000	32985	34250	34250	43950	54750	76000	28950	30000
Weymouth	24500	27000	27500	31000	32000	37000	55000	65000	30000	33500
Truro	21000	25000	24800	30000	29500	38000	63000	80000	25000	35000
Exeter	25250	26250	26000	31000	37000	41500	72000	85000	23500	28000
Barnstaple			22000	24000	28000	30000	54000	59000	20000	27000
Plymouth	25000	28000	25500	33000	33000	40000	50000	75000	24000	30000
St Austell			19000	22000	24000	27500	40000	60000		
Taunton	20500	22500	26000	27500	34000	36000	53000	60000	24000	27500
Torquay/Paignton	23000	24000	28500	30000	33000	35000	55000	79000	27500	35000
Bath	24000	26000	31500	35000	38500	46500	65000	93500	33500	39500
Bristol	20000	22500	26000	28500	29500	36000	51000	72500	26500	29000
Cheltenham	24500	30000	27750	34000	32000	39000	50000	95000	27000	40000
Gloucester	20000	22000	22000	24000	31000	36000	55000	70000	24000	32500
Weston-s-Mare	21000	22000	24000	25750	28000	32500	46000	57000	22000	30000
Swindon	19500	23500	26000	28250	33500	39000	64000	72000	23000	27000
Salisbury	27750	30000	34500	37500	39750	44000	69500	76250	27000	31000
WALES										
Bridgend	16250	18500	19000	22250	25500	30000	44000	59750		
Cardiff	21000	22750	30000	32500	35500	38500	65000	72000	22500	25000
Haverfordwest	15500	16950	19500	20750	26000	28000	60000	62000		
Llanelli	17500	19000	21000	23000	22500	26500	46000	58000		
Merthyr Tydfil			21500	23000	26000	27500				
Pontypridd	17750	18250	18500	22500	19500	27500	31500	52500	16000	20000
Swansea	19000	25000	22000	31000	25000	35000	44000	63000	27000	50000
Abergavenny	21500	24500	27000	29000	33000	37000	58500	63000	26500	32500
Bangor	14000	15000	21000	23000	24000	26000	40000	42000	12000	14000
Colwyn Bay	16000	18000	18500	24000	24000	27500	42500	50000	17500	19500
Newport(Gwent)	18000	21000	22000	24500	27500	31000	52000	62000	22000	25000
Newtown	17500	20000	21000	23000	24000	28500	40000	50000	18000	20000
Wrexham	14250	15500	17000	19000	18500	23500	45000	55000	20500	23500

INLAND REVENUE: VALUATION OFFICE PROPERTY MARKET REPORTS

PRICE RANGES: AUTUMN 1986

7.35 GREAT BRITAIN: TOWNS BY HOUSE TYPE/SIZE - NEW DWELLINGS

£

	1 Bed Starter house estate type		2 Bed Terraced house estate type		3 Bed Semi-detached house estate type		4 Bed Detached house estate type		2 Bed Flat in 2/3 storey block	
	From	To	From	To	From	To	From	To	From	To
SOUTH WEST										
Poole/Bournem'th	29000	32000	33000	35000	38495	49495	63450	84950	28100	32000
Weymouth	26000	28000	29000	32750	34000	39000	58000	70000	32000	35500
Truro	22500	27000	25100	31000	35000	43000	65000	84000	26000	36000
Exeter	26250	27500	27000	32000	37500	43000	74500	88000	24500	32500
Barnstaple			24500	25500	30000	33000	56000	60000	24000	29000
Plymouth	25000	29000	26500	33000	33000	40000	55000	75000	24000	30000
St Austell			20000	24000	28000	31000	45000	60000		
Taunton	22000	24000	27000	29500	36000	38000	53000	70000	24500	38500
Torquay/Paignton		26000	31000	32500	35000	38000	67000	80000	30000	45000
Bath	25750	28000	33250	37500	40000	47500	67500	95000	34500	40000
Bristol	21000	24500	27000	29000	30000	37000	60000	75000	27500	30000
Cheltenham	27000	32000	30000	37000	32500	43000	70000	100000	30000	45000
Gloucester	21000	23000	22000	24000	32000	37000	60000	75000	25500	33500
Weston-s-Mare			27000	29250	30000	35000	55000	65000	34000	38000
Swindon	20500	24000	28000	32000	34000	41000	65000	75000	23000	27000
Salisbury	30000	32250	37000	40000	42500	47000	72500	82000	30000	34000
WALES										
Bridgend	16750	19250	20500	24000	27250	32000	45000	61000		
Cardiff	21000	23000	27500	32500	35500	39000	65000	73000	22500	25000
Haverfordwest	15500	16950	19500	23000	26000	28000	20000	62000		
Llanelli	18000	19500	21500	23500	23000	27000	49000	60000		
Merthyr Tydfil			22500	24000	26000	27500				
Pontypridd	18000	19000	19500	22500	22000	28000	35500	52500	17000	20000
Swansea	19500	25000	22750	32000	29000	45000	47500	72500	27000	50000
Abergavenny	22500	26000	28500	30500	35000	39000	61000	66000	27500	34000
Bangor	14000	15000	21000	23000	24000	26000	40000	42000	12000	14000
Colwyn Bay	16500	18500	19000	24500	25000	28000	45000	52500	18000	20000
Newport(Gwent)	18000	21000	22000	24500	27500	31000	52000	62000	22000	25000
Newtown	18000	21000	22000	24000	25000	29000	40000	52500	18500	21000
Wrexham	15250	16500	18500	21500	20500	25000	45000	55000	20500	23500

PRICE RANGES: SPRING 1984

7.36 GREAT BRITAIN: TOWNS BY HOUSE TYPE/SIZE - NEW DWELLINGS

£

	3 bedroom semi-detached house estate type		3/4 bedroom detached house estate type		Better quality estate detached house		2 bedroom flat in 3 (or more) storey block	
	From	To	From	To	From	To	From	To
SCOTLAND								
Dumfries	23000	30000	31000	35000	55000	60000	25000	35000
Stirling/Kircaldy	32000	34000	37000	42000	55000	70000	20000	24000
Aberdeen	40000	51000	44000	56000	60000	85000	27000	46000
Grampian (Rural)	28000	33000	34000	38000	38000	45000	19000	22000
Inverness	31000	35000	36000	42000	45000	60000	23000	28000
Edinburgh	37500	47500	45000	55000	55000	80000	25000	47500
Ayr	32000	38000	35000	45000	59000	70000	22000	25000
Glasgow	27500	30000	28000	35000			24000	27000
Glasgow suburbs	33000	38000	34000	40000	55000	80000	23500	40000
Greenock	23500	34000	36500		42000	55000	27000	38200
Dundee	30000	35000	37500	45000	55000	70000	28000	35000
Perth	30000	35000	37500	45000	55000	70000	28000	35000

INLAND REVENUE: VALUATION OFFICE PROPERTY MARKET REPORTS

PRICE RANGES: AUTUMN 1984

7.37 GREAT BRITAIN: TOWNS BY HOUSE TYPE/SIZE - NEW DWELLINGS

£

	3 bedroom semi-detached house estate type		3/4 bedroom detached house estate type		Better quality estate detached house		2 bedroom flat in 3 (or more) storey block	
	From	To	From	To	From	To	From	To
SCOTLAND								
Dumfries	23500	30500	32000	36000	55000	65000	25000	35000
Stirling/Kircaldy	32000	36000	37000	45000	55000	75000	20000	24500
Aberdeen	42000	53000	46000	58000	65000	95000	29000	49950
Grampian (Rural)	28000	36000	34000	40000	39000	50000	19500	24000
Inverness	31000	35000	39000	46000	50000	62500	23000	28000
Edinburgh	39000	47500	45000	57500	55000	85000	29000	50000
Ayr	33000	40000	35000	50000	59000	70000	26000	32000
Glasgow	28000	32000	35000	40000	50000	65000	28000	30000
Glasgow suburbs	35300	38000	39150	48850	55000	80000	27300	40250
Dundee	32500	37500	40000	45000	55000	65000	26000	35000
Perth	32500	37500	40000	48000	60000	70000	28000	35000

PRICE RANGES: SPRING 1985

7.38 GREAT BRITAIN: TOWNS BY HOUSE TYPE/SIZE - NEW DWELLINGS

£

	3 bedroom semi-detached house estate type		3/4 bedroom detached house estate type		Better quality estate detached house		2 bedroom flat in 3 (or more) storey block	
	From	To	From	To	From	To	From	To
SCOTLAND								
Dumfries	31000		34000	38000	55000	65000	25000	
Stirling/Kircaldy	32000	37500	39000	50000	53000	75000	23000	25750
Aberdeen	42000	54000	46000	59000	65000	95000	30000	50000
Grampian (Rural)	28500	36500	34000	40000	39000	57000	19500	24500
Inverness	31000	35000	41000	47000	55000		24000	28000
Edinburgh	39000	49000	47500	60000	57500	85000	31000	60000
Ayr	37500	41000	43000	52000	62000	70000	29000	40000
Glasgow	30000	35000	37000	42000	50000	68000	29000	38000
Glasgow suburbs	35750	37000	40000	52000	50000	85000	27500	44000
Dundee	32500	39000	40000	45000	55000	65000	26000	35000
Perth	33000	39000	40000	49000	60000	72500	28000	35000

PRICE RANGES: AUTUMN 1985

7.39 GREAT BRITAIN: TOWNS BY HOUSE TYPE/SIZE - NEW DWELLINGS

£

	3 bedroom semi-detached house estate type		3/4 bedroom detached house estate type		Better quality estate detached house		2 bedroom flat in 3 (or more) storey block	
	From	To	From	To	From	To	From	To
SCOTLAND								
Dumfries	31000		35500	40000	55000	65000	25000	
Stirling/Kircaldy	33000	38500	40000	50000	55000	75000	24000	28000
Aberdeen	41000	54000	46000	59000	65000	95000	30000	50000
Grampian (Rural)	28500	36500	34000	40000	39000	57000	18750	24500
Inverness	33000	37000	44000	49000	60000	80000	25000	28000
Edinburgh	40000	50000	50000	60000	61500	86500	31000	60000
Ayr	39000	41000	43000	52000	62000	70000	29000	40000
Glasgow	32000	37500	42000	46000	50000	75000	31000	42000
Glasgow suburbs	36500	45000	45500	54500	56550	87000	29100	74000
Dundee	32500	39000	43000	49000	60000	70000	27000	36000
Perth	33000	39000	43000	50000	60000	72500	30000	26000

PRICE RANGES: SPRING 1986

7.40 GREAT BRITAIN: TOWNS BY HOUSE TYPE/SIZE - NEW DWELLINGS

£

	3 bedroom semi-detached house estate type		3/4 bedroom detached house estate type		Better quality estate detached house		2 bedroom flat in 3 (or more) storey block	
	From	To	From	To	From	To	From	To
SCOTLAND								
Dumfries	31000		35500	40000	55000	65000	25000	
Dunferm'/K'caldy	33000	38500	42000	52000	58000	75000	23500	26000
Aberdeen	42000	54000	46000	59000	62000	95000	30000	50000
Grampian (Rural)	30000	37000	35000	43000	39000	57000	20500	25500
Inverness	34000	38000	45500	50000	62500	81000	25000	28000
Edinburgh	40000	50000	52000	62000	62000	91000	31000	61000
Ayr	39000	43000	48000	55000	65000	72000	31650	40000
Glasgow	35000	42000	45000	49000	53000	78000	31000	45000
Glasgow (Bearsden	37000	41000	47250	56350	64750	80000	29950	71150
Glasgow (Eastwood	41000	45000	47500	51600	68500	87000	29100	35400
Dundee	35000	40000	43000	50000	60000	70000	27000	36000
Perth	35000	40000	43000	50000	60000	72500	30000	36000
Hamilton	38000	43000	48000	53000	62000	72000	27500	35000

PRICE RANGES: AUTUMN 1986

7.41 GREAT BRITAIN: TOWNS BY HOUSE TYPE/SIZE - NEW DWELLINGS

£

	3 bedroom semi-detached house estate type		3/4 bedroom detached house estate type		Better quality estate detached house		2 bedroom flat in 3 (or more) storey block	
	From	To	From	To	From	To	From	To
SCOTLAND								
Dumfries	34400	38600	39000	46000	65000	72000		
Dunferm'/Falkirk	34000	39000	43000	57500	58000	93000	24000	27000
Aberdeen	40000	54000	46000	59000	60000	95000	29000	50000
Grampian (Rural)	32000	39000	36000	44000	40000	58000	21000	26000
Inverness	34000	38250	45500	51000	57000	81000	24000	26250
Edinburgh	42000	52000	53000	70000	62000	101000	33000	63000
Ayr	40000	44000	50000	57000	65000	72000	31650	40000
Glasgow	35000	43000	45000	50000	54000	80000	31000	47000
Glasgow (Bearsden	37500	42000	47500	59350	64700	82000	29950	76950
Glasgow (Eastwood	45900	49750	49600	53950	75000	106000	34600	56750
Dundee	35000	40000	43000	50000	60000	70000	27000	36000
Perth	35000	40000	43000	50000	60000	72500	30000	36000
Hamilton	40000	44000	48000	54000	62000	75000	27500	37500

PRICE RANGES: AUTUMN 1983

7.42 GREAT BRITAIN:
 TOWNS BY HOUSE TYPE AND AGE OF HOUSE - SECONDHAND DWELLINGS

£

	Pre-1919 terraced house		Interwar semi-detached house/bungalow		Post 1960 semi-detached house/bungalow		Post 1965 detached house		Post 1960 flat in 3 (or more) storey block	
	From	To	From	To	From	To	From	To	From	To
YORKSHIRE AND HUMBERSIDE										
Harrogate	16500	22000	23000	29000	22500	30000	50000	65000	28000	37000
York	15000	20000	21000	26000	22000	28000	45000	65000	25000	30000
Bradford	10500	17000	15750	24500	18000	27000	38500	50000	15500	23000
Calderdale	8500	22000	15000	30000	17500	25000	40000	55000		
Kirklees	9500	15000	16000	22000	18500	23500	43000	53000		
Leeds	8500	20000	18000	27750	20000	30000	40000	62500	17500	30000
Wakefield	13000	15000	18000	24000	19500	25000	45000	58000		
Barnsley	11000	13000	17500	19500	18500	21500	41000	45000	12500	14500
Doncaster	8750	9250	17000	19000	19750	21750	47000	55000		
Grimsby	9500	11000	14500	18000	18500	21500	42500	50000	15000	18000
Hull	8500	15500	20500	25000	21000	25500	41000	47000	15000	22000
Humberside	8000	19000	17000	27500	18000	29500	37500	57000	15000	25750
Rotherham	9500	17000	18000	25000	19000	26500	37500	52000	24000	30000
Sheffield	14000	17000	20000	25500	22000	26500	48000	52000	18000	24000
NORTH WEST										
Bolton	11250	13250	18000	23000	19500	26500	42500	60000	14000	16000
Manchester	9750	13750	19500	22750	22500	26250	45500	55000	18000	22500
Oldham	11000	13000	22000	25000	24000	29000	50000	55000	21000	26000
Rochdale	14000	16000	18000	22500	21000	24000	50000	57000		
Salford	10000	25000	17000	32000	24000	30000	45000	80000	17000	40000
Stockport	13500	17000	22000	25000	23500	28000	44000	55000	19000	29000
Wigan	10250	14250	16000	21000	19000	23500	40000	55000		
Blackburn	7250	12500	18000	25000	20500	26500	46500	61500		
Burnley	9000	17000	17000	25000	20000	27500	37500	60000	11000	14750
Lancaster	13000	20750	18500	25750	20750	27000	42000	62000	21750	36000
Preston	13000	17000	18750	22000	19500	22500	42000	52000	17000	20000
Chester	15000	16000	21000	22000	23500	24500	47000	51000	22000	24000
East Cheshire	13500	24000	19000	27500	20500	29000	40000	63000		31000
Liverpool	14850	17500	19000	24000	21000	25000	41000	50000	16000	17000
St Helens	8000	11500	18500	26000	19000	25000	45000	53000		
Sefton	4250	16500	18750	26750	21000	28500	49000	59500	20000	29000
Warrington	10250	12750	19500	21500	23500	25000	52250	54250	17500	20500
Wirral	9500	13500	19500	25000	19500	26000	47500	60000	17500	25000
NORTHERN										
Newcastle	14000	21000	19000	25000	20000	25000	35000	50000	16250	30000
Northumberland	13000	22500	21000	34000	20000	30000	40000	65000	23000	27500
Sunderland	8000	20000	17000	25000	23000	26500	40000	60000	16000	19000
Tyneside	12500	15500	19000	24000	23500	26500	42500	48000	25000	29000
South Cleveland	12500	18250	20500	25500	20250	28750	46250	57250	11500	15250
North Cleveland	9000	10000	18000	19000	19000	20000	45000	48000	14500	15500
Darlington	10000	13250	19000	23000	25000	29000	60000	70000	23500	29000
Durham	12000	20500	15000	29250	20000	24500	40000	64500		
Carlisle	14000	18000	21000	27000	21000	27000	38000	50000		
South Lakeland	15000	16500	22000	26000	22000	25000	48000	50000		

INLAND REVENUE: VALUATION OFFICE PROPERTY MARKET REPORTS

PRICE RANGES: SPRING 1984

7.43 GREAT BRITAIN:
TOWNS BY HOUSE TYPE AND AGE OF HOUSE - SECONDHAND DWELLINGS

£

	Pre-1919 terraced house		Interwar semi-detached house/bungalow		Post 1960 semi-detached house/bungalow		Post 1965 detached house		Post 1960 flat in 3 (or more) storey block	
	From	To	From	To	From	To	From	To	From	To
YORKSHIRE AND HUMBERSIDE										
Harrogate	17250	22750	23250	30000	23250	30000	51000	67000	28500	37500
York	16000	21000	21000	26000	22000	28000	45000	65000	25000	30000
Bradford	10500	17000	16000	24500	18000	27000	38500	50000	15500	23000
Calderdale	8500	20000	15000	30000	17500	25000	65000	60000		
Kirklees	9750	15250	16000	22000	19000	24000	44000	54000		
Leeds	9000	19000	18500	28000	21000	30000	42000	60000	18000	30000
Wakefield	13200	15500	18000	24000	19500	25000	45000	58000		
Barnsley	11500	13500	18500	21500	19500	22500	42000	46000	13000	15000
Doncaster	9000	9750	17000	19000	20500	22750	47000	55000		
Grimsby	9500	11000	15000	19500	19000	23000	44000	50000	15000	20000
Hull	8600	15500	21000	25000	21500	25000	42500	47500	15000	23000
Humberside	17500	20000	20000	25000	25000	30000	65000	70000	22000	27500
Rotherham	10000	17000	18500	25500	20000	27000	40000	52000		
Sheffield	14500	17500	20500	25500	22500	27000	48000	52000	17000	24000
NORTH WEST										
Bolton	12000	14000	18000	23000	19500	26500	42500	60000	14000	16000
Manchester	10000	14000	19500	23000	23000	27750	45500	55000	18000	22500
Oldham	11000	13000	22000	25000	24000	29000	50000	55000	21000	26000
Rochdale	15000	17000	19000	23000	22000	25000	50000	57000		
Salford	10000	25000	17000	32000	24000	30000	45000	80000	17000	40000
Stockport	16250	17250	23000	24500	27000	29000	55000	60000	24000	29000
Wigan	10500	15000	16000	21500	19000	24000	40000	55000		
Blackburn	7250	12500	18000	25000	20500	26500	46500	61500		
Burnley	9000	17000	17500	25000	20000	28000	40000	60000		
Lancaster	15000	20000	21000	25000	24000	28000	55000	65000	28000	35000
Preston	14000	18000	18750	22000	19500	22500	42000	52000	17000	20000
Chester	15250	16250	21250	22250	23750	24750	47000	51000	22000	24000
East Cheshire	13000	14000	18500	19500	20000	21000	46000	48000		
Liverpool	15250	17750	19750	24500	21760	25500	41000	50000	16500	17500
St Helens	9000	12500	19000	28000	20000	27000	45000	55000		
Sefton	10000	17000	18750	27250	23000	28500	50000	59500	25000	30000
Warrington	10250	12750	19500	21500	23000	25000	52250	54250	17500	20500
Wirral	9750	13750	20000	25500	20000	26500	48000	61000	17500	25000
NORTHERN										
Newcastle	16000	24000	21000	26000	22000	25000	38000	55000	18500	30000
Northumberland	19000	24000	27500	35000	31000	32500	43000	70000		
Sunderland	8250	20750	17250	26000	23500	30000	41000	64000		
Tyneside	13000	16500	19500	24750	24500	27500	45000	52500	26000	30000
North Cleveland	12500	13500	20500	24000	20250	23000	52000	58000	11500	15250
South Cleveland	9500	10500	18500	19500	19500	20000	47000	50000	14500	15500
Darlington	10500	14000	20000	24000	25000	29000	60000	77000	23500	29000
Durham	18500	21250	26000	30500	24000	25000	64000	66000		
Carlisle	14500	16000	21000	24000	22000	25000	38000	42000		
South Lakeland	15000	17000	22000	26000	22500	25500	48000	50000		

INLAND REVENUE: VALUATION OFFICE PROPERTY MARKET REPORTS

PRICE RANGES: AUTUMN 1984

7.44 GREAT BRITAIN:
    TOWNS BY HOUSE TYPE AND AGE OF HOUSE - SECONDHAND DWELLINGS

£

	Pre-1919 terraced house		Interwar semi-detached house/bungalow		Post 1960 semi-detached house/bungalow		Post 1965 detached house		Post 1960 flat in 3 (or more) storey block	
	From	To	From	To	From	To	From	To	From	To
YORKSHIRE AND HUMBERSIDE										
Harrogate	17500	23000	24500	31250	24500	31250	53000	68500	29500	38500
York	18000	23000	21000	26000	25000	29500	50000	65000	25000	30000
Bradford	11000	17750	16750	25500	18750	27000	39500	51000	16000	23000
Halifax	8500	25000	16000	30000	17500	25000	47500	62500	9500	31000
Huddersfield	10500	16000	16500	22500	19500	24500	46000	56000		
Leeds	9000	19500	19000	28750	21500	31000	42500	62000	18500	30000
Wakefield	13500	15750	18250	24500	19500	25250	45000	58000		
Barnsley	11500	13500	18500	22000	19500	22500	42000	46000	13000	15000
Doncaster	9000	9750	17750	20000	21250	23500	47000	55000		
Grimsby	10000	11500	18500	22000	19500	23500	44000	55000	15000	20000
Hull	9000	15500	21500	25500	22000	25500	45000	50000	15500	23000
Beverley	18500	21500	26500	32500	26500	33000	65000	73000	22000	30000
Rotherham	10500	17500	18500	26500	20500	28000	40000	52000		
Sheffield	15500	19000	22000	26000	23500	28000	47000	52500	16000	24000
NORTH WEST										
Bolton	12000	14000	18000	23000	19500	26500	42500	60000	14000	16000
Manchester	10250	14500	20500	24000	23500	28000	47000	56750	15500	22500
Oldham	11500	13500	23000	26000	25000	30000	50000	55000	21000	26000
Bury	15500	17000	19500	23500	23000	25000	50000	58000		
Salford/Trafford	10000	27500	20000	32000	24000	30000	47500	80000	17000	40000
Stockport	16500	17500	24000	25500	28250	30250	62500	67500	24000	29000
Wigan	10500	15500	16000	22000	19000	25000	40000	56000		
Blackburn	7500	13250	19000	26000	22000	27500	48000	65000		
Burnley	9000	17000	17500	25000	20000	28000	40000	60000		
Lancaster	16000	21000	22000	26000	25000	29000	55000	65000	28000	35000
Preston	14000	18000	18750	22000	19500	22500	42000	52000	17000	20000
Chester	16000	17800	21250	23500	25000	26000	51500	53000	22000	24000
Crewe	13500	14500	18500	19500	20000	21000	47000	49000		
Liverpool	12000	18000	21000	26000	22500	27500	42000	50000	17000	23000
St Helens	9000	12500	20000	28000	20000	28000	47500	57500		
Southport	11000	17000	20000	28000	23500	29250	51000	60000	25000	30000
Warrington	10750	13250	20500	22500	25000	27000	53000	56000	18250	21250
Birkenhead	9750	13750	21000	26500	21000	27500	48000	61000	17500	25000
NORTHERN										
Newcastle	16000	24000	21000	28500	23000	26000	40000	56000	20000	35000
Morpeth	20000	25500	27500	36000	31000	33500	43000	72000		
Sunderland	8500	21500	17500	26250	24000	30500	41500	65000		
Tynemouth	13750	17000	20000	25500	25000	28000	46000	53500	26500	31000
Stockton	12500	13500	20500	24000	20250	23000	52000	58000	11500	15250
Middlesbrough	10000	11000	19500	20500	20500	21500	48000	51000	14500	15500
Darlington	10750	14250	20000	24000	26000	30000	62000	79000	23500	29000
Durham	18500	22500	26000	32500	24000	27500	64000	67000		
Carlisle	15500	16500	22000	25000	23000	26000	38000	42000		
Barrow	16000	18500	23000	28000	24500	27000	51000	55000		

PRICE RANGES: SPRING 1985

7.45 GREAT BRITAIN:
TOWNS BY HOUSE TYPE AND AGE OF HOUSE - SECONDHAND DWELLINGS

£

	Pre-1919 terraced house		Interwar semi-detached house/bungalow		Post 1960 semi-detached house/bungalow		Post 1965 detached house		Post 1960 flat in 3 (or more) storey block	
	From	To	From	To	From	To	From	To	From	To
YORKSHIRE AND HUMBERSIDE										
Harrogate	17750	23000	24750	31500	24750	31500	53500	69000	29750	38500
York	18000	23000	23000	28000	26000	31000	55000	65000	25000	30000
Bradford	11250	18000	17250	26000	19250	27500	40500	51750	16250	23000
Halifax	8500	25000	16000	30000	17500	25000	47500	62500	9500	31000
Huddersfield	11000	16500	17250	23250	20500	25000	47000	57000		
Leeds	9500	20000	19000	29000	21500	31500	43000	63000	18500	30000
Wakefield	14000	16250	18500	24500	19750	25750	45000	58000		
Barnsley	11500	13500	18500	22000	19500	23000	42000	46000	13000	15000
Doncaster	9000	9750	18000	20500	21250	23500	47000	55000		
Grimsby	11000	12000	20000	22000	21000	23500	48000	60000	15000	20000
Hull	9500	16000	22000	26000	22000	26500	46000	51000	16000	28750
Beverley	18500	22500	26500	32500	26500	35000	65000	75000	22000	32000
Rotherham	11000	18500	18500	27500	21000	29000	40000	52000		
Sheffield	16500	20000	22000	26000	23500	28000	47000	52500	15500	24000
NORTH WEST										
Bolton	12000	14000	18000	23000	19500	26500	42500	60000	14000	16000
Manchester	10250	14500	20500	24000	23500	28000	47000	56750	15500	22500
Oldham	12000	14000	23000	26000	25000	30000	50000	55000	21000	26000
Bury	15500	17500	19500	24000	23000	26000	50500	60000		
Salford/Trafford	10000	29000	20000	34000	25000	30000	50000	80000	17000	40000
Stockport	16750	17750	24250	25750	28500	30750	63500	68500	25000	29000
Wigan	10750	15750	16250	22250	19250	25250	41000	58000		
Blackburn	9000	15000	19500	28000	22000	29500	46500	64000		
Burnley	9000	17000	17500	26500	21500	30000	40000	60000		
Lancaster	16000	22000	22000	26000	25000	29000	55000	65000	19000	26000
Preston	14000	18000	19000	23000	20000	24000	44000	55000	17000	21000
Chester	16000	18000	21500	23750	25250	26250	52000	53500	22000	24000
Crewe	13500	14500	19000	20000	20500	21500	48000	50000		
Liverpool	12000	18000	21000	26000	23000	28500	43000	52500	17000	23000
St Helens	9000	12500	20000	28000	20000	28000	50000	60000		
Southport	15000	19000	23750	28750	25000	30000	51500	60500	26000	31000
Warrington	11000	14500	20500	22500	25000	27500	53000	56000	18250	21250
Birkenhead	9750	13750	21000	26500	23000	27500	48000	61000	18000	25000
NORTHERN										
Newcastle	16500	25000	21000	28500	23000	27500	40000	56000	20000	35000
Morpeth	22000	26000	28000	36500	31500	34000	44000	73000		
Sunderland	9000	22000	18500	26750	24500	31000	42000	67000		
Whitley Bay	14000	17000	20000	25500	25000	29000	46000	53500	26500	32500
Stockton	12500	13500	20500	24000	20250	23000	52000	60000	12500	16000
Middlesbrough	10000	11500	19500	21000	21000	22000	49000	52000	14500	16000
Darlington	11000	14750	20000	24000	26250	30250	64000	79000	24500	31000
Durham	20000	22500	28000	32500	24000	27500	64000	67000		
Carlisle	16000	19000	22000	24000	24000	27500	38000	42000		
Barrow	16000	19000	25000	31000	24500	30000	51000	55000		

PRICE RANGES: AUTUMN 1985

7.46 GREAT BRITAIN:
TOWNS BY HOUSE TYPE AND AGE OF HOUSE - SECONDHAND DWELLINGS

£

	Pre-1919 terraced house (modernized)		Interwar semi-detached house (modernized)		Post 1960 semi-detached house		Post 1960 detached house		Post 1960 flat in 3 (or more) storey block	
	From	To	From	To	From	To	From	To	From	To
YORKSHIRE AND HUMBERSIDE										
Harrogate	20500	25000	28500	33000	26000	33000	56000	72500	31250	40000
York	22000	27000	25000	29000	26500	31000	59000	70000	25000	30000
Bradford	11750	19000	17750	27000	19750	30000	41500	53000	17000	23000
Halifax	14000	18000	22000	27500	18000	26000	55000	65000	10000	12000
Huddersfield	14000	19000	18500	25000	21000	26000	48000	58000		
Leeds	16500	26000	21500	32000	22000	32500	44000	65000	18950	30000
Wakefield	11000	21000	21950	29000	23000	28500	45000	76500		
Barnsley	14000	16000	21000	23000	19500	23500	44000	48000	14000	16000
Doncaster	12500	14000	19000	21000	22000	24000	47000	55000	15500	16000
Grimsby	13000	16000	20000	24000	22000	28000	45000	60000	25000	30000
Hull	12000	16500	26500	28500	24000	28000	47500	52000	16000	28750
Beverley	22000	26000	29000	35000	27500	35000	65000	75000	25000	32000
Rotherham	14000	19000	22000	28500	22000	30000	42500	52000	20000	25000
Sheffield	19000	22500	24500	28500	25000	30000	48000	55000	15500	24000
NORTH WEST										
Bolton	13000	15500	20000	25500	19500	27000	42500	65000	14000	16000
Manchester	13500	17000	22250	26250	25800	30750	49000	59500	16250	23600
Oldham	15250	17750	24000	27000	25000	30000	50000	56000	21000	26000
Bury	16000	18000	22000	25500	23000	26500	52000	62000	14500	20000
Salford/Trafford	12500	35000	22950	33000	25500	30500	50000	80000	17000	35750
Stockport	17500	24000	25000	30000	25000	31000	59500	68500	22500	29000
Wigan	13500	15500	25000	28000	22500	27000	55000	65000	22000	22000
Blackburn	14000	23000	23100	28000	24000	30000	49000	67000	17500	22500
Burnley	11000	18500	19500	28000	21500	30000	41000	60000		
Lancaster	19000	23000	25000	27000	25000	29000	55000	65000	19000	26000
Preston	16000	20000	26000	29000	27000	31000	54000	60000	22000	26000
Chester	18000	20000	24000	26000	26000	27000	55000	60000	22500	24500
Crewe	14000	15500	19500	22000	20500	23000	50000	60000		
Liverpool	13500	20000	23000	30000	23000	28500	43000	65000	17000	24000
St Helens	14000	19000	23000	30000	22000	29000	50000	60000		
Southport	18500	21500	28250	31500	27000	32000	52000	62000	27500	32500
Warrington	12000	14000	25000	30000	25000	29000	53000	56000	18250	21250
Birkenhead	13500	15000	22500	26500	23500	28500	55000	65000	20000	26000
NORTHERN										
Newcastle	20000	26000	24000	30000	23000	28000	40000	56000	21000	35000
Morpeth	20000	26000	28000	36500	31500	34000	44000	73000		
Sunderland	21000	24000	25000	31500	25000	32000	44000	70000		
Whitley Bay	14500	17500	21000	26750	26000	30500	50000	59000	27000	33500
Stockton	11500	13750	21000	24500	20000	26000	52000	58000	9500	12500
Middlesbrough	13000	15000	25500	27000	22000	23000	50000	52500	15000	16000
Darlington	14000	16500	22000	25000	26250	30250	64000	79000	24500	31000
Durham	23000	26000	34500	38500	24500	28000	65000	68000		
Carlisle	21000	24000	25000	27000	27000	29500	44000	46000		
Barrow	18000	20000	28000	32000	26000	30500	53000	59000		

PRICE RANGES: SPRING 1986

7.47 GREAT BRITAIN:
TOWNS BY HOUSE TYPE AND AGE OF HOUSE - SECONDHAND DWELLINGS

£

	Pre-1919 terraced house (modernized)		Interwar semi-detached house (modernized)		Post 1960 semi-detached house		Post 1960 detached house		Post 1960 flat in 3 (or more) storey block	
	From	To	From	To	From	To	From	To	From	To
YORKSHIRE AND HUMBERSIDE										
Harrogate	19500	24000	28000	35000	26000	35000	56000	72500	27500	40000
York	23000	29000	27000	31000	28000	31500	60000	71000	25000	30000
Bradford	13000	22000	18500	27000	21000	30000	42500	55000	17000	23000
Halifax	15000	19000	22500	28000	18500	27000	56000	65000	10500	12500
Huddersfield	15000	20000	20000	26000	23000	28000	50000	62500		
Leeds	16500	27000	21500	33000	25000	33000	44000	67500	19000	30000
Wakefield	14000	21500	23500	29000	24000	29500	50000	76500		
Barnsley	14000	16000	22500	24500	21000	24500	48000	55000	14500	16500
Doncaster	13000	14500	19500	21500	22500	24500	47000	55000	15500	16000
Grimsby	13000	16000	22000	25000	22000	28000	45000	60000	25000	30000
Hull	12500	16750	26500	28500	24000	28500	49000	53500	16000	28750
Beverley	22000	26000	29000	35000	27500	35000	65000	75000	25000	32000
Rotheram	14000	19000	22500	30000	22500	30000	42500	52000	20000	25000
Sheffield	20000	23000	26000	29000	25000	30000	48000	55000	16000	24000
NORTH WEST										
Bolton	13000	16250	20000	27000	20000	28500	44000	66000	14000	16000
Manchester	14000	23000	23000	27250	25800	30750	49000	59500	16250	23600
Oldham	15250	17750	24000	27000	25000	30000	55000	60000	21000	26000
Bury	16250	18250	22000	25500	23250	27250	52000	62500	14500	21000
Salford/Trafford	14000	37500	25000	37500	25500	37000	52500	82500	18000	41000
Stockport	17500	24250	25000	35000	25500	31750	60000	70250	22500	29500
Wigan	14000	17500	21500	27000	25000	30000	50000	58000		
Blackburn	14500	23500	23750	29000	24500	30750	50000	67500	17600	22750
Burnley	12000	19000	20000	28000	22000	30000	42000	61000		
Lancaster	19500	23500	26000	29000	26000	31000	55000	67000	19000	26000
Preston	16500	20500	26500	30000	27000	31000	54000	60000	22000	26000
Chester	18000	20000	24000	26000	30000	34000	65000	75000	24000	27000
Crewe	14500	16250	19500	24000	21000	24000	52500	65000		
Liverpool	13750	20000	23000	30000	23000	30000	43500	60000	17000	25000
St Helens	14500	19000	24000	30000	24000	29000	50000	60000		
Southport	19000	22000	28250	31500	30000	33500	55500	62000	27500	32500
Warrington	13500	14500	25000	30000	25000	30000	53000	60000	18250	21250
Birkenhead	13500	15500	24000	29000	25500	31000	55000	65000	20000	26000
NORTHERN										
Newcastle	22000	27000	25000	32500	24000	31000	40000	56000	22500	35000
Morpeth	20500	26500	29500	38000	32250	35000	45000	75000		
Sunderland	21500	25000	25500	32000	25000	32000	44500	70000		
Whitley Bay	15000	18500	22000	28000	26000	31000	50000	59000	27000	34000
Stockton	11500	14000	21000	25000	20000	28000	52000	58000	9500	12500
Middlesbrough	13000	15000	25500	27000	22000	24000	50000	53000	15000	16000
Darlington	13500	16750	21750	25000	26500	30500	64000	75000	24500	31000
Durham	23000	26000	26500	34500	24500	28500	65000	68000		
Carlisle	23000	25000	27000	31000	27000	29500	46000	48000		
Barrow	20000	23000	29000	34000	29000	33500	55000	60000		

INLAND REVENUE: VALUATION OFFICE PROPERTY MARKET REPORTS

PRICE RANGES: AUTUMN 1986

7.48 GREAT BRITAIN:
  TOWNS BY HOUSE TYPE AND AGE OF HOUSE - SECONDHAND DWELLINGS

£

	Pre-1919 terraced house (modernized)		Interwar semi-detached house (modernized)		Post 1960 semi-detached house		Post 1960 detached house		Post 1960 flat in 3 (or more) storey block	
	From	To	From	To	From	To	From	To	From	To
YORKSHIRE AND HUMBERSIDE										
Harrogate	19500	24000	28000	36000	26000	35000	62500	77500	27500	40000
York	23000	29500	29250	31500	28000	31950	64000	73500	25000	31250
Bradford	15000	24000	19500	28500	22500	31500	45000	59000	17000	23000
Halifax	15750	20000	23500	29250	20000	28000	58000	67500	11250	13000
Huddersfield	16000	23000	21000	26500	23500	29000	52000	65000		
Leeds	17000	27000	22000	34000	26000	38000	45000	70000	19000	30000
Wakefield	14000	21500	23500	31000	24500	30000	50000	76500	19000	20000
Barnsley	15000	17500	23500	26000	22500	26000	50000	58000	14500	17500
Doncaster	13000	15000	19500	25000	22500	29500	48000	60000	16000	25000
Grimsby	13000	17500	22000	27000	23000	28000	45000	60000	25000	30000
Hull	13000	17500	26500	29000	24500	29250	50000	55000	15000	28750
Beverley	22000	26000	30000	36500	28000	36000	65000	75000	25000	32000
Rotheram	14500	19500	23500	30000	23500	30000	45000	52000	20000	25000
Sheffield	21000	24000	26500	29500	25500	30500	48000	55000	16500	24000
NORTH WEST										
Bolton	13000	16750	20000	28000	20000	30000	46000	70000	14000	16000
Manchester	14500	25850	23500	28500	26500	33000	49000	65500	16600	25000
Oldham	16000	17750	24750	28000	25000	31000	55000	60000	21000	27500
Bury	16750	18750	22500	26250	23500	27750	52000	63500	14000	21750
Salford/Trafford	15000	37500	25000	38000	26500	39000	52500	85000	18000	41000
Stockport	17750	25250	26000	31500	26000	33250	62500	71000	23000	30000
Wigan	14000	18000	21500	27500	25000	30000	50000	58000		
Blackburn	15000	23500	24500	30000	25000	31000	50000	68500	18000	23000
Burnley	12200	19200	22000	30000	24000	32000	44000	63000		
Lancaster	22000	24500	26000	30000	27000	32000	57000	70000	19000	26000
Preston	16500	20500	26500	30000	27000	31500	54000	60000	24000	28000
Chester	19500	24000	24000	27000	32750	34500	65000	85000	26000	29000
Crewe	15000	17500	21000	25000	23000	25500	57000	68500		
Liverpool	14000	20500	23500	31000	23500	32500	43500	60000	17000	25000
St Helens	15000	20000	24500	30000	22000	29500	50000	60000		
Southport	20000	23000	28250	33000	31500	34500	59000	65750	27500	32500
Warrington	15000	17000	26000	30000	26000	30000	55000	62500	18250	21250
Birkenhead	14000	16000	22500	29500	24000	31000	48000	64000	18000	25000
NORTHERN										
Newcastle	21000	27000	24500	36950	25000	31000	42500	56000	22500	35000
Morpeth	22000	28000	30000	40000	32500	36000	47500	80000		
Sunderland	22000	25500	26000	32500	25500	32500	45000	70000		
North Tyneside	16000	20000	22500	28500	26000	31000	50000	59000	27000	34000
Stockton	11500	14500	21000	26000	21000	29000	52000	58000	9500	12500
Middlesbrough	13000	15000	25500	27500	22000	24500	50000	55000	15000	16000
Darlington	14000	17250	21750	25000	26500	30500	64000	75000	24500	31000
Durham	23500	26500	29250	35250	25000	29250	67000	70000		
Carlisle	24000	27000	28000	33000	28000	32000	48000	52000		
Barrow	20500	23500	31000	35500	31000	35500	57000	62000		

PRICE RANGES: AUTUMN 1983

7.49 GREAT BRITAIN:
TOWNS BY HOUSE TYPE AND AGE OF HOUSE – SECONDHAND DWELLINGS

£

	Pre-1919 terraced house		Interwar semi-detached house/bungalow		Post 1960 semi-detached house/bungalow		Post 1965 detached house		Post 1960 flat in 3 (or more) storey block	
	From	To	From	To	From	To	From	To	From	To
EAST MIDLANDS										
Boston	12500	15000	18500	20000	20500	22500	35000	40000		
Lincoln	9000	18500	16500	24000	20000	24500	41000	55000		
Mansfield	6000	8500	16000	23000	17500	27750	40000	60000		
Nottingham	11000	12500	21000	23000	25000	27000	52000	56000	25000	27000
South Notts	8500	16000	16000	24000	18500	26500	45000	75000	14000	20000
Chesterfield	10750	17500	19500	26500	21000	27000	45000	58000		
Derby	9000	14500	16500	25000	17500	22500	42500	55000	12000	16000
Kettering	14500	17500	20000	23000	20000	22000	56000	60000		
Leicester	8500	16000	18000	23000	20000	24000	35000	50000	20000	40000
Northampton	14000	18000	20500	24000	20000	25000	50000	55000	17000	18500
N Leicestershire	14000	18000	18000	24000	20000	25000	50000	65000		
S Leicestershire	12000	16500	18500	22500	18000	24000	40000	52000		
W Derbyshire	13000	19000	19500	27000	20500	28500	40000	50000	16500	27500
WEST MIDLANDS										
Birmingham	12000	16750	24500	31000	24500	31000	52000	72000	16500	26000
Coventry	12000	16500	19500	28750	20500	31000	36000	65000	13500	32500
Dudley	10750	15500	18250	25250	21500	26500	47500	60000	15000	34000
Sandwell	10000	15000	18000	23000	23000	28000	40000	50000	13000	16000
Walsall	11000	13500	17500	23500	21500	27000	41500	52500	12000	19000
Wolverhampton	8000	12500	18500	24000	22500	26500	50000	62500	16000	20000
Lichfield	14000	19500	16500	28500	18250	27500	42500	65000	17000	27000
N Warwickshire	9000	16500	18500	22000	22000	25000	36000	50000	12000	20000
Shropshire	12000	18000	16000	24500	17500	25000	47000	62500		
Stafford	14500	16500	18000	21000	19000	24000	47000	56000		
Stoke-on-Trent	10750	13500	18500	24500	18500	25000	43500	61000		
Warwick	17500	20000	22000	25000	24500	28500	56000	62500	19000	25500
H'ford & W Worcs	17000	19000	21500	25000	23000	26000	48000	56000	17000	21000
E Worcester	13500	19000	18000	25000	19000	25000	47500	73500	16000	25000
EAST ANGLIA										
Cambridge	25000	38000	27000	37500	25000	35000	47000	69000	23000	40000
Peterborough	10000	18000	18000	24000	22000	29000	39000	64000	8000	23000
Ipswich	16000	19000	21500	28000	23500	27000	45000	61000	16000	24000
Bury St Edmunds	15000	22500	25000	35000	22500	30000	40000	55000	17500	22500
N Norfolk	17500	24000	18000	26000	20500	27500	45000	65000	30000	30000
W Norfolk	16500	17500	22500	24000	22500	24000	42000	44000	18000	25000
Norwich	15000	20000	19000	28500	25000	30000	45000	55000	20000	25000

PRICE RANGES: SPRING 1984

7.50 GREAT BRITAIN:
TOWNS BY HOUSE TYPE AND AGE OF HOUSE – SECONDHAND DWELLINGS

£

	Pre-1919 terraced house		Interwar semi-detached house/bungalow		Post 1960 semi-detached house/bungalow		Post 1965 detached house		Post 1960 flat in 3 (or more) storey block	
	From	To	From	To	From	To	From	To	From	To
EAST MIDLANDS										
Boston	12500	15000	18500	21000	20500	24000	37500	45000		
Lincoln	10500	18000	18000	22500	21000	25000	42500	56000		
Mansfield	6500	9500	16500	25000	18250	27000	40000	60000		
Nottingham	11500	13000	21500	23500	25500	27500	52000	56000	25000	27000
South Notts	11000	16000	19000	23000	22500	27000	55000	75000	15000	18000
Chesterfield	12000	17250	19500	26500	21000	27000	45000	59000		
Derby	9000	15000	16500	25000	17500	23000	42500	56000	12000	16000
Kettering	14500	18000	21000	26000	20500	25000	56000	62000		
Leicester	8500	16500	18000	24000	21000	25000	47000	52000	22500	27500
Northampton	14000	18000	21000	25000	22000	26000	50000	60000	17000	18500
N Leicestershire	14500	18500	19000	26000	20000	26000	55000	68000		
S Leicestershire	12500	17000	19000	23500	19000	25000	41000	53000		
W Derbyshire	16000	19000	24500	27500	26500	29500	47500	53500	25000	27500
WEST MIDLANDS										
Birmingham	12000	16750	22500	26500	24500	31000	52000	72000	16500	26000
Coventry	11500	15000	18000	23500	19000	27000	35000	57500	12000	32500
Dudley	11000	17000	18500	26000	22000	27000	49000	65000	15000	35000
Sandwell	10000	15000	18000	23000	23000	28000	40000	50000	13000	16000
Walsall	11000	13500	17500	23500	21500	27000	41500	52500	12000	12000
Wolverhampton	8000	12500	18500	24000	22500	26500	50000	62500	16000	20000
Lichfield	17500	20000	18500	29000	18250	28500	50000	55000	17000	21500
N Warwickshire	9000	16500	18500	22000	22000	25000	36000	50000	13500	20000
Shropshire	14000	18000	17000	25000	20000	26000	52000	63000		
Stafford	14500	17000	18000	22000	20000	25000	48000	57000		
Stoke-on-Trent	11000	14000	18500	25000	19000	25500	44000	61500		
Warwick	18000	20500	22500	25500	25000	29500	57500	65000	19500	26000
H'ford & W Worcs	17500	19500	22000	25000	24000	26500	49000	56000	17250	22250
E Worcester	13500	16000	18000	24000	19000	25000	47500	60000	16000	27500
EAST ANGLIA										
Cambridge	26000	42000	31000	42000	33000	40000	65000	90000	26000	40000
Peterborough	10000	18000	18000	25000	22000	29000	40000	67500	8000	23000
Ipswich	17500	21000	22500	30000	24000	28500	48000	61000	16750	25000
Bury St Edmunds	16000	23500	26250	36750	22500	31500	40000	57500	18500	23500
N Norfolk	18250	25250	19000	26500	22000	28500	48000	65000	16000	32000
W Norfolk	16500	17500	22500	24000	22250	24000	44500	45500	18000	25000
Norwich	16500	22000	20000	30000	24000	30000	45000	60000	20000	25000

7.51 *GREAT BRITAIN:*
TOWNS BY HOUSE TYPE AND AGE OF HOUSE - SECONDHAND DWELLINGS

£

	Pre-1919 terraced house		Interwar semi-detached house/bungalow		Post 1960 semi-detached house/bungalow		Post 1965 detached house		Post 1960 flat in 3 (or more) storey block	
	From	To	From	To	From	To	From	To	From	To
EAST MIDLANDS										
Boston	12500	15000	18000	21000	20500	24000	37500	45000		
Lincoln	11000	18500	18500	23000	21500	25000	45000	57000		
Mansfield	6750	10000	16500	27500	18500	27500	40000	62500		
Nottingham	12000	13500	24000	26000	27500	29500	54000	58000	26000	28000
Carlton (Notts)	13000	17000	20000	24500	24500	28000	60000	80000	16500	19500
Chesterfield	12000	17500	20000	27000	21000	27000	45000	59000		
Derby	9000	15000	17000	25000	18500	23000	42500	56000	12000	16000
Kettering	15000	20000	22000	28000	21000	26000	58000	65000		
Leicester	8600	17000	19500	25500	22750	27000	45000	55000	22500	27500
Northampton	14250	18500	22000	27000	23000	28000	52500	65000	17500	19500
Loughborough	15000	20000	19000	27000	21000	28000	55000	70000		
Hinckley	13000	17500	19500	24000	19500	25500	42000	54000		
Buxton	16500	19500	25000	28000	27250	30000	48250	54500	25000	27500
WEST MIDLANDS										
Birmingham	12250	17000	22750	26750	24750	31250	52500	72500	16500	26000
Coventry	11500	16000	18500	25500	19500	29000	36500	59500	10000	34000
Dudley	11500	17500	19000	27000	22500	28000	50000	70000	15000	35000
Sandwell	10500	15500	18000	23000	23500	28500	42500	52500	13000	16000
Walsall	11250	13750	17500	23500	21500	27000	41500	52500	12000	19000
Wolverhampton	8000	12500	18500	24000	22500	26500	50000	62500	16000	20000
Lichfield	18000	21000	19250	30500	19000	29750	52000	57000	17500	22250
Nuneaton	9000	16500	18500	22000	22000	26500	36000	53000	14000	23000
Shrewsbury	14250	18250	17500	26000	20500	26500	52500	65000		
Stafford	15000	17000	18000	22000	20000	25000	48000	57000		
Stoke-on-Trent	11000	14000	18500	25000	19000	25500	44000	61500		
Leamington Spa	19000	22000	24000	27000	27000	32000	60000	67500	20000	27000
Worcester	17750	19750	22000	26000	24500	27500	49000	57000	17750	22500
Kidderminster	14500	17000	19000	25000	20000	25000	50000	60000	16500	27500
EAST ANGLIA										
Cambridge	28000	45000	32000	43000	33000	40000	68000	93000	27000	43000
Peterborough	10000	18000	18000	26500	22000	29000	40000	80000	10000	25000
Ipswich	18500	22000	23000	31000	25000	30000	50000	65000	17500	26000
Bury St Edmunds	17000	24500	27000	37250	23500	32500	40000	58500	19000	24000
King's Lynn	17000	17500	24500	25000	24000	26000	50000	52000	19000	26000
Norwich	16500	22000	22500	31000	24500	30000	45500	60000	21000	29000

7.52 GREAT BRITAIN:
TOWNS BY HOUSE TYPE AND AGE OF HOUSE - SECONDHAND DWELLINGS

£

	Pre-1919 terraced house		Interwar semi-detached house/bungalow		Post 1960 semi-detached house/bungalow		Post 1965 detached house		Post 1960 flat in 3 (or more) storey block	
	From	To	From	To	From	To	From	To	From	To
EAST MIDLANDS										
Boston	14000	16500	19000	22500	22000	25500	37500	45000		
Lincoln	12500	19000	19500	23000	21500	25000	45000	57500		
Mansfield	7000	10500	17000	27500	19000	28000	40000	62500		
Nottingham	12500	14000	24500	26500	28000	30000	55000	59000	26000	28000
Carlton (Notts)	13500	17500	20500	24500	24500	28500	60000	80000	17000	20000
Chesterfield	12000	17750	20250	27250	21000	27250	45000	59000	17000	24000
Derby	10000	16000	19000	25000	19500	24000	45000	67500	14000	17500
Kettering	15000	20000	22000	28000	21500	27000	58000	65000		
Leicester	8700	17000	20100	26250	23000	27500	46000	57000	22500	27500
Northampton	14500	18500	22500	27500	24000	29000	55000	65000	17500	20000
Loughborough	15000	20000	20000	27000	22000	29000	55000	70000		
Wigston	16000	19000	24000	28000	24500	27000	46000	55000		
Buxton	16500	19500	25000	28000	27250	30000	48250	54500	25000	27500
WEST MIDLANDS										
Birmingham	12500	17000	23250	28500	24750	31500	50000	70000	16500	26000
Coventry	11500	16500	18000	26500	19500	30000	37500	60000	19000	35000
Dudley	11500	17500	19500	27500	22500	28000	50000	70000	15000	35000
Sandwell	10500	15500	18500	24000	24500	29500	42500	52500	14000	17500
Walsall	11500	14000	18000	24000	22250	28000	42000	52500	12000	19000
Wolverhampton	8000	12500	18500	24000	22500	26500	50000	62500	16000	20000
Lichfield	18000	21000	19250	30500	19500	30000	52000	57500	17750	22750
Nuneaton	10000	16500	18500	25000	20000	28500	38000	60000	14000	23000
Shrewsbury	14250	18250	18000	27000	21000	27000	52500	65000	16000	18000
Stafford	16000	19000	18000	22000	21000	26000	48000	57000	14000	15000
Stoke-on-Trent	11000	14000	18500	25000	19000	25500	46000	62000		
Leamington Spa	20000	23000	25000	28000	28000	32500	62500	70000	20000	27000
Worcester	18000	20500	22000	26500	25000	28500	50000	60000	17750	23000
Kidderminster	14500	18000	19000	25000	20000	25000	50000	65000	16500	30000
EAST ANGLIA										
Cambridge	30000	48500	34000	47500	34500	42000	76000	98000	28500	47000
Peterborough	12500	18000	18000	30000	22000	33000	55000	90000	20000	35000
Ipswich	19500	23000	25000	32500	27500	31500	52000	67500	18500	27000
Bury St Edmunds	22500	28000	30000	38000	28500	35000	42500	60000	20000	25000
King's Lynn	16000	19000	24000	33000	23000	30000	50000	65000	23000	35000
Norwich	17000	23000	23000	33500	26000	32500	46000	62500	22000	32000

7.53 *GREAT BRITAIN:*
TOWNS BY HOUSE TYPE AND AGE OF HOUSE - SECONDHAND DWELLINGS

£

	Pre-1919 terraced house (modernised)		Interwar semi-detached house (modernised)		Post 1960 semi-detached house		Post 1960 detached house		Post 1960 flat in 3 (or more) storey block	
	From	To	From	To	From	To	From	To	From	To
EAST MIDLANDS										
Boston	15000	16000	19000	23000	22000	25500	37500	45000		
Lincoln	15000	19750	22000	26000	22000	25000	47500	60000		
Mansfield	10000	11000	17000	27500	19500	28000	40000	62500		
Nottingham	14500	16000	26700	28700	29000	31000	60000	65000	26000	28000
Carlton (Notts)	16000	19500	23000	26000	26000	30000	60000	80000	18000	22000
Chesterfield	13500	19500	22000	28500	21500	27500	45000	59000	17000	24000
Derby	10750	17000	19000	25000	19500	25000	47500	70000	14000	17500
Kettering	15000	20000	24000	29000	24500	28000	60000	70000		
Leicester	17000	20000	24500	28500	25000	28000	50000	60000	18000	19000
Northampton	14500	19000	22500	28500	24000	30000	55000	70000	17000	20500
Loughborough	16000	20500	24000	30000	23000	29000	60000	80000		
Buxton	19500	25000	26000	32000	27500	32500	48500	56500	25500	29000
WEST MIDLANDS										
Birmingham	15000	23750	24750	34000	25000	32000	50000	70000	16500	26000
Coventry	13250	18750	21000	31000	21500	32500	40000	62500	19000	35000
Dudley	15000	18500	23000	28000	24000	30000	52500	75000	15000	35000
Sandwell	13500	18500	23000	29000	25000	30000	45000	55000	14000	17500
Walsall	13000	15500	20500	26500	22750	30000	43250	54000	12250	19500
Wolverhampton	10500	13500	20500	25500	22500	27000	50000	62500	16000	20500
Lichfield	20000	23000	23500	33000	20000	30500	52500	57500	18250	23000
Nuneaton	14000	16500	20000	26000	21000	30000	40000	61000	14000	23000
Shrewsbury	18000	20000	20000	30000	21500	27000	52500	65000	16500	19000
Stafford	16500	19500	19000	23000	22000	27000	48000	60000	14000	16000
Stoke-on-Trent	11000	15500	21000	25500	21500	26000	47000	60000		
Leamington Spa	24000	27000	27500	31000	30000	35000	66000	73000	20000	27000
Worcester	18500	20500	24000	27000	26000	30000	52500	75000	18000	23000
Kidderminster	15500	20000	20000	28000	20000	26000	52500	65000	17000	30000
EAST ANGLIA										
Cambridge	39000	56000	40000	56000	36500	44500	79000	102500	30000	48000
Peterborough	18000	30000	25000	30000	24000	34000	55000	90000	21000	30000
Ipswich	23500	27000	28000	36000	30000	36000	59000	78000	23000	30500
Bury St Edmunds	28500	31500	37000	39000	30000	36000	50000	62000	22500	27500
King's Lynn	18000	20000	27000	35000	24000	31000	50000	65000	23500	35000
Norwich	22500	26500	26000	37500	28000	34000	55000	70000	20000	28000

PRICE RANGES: SPRING 1986

7.54 GREAT BRITAIN:
TOWNS BY HOUSE TYPE AND AGE OF HOUSE - SECONDHAND DWELLINGS

£

	Pre-1919 terraced house (modernized)		Interwar semi-detached house (modernized)		Post 1960 semi-detached house		Post 1960 detached house		Post 1960 flat in 3 (or more) storey block	
	From	To	From	To	From	To	From	To	From	To
EAST MIDLANDS										
Boston	16000	17500	20000	23000	23000	26000	40000	50000		
Lincoln	16000	20000	22500	26500	22500	26000	49500	60000		
Mansfield	10500	12000	17500	28000	20000	28000	42500	67500		
Nottingham	15000	17000	27500	29500	30000	32000	62000	66000	26000	28000
Carlton (Notts)	17000	20000	24000	27500	27000	30000	62500	80000	18000	22000
Chesterfield	13500	20000	22500	29000	22000	25000	45000	60000	17250	24500
Derby	11000	17500	20000	26500	20000	26000	47500	75000	14000	17500
Kettering	22500	25000	26000	29000	26000	30000	65000	75000		
Leicester	18000	20500	28500	33000	26500	30000	55000	65000	18000	20000
Northampton	15000	20000	24000	30000	25000	32500	57500	72500	18000	22000
Loughborough	16000	21000	25000	31000	25000	32000	60000	80000		
Buxton	19500	25000	26000	32500	27500	33500	49500	56500	26000	30000
WEST MIDLANDS										
Birmingham	16000	23750	24750	34000	25000	36000	50000	70000	17000	26000
Coventry	14000	19500	21500	33000	22500	34000	42500	67000	19000	35000
Dudley	15000	19750	23500	29000	25000	31000	52500	75000	15000	35000
Sandwell	13500	18500	23000	29000	25000	30000	45000	55000	14000	17500
Walsall	13250	15750	21000	27000	23250	30500	44000	55000	12500	20000
Wolverhampton	11000	14000	20750	26250	22750	27500	50000	62500	16000	21000
Lichfield	21000	24000	24250	34000	22500	32500	53000	59000	18750	23500
Nuneaton	14000	16500	22000	27500	22000	30000	40000	61000	14500	25000
Shrewsbury	18000	21000	20000	30000	21500	27000	52500	66500	16500	19000
Stafford	17000	20000	20000	24000	23000	28000	48000	60000	15000	17500
Stoke-on-Trent	11500	16500	21000	26000	21000	26000	47000	60000		
Leamington Spa	26000	30000	30000	35000	32500	37500	70000	77000	21000	28000
Worcester	19500	21500	25000	28500	27000	31500	53000	75000	19000	24000
Kidderminster	17000	21500	21500	29000	23000	30000	57000	67500	17000	32000
EAST ANGLIA										
Cambridge	42000	70000	43000	58500	40000	50000	90000	110000	34000	52000
Peterborough	18000	26000	24000	33000	24000	36500	53500	92000	19000	32000
Ipswich	24750	29000	29000	37500	32000	37000	60000	80000	24500	32000
Bury St Edmunds	29500	34000	38500	43500	31500	38000	55000	70000	24000	29500
King's Lynn	18000	24000	27000	37000	26000	32000	50000	65000	23500	35000
Norwich	23000	27000	26500	38000	29000	35000	55000	70000	24000	29000

7.55 GREAT BRITAIN:
TOWNS BY HOUSE TYPE AND AGE OF HOUSE – SECONDHAND DWELLINGS

£

	Pre-1919 terraced house (modernized)		Interwar semi-detached house (modernized)		Post 1960 semi-detached house		Post 1960 detached house		Post 1960 flat in 3 (or more) storey block	
	From	To	From	To	From	To	From	To	From	To
EAST MIDLANDS										
Boston	16500	18500	20500	24000	23500	26500	40000	52500		
Lincoln	16500	24000	23000	28000	24000	27500	52500	62500		
Mansfield	10500	12500	17500	28000	20000	28000	45000	67500		
Nottingham	16000	18250	29000	31000	31000	33500	63000	66000	26000	28000
Carlton (Notts)	17500	20500	25000	28500	28000	31500	65000	82500	18500	22500
Chesterfield	14000	22500	23500	32000	23000	28500	47000	65000	18500	25500
Derby	11500	18000	21000	28000	21000	27500	50000	80000	14500	18000
Kettering	27000	30000	32500	36000	28000	35000	70000	85000		
Leicester	19000	23000	29000	33000	28000	32000	55000	65000	18000	21000
Northampton	17000	23000	26000	33000	26000	35000	57000	75000	18000	23000
Loughborough	17500	23000	26000	33000	27500	34000	62500	82500	16000	18000
Buxton	20500	25500	26500	33000	28500	35000	52500	60000	27500	32000
WEST MIDLANDS										
Birmingham	16250	25000	25250	38000	25000	39500	60000	74000	17000	27000
Coventry	15000	22500	24000	36500	24500	37500	45000	72000	19000	35000
Dudley	16000	21000	24500	30500	27000	33000	57000	80000	15000	35000
Sandwell	14500	20000	24000	30000	26000	31500	46000	57000	15000	18500
Walsall	13500	16250	22000	28000	24000	32000	44750	56000	12750	20500
Wolverhampton	11500	15000	21500	26500	23000	28000	52500	65000	16000	21000
Lichfield	22750	26000	26000	36000	25000	33500	58000	64000	19500	24500
Nuneaton	14500	16500	24500	31000	24500	32500	45000	66000	15500	25000
Shrewsbury	20000	24000	22500	33000	23000	30000	55000	75000	17000	21000
Stafford	18000	21000	21000	26000	24000	29000	50000	65000	16000	18000
Stoke-on-Trent	12250	16500	21000	26000	22000	28000	47000	60000		
Leamington Spa	28000	32000	33000	38000	35000	40000	76000	84000	23000	30000
Worcester	19500	23000	27500	32500	28500	34000	55000	75000	19500	24000
Kidderminster	18000	23000	23000	30000	25000	32500	60000	70000	18000	35000
EAST ANGLIA										
Cambridge	46000	80000	47000	62500	43000	55000	97000	120000	37000	55000
Peterborough	18500	28000	24500	34000	28500	38500	50000	105000	17000	42500
Ipswich	26500	30750	31000	40500	33500	39500	63000	82500	26000	34000
Bury St Edmunds	31500	36500	40000	47500	33500	39750	60000	75000	25500	30000
King's Lynn	19000	26000	30000	40000	29000	35000	52500	67500	24000	36000
Norwich	24500	30000	29000	43000	31000	38500	60000	75000	28000	37000

PRICE RANGES: AUTUMN 1983

7.56 GREAT BRITAIN:
  TOWNS BY HOUSE TYPE AND AGE OF HOUSE - SECONDHAND DWELLINGS

£

	Pre-1919 terraced house		Interwar semi-detached house/bungalow		Post 1960 semi-detached house/bungalow		Post 1965 detached house		Post 1960 flat in 3 (or more) storey block	
	From	To	From	To	From	To	From	To	From	To
INNER LONDON										
Hackney	22500	28000	30000	35500	39000	44000			26500	30000
Tower Hamlets	20000	27500								
Camden	37000	43000							44000	54500
Islington	30000	50000			70000	80000			30000	35000
Bexley/Greenwich	22000	28000	33000	40000	38000	46000	60000	90000	25000	34000
Lambeth	27500	31000	37000	42000					30000	35000
Lewisham	24250	30000	33250	43750	41000	47000	53250	74000	26000	36500
Southwark	24000	28000	35000	42500	37500	45000	100000	150000	28000	36000
H'smith & Fulham	33000	65000							34000	55000
Kens'ton/Chelsea	45000	120000			90000	165000			40000	95000
Wandsworth	32500	47500	40000	55000	46000	67500			33000	70000
S Westminster									55000	120000
N Westminster	33000	36000							47000	73000
OUTER LONDON										
Barking & Newham	23000	25000	26000	35000	30000	33000			24000	26000
Enfield	28000	30000	39000	42500	41000	44000	75000	77500	38000	40000
Haringey	29000	30000	32000	34500	70000	80000	80000	120000	27000	29000
Havering	23000	25000	29500	35000	34500	43000	65000	82000	23000	42000
Redbridge	24000	32000	34000	46000	36000	48000	67000	82000	26000	44000
Waltham Forest	23000	28500	36000	43500					28500	34000
Barnet	27500	37500	38000	46000	37000	48500	65000	90000	37500	47500
Ealing	24000	34000	28500	38000	34000	50000	75000	130000	26000	41000
Harrow	28000	30000	38000	42000	45000	47000	77000	80000	35000	37000
Hillingdon	24000	30000	33000	40000	35000	42000	70000	85000		
Hounslow	30000	51000	33000	50000	35000	47000			28000	38500
Bromley	29000	36500	36500	45000	40500	49500	74000	85000	28500	40000
Croydon	27000	31000	36000	43500	41500	50000	74000	82500	31500	39000
Kingston	30000	35000	40000	48000	50000	55000	100000	110000	35000	45000
Merton	32000	44000	40000	55000	40000	65000	75000	140000	32500	55000
Richmond	37000	50000	40000	55000	45000	60000	80000	130000	35000	50000

PRICE RANGES: SPRING 1984

7.57 GREAT BRITAIN:
TOWNS BY HOUSE TYPE AND AGE OF HOUSE - SECONDHAND DWELLINGS

£

	Pre-1919 terraced house		Interwar semi-detached house/bungalow		Post 1960 semi-detached house/bungalow		Post 1965 detached house		Post 1960 flat in 3 (or more) storey block	
	From	To	From	To	From	To	From	To	From	To
INNER LONDON										
Hackney	23000	28750	31000	36750	40500	45750			27000	30750
Tower Hamlets	21000	28000								
Camden	39000	45000							46000	57000
Bexley/Greenwich	23000	30000	34500	42000	40000	48000	62000	92000	26250	36000
Lambeth	26000	32000	38000	43000					28000	35000
Lewisham	25750	31750	35000	45500	43000	49000	55500	77000	27500	38000
Southwark	25000	29000	35000	42500	37500	45000	100000	150000	29000	37500
H'smith & Fulham	35000	72500							35000	57000
Kens'ton/Chelsea	48000	130000			70000	175000			42500	100000
S Westminster									55000	120000
N Westminster	34000	37000							47000	73000
OUTER LONDON										
Barking & Newham	23500	25500	28500	37000	31500	33500			25000	27000
Enfield	28500	31000	37000	44250	42250	45250	76500	79000	39000	41000
Haringey	29000	31000	33000	35000	75000	85000	85000	125000	27000	29000
Havering	25000	27000	29500	35000	35000	45000	75000	85000	25000	42000
Redbridge	24250	32500	34750	47000	36000	48000			26500	45000
Waltham Forest	24000	29500	36500	44500	40000	50000			29750	35500
Barnet	29000	39000	39500	47500	39500	50500	67500	95000	39000	49500
Ealing	25500	36000	30000	40000	36000	52500	79000	133000	27500	43000
Harrow	31000	32000	42000	44000	46500	48500	80000	82500	38000	39000
Hillingdon	24000	30000	33000	42500	37500	45000	75000	95000		
Hounslow	32750	54500	35000	53000	37000	50000			30500	42000
Bromley	30000	38000	39250	47500	44000	53000	77500	87500	31000	40000
Croydon	27750	34000	38500	45000	42750	51500	76250	85000	32500	40000
Kingston	33000	40000	42000	50000	50000	58000	100000	115000	37000	50000
Merton	33500	50000	41500	57500	41000	75000	77500	145000	35000	70000
Richmond	47500	55000	62500	67500	65000	70000	130000	150000	52500	60000

PRICE RANGES: AUTUMN 1984

7.58 GREAT BRITAIN:
TOWNS BY HOUSE TYPE AND AGE OF HOUSE – SECONDHAND DWELLINGS

£

	Pre-1919 terraced house		Interwar semi-detached house/bungalow		Post 1960 semi-detached house/bungalow		Post 1965 detached house		Post 1960 flat in 3 (or more) storey block	
	From	To	From	To	From	To	From	To	From	To
INNER LONDON										
Tower Hamlets	25000	31000								
Camden	41000	47250							48300	59000
Hackney	24000	30000	32000	39000					28500	32500
Bexley	24500	31500	36000	44000	42000	50000	65000	100000	27500	37500
Lambeth	28000	34000	39500	44500					30000	36500
Lewisham	27000	33500	36750	47750	45000	51500	57750	80000	29000	40000
C'berwell/Peckham	27500	31500	38000	46500	40000	50000	110000	165000	30000	40000
Fulham	35000	82000							35000	65000
Kens'ton/Chelsea	55000	150000			80000	185000			50000	120000
S Westminster									57500	130000
N Westminster	35000	40000							49000	76000
OUTER LONDON										
Romford	29000	32000	32000	42000	39000	49000	80000	97000	27500	65000
Enfield	28500	33500	39000	45500	43000	46500	77500	80500	39000	42000
Haringey	29000	33000	35000	40000					25000	29000
Redbridge	25250	34000	37000	50000	38500	51000			28000	48000
Barnet	34000	42000	43000	52000	42000	53000	80000	110000	41000	54000
Ealing	30000	50000	39000	65000	40000	65000	80000	180000	32000	65000
Harrow	35000	37000	44500	47000	53000	55000	88000	90000	39000	41000
Hillingdon	30000	35000	35000	45000	43000	50000	85000	100000		
Hounslow	35000	63000	38000	65000	42000	52000			34000	48000
Bromley	31000	40000	42000	52000	45000	54000	85000	95000	33500	45000
Croydon/Sutton	29000	36000	42500	52500	45000	55000	80000	95000	33500	42500
Merton/Wandsworth	36000	53000	44500	60000	44500	80000	89000	158000	38000	75000
Kingston	35000	42000	44250	51500	52500	61000	105000	120000	39000	52500

INLAND REVENUE: VALUATION OFFICE PROPERTY MARKET REPORTS

PRICE RANGES: SPRING 1985

7.59 GREAT BRITAIN:
TOWNS BY HOUSE TYPE AND AGE OF HOUSE - SECONDHAND DWELLINGS

£

	Pre-1919 terraced house		Interwar semi-detached house/bungalow		Post 1960 semi-detached house/bungalow		Post 1965 detached house		Post 1960 flat in 3 (or more) storey block	
	From	To	From	To	From	To	From	To	From	To
INNER LONDON										
Tower Hamlets	26000	32000								
Camden	43750	50600							51750	63200
Hackney	25000	32500	35000	42000					28500	32500
Bexley	25000	33000	37000	45750	43500	52000	67000	105000	28500	39000
Lambeth	29000	35000	40000	46000					31000	37000
Lewisham	32000	36000	38500	50000	50000	55000	60000	85000	32000	42000
Southwark	27500	32500	40000	50000	42500	55000	110000	175000	30000	42500
Fulham	40000	86000							40000	75000
Kens'ton/Chelsea	62500	165000			90000	195000			52500	127000
S Westminster									60000	150000
N Westminster	48000	52000							54000	90000
OUTER LONDON										
Romford	31000	34000	34500	45500	41500	52000	90000	120000	30000	65000
Enfield	29500	34000	40000	46500	45000	49000	82500	90000	39000	43000
Redbridge	27000	35000	40000	48000	42000	56000			32000	47000
Barnet	36000	45000	45000	55000	47500	57500	90000	120000	42500	55000
Ealing	35000	50000	39000	65000	40000	65000	80000	200000	32000	65000
Harrow	36000	38000	49000	51500	55000	57000	89000	91000	44000	46500
Hillingdon	33500	38000	36000	50000	43000	51000	85000	100000		
Hounslow	37000	66000	39500	68000	44000	55000			36000	50000
Bromley	32000	41000	45000	55000	46000	56000	75000	105000	35000	45000
Croydon/Sutton	30000	37000	43500	53500	46000	57000	82500	98000	33500	43500
Merton/Wandsworth	38000	56000	46500	62000	47000	84000	95000	168000	40000	79000
Kingston	38500	46500	48500	56000	57000	66500	114000	130000	42500	57000

PRICE RANGES: AUTUMN 1985

7.60 GREAT BRITAIN:
TOWNS BY HOUSE TYPE AND AGE OF HOUSE - SECONDHAND DWELLINGS

£

	Pre-1919 terraced house (modernised)		Interwar semi-detached house (modernised)		Post 1960 semi-detached house		Post 1960 detached house		Post 1960 flat in 3 (or more) storey block	
	From	To	From	To	From	To	From	To	From	To
INNER LONDON										
Tower Hamlets	33000	50000								
Camden	75000	90000							48000	75000
Hackney	45000	55000	50000	57500					30000	36000
Bexley	30000	40000	40000	60000	50000	65000	70000	130000	32000	45000
Lambeth	37000	43000	49000	56000					33500	39000
Lewisham	36000	42000	45000	55000	52000	58000	63000	90000	33000	38000
Southwark	31000	35000	42500	52500	45000	57500	120000	190000	35000	45000
Fulham	75000	95000							45000	80000
Kens'ton/Chelsea	70000	200000			100000	205000			57000	135000
S Westminster									68000	165000
N Westminster	58000	58000							58000	110000
OUTER LONDON										
Romford	35500	39000	42000	55000	46000	54500	94500	125000	32000	69000
Enfield	37500	41500	47500	55000	50000	65000	92500	97500	43000	49000
Redbridge	37000	46000	47000	55000	45000	58000	95000	110000	35000	48000
Barnet	47000	57000	50000	60000	46000	58000	100000	130000	45000	57500
Ealing	39000	55000	45000	75000	45000	75000	80000	250000	35000	65000
Harrow	42500	45000	58000	60000	61000	62500	105000	110000	45000	47500
Hillingdon	40000	55000	45000	65000	53000	60000	90000	135000		
Hounslow	50000	75000	53000	63000	50000	80000	150000	175000	38500	46000
Bromley	37750	47000	50000	59000	53000	62500	76500	115000	38000	50000
Croydon/Sutton	35500	39000	45000	62000	57000	67000	90000	105000	36000	53000
Merton/Wandsworth	50000	65000	53000	72000	52000	90000	105000	185000	44000	85000
Kingston	55000	75000	65000	85000	60000	80000	120500	160000	45000	65000

PRICE RANGES: SPRING 1986

7.61 GREAT BRITAIN:
TOWNS BY HOUSE TYPE AND AGE OF HOUSE - SECONDHAND DWELLINGS

£

	Pre-1919 terraced house (modernized)		Interwar semi-detached house (modernized)		Post 1960 semi-detached house		Post 1960 detached house		Post 1960 flat in 3 (or more) storey block	
	From	To	From	To	From	To	From	To	From	To
INNER LONDON										
T'r Hamlets/N'ham	36000	55000	42500	46000						
Camden	77500	95000							50000	78000
Hackney	45000	60000	52000	60000					30000	36000
Bexley/Greenwich	32000	42000	42500	62500	52500	67500	75000	130000	34000	47500
Lambeth	40750	47500	55000	62500					39000	43000
Lewisham	38000	44000	46000	57500	52000	60000	65000	92000	34500	40000
Southwark	32500	40000	45000	55000	47500	60000	125000	200000	36000	47500
Fulham	80000	100000							50000	90000
Kens'ton/Chelsea	77500	225000			110000	240000			65000	150000
S Westminster									75000	175000
N Westminster	64000	65000							65000	120000
OUTER LONDON										
Romford	40000	45000	45000	60000	50000	60000	100000	130000	35000	70000
Enfield	41000	45000	51000	60000	52000	67500	97500	105000	43000	52000
Redbridge	41000	48000	52000	62000	51000	64000	105000	125000	38000	50000
Barnet	59000	64000	60000	65000	48000	62000	100000	135000	45000	59000
Ealing	50000	65000	50000	80000	50000	80000	90000	200000	38000	70000
Harrow	46000	48500	59000	61000	62000	63500	112000	117000	48000	49500
Hillingdon	44500	58000	50000	67000	55000	69000	100000	165000	42500	50000
Hounslow	50000	90000	55000	75000	55000	85000	150000	180000	39000	50000
Bromley	42500	50000	55000	65000	55000	65000	95000	120000	40000	52000
Croydon/Sutton	41000	46000	51000	68000	58000	68000	100000	130000	38000	58000
Merton/Wandsworth	55000	68500	57950	80000	55000	95000	130000	215000	52000	102500
Kingston	60000	80000	70000	87500	65000	90000	130000	175000	48000	70000

PRICE RANGES: AUTUMN 1986

7.62 GREAT BRITAIN:
   TOWNS BY HOUSE TYPE AND AGE OF HOUSE - SECONDHAND DWELLINGS

£

	Pre-1919 terraced house (modernized)		Interwar semi-detached house (modernized)		Post 1960 semi-detached house		Post 1960 detached house		Post 1960 flat in 3 (or more) storey block	
	From	To	From	To	From	To	From	To	From	To
INNER LONDON										
T'r Hamlets/N'ham	35000	70000	46000	50000						
Camden	90000	115000							70000	100000
Hackney	52500	70000	57500	65000					32500	40000
Bexley/Greenwich	36000	47500	47500	70000	52500	67500	80000	140000	36750	50000
Lambeth	42000	49000	59000	67000					41500	45500
Lewisham	40000	50000	48000	61000	54000	68000	70000	100000	36000	43000
Southwark	40000	55000	50000	65000	55000	70000	125000	200000	40000	55000
Fulham	90000	115000							50000	115000
Kens'ton/Chelsea	90000	260000			125000	265000			70000	157000
S Westminster									82000	190000
N Westminster									75000	140000
OUTER LONDON										
Romford	42500	48000	48000	65000	52000	65000	105000	135000	40000	70000
Enfield	43500	50000	55000	65000	55000	70000	110000	130000	47000	60000
Redbridge	46000	52000	58000	72000	56000	70000	120000	140000	42000	55000
Barnet	65000	75000	65000	72000	60000	71000	110000	150000	50000	65000
Ealing	55000	72000	60000	85000	60000	80000	110000	220000	50000	77000
Harrow	53000	56000	61000	69000	80000	87000	122000	147000	52000	55000
Hillingdon	50000	65000	55000	78000	60000	75000	120000	185000	47000	55000
Hounslow/Feltham	55000	100000	58000	80000	60000	89000	150000	200000	46000	55000
Bromley	48000	54000	60000	67500	60000	67500	105000	135000	45000	58000
Croydon/Sutton	45000	52000	56000	75000	63000	75000	120000	150000	42000	62000
Merton/Wandsworth	62000	75000	65000	90000	60000	100000	145000	230000	60000	105000
Kingston	65000	85000	75000	90000	72000	95000	140000	200000	52000	75000

PRICE RANGES: AUTUMN 1983

7.63 GREAT BRITAIN:
TOWNS BY HOUSE TYPE AND AGE OF HOUSE - SECONDHAND DWELLINGS

£

	Pre-1919 terraced house		Interwar semi-detached house/bungalow		Post 1960 semi-detached house/bungalow		Post 1965 detached house		Post 1960 flat in 3 (or more) storey block	
	From	To	From	To	From	To	From	To	From	To
SOUTH EAST										
Bedford	15000	17500	24500	31000	25500	29500	50000	65000	20500	30500
N Hertfordshire	27500	32000	35000	40000	37500	44000	75000	85000	22000	25000
Luton	18000	22000	27500	40000	28500	40000	65000	80000	20000	27000
St Albans	28000	33000	35000	47500	40000	50000	65000	95000	31500	39500
Watford	27000	30000	36000	40000	41000	48000	73000	88000	32000	42000
Basildon	17500	20500	28000	34000	30000	38000	60000	75000	18000	23000
Chelmsford	21000	29500	26000	39000	28500	39000	58000	95000	20000	30500
Colchester	20000	21000	24000	27000	24000	28000	58500	65000	25000	70000
Harlow	25000	40000	28000	50000	29000	57500	50000	145000	17000	25000
Southend on Sea	20500	22500	27000	31000	27000	34000	62500	67500	22500	31500
Brighton	23000	26000	28000	33000	28000	34000	66000	72500	25000	28000
Canterbury	19500	25000	25000	35000	25000	32500	45000	57500	22000	27000
Eastbourne	20000	25000	28000	33000	30000	37500	50000	65000	27500	33000
East Kent	17700	21000	25500	32750	25500	33750	46000	61500	21500	30750
Maidstone	23000	25000	31000	35000	34000	38000	56000	73000	20500	23500
Medway	17250	19750	24500	27500	25500	29000	48500	53500	17000	19000
Tunbridge Wells	24000	25750	34000	37000	35000	40000	67500	75500	27500	32500
Chichester	23000	32000	25000	45000	30000	37500	55000	85000	30000	36000
Guildford	27500	33000	32000	38000	35000	40000	71000	79000	28000	45000
North Surrey	29000	39000	34000	50000	37000	60000	71000	130000	28000	41000
Reigate	28000	34000	35000	42500	34000	40000	55000	85000	30000	36000
Worthing	22500	29000	27500	35000	30000	36000	62000	72000	24000	30000
East Berkshire	28000	32000	36750	42500	35000	43000	72500	80500	28500	33000
N Bucks	20000	22000	34000	36000	33000	35000	64000	66000	22500	24500
Oxford	28500	37500	30000	45000	31500	46950	55000	100000	25000	42000
W Oxfordshire	17000	28000	22000	40000	24500	36000	42500	62000	20000	28000
Reading	24000	27000	32000	37000	32000	37000	65000	75000	26000	29000
S Bucks	21000	30000	27000	42000	32500	44000	67000	87500	26000	45000
Basingstoke	25500	29500	34000	39500	29500	40000	55000	78000	23500	34000
Portsmouth	14500	17000	22500	24500	25000	29000	55000	60000	23000	39000
Solent	18000	22000	22000	25000	26000	30000	50000	60000	20000	35000
Winchester	22000	28000	26500	36500	28000	37000	55000	70000	29500	35500
Solent (IOW)	17000	20000	21000	25000	23000	26000	45000	50000	22500	32500
Southampton	12000	23000	22000	32000	24000	32000	47000	75000	27000	45000

PRICE RANGES: SPRING 1984

7.64 GREAT BRITAIN:
  TOWNS BY HOUSE TYPE AND AGE OF HOUSE - SECONDHAND DWELLINGS

£

	Pre-1919 terraced house		Interwar semi-detached house/bungalow		Post 1960 semi-detached house/bungalow		Post 1965 detached house		Post 1960 flat in 3 (or more) storey block	
	From	To	From	To	From	To	From	To	From	To
SOUTH EAST										
Bedford	16500	19500	26000	33000	27500	33000	58000	75000	22500	32500
N Hertfordshire	30000	33000	37500	42500	42500	47500	82500	87500	24000	27000
Luton	19000	23000	27500	42500	29000	42500	65000	80000	21000	30000
St Albans	30000	34000	36500	50000	42000	52500	75000	95000	35000	43500
Watford	28000	32000	37000	48000	42000	50000	75000	95000	33000	43000
Basildon	18000	24000	29000	37500	32000	40000	62000	80000	19000	25000
Chelmsford	22000	26000	28000	33000	30000	34000	65000	90000	22500	25000
Colchester	20750	22000	26000	27250	28500	29750	59500	65000	18000	26000
Harlow	32000	40000	35000	55000	38000	57500	90000	145000	40000	70000
Southend on Sea	21000	23000	27500	31500	28000	35000	65000	70000	23000	53000
Brighton	24000	27000	30000	35000	31000	35000	67500	90000	26000	30000
Canterbury	21000	27500	27000	37000	27000	38000	50000	65000	23000	32000
Eastbourne	21500	26500	29000	34000	31000	38000	57500	75000	27500	35000
East Kent	18250	22000	28000	34500	28500	35000	48000	62000	23000	33000
Maidstone	23500	25000	32000	36000	35000	38500	57000	74000	21500	24500
Medway	17000	20000	24500	27500	27500	30000	48500	53500	17500	20000
Tunbridge Wells	27000	30000	37000	40000	38000	43000	74000	83000	30000	35000
Chichester	31000	35000	50000	52000	45000	49000	70000	75000	39000	41000
Guildford	30000	34500	36000	38000	37000	43000	76000	87000	37000	45000
North Surrey	30000	39000	37000	50000	38000	60000	72000	130000	29000	41000
Reigate	29000	37500	35000	50000	34000	47500	70000	105000	25000	39000
Worthing	24000	31000	28500	36000	31000	37000	65000	72000	24500	31000
East Berkshire	31000	36000	39000	46000	40000	48000	77500	90000	32000	37000
N Bucks	20000	22000	36000	38000	34000	36000	72500	77500	24000	26000
Oxford	28500	37500	32000	45000	32000	45000	72500	82500	27500	42500
W Oxfordshire	17000	20000	24000	32000	26000	32500	45000	60000	20000	22000
Reading	26000	29000	34000	40000	34000	40000	70000	80000	28000	31000
S Bucks	22000	33000	29000	41000	34000	41000	70000	88000	29000	38000
Basingstoke	26000	28000	35000	40000	31500	37500	60000	80000	23500	25000
Portsmouth	14500	17000	23500	25500	28500	33000	55000	60000	23000	39000
Solent	22000	24000	23000	26000	27000	35000	54000	64000	20000	35000
Winchester	25000	30000	35000	45000	35000	43000	65000	75000	38000	42000
Solent (IOW)	17500	20000	24000	27000	24000	28000	50000	55000		
Southampton	12000	25000	24000	36000	25000	35000	50000	78000	22000	46000

PRICE RANGES: AUTUMN 1984

7.65 GREAT BRITAIN:
TOWNS BY HOUSE TYPE AND AGE OF HOUSE – SECONDHAND DWELLINGS

£

	Pre-1919 terraced house		Interwar semi-detached house/bungalow		Post 1960 semi-detached house/bungalow		Post 1965 detached house		Post 1960 flat in 3 (or more) storey block	
	From	To	From	To	From	To	From	To	From	To
SOUTH EAST										
Bedford	16500	21000	26000	37500	28000	37500	60000	75000	25000	38500
Hertford	35000	38000	40000	45000	48000	52000	85000	110000		
Luton	21000	27000	27500	47000	31000	47000	70000	90000	22500	35000
St Albans	34000	38000	45000	55000	47500	57500	85000	105000	36000	43000
Watford	29500	34000	39000	50000	44500	53000	78000	95000	35000	45500
Grays	18000	25000	31000	40000	35000	42000	65000	84000	20000	26000
Chelmsford	23000	27250	29500	34750	31500	35750	68000	94500	23750	26250
Colchester	22250	23250	27500	28750	29750	31500	61000	66500	18500	26000
Loughton	35000	42000	40000	55000	42000	58000	88000	145000	40000	70000
Southend on Sea	23000	25000	29000	32000	31000	37500	68000	73000	25000	56000
Brighton	26000	29000	33000	39000	34000	40000	75000	90000		
Canterbury	22000	29000	28500	39000	28500	40000	52500	68250	25000	34000
Eastbourne	23500	28000	31000	36000	33000	40000	60000	90000	29000	36000
Folkestone	19250	23250	29500	36500	29000	36000	50000	65000	23000	35000
Maidstone	24000	26000	36000	38500	36500	41000	65000	80000	22000	25500
Gill'ham/Chatham	18000	21000	26500	29500	31000	34000	52500	60000	17500	20000
Tunbridge Wells	25000	30000	38000	43000	33000	42000	75000	85000	30000	35000
Horsham	31000	37500	50000	55000	45000	49000	70000	78000	39000	42500
Guildford	33500	36000	37500	42500	42500	45000	87000	95000	40000	47500
Walton-on-Thames	40000	50000	45000	55000	50000	70000	80000	170000	40000	60000
Reigate	33000	45000	38000	55000	37000	50000	75000	115000	34000	45000
Worthing	25000	32000	29500	37000	32000	38000	68000	76000	25000	32000
Maidenhead	33000	38000	42000	49000	44000	51000	80000	97500	34000	40000
Aylesbury	24000	26000	37500	42500	37500	40000	75000	80000	26500	28500
Oxford	28500	40000	32000	47000	32000	45000	73000	86000	30000	44000
Banbury	18500	21500	25000	33000	28000	35000	48000	62000	22000	24000
Reading	27500	30000	36000	42000	36000	42000	73500	85000	29000	32500
High Wycombe	27000	34000	35000	45000	37000	46000	75000	90000	33000	39000
Basingstoke	28000	30000	37000	40000	33500	41500	63000	80000	25000	28000
Portsmouth/Havant	16000	18500	25000	30000	31000	36000	60000	67500	24000	39000
Fareham	22000	26000	25000	32000	30000	38000	55000	70000	20000	35000
Winchester	27250	32750	35500	46250	35500	44000	70750	81750	40750	45000
Newport(IOW)	17500	21000	24000	28000	24500	28500	50000	55000		
Southampton	12000	26000	24000	39000	25000	38000	60000	78000	29000	46000

PRICE RANGES: SPRING 1985

7.66 GREAT BRITAIN:
TOWNS BY HOUSE TYPE AND AGE OF HOUSE - SECONDHAND DWELLINGS

£

	Pre-1919 terraced house		Interwar semi-detached house/bungalow		Post 1960 semi-detached house/bungalow		Post 1965 detached house		Post 1960 flat in 3 (or more) storey block	
	From	To	From	To	From	To	From	To	From	To
SOUTH EAST										
Bedford	17000	20000	27000	39000	29000	39000	63000	77500	25000	38500
Hertford	38000	40000	42000	50000	50000	56000	90000	120000	30000	40000
Luton	21000	28000	29000	50000	32000	48000			23000	36000
St Albans	36000	40000	48000	58000	50000	60000	90000	110000	37000	44000
Watford	30500	35000	40000	51500	46500	55000	81000	99000	36500	47250
Grays	19000	26000	32000	42000	35000	44000	65000	88000	21000	26000
Chelmsford	25000	29000	31000	37000	33000	40000	71500	90000	24500	27500
Colchester	22500	24500	28500	30000	30000	33000	62500	67500	19500	27000
Loughton	45000	50000	60000	65000	55000	60000	100000	130000	32500	65000
Southend-on-Sea	24000	26000	30000	33500	32500	39000	70500	76000	26000	58500
Brighton	27000	30000	35000	40000	36000	42000	75000	90000	27500	35000
Canterbury	23500	32000	31000	42000	32500	42500	55000	72500	26500	35500
Eastbourne	24000	28500	31000	37000	33000	41000	65000	95000	29500	37000
Folkestone	20250	24500	30250	37500	31250	38500	53000	69500	24250	36750
Maidstone	25000	28000	37500	41000	37500	43000	70000	85000	23000	26500
Gill'ham/Chatham	19000	25000	30000	38000	34000	41000	54000	65000	20000	23000
Tunbridge Wells	27000	33000	38000	46000	36000	45000	75000	95000	30000	36000
Horsham	32000	37500	50000	57500	45000	49000	72500	87500	39000	42500
Guildford	35000	38000	39000	44000	44000	47500	89000	97500	45000	50000
Walton-on-Thames	41000	51000	47000	56000	51000	70000	85000	180000	42000	61000
Reigate	35000	50000	40000	60000	39000	55000	80000	125000	35000	48000
Worthing	26000	33000	31000	39000	34000	40000	70000	79000	26000	33000
Maidenhead	37000	43000	46000	55000	49000	57000	90000	110000	36000	44000
Aylesbury	27000	30000	40000	45000	40000	46000	78000	100000	28000	30000
Oxford	28000	45000	33000	50000	33000	50000	73000	90000	32000	46000
Banbury	18500	23000	26000	35000	28000	36000	48000	64000	22000	24000
Reading	28000	31000	37000	42000	37000	43000	75000	87000	30000	34000
High Wycombe	27500	36000	36000	48000	38500	48000	80000	97500	34000	40000
Basingstoke	30000	32000	41000	44000	34000	42500	65000	80000	28000	30000
Portsmouth/Havant	19000	24000	27500	33000	33000	38000	63000	67000	24000	40000
Fareham	23000	27000	26000	32000	32000	38000	55000	70000	22000	35000
Winchester	28500	34500	38000	49500	38500	47750	74000	85250	42500	47000
Newport(IOW)	19500	23000	28000	31000	27000	32000	50000	57500		
Southampton	13000	28000	25500	40000	26000	40000	60000	80000	32000	50000

PRICE RANGES: AUTUMN 1985

7.67 GREAT BRITAIN:
TOWNS BY HOUSE TYPE AND AGE OF HOUSE - SECONDHAND DWELLINGS

£

	Pre-1919 terraced house (modernised)		Interwar semi-detached house (modernised)		Post 1960 semi-detached house		Post 1960 detached house		Post 1960 flat in 3 (or more) storey block	
	From	To	From	To	From	To	From	To	From	To
SOUTH EAST										
Bedford	22000	30000	30000	45000	30000	45000	65000	80000	26000	45000
Hertford	40000	50000	45000	55000	54000	59000	95000	125000	32000	46000
Luton	28500	33000	37500	55000	38500	50000	90000	100000	33000	43000
St Albans	42500	46500	56000	64000	56000	64000	110000	130000	40000	50000
Watford	40000	45000	55000	65000	55000	65000	90000	110000	37000	51000
Grays	27000	30000	44000	48000	38000	48000	72000	96000	23000	30000
Chelmsford	27500	32500	35250	41750	35000	42000	75000	95000	26000	29000
Colchester	26000	29000	30000	37000	36000	40000	63000	75000	26000	30000
Loughton/Chigwell	52500	57500	67500	75000	60000	65000	105000	135000	35000	60000
Southend-on-Sea	25500	28000	33500	37000	36000	42000	73500	80000	27000	60000
Brighton	33000	36000	40000	45000	42500	45000	85000	100000	27500	35000
Canterbury	26500	34500	35000	45000	34000	45000	58500	77000	28000	37500
Eastbourne	29000	34000	35000	45000	35000	43000	75000	105000	29500	37000
Folkestone	22000	28000	31500	39500	32500	40000	55500	72500	25250	38250
Maidstone	28000	31000	40000	45000	41000	46000	75000	90000	24000	28000
Gillingham	22000	28000	32000	41000	36000	46000	57000	70000	22000	25000
Tunbridge Wells	30000	35000	41000	48000	40000	49000	78000	95000	30000	38000
Horsham	39000	41000	52000	56000	45000	49000	80000	90000	35000	37500
Guildford	40000	45000	45000	50000	47500	52000	95000	105000	47500	52500
Walton-on-Thames	44500	55750	50000	61500	55500	77700	88750	188500	44500	66500
Reigate	38000	54000	45000	63000	45000	58000	90000	135000	36000	52000
Worthing	32000	37000	42000	48000	38000	44000	80000	88000	31000	37000
Maidenhead	43000	47000	55000	65000	52000	62000	100000	130000	39000	47500
Aylesbury	34000	36000	52000	56000	45000	48000	87000	100000	29000	31000
Oxford	45000	57000	40000	52500	37500	50000	75000	90000	36000	50000
Banbury	23000	24500	29000	35000	28000	37000	50000	65000	22500	24500
Reading	33000	35000	46000	48000	45000	50000	85000	95000	33000	36000
High Wycombe	35000	42000	41000	50000	43000	51000	85000	110000	35000	42000
Basingstoke	33000	35000	45000	50000	42500	50000	70000	85000	30000	33000
Portsmouth/Havant	27500	31500	38000	42500	36000	40000	65000	70000	24000	43000
Fareham	26000	31000	31000	37000	35000	43000	60000	80000	25000	32000
Winchester	39000	47000	48000	57500	42000	52000	80000	97000	45000	55000
Newport(IOW)	21000	25000	30000	35000	30000	35000	52500	62500		
Southampton	24000	26000	31000	34000	32000	42000	57500	85000	34000	52000

PRICE RANGES: SPRING 1986

7.68 GREAT BRITAIN:
TOWNS BY HOUSE TYPE AND AGE OF HOUSE - SECONDHAND DWELLINGS

£

	Pre-1919 terraced house (modernized)		Interwar semi-detached house (modernized)		Post 1960 semi-detached house		Post 1960 detached house		Post 1960 flat in 3 (or more) storey block	
	From	To	From	To	From	To	From	To	From	To
SOUTH EAST										
Bedford	28000	33000	39000	49000	40000	50000	68000	85000	27500	45000
Hertford	45000	55000	52500	62500	55000	62500	100000	130000	35000	40000
Luton	29000	33500	38000	56000	38500	50000	90000	100000	33000	43000
St Albans	45000	55000	60000	70000	60000	70000	115000	140000	42500	52500
Watford	43000	47000	59000	70000	57750	70000	95000	115000	39000	53000
Grays	28000	34000	46000	54000	44000	54000	75000	97500	25000	32000
Chelmsford	30000	35000	38000	45000	37000	44000	80000	100000	28000	32000
Colchester	27000	30000	31000	39000	37000	41000	64000	77000	27000	31000
Loughton/Chigwell	57500	62000	70000	80000	65000	72500	110000	145000	38000	65000
Southend-on-Sea	27000	32500	36000	40000	39000	47000	78000	85000	30000	62500
Brighton	34000	37000	42000	47000	44000	48000	90000	110000	30000	37000
Canterbury	28500	36500	37000	47500	35500	47000	60000	82000	29000	39000
Eastbourne	31000	36000	37000	47000	37000	45000	80000	112500	30000	40000
Folkestone	24000	30000	33000	41500	34000	42000	57500	76000	26500	40000
Maidstone	30000	35000	43000	49000	43000	49000	78000	93000	28000	33000
Gillingham	24000	31000	34000	44000	36000	50000	63000	85000	24000	27000
Tunbridge Wells	32000	40000	44000	55000	40000	50000	85000	110000	33000	42000
Horsham	44000	49000	57000	63000	51000	56000	90000	105000	38000	40500
Guildford	40000	45000	46000	52800	50000	55000	100000	110000	47800	55000
Walton-on-Thames	46000	57000	52500	63000	57000	79000	90000	190000	47000	69000
Reigate	42000	60000	50000	60000	50000	65000	95000	145000	40000	60000
Worthing	33000	36000	48000	51000	40500	44500	84000	88000	34500	37000
Maidenhead	46000	54000	58000	68000	53000	64000	110000	140000	40000	49000
Aylesbury	35000	37000	54000	57000	46000	50000	90000	105000	31000	34000
Oxford	45000	60000	42500	57000	42500	56000	85000	105000	38000	55000
Banbury	24500	26000	31000	37500	30000	38000	54000	68500	24000	26500
Reading	34000	36000	47500	49500	46500	51500	87500	97500	34000	37000
High Wycombe	37000	44000	43000	52000	45000	55000	95000	125000	36000	44000
Basingstoke	36000	39000	48000	54000	44000	53000	75000	90000	32000	35000
Portsmouth/Havant	28000	32000	38000	42500	40000	45000	67500	72000	26000	45000
Fareham	28000	32500	33000	40000	37000	45000	65000	85000	27000	34000
Winchester	41000	49500	50500	60500	45500	56000	84000	105000	47000	57500
Newport(IOW)	21000	25000	30000	35000	31000	35000	57000	70000		
Southampton	26500	30000	31000	36000	32000	42000	57500	86000	25000	45000

7.69 *GREAT BRITAIN:*
TOWNS BY HOUSE TYPE AND AGE OF HOUSE - SECONDHAND DWELLINGS

£

	Pre-1919 terraced house (modernized)		Interwar semi-detached house (modernized)		Post 1960 semi-detached house		Post 1960 detached house		Post 1960 flat in 3 (or more) storey block	
	From	To	From	To	From	To	From	To	From	To
SOUTH EAST										
Bedford	33000	36000	43000	53000	43500	53500	75000	95000	32000	50000
Hertford	47500	57500	55000	65000	60000	67500	110000	125000	37500	42500
Luton	32500	36000	42500	60000	40000	55000	92500	105000	33000	44000
St Albans	52000	60000	65000	75000	64000	74000	125000	145000	48000	58000
Watford	47000	52000	63000	75000	61750	75000	102000	125000	42500	58000
Grays	30000	36000	48000	56000	45000	56000	78000	100000	26000	33000
Chelmsford	31500	37500	40000	48000	39000	46000	84000	105000	29500	33500
Colchester	29500	35000	33000	45000	37000	45000	65000	78000	28000	33000
Loughton/Chigwell	62500	67500	76000	87500	70000	77500	120000	157500	42500	70000
Southend-on-Sea	31000	36000	40000	43000	42500	50000	84000	94000	32500	67500
Brighton	38000	42000	45000	50000	47500	52500	95000	125000	34000	40000
Canterbury	31000	39000	39500	50500	38000	49500	66000	90000	31500	41500
Eastbourne	35000	42000	40000	48000	42000	48000	90000	120000	33000	43000
Folkestone	25000	32000	35000	44000	36000	45000	62500	82000	28000	42500
Maidstone	35000	39000	48000	55000	48000	55000	83000	100000	32000	36000
Gillingham	28000	35000	35000	49000	42000	57000	65000	85000	27000	31000
Tunbridge Wells	36000	46000	47000	60000	50000	68000	85000	120000	35000	48000
Horsham	49000	52500	59000	67000	55000	65000	95000	115000	42500	45000
Guildford	43000	49000	49500	57000	54500	60000	110000	120000	50000	59000
Walton-on-Thames	52500	65000	60000	75000	67000	90000	110000	200000	50000	70000
Reigate	50000	65000	60000	75000	60000	75000	105000	170000	45000	55000
Worthing	37000	40000	50000	56000	43000	48000	90000	100000	37000	41000
Maidenhead	47000	56000	60000	71000	59000	72000	120000	148000	43000	53000
Aylesbury	36000	39000	59500	64000	50000	53000	95000	110000	33000	36000
Oxford	47500	64500	47500	64500	47500	62500	87500	125000	40000	59500
Abingdon	38000	50000	45000	55000	47500	50000	70000	85000	38000	39000
Reading	38000	40000	50000	55000	50000	55000	90000	100000	35000	40000
High Wycombe	39000	47000	46000	58000	49000	60000	95000	135000	39000	48000
Basingstoke	45000	47000	53000	56000	50000	60000	90000	105000	38000	42000
Portsmouth/Havant	30000	35000	43000	48000	42000	47000	68500	75000	28000	47500
Fareham	28500	35000	33500	40500	37000	46000	65000	95000	27000	35000
Winchester	45000	53000	54000	62000	50000	58000	90000	107000	48000	58000
Newport(IOW)	24000	29000	32000	37000	34000	40000	65000	70000		
Southampton	30000	42000	35000	45000	33000	45000	75000	95000	27000	45000

PRICE RANGES: AUTUMN 1983

7.70 GREAT BRITAIN:
TOWNS BY HOUSE TYPE AND AGE OF HOUSE - SECONDHAND DWELLINGS

£

	Pre-1919 terraced house		Interwar semi-detached house/bungalow		Post 1960 semi-detached house/bungalow		Post 1965 detached house		Post 1960 flat in 3 (or more) storey block	
	From	To	From	To	From	To	From	To	From	To
SOUTH WEST										
Bournemouth	21500	23500	24750	29000	26750	28000	63000	70000	23500	30000
West Dorset	22000	28000	26500	31500	28500	34000	47500	60000	28000	31000
Carrick	17500	22500	22000	26000	24500	28750	39000	47500	23500	29500
Exeter	20000	23000	26000	35000	27000	31500	50000	60000	20000	23000
North Devon	17000	20000	25000	30000	23000	27500	48500	65000	16000	25000
Plymouth	18000	22000	25000	29000	28000	33000	55000	65000	18500	28000
Restormel	16500	21000	19000	27000	19500	30000	34000	50000		
Somerset	15500	19500	22000	27000	24000	28000	45000	54000	18500	22000
Torbay	19000	22000	22000	25500	24500	29500	55000		25000	32000
Bath	18000	27000	22000	35000	23000	40000	55000	90000	18500	37500
Bristol	13000	21000	21000	36000	22000	27500	60000	70000	19500	23000
Cheltenham	20000	26000	25000	32000	25000	35000	48000	70000	25000	32500
Gloucester	16000	20000	23000	27000	23000	27500	45000	60000	27500	32500
North West Avon	18000	21000	23000	30000	24500	27500	55000	75000	18500	30000
North Wiltshire	15000	17000	23000	28000	23000	30000	50000	60000	19000	20000
South Wiltshire	21000	26250	26750	33500	28000	35000	52400	65500	19250	24000
WALES										
Afan	10250	15500	14000	22500	16500	24500	26750	47250	8000	13500
Cardiff	14500	20000	27000	32000	29000	36000	52000	64000	23500	28500
West Dyfed	15500	21000	21500	25000	23000	26000	41000	54000	20000	27000
East Dyfed	10500	17000	17000	24000	17500	25000	40000	50000		
Merthyr Tydfil	11000	16000	19000	22000	20000	26000	40000	60000		
Pontypridd	9500	17250	18000	25000	16250	21000	29000	43500		
Swansea	7500	17000	18000	28000	19000	28500	40000	60000	20000	30000
Abergavenny	19000	22000	28000	30000	27000	29000	45000	48000		
Bangor	11500	15750	17000	23000	18500	26250	31500	44000		
Colwyn Bay	9000	16500	17000	25000	19000	26000	30000	50000	13000	40000
Newport	13000	15500	20500	23500	22250	25500	44000	52500		
Welshpool	14000	18000	20000	24000	24000	28000	40000	45000		
Wrexham	8500	11000	12750	19000	14500	23500	34000	54500		

PRICE RANGES: SPRING 1984

7.71 GREAT BRITAIN:
TOWNS BY HOUSE TYPE AND AGE OF HOUSE – SECONDHAND DWELLINGS

£

	Pre-1919 terraced house		Interwar semi-detached house/bungalow		Post 1960 semi-detached house/bungalow		Post 1965 detached house		Post 1960 flat in 3 (or more) storey block	
	From	To	From	To	From	To	From	To	From	To
SOUTH WEST										
Bournemouth	22000	24000	24750	29000	27500	28500	64000	75000	23500	30000
West Dorset	22000	28000	27500	32500	30000	36000	47500	60000	28000	33000
Carrick	19000	24500	25000	29000	26000	32000	47000	56500	26000	32000
Exeter	21000	24000	29000	35000	27500	35000	52500	62500	20000	25000
North Devon	18000	20000	28000	32000	24000	27000	55000	65000	22000	25000
Plymouth	19000	23000	26500	31000	30000	35000	57000	66000	20000	29000
Restormel	17000	22000	19500	28000	20000	30000	40000	60000		
Somerset	17000	19250	24500	27500	26000	28500	51000	56000	21000	23000
Torbay	21000	24000	24500	27500	25500	29500	56000	80000	25000	40000
Bath	22500	28500	23500	36500	25000	42000	65000	92500	26500	40000
Bristol	14000	22000	22000	27000	23000	28500	65000	75000	20000	24000
Cheltenham	22000	27500	25000	32000	26000	36500	50000	75000	28000	35000
Gloucester	16000	20000	23000	27000	23000	29000	50000	70000	22500	32500
North West Avon	19000	22000	24500	32000	25500	29000	60000	80000		
North Wiltshire	16000	18000	23000	28000	24000	31000	50000	60000	19500	22000
South Wiltshire	25000	27500	32000	35000	33250	36500	61750	67750	22750	24750
WALES										
Afan	12500	16500	20000	24000	21000	26000	40000	50000	9500	14000
Cardiff	15000	20000	28000	33000	30000	36500	57000	66500	24000	29000
West Dyfed	15500	21500	21500	25500	23000	26000	42000	55000	20000	27000
East Dyfed	10800	17500	17500	25000	18000	25750	41000	51000		
Merthyr Tydfil	11500	16000			23000	27000	40000	50000		
Pontypridd	8500	17500	18000	25000	18750	27750	32000	51500		
Swansea	8000	18000	19500	29500	20000	31000	43500	65000	21000	32000
Abergavenny	19000	22000	28000	30000	27000	29000	47000	50000		
Bangor	14000	16000	20000	23000	23000	26000	38000	44000		
Colwyn Bay	13500	20000	22000	28000	22500	30000	42500	50000	25000	40000
Newport	14500	16750	22250	24500	23500	27000	50000	58000		
Welshpool	15000	20000	22000	26500	26000	31000	44000	50000		
Wrexham	8500	11000	12750	19000	14500	23500	34000	54500		

INLAND REVENUE: VALUATION OFFICE PROPERTY MARKET REPORTS

PRICE RANGES: AUTUMN 1984

7.72 GREAT BRITAIN:
TOWNS BY HOUSE TYPE AND AGE OF HOUSE - SECONDHAND DWELLINGS

£

	Pre-1919 terraced house		Interwar semi-detached house/bungalow		Post 1960 semi-detached house/bungalow		Post 1965 detached house		Post 1960 flat in 3 (or more) storey block	
	From	To	From	To	From	To	From	To	From	To
SOUTH WEST										
Poole	23000	25500	27500	29250	29000	31500	69500	80000	23500	30000
Weymouth	25000	30000	30000	35000	32500	37500	52500	65000	30000	34000
Truro	20500	26000	26500	30500	28000	34000	50000	60000	28500	35000
Exeter	22000	25000	30000	37000	29000	35000	55000	65000	20000	25000
Barnstaple	19000	22000	27000	30000	25000	28000	50000	65000	20000	25000
Plymouth	20500	25000	28500	33500	32500	37500	61000	71000	21500	30000
St Austell	19000	24000	20000	29000	20000	30000	40000	65000		
Taunton	17750	19750	25500	28500	28000	31000	57000	62000	23000	28000
Torquay/Paignton	22000	25000	25500	28500	27500	31000	58000	85000	25000	40000
Bath	24000	29500	23500	38000	25000	43500	67500	92500	28000	42000
Bristol	14500	22500	23000	28000	24000	29500	67000	77000	20000	25000
Cheltenham	23000	29000	27000	35000	28000	37500	54000	80000	28000	36000
Gloucester	17000	21000	23000	30000	24000	37500	50000	80000	22000	32500
Weston-s-Mare	19500	22500	26000	33000	26500	31000	65000	82000		
Swindon	16500	18500	23750	29000	25000	32000	52000	63000	19750	22500
Salisbury	26500	29000	34000	37500	35250	38750	65000	71500	23750	26000
WALES										
Bridgend	13500	18000	21000	25000	22000	27000	40000	52000	10000	15000
Cardiff	15500	21000	28250	33250	30250	36750	58500	67000	24250	29500
Haverfordwest	15500	22500	21500	26000	23000	26500	45000	55000	20000	27000
Llanelli	9500	16500	17000	25000	17000	25000	43000	52000		
Merthyr Tydfil	12000	16500			23000	27000	40000	50000		
Pontypridd	8500	18000	18500	25750	18750	28250	32000	54800		
Swansea	9000	19000	20000	31000	21000	32500	45000	67500	21000	33000
Abergavenny	19000	23000	28500	30500	28000	30500	47000	50000		
Bangor	15000	17000	21000	24000	23000	26000	38000	44000		
Llandudno	13500	20000	22000	28000	22500	30000	42500	50000	25000	40000
Newport (Gwent)	15250	17500	24000	26500	25000	28750	51500	60000		
Newtown	17000	20000	22000	26500	27500	31000	47000	52000		
Wrexham	13000	16500	16500	23000	18500	24500	38000	54500		

145

PRICE RANGES: SPRING 1985

7.73 GREAT BRITAIN:
TOWNS BY HOUSE TYPE AND AGE OF HOUSE - SECONDHAND DWELLINGS

£

	Pre-1919 terraced house		Interwar semi-detached house/bungalow		Post 1960 semi-detached house/bungalow		Post 1965 detached house		Post 1960 flat in 3 (or more) storey block	
	From	To	From	To	From	To	From	To	From	To
SOUTH WEST										
Poole	28500	34500	38000	49500	38500	47750	74000	85250	42500	47000
Weymouth	26000	31000	31500	36500	34000	39000	55000	65000	31500	36500
Truro	22500	28000	28000	33000	28500	36000	55000	65000	28500	35000
Exeter	23000	26000	31000	39000	31000	39000	56000	67000	21000	26500
Barnstaple	19000	22000	28000	31000	27000	30000	60000	65000	27000	30000
Plymouth	21500	25500	29000	34500	33000	39000	62000	72500	21500	30000
St Austell	19000	25000	20000	29000	21000	30000	42500	67500		
Taunton	18500	23000	26000	29500	28500	32500	59000	68000	23500	29000
Torquay/Paignton	23000	26500	26000	30000	29000	33000	60000	85000	26500	40000
Bath	25000	30000	28000	40000	35000	45000	75000	95000	29500	42500
Bristol	15000	23000	23000	28500	24500	30000	70000	80000	22000	26000
Cheltenham	23000	29000	29000	37000	29000	38500	56000	83000	28000	36000
Gloucester	17250	21250	23500	30500	24250	38000	50000	80000	22000	32500
Weston-s-Mare	20000	24000	27000	34000	27000	32500	67500	85000		
Swindon	18000	20000	28000	33000	29000	36000	60000	71000	21000	23000
Salisbury	27500	30000	35000	38750	36500	40000	67000	73750	24500	26750
WALES										
Bridgend	14000	18500	21000	26000	22000	30000	40000	55000	12000	17000
Cardiff	17000	22000	29000	34500	31500	37500	56750	66750	27000	30000
Haverfordwest	16000	23000	22000	26500	23500	27000	45000	56000	20000	28000
Llanelli	9800	17000	17500	26000	18000	26000	45000	55000		
Merthyr Tydfil	12000	16500			23000	27000	42500	52500		
Pontypridd	8750	18250	18500	26000	19000	28500	32500	54500		
Swansea	9000	20000	21000	31000	22000	34000	47000	70000	22000	45000
Abergavenny	21000	24000	29000	33000	30000	35000	50000	57500		
Bangor	15000	17000	21000	24000	23000	26000	38000	44000		
Llandudno	13500	20000	22000	28000	22500	30000	42500	55000	25000	40000
Newport (Gwent)	15250	18000	24000	27500	25000	29000	51500	60000		
Newtown	17000	20000	22000	28500	27500	31000	47000	52000		
Wrexham	13500	16500	18000	23000	18500	24500	40000	55000		

PRICE RANGES: AUTUMN 1985

7.74 GREAT BRITAIN:
TOWNS BY HOUSE TYPE AND AGE OF HOUSE – SECONDHAND DWELLINGS

£

	Pre-1919 terraced house (modernised)		Interwar semi-detached house (modernised)		Post 1960 semi-detached house		Post 1960 detached house		Post 1960 flat in 3 (or more) storey block	
	From	To	From	To	From	To	From	To	From	To
SOUTH WEST										
Poole	28000	31500	33750	34250	32500	37250	75000	95000	25500	38750
Weymouth	28500	33000	34000	39000	35000	39500	60000	70000	32000	37000
Truro	25000	30000	29500	35000	29000	37000	58000	70000	29500	36000
Exeter	26500	28000	39000	45000	34000	40000	60000	85000	24000	30000
Barnstaple	21000	25000	30000	37000	29000	32000	63000	68000	29000	32000
Plymouth	24500	30000	30500	38000	30000	39000	60000	73000	22000	30000
St Austell	20000	27500	22000	30000	24000	31000	50000	75000		
Taunton	19250	24000	29000	32500	29250	34500	59500	70000	24000	30000
Torquay/Paignton	26000	29000	28500	35000	32000	36000	65000	90000	26500	40000
Bath	28000	31000	33500	42500	36500	46000	75000	96500	29500	43500
Bristol	22000	25000	24000	30000	29000	32500	75000	82000	23000	27000
Cheltenham	26500	35000	33000	40000	29000	40000	58000	87000	30000	38000
Gloucester	18500	23500	27000	33000	24000	34000	50000	80000	22500	32500
Weston-s-Mare	21000	25000	27000	32000	25000	35000	58000	70000	30000	40000
Swindon	22000	26000	33000	40000	30000	38000	65000	80000	21000	24000
Salisbury	28750	31750	38000	42000	39000	43000	70750	78000	26000	28250
WALES										
Bridgend	17000	23000	22000	26000	22500	33000	42000	55000	12500	17500
Cardiff	23250	28500	40500	43000	33500	39000	58000	70000	28000	31000
Haverfordwest	22500	23000	29000	30000	25000	28000	48000	60000	20000	28000
Llanelli	14000	19000	22000	28000	19000	27000	48000	60000		
Merthyr Tydfil	16000	19000			26000	29000	44000	54000		
Pontypridd	14750	18750	18750	26500	19500	29500	32500	55000		
Swansea	16000	26000	25000	36500	23000	36000	48000	73000	22500	45000
Abergavenny	25000	29000	33000	38000	32000	37000	52500	59500		
Bangor	16500	19500	23500	26500	25000	28000	39500	44000	10000	13000
Llandudno	16000	22500	24750	27500	25000	30000	40000	50000	25000	40000
Newport (Gwent)	15500	19000	25000	29000	26750	33000	50000	60000		
Newtown	18500	23000	24000	30000	27500	31000	47000	52000		
Wrexham	14500	17000	20000	25000	22500	27000	42500	57500		

7.75 GREAT BRITAIN:
TOWNS BY HOUSE TYPE AND AGE OF HOUSE - SECONDHAND DWELLINGS

£

	Pre-1919 terraced house (modernized)		Interwar semi-detached house (modernized)		Post 1960 semi-detached house		Post 1960 detached house		Post 1960 flat in 3 (or more) storey block	
	From	To	From	To	From	To	From	To	From	To
SOUTH WEST										
Poole	29500	32500	34000	36500	34750	39750	80000	100000	26250	47500
Weymouth	28500	33500	36000	40000	37500	42500	65000	75000	34000	40000
Truro	25250	31500	29800	36500	29100	37350	58000	70000	29600	36200
Exeter	27750	29500	40000	47500	35750	42000	70000	87500	25250	31500
Barnstaple	22000	26000	33000	38000	30000	35000	64000	70000	30000	35000
Plymouth	25000	30000	30000	38000	30000	39000	60000	75000	23000	42000
St Austell	20000	27500	22500	32500	25000	31000	50000	75000		
Taunton	22000	27500	30000	34000	30500	35000	59500	70000	24000	30000
Torquay/Paignton	27500	30000	31000	37000	33000	37500	65000	90000	26500	40000
Bath	29000	32000	36000	44000	37000	47000	80000	97500	30000	43500
Bristol	19000	24000	28000	34000	30000	35000	77000	85000	24500	29000
Cheltenham	27500	36500	34000	42000	33000	45000	62000	95000	30000	40000
Gloucester	19000	23500	28000	35000	35000	45000	55000	80000	22500	32500
Weston-s-Mare	21000	30000	27500	35000	27000	34500	58000	85000	26000	46000
Swindon	25000	32000	34000	42000	32000	40000	65000	85000	23000	25500
Salisbury	30000	34000	39750	44000	40750	45000	73000	82000	28250	31750
WALES										
Bridgend	17500	24500	22500	28000	22500	33000	42000	57000	15000	20000
Cardiff	24000	29000	41000	43750	33750	39500	60000	71000	28000	32000
Haverfordwest	22500	23500	29000	31000	26000	29000	48000	62000	20000	28000
Llanelli	14500	19500	23000	29000	19000	27000	48000	60000		
Merthyr Tydfil	16750	19750			28000	31000	44000	54000		
Pontypridd	14950	18950	18750	26500	19500	29500	32500	55000		
Swansea	17000	28500	26000	37000	24000	38500	48000	77000	24500	46000
Abergavenny	26000	30000	35000	39000	33000	38000	55000	61000		
Bangor	16500	19500	25000	35000	27500	32000	40000	45000	10000	13000
Colwyn Bay	16000	18000	22500	24500	25000	30000	40000	50000	25000	40000
Newport (Gwent)	20000	23000	28000	33000	28000	34000	55000	70000	22000	25000
Newtown	18500	23000	24000	30000	27500	31000	48000	55000		
Wrexham	14500	17500	21000	26000	22500	27000	43000	57500		

PRICE RANGES: AUTUMN 1986

7.76 GREAT BRITAIN:
   TOWNS BY HOUSE TYPE AND AGE OF HOUSE – SECONDHAND DWELLINGS

£

	Pre-1919 terraced house (modernized)		Interwar semi-detached house (modernized)		Post 1960 semi-detached house		Post 1960 detached house		Post 1960 flat in 3 (or more) storey block	
	From	To	From	To	From	To	From	To	From	To
SOUTH WEST										
Poole/Bournem'th	32000	35000	36000	40000	37500	43000	75000	100000	26750	52500
Weymouth	30000	35500	38000	42500	39500	45000	70000	80000	36000	42500
Truro	26500	32500	30000	37500	30000	38000	60000	75000	30000	37000
Exeter	28000	32000	37000	49000	36500	43500	70000	89000	24000	33000
Barnstaple	25000	29000	37500	43000	35000	39000	68000	73000	33000	38000
Plymouth	25000	30000	30000	40000	31000	42000	65000	77500	25000	42000
St Austell	22500	28500	30000	37500	28000	32500	60000	80000		
Taunton	23500	29000	32000	38000	32500	38000	60000	78000	25000	30000
Torquay/Paignton	29000	34000	36000	41500	37000	42000	70000	95000	30000	45000
Bath	30000	35000	39000	46000	40000	49000	82500	98500	32500	44000
Bristol	19500	24500	29000	35000	32000	37000	78000	86000	25000	30000
Cheltenham	29000	38000	35000	45000	34000	55000	70000	100000	32000	45000
Gloucester	20000	24000	30000	38000	38000	48000	60000	85000	25000	33000
Weston-s-Mare	24500	34500	29000	39000	29750	36000	55000	70000	30000	48000
Swindon	27500	35000	38000	44000	34000	45000	68000	90000	23000	26000
Salisbury	32000	36250	42500	47000	43500	48000	80000	90000	30000	35000
WALES										
Bridgend	18000	25500	23500	30000	23500	35000	44000	58000	15750	21000
Cardiff	24500	30000	39000	44000	37500	43950	60000	71000	28000	32000
Haverfordwest	22500	25000	29000	31000	26500	29000	48000	62000	20000	28000
Llanelli	15000	20000	23500	30000	19500	27500	49000	62000		
Merthyr Tydfil	17000	20000			28000	31000	44000	54000		
Pontypridd	15500	19000	21500	28500	22000	30000	36500	55000		
Swansea	17000	29500	27000	38500	24500	39000	48000	79000	25000	49000
Abergavenny	27000	32000	37000	42000	35000	40000	56500	63000		
Bangor	16500	21500	25000	36000	29000	34000	42000	47000	11000	14000
Colwyn Bay	16000	18000	22500	24500	25000	30000	40000	52500	25000	40000
Newport (Gwent)	20000	24000	27000	32000	28000	34000	55000	70000	22000	25000
Newtown	19000	24000	25000	30000	28000	32000	48000	55000		
Wrexham	15500	19000	22000	28500	22500	29000	43000	60000		

RANGE OF PRICES: SPRING 1984

7.77 GREAT BRITAIN:
    TOWNS BY HOUSE TYPE AND AGE OF HOUSE - SECONDHAND DWELLINGS

£

	2 Bed tenement flat c1900		3/4 Bed semi-detached or terrace c1900		Interwar 4 roomed bungalow		Mid 1960s 3 bed semi-detached house estate type	
	From	To	From	To	From	To	From	To
SCOTLAND								
Dumfries	9000	15000	22000	35000	22500	27500	20000	27000
Stirling/Kircaldy	13000	22000	21000	35000	27000	40000	22000	29000
Aberdeen	26000	34000	40000	70000	50000	65000	40000	60000
Grampian (Rural)			22000	27000	30000	35000	27000	30000
Inverness	13000	20000	22000	30000	35000	42000	24000	30000
Edinburgh	15000	35000	30000	53000	32500	45000	32000	40000
Ayr	14000	19000	28000	35000	30000	35000	28000	35000
Glasgow	17000	19000	37000	45000	35000	38000	28000	30000
Glasgow suburbs	14500	17500	37000	45000	35000	46000	24000	35000
Greenock	14500	18000	25000	42000	37000	50000	26000	32000
Dundee	15000	19000	25000	35000	27500	35000	25000	32500
Perth	14000	17500	28000	35000	27500	40000	25000	32500

	Mid 1960s 3/4 bed detached house estate type		Mid 1960s better quality estate detached house		Mid 1960s 2 bed flat	
	From	To	From	To	From	To
Dumfries	25000	35000	40000	45000	27000	32000
Stirling/Kircaldy	28000	37000	45000	65000		
Aberdeen	50000	65000	65000	85000	40000	45000
Grampian (Rural)	32000	37500	32000	37500		
Inverness	30000	40000	40000	60000	18000	23000
Edinburgh	35000	45000	47500	65000	30000	47000
Ayr	35000	45000	50000	70000	20000	30000
Glasgow	32000	35000	50000	55000	23000	28500
Glasgow suburbs	30000	40000	44000	65000	25000	44000
Greenock	32000	38000	40000	50000	23000	42000
Dundee	32000	38000	45000	60000	22500	27500
Perth	34000	38000	45000	60000	25000	30000

7.78 GREAT BRITAIN:
   TOWNS BY HOUSE TYPE AND AGE OF HOUSE - SECONDHAND DWELLINGS

	2 Bed tenement flat c1900		3/4 Bed semi-detached or terrace c1900		Interwar 4 roomed bungalow		Mid 1960s 3 bed semi-detached ho estate type	
	From	To	From	To	From	To	From	To
SCOTLAND								
Dumfries	9500	17500	23000	37500	22500	28000	20000	27500
Stirling/Kircaldy	13000	22000	21000	35000	27000	40000	22000	29000
Aberdeen	26000	35000	42000	75000	52500	67500	42000	63000
Grampian (Rural)			22000	30000	30000	35000	27000	31000
Inverness	13000	20000	24000	33000	35000	45000	26000	33000
Edinburgh	16000	36000	35000	58000	40000	47000	33000	42000
Ayr	15000	25000	30000	36000	32000	40000	30000	38000
Glasgow	18000	21000	38000	50000	38000	42000	28000	32000
Glasgow suburbs	10000	22000	25500	38000	35000	50000	27000	39000
Dundee	16000	20000	27500	37500	27500	35000	27500	32500
Perth	15000	18500	28500	35000	27500	40000	27500	32500

	Mid 1960s 3/4 bed detached house estate type		Mid 1960s better quality estate detached house		Mid 1960s 2 bed flat	
	From	To	From	To	From	To
Dumfries	26000	36000	40000	45000	27000	32000
Stirling/Kircaldy	28000	37000	45000	65000		
Aberdeen	52500	67500	67500	88000	40000	45000
Grampian (Rural)	32000	38000	32500	40000		
Inverness	30000	40000	45000	60000	18500	24000
Edinburgh	35000	47000	50000	65000	30000	47000
Ayr	35000	48000	50000	70000	23000	32000
Glasgow	35000	42000	50000	65000	28000	32000
Glasgow suburbs	32000	43250	45000	70000	28000	52500
Dundee	32500	38500	50000	60000	22500	27500
Perth	34000	38000	50000	60000	25000	30000

RANGE OF PRICES: SPRING 1985

7.79 GREAT BRITAIN:
    TOWNS BY HOUSE TYPE AND AGE OF HOUSE - SECONDHAND DWELLINGS

£

	2 Bed tenement flat c1900		3/4 Bed semi-detached or terrace c1900		Interwar 4 roomed bungalow		Mid 1960s 3 bed semi-detached house estate type	
	From	To	From	To	From	To	From	To
SCOTLAND								
Dumfries	13000	17500	25000	40000	25000	35000	24000	30000
Stirling/Kircaldy	14000	22000	21000	40000	29000	42500	25000	33000
Aberdeen	26000	36000	42000	75000	52500	70000	42500	65000
Grampian (Rural)			22000	30000	30000	37500	27500	31000
Inverness	13000	21000	25000	35000	36500	47500	27000	35000
Edinburgh	18000	37000	37000	61000	42000	52000	34500	44000
Ayr	15750	26500	32000	38000	34000	42000	30000	38000
Glasgow			40000	50000	40000	44000	28000	35000
Glasgow suburbs	16500	31500	40000	70000	34000	58000	29500	39500
Dundee	16000	21000	27500	37500	27500	35000	27500	35000
Perth	16500	20000	28500	35000	27500	40000	28500	32500

	Mid 1960s 3/4 bed detached house estate type		Mid 1960s better quality estate detached house		Mid 1960s 2 bed flat	
	From	To	From	To	From	To
Dumfries	28000	38000	40000	50000		
Stirling/Kircaldy	33250	46000	50000	67500		
Aberdeen	52500	70000	70000	90000	40000	47500
Grampian (Rural)	32000	38000	33500	42500		
Inverness	31500	42500	45000	63000	19500	25000
Edinburgh	37000	50000	52500	70000	31500	48500
Ayr	37000	50000	50000	70000	25000	35000
Glasgow	35000	45000	50000	65000	28000	32000
Glasgow suburbs	33000	48000	51000	90000	28000	54500
Dundee	34000	40000	50000	65000	24000	29000
Perth	34000	40000	50000	65000	25000	32000

7.80 GREAT BRITAIN:
  TOWNS BY HOUSE TYPE AND AGE OF HOUSE - SECONDHAND DWELLINGS

£

	2 Bed tenement flat c1900		3/4 Bed semi-detached or terrace c1900		Interwar 4 roomed bungalow		Mid 1960s 3 bed semi-detached house estate type	
	From	To	From	To	From	To	From	To
SCOTLAND								
Dumfries	13500	17500	29000	48000	26500	37000	24000	30000
Stirling/Kircaldy	15000	22500	22000	40000	30000	42500	27000	33000
Aberdeen	26000	37500	42000	75000	52500	70000	42500	65000
Grampian (Rural)			22000	31000	30000	37500	27500	31000
Inverness	13500	23000	27500	40000	38000	52000	28000	37500
Edinburgh	20000	38000	41000	63000	43000	54000	36500	47000
Ayr	16500	27000	33500	39000	35000	43000	31000	39000
Glasgow	20000	33000	42500	55000	42000	47500	31500	37000
Glasgow suburbs	17000	32000	41000	72500	35000	61000	29500	40000
Dundee	17000	21000	27500	37500	30000	35000	27500	35000
Perth	16000	20000	28500	35000	30000	40000	28500	35000

	Mid 1960s 3/4 bed detached house estate type		Mid 1960s better quality estate detached house		Mid 1960s 2 bed flat	
	From	To	From	To	From	To
Dumfries	30000	38000	45000	55000		
Stirling/Kircaldy	32500	48500	50000	68000	18500	21500
Aberdeen	52500	70000	70000	90000	40000	47500
Grampian (Rural)	32000	38000	33500	42500		
Inverness	33000	40000	47500	70000	20000	25000
Edinburgh	42000	55000	55000	75000	33000	49000
Ayr	38750	52500	52500	73500	26000	36000
Glasgow	37500	48000	52000	70000	30000	35000
Glasgow suburbs	34000	49000	55000	90000	30000	57000
Dundee	35000	42500	50000	65000	24000	30000
Perth	35000	42500	50000	65000	25000	32000

PRICE RANGES: SPRING 1986

7.81 GREAT BRITAIN:
      TOWNS BY HOUSE TYPE AND AGE OF HOUSE - SECONDHAND DWELLINGS

£

	2 Bed tenement flat c1900		3/4 Bed semi-detached or terrace c1900		Interwar 4 roomed bungalow		Mid 1960s 3 bed semi-detached house estate type	
	From	To	From	To	From	To	From	To
SCOTLAND								
Dumfries	13500	19000	29000	48000	30000	40000	25000	30000
Dunferm'/K'caldy	15000	24000	23500	40000	32000	42500	28000	33000
Aberdeen	26000	39000	43500	77500	54000	72000	42500	65000
Grampian (Rural)			22500	32500	30000	38000	27500	32000
Inverness	14000	24000	29000	42500	40000	57500	29000	39000
Edinburgh	22000	40000	42000	64000	43000	54000	36500	48000
Ayr	17000	28000	34000	40000	36000	45000	32000	40000
Glasgow	21000	35000	42500	57000	43000	56000	33000	41000
Glasgow(Bearsden)	23750	32500	49000	85000	41000	62500	30000	41000
Glasgow(Eastwood)	19000	21500	43500	53500	44000	52500	32000	38000
Dundee	18000	24000	27500	37500	30000	35000	29000	37000
Perth	18000	23000	28500	37500	32000	42500	30000	37000
Hamilton	18000	25000	30000	50000	45000	60000	28000	35000

	Mid 1960s 3/4 bed detached house estate type		Mid 1960s better quality estate detached house		Mid 1960s 2 bed flat	
	From	To	From	To	From	To
Dumfries	30000	38000	45000	55000		
Dunferm'/K'caldy	32500	48500	51000	68000	18500	22500
Aberdeen	53000	72500	72000	92500	40000	48500
Grampian (Rural)	33000	39000	34000	45000		
Inverness	35000	42500	48000	80000	21000	26000
Edinburgh	42000	55000	55000	75000	33500	49000
Ayr	39500	52500	52500	73500	26000	37000
Glasgow	38000	48000	55000	75000	33000	45000
Glasgow(Bearsden)	37000	52000	62000	90000	46500	59000
Glasgow(Eastwood)	35000	43500	70000	84000	33000	41500
Dundee	35000	45000	50000	65000	24000	30000
Perth	35000	45000	50000	68000	25000	33000
Hamilton	35000	45000	55000	65000	25000	35000

7.82 GREAT BRITAIN:
TOWNS BY HOUSE TYPE AND AGE OF HOUSE - SECONDHAND DWELLINGS

£

	2 Bed tenement flat c1900		3/4 Bed semi-detached or terrace c1900		Interwar 4 roomed bungalow		Mid 1960s 3 bed semi-detached house estate type	
	From	To	From	To	From	To	From	To
SCOTLAND								
Dumfries	14500	19500	30000	50000	30000	43000	26000	31000
Dunferm'/Falkirk	18000	25000	25000	40000	35000	45000	29000	37000
Aberdeen	25000	40000	43500	77500	54000	72000	42000	65000
Grampian (Rural)			23000	34000	30000	39000	27500	33000
Inverness	15000	25000	25000	42500	40000	57500	29000	39000
Edinburgh	23000	41000	44000	66000	45000	56000	36500	50000
Ayr	18000	28500	35750	42000	38750	48500	33500	42000
Glasgow	21500	36000	42500	59000	43000	57500	33000	41000
Glasgow(Bearsden)	23750	32500	49000	85000	47000	67500	30000	41000
Glasgow(Eastwood)	20000	22500	45000	54500	45000	56900	33000	39000
Dundee	18000	24000	27500	37500	32500	37500	29000	37000
Perth	18000	24500	28500	37500	32000	42500	30000	37000
Hamilton	19000	27000	30000	50000	45000	60000	28000	35000

	Mid 1960s 3/4 bed detached house estate type		Mid 1960s better quality estate detached house		Mid 1960s 2 bed flat	
	From	To	From	To	From	To
Dumfries	30000	38000	45000	60000		
Dunferm'/Falkirk	32500	49500	51000	75000	19000	24000
Aberdeen	53000	72500	72000	82500	40000	48500
Grampian (Rural)	33000	40000	35000	47500		
Inverness	35000	42500	48000	75000	21000	25000
Edinburgh	43000	58000	58000	77500	33500	50000
Ayr	41500	54500	54000	75500	28000	40000
Glasgow	38500	49500	56000	77000	35000	47500
Glasgow(Bearsden)	37000	52000	62000	90000	46500	59000
Glasgow(Eastwood)	36500	45000	73000	88000	35000	44000
Dundee	35000	45000	50000	65000	24000	30000
Perth	35000	45000	50000	70000	25000	33000
Hamilton	35000	50000	55000	70000	25000	37000

8. Northern Ireland Department of Finance and Personnel (PPRU)

8.1 TECHNICAL DETAILS

(a) Source of data and timing

Northern Ireland Stamp Office data for existing dwellings and building societies' records for new dwellings at mortgage completion stage.

(b) Types of data and periods covered

Average prices: 1978 Q1 to date

Available data

DATA BREAKDOWNS	DATA TYPE AVERAGE PRICES
HOUSE DATA	
All houses	
New/Non-new	*
Type	*
Size	
Age	
LOCAL DATA	
Regions	
Sub-regions	*
Towns	
BUYER DATA	
First-time buyer	
Former owner-occupier	

(c) Frequency

Annual and quarterly

(d) Geographical coverage

Northern Ireland subdivided into seven sub-regions - Belfast, North Down, South Down, South Antrim, North Antrim, Derry and Fermanagh & South Tyrone.

(e) Method of analysis

Existing Houses: Simple averages based on details of all sales of existing houses notified by solicitors to the Stamp Office (Northern Ireland), which passes returns to local Valuation Offices for their use. This information is accessed by the Policy Planning and Research Unit (PPRU) of the Department of Finance and Personnel and details of price, type, ward and district for sales in the preceding quarter are recorded. Any late notifications are collected as part of the next quarter's inquiry and revised results are produced. Sales of houses at non-market prices are excluded.

156

New Houses: Simple averages based on data provided by the largest building societies in Northern Ireland (currently six largest), through the Building Societies Association. About 70 per cent of new houses bought with mortgage loans are covered by this return, but there is no information on the proportion of new houses which are bought by other means.

8.2 LIST OF TABLES

Average prices

8.1 Northern Ireland: new and existing dwellings, type of property. 1978–
8.2 Sub-regions: existing dwellings. 1978–
8.3 Sub-regions: small terraced houses (existing dwellings). 1978–
8.4 Sub-regions: medium/large terraced houses (existing dwellings). 1978–
8.5 Sub-regions: detached houses (existing dwellings). 1978–
8.6 Sub-regions: semi-detached houses and bungalows (existing dwellings). 1978–
8.7 Sub-regions: detached bungalows (existing dwellings). 1978–
8.8 Sub-regions: miscellaneous properties (existing dwellings). 1978–

8.3 CROSS-CLASSIFICATIONS OF DATA

(a) Two-way classifications

Existing dwellings by sub-regions: Table 8.2

(b) Three-way classifications

Existing dwellings by sub-region by type of house: Tables 8.3–8.8

8.4 PUBLICATIONS

(a) Data

PPRU Monitor. Northern Ireland House Prices, Department of Finance and Personnel (PPRU), Belfast. Quarterly
Northern Ireland Annual Abstract of Statistics, Department of Finance and Personnel. HMSO, Belfast. Annual
Northern Ireland Housing Statistics, Department of the Environment (Northern Ireland). HMSO, Belfast. Annual

(b) Description of methodology

None

(c) Supplementary studies

None

NORTHERN IRELAND DEPARTMENT OF FINANCE AND PERSONNEL

AVERAGE PRICES (at completion stage) 1978 –

8.1 NORTHERN IRELAND: NEW AND EXISTING DWELLINGS

£

Year		New	Existing	TYPE OF PROPERTY (EXISTING DWELLINGS)					
				Small Terrace	Medium Terrace	Detached House	Semi-det House/ Bungalow	Detached Bungalow	Other
1982*		24910	20737	9800	16261	34419	20594	29541	15444
1983*		24010	22638	11226	17374	36668	22199	31056	17504
1984*		25951	23509	11748	18219	39005	23408	33010	20540
1985*		28095	24988	13369	19813	42276	25066	34438	19342
1986*		30771	26891	15093	22101	43413	26171	36985	21348
1978	1	18070							
	2	18490	11952	3960	6689	22637	12419	19065	7623
	3	19040	13730	4028	7663	25255	13515	21404	7372
	4	20620	13505	4401	9932	24949	14034	21566	7645
1979	1	21040	14282	5571	10024	24838	14910	22105	9987
	2	21920	15604	5853	10682	26870	16005	24012	7870
	3	22930	17967	7281	12508	29789	17709	26087	7556
	4	25550	18680	7656	13061	32159	18577	28037	8705
1980	1	25640	18241	8240	13624	31825	18857	27201	7953
	2	26610	18815	8859	14137	32121	19207	27691	9479
	3	26860	20373	9089	14533	35108	20092	28154	13558
	4	26600	19063	9040	13554	32614	19624	28242	9009
1981	1	25530	19140	8023	16502	30741	18363	24802	9938
	2	25370	20180	8910	14948	33022	20103	29328	16783
	3	25490	20898	9433	16356	33980	20542	28806	16228
	4	25120	19840	9362	15002	32854	20134	28894	16307
1982	1	25050	19264	8730	16162	33636	19852	28623	15501
	2	24620	20434	9781	16688	33654	20411	29224	13072
	3	25250	21252	10292	15878	34577	20822	29814	16872
	4	24720	21506	10199	16312	35387	21009	30119	15818
1983	1	23650	21451	10428	16190	33886	21495	29784	15549
	2	22790	22320	10779	17240	35323	22048	30875	16653
	3	24250	23895	12064	18808	38992	22642	31782	18571
	4	25090	22697	11478	16936	37780	22505	31553	18659
1984	1	25770	22234	10841	16294	37319	22796	31497	19662
	2	25870	22565	11550	18924	37759	22600	32165	18086
	3	26110	24619	12265	18925	39745	23766	34041	22047
	4	25990	24135	12099	18259	40373	24202	33601	21368
1985	1	27080	23433	12041	19988	41793	23890	32931	19351
	2	27590	24798	13121	19736	42648	24700	34605	16669
	3	28660	26220	14259	19613	42503	26336	35111	19377
	4	28850	24646	13629	20057	41911	24640	34404	21809
1986	1	29300	25965	14147	21454	41994	25130	36030	20378
	2	31880	26120	14648	23023	40089	25818	37559	19967
	3	30750	27716	15708	22316	44941	26656	36295	23342
	4**	30830	27154	14831	21434	45027	26672	38491	21341

* Data for existing dwellings are unpublished figures obtained from Valuation Office records

** Data for existing dwellings have been supplied by PPRU in advance of publication (subject to revision)

NORTHERN IRELAND DEPARTMENT OF FINANCE AND PERSONNEL

AVERAGE PRICES (completion stage) 1978 -

8.2 SUB-REGIONS: EXISTING DWELLINGS

£

Year		Belfast	North Down	South Down	South Antrim	North Antrim	Derry	Fermanagh & South Tyrone
1982		17888	25105	18491	21251	22080	20138	23384
1983		19451	27331	20274	23284	24279	21794	22798
1984		20210	28380	21801	24223	24518	22784	25816
1985		22036	30081	23638	25988	26328	23206	24647
1986		24887	31112	23446	26858	26331	24217	26465
1978	2	14041	13567	16019	14101	8906	13539	11286
	3	15905	17543	8690	15680	12677	14969	16105
	4	10447	17448	12331	15544	15109	14143	15641
1979	1	11972	17988	11869	15504	15894	14351	16196
	2	12800	19816	12606	16280	18054	16228	16344
	3	15751	21049	15416	18430	18799	17976	19319
	4	16321	22840	14932	19514	18350	16660	19763
1980	1	16287	22020	15572	19072	18748	16396	19717
	2	16158	23012	15596	20048	19496	17131	21403
	3	18683	24461	16970	20202	19832	18965	23646
	4	17272	23037	15358	20915	16546	18674	19652
1981	1	15982	21038	13189	19166	17928	16772	18570
	2	17240	24808	17944	20573	22326	19552	22182
	3	18122	25985	18416	21320	20831	19469	23480
	4	16184	24153	18183	20284	22213	20571	23383
1982	1	15787	24392	18117	20206	21667	19456	21941
	2	17659	24661	18433	20283	21680	20104	24780
	3	18549	25479	18469	22058	23030	18923	24123
	4	18921	25603	19118	21986	21881	21673	22658
1983	1	18450	25874	18622	21726	22069	20705	23037
	2	18945	27170	20422	23194	23610	21513	21309
	3	20747	28051	21474	24296	27291	22910	24363
	4	19380	28096	20207	23658	24014	21790	22283
1984	1	18744	26399	20803	23629	22644	22087	24763
	2	19007	28515	21870	24193	24448	21569	25429
	3	21661	29173	23459	24543	25394	23574	26728
	4	20846	28923	20673	24359	25156	23559	25671
1985	1	19640	27442	22479	25230	25984	20526	25928
	2	20811	30843	22995	24543	26272	23355	24674
	3	24260	31640	22923	26879	26069	24017	22893
	4	21707	29364	25160	26513	27095	23955	26177
1986	1	24700	29654	23716	26998	26465	22733	25859
	2	23649	30113	23105	26138	26244	24334	27155
	3	26461	31571	23729	27203	26778	24461	27039
	4	24545	32743	23243	27089	25668	24922	25384

These are unpublished figures obtained from Valuation Office records

159

NORTHERN IRELAND DEPARTMENT OF FINANCE AND PERSONNEL

AVERAGE PRICES (at completion stage) 1978 –

8.3 SUB-REGIONS: SMALL TERRACED HOUSES (EXISTING DWELLINGS)

£

Year		Belfast	North Down	South Down	South Antrim	North Antrim	Derry	Fermanagh & South Tyrone
1982		9161	12931	9065	9930	11127	8745	9402
1983		10167	15144	10911	11553	12759	9519	13834
1984		10971	13983	12467	12531	12900	10697	9947
1985		12489	17432	12199	14529	15067	11657	14402
1986		14585	16468	13930	16780	16158	10635	13962
1978	2	6642	4645	6974	3081	2301	6254	4642
	3	6815	6914	3039	4504	4018	3900	4026
	4	3184	6825	4888	4854	7382	3025	7215
1979	1	4997	7795	4596	4474	7232	3473	7975
	2	5505	7881	4682	5444	8655	4750	6787
	3	6321	9121	6438	7977	10457	4723	7528
	4	7043	10265	5901	7599	10080	4281	7725
1980	1	8485	10066	6530	7973	7690	5600	7469
	2	8391	11610	6673	7533	10643	5880	12691
	3	9126	11456	7168	8599	9422	4188	4850
	4	8600	11589	7617	10061	8495		10103
1981	1	7836	10656	5815	8133	7577	7875	8930
	2	8236	12084	7692	8461	12138	1500	10525
	3	8903	13357	8369	10000	10052	5670	10200
	4	8500	12781	7806	9692	10896	9439	11192
1982	1	8240	12262	8363	7718	10433	7918	10071
	2	9090	12859	9322	10438	10261	7433	6360
	3	9585	13439	8935	10856	10645	9531	13997
	4	9611	12860	9857	10221	12416	9025	6748
1983	1	9580	14079	10460	10889	10820	6600	11194
	2	10310	13192	10031	11256	11727	9200	12290
	3	10392	16880	11810	12332	15308	10033	16851
	4	10351	15539	11059	11746	12767	10682	13021
1984	1	10128	12846	11162	12599	9643	10833	10770
	2	10450	15502	12917	12780	13360	7850	12600
	3	11704	14513	13124	11962	13708	13231	7399
	4	11349	13569	12449	12937	14098	10870	12004
1985	1	11199	13830	11842	13398	14343	9609	13257
	2	12117	16966	11999	14572	15744	9169	14567
	3	13353	21581	10740	15091	14768	13363	14723
	4	12752	17845	13501	14603	15330	12956	13300
1986	1	15584	15763	12885	15447	16655	10147	14873
	2	14064	16067	14230	16506	16071	9503	8175
	3	15258	16836	14321	16929	16341	12797	16362
	4	13716	17058	14016	17658	15799	10356	14046

These are unpublished figures obtained from Valuation Office records

NORTHERN IRELAND DEPARTMENT OF FINANCE AND PERSONNEL

AVERAGE PRICES (at completion stage) 1978 -

8.4 SUB-REGIONS: MEDIUM/LARGE TERRACED HOUSES (EXISTING DWELLINGS)

£

Year		Belfast	North Down	South Down	South Antrim	North Antrim	Derry	Fermanagh & South Tyrone
1982		16115	19308	14366	17495	18348	14009	19643
1983		17620	18637	18056	20142	18620	15302	19960
1984		18000	19394	19881	19880	19292	15456	24059
1985		21446	19564	20901	24219	21182	16917	20419
1986		25742	22021	19224	22250	25943	17925	19528
1978	2	14727	8839	14982	7431	5202	11206	8300
	3	10842	10985	7276	11020	6399	9087	16414
	4	8606	14249	9726	11950	13375	8268	12533
1979	1	9424	11505	9046	12725	11945	9521	11500
	2	10391	12871	7654	14438	15334	10206	7517
	3	11816	13545	13250	15168	14240	9960	18330
	4	13433	15457	15046	14040	11800	10678	12425
1980	1	12496	16759	15265	19000	19033	10987	15195
	2	14045	17278	13245	15300	13625	10557	24389
	3	14822	15085	13734	16100	15237	12876	20417
	4	13624	14968	12255	16372	14011	11125	20750
1981	1	20398	14690	9966	20238	18942	10248	18994
	2	14266	17809	17844	13020	18271	11465	20200
	3	16851	21835	10650	19275	17714	12567	14200
	4	14825	17073	16125	19000	15077	13068	23417
1982	1	15844	18515	13514	17340	20082	14516	19857
	2	16692	21172	12700	18842	18108	13283	17421
	3	15653	18584	15677	14625	18206	14000	30625
	4	16196	18732	16438	18125	17669	14067	18214
1983	1	16141	16776	17604	18970	19854	14670	16815
	2	15255	19113	17711	20612	20500	15959	17333
	3	20425	18892	18767	22321	17000	15928	23690
	4	17439	19786	17988	17558	17108	14526	17550
1984	1	16703	15684	18613		17575	14414	19370
	2	18906	21623	19930	19618	22029	15655	21500
	3	19951	18674	19808	19385	19327	15621	32625
	4	16027	21080	20640	30000	17618	16032	24850
1985	1	22386	20915	19700	19338	21083	16024	19863
	2	21560	19361	26471	31000	21426	16115	21750
	3	22185	18407	17523		21231	18202	19836
	4	19870	25464	22520	28625	20875	17314	20169
1986	1	26879	20579	18850	22250	25042	16660	17300
	2	25791	22092	20667		31222	18760	19385
	3	27392	22709	18191		23615	18108	20817
	4	22853	22129	21333		26896	17921	18339

These are unpublished figures obtained from Valuation Office records

NORTHERN IRELAND DEPARTMENT OF FINANCE AND PERSONNEL

AVERAGE PRICES (at completion stage) 1978 –

8.5 SUB-REGIONS: DETACHED HOUSES (EXISTING DWELLINGS)

£

Year		Belfast	North Down	South Down	South Antrim	North Antrim	Derry	Fermanagh & South Tyrone
1982		38528	35079	29384	31097	30174	31782	29242
1983		38813	39278	31279	33434	34778	33812	26427
1984		41563	42791	31799	33273	37479	34110	35895
1985		45437	46755	36996	37242	39081	36068	29837
1986		48890	46804	36193	38203	36905	35306	35922
1978	2	20913	22843	26153	21154	22813	17607	22573
	3	22732	26703	21867	25776	28323	18574	18844
	4	25961	27874	18738	21076	23927	27938	19426
1979	1	24918	25198	18925	30050	23468	23900	28000
	2	27486	26207	27765	23203	30676	32679	19827
	3	31442	30800	25163	28760	29101	26083	26550
	4	32780	33375	42400	29978	28875	29864	28600
1980	1	35038	31587	32303	27288	29117	25431	42556
	2	34065	36729	24853	27382	27194	28104	16406
	3	37017	37860	28768	30311	30765	32029	33156
	4	36169	34565	25729	28484	25523	29167	23125
1981	1	33287	32452	22524	32471	28623	24507	28696
	2	34740	36989	22765	30348	30853	28127	32250
	3	36140	36643	28560	31018	30504	27967	25667
	4	33020	36991	26073	29954	30152	31289	30560
1982	1	35168	32976	30829	32893	35439	35292	29250
	2	39676	34822	28531	29367	26125	30877	33450
	3	38014	35114	28899	31352	32603	27958	29912
	4	40209	36577	29727	30869	30394	32560	26343
1983	1	36874	37248	24804	32283	28958	30923	28036
	2	37100	38924	35367	31710	31200	30523	25107
	3	40093	39069	34995	34435	45087	33744	31820
	4	40883	41902	29728	35643	33122	38008	24347
1984	1	40400	39962	29548	33870	36639	36591	30639
	2	38319	46700	30447	35221	36015	35842	30054
	3	44092	41763	35780	31464	37505	31428	50673
	4	41784	43757	28531	34303	40188	33433	33623
1985	1	42120	45017	35135	41320	38773	32869	40875
	2	46068	45859	46660	36088	39364	33015	25567
	3	46105	48647	31219	34031	37915	38897	31433
	4	45912	46763	40326	40125	40531	38028	28593
1986	1	45019	49711	35409	39818	38482	28722	37214
	2	45323	39765	37970	37998	35408	37388	37223
	3	51955	48591	36521	39951	37607	33936	34428
	4	51400	50582	34242	35295	36078	39854	36412

These are unpublished figures obtained from Valuation Office records

NORTHERN IRELAND DEPARTMENT OF FINANCE AND PERSONNEL

AVERAGE PRICES (at completion stage)   1978 –

8.6 SUB-REGIONS: SEMI-DETACHED HOUSES, BUNGALOWS (EXISTING DWELLINGS)

£

Year		Belfast	North Down	South Down	South Antrim	North Antrim	Derry	Fermanagh & South Tyrone
1982		20112	21683	19704	20046	21313	21068	19984
1983		22093	22984	21449	21349	22812	22536	20173
1984		23770	24071	21983	22440	23359	23268	22351
1985		25676	26290	22746	24132	24369	23685	22749
1986		27527	27285	23690	24917	24867	23996	22458
1978	2	12557	13370	13364	13743	11277	12798	11927
	3	14212	13861	11080	12656	14591	14519	14918
	4	13205	15334	13710	13793	15521	13329	16358
1979	1	14301	16279	15249	14088	15475	14576	18288
	2	15402	17426	15580	15216	16796	15281	17112
	3	17373	18304	17710	17086	18983	17369	16368
	4	18184	19641	18158	17972	19506	17951	13844
1980	1	18576	19774	18310	18212	20166	17458	19613
	2	18748	19892	17482	20076	18977	18440	24700
	3	19916	21532	18836	19115	19244	19025	21833
	4	19475	20237	18768	19265	20519	19103	19780
1981	1	18897	19027	14918	17875	18121	17894	14614
	2	20299	20699	19943	19343	20017	18915	18722
	3	20315	22114	19200	19669	20136	19620	19932
	4	19738	20593	19615	19348	21993	21009	19533
1982	1	19188	21148	19447	19026	20651	20241	21438
	2	20007	21678	18962	19771	21745	20016	22491
	3	20258	22123	20608	20293	20739	21500	14917
	4	20607	21543	20530	20676	21833	22044	19545
1983	1	21465	22238	21251	20504	21065	22468	16981
	2	21841	22898	21816	21068	22939	22286	19769
	3	22645	23379	22313	21467	22704	22970	22145
	4	22270	23386	20692	22360	23983	22390	19533
1984	1	22720	23466	21867	22050	22830	23436	22735
	2	22406	23917	21448	21838	22907	23018	22734
	3	24386	23812	22766	23024	23783	23844	21986
	4	25188	24829	21560	22631	23725	22568	22108
1985	1	24062	24575	22081	23124	24510	22472	25508
	2	24817	25830	22733	24394	24290	24523	22264
	3	27336	28510	22780	24793	23971	23423	20134
	4	25157	25018	23097	23907	24873	24411	26600
1986	1	26392	26254	23079	24450	23368	23555	21364
	2	26743	27054	23168	24384	25314	23784	24458
	3	28279	27530	24613	25050	25697	24540	22674
	4	28336	28012	24139	25854	24264	23867	21233

These are unpublished figures obtained from Valuation Office records

163

NORTHERN IRELAND DEPARTMENT OF FINANCE AND PERSONNEL

AVERAGE PRICES (at completion stage) 1978 –

8.7 SUB-REGIONS: DETACHED BUNGALOWS (EXISTING DWELLINGS)

£

Year		Belfast	North Down	South Down	South Antrim	North Antrim	Derry	Fermanagh & South Tyrone
1982		33979	31541	27057	27682	27116	27793	27617
1983		33060	33671	28777	30600	28460	29913	26891
1984		39892	35180	29973	33188	30216	31584	29546
1985		39530	37320	32365	35430	32214	31676	29686
1986		41045	41724	34002	37140	32485	33506	31544
1978	2	19796	17816	19633	18865	18896	18703	19303
	3	20630	23123	19793	19525	20862	21227	21175
	4	23327	22372	21391	21367	20071	19980	20156
1979	1	24425	24481	22223	20420	22004	19590	19142
	2	23810	26525	21891	22490	23690	22958	22768
	3	27181	27955	24365	24496	24878	24978	24624
	4	31408	30914	21442	27098	24615	22630	25015
1980	1	31159	29420	27685	26510	24017	23984	24066
	2	30401	29813	24367	27728	26275	24257	25465
	3	32635	29869	24781	27154	26819	26281	26208
	4	31537	30893	24229	28279	24127	26494	24284
1981	1	27032	26845	22891	24300	20845	24983	21033
	2	31886	31655	26718	27458	27240	30088	24333
	3	33914	30705	25875	28282	25982	27264	27543
	4	31383	30320	25798	28588	28530	28409	26050
1982	1	31126	30732	28994	26043	25704	28395	24693
	2	32447	31214	26426	27045	27695	25419	28811
	3	34369	32030	26731	28465	28183	25826	27476
	4	37180	31901	26541	28218	26694	30864	27882
1983	1	32016	31467	27334	28776	28007	29282	26899
	2	33325	33884	29998	30244	28485	28664	25225
	3	32851	34316	29404	31415	28414	31541	29048
	4	33971	35204	27626	31383	28804	30175	25906
1984	1	37349	34184	28683	31199	28062	29640	27972
	2	40639	33829	30338	32981	29360	29322	29640
	3	40311	36071	30647	34272	31879	32701	29875
	4	40774	35566	30154	34012	30958	32481	29900
1985	1	40267	35151	31123	35229	31405	27179	27632
	2	34357	38794	31406	34260	31064	34050	31552
	3	43115	37448	33899	35189	32547	30790	28177
	4	36640	36773	32721	36588	34188	32575	30803
1986	1	40477	41430	33536	36735	31660	31700	30099
	2	41413	40824	34897	37778	33680	35370	31504
	3	42631	39451	31941	37491	32073	32546	32802
	4	38747	47027	36535	36391	32313	34135	30956

These are unpublished figures obtained from Valuation Office records

NORTHERN IRELAND DEPARTMENT OF FINANCE AND PERSONNEL

AVERAGE PRICES (at completion stage) 1978 –

8.8 SUB-REGIONS: MISCELLANEOUS PROPERTIES (EXISTING DWELLINGS)*

£

Year	Belfast	North Down	South Down	South Antrim	North Antrim	Derry	Fermanagh & South Tyrone
1982	21045	19636	11598	11595	15393	10656	12165
1983	21654	21137	11802	11731	14182	16543	18909
1984	21128	25044	23545	11627	16351	18062	19348
1985	20773	18845	23935	25167	18702	17343	15887
1986	23331	22811	20498	15969	18948	17784	20649
1978 2	8086	10000	8568	5057	5312	8063	5748
3	3780	9481	6677	6729	4343	11100	10580
4	7207	8788	7249	6986	4112	4115	8750
1979 1	28000	14520	5236	6494	3406		3567
2	14350	9234	4485	12463	3338	9500	11152
3	21750	8140	6255	6875	4717	12500	7869
4	15514	11417	10348	5840	2721		14100
1980 1	14923	10758	9671	1500	3763	9750	7750
2	7033	13381	5564	7200	6600		
3	27321	16275	8321	14907	4494		2800
4	13810	14991	7416	8036	4519	8075	11576
1981 1	5350	13284	6729	11650	2258		14813
2	23950	15991	13567	10667	18333		19833
3	32200	17426	15620	16183	9875	11000	17583
4	23125	19117	17613	9640	12857	12525	10167
1982 1	18558	20778	10602	14525	10700	17100	10375
2	17667	14979	13378	9139	11120	13000	10800
3	23014	20343	12573	12418	21125	11800	9625
4	23300	23292	10283	11293	15328	7888	16086
1983 1	12188	18735	11000	14695	14405		17568
2	18333	20284	15000	8342	12905	20500	17300
3	29278	21985	10906	10100	15383	11000	17177
4	24093	22672	4250	11436	14094	18014	23569
1984 1	16288	27758	21458	9638	16270	14000	18156
2	21846	24478	15050	10248	16200	14683	16157
3	22750	22200	34973	11836	12356	20558	22031
4	23114	26648	9655	26400	18943	15781	17979
1985 1	12117	20241	35833	16000	15917	16531	21775
2	18333	18632	12846	9000	16571	20375	15151
3	24861	18071	22957	28000	15414	20488	15331
4	22270	19012	29343	29571	24829	13494	14261
1986 1	26082	18733	21150	11250	20222	18889	25646
2	23618	20790	17225	19200	17500	17183	20308
3	25356	26153	21610	16800	16883	18675	19053
4	20267	23969	20762	15250	21500	17339	18492

* Miscellaneous properties include flats, maisonettes and cottages.

These are unpublished figures obtained from Valuation Office records

PART II Institutional Data Sources

9. Abbey National Building Society

9.1 TECHNICAL DETAILS

(a) Source of data and timing

Society's own lending records at the mortgage completion stage for the period 1977 Q4 to 1978 Q2, and at the approval stage subsequently

(b) Types of data and periods covered

Average prices: 1977 Q4 to 1981 Q4
Weighted average prices: 1982 Q1 to date

Available data

DATA BREAKDOWNS	DATA TYPE AVERAGE PRICES
HOUSE DATA	
All houses	*
New/Non-new	(*)
Type	(*)
Size	
Age	(*)
LOCAL DATA	
Regions	*
Sub-regions	
Towns	
BUYER DATA	
First-time buyer	(*)
Former owner-occupier	(*)

(*) These data no longer published

(c) Frequency

Quarterly

(d) Geographical coverage

United Kingdom subdivided into official standard regions (defined in Appendix B)

(e) Method of analysis

Until 1981 Q4 the published series were based on simple averages of house prices. The problem of noncomparability, as discussed in the introductory chapter, was then recognised by the introduction of a weighted average similar to that now employed by the DOE for its weighted index (see Chapter 3). Simple average prices are computed for subsets of houses classified according to particular characteristics and these are then

169

combined in fixed proportions into a single *weighted* average. Subclassifications are made according to type, age group and region. The weights employed are derived from the DOE Five Per Cent Sample Survey results and not from the Society's own mortgage transactions in order to ensure more representative national coverage. All sales, including those at discounted prices, are covered.

9.2 LIST OF TABLES

Average prices and weighted average prices

9.1 United Kingdom: all, age of dwelling, type of buyer, type of house. 1977-
9.2 Regions: all dwellings. 1977-
9.3 Regions: new dwellings. 1977-1984
9.4 Regions: post-1919 dwellings. 1977-1984
9.5 Regions: pre-1919 dwellings. 1977-1984
9.6 Regions: detached houses. 1977-1984
9.7 Regions: semi-detached houses. 1977-1984
9.8 Regions: terraced houses. 1977-1984
9.9 Regions: bungalows. 1977-1984
9.10 Regions: flats and maisonettes. 1977-1984
9.11 Regions: first-time buyers. 1980-1985
9.12 Regions: former owner-occupiers. 1980-1985
9.13 United Kingdom and regions by age of house: detached houses. 1977-1984
9.14 United Kingdom and regions by age of house: semi-detached houses. 1977-1984
9.15 United Kingdom and regions by age of house: terraced houses. 1977-1984
9.16 United Kingdom and regions by age of house: bungalows. 1977-1984
9.17 United Kingdom and regions by age of house: flats and maisonettes. 1977-1984

9.3 CROSS-CLASSIFICATIONS OF DATA

(a) Two-way classifications

Numbers in the grid below refer to the corresponding tables compiled for this data source

(b) Three-way classifications

United Kingdom and regions by type of dwelling, by age of dwelling: Tables 9.13-9.17.

9.4 PUBLICATIONS

(a) Data

Homes - People, Prices and Places. Quarterly from 1978 Q1 to 1984 Q3. and then in a quarterly press release. Abbey National Building Society, London

(b) Description of methodology

None

(c) Supplementary studies

Homes - People, Prices and Places contained two short series of data which we have not reproduced in our tables:

    type of buyer by type of property and by age of property. 1977 Q4-1979 Q4

    type of buyer by region and by new/secondhand. 1980 Q2-1984 Q4

Ad hoc articles published in *Homes - People*, *Prices and Places* are listed below (numbers refer to issue numbers):

1 Average price paid by owner-occupiers and first-time buyers. Comparison of proportions of owner-occupiers and first-time buyers in last quarters of 1976 and 1977.

2 Average prices paid by first-time buyers and owner-occupiers.

    Percentage of first-time buyers and owner-occupiers.

3 Wales and Scotland: regional house prices by first-time buyer, owner-occupier, age of dwelling, type of dwelling.

4 West Midlands and East Midlands. Average house prices and percentage of buyers as above.

    Pre-1919 Houses.

6 South East: average prices in 1st quarter of 1979.

7 First-time buyers and existing borrowers - 2nd quarter 1979.

8 Metropolitan Counties - 3rd quarter 1979.

10 South East: average prices by buyer type.

11 New Homes - 2nd quarter 1980.

ABBEY NATIONAL BUILDING SOCIETY

AVERAGE PRICES (at approval stage) 1977 -

9.1 UNITED KINGDOM: ALL, AGE OF DWELLING, TYPE OF BUYER, TYPE OF HOUSE

| Year | All | AGE OF DWELLING | | | TYPE OF BUYER | |
		New	Post-1919	Pre-1919	First-time	Former Owner-occupier
1977 4*	14092	14601	14691	12399	11547	16879
1978 1*	14473	15227	15015	12659	11701	17417
2*	14842	15741	15385	12939	12633	19345
3	17370	18386	18207	15005	13683	20963
4	18387	19476	19253	15772	14646	22025
1979 1	19418	20577	20364	16567		
2	21263	22357	22445	18131	16519	25443
3	22988	24182	24168	20009	17632	27861
4	23894	25052	25237	20742	18335	29369
1980 1	24370	26158	25413	21344	18859	29725
2	25362	26626	26668	22376	19409	30857
3	25243	26857	26748	21849	19628	30937
4	25192	27018	26663	21894	19660	31387
1981 1	24909	27948	25694	21986	19040	31375
2	25613	28361	26235	23113	18747	32896
3	24501	27937	24947	22006	18456	31840
4**	24143	28214	23400	24037	19818	27865
1982 1	24118	28903	23249	23690	19973	27641
2	24479	28894	23429	25096	20020	28292
3	25396	28804	24896	25118	21492	28741
4	25783	29663	25038	25885	22282	28781
1983 1	26217	30890	25434	26254	22928	29125
2	27428	31955	26503	27911	23670	30752
3	28327	32407	27614	28945	24440	31762
4	29326	33395	28731	30181	25097	33064
1984 1	29182	33637	28461	29417	25003	32882
2	31105	34699	32382	26719	23864	38022
3	31306	34566	32673	26870	23925	38360
4	31483	34573	32936	26979	24270	38365
1985 1	31686				24727	38458
2	32551				25070	39839
3	33660				25948	41175
4	34502					
1986 1	34811					
2	36814					
3	38391					
4	39495					
1987 1	39938					

* Prices at completion stage
** Simple averages before 1981 Q4; weighted averages from 1981 Q4 to date.

£

TYPE OF HOUSE

Detached	Semi-detached	Terraced	Bungalow	Flat/Maisonette
21029	12818	11015	14944	12123
21525	13204	11359	15822	12550
22241	13780	11705	16025	12783
26441	15716	13581	18724	14422
27383	16899	14359	20125	15479
29234	18073	15516	23203	16456
32268	19755	16660	25085	17539
34748	21054	18143	27475	19325
37155	22265	18409	28724	19946
37640	22972	19163	29271	20164
39664	23745	19750	30088	20934
39761	23956	19606	30437	20962
39631	24218	19778	30453	21301
39295	24190	19560	30606	21290
40860	24471	19874	31487	20807
40386	23563	19035	31082	20865
34256	22504	18665	27951	18035
34037	22876	18513	29198	18632
34390	22995	18652	31000	18796
35510	24026	19836	30376	19475
35954	24575	19876	31639	19309
37823	24932	19960	31600	20510
39754	25974	20761	33904	21042
41865	27011	21468	34551	21414
41378	27898	22990	36032	22055
41388	27571	22950	35610	22215
47517	28793	23422	38000	24942
47043	29311	23627	38082	25545
47483	28965	23920	39118	25846

ABBEY NATIONAL BUILDING SOCIETY

AVERAGE PRICES AND WEIGHTED AVERAGE PRICES (at approval stage) 1977 –

9.2 REGIONS: ALL DWELLINGS

Year	North	Yorks & Humberside	North West	East Midlands	West Midlands	East Anglia
1977 4*	11553	10046	11421	11528	12597	13102
1978 1*	12024	10170	11614	11631	12769	13229
2*	12214	10709	12127	11965	13262	13408
3	13464	11329	13529	13033	15607	15370
4	14355	11986	14943	13854	15589	16615
1979 1	13687	13417	15207	15028	17016	17814
2	16290	14451	16660	15559	17835	19280
3	16500	15685	17554	17267	20199	20228
4	17459	16837	18412	17496	20996	21540
1980 1	18192	17478	18842	17917	21861	22683
2	18248	18017	19954	19396	22298	23384
3	18439	18289	20107	19941	21878	23451
4	18163	18138	19705	19830	21508	23842
1981 1	18068	18212	20177	19661	21190	22878
2	18371	19023	20126	20187	21861	23064
3	18128	18084	19267	19835	22746	23429
4	19681	19097	21015	18590	21354	21980
1982 1	18797	18613	21375	19517	21917	22429
2	18672	18803	20830	19248	21120	21277
3	19919	20573	21491	20430	22067	22764
4	19679	20111	21654	18983	21930	23434
1983 1	21114	21099	22143	20190	22580	23733
2	22317	21557	22690	20718	22873	25102
3	22724	22610	23743	21359	23786	26110
4	23518	23147	24506	22351	24878	26485
1984 1	23172	22582	24239	22491	24271	27217
2	23487	24097	25102	25371	26880	30429
3	23714	23937	25391	25344	26757	31017
4	23516	24381	24814	25045	26342	31427
1985 1	23069	24322	24685	25133	25884	31747
2	22685	24044	24797	25894	26591	33114
3	23871	25331	25720	27014	27050	34326
4	23606	24991	26046	27561	27757	34701
1986 1	23886	24513	25812	27721	28046	35416
2						
3	25076	27045	27492	30645	30264	38202
4	25736	26488	27092	30816	31667	41622
1987 1	23902	26101	28573	31754	31282	44707

* Prices at completion stage

174

£

South East	Greater London	South West	Wales	Scotland	Northern Ireland
16330	16321	13619	11637	15076	15469
16602	16871	14290	12112	14956	15693
16958	17540	14563	12362	14994	16476
20738	20220	16870	14283	16802	18489
21970	22039	17518	15195	17309	19122
22854	23584	18211	15619	18122	19539
25273	25982	19929	16627	19185	20507
27586	27677	22118	18952	20760	21934
28863	28702	23267	17767	21471	21934
28728	29763	24060	18972	21129	23234
30325	30219	25250	19713	21933	21718
30066	29849	25525	19525	22424	23067
30064	29869	24604	19075	22207	19209
29631	30047	24588	18821	21438	15120
31309	30751	25401	17690	22473	15030
29870	29114	25554	18744	22241	12481
29383	34348	23919	19300	23472	22088
29081	34415	24518	19205	23553	21561
30111	36015	25248	19625	24684	21541
30927	35066	26191	20643	26397	22180
32105	36950	27316	20766	26445	21572
32671	37612	27462	20306	25453	21481
34681	40446	28782	21895	26414	20823
35778	42480	29674	22358	25695	21828
36493	43826	30349	23101	28673	24054
37238	41788	30141	23133	28823	23479
40252	40275	32412	24286	29942	26237
40732	41678	31886	24164	29728	26066
41330	42392	32442	24112	29779	25977
41404	43722	32484	24304	29790	25836
43393	45275	34097	23722	29978	25423
45195	46503	34982	24194	30173	26166
46723	49221	35466	24702	30910	26856
47318	50573	36561	25428	31259	25597
53497	58073	39404	27341	32320	27578
55363	61398	40506	27370	32568	28196
55607	62897	40842	28651	31586	27322

ABBEY NATIONAL BUILDING SOCIETY

AVERAGE PRICES (at approval stage) 1977-1984

9.3 REGIONS: NEW DWELLINGS

Year	North	Yorks & Humberside	North West	East Midlands	West Midlands	East Anglia
1977 4*	12757	11891	12972	12050	13792	12767
1978 1*	13008	12051	13218	12249	14121	13659
2*	13293	12764	14196	12607	15119	13466
3	14638	14813	16783	14403	18273	15933
4	15579	15459	17625	15920	18116	17120
1979 1	16357	16646	18743	17037	19038	18420
2	17564	17557	20222	18191	20998	20189
3	18798	19104	21754	19583	24722	21185
4	19289	19884	22443	20842	25297	22376
1980 1	20853	20706	23578	20936	26328	24476
2	21246	20943	23897	23691	25654	25127
3	21934	21605	25016	22869	25556	24885
4	21887	21775	24555	23284	25427	25239
1981 1	24644	22697	25066	23499	25611	25044
2	24246	23360	24145	24649	28015	26035
3	26102	22157	23379	24921	28827	25366
4	23762	23532	23469	23156	25745	25081
1982 1	24639	22738	24651	25327	29699	26308
2	24835	24110	24158	24098	25471	26034
3	25683	24273	25613	24733	25820	25957
4	26593	24382	25746	24165	27467	26140
1983 1	27484	26866	27620	25952	26550	26807
2	27120	25852	28588	27309	28198	28241
3	26871	27768	28906	28335	28338	28649
4	28528	28859	29616	27447	31167	30005
1984 1	28447	28626	29587	27325	29332	30397
2	29332	29418	31587	29334	32912	32338
3	29758	29564	31917	30261	32131	34095
4	27981	30244	29698	29218	32539	33859

*   Prices at completion stage

£

South East	Greater London	South West	Wales	Scotland	Northern Ireland
16532	20333	13594	12870	15702	17042
17210	21186	14341	13797	15512	17794
17747	22702	14655	13756	16266	17933
21801	24430	16777	15315	18265	19392
23451	26053	18403	16364	18128	20440
24594	26409	19487	17957	19430	20438
26832	29060	20776	19782	20729	23194
28713	30048	22751	21011	22753	23666
29604	33433	23954	20831	23132	23666
30962	31949	25657	23258	23497	26609
30750	33960	25914	24674	24190	26047
30998	35660	25937	24776	25020	26901
31596	34078	25821	24097	24480	26233
32767	35422	26195	24930	25457	24914
33183	32739	25915	26060	27433	24603
32315	31349	25872	24091	28330	24458
32258	42713	27453	24603	30954	28347
32744	42261	27873	25234	29805	28170
34119	39790	28898	24570	31098	26492
35144	39757	29018	25088	30872	25193
36201	48316	29298	25626	32509	26628
37581	49385	31439	26806	33340	25005
39362	49926	32798	26267	35334	25018
39189	56148	33466	26951	34036	27893
40304	55319	34145	29400	34255	29505
42375	52238	33671	27667	35236	29000
42709	42005	34310	30831	35936	29978
42863	41351	34202	29025	33634	29921
43142	42721	34159	30271	34756	30743

ABBEY NATIONAL BUILDING SOCIETY

AVERAGE PRICES (at approval stage) 1977-1984

9.4 REGIONS: POST-1919 DWELLINGS

Year		North	Yorks & Humberside	North West	East Midlands	West Midlands	East Anglia
1977	4*	12657	10148	12344	12068	12575	13434
1978	1*	12749	10523	12493	12045	13025	13431
	2*	13126	11001	12895	12097	13352	13655
	3	14424	11064	14883	13257	15456	15435
	4	15338	11989	16181	13807	15689	17074
1979	1	14440	13644	15953	15724	17020	18052
	2	18281	15180	17989	15947	18023	19489
	3	17981	16411	19044	18179	19990	20638
	4	19491	18204	20589	18864	20428	21679
1980	1	20226	18131	20478	19011	21116	22160
	2	20260	19229	22084	20260	22858	23704
	3	19990	19962	22098	21230	22633	23730
	4	20059	19535	22432	20611	21750	23879
1981	1	18660	19938	22314	20317	20748	22172
	2	18971	20841	22588	20775	21841	21817
	3	18407	19717	21322	20733	22175	23072
	4	18799	18818	20980	17694	20846	21027
1982	1	17822	18066	21132	18551	20621	21422
	2	17280	17652	20412	18416	20054	19674
	3	18759	20367	21212	20051	21297	21140
	4	18510	19433	21328	17434	20701	21902
1983	1	19706	20454	21537	19182	21841	22773
	2	21388	20766	21936	18915	21589	23313
	3	21464	21854	23140	19656	22627	24886
	4	22449	22267	24122	21380	23852	24682
1984	1	22527	21972	23675	21578	23341	25653
	2	24669	25764	27091	26314	26604	30609
	3	25064	25581	27583	26307	27004	30574
	4	25355	26018	26898	25868	26454	31428

* Prices at completion stage

South East	Greater London	South West	Wales	Scotland	Northern Ireland
16650	17210	13958	12589	16007	15032
16971	17742	14692	12753	15822	14958
17249	18296	15233	13052	16362	15543
21304	22067	17594	15273	18093	17256
22688	23568	18007	16268	18403	17694
23573	25229	18878	16247	19082	18543
26029	27815	21144	17738	20343	19122
28486	29601	23378	19305	21904	21203
29908	30325	23844	18378	22499	21203
29491	31226	25531	19845	22180	22831
31200	31853	26120	21070	23663	20492
31300	31873	25735	20913	23085	20920
31124	31646	24976	21234	23169	17647
30140	31706	24915	20259	20976	13250
31769	32462	25355	17585	21843	12695
30235	30015	25803	19457	21282	10828
28714	33524	23322	18525	21666	20358
28307	33435	23311	18402	21918	20297
28962	35406	23997	19052	22832	19887
30143	35444	25461	20316	24421	21920
31181	37196	26502	20280	24427	20009
31649	38229	25937	19500	22906	21361
33864	40037	27091	21554	24230	21503
35236	42965	28594	22330	23194	19854
35535	44449	29700	22564	27661	22366
36432	41299	29396	22726	27058	21161
41159	42796	33287	25944	31878	26304
41693	43953	32791	26009	32190	25736
42581	45225	33236	25710	31784	25992

ABBEY NATIONAL BUILDING SOCIETY

AVERAGE PRICES (at approval stage) 1977-1984

9.5 REGIONS: PRE-1919 DWELLINGS

Year	North	Yorks & Humberside	North West	East Midlands	West Midlands	East Anglia
1977 4*	8548	8509	8381	9586	11314	12696
1978 1*	9665	8003	8620	9592	9771	12515
2*	9231	8304	9028	10822	10518	12774
3	10297	9086	9220	10627	12695	14580
4	10856	9295	10638	11258	12836	14997
1979 1	10067	9932	10950	10851	14150	16670
2	10878	10446	11781	11884	14173	17741
3	12048	12045	12583	13196	16108	18336
4	12853	12357	12471	11667	18615	20231
1980 1	12613	13467	13047	12694	19247	21642
2	13072	13504	13735	13518	17148	21142
3	14220	13449	14754	14996	17250	21832
4	13506	14190	13738	15305	17340	22656
1981 1	13907	13283	14705	15418	18131	22265
2	14353	13800	14929	15587	17657	23705
3	14528	13474	14616	14434	20042	22776
4	21852	18138	19415	18465	21167	21975
1982 1	18727	18284	20824	18126	20593	23286
2	19531	19999	20050	19158	22139	24133
3	19062	20477	22001	19207	21246	23321
4	18809	21170	22085	19662	21533	25426
1983 1	21526	19595	22038	19142	22697	23304
2	22148	21235	23232	22760	23450	27538
3	24882	22610	25590	20953	25117	27256
4	25118	22982	23687	23633	24560	27934
1984 1	20729	22132	24450	23137	24450	27977
2	18646	18030	18984	20870	23195	28679
3	18616	17735	18820	20058	21774	29792
4	18134	18135	19184	20557	21265	29720

* Prices at completion stage

South East	Greater London	South West	Wales	Scotland	Northern Ireland
15036	14692	13022	9702	13014	14985
14626	15353	13546	10140	12982	12893
15023	15973	13274	10335	12323	17659
18218	17612	15741	11897	14072	24411
18431	19597	15898	12363	15092	22721
18768	21321	16101	12390	15451	22814
21558	23498	17336	13080	15985	16830
24209	25244	19716	16825	17551	21290
25482	26422	21884	15373	18928	21290
25012	27906	20822	15080	18132	17760
27864	28308	23409	15653	18205	19809
26267	27251	24897	15911	19866	28026
26298	27784	23225	15125	19574	17983
26068	27865	23115	15268	19809	15229
28481	28843	25107	15305	20843	16100
26934	27723	24859	16211	20939	15791
29996	31754	25615	17775	23632	22139
28823	32313	25878	16736	24013	19421
31218	34336	26531	18188	25344	24022
30409	35466	25638	19058	25991	20007
32031	35307	28159	18964	25170	19776
33937	36068	28007	18422	26114	19653
34807	39950	29900	20855	26125	14216
36160	41021	29121	20645	26800	19213
40300	42163	30437	22134	27340	22022
37539	42262	30159	22424	28988	23574
36213	36870	29609	19504	24832	18372
36738	38771	28818	19754	24845	19332
36691	38704	29902	19579	25023	17839

ABBEY NATIONAL BUILDING SOCIETY

AVERAGE PRICES (at approval stage) 1977–1984

9.6 REGIONS: DETACHED HOUSES

Year		North	Yorks & Humberside	North West	East Midlands	West Midlands	East Anglia
1977	4*	18726	17911	19202	16666	18523	17769
1978	1*	18661	16735	18888	16374	18375	17750
	2*	20413	18359	19800	17419	19346	18179
	3	21344	20860	23383	18619	22845	21162
	4	24532	20612	24991	20266	22560	23281
1979	1	24422	23002	25401	21655	24872	25142
	2	25176	23604	28645	23504	26563	26289
	3	27999	25949	31159	25538	30402	28083
	4	30856	27807	33513	27366	32357	29493
1980	1	31132	29706	32841	26829	34175	31476
	2	30778	30792	34751	29642	33252	31973
	3	30555	30802	36779	30549	33497	33211
	4	30663	29878	34331	30673	32492	34095
1981	1	32228	31650	35808	29816	33143	32551
	2	32900	31668	36527	31103	35208	34038
	3	34382	31296	34779	32301	37321	33208
	4	29878	28179	32087	26644	29590	29767
1982	1	28355	27834	31702	28778	30355	31842
	2	27898	27510	30865	29171	30401	30327
	3	29333	30708	31963	29462	31030	32273
	4	28157	29364	30816	28680	30895	32816
1983	1	31729	30992	33149	30528	33140	32367
	2	33637	32072	34702	32398	34016	35757
	3	32502	35319	36751	34642	36146	35711
	4	33925	34823	37589	33772	35385	36664
1984	1	32010	33151	36584	33515	34070	36987
	2	40112	38847	42314	37551	40902	42666
	3	40795	38135	42868	37206	39349	43724
	4	40550	37978	40566	37274	39248	43981

* Prices at completion stage

South East	Greater London	South West	Wales	Scotland	Northern Ireland
24360	29323	19218	16840	19814	21430
24933	32443	20604	17114	20248	20339
25567	33823	21535	17510	20768	21856
31892	38395	24725	19667	22697	25964
33195	38005	25356	22186	23655	25475
35154	46007	27365	22259	26224	25485
39356	49864	29110	24339	26113	26256
42438	55677	31511	26244	29281	30003
46349	53798	33897	26820	31515	30003
45311	61305	36037	30530	31061	29029
48287	62836	37878	32018	32610	30454
47489	60934	39177	30748	33849	35573
47820	58825	36983	30145	33072	31402
46658	60881	36473	29239	32709	27987
48627	59360	37796	31926	36619	26743
48030	59058	38824	32578	36324	27851
41295	49530	33677	26934	31903	31696
39981	49689	33481	27034	32561	31727
41766	48270	34278	26659	32534	28349
43122	48182	35624	27935	34469	29300
44795	51588	36489	28346	35562	28883
46351	55353	39551	29174	36365	30169
48511	59425	40653	31995	39327	27219
50573	60325	41772	32005	36095	31199
50721	61438	41144	32936	37848	35139
52319	64097	40538	32847	38830	31265
61751	75229	48805	37019	42908	35452
61389	84484	45070	34946	43012	34076
63429	81325	46378	37179	41551	37088

ABBEY NATIONAL BUILDING SOCIETY

AVERAGE PRICES (at approval stage) 1977-1984

9.7 REGIONS: SEMI-DETACHED HOUSES

Year		North	Yorks & Humberside	North West	East Midlands	West Midlands	East Anglia
1977	4*	11810	9319	10790	9791	11150	10828
1978	1*	12279	9627	11214	9833	11243	11317
	2*	12439	9814	11782	10294	11831	11762
	3	13538	9989	12991	10827	13446	13492
	4	14238	11025	13915	10869	14110	14365
1979	1	14664	12655	14861	12435	15320	14636
	2	18260	13450	16051	12977	15973	16636
	3	17086	14423	17013	14672	17568	17583
	4	17807	15546	17937	15235	18155	18788
1980	1	18789	16279	18590	15665	18956	19523
	2	19822	17208	19806	16273	19646	20650
	3	20114	17891	20103	16915	19771	20638
	4	19861	18166	20509	17438	19961	22020
1981	1	18975	18272	20326	17700	20208	20792
	2	19308	18724	20832	16860	21020	20876
	3	17830	18221	20564	17502	20270	20892
	4	17872	16798	20011	17923	20391	20693
1982	1	17520	17252	20635	18151	20577	21714
	2	17409	17813	20324	17694	19894	20411
	3	18656	19896	21188	18525	20786	20767
	4	19244	19702	21461	17278	20828	21672
1983	1	20145	19729	21839	17651	22124	21828
	2	21844	20173	22282	18442	21798	23026
	3	22419	20951	23283	19223	22596	25128
	4	22774	21639	23614	20854	22766	24652
1984	1	22791	22171	23470	21303	23078	25249
	2	23800	23105	24493	22060	23282	26567
	3	24581	23136	24532	22233	24628	27254
	4	23216	22749	24029	21606	23470	27060

* Prices at completion stage

South East	Greater London	South West	Wales	Scotland	Northern Ireland
14471	18271	12383	10984	14646	11851
14825	19200	12773	11380	14485	12044
15367	20687	13265	11440	15296	13391
18655	24073	15087	12756	16422	13750
20077	26923	16070	13725	16911	15392
21297	28483	17350	14355	17555	15644
22965	31653	18631	15433	19341	15873
25262	32590	20310	17198	20050	18081
26727	34113	22224	16587	21029	18081
27138	35519	22659	17533	21319	19366
28225	36594	22872	18232	21476	19102
28248	35918	23022	18829	22071	19777
28096	36175	23523	19012	22248	17324
28575	36729	23944	17817	20645	15385
28721	36950	23944	17614	21928	13990
28381	36357	23765	17108	21014	12418
27379	32214	21962	17714	21591	19682
27725	32748	22786	19094	22165	19927
28214	32545	23677	18495	23642	20486
28467	35062	24378	19653	24808	21002
29506	36582	26603	19735	24801	21216
30262	37710	24994	19711	25444	20868
32369	39736	26159	20837	25614	19759
33547	42089	27413	21615	25316	20737
34477	42915	28755	22316	27823	22405
34970	36653	28610	22854	27450	23131
37127	48931	30021	22610	30589	22002
38135	49843	29910	23827	29710	22730
38158	50510	29847	22703	30486	22941

ABBEY NATIONAL BUILDING SOCIETY

AVERAGE PRICES (at approval stage) 1977-1984

9.8 REGIONS: TERRACED HOUSES

Year	North	Yorks & Humberside	North West	East Midlands	West Midlands	East Anglia
1977 4*	8347	6282	7266	7409	8418	9280
1978 1*	8995	6744	7562	7508	8592	9552
2*	8655	7020	7537	7456	8757	9826
3	10226	7097	8436	8515	10090	10384
4	10078	7796	9381	8652	10285	11738
1979 1	9994	8555	9545	9293	11283	12287
2	11068	9606	10106	9359	11708	14406
3	11080	10322	11073	9821	12473	14451
4	12315	10501	11234	9840	13285	14843
1980 1	12432	11265	11553	10400	14253	16152
2	12080	12115	12266	11007	14410	17136
3	12535	11914	12677	11941	15037	16279
4	13057	11936	12607	12256	14951	16961
1981 1	12779	11874	13371	12255	14370	16910
2	12254	11995	12882	12291	14578	15570
3	12950	12192	12983	12131	14634	17809
4	13687	12674	14056	13117	15941	17824
1982 1	13455	12835	13577	13897	17205	17668
2	13487	13066	13801	13216	14794	15611
3	14307	14285	14380	14388	16453	17962
4	13962	14106	15022	13143	16281	18515
1983 1	14806	15153	14776	14583	15752	19382
2	15725	15439	14714	14141	15820	19679
3	16299	15076	15298	14513	16505	21430
4	17742	16455	16452	16335	18109	22604
1984 1	17328	15877	16580	15836	17401	22677
2	16892	15772	16311	16282	18256	21582
3	16811	15817	16139	16678	17193	22499
4	16498	16075	16442	16432	16984	23734

* Prices at completion stage

£

South East	Greater London	South West	Wales	Scotland	Northern Ireland
12510	15436	10191	8433	12441	8878
12753	15503	10673	8787	13318	9741
13248	16515	11015	9114	13342	12925
15463	18964	12471	10146	14678	11063
16574	20317	12680	10294	15187	11162
17884	22523	13405	10973	15211	10191
18953	24435	14797	11180	16477	12430
20837	26379	16309	14509	17900	14240
21480	27469	17493	11757	18278	14240
22246	28473	17240	12632	18048	14511
22815	28901	19056	13091	19164	12605
23131	28641	19120	13594	18579	13063
22915	28905	18938	13684	19345	11819
22906	29008	18752	13743	15710	10284
23842	30025	20195	12655	16450	8299
23356	28483	19435	13385	16172	7894
24035	28897	19653	14428	18672	15260
23556	28194	19716	14333	18913	13839
24298	29027	20716	15023	19932	15691
25225	30330	21186	15894	22245	15623
25714	30912	21596	15528	20897	16079
26518	31265	21838	14442	17980	13975
28342	33203	23222	16069	17903	13943
29153	35574	24399	16760	17478	13567
29926	36878	24912	17234	23725	14517
30424	37258	24209	17116	24243	14982
30644	38911	23942	17586	25210	15128
31307	39928	24297	17392	23760	15026
31218	40621	25626	17199	25345	16057

ABBEY NATIONAL BUILDING SOCIETY

AVERAGE PRICES (at approval stage) 1977-1984

9.9 REGIONS: BUNGALOWS

Year	North	Yorks & Humberside	North West	East Midlands	West Midlands	East Anglia
1977 4*	14123	12335	14373	12545	14095	12225
1978 1*	15395	12745	13966	13565	15737	13000
2*	15209	12841	15925	13256	15469	13498
3	16833	15334	17468	14005	17983	14607
4	18445	16305	18772	15145	19060	16215
1979 1	20227	18778	23085	17075	12245	19617
2	25035	21255	23871	18572	23144	19603
3	24772	22409	26065	21014	27060	20446
4	26067	24636	26401	22507	27682	23305
1980 1	27095	23360	28550	25135	29333	22714
2	25105	22582	27778	22776	30515	24688
3	26910	25844	27787	25412	28952	24606
4	26470	23881	29382	24692	26644	24139
1981 1	27697	25117	31292	23513	28831	22638
2	34681	26702	29599	23561	31494	24161
3	31164	25290	30418	24056	31843	25809
4	25230	24446	25918	24055	25671	24359
1982 1	25048	23980	29286	25490	27441	23374
2	24244	24870	27044	26165	28744	25624
3	26585	25167	27502	26394	29432	26634
4	25757	25107	28850	24729	28211	27495
1983 1	27613	27753	28446	26923	28862	26843
2	28186	29326	29938	28067	30504	28227
3	30718	30296	32876	26758	30408	28740
4	31540	30321	31310	27487	37242	28616
1984 1	31857	28609	32263	27764	34691	31421
2	33507	34013	35285	32856	37390	31723
3	32487	33213	39154	31264	36205	31410
4	37969	37916	36432	31105	39818	31199

* Prices at completion stage

£

South East	Greater London	South West	Wales	Scotland	Northern Ireland
17294	20289	14529	13066	17271	16605
17715	20599	16327	13261	17592	17977
18183	21171	16410	13396	17847	17146
21950	25098	18458	15549	20779	18478
24828	29481	19673	16685	19851	19874
28593	40259	21820	17920	22558	21984
30136	38728	23846	20026	25859	23242
33916	39116	27888	20689	27254	24682
35185	41036	27784	21743	28653	24682
35729	37755	29847	21958	28167	28837
37201	39668	30289	24301	30952	26115
36939	45375	30257	23191	30743	28662
37415	46651	30633	23676	29309	27998
36292	44441	29853	25102	33496	25771
39185	46306	29726	23606	31077	26401
37701	49391	31139	24724	31478	22958
31621	35851	26325	24125	29467	26969
33297	39395	28603	23527	27575	27611
35453	53731	28845	24480	30902	26212
36904	34063	30724	23828	31583	27246
40251	40253	30496	24178	33235	26621
38609	37037	32287	26036	31766	26510
41594	45257	35071	26289	33251	25932
41802	47861	33215	26912	33508	28128
43325	52170	36334	26558	33655	26660
44096	45970	36534	26137	33344	29224
48711	60522	38941	29015	39677	31290
48742	60699	40283	28370	40020	30827
51029	74455	39059	28276	38876	29746

ABBEY NATIONAL BUILDING SOCIETY

AVERAGE PRICES (at approval stage) 1977-1984

9.10 REGIONS: FLATS & MAISONETTES

Year		North	Yorks & Humberside	North West	East Midlands	West Midlands	East Anglia
1977	4*	8108	9762	10606	8631	10933	10717
1978	1*	8409	10218	10697	7176	9310	7775
	2*	8243	9970	11351	10715	9064	9248
	3	9060	9672	12506	9521	11885	10390
	4	8557	10637	13627	11298	11172	10639
1979	1	8885	11221	12547	9785	12496	11209
	2	8528	10046	12894	10705	12989	11837
	3	10313	12584	14995	12783	15692	11075
	4	10532	24740	13948	10399	15504	15324
1980	1	11288	15752	16990	11652	15327	14794
	2	11241	14976	17656	12988	16439	16340
	3	12396	15849	17331	12741	16822	15667
	4	10484	15557	17494	13770	16500	17147
1981	1	11822	15353	16893	14034	12232	17398
	2	10682	14867	16937	14467	9872	15793
	3	13001	14214	11629	13272	14283	15698
	4	13249	19315	13055	11084	16261	17324
1982	1	11800	15160	16909	14805	16528	17409
	2	12634	14262	15514	13712	16343	17171
	3	13365	15259	15976	18611	15896	16820
	4	13278	14480	15828	14480	16421	17099
1983	1	14975	17720	18318	16990	16764	20518
	2	14151	16365	18203	16303	17240	21137
	3	14963	18452	17035	15832	17682	18985
	4	13305	18345	20171	16332	18367	18913
1984	1	15126	17621	18485	18223	18496	20944
	2	14495	17525	17717	17554	17709	21684
	3	14454	18725	18607	16075	17579	22070
	4	14160	17908	22487	16021	16967	21283

* Prices at completion stage

South East	Greater London	South West	Wales	Scotland	Northern Ireland
11872	13276	12135	9946	10180	
12338	13925	12388	11474	10090	
12825	14123	13132	11185	10589	
14143	16085	13075	12692	11285	29500
15304	17569	14222	15217	11922	
16217	18835	14656	9406	12714	
17127	20313	15696	13685	13492	
19078	22188	16120	15703	14554	
19958	22971	18030	14663	14430	
20292	23453	18307	16564	14364	
20746	24096	18785	19002	14991	
20446	24253	19294	16497	15943	
21060	24269	19759	14257	16073	
21319	24505	18461	14189	16769	
20629	24938	16536	7137	16389	
20738	23499	18651	13915	17380	
21208	26553	17399	15648	17466	24311
22035	26044	21173	12548	18542	
22990	26207	20802	17134	19053	
22929	26760	20940	19261	19297	
23272	27308	22522	20221	19599	15260
24567	28144	21938	17220	18574	20131
25492	29779	22532	19047	20586	25288
26046	30949	23645	18476	22063	22610
26242	32122	22888	20946	21810	32709
26743	31721	24532	20452	21192	25010
26635	31139	22075	19828	20471	
27121	32076	23070	20779	20812	
27196	32922	22096	18961	21029	24571

ABBEY NATIONAL BUILDING SOCIETY

AVERAGE PRICES (at approval stage) 1980-1985

9.11 REGIONS: FIRST-TIME BUYERS

Year		North	Yorks & Humberside	North West	East Midlands	West Midlands	East Anglia
1980	1	13669	13405	14173	13616	16495	17735
	2	13339	13506	14503	14028	15752	18134
	3	14081	13771	15172	14226	16835	18501
	4	14273	13774	15537	14802	16841	18818
1981	1	13957	13589	15377	14638	15793	17931
	2	13356	13468	14818	14015	14835	16617
	3	13361	13721	14694	14913	15710	17487
	4	16512	15910	17799	15684	17271	18536
1982	1	15677	15492	18476	16161	18451	18176
	2	14394	15000	16347	16019	17922	19035
	3	16506	17921	18042	17631	18755	19931
	4	17272	17111	18281	16495	18603	20325
1983	1	18342	18185	19235	17586	19939	21493
	2	19690	18405	19487	18600	20276	21631
	3	19745	20173	20250	19173	20559	22420
	4	19909	19846	21429	19506	21829	22757
1984	1	19961	20320	21301	19702	21228	23247
	2	18412	17924	19015	19342	19833	23072
	3	18439	18248	19061	19288	19880	23803
	4	18195	18524	18834	18763	19547	24036
1985	1	18246	18432	20009	19049	19817	25518
	2	18364	18679	19033	19132	19742	26219
	3	18278	19305	19556	20584	20610	26475
	4	17873					

£

South East	Greater London	South West	Wales	Scotland	Northern Ireland
21564	24450	18729	14408	16556	20595
22330	24657	19938	15579	16659	18401
22561	24905	19796	15603	17694	18779
22448	24816	19413	15371	17177	15388
22128	24705	19200	14786	16100	12614
22183	25122	18763	13359	15977	12080
21947	24261	19055	14305	16137	9969
24091	27979	18947	15716	18135	19441
23973	28241	20591	15738	18717	18696
24637	30178	20697	15741	19528	18473
26215	28940	22489	17680	22072	19102
27935	32429	24199	17515	22705	19100
28194	33342	24097	18203	22711	19760
29277	35599	24415	18575	23085	18908
29862	36902	25598	19254	23111	20026
30549	38184	26288	19234	23770	21161
31691	34152	26175	20210	24613	20653
30142	33427	25161	19553	23228	22155
29984	34320	24804	19693	22714	21994
30646	35684	25982	19378	23292	21978
30892	36598	25203	20174	23464	21252
31907	37327	26285	19538	24105	21754
33482	39312	26906	19605	23741	21391
	40706				

ABBEY NATIONAL BUILDING SOCIETY

AVERAGE PRICES (at approval stage) 1980-1985

9.12 REGIONS: FORMER OWNER-OCCUPIERS

Year		North	Yorks & Humberside	North West	East Midlands	West Midlands	East Anglia
1980	1	22177	21508	24552	22767	26739	26548
	2	22430	22281	24762	24140	27403	27531
	3	22542	22642	25323	25487	27100	27942
	4	22739	22475	24613	25538	26761	28884
1981	1	23374	23028	25754	25096	27517	28193
	2	24148	23589	26071	26784	29281	29286
	3	24867	22561	24675	25885	30987	29716
	4	23087	22040	23732	21215	24805	24919
1982	1	22285	21470	23913	22521	24776	25633
	2	23456	22283	24753	22164	23757	22952
	3	23736	23000	24508	22960	24798	24879
	4	22370	22857	24606	21209	24674	25756
1983	1	24251	23799	24859	22636	24785	25361
	2	25316	24479	25682	22688	25040	27626
	3	26096	24868	27006	23394	26480	28793
	4	27640	26206	27381	24998	27423	29195
1984	1	26808	24679	26983	25087	26812	30104
	2	29596	29675	31352	30994	33461	35934
	3	30042	29098	31858	31102	33253	36274
	4	29876	29672	30892	31026	32688	36951
1985	1	29134	29523	29815	30479	31865	36446
	2	28048	28881	31105	31834	33345	38305
	3	30802	30780	32445	32672	33404	39942

£

South East	Greater London	South West	Wales	Scotland	Northern Ireland
34328	37349	28103	23859	25894	26575
36273	39038	29438	24116	27051	26252
36169	37782	30215	24370	27522	30425
36812	38403	29781	23887	27858	29712
35447	38723	29411	24487	29081	27329
38284	39174	30968	25267	29938	28171
36713	38590	30894	25120	30316	27338
33138	42727	27596	22473	28537	23942
32566	42042	27244	22372	28326	24102
33846	43533	28408	23173	29772	24497
34142	43147	28761	23350	30666	25145
34951	42915	29479	23735	30137	23953
35821	43366	29840	22409	28206	23371
38482	46948	31867	25215	29757	23072
39940	49996	32554	25463	28289	23807
40675	51394	33217	26968	33596	27302
41140	52078	32943	26056	33050	26916
47746	51500	38084	30234	37165	32205
48700	53786	37369	29787	37273	31298
49239	53438	37496	30078	36759	31325
49345	55192	38198	29663	36973	32815
52081	57991	40228	29117	36795	30794
54056	58080	41325	30102	37638	33560

ABBEY NATIONAL BUILDING SOCIETY

AVERAGE PRICES (at approval stage) 1977–1984

9.13 UNITED KINGDOM AND REGIONS BY AGE OF HOUSE: DETACHED HOUSES

Year	UNITED KINGDOM			NORTH			YORKS & HUMBERSIDE			NORTH WEST		
	New	Post-1919	Pre-1919	New	Post-1919	Pre-1919	New	Post-1919	Pre-1919	New	Post-1919	Pre-1919
1977 4*	19658	21155	23062	16493	20204	21445	16209	17266	23305	17586	19234	24621
1978 1*	20336	21706	23492	16782	18808	26189	15658	16660	19631	17959	19152	20181
2*	20706	22763	23941	18792	19710	32131	16311	19604	19885	18502	20506	22311
3	23792	27673	27983	18949	22860	24679	19084	22155	21199	21759	23509	30514
4	25118	28650	28147	22462	24148	37636	19766	21414	20015	23695	24639	32031
1979 1	26603	30937	30445	22753	24883	29900	21232	24540	26764	24120	25895	28221
2	28768	34052	34991	23697	26530	26136	23020	23587	26517	26852	29186	32491
3	30844	36619	36985	26147	28694	32134	24564	27101	25170	28195	32687	35370
4	32113	39775	39289	28164	32210	29439	24732	30009	28295	30435	35420	35410
1980 1	33695	39602	40816	27935	33050	34645	26613	31608	33503	31617	33868	32893
2	34023	41975	45499	27771	32736	32450	28365	31935	33562	31445	35899	45592
3	34910	41507	43653	26675	30769	39232	28804	31230	33472	34419	36899	45390
4	35372	41256	42850	28342	30807	38136	27490	30020	33463	31345	36050	39268
1981 1	36150	40546	41554	31399	31740	36870	28867	32855	34992	32591	36341	45801
2	36931	42053	43926	30299	33335	40341	30496	31292	36269	32681	36922	47820
3	37578	41269	42276	35479	35031	28042	30069	32182	30452	31780	34417	49848
4	34612	34279	35123	29713	29308	33648	28947	29299	25168	28181	34009	33384
1982 1	34234	33858	34763	30167	27583	28126	27714	27773	28517	28975	32330	35139
2	33992	34429	36450	29522	26942	28743	28573	26874	27583	28696	32240	29273
3	34219	36388	36978	31677	28433	28503	29633	31702	30521	29894	32733	32249
4	35554	35925	38132	31679	26475	26632	29225	29052	31232	31086	30151	36341
1983 1	37076	38898	38315	33306	30858	31176	31295	31865	28355	33824	33903	35753
2	38934	40027	40991	33152	33386	36243	30301	33268	27085	35738	34217	36659
3	39451	41612	44554	31127	32982	41786	33790	34200	40929	34554	36169	44772
4	40010	41749	43657	32449	34675	34513	32393	34698	39461	36770	38365	38659
1984 1	40433	41763	43344	33131	31742	29773	35871	32299	31970	36582	35501	44218
2	45259	47479	51228	36504	39938	52067	37050	39216	41392	40492	41905	49415
3	44998	46995	50532	36926	42869	43153	36339	37751	44631	40741	42180	54034
4	44795	48131	49298	37739	41053	47002	35335	38395	42386	36204	41001	49570

* Prices at completion stage

196

EAST MIDLANDS			WEST MIDLANDS			EAST ANGLIA		
New	Post-1919	Pre-1919	New	Post-1919	Pre-1919	New	Post-1919	Pre-1919
15262	16859	19041	17432	18533	20763	16563	17530	21216
15864	15842	20771	18110	18554	18299	17141	17527	19695
15918	16795	24139	18773	19415	21023	16403	17788	23517
17447	19205	20589	22165	23948	21673	19999	21503	22379
19276	20501	22818	21228	22844	25592	21520	24285	24977
21275	21985	21424	22762	26467	27717	22856	25498	28865
21801	22923	35618	24750	27468	29980	24562	27202	27892
23592	25755	29776	29188	31690	30041	25803	29974	28997
25644	29999	25062	29688	32724	39754	26887	29288	35984
24275	27947	30023	32433	33440	41462	29408	31241	37443
28535	29934	32608	31026	35832	33888	28687	33250	35884
28079	31533	34163	30573	34217	41661	30098	33829	37022
29437	31316	32524	30322	34331	35038	32442	32366	39612
29104	29089	34667	31829	33038	37901	31222	30922	39768
30669	30442	34904	33777	36180	35794	30522	33488	42376
34206	30948	33345	36386	35790	44514	32491	32391	37117
28800	24916	28322	29777	29908	32435	30471	29728	28725
31427	27368	28770	31745	29444	31119	33479	29965	34313
28558	27919	34980	30406	30147	31796	31340	29630	30697
29814	29146	29395	31082	30607	32899	30455	31803	39703
29395	28328	30246	32116	29259	34216	30403	32259	42657
31878	30570	27648	32195	33155	35862	32251	32743	30990
33856	31407	32682	34879	32687	38284	34918	35094	39449
37227	33272	33081	34876	35789	40227	35030	34943	39783
34757	32635	35059	35998	34015	38946	36226	34492	44100
32984	32531	38249	34820	34131	31004	36307	36298	40320
37439	35988	44108	41921	39856	43390	40954	41566	47504
39272	36267	37776	40328	38526	40867	43523	41550	50002
38275	35696	42138	39562	38691	41144	42584	43365	47280

ABBEY NATIONAL BUILDING SOCIETY

AVERAGE PRICES (at approval stage) 1977-1984

9.13 UNITED KINGDOM AND REGIONS BY AGE OF HOUSE: DETACHED HOUSES (continued)

Year	SOUTH EAST			GREATER LONDON			SOUTH WEST			WALES		
	New	Post-1919	Pre-1919	New	Post-1919	Pre-1919	New	Post-1919	Pre-1919	New	Post-1919	Pre-1919
1977 4*	23342	23889	28453	36515	29701	24867	18494	19103	20080	17457	16711	16540
1978 1*	23392	25096	28536	32853	31808	34411	19903	20036	22595	18574	17277	15447
2*	24601	25425	28636	36773	34811	26076	19827	21756	23506	17425	17940	16799
3	29385	32362	35135	39033	39979	32659	22521	25419	25832	19128	20077	19504
4	30892	34364	33657	41511	38455	34007	24905	24892	26885	20712	24030	20781
1979 1	33276	36398	34686	48060	46764	42507	25176	27719	30668	22233	22120	20155
2	35136	40873	44402	48164	51289	45943	27088	30495	29836	25590	24461	22190
3	37468	43285	50397	51019	58811	48441	30317	32005	32521	27164	26303	24462
4	39461	48338	53075	64625	55519	43084	31153	34470	36555	25940	27958	26007
1980 1	40921	46716	52081	57919	62000	59796	34469	36925	36883	28569	33926	27579
2	39964	49882	61973	57400	63709	62286	33692	40039	40248	33026	31357	31769
3	41479	49123	53160	68378	63118	49169	34233	37896	47340	30875	30897	30289
4	42962	48677	53809	63314	59676	54150	34500	35868	42560	31950	31378	26040
1981 1	43486	47640	49523	61492	61930	57291	33765	36439	40575	31670	29624	25997
2	43200	49660	55558	56028	61874	52082	35624	37387	41239	35772	31776	28615
3	44098	48821	52985	54954	61664	52503	35227	38760	43457	31764	33453	31588
4	39977	41158	45151	70690	48942	40166	34591	31306	38699	27511	28018	24557
1982 1	38886	39980	43000	62795	49427	40157	33302	33014	34918	29628	25521	26586
2	39753	41853	48021	44465	52241	50870	34757	34160	34248	28536	27083	23757
3	41740	43633	46273	45241	51840	48640	34242	36176	36944	29586	28454	25558
4	43474	44972	49081	62019	52518	45195	34869	36306	39914	30962	28413	25229
1983 1	44164	47475	50395	70939	61812	45296	37715	39383	43185	34133	27455	27324
2	47202	49414	50176	57880	58837	61738	39572	40167	43146	32336	32085	32333
3	46773	52524	55466	77541	62078	57132	41056	42466	42357	30841	32830	32811
4	47923	51026	56846	69997	63955	53304	41013	40096	44044	36962	31491	30985
1984 1	50318	52990	57169	67618	66207	59064	40064	41008	41288	33434	31840	33368
2	58117	61257	69627	67173	79580	61287	48856	47478	52231	41503	37402	32757
3	59315	60134	70241	62400	87333	81073	46100	44697	44852	37409	35490	31945
4	60488	63453	67901	73293	84185	73244	45394	47584	44355	39149	37996	34021

* Prices at completion stage

198

£

SCOTLAND			NORTHERN IRELAND		
New	Post-1919	Pre-1919	New	Post-1919	Pre-1919
19329	19917	20472	22673	21031	20795
19416	20955	20061	23190	19343	16700
20025	22019	19542	25468	19202	25750
22315	22908	22976	24743	23243	44357
23388	24113	23322	23780	25144	29158
25640	26087	27720	25250	21754	34813
25570	27086	25229	29210	24497	22490
29091	29931	28454	32396	29773	27775
30267	31103	33287	32396	29773	27775
30397	30368	33457	26708	33457	20986
32111	33331	32050	35240	27558	30486
33807	32826	35269	31005	33323	46484
34117	31666	35157	39025	31579	26292
35840	31116	33114	33195	28425	21978
38581	36406	35249	28611	27008	21797
37825	37146	33371	33090	27432	22631
38265	30335	27368	36116	28100	36085
34618	31898	32730	35045	32064	25924
36909	29175	33631	30322	29285	25608
35963	32765	35109	28828	32919	22716
39343	33461	32569	30217	28294	26888
39431	33608	36704	26943	34134	28222
44721	37558	34919	29289	29237	18456
41234	32256	34240	32682	31360	25999
41220	36898	35064	36229	34180	34816
42281	37210	37780	34718	26529	30751
45635	41192	44014	38768	35720	26474
42682	43170	42975	37318	32418	37302
45272	40723	40107	42340	38224	25104

ABBEY NATIONAL BUILDING SOCIETY

AVERAGE PRICES (at approval stage) 1977-1984

9.14 UNITED KINGDOM AND REGIONS BY AGE OF HOUSE: SEMI-DETACHED HOUSES

Year	UNITED KINGDOM			NORTH			YORKS & HUMBERSIDE			NORTH WEST		
	New	Post-1919	Pre-1919	New	Post-1919	Pre-1919	New	Post-1919	Pre-1919	New	Post-1919	Pre-1919
1977 4*	12020	12890	13616	11256	11817	14789	10034	8958	10711	10528	10897	10572
1978 1*	12409	13181	14540	11633	12395	14151	10176	9392	11153	10973	11134	12504
2*	13073	13706	15337	11983	12486	14964	10706	9573	10721	11683	11612	13289
3	14657	15733	16812	12947	13682	15100	12547	9145	14116	12943	13153	12102
4	15570	16904	18493	14182	14140	16486	12460	10577	13959	13497	14087	13508
1979 1	16394	18273	19410	15052	14498	15300	12970	12439	14514	15078	14792	15076
2	17569	20010	21158	15314	19363	18077	13627	13427	13346	15022	16151	16924
3	19157	20938	23736	16149	16929	24873	14176	14284	16308	16072	17067	17969
4	19841	22212	25445	16788	17356	38571	16208	15172	18348	16932	17861	20879
1980 1	20644	22803	26532	18239	18614	22727	15917	16053	18937	17385	18481	21666
2	21205	23515	27951	18292	19895	26684	16880	17142	18563	18509	19944	22294
3	21660	23955	26542	19811	19894	23633	17002	17853	20263	18872	20046	23054
4	21848	24175	26887	19115	19618	27603	17617	18003	20380	20378	20419	21416
1981 1	22716	23817	27632	20974	18309	22635	18348	18007	20711	19878	20425	20223
2	22746	24035	28421	20092	18836	25518	18672	18436	21756	19630	20847	22231
3	22262	23148	27042	20970	17017	25425	17884	18100	20370	20090	20545	21434
4	23741	22074	23772	19590	17347	21309	20317	16098	18099	21271	19794	19878
1982 1	24429	22447	24256	22498	16564	22823	19045	16698	20262	21520	20324	21827
2	24295	22414	25326	21476	16679	22511	19946	17251	20276	20276	20280	20813
3	24033	23940	24704	20277	18313	20192	20472	19631	21439	22177	20953	21908
4	24419	24383	25968	22650	18532	20855	20393	19371	21772	21496	21320	22502
1983 1	25398	24535	27102	22765	19537	25065	21020	19224	22689	22236	21618	23612
2	25803	25689	28090	22432	21502	25196	21045	19693	23620	22240	21858	25200
3	26454	26723	29251	22739	21865	29022	21305	20637	22550	23441	22657	27483
4	27274	27636	29945	23064	22280	28140	23146	21201	23530	22793	23449	25908
1984 1	27610	27152	29994	24068	22565	23390	23096	21727	24345	24181	23245	23938
2	27143	28444	32152	23845	23562	26896	23231	22741	26727	23331	24514	25404
3	26803	28962	33396	25584	23821	32492	22482	23098	24179	23302	24527	25704
4	27139	28553	32820	22213	22966	28846	23638	22094	28601	23626	23877	25574

* Prices at completion stage

£

EAST MIDLANDS			WEST MIDLANDS			EAST ANGLIA		
New	Post-1919	Pre-1919	New	Post-1919	Pre-1919	New	Post-1919	Pre-1919
9806	9676	10413	11046	11092	11846	10823	10946	10512
9927	9898	9168	11046	11355	10889	10923	11186	12191
10306	9911	12357	11865	11822	11821	11400	11966	11586
11968	10251	11864	13161	13346	14545	13114	13299	14692
12237	10524	10595	14418	13963	14677	13991	14093	15431
12726	12656	11075	14462	15228	18378	15007	14260	15829
13643	12952	12348	15687	16049	15873	17691	16179	16702
15991	14439	14267	17203	17314	19848	16573	17800	17980
14926	15310	15408	17880	17886	20298	18305	19365	17228
16161	15799	13599	19207	18700	21245	18944	19218	21962
17025	16340	15078	17890	19718	22885	20166	20577	21355
17682	16891	15962	19554	19595	22067	20824	20316	21524
17259	17215	18794	19711	19882	20950	19798	22663	22269
18457	17430	18118	20106	20093	21413	20366	19929	23757
18310	16843	15304	20267	20989	22056	21871	19951	24105
18265	17156	17882	19904	19526	26429	19838	20138	23747
18256	17780	18558	21876	19818	22749	21458	20271	21801
20778	17877	17301	21526	20092	22745	21362	21178	24251
19931	17217	18118	21766	19359	21778	21429	19194	25060
20158	18315	18090	22629	20479	20689	21107	20610	20860
19886	16799	17358	22382	20357	22276	22452	21073	23327
19978	17012	19156	23703	21731	23234	22367	21721	22267
21339	17325	23648	23704	21417	22365	23053	22372	25875
21881	18448	20998	23394	21901	25300	24207	24781	26541
21997	20404	22123	23795	22472	23359	25645	24041	25886
22051	20947	22956	25029	22512	25898	24794	25180	25858
22294	21872	22888	22815	23185	24850	24746	26646	27691
21663	22315	22318	22922	24563	27593	26171	26847	29605
21682	21582	21668	24164	23147	25590	25751	27057	28088

AVERAGE PRICES (at approval stage) 1977-1984

9.14 UNITED KINGDOM AND REGIONS BY AGE OF HOUSE:
SEMI-DETACHED HOUSES (continued)

Year	SOUTH EAST			GREATER LONDON			SOUTH WEST			WALES		
	New	Post- 1919	Pre- 1919	New	Post- 1919	Pre- 1919	New	Post- 1919	Pre- 1919	New	Post- 1919	Pre- 1919
1977 4*	13738	14693	14277	17447	18237	18483	12065	12316	13050	11556	11016	10022
1978 1*	14341	14958	15797	19228	18915	20392	12481	12466	14040	11523	11398	11104
2*	15101	15386	15706	19804	20719	20630	12878	13080	14616	11258	11589	10966
3	18307	18817	18302	21060	24602	22476	15153	14882	15617	11977	13122	11883
4	19216	20294	19923	37356	26836	26564	15531	16116	16647	13881	13728	13423
1979 1	20167	21722	20398	24038	28532	28605	17216	17316	17645	14466	14549	13120
2	21294	23314	22871	27790	31604	32413	17924	18787	19092	15853	15473	14687
3	23953	25487	25507	36255	32015	34119	18893	19995	22632	16866	17548	15845
4	24939	26974	27091	40592	33560	35508	20559	21362	27941	17727	16038	17543
1980 1	25519	27452	27138	40411	33943	40306	21680	22600	24075	19208	17399	15778
2	26883	28117	29685	31317	34893	42998	21923	22253	26236	19582	18168	17243
3	26189	28442	28993	30443	35989	36098	21671	22975	25124	21854	18221	18569
4	27023	28314	28039	30564	35616	38605	21805	23147	26716	19416	19048	18496
1981 1	27255	28416	30260	37744	36581	37122	22354	23414	27195	19323	17731	16987
2	27113	28448	31210	30712	36683	38753	22401	23437	27149	20545	17279	16852
3	27154	28287	29642	32390	36157	37431	22914	23173	26675	19688	16584	17735
4	27115	27157	28660	33044	32013	32364	22379	21264	24145	22321	16983	17014
1982 1	27642	27508	28924	34610	32676	31993	23948	22117	24801	24245	18707	16773
2	28438	27703	30698	32446	32129	34602	24900	22689	26818	21427	17917	19546
3	28219	28307	29931	35791	35196	34611	24605	24117	25117	21216	19695	18185
4	29244	29233	31604	35285	36819	36505	25203	26241	28745	21592	19545	19102
1983 1	31903	29571	32705	34872	37498	39068	25229	24123	28456	21176	19544	19697
2	31804	32101	34456	43744	39764	39497	26563	25457	28384	22513	20714	20548
3	32746	33199	36212	40998	42513	41397	27356	26927	28692	23594	21148	22814
4	34121	33934	37520	44365	42520	44528	27595	28729	29742	23537	22121	22373
1984 1	34561	34688	36945	40404	35000	45407	27759	28258	30519	22264	22492	24601
2	35371	37160	37983	42839	48516	51043	27277	29812	33133	24292	22897	19968
3	34483	38265	39663	49589	49304	52048	28046	29018	34794	24141	24183	21914
4	35351	38227	39457	43928	50417	51347	28535	29599	31878	25434	22587	21134

* Prices at completion stage

£

SCOTLAND			NORTHERN IRELAND		
New	Post-1919	Pre-1919	New	Post-1919	Pre-1919
13809	14722	16284	12066	11691	14192
13823	14433	16225	12388	11857	17350
14335	15335	18104	12804	13231	22625
15560	16320	18453	13938	13823	10300
16315	17106	18036	15326	14925	21480
16960	17379	20259	15924	15573	15200
18248	19213	23519	15892	15889	14925
19222	20158	22057	17504	17859	23725
19825	21506	22171	17504	17859	23725
20487	20945	24707	19371	19118	22500
20510	21309	25199	20461	18707	23653
22781	21448	23544	21755	18552	30036
21536	21637	25817	20754	16589	22750
22484	19105	29116	21167	14097	26208
23976	20253	27854	20445	12305	13944
24156	19861	22892	20039	11339	19175
25079	20581	24252	21419	19273	21082
25826	21165	24985	21771	19660	18307
26295	22584	25811	22957	19785	31962
26516	24400	24529	21422	20435	23230
25981	24194	25705	23491	20668	20802
27059	24765	26787	22123	20200	23689
26678	25226	26799	21035	20284	12667
27494	24731	25549	22774	20138	21861
28970	27305	29012	23478	21867	23659
29836	26852	28288	22975	22688	27614
33739	29527	31471	23029	21698	25830
29757	28749	33643	23373	22608	
30305	29675	34057	24052	22626	24796

ABBEY NATIONAL BUILDING SOCIETY

AVERAGE PRICES (at approval stage) 1977-1984

9.15 UNITED KINGDOM AND REGIONS BY AGE OF HOUSE: TERRACED HOUSES

Year	UNITED KINGDOM New	Post-1919	Pre-1919	NORTH New	Post-1919	Pre-1919	YORKS & HUMBERSIDE New	Post-1919	Pre-1919	NORTH WEST New	Post-1919	Pre-1919
1977 4*	12182	12257	9717	11144	9170	7505	8837	5579	6233	9899	8209	6676
1978 1*	12476	12629	9992	11397	9139	8353	9429	6703	6401	9991	8919	6701
2*	13342	12684	10405	11385	9119	7805	9819	6738	6776	10355	8507	6826
3	15122	15075	12051	12101	11497	8940	10871	6574	6905	13758	10255	7448
4	16086	16070	12584	12886	10184	9334	11333	6912	7762	12948	11520	8357
1979 1	17387	17113	13605	12928	10360	8995	11839	9137	7757	14382	10403	8843
2	17909	18863	14626	14623	11549	9684	12605	10563	8682	15194	11408	9408
3	19823	20367	16134	14673	12450	10003	13245	10990	9687	19468	12097	10319
4	20748	20653	16269	15806	13246	11437	14340	11732	9625	16816	13954	10050
1980 1	21280	20923	17426	15887	15364	10600	14305	12040	10345	15898	13548	10564
2	21930	21902	17902	15900	13255	11253	15865	13207	11095	17640	14432	11295
3	22032	22079	17492	17706	13678	11645	16855	13279	10830	16716	14856	11853
4	22039	21971	17924	17817	15365	11692	16440	13216	11099	16509	15314	11687
1981 1	22557	20686	18126	18183	13194	12040	18410	13776	10827	17983	15297	12382
2	22975	20511	18856	12342	12017	9138	13540	14610	18190	16826	14147	12176
3	23659	19168	18149	19412	12024	13091	16138	12803	11687	17074	13356	12610
4	22738	18583	18073	18243	14181	12860	18546	12971	11660	18348	14911	13182
1982 1	24220	18259	18025	17402	13302	12972	16690	13284	12084	17831	14610	12645
2	22538	18135	19020	18864	12618	13471	16448	13003	12724	20632	13760	13188
3	22339	19956	19632	19249	13284	14171	17509	15490	13442	23092	15291	13274
4	23390	19758	19694	20367	13667	13289	17804	15048	13270	20111	16160	14145
1983 1	24699	19633	19988	21094	13947	14518	27687	14822	14064	22439	15061	14024
2	24076	20494	20969	19970	15307	15420	20993	14949	15243	20069	15108	14129
3	21608	21552	21599	20858	15435	16275	20155	15874	14333	24353	16601	14013
4	26036	23501	22222	27671	16875	16928	27340	16476	15443	22318	17187	15633
1984 1	25663	23345	22496	20953	17745	16639	22958	17124	14611	22339	17311	15781
2	27459	25523	21376	20805	17263	16423	20066	16895	14885	22234	17456	15692
3	27789	25895	21448	20554	17546	16194	20083	17392	14692	21413	17275	15546
4	27481	26305	21739	20229	17173	15909	22199	18084	14594	21809	17391	15913

* Prices at completion stage

EAST MIDLANDS			WEST MIDLANDS			EAST ANGLIA		
New	Post-1919	Pre-1919	New	Post-1919	Pre-1919	New	Post-1919	Pre-1919
9546	8110	6417	10216	8975	7753	9555	9633	8854
9760	7880	6559	10277	9547	7398	10045	10149	8994
9827	7668	6573	11036	9781	7393	10814	10632	8770
10991	9437	6946	12550	10992	9148	10965	10437	9725
11967	8746	7752	13839	11380	9138	12759	11660	11453
12045	10317	8079	18056	12361	9377	13097	13326	11365
12750	11155	7828	15297	13442	10272	14506	15254	13764
14183	10686	8645	17412	13942	11083	15185	14732	14013
19400	11092	7933	16308	14549	12174	16102	14889	14371
15215	12302	8776	18703	15475	12638	17058	16622	15566
15225	13071	9567	17794	16089	13025	21775	17951	15012
15777	13305	10798	18147	19335	12782	18267	16635	15550
16062	13594	10999	18715	16156	13840	18706	17271	16277
16910	13710	10904	17582	15450	12870	19071	16772	16378
18095	13475	11016	18325	15897	13409	18314	14054	16900
16917	13413	11100	19868	16137	13317	19948	16886	17994
17408	13424	12359	22300	16484	13979	19857	16691	18373
18067	14476	13154	43237	15896	14003	20429	18241	16966
18064	14150	12242	17541	14211	15134	19011	14929	18406
18051	15497	13442	17894	16442	16220	19084	17045	18757
18249	11924	13105	24230	16017	15079	20900	17327	20371
19426	14197	14101	18559	16096	15074	21694	19018	19498
19283	13459	14232	20994	15254	16414	21845	18771	20129
19630	13633	14557	21602	16352	15995	20863	21000	21720
19316	17194	15515	21114	19394	16777	25122	21416	23085
20283	16931	14640	19984	17613	16868	24459	21587	23160
19508	17942	15047	20061	18108	18191	22683	22085	20996
24322	17135	15418	20821	18108	16157	24325	21943	22534
20571	17416	15397	20506	18275	15678	25317	24491	22868

ABBEY NATIONAL BUILDING SOCIETY

AVERAGE PRICES (at approval stage) 1977-1984

9.15 UNITED KINGDOM AND REGIONS BY AGE OF HOUSE: TERRACED HOUSES (continued)

Year	SOUTH EAST			GREATER LONDON			SOUTH WEST			WALES		
	New	Post- 1919	Pre- 1919	New	Post- 1919	Pre- 1919	New	Post- 1919	Pre- 1919	New	Post- 1919	Pre- 1919
1977 4*	13320	13110	11054	22659	16180	14483	10789	10525	9636	9511	9556	8052
1978 1*	13625	13520	10985	18080	16505	14535	11306	10814	10292	10088	10021	8160
2*	14701	13784	11521	20354	16763	16084	12106	11479	10070	12037	10270	8278
3	16756	16501	13532	25031	20197	17676	13137	12896	11928	11165	12064	9402
4	18253	17760	14072	24223	21657	19001	13830	13211	11861	11892	11955	9557
1979 1	19316	19076	15077	26084	23474	21514	15358	13979	12302	12879	11960	10230
2	19725	20467	16488	26885	25605	23349	16403	16104	13314	12667	13395	10432
3	22351	22027	18730	28717	27813	25058	16469	19088	14566	15054	13101	15046
4	23115	22728	19231	29767	27853	27011	18384	18684	16435	15196	11572	11528
1980 1	24354	23206	20301	31683	28877	28029	18901	18272	16179	17740	12813	12067
2	23749	24069	21087	36522	30026	27905	21447	19321	18084	17475	14113	12365
3	24663	24445	20929	37872	29488	27703	20556	19452	18369	17405	14567	13078
4	24513	24296	20630	34446	29660	28208	20874	19212	18111	16854	15520	12966
1981 1	24880	23479	21385	33387	29714	28299	20796	18467	18496	15841	15126	13255
2	25590	24515	22203	32409	31004	29231	21680	19618	20147	16290	11274	13138
3	26731	23271	22165	32108	28507	28191	20329	19551	18955	19266	13092	13297
4	26090	24275	22771	33110	27624	29246	21290	18917	19900	21293	13932	13620
1982 1	26882	23505	22525	31767	27100	28715	20903	18822	20397	18645	14502	14030
2	27781	23573	25052	31759	28023	29525	22092	19871	21423	21057	15194	14490
3	26806	25381	24816	34900	30312	30325	22840	20875	21199	22004	16071	15105
4	28155	25649	25287	34025	30840	31190	22942	21274	21590	21300	15728	14770
1983 1	29312	26453	26097	32724	30946	31885	23709	20889	22723	21411	13926	14683
2	30234	28769	27044	38627	33197	33339	24524	21773	24328	18755	16561	15674
3	30365	29734	27990	38247	35814	35489	24151	23794	24955	23113	17753	15961
4	32192	30552	28381	37614	37141	36888	25185	26285	23755	20517	18274	16556
1984 1	33142	31289	28440	42821	37018	37447	24263	24685	23862	20435	18181	16499
2	32404	31612	28847	42715	39757	37918	25127	24338	23359	26210	18530	16703
3	32358	32809	29017	43151	39725	39859	25272	24924	23580	21706	18402	16773
4	31848	32553	29274	43461	41348	39799	25085	24839	26371	21983	19054	16273

* Prices at completion stage

206

SCOTLAND			NORTHERN IRELAND		
New	Post-1919	Pre-1919	New	Post-1919	Pre-1919
12678	12948	11744		8280	10375
13473	13723	12723		9393	10321
14102	13555	12657		12411	13814
15012	14262	14889	12250	9300	12694
14917	15465	15080		11343	10800
14773	16521	13808		9679	11088
16497	16944	15752		12267	13000
19059	17695	17660		13457	15350
17735	17495	19679	13000	13457	15350
18119	17354	19169	12500	14482	14620
20685	17648	20449	17625	12369	12195
19342	17142	20376	17257	11729	14785
19727	18025	21783	16481	10404	14637
20742	13858	19760	18772	9375	12257
22226	13681	23737	17637	7199	12807
22051	13426	23590	16500	7205	14072
24971	17086	21130	23076	14084	14586
23891	16700	21998	16980	12817	15713
23273	18693	21941	22873	12394	16395
24837	19661	24629	20168	15229	14677
26339	18590	22794	23684	13904	15300
29776	15338	21452	21486	14830	12093
27319	15402	23181	17400	15826	12255
25560	15012	25307	22704	11589	12858
26172	23040	24277	17042	14261	14334
27884	21750	28535	20914	13444	16059
28326	22782	27409	21007	14618	15193
27105	22025	24779		14217	16007
27351	23491	27210		17565	14226

ABBEY NATIONAL BUILDING SOCIETY
AVERAGE PRICES (at approval stage) 1977-1984

9.16 UNITED KINGDOM AND REGIONS BY AGE OF HOUSE: BUNGALOWS

Year	UNITED KINGDOM			NORTH			YORKS & HUMBERSIDE			NORTH WEST		
	New	Post-1919	Pre-1919	New	Post-1919	Pre-1919	New	Post-1919	Pre-1919	New	Post-1919	Pre-1919
1977 4*	14123	15177	15233	14014	14220	13770	11620	12710	11750	15357	14118	11500
1978 1*	15433	15957	15739	17576	15177	9500	12244	13071		13877	14090	8423
2*	15503	16235	15456	14267	15788	9000	12582	13102	9333	15673	15811	22090
3	17657	19089	19965	17416	16755	13425	15132	15360	17375	18662	16881	32500
4	19154	20458	22982	17521	19039	14333	16007	16187	25667	17743	19318	13248
1979 1	21151	23956	26250	19999	20933	14750	17737	20107	18759	22022	23145	40725
2	23348	25769	25768	22565	27619	15000	18082	23867	19583	23174	24412	
3	24232	28974	25318	20567	26535	17300	21431	23057	26962	22648	27654	27237
4	26297	29408	32027	24215	27222	17425	19266	27445		25909	26908	14037
1980 1	27993	29801	29030	27363	27023	25000	23334	23055	30998	25911	29653	36750
2	27399	31110	29748	24599	24982	36500	21035	23972	21325	26980	28142	32000
3	29368	30798	30537	30527	25463	38500	24906	26476	17000	26018	28612	24516
4	27716	31158	32407	24429	27043	30500	23885	23940	20147	27634	29671	43250
1981 1	28741	31294	28596	27678	27840	25943	24241	25276	34500	30400	31659	34000
2	30336	31817	31564	33024	34630	42620	24153	28079	18711	27743	30434	
3	29142	31696	30321	28104	30911	45750	24642	26005	16817	28124	30679	40813
4	28891	27883	29088	25750	23935	37445	23943	24571	29625	23972	27142	16715
1982 1	30335	29085	26706	24860	26371	13586	24368	24105	17874	28066	29802	25267
2	31589	31161	27901	28194	23390	19025	24650	24842	26641	24228	27611	39950
3	31809	30033	30505	29611	25915	21731	25738	24862	34375	25372	27723	51333
4	32017	32152	30122	30277	24441	23455	25858	24698	34031	27500	29229	32500
1983 1	31952	31562	32567	30281	27101	26187	26570	28151	12000	26300	29103	24136
2	34335	33934	37023	27056	29883	19502	29010	29372	34738	30503	29666	39600
3	33752	35123	37628	31834	29037	50000	30833	30271	30875	29686	33651	38725
4	36428	36241	46162	29678	31582	30500	33361	30341	23454	32571	31220	18000
1984 1	36311	35553	36506	32524	32845	16484	26619	29190	28950	30111	32756	37733
2	36441	38403	37752	39403	32097		30190	35490	30871	36137	34934	50899
3	35966	38645	37321	40115	31156		31613	33810		39054	39259	29416
4	36457	39707	43433	33506	38748		34496	38989	50890	37080	36264	43745

```
*  Prices at completion stage
```

£

EAST MIDLANDS			WEST MIDLANDS			EAST ANGLIA		
New	Post-1919	Pre-1919	New	Post-1919	Pre-1919	New	Post-1919	Pre-1919
12740	12282	16060	14213	14181	9500	11735	12422	
12430	14193	12867	15418	15866		13064	13019	9250
14275	12603	25000	13649	16561	14750	13539	13411	20000
12361	14854	12125	18385	17601	23375	14176	14984	9167
13410	16135	12000	19780	18879	11000	15967	16323	17000
16353	17021	39000	18978	22844	37333	16939	20357	22800
18771	18487	19250	22358	24251	12416	17946	20141	22400
19060	22349	18408	24234	28275	35000	19405	21039	16455
22665	22621	17975	27234	26527	39625	22247	23359	33750
33028	22142	31750	27313	30426	33875	24301	22269	17125
23302	22673	15750	29545	31071	30000	25973	23886	29750
24554	25569	30250	27810	30837	23590	24015	24521	28187
24098	24339	42000	26922	24720	69750	23202	23840	42833
21539	24716	14333	28629	29056	25983	22816	22945	15050
25091	21866	52167	28383	32710	25375	27600	23280	
24712	23794		32288	31695		23737	26311	19750
25211	23703	24828	29424	25291	23723	24824	24217	20000
24685	25749		28913	26968		22887	23566	23125
27019	25889		28509	29448	20687	30155	24333	18639
27103	26218	23845	28409	29887	27850	31037	24866	20911
25368	24431	32000	30013	27832	20240	30019	26266	23500
27642	26527	39167	27846	29142	34250	26964	26870	26500
31182	26991	31750	28792	30807	39833	28600	27751	27960
27567	26359	30000	28823	30632	46750	28474	28445	49983
28442	26746	45833	45169	34455	35910	27750	28980	33000
31403	26261	31564	34415	34663	39514	29842	31947	38803
34866	32393		40861	36599		28557	32299	
31164	31299		36279	36181		28638	31915	
30482	31324		44907	38659		30048	31406	31649

AVERAGE PRICES (at approval stage) 1977-1984

9.16 UNITED KINGDOM AND REGIONS BY AGE OF HOUSE: BUNGALOWS (continued)

Year	SOUTH EAST			GREATER LONDON			SOUTH WEST			WALES		
	New	Post-1919	Pre-1919	New	Post-1919	Pre-1919	New	Post-1919	Pre-1919	New	Post-1919	Pre-1919
1977 4*	16875	17335	17994	14950	20784	12800	13066	14631	24400	12190	13343	13550
1978 1*	18459	17528	19525	14995	20649	21817	16021	16380	18433	12955	13468	12094
2*	19422	17987	14250	25024	20849	17995	15329	16847	12083	13407	13421	11000
3	20807	21990	26450	31188	24531		17145	18793	20833	14614	15925	13250
4	26420	24104	34188	32875	29860	22800	17578	20599	19425	16492	16793	16375
1979 1	28043	28213	37305	48333	38984		21531	21975	19650	18504	17599	17500
2	32001	29872	28317	46750	32181	68791	22866	24007	25830	18987	20933	17977
3	33923	33733	39066	48676	40571	20290	25548	28701	25458	18834	22161	19055
4	34640	34420	49227		39963	49983	25481	28086	39500	19955	23616	11174
1980 1	35240	35793	36069	26117	39275	40250	27766	30431	28562	22467	22097	12983
2	36988	36854	49654	85750	39739	27387	27237	30722	34166	21057	26735	21315
3	39058	36561	37861	54000	44405	54625	32232	29969	27690	21991	23874	20258
4	33882	37941	35394	53625	42261	77590	28854	31144	20000	24410	24277	18649
1981 1	35894	35917	44623	67000	42777	40000	28178	29999	33883	23049	26670	18425
2	41802	38666	42794	62375	44972	56250	29654	29591	40167	23691	24282	15606
3	37369	37464	42992	40000	49209	57833	29556	30763	41814	25148	25471	15594
4	29965	31992	38688	44626	34976	27233	26858	26145	32490	26420	23472	22368
1982 1	33932	33149	31188	46430	38004	37370	28817	28362	36765	25350	23211	17085
2	38017	34796	32929	65225	53972	26871	29375	28548	34255	24534	25701	16473
3	41657	35434	31571		34076	46000	31254	30607	28104	25059	23757	21092
4	39853	40836	35198	54194	43195	34635	30979	30092	33830	24760	24682	18771
1983 1	40396	37779	50656	34034	36909	29417	34724	31817	25462	23914	27196	14995
2	43590	40581	48631	63500	45764	36703	36792	34270	47279	26264	26507	22775
3	42180	41491	45271	44784	51985	41013	34203	33057	29114	25274	27827	15533
4	42165	42058	82932	61225	57625	43870	39536	34904	41313	28236	26023	27114
1984 1	47447	42375	52393	44693	47057	28850	38748	35558	38423	28329	26222	20878
2	52630	48123	53739	77033	59930		38858	38852	52674	28556	29401	24724
3	50458	48580	47839		60699		46825	39430		28587	28489	24372
4	46781	51227	62472		74455		44406	37940	56869	30123	27681	26439

* Prices at completion stage

£

SCOTLAND			NORTHERN IRELAND		
New	Post-1919	Pre-1919	New	Post-1919	Pre-1919
16229	18114	11190	16760	16629	11375
16816	18290	15696	18125	17977	8200
17043	18531	17856	17025	17270	
20090	21492	15514	18521	18526	13371
19126	20326	21667	21337	18493	17000
22172	23537	19171	21115	23384	13500
25833	26679	20523	23479	23478	12250
26588	28498	22896	23208	26716	21906
28657	29379	23268	23208	26716	21906
28649	28113	26577	30270	28000	22000
29018	32369	25667	25971	26175	30000
32479	30549	27565	30195	26694	39401
29771	29630	25821	28978	27498	22933
32013	36254	20683	29829	22927	19307
32350	31010	27223	29643	24896	22125
32373	31562	28995	26351	23367	13416
32112	28723	28303	28039	26955	24059
31950	27078	17682	29407	27164	23669
34253	30431	27452	27079	27211	15228
33081	31603	27294	28337	27096	22716
34280	34627	24576	27032	27200	20902
33779	31550	29745	28852	26802	16740
35198	34243	25181	28941	25369	17961
36150	33140	29573	29360	28697	18717
34224	35056	25484	29731	25815	21028
35848	34293	27110	29699	29741	23253
40133	40144	29110	29932	32648	21288
38177	41169	33157	29713	31676	24986
38726	38982	38118	30686	29485	21376

ABBEY NATIONAL BUILDING SOCIETY

AVERAGE PRICES (at approval stage) 1977-1984

9.17 UNITED KINGDOM AND REGIONS BY AGE OF HOUSE: FLATS & MAISONETTES

Year	UNITED KINGDOM			NORTH			YORKS & HUMBERSIDE			NORTH WEST		
	New	Post-1919	Pre-1919	New	Post-1919	Pre-1919	New	Post-1919	Pre-1919	New	Post-1919	Pre-1919
1977 4*	12669	12213	11741	8619	8065	8002	7864	10470	11833	10494	10756	9700
1978 1*	12102	12689	12506	9058	8293	7281	9526	10397	13450	10478	10119	13700
2*	13183	13043	12281	9271	8336	6456	9006	11050	20000	9808	12027	14079
3	14814	14842	13775	12402	8083	7706	8666	10750		13949	12080	9588
4	15604	15679	15144	9400	9556	6708	8938	13853	7000	14270	13383	7500
1979 1	16090	16903	15920	10957	8799	7182	10018	12500	11440	13144	11872	14083
2	17209	17827	17241	10877	8563	7826	9390	10441	11916	14187	12632	5840
3	20563	19593	18723	12182	11251	8683	11996	12303	15737	15084	15193	12750
4	20620	20018	19719	13330	10800	8150	13683	16223	9482	14778	13203	13050
1980 1	21158	20653	19366	15781	11329	8700	17268	14195	19100	19135	16636	13737
2	21689	20843	20860	15274	10768	9817	15797	13800	14483	14129	18423	19415
3	21619	21170	20592	12585	12190	12608	15409	15258	20333	20032	17637	14418
4	22223	21542	20854	14991	10903	9262	17260	15405	13635	19221	16054	20890
1981 1	22489	20920	21448	21833	12340	10760	15232	15755	14337	17966	16898	14627
2	21670	19480	22083	12342	12017	9138	13540	14610	18190	16288	16062	22891
3	22555	20101	21374	13211	14800	11523	14662	14269	13200	14882	10154	10421
4	21165	17721	17301	13516	13027	13457	14875	21734	19455	15046	12775	12834
1982 1	20998	18357	18512	13038	12054	11257	15363	16017	14036	16707	17812	14908
2	22866	17930	21909	12943	12074	13130	30478	11469	23688	18141	15331	13961
3	20258	19488	19698	13254	14731	11988	17025	14883	15909	17431	15318	18759
4	21291	18931	20945	14221	14881	11626	21380	12231	21275	16713	15551	16538
1983 1	22255	20373	20129	14592	14789	15347	17817	17962	16789	22380	17648	19204
2	21757	20642	22600	17869	14267	13690	18618	15811	17499	21169	18115	17617
3	23148	21300	21331	16502	14798	15064	23895	18324	16739	20965	16092	20516
4	22427	21979	23075	17141	13680	12442	19815	17779	18945	18152	20005	21018
1984 1	23705	22002	22150	22401	14294	14429	19262	15791	20566	19280	19063	16786
2	25396	25178	24569	18577	14289	13659	17641	16490	23312	19457	16619	22167
3	25908	25965	24991	16144	14534	13833	24706	16365	21875	18097	18756	18951
4	25994	26242	25371	14606	14271	13806	19363	16778	21575	19223	23688	22387

* Prices at completion stage

EAST MIDLANDS			WEST MIDLANDS			EAST ANGLIA		
New	Post-1919	Pre-1919	New	Post-1919	Pre-1919	New	Post-1919	Pre-1919
7884	7807		13224	9681	9250	7913	12325	
7661	7150	5150	9228	9425	7267	8630	6920	
8805	13390		12763	8811	9500	9017	9525	
13200	8518		12875	11418	21588	10136	10283	11375
	11408	10800	11331	11132	11300	9642	9336	22750
8971	8733	22500	14030	12444	9488	9723	10681	16123
14020	9325		16091	12512	12435	12708	11209	15750
15225	11029	13525	39884	12603	12481	11283	11433	9316
6999	12288		16955	14377	31816		17208	11180
12486	11322	12275	19245	14785	12343	16025	15495	11010
14591	12179	13012	18277	16140	16400	25897	14755	20533
13482	12422	12691	20656	15571	16546	17330	15633	8000
16679	13340	11225	18509	16122	14900	16861	16967	18078
15115	12895	19500	17173	10893	17734	15929	17519	25000
13363	15914	14625	17491	8996	10360	16430	14492	20750
13883	12966		17086	13580	15733	14492	15789	20100
13919	10528	11717	16893	16270	13325	16050	17403	
23303	12164	18716	16525	16681	16141	15944	15665	21380
13617	13064	16217	19856	15352	31032	16198	15166	33415
15600	19547	20021	16482	15847	15851	20284	14223	20357
18407	12191	24965	18469	15683	18990	15459	17630	12267
16215	18029	12932	15089	16496	19263	19042	18970	24088
16239	14959	32500	15905	17083	18494	17453	18513	37852
15742	15672	15812	18139	17484	19880	22057	18688	16187
16158	15555	30000	18250	17479	21078	21697	17985	22040
16622	17209	19981	19324	17689	20925	28477	17944	21532
17604	17351	25533	18337	16856	25795	25101	20091	23125
18394	15400		18346	17472	17432	25207	20755	
17767	15652	13954	18979	16058	22886	23475	20731	17970

AVERAGE PRICES (at approval stage) 1977-1984

9.17 UNITED KINGDOM AND REGIONS BY AGE OF HOUSE:
FLATS & MAISONETTES (continued)

Year	SOUTH EAST			GREATER LONDON			SOUTH WEST			WALES		
	New	Post-1919	Pre-1919	New	Post-1919	Pre-1919	New	Post-1919	Pre-1919	New	Post-1919	Pre-1919
1977 4*	12271	11946	10272	15322	13352	12898	16285	10578	9329	10135	10931	
1978 1*	12338	12566	11081	16416	13949	13690	11125	13195	12671	14598	11190	7500
2*	13091	12996	11397	17516	13994	13884	13753	13652	11750	13350	10636	9875
3	14333	14281	13293	19035	16744	15128	13367	13573	11996	13288	11665	14663
4	15410	15491	14229	21041	17486	17166	15228	13739	14968	11788	16006	16983
1979 1	16692	16622	14192	20387	19378	18110	13680	14928	14686	8750	8025	13875
2	18124	17445	15159	23385	20595	19850	15483	16093	15245	8950	15093	10425
3	20526	19483	16785	25976	22559	21506	15849	16541	15460	14297	13835	21000
4	21817	20349	16974	27014	22924	22669	17928	17195	19402	17375	14083	15208
1980 1	21698	20597	17962	25753	23782	22949	24729	17922	16805	11800	18466	13475
2	22804	20527	19740	26357	23491	24369	20252	17720	19502	22500	19186	15875
3	22532	20827	17888	26937	24152	24120	24015	19019	17751	16890	16806	14850
4	23522	21148	19216	26519	24445	23962	19976	19244	20211	17443	14799	11630
1981 1	24779	21496	19056	28394	24226	24426	19641	17904	18622		14442	13355
2	23605	20343	19238	28646	23961	25414	17077	14379	19725		6574	12500
3	22955	20568	19347	28067	22274	24165	20522	17766	19307	16550	13295	9833
4	27335	20739	19199	31546	26165	25334	21796	15414	19619	15508	15345	15987
1982 1	23982	21802	21918	29895	24452	26745	22752	20534	21762	15210	13157	7666
2	25684	22973	21969	31419	24458	26761	21710	20043	21582	19626	15494	17332
3	23620	23533	21265	30923	25342	27885	21869	21626	19781	18484	19041	21946
4	26892	22951	22574	30720	26748	27661	20094	24025	21694	19366	19564	21530
1983 1	28431	24765	22729	36533	27675	28274	24257	21745	21590	18877	18169	15093
2	27712	25532	24689	32782	28110	30826	21577	22664	23028	17750	19472	18724
3	26924	26750	23774	40238	29295	31952	26991	23644	22879	27498	19588	13638
4	27616	26559	25015	34565	31946	32184	21681	22854	23314	25860	20736	21083
1984 1	29144	27238	24853	33751	31064	32160	24183	24572	24534	26314	20708	18350
2	27399	27553	23440	35279	30650	31178	21700	21360	23216	27292	18416	15728
3	28052	28132	23541	34625	31601	32263	22313	23626	22832	28663	18970	23786
4	28191	27856	24600	35422	32827	32758	21752	22135	22260	23326	18212	19362

```
*  Prices at completion stage
```

£

SCOTLAND			NORTHERN IRELAND		
New	Post-1919	Pre-1919	New	Post-1919	Pre-1919
12355	11311	9720			
11402	10526	9685			
13168	11569	9979			
12394	12334	10881			29500
12672	12441	11658			
15988	13301	11928			
14981	14495	12860			
15601	15131	14211			
15312	14473	14325			
16346	14804	14031			
17644	16507	14319			
18635	15987	15481			
18176	17035	15575			
19297	16140	16527			
20679	15547	16009			
22077	16868	16998			
22780	16095	16953			
23085	19574	17619			
23347	19279	18377			
24154	19029	18371			
24553	19398	18644	21514	13250	15000
23854	16841	18963	20818		20000
25264	19752	20185	21092	36500	17000
26479	21739	21445	22313		22667
25394	22711	21001	23356	36000	
24586	22527	20229	22681	25387	
23627	22006	19761			
24113	22765	19973			
25903	22656	20142	24571		

10. Anglia Building Society

10.1 TECHNICAL DETAILS

(a) Source of data and timing

Society's own records of prices at the valuation stage

(b) Types of data and periods covered

Percentage price changes: 1969 to date
Index of average prices: 1974 to date

Because of inconsistencies in the presentation of the published data for the United Kingdom before 1974 and for the regions before 1983, we have not reproduced the earlier data.

Available data

DATA BREAKDOWNS	DATA TYPES	
	INDEX NUMBERS	PERCENTAGE CHANGES
HOUSE DATA		
All houses		*
New/Non-new	*	*
Type		
Size		
Age	*	*
LOCAL DATA		
Regions		*
Sub-regions		*
Towns		*
BUYER DATA		
First-time buyer		
Former owner-occupier		

(c) Frequency

Percentage price changes: biannual since 1983, previously annual

Index of average prices: annual

(d) Geographical coverage

United Kingdom subdivided into regions and selected sub-regions and towns (termed survey areas by the Society). The number of survey areas has increased with time, there being 30 at present (for details see Tables 10.4 and 10.5).

(e) Method of analysis

Valuations are based on capitalized 1939 rental values of properties (related to floor area, type of property and characteristics). A post-war multiple (pwm) is applied to this 1939 valuation to provide a current valuation for each property. The pwm is taken as the multiple currently obtaining in each corresponding region as based on surveyors' experience.

The above valuation (which is referred to as the "old" system) is compared with and checked against a new "direct" system of valuation, whereby an adjustment (devaluation) is made to the recorded selling price of each house by one of the Society's valuers. This devaluation technique is used to make allowance for variations in house attributes which would otherwise make comparisons of property prices inappropriate. Due allowance is made in the devaluation for such factors as fixtures and fittings, garages, central heating, environmental factors, etc., which may have affected prices. The worth of these items is then discounted from the respective figures before inclusion in the data. By such means the analysis of house prices is keyed to a common base.

All sales at non-market prices, such as those to sitting tenants and council house tenants, are excluded from the analyses.

10.2 LIST OF TABLES

Percentage price changes

10.1 United Kingdom: age of dwelling. 1974-
10.2 Regions: age of dwelling. 1973-1982
10.3 Regions: age of dwelling. 1983-
10.4 Survey areas: age of dwelling. 1983-1985
10.5 Survey areas: age of dwelling. 1986-

Index of average prices

10.1 United Kingdom: age of dwelling. 1974-

10.3 CROSS-CLASSIFICATIONS OF DATA

(a) Two-way classifications

Numbers in the grid below refer to the corresponding tables compiled for this data source

(b) Three-way classifications

None

ANGLIA BUILDING SOCIETY

10.4 PUBLICATIONS

(a) Data

Housing Market biannual (previously *Voice of Anglia*). Anglia Building Society, Northampton

(b) Description of methodology

None

(c) Supplementary studies

None

ANGLIA BUILDING SOCIETY

PERCENTAGE PRICE CHANGES AND INDEX (at valuation stage) 1974–

10.1 UNITED KINGDOM: AGE OF DWELLING

Year	PERCENTAGE PRICE CHANGES				INDEX (31 December 1973 = 100)		
	All	New	Post-1919	Pre-1919	New	Post-1919	Pre-1919
1974		2.0	2.0	3.0	102.0	102.0	103.0
1975		8.0	7.0	7.0	110.2	109.1	110.2
1976		10.2	7.8	6.2	121.4	117.7	117.0
1977		7.5	6.6	7.3	130.5	125.4	125.6
1978		31.5	30.0	24.5	171.6	163.0	156.3
1979		35.0	32.0	33.0	231.0	215.2	207.9
1980		8.8	8.4	14.6	252.0	233.3	238.3
1981		7.8	2.6	5.7	271.7	239.3	251.9
1982		6.2	5.5	4.1	288.5	252.5	262.2
1983	9.0	8.5	8.2	9.5	313.0	273.2	287.1
1984	8.6	7.9	9.0	8.9	337.4	297.8	312.7
1985	10.2	9.5	10.2	10.9	369.5	328.1	346.7
1986	17.2	17.1	16.7	17.9	432.7	382.9	408.8

ANGLIA BUILDING SOCIETY

PERCENTAGE PRICE CHANGES (at valuation stage) 1973-1982

10.2 REGIONS: AGE OF DWELLING

Year	North Eastern	North Western	Midlands	East Midlands	West Midlands	East Anglia	London & South East
NEW DWELLINGS							
1973	15.0	22.0	16.0	1.0	16.0	24.0	17.0
1974	2.0	8.0	(0.5)	(2.5)	4.0	1.5	(2.0)
1975	6.0	8.0	8.0	6.8	12.0	4.5	7.5
1976	11.7	10.7	6.8	7.4	9.7	9.0	10.3
1977	6.3	10.7	8.3	3.0	7.0	6.2	7.9
1978	32.1	30.4	32.4	22.5	44.0	32.3	38.0
1979	26.0	37.0	33.0	40.0	48.0	36.0	30.0
1980	9.0	10.0	8.5	7.9	10.5	6.3	6.5
1981	13.3	7.3	13.8	9.0	0.0	6.8	5.8
1982	5.7	0.7	6.0	4.1	0.0	4.0	5.1
POST-1919 RESALES							
1973	18.0	23.0	11.0	0.0	15.0	12.0	9.0
1974	1.5	6.0	(1.0)	(1.8)	4.0	(3.0)	(1.0)
1975	4.0	9.0	5.5	6.0	8.0	6.5	4.5
1976	8.2	7.3	5.1	5.6	7.9	6.8	7.2
1977	6.2	13.0	6.0	4.0	8.5	3.7	4.3
1978	23.5	30.6	30.8	24.9	29.8	38.2	53.0
1979	28.0	32.0	31.0	36.0	37.0	27.0	28.0
1980	13.4	1.0	12.3	9.0	6.2	8.2	4.0
1981	0.8	4.2	2.3	3.2	6.9	2.9	0.5
1982	5.8	2.8	3.9	4.7	(2.7)	8.0	7.7
PRE-1919 RESALES							
1973	20.0	37.0	14.0	12.0	21.0	21.0	8.0
1974	5.0	9.0	2.0	(1.5)	6.0	4.0	3.0
1975	4.0	6.5	5.5	5.5	6.5	6.5	6.0
1976	7.7	4.0	5.6	3.0	6.6	7.1	2.0
1977	5.6	14.5	(1.2)	0.0	7.0	6.5	4.8
1978	12.4	11.8	21.9	17.0	13.9	29.0	44.3
1979	23.0	48.0	21.0	33.0	30.0	35.0	40.0
1980	14.0	6.5	33.4	19.5	7.5	11.9	8.4
1981	6.4	4.8	5.8	4.7	11.5	9.7	0.1
1982	10.2	5.5	5.8	5.5	5.4	5.4	4.7

Figures in brackets are negative

| | | | £ |
North London	South West Midlands	Western	Scotland
6.0	2.0	11.0	12.0
(4.0)	(2.5)	5.0	8.0
5.0	7.0	10.0	12.0
5.4	8.7	12.3	20.0
	6.1	8.0	12.0
51.9	30.0	23.4	14.0
34.0	37.0	36.0	30.0
4.8	2.1	17.0	14.5
8.3	5.6	0.0	8.9
7.2	11.8	2.4	14.4
2.0	4.0	19.0	23.0
(2.0)	(1.5)	2.5	5.0
6.0	7.0	10.0	10.0
7.8	4.8	7.0	18.4
6.3	5.0	7.5	7.7
47.2	30.2	24.2	14.8
30.0	35.0	36.0	27.0
9.3	4.1	12.0	15.0
1.4	5.2	3.7	3.7
8.4	4.2	0.4	6.8
2.0	7.0	40.0	50.0
(3.5)	1.0	7.0	6.5
3.0	11.5	11.5	10.0
9.0	4.1	6.1	13.1
6.7	4.5	12.0	20.0
51.2	29.4	17.5	13.4
34.0	37.0	21.0	33.0
17.0	9.1	33.5	0.0
7.7	7.2	21.8	11.8
4.2	(5.2)	4.2	(5.6)

ANGLIA BUILDING SOCIETY

PERCENTAGE PRICE CHANGES (at valuation stage) 1983–

10.3 REGIONS: AGE OF DWELLING

Year	North & Yorkshire	North West	North East Midlands	East Midlands	West Midlands	South Midlands	East Anglia
NEW DWELLINGS							
1983	1.1	4.0	5.0	15.2	4.8	13.9	11.2
1984	9.0	5.2	3.2	9.8	6.2	10.0	11.0
1985	10.0	2.5	7.3	8.6	6.8	15.0	12.3
1986	13.0	10.9	7.9	19.1	11.5	16.0	20.0
POST-1919 RESALES							
1983	3.6	5.1	5.5	8.1	7.2	11.0	9.2
1984	1.0	1.4	8.2	9.6	3.4	18.0	10.2
1985	10.0	3.4	5.0	11.8	7.8	12.0	16.7
1986	13.0	10.1	8.9	20.6	10.2	15.3	16.4
PRE-1919 RESALES							
1983	5.8	5.2	2.1	8.3	5.1	9.4	9.3
1984	8.0	3.6	5.9	8.0	3.4	21.0	13.3
1985	9.0	0.0	9.0	10.8	6.8	10.0	12.4
1986	10.0	10.5	8.8	20.9	11.4	17.4	21.4

London & South East	South	South West	Scotland	Northern Ireland
8.2	8.7	-	4.9	(2.0)
9.7	7.7	7.0	2.3	(1.7)
12.1	12.8	6.9	3.6	6.0
22.5	20.0	15.0	8.0	5.0
10.9	9.4	6.0	2.0	4.5
11.3	11.2	5.0	13.9	1.9
11.2	14.1	9.6	0.2	2.8
23.4	15.8	18.0	11.0	0.1
14.3	10.1	12.0	14.6	3.2
10.3	11.5	5.0	14.0	4.6
15.7	10.8	2.4	2.0	1.5
23.4	24.3	14.0	5.0	1.0

ANGLIA BUILDING SOCIETY

PERCENTAGE PRICE CHANGES (at valuation stage) 1983-1985

10.4 SURVEY AREAS: AGE OF DWELLING

Year	North & Yorkshire			Cheshire & South Lancashire			North Lancashire			Nottinghamshire & South Yorkshire			Lincolnshire		
	N	M	O	N	M	O	N	M	O	N	M	O	N	M	O
1983	1.0	3.5	6.0	5.0	5.5	9.0	3.0	6.0	3.0	1.0	4.5	1.0	10.0	6.5	5.0
1984	9.0	1.0	8.0	4.4	2.5	4.8	6.1	0.4	2.5	5.0	8.0	4.0	1.5	8.5	7.8
1985	10.0	10.0	9.0	(2.0)	3.7	0.0	4.5	3.0	0.0	8.0	6.3	12.0	6.7	3.6	6.1

Year	Birmingham			Western			Cambridge			Suffolk			Norfolk		
	N	M	O	N	M	O	N	M	O	N	M	O	N	M	O
1983	7.5	6.0	5.0	2.5	8.0	5.5	10.0	7.5	7.0	14.0	10.0	10.0	9.5	10.0	10.5
1984	0.5	1.5	0.8	12.0	5.4	6.0	10.4	9.2	11.2	11.6	15.0	16.5	11.1	6.4	12.2
1985	5.5	7.5	4.1	8.0	8.0	9.5	14.3	20.2	17.3	14.0	19.0	13.0	8.5	11.0	7.0

Year	Mid Surrey & South London			North London, Middlesex, Herts			East Sussex			North Kent & South East London			Berks, West Surrey & North Hampshire		
	N	M	O	N	M	O	N	M	O	N	M	O	N	M	O
1983	18.0	17.0	16.5	8.5	15.5	8.0	4.0	11.0	22.0	-	14.5	16.0	13.5	15.0	12.5
1984	7.0	11.2	11.9	15.6	17.0	15.2	13.3	11.8	3.3	-	12.5	18.0	11.0	11.0	12.0
1985	9.5	10.3	17.6	22.0	17.0	16.0	8.0	7.0	18.0	-	10.0	15.0	14.0	15.0	12.5

N = New properties
M = Modern (post-1919) resales
O = Older (pre-1919) resales

Figures in brackets are negative

Hinckley			Northamptonshire			Bedford			Midlands			Leicester		
N	M	O	N	M	O	N	M	O	N	M	O	N	M	O
1.5	6.0	4.5	15.0	7.0	10.0	14.5	11.5	11.0	18.0	6.0	8.0	22.0	6.0	10.5
11.7	6.3	0.3	1.2	12.0	12.2	15.9	12.0	15.2	6.9	6.7	4.6	13.2	11.3	7.6
4.7	7.8	5.1	13.8	7.8	9.8	10.0	18.4	18.6	8.5	18.0	17.5	6.0	6.8	3.0

South Midlands			Essex			Thanet			Medway Towns			Kent Weald		
N	M	O	N	M	O	N	M	O	N	M	O	N	M	O
13.5	10.0	9.5	7.5	10.0	21.0	10.0	6.5	11.5	10.0	4.0	10.0	10.0	8.0	9.0
10.0	18.0	21.0	4.2	6.6	13.0	3.8	2.1	10.0	14.0	17.5	4.0	10.0	12.0	7.0
15.0	12.0	10.0	15.0	6.0	15.0	10.0	18.0	18.0	12.1	10.1	10.8	8.0	11.0	15.0

Hampshire			West Sussex			South West		
N	M	O	N	M	O	N	M	O
4.0	2.5	3.0	5.0	10.5	15.0	15.0	6.0	12.0
5.0	8.0	12.0	7.1	14.7	10.5	7.0	5.0	5.0
10.0	9.0	10.0	14.5	18.3	9.8	6.9	9.6	2.4

ANGLIA BUILDING SOCIETY

PERCENTAGE PRICE CHANGES (at valuation stage) 1986–

10.5 SURVEY AREAS: AGE OF DWELLING

Year	North & Yorkshire			Cheshire & South Lancashire			North Lancashire			Nottinghamshire & South Yorkshire			Lincolnshire		
	N	M	O	N	M	O	N	M	O	N	M	O	N	M	O
1986	13.0	13.0	10.0	17.2	8.2	8.0	4.5	12.0	13.0	-	-	-	9.8	10.6	10.6

Year	Birmingham			Western			Cambridge			Suffolk			Norfolk		
	N	M	O	N	M	O	N	M	O	N	M	O	N	M	O
1986	11.2	11.3	13.8	11.8	9.1	9.1	28.5	18.8	18.7	17.0	10.0	23.0	14.5	20.5	22.5

Year	Mid Surrey			North Kent			North London, Middlesex, Herts			East Sussex			Maidenhead		
	N	M	O	N	M	O	N	M	O	N	M	O	N	M	O
1986	24.0	30.0	21.0	18.0	18.0	27.0	22.0	22.0	25.0	37.0	23.0	26.0	-	-	-

N = New properties
M = Modern (post-1919) resales
O = Older (pre-1919) resales

Figures in brackets are negative

Hinckley			Northamptonshire			Bedford/ Milton Keynes			Midlands			Leicester		
N	M	O	N	M	O	N	M	O	N	M	O	N	M	O
11.1	13.5	11.5	20.0	27.0	30.0	27.0	23.5	21.0	20.5	22.2	29.1	17.0	17.0	13.0

South Midlands			Essex			Thanet			Medway Towns			Kent Weald		
N	M	O	N	M	O	N	M	O	N	M	O	N	M	O
16.0	15.3	17.4	20.0	28.0	21.0	11.0	18.0	19.0	24.0	21.0	23.0	24.0	27.0	25.0

Waverley			South Hampshire			West Sussex			South West		
N	M	O	N	M	O	N	M	O	N	M	O
22.0	20.0	22.0	23.0	12.0	24.0	15.0	15.5	27.0	15.0	18.0	14.0

11. Halifax Building Society

11.1 TECHNICAL DETAILS

(a) Source of data and timing

Society's own lending records at the mortgage approval stage

(b) Types of data and periods covered

Current data:

Average prices: 1983 to date
Standardized index: 1983 to date

Historical data:

Average prices: Jan 1975-Dec 1982, monthly
                  1976 Q1- 1982 Q4, quarterly
Index: June 1975-July 1983, monthly

Available data - current

DATA BREAKDOWNS	DATA TYPES	
	AVERAGE PRICES	INDEX NUMBERS
HOUSE DATA		
All houses	*	*
New/Non-new	*	*
Type	*	
Size		
Age	*	
LOCAL DATA		
Regions	*	*
Sub-regions		
Towns		
BUYER DATA		
First-time buyer	*	*
Former owner-occupier	*	*

HALIFAX BUILDING SOCIETY

Available data - historical

DATA BREAKDOWNS	DATA TYPES	
	AVERAGE PRICES	INDEX NUMBERS
HOUSE DATA		
All houses	*	
New/Non-new	*	[*]
Type		
Size		
Age		
LOCAL DATA		
Regions	*	
Sub-regions		
Towns		
BUYER DATA		
First-time buyer		
Former owner-occupier		

[*] Non-new property only

(c) Frequency

Current data: average prices - monthly and quarterly
  standardized index - monthly and quarterly
Historical data: average prices - monthly and quarterly
  index - monthly

(d) Geographical coverage

United Kingdom, subdivided into official standard regions (defined in Appendix B)

(e) Method of analysis

Current data

Average prices: simple averages, excluding properties sold at non-market prices.

Standardized index: the indices are standardised to take account of the influence of changes in the composition of dwellings mortgaged in each time period according to thirteen characteristics as follows:

Location: official standard regions

Type of property:
  house
  bungalow
  converted flat or maisonette
  purpose-built flat or maisonette

Each type of property is sub-classified as follows:
  semi-detached
  detached
  terraced

Age: estimated age in years

Tenure: freehold/leasehold

Number of habitable rooms

Number of bathrooms

Number of separate toilets

Central heating: none, full, partial

Number of garages

Number of garage spaces

Garden (yes/no)

Land (area of land if greater than one acre).

Road charge liability (amount).

Estimates are made in each time period of the influence of each characteristic on prices using multiple regression analysis. These estimates may be regarded as "characteristics prices". The indices are derived by comparing base-weighted averages of the characteristics prices with average prices in the base period (1983).

The formula is as follows:

$$I_{t_n} = \frac{\exp(\Sigma b_{jt_n} Q_{jt_0})}{\exp(\Sigma b_{jt_0} Q_{jt_0})} \times 100$$

where I_{t_n} is the index for the current period

where b_j are regression coefficients for each characteristic

where Q_{jt_0} are the weights and represent the proportions of the qualitative variables and the means of the quantitative variables present in the base period.

Properties which are not for private occupation and those that are likely to have been sold at non-market or discounted prices are excluded from the analysis.

Detailed descriptions of the methodology are given in the references cited in 11.4(b).

Historical data

Average prices and indices: The series of average prices for the United Kingdom shown in Tables 11.8-11.11 include previously unpublished data supplied by the Society. The prices are simple, unadjusted averages, excluding properties sold at non-market prices, and are calculated on the same basis as those currently produced by the Society. They, therefore, form a continuous series of unadjusted average house prices from 1975.

The series of average prices and an index, shown in Table 11.12 were originally published as the "Times/Halifax house price index", which appeared monthly in *The Times*.

11.2 LIST OF TABLES

Average prices (current series)

11.1 United Kingdom: all dwellings, age of dwelling, type of buyer, type of dwelling. 1983-
11.2 Regions: all dwellings. 1984-
11.3 Regions: age of dwelling. 1984-
11.4 Regions: type of dwelling. 1984-
11.5 United Kingdom and regions by age of house: type of dwelling. 1984-

Standardized index (current series)

11.6 United Kingdom: all, new, and existing dwellings, type of buyer. 1983-
11.7 Regions: all, new and existing dwellings. 1983-

Average prices (historical series)

11.8   United Kingdom: all, new and existing dwellings. 1975-1982 - monthly
11.9   United Kingdom and regions: all dwellings. 1976-1982 - quarterly
11.10   United Kingdom and regions: new dwellings. 1976-1982 - quarterly
11.11   United Kingdom and regions: existing dwellings. 1976-1982 - quarterly
11.12   Great Britain: existing dwellings. June 1975-July 1983 - monthly

Index (historical series)

11.12   Great Britain: existing dwellings. June 1975-July 1983 - monthly

11.3   CROSS-CLASSIFICATIONS OF DATA

(a)   Two-way classifications

Numbers in the grids below refer to the corresponding tables compiled for this data source

Average prices and standardized index(*) - current series

Average prices - historical series

(b)   Three-way classifications

Average prices (current series):

Regions by age of dwelling by type of dwelling: Table 11.5

11.4 PUBLICATIONS

(a) Data

Monthly press release and quarterly *Regional Bulletin*. Halifax Building Society, Halifax. Until 1983 the data on average prices were published in *The Times* under the title "Times/Halifax house price index".

(b) Description of methodology

Fleming, M.C. and Nellis, J.G., (1984) *The Halifax House Price Index: Technical Details*. Halifax Building Society, Halifax (available free from the Society).

Fleming, M.C. and Nellis, J.G., (1985) "The application of hedonic indexing methods: a study of house prices in the United Kingdom", *Statistical Journal of the United Nations Economic Commission for Europe*, **3**, pp. 249-70.

(c) Supplementary studies

Loans for council house purchase *Regional Bulletin No. 4* (1984 Q4).

Loans for new houses. *Regional Bulletin No. 5* (1985 Q1)

House prices - the North/South divide. *Regional Bulletin No. 6* (1985 Q2)

Halifax loans for council house purchase. *Regional Bulletin No. 8* (1985 Q4)

House prices - the North/South divide. *Regional Bulletin No. 9* (1986 Q1)

Percentage changes in house prices from first quarter 1983. *Regional Bulletin No. 12* (1986 Q4)

HALIFAX BUILDING SOCIETY

AVERAGE PRICES (at approval stage) 1983 –

11.1 UNITED KINGDOM:
    ALL DWELLINGS, AGE OF DWELLING, TYPE OF BUYER AND TYPE OF DWELLING

Year		All	AGE OF DWELLNG					TYPE OF BUYER	
			Pre- 1919	1919- 1945	1946- 1960	Post- 1960	New	First-time Buyer	Former Owner- occupier
1983	1	29594					34168	21397	34968
	2	31200					34953	22173	36455
	3	32103					35642	22643	37461
	4	30821					34473	22676	36044
1984	1	29614	25009	30974	33282	30674	33797	22386	35550
	2	30688	26243	32118	34898	31841	33812	23258	36799
	3	31735	27765	32943	36723	32783	34427	23926	37853
	4	31919	27793	33020	36456	33247	34299	24142	37501
1985	1	31529	27033	32728	35236	32696	35059	24105	39967
	2	32683	28307	34268	36760	33591	36292	24464	38484
	3	32678	28386	34458	36731	33627	37347	24930	39041
	4	34407	29992	36222	38325	35113	40122	25737	41205
1986	1	35164	30799	37862	38468	35619	40892	26453	42147
	2	38266	34143	41203	42383	37814	44492	28029	44953
	3	40475	36528	43889	44089	39947	46566	29607	46856
	4	41285	37329	44180	43792	40852	47710	30751	47485
1987	1	43278	38943	44851	46230	42936	51454	32237	49189

£

TYPE OF DWELLING

Detached house	Semi-detached house	Terraced house	Bungalow	Flat/Maisonette
46314	27974	22205	33236	25875
48219	28800	23281	34771	26661
49438	29761	24106	36197	27105
49133	29940	24314	35955	28040
48692	29717	24221	35936	28578
51254	30911	24858	37178	29282
53073	30913	24943	37682	29034
55997	32461	26129	38833	30826
57123	33166	27046	39066	32076
60506	35234	29206	41165	35220
62746	37244	30957	43594	37138
62909	37873	32160	43132	38914
64484	39259	34102	44691	42724

235

HALIFAX BUILDING SOCIETY

AVERAGE PRICES (at approval stage) 1984 –

11.2 REGIONS: ALL DWELLINGS

Year		North	Yorks & Humberside	North West	East Midlands	West Midlands	East Anglia
1984	1	23913	22255	23794	24143	26511	29634
	2	24256	23247	24653	25944	27191	30404
	3	24867	23407	25868	26075	28197	32250
	4	25964	24023	25698	26617	27957	33046
1985	1	25028	22995	25103	26869	27723	32054
	2	24752	23818	25751	27213	28587	33594
	3	24011	23662	25981	26812	27355	33440
	4	24359	24007	26635	27668	28233	34595
1986	1	23895	23966	27439	27407	27834	35407
	2	25280	26028	29361	28414	29894	38021
	3	26684	26717	30387	30515	31337	40169
	4	27034	26778	31407	31227	33297	42432
1987	1	28354	27865	31666	32645	33285	44550

South East	Greater London	South West	Wales	Scotland	Northern Ireland
38700	40163	32176	24807	28275	25467
39929	41220	32490	24727	29396	25203
41466	42506	33474	26607	28967	26398
42024	43589	34985	26263	29865	26114
42908	44799	34140	25873	29547	26083
44636	48171	35596	25529	30413	26299
44765	49105	35600	25478	30015	27329
47889	52988	36653	26040	29491	27735
48853	55534	36834	25692	28851	27193
53814	60604	38909	27377	31280	29245
56865	64622	41844	29720	31952	29944
58736	65035	42816	29802	32133	29836
62061	69092	44610	30164	34681	29592

HALIFAX BUILDING SOCIETY

AVERAGE PRICES (at approval stage) 1984 –

11.3 REGIONS: AGE OF DWELLING

Year		North	Yorks & Humberside	North West	East Midlands	West Midlands	East Anglia
PRE-1919 DWELLINGS							
1984	1	18907	16955	17595	18848	22285	26911
	2	18965	17858	18548	21066	24360	28551
	3	18838	18299	19982	21288	25837	30534
	4	20308	18754	20029	21138	23868	30384
1985	1	19870	17578	18850	21596	23050	28545
	2	20137	18291	19379	21154	24934	31178
	3	19051	18499	20066	22114	23528	31148
	4	19727	18847	20355	22353	23906	30491
1986	1	18744	18715	20756	22519	23811	32067
	2	19955	20736	22890	23174	25358	35808
	3	21596	20818	23608	24695	27729	37708
	4	21624	21283	24012	26127	29244	39973
1987	1	23101	22194	25254	24673	27708	41635
1919-1945 DWELLINGS							
1984	1	22139	21858	25172	23425	26594	29947
	2	23811	22579	25425	25042	25443	30512
	3	24305	23208	26269	25240	26375	34639
	4	26071	23032	26598	25669	26345	35710
1985	1	24257	22908	25716	24724	25993	34575
	2	23085	23881	26902	26021	26848	33152
	3	23086	23121	26682	25705	27154	33660
	4	23972	23431	26616	27008	27889	34697
1986	1	23401	23632	28032	26389	26897	34393
	2	24886	25755	29353	28222	28562	39193
	3	25894	26659	31072	29457	30484	42703
	4	26200	26075	31382	30489	32212	42673
1987	1	26230	26708	30914	31294	30666	44505
1946-1960 DWELLINGS							
1984	1	27724	23818	28255	25650	29605	33162
	2	27469	25612	30080	27453	30878	31946
	3	29323	26733	30145	28568	32694	36338
	4	29705	26528	30505	29668	31659	34870
1985	1	28573	25533	29204	29054	29963	36679
	2	27879	25550	29144	29573	31490	36888
	3	27321	25578	31258	29515	30109	35742
	4	28502	26519	30934	28790	31235	37785
1986	1	26354	24937	29765	26672	29150	38766
	2	28422	27177	32362	29551	33795	40549
	3	28424	28945	35237	31488	35098	40915
	4	27907	28059	33983	30747	35618	41138
1987	1	29763	28797	32868	34219	36293	44797

South East	Greater London	South West	Wales	Scotland	Northern Ireland
					£
33291	37481	29230	20332	23522	20440
34900	37830	29610	20338	25360	19960
36812	39678	31172	22000	25187	21349
38069	40498	32929	21989	26096	22333
38712	41438	32065	22322	25669	20918
39938	45551	33196	21030	26536	20656
39491	46181	33819	21588	26206	23061
42725	51287	34664	21572	24919	21840
43048	53875	34044	21329	24211	21414
48107	59009	36295	22386	27338	25699
51705	62722	40085	24786	27930	24587
53907	62845	40746	24448	27920	24842
55265	67322	42437	23980	31085	25352
40893	43032	33404	24599	30134	20211
42897	44818	34043	25518	30650	21015
45079	45747	35647	26936	30098	23080
44439	47810	36988	26306	31042	20879
44994	50048	36275	25326	31280	20769
46923	52859	38149	27719	34388	22764
48263	53306	38256	27581	33725	22197
52052	55680	37897	26332	33162	22196
53741	58809	41415	26073	31148	22472
57945	63814	34109	28124	34636	24629
61229	68145	44793	29957	37199	26178
64126	68435	46211	33194	35905	24689
65115	71638	46580	32845	36493	23311
41984	44478	34282	30289	32804	23376
44329	46504	37074	31359	35559	28535
47412	46891	37741	31393	35302	26789
47471	50050	37981	28978	36660	28151
47592	47406	37211	28229	31686	25704
49595	53017	40609	30126	33520	27633
50021	53250	40853	28961	32884	27791
53917	57068	40254	29010	31398	30119
56259	56779	41198	26776	30809	28450
60499	63321	45006	32207	34965	30457
62128	67940	45606	34077	35874	30285
63585	66913	46623	35787	33245	28681
66310	70604	46742	35151	35474	30165

HALIFAX BUILDING SOCIETY

AVERAGE PRICES (at approval stage) 1984 –

11.3 REGIONS: AGE OF DWELLING (continued)

Year		North	Yorks & Humberside	North West	East Midlands	West Midlands	East Anglia
POST-1960 (NON-NEW) DWELLINGS							
1984	1	26233	25181	26669	26309	26632	30167
	2	26635	26623	27737	27972	26924	30647
	3	27852	26642	29298	28268	28114	32326
	4	28894	27688	28676	28726	28921	32992
1985	1	27431	26552	28358	28904	28045	32018
	2	27585	27452	28888	29183	28757	33629
	3	27785	27617	29038	29077	27160	33240
	4	27295	27891	29758	29810	27923	35320
1986	1	27071	27541	30806	29431	27897	35877
	2	28912	29283	32094	30014	29471	37682
	3	29837	30446	32704	32422	30709	39936
	4	30408	29946	34349	32803	32152	42693
1987	1	31436	31081	33754	34962	33601	44178
NEW DWELLINGS							
1984	1	31403	28484	30079	29550	30841	32016
	2	30689	28893	29657	30467	31982	32003
	3	31344	28305	29741	30472	32465	32304
	4	30946	30206	29344	31186	31129	35085
1985	1	32037	28691	30705	31548	34014	34366
	2	31106	30157	31664	33288	34617	36965
	3	32357	31478	33225	31198	34448	38068
	4	33132	31979	36209	34866	36238	38880
1986	1	34604	31979	36914	34488	36204	39761
	2	34917	32826	37418	36335	40175	41721
	3	37918	34541	39555	39776	40610	44106
	4	37679	35011	40966	38868	45183	46721
1987	1	38860	37096	44762	42338	44367	48998

£

South East	Greater London	South West	Wales	Scotland	Northern Ireland
38870	39670	32757	26237	30361	26928
40028	41547	33013	26212	31928	28260
41232	43337	33570	28332	31094	30061
42161	42472	35181	27977	32533	30265
42570	44681	34304	27939	31563	30215
44403	44872	35328	27591	32365	29901
44477	47909	35421	27315	31739	31640
46640	50785	36091	28150	32289	31286
47807	53878	36029	28376	31457	29410
52084	56270	37623	30153	32529	30923
55207	61716	40764	32203	32937	31360
56792	62299	40985	31849	34102	30705
61323	65532	43163	31220	35489	31927
42175	42435	34507	29271	31235	29412
41522	42329	34010	27779	30996	27597
42168	42352	35006	30998	31609	28361
42056	42427	35723	31140	30851	28720
44732	43015	34808	28612	31186	27890
46541	46508	36718	28509	31973	29110
48452	48982	35862	28531	33719	30630
52447	54214	40164	33337	33835	30890
54386	55223	40242	32694	34820	30513
61193	63850	43275	32652	36980	31756
64942	64280	45840	36466	38276	33313
65393	70348	48845	35909	37488	34210
69914	76985	50941	42134	40723	33096

HALIFAX BUILDING SOCIETY

AVERAGE PRICES (at approval stage) 1984 –

11.4 REGIONS: TYPE OF DWELLING

Year		North	Yorks & Humberside	North West	East Midlands	West Midlands	East Anglia
DETACHED HOUSES							
1984	1	42210	36561	41893	36555	40558	42197
	2	41617	38422	44077	38836	41712	43202
	3	41136	39090	44545	38904	42904	46499
	4	41437	39973	44069	38782	41107	46913
1985	1	40817	37521	42765	40593	41698	44878
	2	40230	39977	44949	40315	44417	48295
	3	41978	41099	46501	41653	44561	48208
	4	42531	42049	48481	43428	45568	49302
1986	1	42717	41329	48489	43812	44864	52620
	2	45400	44500	50049	44556	47314	56271
	3	46815	44065	52396	46605	49414	57632
	4	45471	44257	53479	47309	51038	60147
1987	1	47618	46377	52450	48377	51586	60952
SEMI-DETACHED HOUSES							
1984	1	24568	22116	23853	21577	23385	25792
	2	25462	22667	24467	22292	23657	26783
	3	25748	23061	24789	22734	24334	27421
	4	26808	23607	25282	22911	24518	28263
1985	1	26195	23270	25007	23390	24550	28019
	2	26151	23893	25911	23623	25092	29528
	3	26115	23899	25851	24058	24887	30250
	4	27108	24291	26308	24633	25445	30983
1986	1	26437	24460	26653	24533	25309	31201
	2	27521	25674	27840	25629	26674	33958
	3	28333	26317	28399	26460	27500	35381
	4	27971	26195	29252	27266	28615	37835
1987	1	28577	27152	29831	28364	29210	39653
TERRACED HOUSES							
1984	1	17176	14959	15833	15597	17298	20516
	2	17980	15485	15904	16436	17860	21729
	3	18122	15700	16876	16474	18134	22193
	4	18941	15853	17057	17031	18298	23209
1985	1	18681	16035	17160	17502	18378	23833
	2	18993	16411	17186	17862	19008	24985
	3	18298	16322	17330	18146	18344	24851
	4	18760	16815	17513	17969	19114	25670
1986	1	18317	17018	18135	19016	19626	26904
	2	18665	17662	19004	19363	19843	28061
	3	19741	18389	19567	20080	20696	29020
	4	19991	18499	19673	21296	21317	30614
1987	1	21256	19168	20600	21690	21711	33189

£

South East	Greater London	South West	Wales	Scotland	Northern Ireland
59738	81830	45902	38286	41036	39333
62753	85334	48048	38174	44816	38585
65688	84666	49946	39912	43790	38662
65798	89885	51742	40793	43538	41771
65055	94073	50024	39033	41695	38811
70107	93882	53720	39425	47299	41145
73750	98889	56208	40182	46384	45277
77581	104907	56971	42021	47663	44460
79791	115549	55891	41207	46276	41477
84662	119476	59838	42339	48855	46993
90790	124494	63107	46481	48926	45699
92423	129370	64456	45965	48009	44555
93261	137929	65018	46764	49846	44843
36387	48430	29587	23129	29862	23138
37163	49263	30203	23614	31040	23477
38762	51880	30781	24615	31029	24250
39464	52329	31881	23955	31259	24611
40905	54997	32080	24099	31108	24871
41735	58936	33058	24328	32800	25140
42760	59800	33292	24772	32239	25473
45125	62789	33855	25097	32499	24981
45866	67010	35209	25240	32780	25509
49621	70258	36291	26468	33475	26965
52225	76215	38536	27459	33176	27156
55205	76840	40150	27823	33643	27396
57776	80914	41144	28362	35520	26733
29384	39266	24115	17699	26768	15980
30457	40687	24677	18253	27267	15772
31206	41940	25220	18693	28284	16303
32377	42940	26206	18734	28401	15651
33177	44186	26752	19576	26571	16947
34489	46807	27022	18818	28165	15838
34160	49407	27580	19288	28311	16151
36160	52252	28375	19501	28844	16845
37374	55468	28761	18883	27745	16888
40255	59224	29892	19900	28502	18918
42572	62760	31969	20829	28534	18703
45002	64949	32369	20463	30596	18555
48440	68882	34974	20839	31356	18835

HALIFAX BUILDING SOCIETY

AVERAGE PRICES (at approval stage) 1984 –

11.4 REGIONS: TYPE OF DWELLING (continued)

Year		North	Yorks & Humberside	North West	East Midlands	West Midlands	East Anglia
BUNGALOWS							
1984	1	28533	27997	30836	29681	32597	31131
	2	30549	29106	31673	30686	33829	30649
	3	32774	29700	33700	31796	35294	31700
	4	32235	30859	32800	31757	34967	32577
1985	1	31586	29735	32776	30650	36220	32916
	2	32857	31028	33358	32033	36308	34329
	3	31782	31097	33821	31417	37790	34464
	4	32874	31305	34216	34377	39950	35795
1986	1	33684	30978	35016	32887	35429	37025
	2	34310	32500	35866	33897	38323	37523
	3	34557	34726	38255	36926	39070	40666
	4	35122	33311	37724	37022	44336	42338
1987	1	35756	34031	39019	38490	42239	45135
FLATS AND MAISONETTES							
1984	1	13962	18253	19569	16037	17625	19450
	2	14679	18170	19891	17796	18600	20746
	3	15319	17781	20096	18871	18379	24492
	4	15107	19859	20364		18999	23078
1985	1	15957	19038	20146	19803	20213	20539
	2	15191	18339	19596	18244	18608	21453
	3	15033	19362	19327	17245	17843	24083
	4	15218	19248	20599	20498	18000	24877
1986	1	15620	18987	21974	19490	17936	23938
	2	16396	19067	21377	18619	19075	24785
	3	16699	19176	23269	20454	18851	26009
	4	17294	19596	22172	24113	20686	27875
1987	1	17876	20596	22939	20850	20940	28985

					£
South East	Greater London	South West	Wales	Scotland	Northern Ireland
43536	54150	36301	27712	33367	29048
46888	54572	39103	27490	34921	29475
49481	59800	39912	28506	34308	31251
48883	61047	39750	28473	34813	30201
49695	59867	40279	29856	35372	30645
50779	68874	41060	28887	37982	30294
53685	62770	41423	29231	37012	32287
56376	67413	42425	29162	38072	31102
55799	67519	43111	31126	36231	31619
59724	78433	45081	30402	38314	31946
64576	82157	47570	33647	39059	32641
66268	81309	50224	33368	38529	32660
68157	80366	49584	34382	40354	32200
25846	31768	23492	18201	20964	
26941	32750	22354	20241	21715	
27558	33398	23524	22703	21892	
28056	34640	23971	19859	22766	
28814	35960	24851	20021	22976	
29134	39102	26282	19233	22773	
29735	39274	25442	19983	22593	
30999	43601	24907	21062	22422	
31712	44951	25627	21767	22087	
32889	50155	27585	21103	23521	
35141	52750	28644	21817	23339	
37908	53965	29906	22617	24455	
40944	57323	31505		25203	

HALIFAX BUILDING SOCIETY

AVERAGE PRICES (at approval stage) 1984 –

11.5 UNITED KINGDOM AND REGIONS BY AGE OF HOUSE:
TYPE OF DWELLING

Year	UNITED KINGDOM					NORTH				
	Pre-1919	1919-1945	1946-1960	Post-1960	New	Pre-1919	1919-1945	1946-1960	Post-1960	New
DETACHED HOUSES										
1984 1	50061	52168	53227	42738	46262	47699			38136	42846
2	52486	54424	55052	44421	47838	47947	48843		37798	43160
3	55020	55625	56536	45266	47881	43048			40332	38851
4	55069	53859	57412	45380	47718	46045			39628	39151
1985 1	52693	56150	57567	44988	48304				38884	39803
2	54917	59058	62044	47114	49883	43976			39490	39289
3	58733	62111	62881	48468	50849	47730			40772	39210
4	62818	65720	66769	50774	53975	48387			39576	42116
1986 1	65276	69067	71400	52226	54195				40793	41356
2	68277	73697	74159	54637	58048	54796			42967	42063
3	71119	75129	73546	56755	60142	55681			42231	47496
4	71643	74243	76278	57255	60780	51274			42332	45324
1987 1	72553	74557	76009	59738	63607				45417	46911
SEMI-DETACHED HOUSES										
1984 1	32608	28615	28403	26028	26526	31348	23269	25654	24215	24482
2	32558	29975	29285	26858	26778	30074	25658	25522	24976	24585
3	34448	30352	30789	27618	27526	28531	26243	26267	25021	25157
4	34784	30756	30647	27817	27272	32537	27234	26764	25869	25592
1985 1	34343	30651	29857	27848	27734	28859	26560	27297	25330	26020
2	36361	32169	31019	28399	28288	31677	25200	26981	25559	26303
3	35947	31796	30878	28516	29355	31091	25823	25175	25874	26383
4	39349	33357	32201	29443	30133	38887	26943	26274	25888	26313
1986 1	39976	34836	32173	30385	30263	31178	26066	26091	26032	26494
2	43130	37692	34323	31517	31594	32115	27922	27010	27073	26319
3	46235	39499	36003	32966	33297	35269	29042	26721	27449	28009
4	45789	40313	36474	33979	33970	34143	27773	27128	27470	27548
1987 1	47953	40854	38811	35598	36980	36193	27708	29791	27574	28760
TERRACED HOUSES										
1984 1	19652	24434	25584	26374	27697	16210	17056		20126	21443
2	20532	25559	25550	27319	28193	17141	17166		20889	21748
3	21653	25969	27553	28127	28278	17277	17131		21770	23998
4	21658	26376	27835	29084	28369	18328	18243		21642	23661
1985 1	21473	26067	28208	28471	30006	18137	17383		21759	22618
2	22352	26687	27257	29110	29713	18409	17336		21588	24075
3	22486	26979	27363	28996	30735	17546	17765		21495	24637
4	23506	28364	28391	30292	32866	18106	18210		21928	23791
1986 1	24139	30677	27919	30794	34707	17842	18075		21673	
2	26155	32716	30781	32800	37292	18001	18482	18520	21817	
3	27866	35603	33941	34318	39425	19500	18382		22041	
4	28745	36817	34480	36108	39355	19315	19309		23197	
1987 1	30238	38522	35805	38532	44755	20546	19981		25008	

YORKSHIRE & HUMBERSIDE

Pre-1919	1919-1945	1946-1960	Post-1960	New
38995	40620	40336	34927	36029
44296	42150	43630	36404	36854
47286	41926	44051	36224	36771
50083	40968	44348	37607	37799
38411	44268	42059	35830	36147
45729	47731	44573	37147	38492
46131	43978	45362	38984	40061
46127	43438	50939	40027	41428
50317	41576	42824	39535	40224
54990	52336	53249	40831	41702
48961	48105	51770	42386	41499
51481	44546		41868	44041
55397	49386	55873	43243	46355
26512	21413	21160	21954	22573
24614	22261	21937	22510	23954
25004	22495	23295	23139	22758
28494	22979	23048	23447	23093
26680	22576	22795	23306	23265
26927	23593	22508	23907	24437
27505	23283	22727	23973	23961
28725	23697	23326	24175	24406
26999	24002	22335	24813	24750
30241	25690	23604	25333	25356
31484	26135	24735	25811	25536
31308	25789	23872	25909	27004
33009	26652	25067	26896	27086
14175	15320	15916	17745	20719
14779	15661		18409	21125
14814	16365	15823	18807	21897
15117	16484		19049	21808
15219	16492		19456	22458
15646	16697	16123	19649	22547
15607	16764	17366	19705	22232
16196	17136	18050	19669	22567
16167	17617	17695	19984	24539
16962	18165	19439	20518	22345
17622	18941	19387	21312	26560
17840	18953	20169	21100	23504
18470	19019	20122	21501	26701

NORTH WEST

Pre-1919	1919-1945	1946-1960	Post-1960	New
53567	46889	49711	37703	41543
57440	48694	51890	39292	43660
55331	52794	48192	40652	41886
55345	49962	49919	39388	43467
50343	48457	46846	39776	43657
54129	48407	52585	41870	43344
57364	52615	56130	42499	43898
65096	52087	55362	44598	46815
59269	52845	57214	44973	48228
68024	56438	57214	46234	47081
64959	62229	60008	47338	50190
67348	63575		50068	48441
69251	61018	59362	47072	53286
27138	24186	25068	22340	23889
27440	24477	26144	23331	23475
28179	24669	26081	23509	24065
29989	25106	26171	24067	23979
27468	24973	25478	24287	24467
28721	26312	27007	24452	25036
29247	25662	27361	24369	25827
30819	26072	27322	24705	26513
29997	26906	26749	25467	26327
32310	28044	28473	26267	27422
34155	28531	29766	26506	26751
35771	29510	28963	27173	27760
38909	29420	29109	27975	29944
14866	17295	17272	19758	22524
14938	16757	17882	19633	21877
15933	17707	17983	20538	21143
16194	17272	19122	21270	20569
16152	18433	20209	20601	21938
16252	17702	19218	20871	23254
16479	17766	19775	20796	23928
16708	17781	18755	21604	25216
17332	18696	19130	21482	25570
18240	19182	20157	22047	25142
18666	19939	19199	22936	27833
18629	20036	21867	23266	28445
19648	20498	21328	24025	30419

EAST MIDLANDS

Pre-1919	1919-1945	1946-1960	Post-1960	New
40334	34201	36038	34636	39337
43908	38829	38571	36638	40686
42415	39916	38797	36656	40472
38939	38153	40676	36679	43726
46805	37705	43928	38092	43318
43038	40990	42539	37793	42965
48560	41652	46295	39025	40741
52331	42107	44344	40141	45351
53068	44439	43851	40675	45102
49722	44360	47281	41297	48048
51324	45188	46865	44273	49424
52758	47079	46328	44869	48895
53814	48782	50413	45756	50693
21901	21582	20695	21749	21304
24131	21421	21465	22427	22145
24518	21868	22450	22926	22239
23795	21987	22884	23229	22894
24977	22215	24002	23717	22752
22650	23538	24418	23956	23232
25283	23214	23832	24318	23789
27146	24190	23838	24208	24728
24347	23689	23103	25371	24951
26084	25372	24164	25895	25904
27830	25603	25761	26687	26421
28204	26511	26623	27580	27435
28290	27298	27699	29047	29089
14394	16028		18516	20771
15187	16182	17844	19285	21442
15372	16840		19279	21034
15854	16231		19375	22450
16389	16430		20065	22126
16821	17216		20343	21757
17038	18339	17400	20594	22797
16988	18140	18665	20680	22036
18048	18683	18912	21468	22715
18447	19284	18754	21326	23959
19319	19279		22005	25408
20380	20026		23580	26016
20523	22524			25343

HALIFAX BUILDING SOCIETY

AVERAGE PRICES (at approval stage) 1984 –

11.5 UNITED KINGDOM AND REGIONS BY AGE OF HOUSE: TYPE OF DWELLING (continued)

Year	WEST MIDLANDS					EAST ANGLIA				
	Pre-1919	1919-1945	1946-1960	Post-1960	New	Pre-1919	1919-1945	1946-1960	Post-1960	New
DETACHED HOUSES										
1984 1	46628	46235	44260	37059	40328	51208	41456		38835	42107
2	51688	43844	48152	37234	42129	49688	43397		40278	42740
3	51935	45140	48503	38486	42406	55340	52209		43265	42672
4	46511	42822	47022	38838	40205	55980	47866		44584	45543
1985 1	45528	45383	47013	38423	43645	50621			41649	45525
2	49427	44835	55830	41272	44143	52603			45227	47600
3	52805	51275	53342	39210	45283	57656	44772		45695	47751
4	51791	51130	51698	41820	44878	54069	50962		47543	48771
1986 1	53297	50937	53781	41516	44452	61764			49521	53634
2	57485	50936	56807	43166	47253	67690	61251		51849	55303
3	62752	52521	57592	44431	48693	66940	65426		53676	56521
4	63949	56608	59471	44503	51958	70718			55492	62811
1987 1	62610	54399	59512	49028	50270	72992			57727	61166
SEMI-DETACHED HOUSES										
1984 1	27301	23210	24065	22336	23354	27583	25750		25476	23746
2	27218	23331	25154	22556	23846	27917	27674	26809	26432	25264
3	28186	24130	26017	22996	23514	29556	29233		26296	25511
4	28066	23791	26326	23734	23797	29841	29712		27223	26288
1985 1	25597	24292	26979	23736	24760	28048	31598		27781	26002
2	28280	25189	26384	23753	24693	32855	30050	29241	28516	27068
3	27952	24863	26452	23628	25027	32956	31000		29201	27915
4	28262	25393	27420	24098	24848	31686	31822	31448	30505	30176
1986 1	28366	25230	25964	24711	24668	32897	31364	31070	31850	29232
2	30195	26701	28979	25397	25970	37893	34211	32733	32574	32593
3	30721	27503	29800	26226	26362	39407	36727	32402	33666	33302
4	33790	28738	28374	27138	28972	40750	40011	37939	37342	32321
1987 1	34480	28167	30288	28462	28583	43150	42437		38619	36139
TERRACED HOUSES										
1984 1	15834	17117		19879	21302	19417			23148	22255
2	16634	17560	18405	19835	22010	21132			22425	23669
3	16895	17445		20866	23357	21432			23435	23933
4	16959	18025		21590	21465	22581			24147	25006
1985 1	17284	17175		20874	22367	22583			25373	
2	17692	18332	20255	21427	24203	23720			26873	28245
3	17036	18458	18619	20969	22970	24246			25850	25741
4	18022	18760	20957	21277	22635	24316	24765		27126	29025
1986 1	18248	19105	19297	21814	25848	25912			27932	29484
2	18202	20174	20927	22363	26023	27192			29176	30449
3	19649	20595	22251	22443		28111			30214	29962
4	19540	20885		24139		29311			31718	32664
1987 1	20051	21757		24340		32496			33468	37481

SOUTH EAST					GREATER LONDON					SOUTH WEST				
Pre-1919	1919-1945	1946-1960	Post-1960	New	Pre-1919	1919-1945	1946-1960	Post-1960	New	Pre-1919	1919-1945	1946-1960	Post-1960	New
65442	65051	66555	56535	58525	86139	84007	77895	75739	82917	47832	45588	45249	44924	46195
72265	66136	72181	58977	61116	81678	91365	77451	85997	81172	48127	48386	52556	47533	47658
78647	72125	75516	60989	60548	89515	84250	82544	91682	71119	53620	48544	53421	47361	50241
79478	67431	77900	61631	61656	80969	89662				56953	50640		48689	51155
75336	69967	78201	60868	62281		98435				52228	52006		47588	50171
83773	76246	81893	64988	65698		96824	87757	87131		54489	56268	58603	52140	52700
91354	80631	84782	67722	68869	85785	104497	94738	98465		61280	56990	64059	53007	54792
95329	86403	88855	69972	73914	99605	108984	106415	108496		62587	54746	61371	53616	57142
101619	89534	100179	72488	73927	120845	123075	106186	109643		58961	61018	56725	53337	55242
100546	96886	101418	77390	80642	131524	121666	120892	106853	115796	64237	67824	67254	56162	56890
110039	102629	101472	82613	87197	134169	127578	123890	114156		71925	63560	73146	58701	60681
118300	102562	110627	83442	87551		135309		126923		70242	68835	72590	60271	63236
107819	101713	106709	88046	91441		131390		133077	144222	69787	69199		62435	63981
37834	36768	38012	35356	34816	53099	47767	43834	46593		30777	30276	31321	28832	27743
38573	38948	39140	35859	33820	49450	50126	47729	47676	41175	32666	31314	30665	29219	27877
40238	39698	41904	37287	35760	56016	51766	48203	49502	41425	33268	31603	31892	29640	28875
41838	40871	42459	37781	35201	53852	53152	50871	47848	40018	33895	33853	32476	30525	29863
43628	42667	42223	39083	37373	58823	55141	51025	53286	47084	36464	32991	32015	30946	28659
45183	42732	44041	39791	37224	63295	59733	52743	50964	50560	37086	34425	33225	31638	29883
46000	43494	44244	40768	39517	62881	60261	53250	53538	56932	35873	34506	34059	32301	31058
49894	46090	46682	42433	40820	69741	61734	59830	55701	55311	37035	34926	33486	32691	30981
49428	48244	47873	43554	41763	75820	66225	56073	62281		39466	36784	36986	33292	32242
55984	51174	51240	46264	46731	77969	70052	62604	59062	60552	40159	38229	35594	34592	33738
59206	52909	53671	48770	49698	85758	75458	65543	69729	66337	43743	39269	37190	36476	35839
58913	58170	57144	52182	49989	83073	77509	69512	68728	65221	46729	42082	37604	37490	36832
61949	59893	58760	55339	55610	87445	81811	71303	70591		47354	42719	40193	39378	37368
26916	28109	30641	31460	31545	39553	37430	36789	43586	40916	23653	23510		24967	24512
28052	29436	31327	32284	32317	39974	39641	37546	47681	42026	24246	24703		24975	25600
29148	30885	32540	33188	31747	41993	40330	41314	46412	42729	24687	25809	25892	25409	26489
30309	31285	34036	34411	32604	42783	42344	40038	47807	41130	25823	26585		26757	26239
31133	31987	34741	34594	34699	43744	43795	41317	47561	44740	26522	26814		26950	27197
32004	33340	35833	36844	35162	47624	45807	42489	48928	44152	26659	26644		27535	27336
31694	33565	35398	35996	37327	50476	46602	48106	52760	49276	28221	26973	27017	27349	26002
34152	34618	36372	37742	38851	54507	48146	47182	52672	57140	28671	28850	27294	28160	27581
34708	36603	37926	38754	42679	57656	51353	46290	57346	64308	28434	30055		28944	29275
38363	37970	39859	41774	42829	60671	54626	51805	63138	71422	29952	30161	29409	29838	29735
40287	42648	44097	43898	45592	65202	58233	56679	64635	68016	32363	31441	31532	31165	33005
42934	44915	44294	46376	47206	68113	60675	55090	65131	68442	32324	31645		32472	32993
46173	47266	51185	49693	51191	72438	63718	57819	68918	76199	35400	34105		34571	36073

HALIFAX BUILDING SOCIETY

AVERAGE PRICES (at approval stage) 1984 –

11.5 UNITED KINGDOM AND REGIONS BY AGE OF HOUSE:
TYPE OF DWELLING (continued)

£

Year	WALES Pre-1919	1919-1945	1946-1960	Post-1960	New	SCOTLAND Pre-1919	1919-1945	1946-1960	Post-1960	New	NORTHERN IRELAND Pre-1919	1919-1945	1946-1960	Post-1960	New
DETACHED HOUSES															
1984 1	38452	39972		35814	41284	39161			39730	44003					44255
2	34462	40500		6595	43277	42792	51627		43798	47511				37271	40085
3	37171	39561		38720	45920	42602			41545	50213		41035		37007	
4	38289	44811		38869	46376	42028			43892	44968				40536	
1985 1	39216			38143	46069	37802			41603	44443					
2	36355	43637		38451	41100	43186			46486	53820				38996	
3	37897	43522		38712	42793	44281			45767	47812				42960	
4	39345			40354	49317	46531			45607	50151				45670	45208
1986 1	39943			40281	45161	39510			46338	54389					39737
2	38990	38304		43219	44017	47255			46614	51732				46364	48551
3	46748	45549		44702	50240	48016			46412	54487				45151	
4	43819	47424		46666	45172	42803			47491	53796				40268	49780
1987 1	43331			43348	53981	47712			47973	56300				44633	
SEMI-DETACHED HOUSES															
1984 1	23568	22750	25879	22508	24699	30394	32056		28742	30816	21956			23105	23380
2	22581	24624	29781	22510	23719	34117	33550	29856	29871	30751	22160	23752		23817	23444
3	24409	25650	29565	23306	24925	32741	34988	32115	29538	31265	22420	24387		24495	24088
4	23530	24245	27589	23254	24988	32368	34309	34762	29865	31005	22911	25665		24459	24838
1985 1	23421	24869		23648	23077	34600	30878		30240	30489	22226	26540		25053	24405
2	23900	25474	26751	23311	25498	36066	37484	33575	30880	30724	24774	25072		25534	24973
3	24780	26595	27832	23457	23887	34579	35780	33297	30663	32078	24548	25364		25328	25297
4	23681	26588	28340	24087	26433	35415	34569	31435	31103	32434	23526	26038		24775	25672
1986 1	23717	26470	27127	25111	25004	35496	34558	33480	31094	34345	24184			25434	25999
2	25891	28397	27816	25806	25295	38029	35799	33084	31600	33160	28227	26313		25932	26147
3	26861	28446	27862	26944	28277	35884	37834	34295	31437	33264	28315	25937		25891	26895
4	29810	28512	30965	26457	26841	36808	35488	32649	31970	34615				26479	27493
1987 1	26978	30830	32640	27058	29058	41149	37133		33015	35596	25018			27008	27573
TERRACED HOUSES															
1984 1	16409	18324		21435	22606	29775			23864	28061	15398	14386			
2	16882	19519		20880	22098	28998	28286		25361	29196	15405	14470			
3	17427	19840		20803	23311	30624	29186		26460	28513	16374	14185			
4	17439	19250		22931	21647	29207			27563	28221	14996	14099			
1985 1	18883	18859		22385	21613	26196			25514	27907	16896	15489			
2	17758	19692		21470	22329	30996	29183		26198	28397	15624	14378			
3	18025	20959		22682	22298	31270	31032		26355	28758	16232	14810			
4	18491	20830		22042	23864	32014	33057	26932	29110	16595	15791				
1986 1	18103	19480		21902	22796	27672			26274	29531	16667	15267			
2	18989	21431		23433	23599	31378	30838		25881	31311	18508	17007		20614	
3	19724	22694		24409		30062	29680		26550	32445	18845	16729		19517	
4	19468			23309		35512			28264	29633	18387	16211			
1987 1	19544	25237		23432		34968			27808		18929	16923			

Year	Pre-1919	1919-1945	1946-1960	Post-1960	New	Pre-1919	1919-1945	1946-1960	Post-1960	New
BUNGALOWS										
1984 1	30466	37273	37013	31282	33260		24332		27508	35947
2	32302	37908	39314	33234	33341		26646	34314	30053	34543
3	32676	39989	41412	33966	35744		27705	34271	33065	40158
4	30041	40099	40936	34368	34571		31026		33158	35310
1985 1	33973	39423	40653	34211	34866		29662		30406	37462
2	34031	40217	41474	35247	36747		29663	35116	32935	38869
3	30621	41550	42577	35560	36943		24603		33129	38608
4	32264	43431	42975	36861	37877		28771	36666	32094	38210
1986 1	37261	44552	45770	36736	38229		25213		34302	39727
2	36782	45349	49197	38873	39629		24873		35696	40521
3	39349	51054	51138	40809	40459		30540		34418	40873
4	34793	50355	51179	40482	41168		29500		36125	39045
1987 1	41866	52548	53301	41677	42238		28852		36591	39565
FLATS AND MAISONETTES										
1984 1	26448	26210	26985	25049	25296	13299	12011		15464	
2	27205	26629	28405	25597	26623	14172	13052		15177	
3	27458	27168	27734	26237	27313	14248	14194		16222	
4	28670	27768	29174	27181	27580	13836			15584	
1985 1	29869	28856	29008	26711	28061	15701			17041	
2	30644	29897	30737	26841	29133	14776	14021		15717	
3	30030	30512	27840	26765	30002	14599	14207		15736	
4	31935	31256	30825	28135	32707	14573	14597		16106	
1986 1	33593	33362	30863	29019	33485	15080	14873		16423	
2	37231	38181	36909	30383	37732	16611	15398		16026	
3	38971	39365	37322	33063	39435	16517	15119		16467	
4	40448	40339	37347	34850	43930	17652	15745		16579	
1987 1	45502	43464	45708	36946	46730	17746			17711	

HALIFAX BUILDING SOCIETY

AVERAGE PRICES (at approval stage) 1984 –

11.5 UNITED KINGDOM AND REGIONS BY AGE OF HOUSE: TYPE OF DWELLING (continued)

		YORKSHIRE & HUMBERSIDE					NORTH WEST				
		Pre-1919	1919-1945	1946-1960	Post-1960	New	Pre-1919	1919-1945	1946-1960	Post-1960	New
BUNGALOWS											
1984	1		31278	29629	26595	30139		31570	32375	29800	33415
	2		30617	31928	28236	29744		32375	33936	30379	34124
	3		32113	32292	28377	30962		36493	35553	32115	36281
	4		31838	33475	30307	30592		36143	34523	31537	34390
1985	1		28368	31431	29294	30838		34353	36752	30945	35732
	2		30964	32391	30581	32047		38783	32990	31844	36176
	3		32424	31115	30668	32653		36011	36095	31979	35926
	4		32192	31129	30817	32442		35735	34347	32264	38800
1986	1		34147	34151	29745	33081		34132	36349	33895	40115
	2		33315	33504	32224	32541		35223	40226	35009	36472
	3		38233	37891	33789	35298		39658	43579	36773	39226
	4		37195	37905	31888	34378		37235	45323	36251	40027
1987	1		37361	35524	32792	36621		42511	38024	37493	42625
FLATS AND MAISONETTES											
1984	1				17229	20593	17799			19000	20953
	2	19811			16083	21142				18732	21372
	3				16965	18967				20934	19990
	4				18556					19931	21024
1985	1				16785					19115	21757
	2				16907		20765			19752	20055
	3	21206			17816		18867			19452	21196
	4	22079			17415		19526			19791	25086
1986	1	20604			17128		22759			21100	23410
	2	20934			18174		21108			21047	
	3	17881			18919		27759			21807	
	4	19864			19191	20499				20510	
1987	1				19358					20602	

EAST MIDLANDS					WEST MIDLANDS					EAST ANGLIA				
Pre-1919	1919-1945	1946-1960	Post-1960	New	Pre-1919	1919-1945	1946-1960	Post-1960	New	Pre-1919	1919-1945	1946-1960	Post-1960	New
	30671	31114	28906	30695			36023	30536	33842	29802			30521	30735
	32403	31852	30481	29735		33424	35656	33107	35520	35583	31019		29872	31335
	29065	34015	31216	33716				33442	35432	33511	35126		30804	30599
			30759	31659				33716					31454	
		29841	31338	29750				34715			34450		32124	
	30018	34283	31024	35415		37851		35120	36351		35243		33939	36554
	30125	31206	31530	32556			42994	36365	40960	35193	37700		32676	39986
	32317	34341	33788	37965			38286	33075	41281		38450		35159	
	31882	36778	32569	32963		37623		33635	38668				35868	39271
	40436	36011	33386	35628				35432		34051	38766		37278	39924
	38621		35172	39651			44569	36198	42129	39088	43042		40535	41839
			34798	42595				39877	53998					41865
			38343	40277				40143			49352		43431	
			16161					17424	18580					
			17088					17398	20111				20471	21700
			16483					17525	19431				22683	
								17333	20367					
								19049	20816					
								18402	19967				20798	
			16859		16904			17508	17683				21946	
			17418					17508					23158	
			16319					17654					23580	
			17959		24799			18348					22586	
			19136					18408					25591	
			21827					19675					26375	
			20081					20287						

HALIFAX BUILDING SOCIETY

AVERAGE PRICES (at approval stage) 1984 –

11.5 UNITED KINGDOM AND REGIONS BY AGE OF HOUSE: TYPE OF DWELLING (continued)

	SOUTH EAST					GREATER LONDON					SOUTH WEST				
	Pre-1919	1919-1945	1946-1960	Post-1960	New	Pre-1919	1919-1945	1946-1960	Post-1960	New	Pre-1919	1919-1945	1946-1960	Post-1960	New
BUNGALOWS															
1984 1		43616	43542	41840	51600		50195				35530	37019	35380		41579
2		45139	46967	47602	47984		49447				38088	40608	38869		41217
3		48881	50030	48591	51838		54489				39601	43046	39722		38721
4		48221	49095	48815	50868		55226				37506	39377	39741		43576
1985 1		47989	50984	49418	51583		56344				37690	42407	41411		36799
2		46804	51535	51421	58590		63998				39953	43311	39917		44180
3		51367	54622	54585	58075		61004				40891	44430	40661		41593
4		53207	59791	56047	57285		63557				42180	48365	41823		44943
1986 1		54994	55261	55453	59364		61221				42381	44549	42044		42118
2		57130	62653	58715	64718		73935				42572	48605	44636		45691
3		62725	64036	64192	66867		78405				48782	51380	46943		45421
4			66341	68118	64319	71785				72076	49598	56780	48188		54655
1987 1		68313	70918	66171	65681		81434				47128	55540	48207		53050
FLATS AND MAISONETTES															
1984 1	23498	23512	26746	26751	27114	31772	29784	33916	32151	33683	23490			23347	24107
2	24270	24976	27513	27531	28677	32744	31468	32574	32967	35200	22228	19436		23268	22437
3	25597	26256	26701	27941	29673	33239	31625	32536	34893	35561	24135			22882	23609
4	24938	25843	28935	29682	28901	35048	32070	32781	34805	36820	23053			24169	24528
1985 1	26508	27673	29122	29446	30546	36270	33535	36159	36280	36716	25523			24879	24134
2	26709	27767	31085	29862	30954	39900	36265	40592	38076	40229	27623			26324	24545
3	27144	27862	30833	30689	32800	39824	37040	36487	39396	40931	26491			24058	25398
4	28700	28846	31701	31993	34087	44814	39010	41555	42390	46662	25235			24238	27279
1986 1	29224	29053	33115	32661	35747	46157	41693	41928	44020	45033	26888			23458	27070
2	30264	31635	36343	33395	37852	52071	47548	50033	46725	49621	28558			24727	36077
3	31778	33538	37525	36179	41388	54311	48617	51566	51330	52877	29074			27645	29977
4	34234	35933	38744	38685	44273	55166	48230	50900	51873	63473	31567			27851	
1987 1	38996	39010	42078	41415	44204	58667	52292	55812	55185	63486	32691			28196	

£

WALES					SCOTLAND					NORTHERN IRELAND				
Pre-1919	1919-1945	1946-1960	Post-1960	New	Pre-1919	1919-1945	1946-1960	Post-1960	New	Pre-1919	1919-1945	1946-1960	Post-1960	New
			26434	29846		34300		33673	33795				28744	29048
	25740	28837	27526	27901	25161	37781	43747	34492	34465				31026	27537
	27970	29079	28011	31279	27578	37210	42570	33241	35094				32562	30179
			28768		27886	39305	40129	34599	34171				32325	29013
			29877			39363		34388	36572				33434	28753
			28915			41770	42068	36962	37521				32196	28914
	27182		29300	31736	28004	40662	41688	35851	40108				34670	31323
	24807		29286	32276	25872	42394		38515	39157				31730	31019
			29723	36692	26360	41194		35166	38012				31806	31663
	27712		29766	33837	28845	41139		37840	41128				32933	31792
		40565	34217	32919	31303	44810	43154	37501	41706				33537	33214
			32259	33583	24876	43651		39018	39901				33694	32830
			32886			43051		39707	41506				33587	32063
			20068		19623	22664		22896	23716					
					21056	22303		22129	23870					
					21196	22048		22796	24684					
					22105	23064		22919	25101					
					22440	23199		22655	25154					
					22351	24797		21853	24864					
			21352		22111	23849	19182	22783	26271					
			19615		21550	23786	19971	23267	27081					
					21358	23834	19522	22138	26514					
			21758		22978	24861		22939	28636					
					22945	25782		22499	28867					
			22555		23780	26292		23934	30509					
					24371	24540		25040	32533					

HALIFAX BUILDING SOCIETY

STANDARDISED INDEX (at approval stage) 1983 –

11.6 UNITED KINGDOM:
ALL, NEW AND EXISTING DWELLINGS, TYPE OF BUYER

1983 = 100

Year	All	New	Existing	First-time Buyer	Former Owner-occupier
				TYPE OF BUYER	
1983	100.0	100.0	100.0	100.0	100.0
1984	107.2	106.9	107.1	107.6	107.3
1985	117.0	115.4	117.3	117.4	116.7
1986	129.9	126.6	130.6	129.6	129.3
1983 1	95.9	96.5	96.0	96.7	95.8
2	99.9	100.3	99.8	99.6	99.9
3	102.2	101.1	102.3	101.6	102.4
4	102.4	102.4	102.3	102.6	102.2
1984 1	102.9	103.7	102.7	103.8	103.0
2	106.5	106.9	106.3	106.8	106.7
3	109.2	108.2	109.2	109.4	109.3
4	111.0	109.3	111.0	111.3	110.5
1985 1	112.2	110.9	112.3	113.4	111.3
2	115.9	113.8	116.2	116.0	115.4
3	117.6	116.4	117.9	118.0	117.5
4	120.7	119.6	121.0	120.7	120.9
1986 1	122.5	120.9	123.0	123.7	122.2
2	128.6	125.2	129.4	128.4	128.0
3	133.1	129.5	134.0	132.7	132.3
4	136.9	132.6	137.8	136.5	135.9
1987 1	140.6	136.5	141.6	140.7	139.1

Year		All	New	Existing	TYPE OF BUYER	
					First-time Buyer	Former Owner-occupier
1983	Jan	94.8	96.1	94.7	95.6	94.9
	Feb	95.7	96.3	95.9	96.8	95.5
	Mar	96.9	97.0	97.0	97.4	96.7
	Apr	98.5	99.2	98.4	98.5	98.4
	May	100.3	101.1	100.3	99.8	100.3
	Jun	100.9	100.6	100.7	100.5	100.9
	Jul	102.1	100.9	102.2	101.8	102.0
	Aug	102.3	100.4	102.5	101.4	102.6
	Sep	102.2	101.9	102.3	101.6	102.6
	Oct	102.5	102.2	102.7	102.5	102.4
	Nov	102.4	102.4	102.4	102.4	102.2
	Dec	102.2	102.9	101.9	102.8	102.1
1984	Jan	101.7	102.6	101.5	102.4	102.2
	Feb	102.5	104.0	102.1	103.7	102.5
	Mar	104.0	104.5	103.9	104.9	103.9
	Apr	104.8	106.5	104.5	105.4	105.0
	May	106.4	107.0	106.2	106.9	106.5
	Jun	107.8	106.9	107.7	107.8	108.1
	Jul	108.9	107.7	108.9	108.9	109.1
	Aug	108.9	108.7	108.8	109.1	109.2
	Sep	110.0	108.5	110.0	110.5	109.7
	Oct	110.5	108.4	110.6	110.9	110.1
	Nov	111.4	109.6	111.2	111.8	110.6
	Dec	111.4	110.2	111.3	111.4	111.0
1985	Jan	111.3	110.9	111.3	112.5	110.8
	Feb	111.9	110.5	112.1	113.5	110.9
	Mar	113.1	111.1	113.4	114.1	112.1
	Apr	115.2	114.2	115.3	115.2	114.9
	May	115.7	113.5	116.1	116.2	115.1
	Jun	116.7	113.4	117.1	116.6	116.3
	Jul	116.4	115.5	116.6	117.0	116.1
	Aug	117.2	116.1	117.6	117.2	117.5
	Sep	118.9	117.3	119.3	119.4	118.8
	Oct	119.8	118.0	120.3	119.8	120.0
	Nov	120.5	119.7	120.8	120.8	120.7
	Dec	122.2	122.1	122.3	121.9	122.7
1986	Jan	121.0	120.3	121.4	122.3	120.7
	Feb	122.3	119.8	122.8	124.0	121.6
	Mar	124.0	122.5	124.6	124.6	123.9
	Apr	126.7	122.7	127.6	126.9	126.0
	May	128.4	125.4	129.1	128.1	127.8
	Jun	130.8	127.5	131.5	130.3	130.1
	Jul	132.3	128.3	133.3	131.7	131.5
	Aug	133.1	130.7	133.9	132.5	132.4
	Sep	134.1	129.8	135.1	134.2	133.1
	Oct	136.1	131.4	137.1	135.9	135.1
	Nov	136.9	132.5	137.8	136.6	135.7
	Dec	138.3	134.4	138.9	137.2	137.3
1987	Jan	137.4	134.7	138.2	138.0	136.2
	Feb	140.6	136.6	141.5	141.9	138.8
	Mar	142.9	137.6	144.2	141.9	141.2

HALIFAX BUILDING SOCIETY

STANDARDISED INDEX (at approval stage) 1983 –

11.7 REGIONS: ALL, NEW AND EXISTING DWELLINGS

Year		North	Yorks & Humberside	North West	East Midlands	West Midlands	East Anglia
ALL DWELLINGS							
1983		100.0	100.0	100.0	100.0	100.0	100.0
1984		104.8	106.1	103.9	106.9	103.9	108.4
1985		109.6	112.0	110.1	116.6	109.7	121.2
1986		114.5	119.6	118.9	126.8	119.4	138.9
1983	1	96.5	96.2	96.5	95.5	97.1	95.1
	2	98.8	100.2	100.2	100.4	101.2	99.2
	3	102.4	101.7	101.8	102.5	101.7	101.7
	4	102.6	102.2	101.5	102.0	100.2	104.2
1984	1	101.3	102.9	100.7	102.6	100.5	104.2
	2	104.3	105.7	103.3	106.8	103.6	107.0
	3	105.6	107.3	105.6	108.7	105.6	110.4
	4	108.5	108.7	106.7	110.4	106.6	113.3
1985	1	109.2	108.2	106.9	112.9	106.3	115.3
	2	109.7	111.5	109.2	115.3	109.5	120.9
	3	109.1	112.6	110.6	117.0	109.4	121.6
	4	110.3	114.3	113.1	119.8	112.4	125.1
1986	1	111.1	114.8	114.7	120.7	113.3	129.7
	2	113.9	119.5	119.0	124.9	118.0	137.6
	3	116.7	122.3	120.8	129.1	121.5	142.1
	4	116.9	122.6	121.6	133.6	126.2	149.0
1987	1	120.2	126.4	122.6	136.7	126.9	155.5
NEW DWELLINGS							
1983		100.0	100.0	100.0	100.0	100.0	100.0
1984		105.2	106.0	103.1	107.5	105.8	108.6
1985		107.4	111.6	109.4	116.3	110.8	121.8
1986		112.2	116.9	114.4	124.7	119.3	138.0
1983	1	96.2	96.3	96.2	95.6	97.2	95.7
	2	99.8	100.7	101.7	99.5	98.0	99.2
	3	102.4	101.0	100.3	102.4	100.6	100.5
	4	100.2	102.1	101.4	102.6	104.2	103.2
1984	1	104.9	103.0	102.3	104.1	102.8	104.6
	2	105.1	107.2	103.6	106.5	105.8	107.8
	3	104.8	107.0	103.1	109.7	107.9	110.5
	4	106.9	106.8	104.0	110.4	106.8	113.3
1985	1	107.2	108.2	106.9	112.7	107.9	114.4
	2	107.8	110.9	107.4	115.3	109.8	121.3
	3	108.0	112.3	109.3	115.3	110.8	123.8
	4	107.0	113.8	113.2	121.0	113.7	125.6
1986	1	109.6	114.1	113.1	117.8	112.4	128.2
	2	111.8	115.8	113.6	123.3	118.4	137.9
	3	114.8	119.0	116.5	126.6	121.2	139.8
	4	113.1	119.6	115.4	131.3	127.4	149.3
1987	1	117.4	124.1	116.7	136.1	123.7	151.6

South East	Greater London	South West	Wales	Scotland	Northern Ireland
100.0	100.0	100.0	100.0	100.0	100.0
109.7	111.6	106.3	104.5	109.1	107.9
123.9	131.2	117.7	111.1	115.9	114.1
144.3	159.6	131.6	118.3	119.9	121.4
95.6	95.7	96.5	96.4	94.4	96.3
99.2	99.2	100.2	102.2	102.9	102.5
102.8	102.6	101.8	102.2	102.9	102.5
103.3	103.2	101.7	100.4	103.6	101.4
104.4	105.9	102.0	100.9	103.8	103.4
108.6	110.3	105.2	104.1	109.1	107.2
112.5	114.0	108.4	107.3	110.1	111.4
114.8	117.8	110.9	105.7	112.4	111.4
116.8	121.4	112.5	108.3	111.9	112.9
121.9	128.2	116.6	109.2	116.7	113.4
124.6	132.7	118.9	112.6	116.3	114.8
129.8	139.3	121.0	113.2	117.5	114.9
133.1	145.1	123.2	112.0	115.4	115.2
141.7	156.2	129.5	117.0	120.1	124.9
149.5	166.6	135.2	122.2	121.1	123.2
157.1	174.1	139.7	123.4	123.3	122.1
165.1	182.9	143.0	125.6	124.5	121.8
100.0	100.0	100.0	100.0	100.0	100.0
109.2	107.8	106.7	105.5	106.8	108.9
122.1	123.2	115.3	111.4	113.6	115.4
141.7	151.1	127.3	117.7	120.3	121.4
95.9	97.1	97.7	96.4	98.0	95.9
100.2	101.9	98.9	103.8	99.2	101.5
101.8	101.8	102.2	98.1	100.0	100.8
103.5	99.8	102.0	101.9	103.3	101.5
105.6	104.6	102.8	101.2	102.2	106.5
109.0	106.9	106.3	104.7	107.6	107.8
110.2	109.2	108.7	108.6	108.7	111.1
112.6	112.6	109.8	107.4	109.2	112.7
114.8	116.4	111.2	106.7	109.6	108.9
118.7	117.2	114.3	109.2	112.8	112.9
124.9	125.3	115.4	110.6	115.0	117.2
127.8	135.2	119.9	115.2	117.3	120.5
131.9	137.2	121.0	116.9	116.7	117.2
139.3	149.6	126.3	115.8	120.6	118.7
147.2	157.8	129.6	121.1	121.5	124.2
152.5	164.5	135.0	119.2	123.0	127.9
160.1	169.2	139.6	130.2	125.1	123.9

HALIFAX BUILDING SOCIETY

STANDARDISED INDEX (at approval stage) 1983 –

11.7 REGIONS: ALL, NEW AND EXISTING DWELLINGS (continued)

Year	North	Yorks & Humberside	North West	East Midlands	West Midlands	East Anglia
EXISTING DWELLINGS						
1983	100.0	100.0	100.0	100.0	100.0	100.0
1984	104.7	105.9	103.8	106.7	103.6	108.1
1985	110.1	112.0	110.4	116.6	109.9	121.2
1986	115.3	120.1	119.7	127.3	120.2	139.2
1983 1	96.6	96.3	96.8	95.6	97.1	95.2
2	98.6	100.0	100.0	100.5	101.5	99.3
3	102.4	101.8	102.0	102.3	102.1	102.0
4	102.9	102.1	101.4	102.1	99.4	104.1
1984 1	100.8	102.8	100.5	102.1	100.1	104.0
2	104.2	105.3	103.1	106.9	103.3	106.4
3	105.9	107.0	105.6	108.6	105.4	110.3
4	108.6	108.6	106.7	110.1	106.4	113.1
1985 1	109.9	108.1	107.0	112.8	106.1	115.1
2	110.0	111.5	109.6	115.3	109.6	120.9
3	109.5	112.7	111.1	117.3	109.6	121.4
4	111.0	114.5	113.3	119.7	112.8	125.0
1986 1	111.9	115.0	115.1	121.4	113.9	130.0
2	114.7	120.2	119.9	125.3	118.9	137.6
3	117.3	122.8	121.7	129.9	122.7	142.6
4	117.9	123.1	122.7	133.9	126.6	148.9
1987 1	121.3	126.7	123.7	137.4	128.5	156.2

South East	Greater London	South West	Wales	Scotland	Northern Ireland
100.0	100.0	100.0	100.0	100.0	100.0
109.7	111.8	106.2	104.1	109.5	107.5
124.3	131.5	118.2	111.1	116.3	114.0
145.0	160.1	132.6	118.8	120.1	122.1
95.5	95.7	96.4	96.6	93.9	96.1
99.1	99.1	100.3	100.3	99.0	99.0
103.0	102.6	101.6	103.0	103.4	103.3
103.3	103.3	101.8	100.3	103.7	102.3
104.3	105.8	102.0	100.5	104.3	102.6
108.5	110.4	105.2	103.9	109.3	107.1
112.8	114.3	108.3	106.6	110.5	110.3
114.9	117.9	110.9	105.4	112.6	110.3
117.2	121.5	112.9	108.5	112.3	114.2
122.5	128.6	117.1	109.3	117.6	113.7
124.7	132.9	119.7	112.8	116.6	114.6
130.1	139.4	121.4	112.9	117.7	113.4
133.5	145.6	123.8	111.8	115.3	115.2
142.3	156.5	130.5	117.2	120.3	127.5
150.2	167.2	136.5	122.8	121.3	123.6
158.1	174.5	140.8	124.7	123.7	121.1
166.2	183.6	144.3	125.2	124.3	122.6

HALIFAX BUILDING SOCIETY

TIMES/HALIFAX SERIES OF AVERAGE PRICES (at approval stage) 1975-1982

11.8 UNITED KINGDOM: ALL, NEW AND EXISTING DWELLINGS - MONTHLY

£

Year		All	New	Existing	Year		All	New	Existing
1975	Jan	11508	12057	11396	1979	Jan	18337	21115	17924
	Feb	11229	11764	11115		Feb	18724	21868	18211
	Mar	11857	12640	11697		Mar	19272	22173	18841
	Apr	12077	12632	11967		Apr	19944	22874	19521
	May	12368	12907	12265		May	20532	23169	20175
	Jun	12712	13197	12625		Jun	20971	23252	20664
	Jul	12781	13174	12719		Jul	21857	23935	21576
	Aug	12822	13294	12747		Aug	22090	24989	21721
	Sep	12626	13106	12547		Sep	21864	24087	21576
	Oct	12747	13268	12670		Oct	22394	25315	22005
	Nov	12631	13167	12546		Nov	22739	25123	22418
	Dec	12648	13488	12513		Dec	22689	26261	22215
1976	Jan	12868	13696	12723	1980	Jan	22980	26700	22440
	Feb	12740	13491	12606		Feb	22956	27232	22345
	Mar	13025	13877	12866		Mar	23496	28105	22839
	Apr	13390	13937	13285		Apr	24103	28877	23471
	May	13538	14244	13409		May	24548	29250	23919
	Jun	13664	14476	13521		Jun	25008	28615	24568
	Jul	13936	14482	13843		Jul	25243	29648	24748
	Aug	13751	14584	13608		Aug	24971	29866	24450
	Sep	13665	14485	13532		Sep	25013	29909	24481
	Oct	13499	14397	13355		Oct	24924	29694	24409
	Nov	13678	14383	13564		Nov	24982	29507	24493
	Dec	13594	14659	13421		Dec	24963	30797	24356
1977	Jan	13565	14855	13351	1981	Jan	24930	30270	24341
	Feb	13305	14566	13107		Feb	25289	30961	24631
	Mar	13407	14742	13198		Mar	25451	30012	24913
	Apr	13796	14953	13614		Apr	25848	31306	25226
	May	13823	15092	13635		May	25880	31141	25317
	Jun	14188	15367	14021		Jun	25813	30620	25310
	Jul	14309	15544	14137		Jul	25781	30318	25314
	Aug	14437	15938	14239		Aug	25171	29894	24665
	Sep	14453	15881	14264		Sep	24575	29113	24105
	Oct	14606	15958	14409		Oct	23952	28886	23436
	Nov	14799	16344	14583		Nov	24205	29398	23615
	Dec	15006	17179	14703		Dec	24725	30043	24061
1978	Jan	15189	17491	14828	1982	Jan	24179	30650	23493
	Feb	14967	17189	14607		Feb	23983	30336	23293
	Mar	15626	17843	15235		Mar	24494	30235	23878
	Apr	15743	18105	15337		Apr	25333	30590	24781
	May	15827	18095	15467		May	26037	31156	25479
	Jun	16690	18703	16390		Jun	26430	31857	25884
	Jul	17379	19320	17102		Jul	26920	31039	26528
	Aug	17572	19821	17255		Aug	27770	32340	27264
	Sep	17753	19312	17533		Sep	27634	31798	27193
	Oct	17679	20513	17306		Oct	27717	33685	27067
	Nov	18111	20439	17785		Nov	27920	32117	27439
	Dec	18243	21309	17818		Dec	27447	31786	26921

HALIFAX BUILDING SOCIETY

TIMES/HALIFAX SERIES OF AVERAGE PRICES (at approval stage) 1976-1982

11.9 UNITED KINGDOM AND REGIONS: ALL DWELLINGS - QUARTERLY

Year		United Kingdom	North	Yorks & Humberside	North West	East Midlands	West Midlands
1976	1	12892	10271	9576	10485	10542	12784
	2	13532	10811	10249	11143	11173	13382
	3	13780	11375	10447	11410	11774	13584
	4	13592	11161	10356	11206	11474	13642
1977	1	13419	11388	9922	10952	11220	13189
	2	13937	12064	10504	11593	11523	13943
	3	14401	12317	10749	12105	11869	14223
	4	14794	12844	11069	12529	12147	14824
1978	1	15264	13347	11549	12741	12402	14539
	2	16100	13739	11999	13573	12952	15671
	3	17571	14585	12731	14725	14080	16682
	4	17993	15152	13040	15209	14648	17071
1979	1	18815	15312	13553	15930	14796	17740
	2	20495	16483	14250	17298	16177	19266
	3	21938	17495	15340	18380	17751	19777
	4	22598	17568	16312	19103	18067	20561
1980	1	23164	18015	16974	19200	18769	21497
	2	24560	18706	18106	20371	19463	22591
	3	25083	19415	18059	21044	20207	23719
	4	24955	19321	18631	20801	20407	23096
1981	1	25253	19752	18603	21264	20824	23518
	2	25846	19764	19499	22013	21685	24028
	3	25181	19471	19449	21781	21092	23543
	4	24259	18743	18175	20843	21021	22648
1982	1	24258	18108	17461	20873	20197	22804
	2	25939	19969	19376	21609	21665	23423
	3	27439	21410	20520	22795	22667	24989
	4	27709	21686	19998	22270	23058	25666

£

East Anglia	South East	Greater London	South West	Wales	Scotland	Northern Ireland
12542	16756	16243	13553	10861	12888	10701
12656	17564	16688	14180	10974	13805	12661
13013	17497	16704	14029	11741	14257	13747
12791	17129	17073	14067	11396	13621	14296
12442	17143	17037	13843	11349	13513	14230
13105	17550	17141	14220	12047	14455	15101
13487	18339	17432	14811	12564	14818	15679
13395	18798	18258	15294	12761	14996	15576
13715	19484	19376	15694	12927	15436	15420
14342	20672	20237	16319	13976	16680	17212
15813	22785	22433	17897	14730	17168	19470
16276	23182	23071	18573	15165	17439	19749
17184	24396	24422	19660	16046	17651	19575
18352	26851	27294	21534	17345	19263	21775
20841	29093	29483	23030	17879	20499	23110
21595	30115	30697	24181	18504	20753	22260
22390	30995	31512	24781	19713	20386	22350
23140	32683	33155	26522	19857	22336	23499
24261	33200	33345	26910	20435	23160	21893
24013	32980	32952	26691	21283	22502	20054
24309	33272	33582	26550	19804	22264	20706
24334	34091	34021	27656	20853	23538	22342
24345	33375	33161	27663	20250	24137	21271
24621	32798	32707	26990	19510	23478	21129
23829	33133	34511	26345	19366	23269	21151
25255	35750	34978	27990	21214	24048	22319
26942	37113	36650	29649	21923	26074	22004
27032	37627	37384	30193	22704	25615	22429

265

HALIFAX BUILDING SOCIETY

TIMES/HALIFAX SERIES OF AVERAGE PRICES (at approval stage) 1976-1982

11.10 UNITED KINGDOM AND REGIONS: NEW DWELLINGS - QUARTERLY

Year		United Kingdom	North	Yorks & Humberside	North West	East Midlands	West Midlands
1976	1	13709	11836	10862	12245	11541	13647
	2	14215	12294	11363	12420	11878	14624
	3	14517	12673	11771	13004	12633	14776
	4	14467	13213	11973	12821	12559	13884
1977	1	14719	13141	12000	12738	12357	14469
	2	15137	14349	12718	13940	12722	15024
	3	15787	14461	13431	14003	13269	16468
	4	16451	15120	13718	14918	13741	16299
1978	1	17515	16192	14250	16341	14702	17927
	2	18298	16376	15366	17773	15283	18693
	3	19485	17135	15726	18603	16506	19175
	4	20713	18479	16839	19040	17456	21183
1979	1	21761	18750	17854	20131	17718	22286
	2	23100	19600	17954	21713	19124	23612
	3	24329	20805	19229	23164	20455	25127
	4	25509	21025	21286	23907	21314	25963
1980	1	27393	23239	21560	25170	24133	28314
	2	28917	23529	24057	26548	24209	30118
	3	29800	24585	24018	27736	25642	29287
	4	29940	25739	26295	28309	26169	28787
1981	1	30398	27076	25709	29520	27577	28893
	2	31026	27503	26487	30040	27336	30190
	3	29777	28527	25696	28300	25965	29927
	4	29421	27121	26014	27004	26133	28754
1982	1	30363	27433	25662	29578	25744	29024
	2	31201	29126	27396	29849	27541	29346
	3	31749	30422	26498	29724	27396	30936
	4	32508	28629	26417	30034	27232	31164

£

East Anglia	South East	Greater London	South West	Wales	Scotland	Northern Ireland
12567	17865	21438	13756	12102	13778	13458
12647	18731	21010	14415	11610	14836	15089
13046	18494	19600	14076	12807	14984	16089
12448	18028	20401	13710	12318	15694	17287
12333	19022	21533	14122	12376	15500	17006
13190	18798	20680	14327	12952	15988	18840
13163	19685	22120	15151	13633	16812	18758
13151	20559	22865	15694	13431	17002	19458
15305	21597	23389	16492	14907	17427	19912
14779	22773	25699	16992	15531	18336	20823
16158	24785	29907	18435	15719	18811	21704
17278	26350	27575	20534	17148	20303	21616
19080	27523	30414	21431	18666	19911	23994
20560	30104	32838	22523	19955	20675	27351
22076	31644	32242	24263	20071	21891	27270
24056	33565	37503	25192	22613	22822	26711
25487	34202	39356	27861	23832	23826	30249
25805	36151	36710	28851	25448	25120	30041
27377	37760	40121	28903	26084	27468	27291
27332	36408	46343	29641	27458	26436	26120
27952	36670	37613	29486	25608	28179	26472
26237	38608	42110	29267	27823	29398	27606
26066	36166	35612	30309	26242	28817	24671
28570	35612	35658	29282	24804	28841	24607
27976	36882	38055	28759	27200	28875	25375
28722	37760	36275	31294	28528	29481	24001
28758	38945	37255	32126	27335	29597	25622
30285	41326	37858	32244	26699	29710	26325

HALIFAX BUILDING SOCIETY

TIMES/HALIFAX SERIES OF AVERAGE PRICES (approval stage) 1976-1982

11.11 UNITED KINGDOM AND REGIONS: EXISTING DWELLINGS - QUARTERLY

Year	United Kingdom	North	Yorks & Humberside	North West	East Midlands	West Midlands
1976 1	12745	9956	9287	10190	10341	12614
2	13407	10499	9995	10911	11023	13171
3	13656	11150	10171	11151	11600	13407
4	13450	10802	10060	10971	11275	13603
1977 1	13212	11069	9550	10694	11008	12985
2	13759	11688	10134	11248	11318	13778
3	14215	11946	10361	11845	11678	13929
4	14559	12515	10667	12201	11915	14637
1978 1	14891	12848	11069	12238	12017	13976
2	15750	13304	11389	12977	12578	15235
3	17300	14173	12272	14213	13681	16369
4	17622	14678	12526	14747	14174	16539
1979 1	18363	14777	12921	15365	14259	17097
2	20136	16041	13717	16711	15710	18692
3	21625	17003	14819	17818	17329	19123
4	22209	17040	15619	18506	17542	19889
1980 1	22557	17189	16375	18408	17944	20540
2	23997	18094	17405	19677	18781	21564
3	24568	18903	17497	20394	19545	22919
4	24422	18763	17996	20026	19685	22385
1981 1	24660	19084	17893	20422	19834	22750
2	25283	19080	18823	21234	20932	23228
3	24701	18761	18873	21213	20500	22728
4	23673	18130	17494	20229	20360	21829
1982 1	23602	17458	16805	20049	19529	22040
2	25388	19231	18666	20963	20965	22749
3	26992	20634	19983	22297	22069	24314
4	27158	21016	19414	21571	22536	24955

£

East Anglia	South East	Greater London	South West	Wales	Scotland	Northern Ireland
12535	16575	16045	13510	10580	12654	10144
12659	17370	16516	14127	10820	13532	12066
13005	17340	16601	14020	11486	14080	13302
12874	16981	16963	14136	11184	13190	13584
12471	16835	16899	13794	11131	13122	13610
13083	17377	17019	14203	11868	14138	14294
13541	18160	17321	14760	12341	14483	15116
13444	18531	18106	15228	12653	14575	14909
13301	19121	19201	15521	12561	14885	14456
14236	20321	20103	16187	13639	16319	16198
15751	22467	22240	17802	14561	16817	19053
16096	22732	22994	18220	14782	16878	19390
16744	23907	24236	19324	15533	17052	18373
18008	26398	27178	21380	16867	18941	20728
20615	28770	29430	22828	17525	20205	22294
21136	29690	30562	23999	17857	20306	21763
21721	30483	31258	24251	19074	19687	20927
22718	32180	33045	26149	19094	21831	22292
23764	32658	33203	26651	19796	22541	20862
23458	32592	32661	26246	20608	21907	19097
23586	32839	33462	26120	19176	21425	19782
23984	33583	33817	27420	20246	22665	21234
24089	33061	33073	27317	19667	23432	20618
23861	32425	32556	26696	18953	22584	20390
23160	32654	34316	26000	18697	22366	20406
24754	35499	34917	27534	20494	23276	21971
26665	36885	36623	29343	21390	25525	21392
26468	37138	37357	29856	22272	25010	21733

HALIFAX BUILDING SOCIETY

TIMES/HALIFAX SERIES (at approval stage) June 1975 – July 1983

11.12 GREAT BRITAIN: EXISTING DWELLINGS

Date		Index (Dec 1977 = 100)	Average Price (£)	Date		Index (Dec 1977 = 100)	Average Price (£)
		Unadjusted				Seasonally adjusted	
1975	Jun	86.0	12646	1978	Mar	105.6	15579
	Sep	85.4	12562		Jun	109.3	16133
	Dec	85.3	12533		Sep	118.2	17450
					Oct	117.4	17326
1976	Mar	87.7	12896		Nov	119.9	17691
	Jun	92.1	13544		Dec	121.1	17866
	Sep	92.0	13531				
	Dec	91.2	13413	1979	Jan	122.9	18132
					Feb	127.8	18783
1977	Jan	90.7	13340		Mar	130.5	19259
	Feb	89.1	13105		Apr	131.7	19441
	Mar	89.8	13197		May	136.2	20094
	Apr	92.6	13617		Jun	138.4	20341
	May	92.7	13630		Jul	142.6	21038
	Jun	95.3	14011		Aug	145.2	21427
	Jul	96.1	14122		Sep	145.5	21480
	Aug	96.8	14234		Oct	149.5	22065
	Sep	96.9	14249		Nov	151.4	22339
	Oct	98.0	14402		Dec	151.0	22291
	Nov	99.2	14580				
	Dec	100.0	14701	1980	Jan	154.2	22754
					Feb	156.2	23052
1978	Jan	100.8	14824		Mar	158.2	23352
	Feb	99.4	14610		Apr	158.6	23406
	Mar	103.7	15248		May	161.7	23866
	Apr	104.3	15334		Jun	164.0	24205
	May	105.2	15465		Jul	163.7	24165
	Jun	111.4	16381		Aug	164.0	24204
	Jul	116.2	17084		Sep	165.8	24473
	Aug	117.2	17229		Oct	166.4	24556
	Sep	119.2	17522		Nov	166.0	24499
	Oct	117.5	17279		Dec	166.2	24523
				1981	Jan	167.7	24752
					Feb	172.6	25472
					Mar	172.9	25511
					Apr	170.5	25164
					May	171.5	25304
					Jun	169.5	25003
					Jul	167.9	24779
					Aug	165.5	24424
					Sep	163.1	24064
					Oct	159.7	23562
					Nov	159.0	23553
					Dec	164.1	24217
				1982	Jan	163.1	24072
					Feb	162.6	23999
					Mar	165.2	24382
					Apr	169.1	24949
					May	171.5	25309
					Jun	172.3	25429
					Jul	174.5	25745
					Aug	181.9	26849
					Sep	183.6	27101
					Oct	184.2	27178
					Nov	186.8	27560
					Dec	186.0	27451
				1983	Jan	182.0	26858
					Mar	185.0	27300
					Apr	188.4	27796
					May	190.5	28108
					Jun	193.3	28525
					Jul	196.6	29012

12. Incorporated Society of Valuers and Auctioneers

12.1 TECHNICAL DETAILS

(a) Source of data and timing

Valuations of *typical* properties made by members of the ISVA

(b) Types of data and periods covered

Average prices: April 1978 to date
Index: April 1978 to date

Available data

DATA BREAKDOWNS	DATA TYPES	
	AVERAGE PRICES	INDEX NUMBERS
HOUSE DATA		
All houses	*	*
New/Non-new		
Type	*	
Size		
Age		
LOCAL DATA		
Regions	*	
Sub-regions		
Towns		
BUYER DATA		
First-time buyer		
Former owner-occupier		

c) Frequency

Quarterly

(d) Geographical coverage

England, subdivided into five regions - South East, West, Midlands, North West and North East

(e) Method of analysis

Both an index and an average price series are derived for England from valuations of *typical* houses by members of the ISVA (estate agents, valuers and surveyors).

INCORPORATED SOCIETY OF VALUERS AND AUTIONEERS (ISVA)

12.2 LIST OF TABLES

Average prices

12.1   England: all dwellings and type of dwelling. 1978–
12.2   England - Regions: all dwellings. 1978–

Index

12.3   England: all dwellings. 1978–

12.3 CROSS-CLASSIFICATIONS OF DATA

None

12.4 PUBLICATIONS

(a) Data

The Valuer, Journal of the Incorporated Society of Valuers and Auctioneers. ISVA, London. Ten issues per year.

(b) Description of methodology

None

(c) Supplementary studies

None

INCORPORATED SOCIETY OF VALUERS AND AUCTIONEERS

AVERAGE PRICES (valuations of typical properties) 1978 –

12.1 ENGLAND: ALL DWELLINGS AND TYPE OF DWELLING

£

Year		All	TYPE OF DWELLING (see key below)					
			A	B	C	D	E	F
1978	Apr	17667	9855	12971	12520	15933	20778	22762
	Jul	18680						
	Oct	19555						
1979	Jan	20897						
	Apr	22534	12494	16679	15947	20423	27277	42556
	Jul	24452	13652	18003	17206	22477	29777	46122
	Oct	25934	14591	19072	18183	23441	31587	28881
1980	Jan	26650	15224	19536	18611	24103	32291	50045
	Apr	27216	15652	19918	18976	24378	32351	50885
	Jul	27466	15860	19941	19105	24615	32292	51255
	Oct	27631	16404	20147	19319	24644	32230	51306
1981	Jan	28058	16784	20823	19798	25484	32877	52351
	Jun	29578	17417	21449	21464	27420	35246	54400
	Oct	29040	17560	21760	20437	26363	34000	53377
1982	Jan	29376	17628	21452	19822	27063	32950	53110
	Jun	30430	18728	22064	21619	27800	35839	55973
	Sep	30834	19323	22607	21380	28185	35482	56305
	Dec	30988	19728	22607	21598	28255	35163	56474
1983	Mar	31529	20088	23686	23379	28639	36108	56475
	Jun	32608	20285	23548	23401	28926	37485	60775
	Oct	33740	21197	24417	23420	31066	38931	62659
	Dec	34148	21740	25092	23655	32232	39734	64092
1984	Mar	35014	22185	25717	24128	32554	41872	64803
	Jun	36348	23210	27020	24516	33188	43172	66877
	Oct	36937	24057	27476	25156	33487	43850	67255
	Dec	37331	24423	27613	25361	33862	44431	67754
1985	Mar	38157	25141	28398	25846	34585	45243	69004
	Jun	38968	25676	28849	26234	35250	46301	70550
	Oct	40159						
	Dec	41013						
1986	Mar	42084						
	Jun	43309						

Key to dwelling types:

A Pre-1914 mid-terrace house, modernised with bathroom and inside lavatory. Three bedrooms.
   A total of 800 sq ft of living space.

B Modern mid-terrace house with garage or parking space. Three bedrooms, two reception rooms
   or through living room and totalling around 850 sq ft.

C Post-war two-bedroom flat with garage in purpose-built block with 650 sq ft of living space.

D Mid-1930s semi-detached house with three bedrooms, a garage and central heating.
   Around 900 sq ft in all.

E Modern detached three-bedroom house with garage, cloakroom, central heating and typical
   sized garden for the area. Living area of 1,100 sq ft.

F Modern detached four-bedroom house with two bathrooms, two garages, cloakroom, two reception
   rooms, central heating and typical garden for its size in the area. A total of 1,500 sq ft
   of living space.

INCORPORATED SOCIETY OF VALUERS AND AUCTIONEERS

AVERAGE PRICES (valuations of typical properties) 1978 –

12.2 ENGLAND - REGIONS: ALL DWELLINGS

£

Year		South East	West	Midlands	North West	North East
1978	Apr	21346	16993	15149	16501	16013
1979	Apr	27847	21358	18919	21453	19060
	Jul	29911	23589	20684	23114	20718
	Oct	31465	25560	21895	24244	22079
1980	Jan	31898	26499	22790	25233	22711
	Apr	32666	27047	23597	25755	23356
	Jul	32649	27272	23744	25875	23584
	Oct	32882	27425	23793	25850	23681
1981	Jan	33680	27517	24181	26078	23802
	Jun	37634	29407	24095	25490	25183
	Oct	35569	29241	23764	25245	24769
1982	Jan	36645	29235	23835	25288	24975
	Jun	38557	28739	23803	25853	25628
	Sep	38685	30087	24654	26472	25610
	Dec	39072	31136	24656	26737	25482
1983	Mar	40138	32276	26734	27380	25600
	Jun	39672	32569	26649	31535	28555
	Oct	41792	33217	26361	30100	26533
	Dec	45160	33729	25911	29394	27306
1984	Mar	46740	34235	26108	29688	28618
	Jun	48656	35248	27110	30709	29628
	Oct	49852	36044	27715	30850	29683
	Dec	50455	36068	27965	31404	29819
1985	Mar	51728	36946	28501	31945	30274
	Jun	52924	37721	29021	32432	30697
	Oct	54823	39051	29949	32997	31584
	Dec	56254	39636	30614	33563	32161
1986	Mar	57821	40622	31324	34364	32765
	Jun	59726	41678	32114	35233	33381

INCORPORATED SOCIETY OF VALUERS AND AUCTIONEERS

INDEX (valuations of typical properties) 1978 –

12.3 ENGLAND: ALL DWELLINGS

Year		Index (April 1978 = 100)
1978	Apr	100.0
	Jul	105.7
	Oct	110.7
1979	Jan	118.3
	Apr	127.5
	Jul	138.4
	Oct	146.8
1980	Jan	150.8
	Apr	154.0
	Jul	155.4
	Oct	156.4
1981	Jan	158.8
	Jun	167.4
	Oct	164.4
1982	Jan	166.3
	Jun	172.2
	Sep	174.5
	Dec	175.4
1983	Mar	178.5
	Jun	184.6
	Oct	191.0
	Dec	193.3
1984	Mar	198.2
	Jun	205.7
	Oct	209.0
	Dec	211.2
1985	Mar	215.9
	Jun	220.5
	Oct	227.3
	Dec	232.1
1986	Mar	238.2
	Jun	245.1

13. Leeds Permanent Building Society

13.1 TECHNICAL DETAILS

(a) Source of data and timing

Society's own lending records at the mortgage approval stage

(b) Types of data and periods covered

Simple average prices: 1978 Q2 - 1983 Q3
Weighted average prices: 1983 Q4 to date

Available data

DATA BREAKDOWNS	DATA TYPES	
	SIMPLE AVERAGE	WEIGHTED AVERAGE
HOUSE DATA		
All houses	(*)	*
New/Non-new	(*)	
Type	*	
Size		
Age	(*)	
LOCAL DATA		
Regions	*	*
Sub-regions		
Towns		
BUYER DATA		
First-time buyer		
Former owner-occupier		

(*) These data no longer published

(c) Frequency

Quarterly

(d) Geographical coverage

United Kingdom and official standard regions (defined in Appendix B)

(e) Method of analysis

Simple average prices: simple averages produced from 1978 to 1983 Q3, and continued thereafter only for house types by region.

Weighted average prices: from 1983 Q4 the prices for all houses at both national and regional levels have been derived as a weighted average. Fixed weights are used which relate to the distribution of mortgages by region and type of dwelling obtained by the Department of the Environment in their Five Per Cent Sample Survey in 1980 (see Chapter 3). Both series of house prices exclude sales at non-market prices.

13.2 LIST OF TABLES

Simple average and weighted average prices

13.1   United Kingdom: all, age and type of dwelling. 1978-
13.2   Regions: all dwellings. 1980-

Weighted average prices

13.3   Regions: type of dwelling. 1983-

13.3 CROSS-CLASSIFICATIONS OF DATA

(a) Two-way classifications

Numbers in the grid below refer to the corresponding tables compiled for this data source.

(b) Three-way classifications

None

13.4 PUBLICATIONS

(a) Data

Housing Finance (formerly *House Prices*). Quarterly from 1980 Q1 to date. Leeds Permanent Building Society, Leeds

(b) Description of methodology

None

(c) Supplementary studies

A regular commentary on aspects of the housing market is published in *Housing Finance*, including occasional reference to weighted average house prices in connection with first-time buyers and former owner-occupiers.

LEEDS PERMANENT BUILDING SOCIETY

AVERAGE PRICES (at approval stage) 1978 –

13.1 UNITED KINGDOM: ALL, AGE AND TYPE OF DWELLING

Year	All	AGE OF DWELLING				
		New	Pre-1919	1919-1945	Post-1945	All non-new
1978 2	16459	17709	14239	16955	16770	16096
3	16964	17517	14618	17632	17602	16795
4	17946	18526	15382	18884	18506	17768
1979 1	18864	19925	15934	19782	19295	18557
2	20472	21515	16734	21608	21196	20177
3	21944	22709	19002	23292	22585	21746
4	22943	23968	19862	24205	23609	22671
1980 1	23249	25275	19415	24183	24315	22715
2	23974	26170	19724	25478	25070	23409
3	24032	27081	20080	25269	25008	23407
4	24374	26472	20675	26199	25155	23867
1981 1	23764	26583	19700	24647	25269	23277
2	24194	26563	20409	25286	25292	23756
3	24262	26254	20413	25168	25625	23911
4	22774	24784	18734	23870	24574	22376
1982 1	22735	24922	18546	23718	24156	22303
2	24208	26085	20030	25215	25971	23926
3	25319	27419	21146	26568	27188	25017
4	25648	28700	21028	26806	27510	25029
1983 1	26320	29183	21612	28053	27985	25887
2	27348	30397	22523	28696	29044	26897
3	28592	31824	23772	30075	30140	28082
4	29106					
1984 1	29331					
2	30317					
3	31347					
4	31116					
1985 1	31489					
2	32628					
3	33692					
4	34955					
1986 1	35603					
2	36235					
3	38586					
4	40022					
1987 1	39946					

£

TYPE OF DWELLING				
Detached	Semi-detached	Terraced	Bungalow	Flat
40117	24805	19561	29563	21632
41086	25603	20340	29885	22004
42288	26176	21005	30779	22684
43906	27129	21680	32442	23691
44366	27071	21904	32641	23366
43605	27682	22097	33485	23841
44932	28460	23195	34236	24687
47270	29184	23728	35537	25389
46683	29004	23729	35039	25262
47001	29538	23989	35246	25733
49070	30449	24641	36963	26672
50822	31310	25732	37466	27446
52492	32320	26949	38499	29106
53861	32547	27253	39059	30881
54645	33541	27707	39077	31135
57606	35653	29754	42584	32826
58933	36626	31372	44110	35417
58432	36698	31700	42835	35641

LEEDS PERMANENT BUILDING SOCIETY

AVERAGE PRICES (at approval stage) 1980 –

13.2 REGIONS: ALL DWELLINGS

Year		North	Yorks & Humberside	North West	East Midlands	West Midlands	East Anglia
1980	1	18151	18365	18727	18777	21247	24943
	2	18586	19286	19429	19103	21998	23594
	3	18830	19216	20040	19863	21896	23203
	4	18197	19479	20022	19848	22376	23730
1981	1	17879	19962	19500	19787	21175	23113
	2	20240	19507	19998	19524	22511	23606
	3	19911	19482	19927	20677	22430	22892
	4	18200	19470	19309	19782	20406	22451
1982	1	17870	19043	19595	18863	20212	22343
	2	19072	19791	20944	20187	21224	23152
	3	20038	20275	21972	21777	21718	23981
	4	20846	20884	22187	21126	22132	25444
1983	1	21274	20745	22361	22363	23165	26419
	2	21408	22034	23663	23857	24048	27846
	3	22522	23699	23760	24669	24586	29640
	4	22596	22917	23856	23653	25240	29302
1984	1	22280	23058	23852	24276	24971	29227
	2	22604	24034	24523	24325	25409	30434
	3	22983	24503	25301	24954	25822	31396
	4	23347	23871	24874	24983	25763	29939
1985	1	23013	23813	26257	24282	25451	30617
	2	23542	24392	25488	24924	26297	32012
	3	24435	25008	26679	26365	27128	33939
	4	25010	25718	27433	26942	27791	35173
1986	1	24733	26316	27185	27180	27888	35188
	2	25079	26547	27776	28011	29048	36083
	3	25709	28148	29282	29186	30910	38664
	4	26472	27872	29066	30545	31404	41327
1987	1	26091	27794	28870	31012	31312	40432

South East	Greater London	South West	Wales	Scotland	Northern Ireland
29892	31630	24359	19779	21356	22207
30542	32287	25557	19813	21492	23329
31329	32440	25498	18774	21596	23054
31237	32157	25263	19914	21980	24100
29887	30241	25262	19339	22496	21908
30181	30925	26288	19234	22785	22378
29715	31181	25960	20401	24337	23120
27555	29293	25041	19166	23165	22494
28295	29894	23536	19592	23380	21177
30360	32041	25102	20790	23915	22389
32805	33017	27103	20651	24677	24146
33482	33545	27140	21026	24625	24011
34627	34646	28099	21764	24900	24057
36055	35699	28675	22664	25448	24340
37390	37347	30245	23285	26791	25212
37485	36793	30665	23976	28027	26522
37174	37851	31866	25272	28238	27354
38937	40395	32275	24719	29307	27747
40765	41674	33384	26778	30115	27529
40502	42299	33145	25345	30203	27378
41590	43150	33745	25471	29371	27119
43424	46025	35437	26635	30577	28220
45109	48048	35470	25709	31057	28420
47111	51191	36567	26885	31951	28459
48055	54659	37335	27224	31867	29976
49309	53923	38469	27556	31832	29302
53316	59019	40832	28794	32452	29194
55984	62269	42130	28745	34691	31307
55259	64720	42149	29189	33570	30973

LEEDS PERMANENT BUILDING SOCIETY

AVERAGE PRICES (at approval stage) 1983 –

13.3 REGIONS: TYPE OF DWELLING

Year	North	Yorks & Humberside	North West	East Midlands	West Midlands	East Anglia
DETACHED HOUSES						
1983 4	39784	37572	40394	35865	37847	38779
1984 1	38698	36865	39157	36214	37095	39464
2	38254	38462	39658	35521	37961	41532
3	40081	39616	40994	36664	38270	41758
4	40343	38269	41928	36851	38490	41550
1985 1	37463	37724	44102	35351	36799	41818
2	40614	38797	41200	36086	38057	44547
3	40303	39003	43174	39289	40085	45110
4	42625	41217	45286	40345	41812	46758
1986 1	42809	41734	46312	41197	42107	46950
2	41590	41567	48257	41883	43856	48465
3	42810	45713	48871	43962	46691	52761
4	43402	44369	47003	44771	47702	55460
1987 1	44369	42910	47554	45985	47117	54722
SEMI-DETACHED HOUSES						
1983 4	24469	22290	23308	20885	22345	27152
1984 1	23878	22665	23383	21659	22226	26062
2	24129	23504	24395	21722	22617	26376
3	24474	23700	24843	22553	22918	27588
4	24906	23312	24221	22130	22572	26108
1985 1	24556	23717	25581	21641	23062	26854
2	25429	23894	25080	22655	23569	27806
3	25253	25076	26295	22653	24097	31300
4	25954	25358	26892	23875	24690	30787
1986 1	27066	25938	26176	23472	24928	31637
2	26998	25862	26363	24579	25650	33317
3	27313	27319	28582	25314	26966	34913
4	28263	27357	28319	26916	27264	37464
1987 1	27672	27323	28377	27307	27903	35883
TERRACED HOUSES						
1983 4	15708	15288	15375	14924	16236	20258
1984 1	15991	15517	15520	15238	15983	20428
2	16000	16663	16053	15860	16607	21994
3	16716	16930	16653	16208	16682	22560
4	17298	16421	16115	16258	17143	21200
1985 1	16976	16384	16630	16073	17119	21807
2	16813	16768	16893	16343	17694	22701
3	18451	17462	17512	17900	18065	23618
4	18745	18086	17551	17301	17697	25642
1986 1	17451	18314	17694	17752	18162	25044
2	18553	18640	17939	18225	18991	26236
3	18963	19358	18865	18997	19540	27545
4	19760	19379	19496	20175	19339	29723
1987 1	19347	19144	19079	20568	20078	30206

					£

South East	Greater London	South West	Wales	Scotland	Northern Ireland
57384	66486	43845	36215	40378	38900
54028	67359	45597	38867	40665	39556
57321	77149	44906	36627	42270	39077
62282	80081	48417	42191	42189	36779
60658	81786	47205	36825	43664	37876
63199	81691	48116	38201	40494	37306
66395	87350	51724	42596	43971	40329
69623	93634	50905	41412	44787	38244
72327	92936	52299	38804	46639	39602
73369	109731	54269	43742	46923	41263
75025	98822	56129	43718	45283	40739
79825	109535	59497	43094	44540	38915
83542	105423	57338	43485	50681	46253
81668	108469	58290	45505	47533	44579
34563	44014	28301	22612	28253	22601
35639	46545	29609	23917	29370	22439
36906	48371	30932	23813	29273	23859
37935	51309	30348	25123	31083	23418
38217	51841	30287	23571	31546	24170
39275	52812	31792	22833	30309	24545
40876	57492	32383	23351	31770	24523
42237	57734	33759	22890	32020	24871
43567	61646	34257	25812	32970	24428
44313	63898	33577	24821	32693	25683
46797	65718	34745	25602	32845	26058
50415	71190	37109	27297	34025	26114
51892	75733	39178	26583	34277	26298
52086	75490	39547	25995	34343	26777
28250	36045	23298	17373	25246	14340
28415	36711	23432	17772	24040	16707
29915	39597	24338	17496	25297	15840
30488	40324	24855	18202	26789	16251
30475	41391	24994	18076	26103	16414
30765	42335	25162	18199	26735	17196
31548	45010	25441	18247	26499	18030
33252	46825	25919	18325	27212	17755
35622	51117	26884	18959	27611	16232
35788	52898	27649	19197	27149	16788
36620	51748	28360	19571	27822	17226
39994	57964	30459	20260	28159	17990
43250	60796	32397	20996	30196	18692
42768	65364	31959	21747	28983	18302

LEEDS PERMANENT BUILDING SOCIETY

AVERAGE PRICES (at approval stage) 1983 –

13.3 REGIONS: TYPE OF DWELLING (continued)

Year	North	Yorks & Humberside	North West	East Midlands	West Midlands	East Anglia
BUNGALOWS						
1983 4	29259	28373	28157	27110	31832	30702
1984 1	27967	28840	30078	28456	32765	30529
2	30938	28878	30275	28911	30727	30714
3	30025	30015	31975	28514	34825	33937
4	29318	29103	30275	29622	33366	29699
1985 1	31283	28374	34171	28601	31704	31309
2	30341	30101	31756	28856	34676	31776
3	34781	29269	34172	30491	34539	35617
4	33706	29503	34697	31213	35169	37490
1986 1	31768	31489	33447	31628	33283	36727
2	32225	33088	35369	32539	35310	34735
3	34733	34269	37161	34200	43313	38025
4	34626	33663	37134	36383	45870	41528
1987 1	32961	35928	34572	35572	40197	39179
FLATS						
1983 4	13806	18947	19366	14735	17388	22129
1984 1	14139	17524	19006	17194	16965	20299
2	14339	18895	18050	15372	17632	24303
3	13426	19743	20634	15306	16840	22076
4	13745	20370	18884	15205	16845	21991
1985 1	14641	17949	19589	16461	17541	21433
2	15057	19540	20175	15667	17714	21652
3	14347	19245	19359	19608	18058	22673
4	15263	19730	24427	15178	18558	26333
1986 1	15035	20229	19957	15430	17462	27109
2	15591	19618	18344	18750	19317	23643
3	15659	21612	21443	18692	19396	24569
4	16698	20174	21600	20883	19513	29674
1987 1	17200	20428	21731	21488	19226	26295

South East	Greater London	South West	Wales	Scotland	Northern Ireland
					£
41958	51227	35421	26120	33653	28303
41890	55602	38305	27762	34120	29316
43312	51654	38230	28071	37242	29918
44885	58147	39774	29722	37030	31008
45884	52114	40084	31502	36044	28922
46889	45436	39357	31835	35716	27713
50944	51905	44199	32682	36624	28822
50205	57659	41872	28730	38497	30630
51000	60373	44562	32479	39356	31036
55201	54581	45607	29072	38454	33190
53648	60454	46857	28675	37162	30786
61199	68632	48873	33390	38976	31243
62965	73652	51423	32202	41985	32535
61076	75398	51265	31748	39916	32279
23882	29031	21547	19141	19276	14950
25035	29604	22965	19000	19174	28500
25692	31380	21125	17150	19806	23575
26637	32033	23506	24200	20430	22430
26118	32293	23045	19289	20292	18300
26414	33327	22921	19260	20237	23364
27161	34934	24354	18306	20717	19900
28039	37079	23050	12500	20400	21180
30215	39537	23492	19203	20934	17950
31324	43829	26247	21793	21378	30075
31548	43334	26403	22950	22423	25850
33809	46212	26660	20459	22868	23814
36402	50147	32523	20916	24262	26170
35860	51835	29706	23926	23810	25388

14. National House-Building Council

14.1 TECHNICAL DETAILS

(a) Source of data and timing

Actual sales prices: based on returns for new houses at the mortgage completion stage - for further details see (e) below

Estimated start prices: NHBC records of expected selling prices of new houses, assessed when building has just started.

(b) Types of data and periods covered

Average prices of new houses sold (actual): 1980 Q4 to date
Average prices of new houses started (estimates): 1980 Q1 to date

Available data

DATA BREAKDOWNS	DATA TYPES	
	ACTUAL PRICES	ESTIMATED PRICES
HOUSE DATA		
All houses		
New	*	*
Type		*
Size		
Age		
LOCAL DATA		
Regions	*	*
Sub-regions		
Towns		
BUYER DATA		
First-time buyer		
Former owner-occupier		

(c) Frequency

Quarterly

(d) Geographical coverage

Actual sales prices: official standard regions of England and Wales (defined in Appendix B).

Estimated selling prices of houses started: Great Britain subdivided into official standard regions - see Appendix B.

(e) **Method of analysis**

As stated above, two separate series are regularly published dealing with average prices of new houses:

(i) simple average prices of new houses sold by housebuilders registered with the NHBC based on returns made by the solicitors acting for purchasers at the completion stage of the sale;

(ii) simple averages of the *estimated* selling prices of new dwellings *started* by housebuilders registered with the NHBC. The estimates are made by builders when they apply to register a dwelling with the NHBC. The series represents, therefore, selling prices anticipated at the time of application (there are safeguards against underestimating price). Builders are requested to register dwellings at least twenty-one days before building starts; most applications are made slightly earlier. All published prices are rounded to the nearest £1000.

14.2 LIST OF TABLES

Average sales prices (actual)

14.1 Regions: new dwellings. 1980–

Estimated start prices

14.2 Regions: new dwellings. 1980–
14.3 Great Britain, England, Wales, Scotland: new dwellings by house type. 1981–

14.3 CROSS-CLASSIFICATIONS OF DATA

(a) **Two-way classifications**

Average sales prices (actual): New dwellings by region. Table 14.1

Estimated start prices: New dwellings by region. Table 14.2

(b) **Three-way classifications**

New dwellings by region by house type (estimated prices): Table 14.3

14.4 PUBLICATIONS

(a) **Data**

Private House-Building Statistics. National House-Building Council, Amersham. Quarterly since 1981 Q4

(b) **Description of methodology**

None

(c) **Supplementary studies**

None

NATIONAL HOUSE-BUILDING COUNCIL

AVERAGE SALES PRICES (at completion stage) 1980 –

14.1 REGIONS: NEW DWELLINGS

Year		North	Yorks & Humberside	North West	East Midlands	West Midlands	East Anglia
1981		27000	25000	28000	26000	28000	27000
1982		26000	25000	27000	25000	27000	27000
1983		28000	27000	28000	27000	29000	29000
1984		30000	29000	29000	29000	31000	33000
1985		33000	32000	32000	33000	34000	38000
1986		36000	34000	37000	38000	39000	41000
1980	4	24000	24000	27000	24000	26000	27000
1981	1	25000	26000	28000	26000	27000	28000
	2	27000	25000	27000	25000	27000	26000
	3	27000	25000	28000	26000	28000	27000
	4	27000	25000	27000	26000	28000	27000
1982	1	26000	24000	27000	25000	27000	26000
	2	26000	25000	26000	25000	27000	27000
	3	26000	25000	28000	26000	28000	27000
	4	27000	25000	27000	26000	27000	28000
1983	1	28000	26000	27000	26000	28000	29000
	2	28000	26000	28000	27000	28000	30000
	3	29000	28000	29000	28000	30000	30000
	4	28000	27000	29000	28000	30000	29000
1984	1	30000	28000	28000	28000	30000	31000
	2	30000	28000	29000	29000	31000	32000
	3	29000	29000	31000	29000	33000	34000
	4	32000	29000	29000	30000	32000	34000
1985	1	33000	31000	30000	31000	32000	35000
	2	30000	33000	30000	31000	33000	40000
	3	33000	32000	32000	34000	35000	39000
	4	35000	31000	32000	35000	35000	39000
1986	1	35000	32000	35000	35000	37000	40000
	2	35000	33000	36000	37000	38000	40000
	3	38000	35000	39000	39000	40000	42000
	4	37000	35000	39000	38000	43000	45000
1987	1	41000	37000	39000	39000	42000	46000

				£

South East	Greater London	South West	England	Wales
35000	41000	29000	30000	26000
35000	39000	29000	30000	28000
38000	42000	31000	33000	27000
42000	47000	35000	36000	30000
47000	54000	38000	40000	31000
57000	61000	46000	48000	36000
34000		28000	29000	25000
35000	42000	29000	30000	26000
35000	43000	29000	30000	26000
37000	42000	30000	31000	26000
35000	38000	29000	30000	26000
34000	38000	28000	29000	27000
34000	39000	29000	30000	27000
36000	38000	30000	31000	29000
35000	40000	30000	31000	28000
37000	40000	30000	31000	26000
37000	42000	32000	33000	28000
39000	44000	33000	34000	29000
39000	43000	32000	34000	28000
40000	44000	32000	34000	28000
42000	44000	34000	36000	29000
42000	49000	36000	37000	31000
43000	50000	37000	37000	31000
45000	56000	36000	40000	31000
46000	52000	39000	40000	29000
47000	54000	40000	41000	32000
49000	56000	40000	42000	32000
51000	57000	41000	44000	33000
56000	62000	44000	46000	35000
60000	60000	47000	49000	38000
59000	62000	47000	50000	35000
63000	64000	51000	52000	38000

NATIONAL HOUSE-BUILDING COUNCIL

ESTIMATED PRICES AT BUILDING START STAGE 1980 –

14.2 REGIONS: NEW DWELLINGS

Year		Great Britain	North	Yorks & Humberside	North West	East Midlands	West Midlands	East Anglia
1980		29000	27000	24000	28000	25000	27000	26000
1981		30000	26000	25000	27000	26000	27000	27000
1982		30000	27000	25000	26000	26000	26000	27000
1983		33000	29000	28000	28000	28000	30000	30000
1984		37000	32000	31000	31000	32000	33000	35000
1985		42000	35000	33000	35000	36000	39000	40000
1986		50000	39000	36000	39000	40000	43000	45000
1980	1	28000	25000	23000	28000	24000	26000	25000
	2	29000	28000	26000	29000	25000	27000	27000
	3	29000	27000	24000	28000	25000	26000	26000
	4	28000	27000	23000	26000	24000	27000	25000
1981	1	30000	27000	24000	26000	25000	27000	26000
	2	30000	25000	25000	27000	26000	28000	28000
	3	30000	28000	25000	28000	26000	26000	26000
	4	29000	26000	24000	25000	25000	27000	26000
1982	1	29000	26000	23000	25000	25000	25000	26000
	2	29000	26000	25000	27000	26000	27000	27000
	3	30000	29000	25000	25000	26000	27000	27000
	4	30000	26000	25000	26000	27000	27000	28000
1983	1	32000	27000	26000	27000	27000	28000	28000
	2	33000	29000	27000	29000	28000	30000	31000
	3	33000	29000	28000	28000	30000	30000	31000
	4	34000	30000	29000	29000	30000	30000	30000
1984	1	36000	29000	30000	30000	31000	31000	34000
	2	36000	30000	30000	31000	32000	33000	36000
	3	38000	34000	32000	32000	34000	33000	33000
	4	38000	32000	32000	33000	33000	35000	36000
1985	1	43000	34000	32000	33000	35000	39000	40000
	2	41000	33000	33000	35000	34000	36000	38000
	3	42000	36000	33000	36000	38000	39000	39000
	4	44000	36000	34000	37000	37000	40000	41000
1986	1	46000	38000	36000	37000	37000	40000	43000
	2	49000	38000	37000	39000	40000	42000	45000
	3	51000	41000	36000	40000	40000	44000	46000
	4	53000	40000	38000	42000	42000	48000	48000
1987	1	52000	40000	39000	42000	44000	47000	50000

South East	Greater London	South West	England	Wales
34000		28000	29000	25000
35000	39000	29000	30000	26000
35000	36000	29000	30000	25000
39000	44000	32000	33000	27000
44000	45000	37000	38000	31000
50000	56000	42000	44000	34000
60000	73000	47000	51000	37000
34000		28000	29000	25000
35000		28000	30000	27000
34000		28000	29000	26000
34000		27000	27000	25000
36000	49000	29000	30000	25000
36000	38000	30000	30000	27000
34000	35000	28000	30000	27000
35000	36000	29000	29000	25000
34000	40000	28000	29000	24000
34000	35000	29000	30000	25000
37000	33000	30000	30000	26000
36000	37000	30000	31000	25000
37000	44000	30000	32000	25000
39000	43000	33000	34000	28000
39000	40000	33000	34000	27000
40000	48000	35000	35000	29000
43000	43000	36000	37000	29000
43000	44000	36000	37000	31000
44000	49000	37000	38000	30000
47000	47000	37000	39000	32000
50000	67000	40000	44000	33000
50000	52000	40000	42000	34000
51000	50000	41000	43000	34000
52000	56000	45000	45000	35000
56000	62000	45000	48000	36000
57000	76000	47000	50000	38000
62000	76000	48000	52000	36000
67000	74000	49000	55000	38000
66000	77000	50000	55000	37000

291

NATIONAL HOUSE-BUILDING COUNCIL

ESTIMATED PRICES AT BUILDING START STAGE 1982 –

14.3 GREAT BRITAIN, ENGLAND, WALES, SCOTLAND: NEW DWELLINGS BY HOUSE TYPE

£

Year	Detached Houses	Detached Bungalows	Semi-det Houses	Terraced Houses	Attached Bungalows	Flats & Maisonettes
GREAT BRITAIN						
1982	42000	35000	24000	24000	22000	24000
1983	47000	38000	26000	27000	25000	27000
1984	51000	41000	28000	30000	27000	30000
1985	57000	45000	31000	35000	31000	37000
1986	65000	49000	34000	42000	33000	45000
1981 4	41000	33000	24000	23000	22000	24000
1982 1	42000	34000	23000	24000	21000	23000
2	41000	34000	24000	24000	22000	24000
3	43000	35000	24000	24000	22000	23000
4	43000	36000	24000	25000	23000	25000
1983 1	45000	36000	25000	26000	24000	26000
2	47000	38000	26000	26000	24000	28000
3	47000	39000	26000	27000	25000	26000
4	49000	40000	27000	27000	26000	28000
1984 1	50000	41000	27000	30000	26000	28000
2	50000	40000	27000	30000	27000	29000
3	52000	41000	28000	30000	27000	31000
4	53000	42000	28000	31000	28000	31000
1985 1	57000	44000	30000	34000	30000	38000
2	55000	44000	30000	34000	30000	36000
3	57000	45000	31000	36000	30000	35000
4	58000	46000	34000	36000	33000	37000
1986 1	62000	47000	33000	38000	33000	41000
2	63000	48000	34000	40000	33000	46000
3	65000	49000	35000	45000	32000	48000
4	71000	51000	35000	45000	35000	44000
1987 1	71000	52000	36000	46000	36000	49000

£

Year		Detached Houses	Detached Bungalows	Semi-det Houses	Terraced Houses	Attached Bungalows	Flats & Maisonettes
ENGLAND							
1982		43000	35000	24000	24000	22000	24000
1983		47000	39000	26000	27000	25000	27000
1984		52000	42000	28000	30000	27000	30000
1985		58000	46000	31000	35000	31000	37000
1986		65000	50000	35000	43000	33000	46000
1981	4	41000	34000	23000	23000	21000	24000
1982	1	43000	34000	23000	24000	21000	23000
	2	42000	35000	23000	24000	21000	23000
	3	43000	35000	24000	25000	22000	23000
	4	43000	37000	24000	25000	23000	25000
1983	1	45000	37000	25000	26000	24000	27000
	2	47000	38000	25000	27000	24000	28000
	3	48000	40000	26000	27000	25000	26000
	4	49000	40000	27000	28000	25000	29000
1984	1	50000	42000	27000	30000	25000	29000
	2	51000	41000	27000	30000	26000	30000
	3	53000	42000	28000	30000	27000	32000
	4	53000	43000	28000	31000	28000	31000
1985	1	58000	45000	30000	34000	30000	39000
	2	56000	45000	30000	34000	30000	36000
	3	58000	46000	31000	36000	29000	36000
	4	59000	47000	34000	37000	33000	37000
1986	1	63000	47000	33000	39000	33000	42000
	2	64000	49000	35000	41000	33000	48000
	3	66000	51000	35000	47000	33000	50000
	4	72000	52000	36000	47000	35000	46000
1987	1	72000	54000	37000	48000	37000	50000

NATIONAL HOUSE-BUILDING COUNCIL

ESTIMATED PRICES AT BUILDING START STAGE 1982 –

14.3 GREAT BRITAIN, ENGLAND, WALES, SCOTLAND:
NEW DWELLINGS BY HOUSE TYPE (continued)

£

Year		Detached Houses	Detached Bungalows	Semi-det Houses	Terraced Houses	Attached Bungalows	Flats & Maisonettes
WALES							
1982		37000	27000	22000	19000	20000	19000
1983		40000	30000	23000	20000	22000	22000
1984		43000	33000	26000	23000	25000	26000
1985		47000	36000	28000	26000	27000	30000
1986		50000	40000	26000	27000	29000	33000
1981	4	33000	28000	22000	19000	19000	21000
1982	1	37000	27000	22000	19000	20000	19000
	2	36000	27000	22000	20000	19000	21000
	3	39000	28000	21000	20000	22000	19000
	4	37000	27000	22000	19000	20000	19000
1983	1	39000	28000	22000	19000	22000	22000
	2	40000	30000	23000	21000	22000	23000
	3	41000	29000	23000	20000	23000	21000
	4	41000	32000	23000	22000	23000	22000
1984	1	40000	32000	26000	24000	25000	25000
	2	43000	34000	24000	22000	24000	24000
	3	44000	31000	25000	23000	24000	27000
	4	45000	33000	27000	25000	27000	29000
1985	1	47000	36000	27000	23000	26000	30000
	2	46000	36000	28000	27000	27000	27000
	3	47000	36000	28000	26000	24000	32000
	4	46000	37000	28000	26000	29000	29000
1986	1	49000	40000	26000	28000	27000	32000
	2	50000	39000	28000	27000	27000	38000
	3	50000	40000	27000	27000	29000	31000
	4	53000	42000	23000	27000	33000	42000
1987	1	53000	42000	26000	27000	28000	32000

Year		Detached Houses	Detached Bungalows	Semi-det Houses	Terraced Houses	Attached Bungalows	Flats & Maisonettes
SCOTLAND							
1982		40000	37000	28000	25000	24000	25000
1983		44000	37000	29000	27000	27000	25000
1984		47000	42000	31000	30000	30000	28000
1985		51000	43000	33000	32000	32000	34000
1986		52000	44000	35000	34000	33000	34000
1981	4	38000	36000	27000	26000	23000	25000
1982	1	38000	36000	27000	25000	24000	23000
	2	37000	35000	27000	24000	25000	27000
	3	46000	39000	31000	26000	24000	24000
	4	42000	37000	27000	27000	25000	24000
1983	1	40000	36000	28000	27000	25000	25000
	2	46000	36000	29000	28000	27000	26000
	3	46000	38000	31000	27000	27000	25000
	4	41000	40000	30000	27000	28000	26000
1984	1	47000	42000	29000	29000	28000	26000
	2	50000	42000	31000	31000	30000	28000
	3	45000	41000	32000	29000	31000	29000
	4	47000	44000	31000	30000	30000	29000
1985	1	56000	44000	33000	31000	31000	33000
	2	46000	43000	32000	30000	30000	33000
	3	49000	43000	33000	33000	34000	34000
	4	53000	43000	33000	32000	33000	36000
1986	1	48000	45000	34000	32000	35000	33000
	2	53000	44000	34000	35000	32000	35000
	3	56000	43000	37000	34000	31000	35000
	4	54000	47000	35000	34000	35000	33000
1987	1	57000	47000	36000	33000	34000	35000

15. Nationwide Building Society

15.1 TECHNICAL DETAILS

(a) Source of data and timing

Society's own lending records at the mortgage approval stage

(b) Types of data and periods covered

Average prices: 1952 to date

Index of average prices: 1946 to date.

An index of price ranges was published up to 1968 Q4 and an index of average prices by class of house, based on building standards and age, was published up to 1962 Q4. These have not been reproduced here.

Some of the figures for periods before 1977 Q4 are revised figures previously unpublished by the Society and they therefore differ from figures published in the bulletins at this time. In addition, an Appendix Table at the end of this chapter gives long-run quarterly series of average prices for all, new, modern and older dwellings (from 1952 Q4 to date) and corresponding index numbers (from 1946 to date). These data represent "final" figures as opposed to those regularly published in the Society's bulletins which are compiled and reported before the final figures become available. The Table also provides information for a longer time period than is available from the published bulletins.

Available data

DATA BREAKDOWNS	DATA TYPES	
	AVERAGE PRICES	INDEX NUMBERS
HOUSE DATA		
All houses	*	*
New/Non-new	*	*
Type	*	
Size		
Age	*	*
LOCAL DATA		
Regions	*	
Sub-regions		
Towns		
BUYER DATA		
First-time buyer	*	
Former owner-occupier	*	

(c) Frequency

Average prices: annual 1952-1959, quarterly 1960 Q1 to date previously unpublished (quarterly average prices, back to 1952, are included in an Appendix Table to this chapter). The Society published average prices six-monthly from 1959 Q4 to 1973 Q4

and quarterly thereafter. Unpublished data provided by the Society are reproduced in Tables 15.14 and 15.15 giving annual figures prior to 1960 and quarterly thereafter.

Index of average prices: annually from 1952-1976 (Q4 only for each year) and then quarterly, but previously unpublished quarterly figures from 1952 are included in the Appendix Table referred to above (see pages 301-303).

(d) Geographical coverage

United Kingdom subdivided into regions. The regional breakdown is currently by official standard regions (defined in Appendix B). Prior to 1977 Q4, Nationwide regions differed from these regions in that they were based on branch office territories (these were subject to occasional changes). The regional figures back to 1976 Q1 shown in this volume have been reworked according to official standard regions. In 1971 Q4 Wales was defined as a separate entity whereas before it had been subdivided between the regions defined as South West, Midlands and North West (the present counties of Gwent, Glamorgan and Dyfed were part of South West; Powys part of Midlands; Gwynedd and Clwyd part of North West).

(e) Method of analysis

Average prices and index of average prices: based on the Society's mortgage lending records for the purchase of dwellings for owner-occupation but excluding the following categories:

exceptionally large dwellings (those with a floor space over 2,200 sq ft, or 6 or more bedrooms);

dwellings at the extreme ends of the price range (measured both in terms of actual price and price per sq ft);

sales to sitting tenants and other sales below market price;

dwellings built before 1800.

Except for the figures analysed by buyer type (first-time buyer and former owner-occupier) the figures do *not* represent simple average prices. They represent *weighted* averages (calculated as an average price per square foot x average size) weighted by region and property type. The weights for house size and type are based on the properties on which the Nationwide has approved loans over the previous eight years within each region. The regional weights employed for deriving UK figures are based on official (DOE) estimates of the stock of owner-occupied dwellings in each region. This is done to eliminate any unrepresentativeness in the regional pattern of Nationwide lending.

The present method of calculation was introduced in 1977 Q4 and carried back to 1973 Q4. Previously no weighting pattern was employed, except that the influence of house size was allowed for by analysing average prices per square foot. The latter was introduced from 1959 Q4. Indices for the period 1946-1952 are based on surveyors' estimates.

All figures have been rounded to the nearest £10.

15.2 LIST OF TABLES

Average prices (current series; see also Appendix Table)

15.1   United Kingdom: all, age of dwelling, type of buyer, type of house. 1968-
15.2   Regions: all dwellings. 1976-
15.3   Regions: new dwellings. 1976-
15.4   Regions: modern dwellings. 1976-
15.5   Regions: older dwellings. 1976-
15.6   Regions: detached houses. 1976-
15.7   Regions: semi-detached houses. 1976-
15.8   Regions: terraced houses. 1976-
15.9   Regions: bungalows, flats and maisonettes. 1976-

15.10 United Kingdom and regions by age of house: detached houses. 1976-
15.11 United Kingdom and regions by age of house: semi-detached houses. 1976-
15.12 United Kingdom and regions by age of house: terraced houses. 1976-
15.13 United Kingdom and regions by age of house: bungalows, flats and maisonettes. 1976-

Average prices (historical series; see also Appendix Table)

15.14 Regions: new dwellings. 1954-1975
15.15 Regions: existing dwellings. 1952-1975
15.16 Regions: type of buyer. 1977-1981

Index of average prices (see also Appendix Table)

15.17 United Kingdom: all, new, modern and older. 1946-

15.3 CROSS-CLASSIFICATIONS OF DATA

(a) Two-way classifications

Numbers in the grid below refer to the corresponding tables compiled for this data source

ALL HOUSES	NEW	NON-NEW	AGE	TYPE	SIZE	REGIONS	SUB-REGIONS	TOWNS	FTB/FOO
	15.10-15.13		15.10-15.13						
15.2	15.3, 15.14	15.15	15.4-15.5	15.6-15.9					
						15.16			
HOUSE DATA						**LOCAL DATA**			**BUYER TYPE**

(b) Three-way classifications

House type by region by age of house: Tables 15.10 - 15.13

15.4 PUBLICATIONS

(a) Data

The following are published by the Nationwide Building Society (formerly the Co-operative Permanent Building Society), London:

Occasional Bulletin. Quarterly from Jan 1952-Oct 1977
Housing Trends. Quarterly from Jan 1978-Jan 1981
House Prices. Quarterly from April 1981 to date

(b) Description of methodology

None

(c) Supplementary studies

The Nationwide Building Society has published a large number of supplementary studies. The following is a list of titles published to date:

Who Buys Houses. Bulletin Nos: 38, 59, (supplement to 59), 87, 111, and 124 (Jul 1960 to Dec 1974)

What Houses are People Buying. Bulletin Nos: 51, 75, 97 (Oct 1962 to Oct 1970)

Newly Built Houses. An Analysis of 2,802 New Houses and the People Who Bought Them. Bulletin No: 72 (April 1966)

A Regional Comparison of Average House Prices and Incomes. Bulletin Nos: 76, 100, 112 (Dec 1966 to Oct 1972)

Central Heating. Bulletin No: 98 (Nov 1970)

Why do People Move? Bulletin No: 99 (Nov 1970)

The House Buyer's Choice. Bulletin No: 113 (Dec 1972)

House Prices Over the Past Thirty Years. June 1976, April 1985

First Homes. 1979

Home Owners on the Move. 1979

First-time Home Buyers in 1980

More First-time Buyers. 1981

House Buyers Moving. Sep 1982

Home Buying in London. Press Release 1983

Nationwide Lending to Council House Tenants. Press Briefing 1983

Lending to Women. September 1984 and February 1986

Lending in the Major Conurbations. November 1984

Lending to Older Borrowers (compared with all borrowers). December 1985

Housing as an Investment. April 1986

Are First-time Buyers being Prevented from Entering the Owner-occupied Housing Market?. July 1986

House Prices in Europe. Jan 1987

Local Area Housing Statistics. 1985:

South West England	Northern England
The Solent Area of Hampshire	London Boroughs
London and the Home Counties	Buckinghamshire
Scotland	West Midlands County
Wales	North West England
Yorkshire and Humberside	Berkshire
East Midlands	

Local Area Housing Statistics. 1986:

South West England	South Coast Counties
Surrey	Merseyside
Greater Manchester	Kent
East Anglia	South Yorkshire
Hertfordshire	Wales
West Midlands Region	Northern Ireland
Greater Glasgow	London Boroughs
Essex	

Local Area Housing Statistics. 1987:

Wiltshire
Avon
Lancashire
Bedfordshire
Nottinghamshire

APPENDIX TABLE

NATIONWIDE BUILDING SOCIETY

AVERAGE PRICES AND INDEX NUMBERS (at approval stage) 1946-

UNITED KINGDOM: ALL, NEW, MODERN, OLDER

Year	AVERAGE PRICES				INDEX (1973 Q4 = 100)			
	All	New	Modern	Older	All	New	Modern	Older
1946 Q4						15	16	14
1947 Q4							20	16
1948 Q4							19	16
1949 Q4							21	18
1950 Q4							21	18
1951 Q4							23	20
1952 Q4	2030	2090	2260	1700	21	21	22	19
1953 1	2030	2090	2240	1720	21	21	21	20
2	2030	2090	2240	1720	21	21	21	20
3	2020	2100	2240	1700	21	21	21	19
4	2010	2100	2210	1720	21	21	21	20
1954 1	2000	2100	2190	1700	20	21	21	19
2	2010	2100	2220	1690	21	21	21	19
3	2000	2110	2180	1700	20	21	21	19
4	1990	2110	2170	1690	20	21	21	19
1955 1	2040	2150	2220	1750	21	21	21	20
2	2080	2200	2280	1760	21	22	22	20
3	2080	2200	2280	1770	21	22	22	20
4	2080	2200	2270	1770	21	22	22	20
1956 1	2120	2260	2330	1780	22	22	22	20
2	2150	2300	2360	1820	22	23	23	21
3	2150	2300	2360	1820	22	23	23	21
4	2150	2310	2350	1820	22	23	23	21
1957 1	2170	2330	2360	1850	22	23	23	21
2	2170	2350	2350	1860	22	23	23	21
3	2180	2360	2360	1860	22	23	23	21
4	2180	2380	2360	1860	22	24	23	21
1958 1	2200	2390	2370	1880	23	24	23	21
2	2200	2390	2360	1890	23	24	23	22
3	2210	2400	2390	1890	23	24	23	22
4	2220	2410	2400	1900	23	24	23	22
1959 1	2230	2420	2400	1920	23	24	23	22
2	2260	2440	2430	1950	23	24	23	22
3	2280	2470	2450	1960	23	25	23	22
4	2330	2540	2510	1990	24	25	24	23
1960 1	2350	2580	2530	2020	24	26	24	23
2	2400	2640	2570	2070	25	26	25	24
3	2470	2700	2670	2110	25	27	26	24
4	2500	2740	2690	2150	26	27	26	25
1961 1	2580	2870	2780	2190	26	28	27	25
2	2620	2900	2800	2260	27	29	27	26
3	2650	2910	2820	2310	27	29	27	26
4	2730	2950	2930	2360	28	29	28	27
1962 1	2740	2970	2940	2370	28	29	28	27
2	2790	3060	2980	2420	29	30	29	28
3	2840	3100	3030	2460	29	31	29	28
4	2870	3130	3050	2500	29	31	29	29
1963 1	2950	3160	3170	2560	30	31	30	29
2	3030	3230	3270	2630	31	32	31	30
3	3060	3260	3310	2650	31	32	32	30
4	3160	3300	3440	2740	32	33	33	31
1964 1	3220	3350	3470	2820	33	33	33	32
2	3320	3430	3600	2880	34	34	35	33
3	3370	3550	3630	2940	35	35	35	34
4	3420	3570	3730	2940	35	35	36	34

APPENDIX TABLE

NATIONWIDE BUILDING SOCIETY

AVERAGE PRICES AND INDEX NUMBERS (at approval stage) 1946–

UNITED KINGDOM: ALL, NEW, MODERN, OLDER (continued)

Year	AVERAGE PRICES					INDEX (1973 Q4 = 100)			
	All	New	Modern	Older		All	New	Modern	Older
1965 1	3510	3670	3890	2950		36	36	37	34
2	3590	3770	3910	3100		37	37	37	35
3	3630	3810	3930	3140		37	38	38	36
4	3670	3830	4020	3150		38	38	39	36
1966 1	3720	3860	4090	3160		38	38	39	36
2	3820	3960	4170	3300		39	39	40	38
3	3820	4030	4200	3230		39	40	40	37
4	3850	4080	4170	3310		39	40	40	38
1967 1	3910	4150	4260	3340		40	41	41	38
2	3970	4190	4340	3390		41	42	42	39
3	4040	4210	4410	3490		41	42	42	40
4	4120	4300	4480	3570		42	43	43	41
1968 1	4190	4310	4570	3650		43	43	44	42
2	4290	4460	4680	3710		44	44	45	42
3	4350	4570	4700	3790		45	45	45	43
4	4390	4620	4740	3820		45	46	45	44
1969 1	4450	4620	4820	3900		46	46	46	44
2	4510	4660	4900	3940		46	46	47	45
3	4540	4760	4890	3990		47	47	47	45
4	4630	4810	5010	4050		47	48	48	46
1970 1	4700	4900	5060	4140		48	49	49	47
2	4780	4910	5170	4210		49	49	50	48
3	4840	5040	5180	4290		50	50	50	49
4	4920	5120	5280	4360		50	51	51	50
1971 1	5090	5310	5470	4510		52	53	52	51
2	5270	5540	5670	4640		54	55	54	53
3	5630	5870	6050	4990		58	58	58	57
4	5940	6190	6430	5210		61	61	62	59
1972 1	6450	6680	6940	5730		66	66	67	65
2	7040	7210	7650	6170		72	72	73	70
3	7940	8330	8540	6980		81	83	82	80
4	8460	9020	9040	7460		87	89	87	85
1973 1	8850	9400	9450	7480		91	93	91	85
2	9310	9770	10020	8200		95	97	96	94
3	9680	10030	10430	8550		99	100	100	97
4	9760	10080	10430	8770		100	100	100	100
1974 1	9920	10220	10610	8920		102	101	102	102
2	10020	10340	10650	9080		103	103	102	104
3	10140	10410	10740	9270		104	103	103	106
4	10200	10570	10800	9320		105	105	104	106
1975 1	10380	10710	10920	9550		106	106	105	109
2	10720	11150	11290	9800		110	111	108	112
3	10970	11480	11550	10010		112	114	111	114
4	11280	11950	11900	10210		116	119	114	116
1976 1	11510	12240	12130	10420		118	121	116	119
2	11730	12540	12310	10650		120	124	118	121
3	11990	12850	12660	10770		123	127	121	123
4	12200	13190	12810	10990		125	131	123	125
1977 1	12400	13470	13000	11190		127	134	125	128
2	12680	13880	13270	11400		130	138	127	130
3	12960	14220	13540	11670		133	141	130	133
4	13140	14660	13710	11760		135	145	131	134

Year	AVERAGE PRICES					INDEX (1973 Q4 = 100)			
	All	New	Modern	Older		All	New	Modern	Older
1978 1	13810	15320	14420	12380		141	152	138	141
2	14480	15980	15140	12990		148	159	145	148
3	15900	17470	16810	14140		163	173	161	161
4	16810	18440	17780	15010		172	183	170	171
1979 1	17780	19690	18720	15970		182	195	179	182
2	19060	20840	20080	17240		195	207	193	197
3	20470	22470	21440	18690		210	223	206	213
4	21950	23750	23090	20100		225	236	221	229
1980 1	22660	25310	23760	20590		232	251	228	235
2	23330	26210	24420	21230		239	260	234	242
3	23610	26650	24680	21520		242	264	237	245
4	23470	26790	24510	21390		240	266	235	244
1981 1	23760	27710	24950	21460		243	275	239	245
2	24080	28170	25300	21840		247	279	243	249
3	24170	28070	25540	21860		248	278	245	249
4	23780	28690	25050	21350		244	285	240	243
1982 1	24140	29190	25290	21750		247	290	242	248
2	24660	29480	26010	22270		253	292	249	254
3	24950	29750	26500	22490		256	295	254	256
4	25560	30430	27130	23130		262	302	260	264
1983 1	26280	30800	27980	23800		269	306	268	271
2	27410	32240	29200	24750		281	320	280	282
3	28240	33000	30030	25560		289	327	288	291
4	28690	33860	30470	25900		294	336	292	295
1984 1	29900	34930	31690	27120		306	347	304	309
2	31060	35820	32790	28340		318	355	314	323
3	31550	36040	33260	28920		323	358	319	330
4	33060	37910	34940	30110		339	376	335	343
1985 1	34160	39910	36150	30740		350	396	347	351
2	34970	40480	36940	31640		358	402	354	361
3	35350	41430	37380	32070		362	411	358	366
4	36190	42980	37750	32720		371	426	362	373
1986 1	37060	44080	38630	33380		380	437	370	381
2	38470	45380	39960	34930		394	450	383	398
3	39830	46810	41380	36210		408	464	397	413
4	41360	48310	42910	37690		424	479	411	430
1987 1	43350	50090	44780	39650		444	497	429	452

NATIONWIDE BUILDING SOCIETY

AVERAGE PRICES (at approval stage) 1968 -

15.1 UNITED KINGDOM:
ALL, AGE OF DWELLING, TYPE OF BUYER, TYPE OF HOUSE

£

Year		All	AGE OF DWELLING			TYPE OF BUYER		TYPE OF HOUSE			
			New	Modern	Older	First-time Buyer	Former Owner-occupier	Detached	Semi-detached	Terraced	Other
1968	2		4530								
	4		4680								
1969	2		4820								
	4		4800	5080	3780						
1970	2		4980	5310	3990						
	4		5110	5650	4230						
1971	2		5540	6130	4460						
	4		6170	6810	5160						
1972	2		6920	7950	6010						
	4		8730	9730	8090						
1973	2		9650	10460	8630						
	4	9770	9780	10520	8880	8830	12490				
1974	1	9690	9870	10520	9880						
	2	9860	10200	10530	9240						
	3	9950	10670	10150	8760						
	4	10070	10780	10430	8860	9600	12880				
1975	1	10310	11290	10730	9410						
	2	10630	11840	11300	10230						
	3	11030	12440	12040	10890						
	4	11340	12600	12800	10640	10130	14510				
1976	1	11410	12260	12020	10900			15510	10730	9320	11500
	2	11800	12810	12330	10230			16040	11070	9700	11860
	3	12040	13310	12870	10660			16420	11270	9820	12230
	4	12250	13620	12850	10980	10860	15560	16770	11550	9890	12350
1977	1	12460	13590	12870	10710	10800	15680	17050	11730	10120	12510
	2	12740	13900	13350	11120	11010	15970	17500	11980	10270	12850
	3	13020	14410	13590	11480	11230	16400	17850	12280	10490	13120
	4	13200	14630	13780	11790	11390	16370	18260	12440	10520	13310
1978	1	13850	15310	14490	12370	11620	16930	18950	13160	11080	13950
	2	14380	15880	15060	12860	12020	17960	19850	13650	11450	14450
	3	15740	17260	16610	14030	12760	20080	21960	14960	12470	15780
	4	16660	18250	17650	14850	13650	21110	23420	15840	13160	16700
1979	1	17520	19320	18430	15780	14410	21740	24400	16740	13980	17530
	2	18870	20670	19860	17070	15200	23240	26100	17990	15200	18930
	3	20250	22220	21260	18420	16430	25480	28160	19390	16270	20210
	4	21540	23420	22680	19670	17680	27910	29910	20600	17420	21600
1980	1	22500	24970	23600	20480	18160	28780	31400	21530	18110	22530
	2	23270	26050	24370	21200	18410	29040	32820	22310	18690	23170
	3	23600	26650	24650	21520	18870	29670	33320	22700	18850	23570
	4	23480	26790	24480	21440	19090	29310	33080	22740	18940	23270
1981	1	23620	27400	24840	21340	19190	29600	33420	23110	18910	23510
	2	24160	28250	25340	21890	18450	30190	34240	23740	19290	24270
	3	24170	27980	25530	21860	19120	29930	34580	23800	19110	24420
	4	23740	28360	25080	21320	18830	28750	34580	23500	18550	23960
1982	1	24040	29070	25200	21650	19790	29400	34680	23700	19010	24280
	2	24670	29460	26020	22290	20290	31310	36240	24390	19370	25080
	3	24910	29600	26500	22440	20470	32350	36430	24720	19660	25220
	4	25530	30230	27120	23130	21730	32950	37190	25300	20200	25940

£

Year	All	AGE OF PROPERTY			TYPE OF BUYER		TYPE OF HOUSE			
		New	Modern	Older	First- time Buyer	Former Owner- occupier	Detached	Semi- detached	Terraced	Other
1983 1	26110	30670	27880	23560	22070	34520	37970	25760	20670	26430
2	27340	32160	29140	24680	22490	36370	39880	26840	21600	27350
3	28200	32990	29980	25530	23060	37140	41100	27580	21960	28240
4	28720	33850	30520	25930	23230	37820	41900	27740	22270	28980
1984 1	29690	34710	31510	26880	24760	39090	43170	28560	23060	29770
2	31370	36520	33250	28430	27030	42910	45540	30050	24200	31170
3	31460	36070	33120	28840	27440	43190	45740	30100	24280	31140
4	32810	37440	34680	29930	27300	41520	46890	31280	25110	32840
1985 1	33850	39310	35840	30420	29540	44970	50390	33780	25990	33300
2	34860	40390	36880	31500	30460	46260	52450	34590	27330	33850
3	35450	41380	37310	32000	29590	46450	53130	35340	27610	34980
4	36250	43030	37810	32820	30550	46230	54410	35930	28320	35730
1986 1	36820	43820	38360	33190	31400	46230	54470	36560	29040	36080
2	38180	45080	39830	34530	33010	50110	56860	37900	30200	37200
3	39640	46630	41200	36020	32310	51600	59480	39300	31380	38680
4	41150	48190	42770	37470	33280	53250	61800	41210	32460	39900
1987 1	42910	49650	44230	39300	33860	54820	63570	42720	34700	41090

NATIONWIDE BUILDING SOCIETY

AVERAGE PRICES (at approval stage) 1976 –

15.2 REGIONS: ALL DWELLINGS

Year		Northern	Yorks & Humberside	North West	East Midlands	West Midlands	East Anglia
1976	1	9550	9310	9630	9360	10820	10940
	2	9860	9630	9840	9700	11220	11200
	3	10120	9940	10090	9870	11420	11400
	4	10570	10180	10390	10090	11660	11640
1977	1	10810	10300	10710	10190	11840	11650
	2	11170	10520	11060	10500	12180	11940
	3	11410	10730	11350	10650	12510	12280
	4	11520	11130	11520	10740	12540	12490
1978	1	11900	11610	12180	11230	13260	13100
	2	12370	10900	12440	11430	13510	13310
	3	13190	12570	13390	12490	14880	14230
	4	13570	13110	14320	13030	16150	15100
1979	1	14160	13650	15210	13900	16800	16040
	2	14960	14350	16290	14940	17500	17340
	3	16100	15720	17360	15870	18980	18900
	4	16740	16620	18270	16490	20110	20560
1980	1	17630	17220	19220	17560	21060	21820
	2	18110	18130	20120	18610	21660	23190
	3	18650	18770	20840	19170	21840	23290
	4	18610	18750	20520	19130	21540	23620
1981	1	18200	19260	20560	19320	22030	23600
	2	19120	19340	21150	19640	22430	24150
	3	19190	19390	21010	20110	22500	23800
	4	18890	18960	20610	19960	21780	24200
1982	1	19290	19350	20530	19680	21970	23180
	2	19700	19580	21200	20370	22340	24180
	3	20320	19530	21060	20290	22120	24880
	4	21000	20080	21540	21150	22740	25740
1983	1	20810	20370	21740	21280	23600	25990
	2	21870	21230	22490	22460	23860	27120
	3	22690	21670	22930	22710	24700	28290
	4	23230	21820	23380	23010	24530	28700
1984	1	23140	22480	23860	23710	25510	29650
	2	24510	23490	25450	25110	26910	31290
	3	24360	23560	25020	24760	26880	31200
	4	25440	25020	26610	26040	28310	32700
1985	1	26080	25290	26990	26920	28910	33860
	2	26290	26030	27660	27730	29410	35530
	3	26750	25760	28040	27760	29910	36400
	4	27050	26650	27920	28220	30330	37100
1986	1	26580	26610	28520	28970	29960	37510
	2	27800	27080	29140	30410	30650	39710
	3	27550	27320	29760	30880	31140	40180
	4	27820	27960	29780	32500	32560	42670
1987	1	28100	29080	30730	33720	33300	44170

£

Outer South East	Outer Metrop	Greater London	South West	Wales	Scotland	Northern Ireland
12380	14840	13930	11430	10130	12180	11620
12570	15480	14330	11960	10500	12780	12360
12840	15730	14470	12210	10630	13180	13030
12890	15870	14660	12280	10840	13450	13430
13070	15960	15040	12520	11010	13620	13850
13310	16240	15180	12790	11160	13910	14570
13640	16610	15350	12960	11470	14370	15160
13920	16740	15710	13150	11540	14350	15240
14550	17640	16590	13800	11940	14850	16340
15110	18630	17500	14420	12410	15370	17200
16740	20840	19490	15850	13480	16510	18680
17880	22470	20620	16550	14130	17100	19280
18950	23090	22050	17570	15150	17600	19710
20540	25030	24560	19030	16460	18480	20700
22430	26940	25950	20480	17480	19530	21930
24060	28570	27640	22200	18720	21400	22460
25480	30250	28430	23060	19190	21440	23590
26090	30770	29400	23710	19880	22150	24080
26450	31110	29300	24120	19940	22270	23700
26070	30750	29270	24160	20110	22750	22890
26230	31170	29330	24390	20080	22340	22750
26960	31700	29720	25260	20200	23570	23020
26850	31660	30070	24830	20290	23660	22030
26350	31410	29430	24250	19810	23310	21780
26540	31760	30020	24720	20530	24180	22170
27380	32610	30990	25230	20930	25000	21930
27850	33470	31120	25840	21590	24810	21970
28410	34510	31980	25930	22060	25480	22180
29550	35510	32490	27330	22320	25620	22390
31300	37820	34500	28460	22900	27000	22970
32560	39090	36160	29450	23330	27580	23050
32930	40780	37160	29990	23660	28330	23700
34690	42410	39060	30930	24380	28170	24140
36730	45030	41360	32250	25810	29830	24830
36840	45640	41740	32780	25910	29660	25180
38200	46630	43650	34290	26500	30830	25680
39430	48640	46310	35170	26870	31520	26170
41140	50300	48360	35560	27720	31890	26450
41440	51710	49840	36640	27680	32130	27070
42570	53280	52100	37200	28120	32520	27080
43690	54030	53890	38060	28630	32450	27130
45810	56280	56210	39710	28950	33170	27930
48010	59880	60100	41470	29810	33740	28350
49840	63490	64160	42460	30220	33620	27510
51720	68040	68310	44090	30580	34090	27390

NATIONWIDE BUILDING SOCIETY

AVERAGE PRICES (at approval stage) 1976 –

15.3 REGIONS: NEW DWELLINGS

Year		Northern	Yorks & Humberside	North West	East Midlands	West Midlands	East Anglia
1976	1	11290	10370	11120	10210	12290	11450
	2	11650	10710	11500	10560	12640	11830
	3	12040	11040	11800	10790	12890	12190
	4	12130	11420	12220	11250	13520	12280
1977	1	12550	11660	12630	11350	13890	12330
	2	13250	11960	13070	11640	14190	13170
	3	13510	12250	13360	11830	14120	13600
	4	13790	12570	13710	12100	14990	13570
1978	1	14000	13490	14520	12550	15440	14090
	2	14770	13820	14720	13140	16000	14380
	3	15680	14890	16190	14360	17340	15730
	4	16090	16030	17500	15350	18650	16600
1979	1	17240	16920	18370	16290	19910	18200
	2	18160	16610	20310	17750	20530	19500
	3	19610	18630	21620	19060	22990	21240
	4	20260	19810	22240	19710	23580	22800
1980	1	21650	20810	23660	21010	26040	25170
	2	22540	22770	25470	22270	25740	25810
	3	23020	23040	25610	22860	26470	26580
	4	23420	23390	26120	23840	26290	26230
1981	1	23430	23460	26690	24510	27710	26770
	2	24250	24610	27490	24820	28080	28310
	3	24680	23860	26940	26160	27960	27160
	4	24800	24920	27280	25890	28300	27570
1982	1	25650	26230	27480	25750	29170	26600
	2	25770	26050	28300	26500	28840	27560
	3	27280	26120	28770	25840	28310	28660
	4	26970	26080	30030	26390	28630	28820
1983	1	27870	26750	30420	26660	30060	27920
	2	28730	27460	30520	28250	30300	29950
	3	28400	28210	31360	28740	30940	30030
	4	30550	30310	31110	30100	31910	31090
1984	1	31490	30130	31610	29450	31780	31070
	2	31460	32170	33820	31500	33630	34100
	3	31350	31750	33080	31070	32700	34950
	4	32610	34590	34200	32700	34790	34330
1985	1	32600	33270	36880	33730	36620	37400
	2	32280	34610	35930	33050	36930	38810
	3	33670	33680	36520	34820	37150	40610
	4	34170	34100	37810	35700	39320	40550
1986	1	35000	35370	37740	36240	37570	41520
	2	35680	36290	38560	37810	38660	44210
	3	36560	36650	39100	38310	40400	44550
	4	37260	37470	38230	40830	41600	47520
1987	1	35410	37900	42370	44220	41750	50240

Outer South East	Outer Metrop	Greater London	South West	Wales	Scotland	Northern Ireland
13090	16140	16770	11580	11270	13360	12950
13230	16900	17170	11800	11610	13530	13420
13770	17150	17500	11930	11790	13830	14040
13870	17510	18070	12050	12160	14410	14380
14070	17480	18200	12460	12480	14620	15310
14450	17830	19420	12840	12620	14810	16560
14930	18230	20350	13220	12840	15570	16720
15430	18880	20300	13550	13490	15750	17270
15910	19910	21110	14170	14180	16240	18760
16520	21150	22370	14700	14560	16710	19500
18280	22860	24280	16180	15060	18140	20330
19470	23660	26220	17070	16070	18760	20970
20630	24950	28100	18140	17720	19280	21990
22660	27480	31300	19640	19300	20160	22890
24900	29600	32190	21080	20110	20620	23380
26560	30720	33000	22900	21530	22840	23900
28240	33080	34020	24710	22590	22850	26500
29130	33900	34760	25420	24160	24220	27540
30080	35020	35830	26310	24430	94910	27270
29640	35070	37410	25740	24530	25970	26100
30280	36460	36950	26900	25140	25520	26010
31010	37920	39020	27470	25840	26310	26540
30590	36700	40100	27890	25920	26270	24740
30930	37280	41900	27490	25620	27580	24820
32350	37730	41480	28470	26900	28670	25360
31410	39320	40960	27980	27650	30330	26060
31660	40090	40630	28360	26520	30560	24470
33330	39750	39950	28970	26870	31660	26100
33910	40060	38690	29990	27630	30600	25020
37310	42180	40490	32010	28270	31660	26140
38060	43760	40910	33260	28950	32930	26310
38910	45260	40020	33510	28310	33760	27310
41280	47860	41350	34640	31320	33440	27530
42590	50450	46260	35760	32240	34480	28410
43740	49290	43160	36400	31670	32770	27800
43950	50760	46460	38480	31690	34560	28530
45220	53460	46140	38760	31530	34950	29040
47050	54070	52040	39410	32790	35540	29110
48000	56430	52870	40830	34000	36320	30760
50490	59330	57210	41570	34050	37460	30770
52270	58830	61380	41620	36010	38420	30190
53280	63090	60380	44700	35790	38220	31560
56960	66910	61580	45860	38730	38790	31440
58470	70460	66500	47910	36840	38680	32030
60410	73950	66880	48800	37350	37620	31860

NATIONWIDE BUILDING SOCIETY

AVERAGE PRICES (at approval stage) 1976 –

15.4 REGIONS: MODERN DWELLINGS

Year		Northern	Yorks & Humberside	North West	East Midlands	West Midlands	East Anglia
1976	1	10720	10370	10410	10350	11000	11520
	2	10790	10430	10570	10830	11430	11660
	3	11170	10860	10890	10830	11710	12040
	4	11880	11080	11220	10950	11820	12190
1977	1	12140	11180	11540	11110	11990	12170
	2	12340	11430	11950	11310	12400	12380
	3	12640	11650	12090	11620	12650	12660
	4	12680	12190	12410	11620	12580	13080
1978	1	13300	12660	13140	12240	13500	13720
	2	13750	13030	13520	12350	13700	13920
	3	14740	13900	14650	13690	15220	15020
	4	15450	14350	15810	14090	16690	16170
1979	1	15820	14850	16710	15310	17300	17120
	2	16530	16120	18280	16490	18170	18010
	3	18140	17750	19270	17210	19400	19660
	4	18900	18600	20510	18010	20930	21440
1980	1	19790	19600	21430	19030	21640	22550
	2	20200	20040	22120	20350	22470	24470
	3	21090	21040	22850	20930	22430	24310
	4	20650	20700	22410	20770	21970	25000
1981	1	21100	21910	22650	20990	22510	24620
	2	21680	21940	23630	21070	22990	24470
	3	21480	22580	23420	21690	23430	24500
	4	21300	21470	23570	21300	22310	25570
1982	1	21560	21880	22960	21180	22220	24300
	2	21640	22410	24260	21940	23220	25120
	3	23250	22350	23930	21970	23160	25620
	4	23870	23030	24630	23220	23950	26650
1983	1	23310	23930	24730	23590	24580	27370
	2	24750	24300	25830	24380	25110	28840
	3	25730	24800	26320	24890	25920	29360
	4	26180	25440	27130	25090	25500	30300
1984	1	26350	26280	27410	26200	26770	31120
	2	28080	26970	29510	27170	27540	32000
	3	27340	27200	28580	26750	27690	31710
	4	28230	28550	30160	28550	29240	34440
1985	1	29080	28940	30100	29430	29730	34790
	2	29530	29990	31520	30190	30500	35600
	3	29990	29070	31900	30610	30790	38100
	4	29630	30120	31040	30580	31330	38050
1986	1	28880	29870	31760	30820	30660	39730
	2	30830	29750	32760	32580	31360	40660
	3	30230	30420	33400	32760	31780	41260
	4	30100	31680	33280	34840	33250	44280
1987	1	29790	32040	33240	35000	35050	44760

						£
Outer South East	Outer Metrop	Greater London	South West	Wales	Scotland	Northern Ireland
12870	15030	15090	11940	11110	13340	11110
13100	15700	15410	12380	11490	14170	11890
13430	15950	15710	12830	11680	14630	12630
13370	16060	15700	12880	11890	14600	13220
13560	16150	16070	13110	11970	14820	13400
13750	16390	16350	13230	12330	15150	13770
14060	16710	16550	13430	12600	15470	14500
14340	16840	16800	13650	12620	15320	14330
15100	17650	17740	14300	12990	15890	15300
15780	18840	18600	14990	13610	16650	16230
17560	21350	21030	16760	14990	17700	18200
18980	23270	22290	17440	15550	18420	18670
20050	23710	24050	18200	16480	18780	18880
21820	25660	25990	19990	18090	19610	19900
22420	27500	27450	21480	18710	21190	21770
25200	29420	29280	23270	20480	22640	22520
26660	30950	30100	23960	20580	22400	23310
26970	31540	30720	24940	21710	22920	23770
27130	31430	31010	24980	21820	22780	23510
26810	31000	30270	25340	21880	23680	23530
27050	31820	30740	25110	22530	23940	23390
28000	31710	30820	26220	22090	25070	24010
27980	32100	31470	25470	22900	25070	23910
27480	31650	30430	25490	21900	24400	23740
27380	31980	31760	25270	22460	25610	24150
28330	33020	31990	26250	23040	26480	23580
28880	34110	33200	26900	24050	26360	25210
29420	34800	33140	26810	24480	27290	25040
30590	36140	34080	28090	25050	27840	25800
32270	38360	36040	29270	26190	28970	26510
33980	39890	37430	29870	26310	29560	26140
34250	41600	38420	30410	26850	29790	27370
35740	43130	40230	31870	26940	29710	27560
38170	45670	43070	33320	29070	32410	28090
37810	45700	42530	33900	29440	32080	29290
39530	47970	44090	35250	29580	33780	29390
41040	49420	47240	36240	30140	34330	29300
42570	51240	49060	36300	31010	33990	30210
42760	51980	49810	37200	30790	34690	30140
43400	53120	51570	37970	31720	34570	29630
44570	55030	52560	39300	31060	34390	29710
47400	56640	56220	40130	31670	35300	30730
49190	60180	59970	42100	32510	35100	31130
50660	63260	64760	42920	32850	35480	29560
53700	67910	66710	44930	33770	35830	29170

NATIONWIDE BUILDING SOCIETY

AVERAGE PRICES (at approval stage) 1976 –

15.5 REGIONS: OLDER DWELLINGS

Year		Northern	Yorks & Humberside	North West	East Midlands	West Midlands	East Anglia
1976	1	7330	7160	8170	7380	9560	9500
	2	7890	7830	8370	7520	9910	9880
	3	7930	7960	8500	7900	9920	9660
	4	8310	8140	8720	8120	10220	10160
1977	1	8410	8240	9010	8130	10300	10210
	2	8770	8350	9250	8620	10520	10210
	3	8930	8490	9730	8520	11240	10610
	4	9010	8760	9650	8630	11010	10610
1978	1	9250	8970	10170	8950	11450	11250
	2	9590	9190	10400	9100	11800	11430
	3	10180	9580	11080	9630	12980	11810
	4	10350	10040	11720	10170	13890	12240
1979	1	11020	10610	12660	10540	14410	12710
	2	11870	11240	13050	11150	14950	14720
	3	12530	12060	14220	12360	16520	16100
	4	13120	13040	14960	12860	17260	17640
1980	1	13990	13220	15820	13850	17980	18330
	2	14490	14320	16770	14640	18710	19440
	3	14850	14860	17690	15320	19070	19610
	4	15070	15210	17340	15090	19020	19890
1981	1	14030	15440	17270	15250	19220	20230
	2	15490	15400	17660	16020	19590	21150
	3	15750	15360	17820	16060	19340	20810
	4	15400	15180	17010	16290	18870	20410
1982	1	15830	15280	17230	15790	19180	19710
	2	16680	15640	17730	16690	19070	21170
	3	16400	15770	17800	16830	18820	22020
	4	17480	16560	18030	17490	19360	23060
1983	1	17390	16360	18340	17330	20290	23140
	2	18090	17630	19100	18840	20250	23290
	3	18830	17900	19400	18690	21130	25910
	4	19130	17420	19640	18710	20890	25090
1984	1	18580	18110	20240	19250	21810	26600
	2	19920	19030	21240	20890	23870	28730
	3	20320	19060	21220	20610	23920	28500
	4	21470	20250	22720	20920	24930	28870
1985	1	21910	20790	23220	21880	25190	30550
	2	22080	21110	23580	23250	25490	33770
	3	22410	21410	23800	22200	26300	31450
	4	23110	22070	23820	23050	25880	33690
1986	1	22470	21710	24280	24360	26330	31780
	2	23210	22620	24590	25420	26870	35680
	3	23020	22600	25250	26160	27040	36020
	4	23470	22540	25430	26810	28450	37390
1987	1	24850	24540	26580	28580	27960	39930

Outer South East	Outer Metrop	Greater London	South West	Wales	Scotland	Northern Ireland
11170	13660	13360	10480	8630	10180	10880
11320	14130	13790	11370	9000	10850	12130
11330	14370	13860	11380	9050	11260	12540
11550	14480	14120	11420	9210	11610	12110
11700	14650	14520	11580	9410	11700	12570
11940	14950	14560	12020	9340	12030	13640
12210	15400	14700	11990	9720	12410	14580
12360	15200	15110	12030	9610	12380	14770
12870	16220	15970	12720	9910	12820	15540
13250	16720	16940	13310	10240	13100	16670
14650	18670	18830	14220	11200	14130	17140
15400	20350	19950	14910	11780	14630	18230
16520	20990	21320	16340	12650	15290	18360
17700	22700	24000	17380	13610	16230	19110
19570	24720	25420	18830	15150	17170	19210
21410	26200	27110	20480	15840	19280	19230
22740	27860	27920	21070	16480	19610	19160
23660	28220	29000	21390	16530	20130	19480
24020	28970	28760	22020	16640	20120	19280
23710	28630	28870	22050	17230	19950	17630
23630	28240	28870	22420	16700	19050	17890
24160	29390	29320	23180	17160	20690	17830
24120	29310	29610	22730	16790	21040	16630
23280	29140	29010	21500	16760	20340	16300
23360	29480	29450	22520	17470	20760	16510
24800	29910	30310	22950	17770	21400	16340
25330	30560	30520	23670	18660	21190	16060
25630	32600	31590	23830	19230	21690	16230
26860	33240	31980	25490	19080	21840	16900
28140	35690	33980	26230	19190	23550	17020
28860	36430	35710	27580	19860	23990	17420
29170	38150	36770	28200	20190	25190	16990
31080	39580	38700	28460	21030	24950	17760
32650	42270	40770	29710	21960	25680	18150
33150	44380	41510	30150	21990	26190	18270
34290	43160	43430	31630	22940	26590	18620
35160	45850	46110	32540	23160	27540	19910
37040	47660	48040	33230	23850	28570	19850
37360	49760	49730	34380	23750	28140	20300
38610	51500	52040	34550	23760	28630	20650
39400	50850	53940	35120	24820	28170	21010
40950	53420	56060	37200	25050	29160	21190
43180	57080	60070	38970	25430	30520	22170
45630	61540	63920	39720	26320	29860	20770
45850	66320	68760	41180	26180	31070	21120

£

NATIONWIDE BUILDING SOCIETY

AVERAGE PRICES (at approval stage) 1976 –

15.6 REGIONS: DETACHED HOUSES

Year		Northern	Yorks & Humberside	North West	East Midlands	West Midlands	East Anglia
1976	1	14700	13850	14390	12350	14450	14120
	2	15000	14120	14590	12800	14990	14290
	3	16050	14720	15000	12980	15650	14540
	4	16660	14990	15650	13420	15980	14790
1977	1	16360	15130	16410	13530	16390	14800
	2	17420	15570	16790	13920	16680	15420
	3	17560	15820	17160	14060	16970	15850
	4	17790	16350	17590	14510	17180	16200
1978	1	17880	17290	18380	14730	18010	16660
	2	18800	17660	18760	15130	18450	16930
	3	20180	18940	21010	17020	20270	19140
	4	21120	20110	22850	17750	22830	20180
1979	1	22080	20830	23670	19240	23640	21800
	2	22570	21360	25320	20740	24610	22740
	3	24700	23620	27760	21950	26500	25140
	4	26400	25210	28700	23580	28070	27100
1980	1	27740	26020	29930	24810	29910	29360
	2	28680	27310	31440	26280	31170	31800
	3	30150	28000	31740	27100	31050	31590
	4	29140	28510	31040	26950	30550	31650
1981	1	30170	28190	31770	27740	31070	32070
	2	29320	29420	32910	28100	31700	33730
	3	30050	29480	32260	29390	32600	31880
	4	29750	29750	32610	29200	32040	32420
1982	1	30290	30010	32270	28700	32390	31820
	2	31250	31670	34260	29840	33390	33600
	3	33700	31040	34440	29640	32390	33840
	4	32550	31220	34550	31370	33770	35330
1983	1	32580	32770	35000	31000	34570	34770
	2	34530	33420	37150	31510	35270	36450
	3	34090	34480	37780	32850	36330	37420
	4	36520	34290	37660	33730	36280	38060
1984	1	35720	35550	38860	33950	37570	40630
	2	37280	38370	42030	37100	39110	41530
	3	38330	37680	41920	36130	39370	40200
	4	39040	39710	42440	37350	40740	42380
1985	1	40490	39450	42060	38750	41850	43740
	2	39560	40890	44970	40100	42860	46370
	3	42000	40280	44500	39850	42760	48550
	4	40850	40710	44750	40850	44110	47530
1986	1	39640	40850	46510	40120	43280	49920
	2	42540	42610	47780	42980	44310	52210
	3	44260	42510	47990	43450	45430	52860
	4	43450	42190	47810	44930	48050	55920
1987	1	41960	43830	49670	47840	48270	57470

£

Outer South East	Outer Metrop	Greater London	South West	Wales	Scotland	Northern Ireland
16860	20760	22460	14800	13660	16140	14530
16930	22270	22160	15520	14150	16900	15860
17560	22000	23070	15730	14550	17310	15970
17590	22390	23740	16080	14650	17400	16970
17910	22530	23560	16440	15070	17640	17170
18260	22900	25030	16890	15540	18020	18090
18690	23310	25160	17390	15760	18410	19250
19370	23730	25840	17540	16120	18810	19990
20040	24890	26930	18420	16360	19180	19680
21320	27490	29920	19330	16980	19790	21630
23720	30410	33120	21920	18630	21700	24050
25320	32800	33900	22850	19880	22590	24010
26340	33350	36460	24250	21310	22670	25660
29180	36670	39910	26560	22400	23770	27090
31470	39470	44410	28370	24080	25090	28020
33300	41360	45760	30520	27110	27820	28590
35440	44060	45920	31750	26870	28460	29920
36660	45200	49460	32700	28420	29310	31230
37190	45660	50480	33470	28460	31020	31780
37100	44800	50910	32860	28390	30640	32450
36750	46150	48840	33140	28650	30200	31240
37900	46350	50080	34680	28370	31280	30980
37850	45740	50870	33460	29980	33870	30210
37700	47160	53890	34530	28610	32800	30000
37680	47720	50760	34230	30190	33360	31580
40050	49370	53520	35510	31660	35080	31250
39080	50310	55890	36660	32230	35510	32040
39980	51240	55250	36720	33500	35620	31580
42180	52510	55640	38330	33680	34640	32310
44620	55730	61590	40100	34250	37840	34270
46010	58690	59870	41490	35030	38720	32580
46640	61510	66640	42100	34520	38840	33560
49830	62500	66680	43550	36130	37170	33780
51930	65380	70030	44170	39380	41830	37150
52190	67170	71730	45450	38540	40710	38180
54360	68150	73200	46070	38650	41830	38530
54660	71260	79080	47540	40080	43590	39020
58080	73140	82830	49570	42170	45060	39490
58630	75890	85110	50630	41790	45080	37110
59270	79590	89610	51840	40560	46280	39300
61220	78170	88820	53190	40860	44080	37600
64040	81760	92910	55630	41040	46690	40250
67820	88160	100820	57530	44640	47490	41320
70790	93080	112230	59000	40750	47020	40450
71460	100700	110600	61570	45080	47770	39190

NATIONWIDE BUILDING SOCIETY

AVERAGE PRICES (at approval stage) 1976 –

15.7 REGIONS: SEMI-DETACHED HOUSES

Year		Northern	Yorks & Humberside	North West	East Midlands	West Midlands	East Anglia
1976	1	9890	8770	9210	8560	9920	9800
	2	10290	9060	9330	8810	10250	10290
	3	10460	9320	9540	9050	10300	10500
	4	10960	9620	9930	9130	10600	10700
1977	1	11260	9790	10210	9110	10700	10590
	2	11530	9820	10540	9400	11070	10750
	3	11850	10100	10800	9520	11370	10840
	4	11900	10580	10990	9580	11380	11180
1978	1	12830	11010	11770	10200	12160	11970
	2	12940	11300	11940	10380	12340	12060
	3	14010	11890	12790	11270	14040	12290
	4	14420	12520	13710	11690	14750	13890
1979	1	14830	12930	14790	12400	15590	14290
	2	15880	13890	15640	13320	16030	15530
	3	17040	15200	16790	14380	17520	16980
	4	17700	15760	17750	14520	18730	18840
1980	1	18480	16810	18740	15550	19580	19700
	2	19410	17800	19660	16950	20020	20430
	3	19700	18080	20520	17110	20360	20480
	4	19890	18390	20240	17530	20250	21150
1981	1	19450	19430	20490	18020	21080	21240
	2	21270	19310	21110	18280	21480	21630
	3	20480	19960	21030	18540	21030	21960
	4	20530	18880	20670	18990	20520	22290
1982	1	21350	19040	20820	18120	20990	21450
	2	21290	19610	21660	19070	21360	21640
	3	21880	20170	21470	18720	21530	22740
	4	22820	20560	22370	20000	21610	23670
1983	1	22700	20520	22660	19950	22070	24170
	2	23410	21780	22780	21350	22480	24030
	3	24210	21780	23060	21220	22850	25630
	4	24390	21850	23380	20640	22680	24850
1984	1	24080	22290	23750	21640	23190	25560
	2	25610	22970	24970	22200	24230	27700
	3	24920	23540	24470	22070	24050	28020
	4	26050	24040	26050	22980	24850	29960
1985	1	26810	25300	26630	24340	25690	30950
	2	27700	25790	27160	24660	26250	29940
	3	28200	25100	27230	24790	27060	31290
	4	27550	25880	27480	25790	27600	32340
1986	1	27850	25900	27560	26900	27300	32410
	2	28700	26090	28250	27360	27890	35260
	3	27310	26420	29020	27630	28130	35520
	4	28660	28130	29590	29720	29360	38220
1987	1	28750	29130	29640	29340	30190	40980

£

Outer South East	Outer Metrop	Greater London	South West	Wales	Scotland	Northern Ireland
11590	13560	15440	10880	9820	12130	9090
11750	14050	15920	11380	10140	12780	9570
11880	14440	16070	11550	10240	13090	9960
12010	14580	16630	11520	10590	13600	10390
12140	14580	17100	11710	10610	13910	11030
12300	14940	17150	11990	10870	14050	11370
12720	15360	17370	12250	11230	14470	11910
12870	15420	17990	12430	11110	14380	11360
13580	16330	19040	12960	11560	14740	12450
14140	17340	20450	13690	12090	15040	13480
15640	19520	23180	14820	13110	16290	14450
16860	21050	24350	15710	13510	17150	15260
17950	22060	25880	16830	14510	17710	15740
19640	24170	28950	18000	15960	18380	16380
21700	25940	30320	19480	17230	19780	17850
23400	27650	32250	21510	17720	21480	18980
24630	29040	33360	22550	18320	21450	19160
25010	29600	34190	22860	19430	22400	20320
25410	30260	33970	23470	19630	22240	20060
25520	29610	33980	23770	19630	22820	19920
26080	30220	34530	23950	19600	22920	19880
26040	31120	35640	24820	20080	23420	20340
26110	31590	36340	24330	19950	23050	20350
25520	31110	35780	24380	20020	23670	19810
25770	30990	36400	24250	20540	24870	20340
26190	32420	37090	25100	21440	25870	19820
27010	32980	37810	25350	21700	25430	21070
27670	34220	37970	25290	21790	25900	20820
28010	34770	39400	26240	22180	26620	21370
29920	36740	41790	27080	23560	27850	21480
30480	37710	44740	28530	23490	28510	21870
31070	38760	45370	28640	23410	29230	21980
32110	40720	47280	29050	24800	29080	22550
33980	42600	50950	30250	25590	31180	22980
34020	43400	50420	30570	26810	30800	23530
35450	44320	52890	31910	25890	32560	24240
36980	46890	56020	33620	26280	32900	24590
38750	49010	57780	33130	27060	33340	25260
39380	49890	60490	35030	26400	33400	25590
40300	51430	61550	34990	27040	33650	25090
41530	52020	63520	35850	28000	33790	25410
43190	55240	66810	36970	28340	34000	25420
46110	58210	71630	38560	28120	34540	25550
46950	62500	74980	40730	30490	34970	25340
49710	65870	80940	41190	29420	34810	25580

NATIONWIDE BUILDING SOCIETY

AVERAGE PRICES (at approval stage) 1976 –

15.8 REGIONS: TERRACED HOUSES

Year		Northern	Yorks & Humberside	North West	East Midlands	West Midlands	East Anglia
1976	1	6880	6450	6690	6230	7950	8640
	2	7120	6990	7010	6560	8250	8560
	3	7230	6990	7230	6560	8260	8370
	4	7630	7120	7140	6530	8190	8880
1977	1	7870	7110	7280	6910	8280	8880
	2	8110	7310	7450	7260	8610	8970
	3	8370	7420	7930	7250	8960	9420
	4	8330	7560	7730	7100	8900	9220
1978	1	8260	7750	8130	7570	9390	9750
	2	9000	8160	8390	7510	9330	10100
	3	9420	8320	8900	7780	9830	10100
	4	9420	8640	9070	8220	10570	10340
1979	1	10200	8880	9740	8380	11110	11540
	2	10730	9400	10530	8880	12050	12980
	3	11340	10280	11340	9900	13110	13720
	4	11520	11260	11930	10380	13690	14930
1980	1	12370	11380	12580	11200	14530	15350
	2	12850	12000	13400	11670	14940	16300
	3	12970	12690	13990	12750	15310	16930
	4	13400	12930	13960	12440	15590	17820
1981	1	12890	12880	14120	12380	15750	17600
	2	13470	13180	14280	13320	16280	18060
	3	14430	13100	14690	13410	16020	17700
	4	14050	13050	14050	13300	15560	17900
1982	1	14150	13320	14140	13310	15280	16890
	2	15150	13310	14360	13750	15490	18380
	3	14830	13230	14780	13920	15120	18840
	4	16010	14300	14730	14170	15640	19230
1983	1	15300	14030	15150	14320	16930	19780
	2	16260	14890	15630	15660	16100	20950
	3	16760	15170	15830	15190	17070	21750
	4	16590	14890	16060	15740	16710	21210
1984	1	16770	15290	16180	15610	17650	21760
	2	17310	15350	17000	16850	18810	23300
	3	17740	15410	16560	16150	18120	23620
	4	18600	16700	17250	16740	19500	23440
1985	1	19030	16320	17990	17240	19530	24660
	2	19550	17710	18120	18970	19600	29770
	3	18980	17860	19110	18500	20290	26830
	4	20590	18210	18590	18250	19830	28800
1986	1	19290	18310	18970	19760	20250	27470
	2	20510	18520	18900	21010	20870	30390
	3	20290	18550	19730	22270	21070	30860
	4	20400	19280	18950	22330	21870	31340
1987	1	21490	20060	20650	24100	22580	33770

Outer South East	Outer Metrop	Greater London	South West	Wales	Scotland	Northern Ireland
10140	12250	12910	9280	7790	10570	7790
10340	12410	13510	9690	8080	11780	8420
10540	12780	13470	10010	8080	12000	8510
10650	12890	13560	9940	8190	12140	9100
10810	13050	14120	10050	8450	12550	9130
11050	12980	14150	10380	8230	12730	9810
11150	13370	14330	10260	8600	13130	10260
11330	13370	14650	10160	8490	13060	10930
11900	14180	15560	10940	8900	13200	11560
12070	14630	16060	11480	9130	13490	12000
13370	16440	18170	12300	10120	14310	12620
14030	18000	19500	12580	10550	15920	13140
15220	18550	20840	13790	11360	16000	13110
16320	19700	23600	14960	12080	16850	14020
17620	21640	24880	15970	12620	17730	13800
19400	23140	26550	17640	13590	19270	14010
20630	24230	27200	18100	14310	19950	14330
21360	24550	28410	19000	14180	21080	14070
21190	24450	28360	19250	14270	20010	14550
20600	24750	28640	19340	15260	21090	13520
20930	25060	28540	19870	15170	21180	13150
21810	25790	28630	20400	15520	21090	13080
21580	25450	29230	20550	15360	21710	12840
20850	24450	27680	19170	14920	21730	12900
21020	25220	29050	20110	15580	22670	12550
21980	25990	29800	20100	15650	21900	13270
22720	26830	30440	20470	16550	21690	11860
23070	27720	31480	20500	17070	24050	12700
23970	28990	31590	21820	16780	24050	13330
24990	30440	34010	23190	16990	24810	14380
25790	30360	35090	22760	17380	25320	15160
25810	31730	36300	23150	18060	25580	15130
27460	32660	38820	23890	18000	26010	14870
28810	35160	40210	24670	18780	27710	15360
28640	35320	41200	25380	18520	28560	15490
29370	35280	42100	26180	19570	28870	15370
30950	37500	45020	26740	19510	28150	16350
32780	39290	47650	27460	20120	29720	16570
31900	40350	49020	28420	20580	29000	16930
34370	40980	50630	29070	21420	29810	17660
35150	43070	53410	29810	21650	28830	17390
37130	44810	55230	31340	22220	30140	17890
37890	47290	58800	32870	22310	31490	18100
40080	50580	63610	32600	22710	30460	17010
41670	55860	69100	34690	22990	32040	17620

NATIONWIDE BUILDING SOCIETY

AVERAGE PRICES (at approval stage) 1976 –

15.9 REGIONS: BUNGALOWS, FLATS AND MAISONETTES

Year		Northern	Yorks & Humberside	North West	East Midlands	West Midlands	East Anglia
1976	1	10060	10120	10480	9910	10720	10470
	2	10310	10240	10800	10310	11240	10850
	3	10420	10840	10970	10500	11310	11350
	4	10730	11100	11270	10980	11660	11380
1977	1	11240	11310	11510	11010	11690	11550
	2	11520	11760	12200	11180	12130	11750
	3	11550	11940	12200	11640	12560	12190
	4	12100	12420	12610	11430	12410	12440
1978	1	12230	12970	13190	12100	13030	13090
	2	12580	12850	13750	12390	13420	13450
	3	13280	14110	14700	13300	14500	14560
	4	14370	14240	16100	14290	16050	15010
1979	1	14710	15620	17020	15300	16060	15560
	2	15740	16130	18920	16230	17020	17290
	3	17570	17550	18800	16670	18720	18840
	4	18210	18660	20340	17590	19520	20210
1980	1	19590	19140	21760	19060	19740	21380
	2	19040	20320	22380	20440	20920	22850
	3	21010	21950	23410	21310	21400	23360
	4	19850	20890	23540	21610	20340	23100
1981	1	19360	23070	22420	21460	21390	23190
	2	21210	22850	24480	21940	21810	22730
	3	20730	22130	24180	22870	23260	24310
	4	20530	23370	24610	21620	22020	25270
1982	1	20720	23810	23410	22780	22040	23210
	2	20800	23600	25220	23690	22630	24210
	3	22490	23800	24300	23930	23030	25020
	4	22180	24260	25920	23810	24100	25520
1983	1	21650	25350	25470	24470	23950	26100
	2	23550	25140	26820	25220	24850	27590
	3	23540	25100	26800	25400	25160	28080
	4	25970	26920	28610	25470	24320	30200
1984	1	25370	27650	29280	27120	25160	29130
	2	27010	28170	29970	26700	25670	30680
	3	25350	27900	29370	27450	27090	31410
	4	26280	29570	31960	29560	28420	32790
1985	1	26290	30470	32540	29180	28340	33900
	2	26760	29710	32720	29600	29590	33980
	3	28570	29860	33080	31030	30720	37300
	4	29340	32410	31560	30750	30520	38840
1986	1	29620	30970	32250	31440	29130	38910
	2	30180	31370	33640	33550	29390	38720
	3	30270	32820	34030	32640	29930	39510
	4	29240	31640	34530	35710	30730	43720
1987	1	29660	33430	35290	36590	32300	41910

£

Outer South East	Outer Metrop	Greater London	South West	Wales	Scotland	Northern Ireland
12480	13730	12430	11970	10790	11160	12680
12870	14260	12540	12520	11230	11530	13410
13080	14740	12830	12870	11360	12020	14540
12920	14600	12710	12990	11600	12250	14660
13010	14700	12800	13410	11670	12260	15060
13310	15300	12960	13330	11850	12630	15980
13750	15460	13100	13450	12030	13150	16380
13970	15510	13180	14160	12470	13030	16620
14490	16170	13800	14570	12900	13730	18320
15030	16340	14690	15010	13640	14370	18810
16880	19010	15950	16780	14410	15280	20200
18320	20500	17030	17830	15080	15410	20780
19340	20680	18630	18240	16000	16110	20830
20360	22300	20430	20100	18220	17060	22120
22590	23670	21790	22290	18660	17880	23650
23790	25530	23570	23400	20210	19600	23960
25050	27400	24520	24330	20730	19300	26070
25020	27570	25170	25080	21520	19970	26160
26160	27760	24850	24900	22050	20040	25630
25190	27780	24310	25300	22310	20390	24410
25240	27650	24620	25280	23240	19700	25370
26640	27710	24960	26280	23050	21740	26530
26470	28190	24900	25560	23190	21240	24940
26280	28540	25030	24020	22940	20600	25450
26600	28750	25050	25410	23340	21370	25650
26780	28710	26630	26290	22890	22450	25770
27410	29970	25750	26960	23940	22420	26140
27540	30800	26930	27250	24140	23050	27210
28950	31060	27280	28840	25030	23310	26970
29920	33231	28170	28440	24860	24420	27260
31790	34000	29820	29740	25490	24960	27050
31350	35160	30250	30350	26240	26020	28290
32200	36890	31550	31210	26230	26150	29170
34790	39070	33550	33310	28030	26800	29190
34670	38550	33770	32990	27930	26700	29360
35160	40120	36050	36280	29610	27750	29850
37190	40860	38170	36160	29260	28780	29990
37270	42680	39930	36350	29420	28600	30420
38870	44820	40730	37070	30320	29080	32280
39590	45610	44010	38020	31640	29040	30900
40440	47220	44890	38890	31480	29570	31170
42800	47680	47240	40330	31450	29970	32470
44410	51500	50720	42570	33180	30390	33410
46300	53350	53670	43890	34380	30280	31920
48610	55240	56170	45370	32930	30740	31580

NATIONWIDE BUILDING SOCIETY

AVERAGE PRICES (at approval stage) 1976 –

15.10 UNITED KINGDOM AND REGIONS BY AGE OF HOUSE: DETACHED HOUSES

Year	UNITED KINGDOM			NORTHERN			YORKS & HUMBERSIDE			NORTH WEST		
	New	Modern	Older	New	Modern	Older	New	Modern	Older	New	Modern	Older
1976 1	15700	15650	14910	15000	14880	12950	13110	14520	13010	14440	14430	14130
2	16080	16230	15510	15160	15220	13540	13890	14220	14360	14530	14590	14750
3	16350	16660	15890	15820	16360	15740	14420	15070	14060	14900	15210	14520
4	16910	16930	16160	15910	17640	15730	14550	15500	13990	15640	15800	15130
1977 1	17200	17130	16630	15740	17350	14910	14570	15560	14880	16190	16310	17220
2	17870	17520	16960	17580	17790	15440	15390	15860	14830	16700	16880	16650
3	18300	17800	17370	17840	18020	14820	15780	16240	14050	17190	16940	17830
4	18890	18150	17670	18430	17860		16340	16640	15080	17520	17760	17130
1978 1	19520	18950	18150	17970	18390		17550	17530	15490	18130	18830	17400
2	20400	19790	19270	19260	19180		17750	17800	16780	18390	19120	18250
3	22220	21940	21630	19980	20730		19400	19140	16850	20450	21450	20710
4	23580	23490	23000	21030	21710		20350	20470	17790	22290	23190	22880
1979 1	24660	24430	23970	22010	22490	20020	20720	20920	20740	23150	24190	23030
2	26170	26360	25370	23500	22280	19800	19550	22840	21100	26070	25850	21970
3	28120	28340	27770	25080	24820	22370	23320	24570	20670	27430	28510	25970
4	29440	30330	29620	26460	26820	23660	24960	26110	22630	28360	29540	26500
1980 1	31430	31840	30310	28550	27510	25260	25640	27220	23030	29550	30460	28960
2	32500	33240	32390	30090	27800	26740	28310	27880	22560	31480	31690	30470
3	32990	33630	33170	31140	29720	28050	27620	28700	26920	30720	32100	33420
4	32760	33410	32860	29800	28800	27960	28480	28830	27590	31170	30600	32160
1981 1	33930	33420	32720	30520	30360		28370	28460	26900	32580	31320	30880
2	34420	34310	33770	30220	29470	24680	30390	29350	27210	32490	33420	32440
3	34330	34550	34000	31190	29540		29050	30960	25960	32490	32270	31530
4	34850	34310	34790	31500	28960	26710	30280	29770	28410	32940	32310	32710
1982 1	35490	34180	34500	32600	29190		30500	30490	27170	32090	31920	34010
2	36690	36020	36060	33310	30490		32440	31360	30930	34350	34470	33370
3	36810	36190	36460	36040	33530		31450	30660	31680	34330	34450	34650
4	38040	36410	38000	34330	32330	27550	31930	30420	32980	36100	33330	35280
1983 1	38700	37270	38830	35600	31770	27630	32200	33260	31870	37430	33280	36090
2	40820	39500	39780	37260	33970	29890	32110	33420	35510	38800	36450	36830
3	41970	40490	41730	35120	33800	32830	35060	34050	35170	41490	36780	35900
4	43520	40910	42780		36060		37480	33020	34310	40940	37120	35310
1984 1	44590	42000	44760	37490	35340		36180	34980	36710	41920	37340	40250
2	46970	44410	47070	38900	36500	37980	41720	36740	39860	45280	40480	43440
3	46630	44540	48090	36980	39300		40950	36970	35940	44210	40060	45490
4	47430	46250	48100	38110	39340		43880	38480	38600	44830	40640	46030
1985 1	51770	49710	50590	40110	41260	36950	41900	38020	41630	48230	38820	46160
2	54850	52190	52110	39180	40520	35210	45240	39900	38500	45710	43390	49350
3	54220	52140	54210	42120	41490	44310	41520	39740	40460	45690	43520	46210
4	56180	53820	54450	41160	39800		41470	40000	42020	47840	43180	45420
1986 1	56660	53940	54340	43160	37600		43170	40260		46800	44420	53100
2	59820	56070	57000	44790	41510		44290	41060	45260	49250	46290	50530
3	61510	58270	60790	44590	43860		42630	41680	45290	48730	46560	51710
4	63910	62130	61920	49590	41560		46960	40980	38230	46840	46430	54140
1987 1	66280	62140	63700		41950			42640		51160	48410	51580

£

EAST MIDLANDS			WEST MIDLANDS			EAST ANGLIA		
New	Modern	Older	New	Modern	Older	New	Modern	Older
12320	12650	11310	14530	14310	14780	14220	14300	13400
12650	13360	11060	15060	14900	15190	14410	14270	14150
12930	13320	11880	15600	15570	15980	15220	14300	14110
13990	13360	12770	16530	15680	16090	14890	15030	13860
13850	13690	12480	17100	16200	15900	14570	14990	14580
14630	13860	13070	17380	16350	16630	16310	15280	14370
14740	14020	13200	17340	16690	17310	16990	15470	15120
15290	14350	13920	18550	16470	17310	16540	15960	16360
14930	15030	13410	19020	17720	17360	16860	16530	16750
16480	14900	14040	19470	17900	18680	17420	16870	16350
17690	17400	14760	21320	19560	20870	20030	18680	19080
18900	17590	16600	23300	22650	22640	20980	20210	18820
20200	19390	17380	24270	23460	23130	22290	22180	19920
21880	20940	18490	25030	24570	24020	23300	22400	22710
23280	22130	19500	27980	25740	26280	26530	24860	23550
24410	24050	21110	28190	28050	27930	27880	26730	26730
25770	25040	22660	31660	29400	28190	30730	29320	27060
27200	26560	24150	30730	31360	31450	30990	32800	30710
27590	26970	26640	31570	30570	31440	32270	32110	28970
27860	27240	24790	30210	30120	32390	32020	33210	26770
29430	27430	25770	32660	30390	29870	32650	32130	29180
29690	27590	26820	32690	31530	30170	35180	33190	32260
32000	28550	27410	31900	32600	34030	31760	32220	31210
31750	27420	29650	33080	30470	34080	32400	32120	33280
31470	27810	26660	34280	29810	35420	31120	32600	31110
32470	28540	29220	33650	33360	32890	33680	33710	33150
31450	28930	29010	33230	31570	33120	35300	32840	34020
34110	30210	31130	34010	32600	37090	35720	34960	35720
34390	30010	29760	36250	32650	37920	33840	34980	35610
35320	31040	28750	37300	34350	34700	37720	36820	33480
35600	32280	31600	38430	34800	38190	37310	37660	36870
37650	32890	32130	40100	34360	36620	39190	38120	36400
37290	33750	30970	39260	36250	39290	40220	39720	44050
39630	35560	39210	41320	37250	41800	42540	40460	43520
38220	34980	37530	39660	37560	44870	44110	38470	40140
40280	36690	36270	41830	39530	42870	42220	41990	43980
42810	37780	37290	44190	40170	43830	46320	42010	45770
41660	39890	38970	45420	41210	44220	47550	44890	49570
44080	38750	38190	43960	41050	46300	49420	48350	47770
45220	39750	38510	45730	42730	45730	49630	45800	49590
44350	38860	38300	43790	42450	45040	49380	50640	48520
46060	42420	40630	46390	42650	46080	52590	50960	55600
46700	43010	40570	48360	42970	48300	53470	52200	54030
50120	43970	40940	50400	45850	51100	57180	55680	54500
55750	44590	47260	49410	47960	47270	60660	57480	

NATIONWIDE BUILDING SOCIETY

AVERAGE PRICES (at approval stage) 1976 –

15.10 UNITED KINGDOM AND REGIONS BY AGE OF HOUSE: DETACHED HOUSES (continued)

Year	OUTER SOUTH EAST New	Modern	Older	OUTER METROPOLITAN New	Modern	Older	GREATER LONDON New	Modern	Older	SOUTH WEST New	Modern	Older
1976 1	17770	16830	15860	21370	20800	19840	24840	24320	20540	16160	15030	13440
2	17410	17140	15820	22740	22670	20620	25190	24170	20010	16000	15830	14650
3	18120	17700	16540	22190	22380	20770	26040	25530	20530	15880	16210	14830
4	18070	17600	17010	22950	22450	21530	25700	25890	21620	16440	16660	14830
1977 1	18730	17880	17050	22980	22530	21940	26800	25200	21690	17070	16660	15600
2	19030	18360	17090	23550	22840	22180	30870	26900	22620	17770	16880	16270
3	19790	18590	17660	24300	23180	22350	30900	26960	22680	18600	17500	16310
4	20600	19460	17710	24780	23590	22700		27250	23850	18990	17440	16650
1978 1	21560	19990	18370	26000	24590	24230		30030	23440	20120	18410	17200
2	22520	21130	20430	29050	27520	25460		32470	26830	20230	19500	18390
3	24550	23840	22420	31240	30150	30000		33970	31430	22570	22350	20760
4	26040	25690	23510	32420	32760	33340		35420	31400	24400	23270	21030
1979 1	27570	25950	25730	34140	32990	33300		40040	32430	25940	24160	23010
2	30060	29650	27000	37420	36700	35650		41110	37530	26790	27090	25600
3	32430	31650	29790	39170	39530	39720		45010	42960	28180	29750	26610
4	33540	33570	32380	40200	41640	42200		47760	42890	30210	31720	29130
1980 1	36520	36190	32380	43950	44070	44200		47500	43720	32450	32930	29210
2	36690	36630	36690	43730	45470	46710		50500	47560	32350	34200	30920
3	37830	37220	36190	44310	46180	46390		53240	47950	33610	34900	31200
4	37740	36940	36490	44220	44490	46480		54490	47710	31960	35540	29940
1981 1	37360	36230	37000	46110	46380	45610		52740	45500	34120	34530	29960
2	37900	38480	36650	46020	45310	49480		52160	47930	34870	35910	32650
3	37950	37820	37780	43750	46340	47180		54370	47730	36050	33570	30310
4	37510	38730	35700	45660	46880	50070		57090	51040	35480	36760	30270
1982 1	40300	36740	36030	47180	47760	48420	57750	54950	47200	36320	34430	31660
2	39660	39690	40990	49140	48690	51450	60790	58630	49320	37420	36520	32070
3	39950	38830	38540	50230	50880	48970	62760	60910	51980	37570	37750	34250
4	42430	39480	38160	50500	50870	53060	61860	56360	53630	38390	36760	35280
1983 1	42850	41750	42490	49920	52820	54660	61590	59620	52520	40030	38190	37120
2	46030	43500	46010	53770	56020	57070	69010	63380	59410	42080	40700	37560
3	46500	45690	46310	55350	58690	62180	66100	62250	57540	44830	41070	39350
4	47290	46200	47130	60990	60660	64290		66350	66200	43590	41170	42260
1984 1	51620	48130	52630	62480	61820	64370		68810	65510	45130	42720	43520
2	52680	51260	53040	65450	64870	66740	77080	71580	68050	46350	44420	41890
3	53860	50820	54250	66500	66430	69900	69240	75280	70080	47070	45070	44690
4	54750	54220	54270	65180	69440	67440		75570	72490	47650	45800	45130
1985 1	56210	54770	52270	71030	70280	74190	71520	80160	79730	49450	47880	45330
2	59040	58510	55460	71900	72360	76530	91810	85950	79390	51440	48950	48930
3	59720	58270	58190	74740	73620	83370	81330	84750	85980	52920	49160	50930
4	62660	58160	57620	78590	78280	84270	88730	91640	88530	54320	50920	50920
1986 1	64830	59530	60820	74600	78570	81090		89800	87030	54430	53540	51380
2	65200	63240	64640	82160	80320	85320	10830	95470	89770	58960	53370	56020
3	70950	65620	69730	86840	87400	91760	103210	101650	99900	60020	54990	59300
4	73580	67760	75510	89090	91020	103540	114790	127850	102200	61640	56750	60110
1987 1	76020	70670	67310	98320	98140	110770		107100	111640	63940	60000	61850

WALES			SCOTLAND			NORTHERN IRELAND		
New	Modern	Older	New	Modern	Older	New	Modern	Older
14890	14290	11500	17120	16430	13790	15670	14240	14090
15220	14650	12340	17450	17380	14840	16250	15270	17170
15140	15400	12580	17230	18170	15510	16690	15270	17270
15740	15360	12470	18090	18130	14570	18750	16570	16140
16300	15570	13120	18220	18130	15510	19560	16710	15870
16440	16540	13060	18510	18740	15530	20520	16950	18750
16180	16460	14200	19220	18860	15980	20040	18460	20720
16730	16940	14220	20340	18980	15750	21120	19090	21430
17880	16700	14430	20170	19040	17740		18090	
18520	17540	14600	20500	19830	18510	22940	20350	23800
19340	19680	16190	22500	21530	20710	24910	23870	23550
20470	20750	17850	24130	22180	21020	24440	23570	24710
22760	22510	18000	24260	21670	22250	25760	25500	26000
24440	23470	18380	25140	23310	22540	29710	25360	28110
25170	23330	23990	25730	25780	22760	27710	27540	30330
28330	27430	25200	27880	28040	27300	29150	27520	30530
28760	27930	23150	28130	29120	27720	30910	28970	30500
31430	29150	23980	29540	29630	28300		30130	
31520	28810	24160	31120	30010	28450	34570	29610	31680
30390	29960	23740	31210	30210	30480	36330	30330	31050
32440	30080	22560	31200	30500	27590			
30840	29160	24480	32060	32260	27220	32400	30020	
30380	31900		36750	32260	32490		29630	
	28900	25160	36530	30840	31020	29780	29660	31030
32670	30320	27220	36020	32640	30320	33050	30500	32130
33390	32320	28720	37540	34500	32320	34990	29310	
32660	33090	30260	39140	34100	33940	33660	30660	33490
33460	33730	33120	41840	34180	31770	34870	30660	30600
36580	33300	31920	38840	33850	31840	33080	31260	33970
36530	36050	28860	43010	36720	34910	35610	35890	28790
37430	34900	33540	42290	38860	34530	32510	33230	
35970	36550	29640	43150	37530	38290		33890	30100
41580	36280	32150	42930	36310	34300	38690	33620	
41320	41170	34380	47110	41460	38220	38910	36680	36180
39690	39680	35420	46110	40570	36330	38490	38920	
42560	39010	35190	42300	43490	36560	41520	37390	
41910	40140	38700	47160	44280	38190			
43050	42590	40640	50850	43960	42810	41930	39040	
45940	41630	38860	49730	44130	42980	41570	35170	
42850	43880	31950	50070	44660	46320	42110	39630	34830
44810	41240	36590	50850	43230	37890	37820	39070	
44890	42280	35260	53880	44930	42630	41640	40740	37370
50860	43820	40880	54990	44210	47550	38630	41960	43460
43730	42940	33780	51750	45060	46400	42560	39300	
45100	45860	43510	49920	46570	48430		39140	

15.11 UNITED KINGDOM AND REGIONS BY AGE OF HOUSE:
SEMI-DETACHED HOUSES

Year	UNITED KINGDOM			NORTHERN			YORKS & HUMBERSIDE			NORTH WEST		
	New	Modern	Older	New	Modern	Older	New	Modern	Older	New	Modern	Older
1976 1	10070	10800	10900	9700	10360	9040	9090	9020	8150	8870	9280	9240
2	10430	11070	11330	9950	10500	10140	8780	9260	8830	9270	9360	9310
3	10650	11330	11430	10370	10660	10120	9400	9390	9160	9460	9660	9420
4	10930	11510	11890	10570	11400	10370	9290	9680	9660	9760	9980	9930
1977 1	11280	11660	12050	11080	11780	10310	9960	9790	9720	10260	10220	10170
2	11490	11920	12270	11320	11870	10990	9670	9990	9580	10580	10580	10490
3	11770	12210	12590	11410	12240	11420	10120	10100	10080	10890	10770	10790
4	12130	12320	12760	11800	12290	11120	10670	10580	10510	11130	10940	11010
1978 1	12710	13010	13590	12340	13130	12620	10700	11110	10980	12320	11560	11860
2	13120	13520	14070	12890	13360	12050	11140	11680	10650	12200	11720	12130
3	14160	14820	15480	13410	14540	13340	11320	12100	11750	13260	12740	12720
4	14890	15730	16360	13650	14980	13830	12670	12470	12560	13870	13820	13530
1979 1	15820	16480	17420	14550	15410	13900	13870	12620	13100	14630	14640	15000
2	16810	17660	18860	15470	15740	16420	13610	13780	14180	15300	15930	15420
3	18140	18850	20530	17100	17070	16940	14450	15400	15160	16130	16820	16920
4	19020	20150	21680	17020	17610	18260	15160	15950	15650	16620	17950	17810
1980 1	20180	20860	22820	17960	18390	18930	16960	17130	16270	17790	18870	18810
2	21000	21610	23580	18720	19700	19320	18500	17530	17960	19140	19450	19990
3	21330	21930	24070	18680	20050	19730	17820	18180	18030	19920	20230	20940
4	21640	21880	24080	20310	20110	19270	17910	18430	18480	19350	20120	20550
1981 1	21940	22550	24230	19870	20380	17740	19110	19640	19240	20080	20450	20600
2	22830	22820	25060	21070	21300	21320	19480	19500	19020	21500	20580	21510
3	22610	23000	25020	20840	20700	19970	18420	20480	19650	20990	20730	21300
4	23090	22730	24480	22020	20560	19880	19320	18920	18720	20560	20920	20480
1982 1	23930	22680	24790	22800	21250	20910	21320	19010	18530	22270	20540	20790
2	23880	23300	25760	21560	21100	21480	19830	19510	19700	21560	21200	22070
3	24570	23750	25860	22790	21770	21780	22140	19820	20230	23430	21010	21570
4	24980	24280	26530	23280	23130	22250	21390	20580	20380	24290	22170	22280
1983 1	25550	24920	26770	23830	22370	22950	22130	20770	19920	25170	22320	22630
2	26150	25630	28380	24740	22790	24110	22250	21360	22240	23540	22230	23150
3	27280	26130	29310	24910	24130	24210	23050	21280	22190	24100	22390	23530
4	27450	26440	29290	27070	23820	24770	23960	22260	21060	23410	23010	23690
1984 1	27830	27190	30270		24470	22690		22610	21880	23340	23230	24250
2	28220	28600	32030		25830	25360	23350	22650	23310	24700	24940	25020
3	28000	28360	32460		24090	25830		23150	24150		23850	25030
4	29530	29450	33670	27180	25530	26670	22920	24140	24060		24920	27120
1985 1	32640	33030	34530	24450	26260	28130	25850	24690	25950	26480	25830	27340
2	33750	33760	35580	26610	27330	28500	25150	25660	26020	26810	26110	28110
3	34510	34520	36110		27190	30020		24780	25340	26560	26620	27850
4	35360	34630	37070		27100	27520		24990	26760	27910	26170	28580
1986 1	37090	35550	37310		26790	28780	27310	25890	25650	28010	26490	28440
2	37500	36940	38840		28290	29150		25030	26870	27400	27340	29180
3	38160	38280	40110		26760	27220	27080	25500	27470	28520	28050	29950
4	40100	39960	42360		28440	29750		27820	27970	27210	28020	31340
1987 1	39830	41220	44250		27070	32210		27630	30680		27680	31140

£

EAST MIDLANDS			WEST MIDLANDS			EAST ANGLIA		
New	Modern	Older	New	Modern	Older	New	Modern	Older
8760	8950	7810	9760	9940	9940	9380	10160	9500
8860	9330	7920	10110	10270	10240	10260	10300	10290
8960	9400	8490	10060	10430	10050	10420	10760	10150
9080	9280	8900	10250	10600	10740	10130	10750	10940
9270	9430	8500	10360	10700	10840	10400	10500	10830
9120	9720	9000	10720	11210	10840	10820	10910	10490
9270	9910	8980	10670	11370	11660	10650	10970	10750
9810	9840	9040	11360	11490	11110	11010	11590	10660
10570	10460	9590	11760	12230	12160	12240	12060	11690
10260	10670	9920	12330	12340	12360	12270	12440	11320
11710	11520	10630	12940	13990	14540	12710	12420	11860
12640	11890	10920	13710	14750	15120	13490	14390	13360
12680	12950	11360	14840	15570	15900	14980	15080	12670
13730	14010	12020	14870	16260	15930	15670	16010	14720
15350	14620	13660	17060	17340	17990	16410	17500	16500
15040	15090	13470	17760	18870	18740	18300	19660	17840
15880	15940	14840	18720	19620	19770	20430	19720	19310
17250	17510	16010	19290	19840	20570	21170	20500	19960
17740	18180	15400	19620	20170	20910	21050	20480	20200
18880	18130	16260	20410	19870	20830	21130	21080	21250
18960	18350	17300	20980	20860	21480	20760	21560	20980
19540	18640	17430	21110	21080	22220	21550	21580	21730
20130	19010	17470	22120	20840	21020	21750	21140	23360
21030	19210	18120	21350	20630	20120	22090	22750	21700
20590	18490	16930	21870	20590	21380	21450	21460	21440
20330	19470	18220	22450	20570	22260	21060	21390	22270
20120	18960	18080	22490	21050	21990	22630	22030	23820
20620	20180	19650	22030	21450	21750	22880	22700	25390
19640	20710	19100	23070	21920	22060	22920	24390	24320
21600	21390	21260	22010	22010	23320	23220	24060	24310
22380	21150	21090	22720	22470	23480	23970	24730	27520
22420	20870	19990	22250	22420	23190	23790	24460	25830
21260	22150	21070	24720	22940	23220	24240	25960	25440
22290	22500	21830	23730	23570	25380		26710	30210
22290	21740	22420	23250	23490	25090		27300	29340
23170	23440	22390	24570	24270	25790	27080	30000	30830
23550	24630	24140	26140	25290	26200	29480	30040	32820
24590	24790	24520	24550	25600	27570	28040	29970	30550
25120	25540	23800	26420	26430	28150	31390	32310	29770
26460	25720	25730	30310	27080	27790	27590	33040	33150
27100	27000	26730	27490	26530	28450	32390	32890	31700
27770	27400	27220	27450	27250	28950	33860	35010	36190
27670	27900	27270	26660	27790	28970	34450	35690	35670
29850	30630	28500	28040	29120	30000	34880	38180	39560
29050	29330	29410	28040	30140	30720	38150	39610	44170

15.11 UNITED KINGDOM AND REGIONS BY AGE OF HOUSE:
SEMI-DETACHED HOUSES (continued)

Year		OUTER SOUTH EAST			OUTER METROPOLITAN			GREATER LONDON			SOUTH WEST		
		New	Modern	Older	New	Modern	Older	New	Modern	Older	New	Modern	Older
1976	1	11460	11760	11350	13280	13840	13120	16320	16250	15080	10210	11190	10710
	2	11870	11940	11350	13950	14230	13730	13280	16760	15560	10780	11390	11800
	3	11900	12160	11370	14640	14700	13880	13170	16900	15710	10910	11790	11490
	4	12290	12170	11600	15000	14920	13800	18130	17060	16420	10900	11630	11730
1977	1	12220	12430	11600	14820	14830	14030	17470	17470	16940	11400	11760	11830
	2	13080	12400	11780	15430	15030	14620	19890	17630	16890	11880	12020	12010
	3	13270	12740	12430	15360	15450	15190	20310	18230	16940	12160	12280	12230
	4	13580	12740	12780	16050	15610	14860	19670	18610	17690	12470	12270	12730
1978	1	14120	13640	13230	16650	16420	16080		19400	18840	12830	12930	13120
	2	14630	14510	13270	17700	17620	16720		20300	20470	13180	13810	13760
	3	16100	15990	14850	19620	20080	18540		23460	23040	14350	15070	14580
	4	17050	17300	16060	19660	21950	20000		25430	23980	15280	15830	15700
1979	1	17930	18560	16980	21020	22790	21210		26580	25640	16030	16960	17040
	2	20000	20020	18870	23320	24580	23770		29650	28730	17320	18210	18000
	3	22360	22070	20870	25200	26070	25930		30310	30290	18450	19250	20480
	4	22820	23830	22980	26900	27970	27380		31940	32320	20470	21710	21750
1980	1	24050	24760	24660	28340	29050	29190		33860	33260	22550	22080	23320
	2	24390	25560	24520	28590	30120	29160		34680	34120	22490	22760	23230
	3	25230	25170	25810	28930	29890	31060		33900	33990	22970	23410	23850
	4	23930	25300	26390	30360	29360	29750		33560	34040	23200	23380	24650
1981	1	25960	26220	25940	29460	30690	29820	36990	35300	34400	23020	23590	24990
	2	25900	26030	26100	31960	31180	30870	36760	34980	35720	23480	24440	26090
	3	25160	26690	25700	31670	31470	31710	37380	36230	36340	24250	24010	24860
	4	26590	25630	25020	31930	30860	31260	36330	34390	35970	24360	24360	24420
1982	1	27050	25910	25170	31340	30640	31340	34170	37520	36270	23760	23760	24630
	2	25580	25990	26650	34010	32370	32180	34580	36650	37180	25210	24880	25370
	3	26730	26830	27350	36150	32770	32740	35830	38990	37670	24350	25590	25430
	4	27830	27330	28100	34690	33720	34770	38390	36920	38110	25290	24860	25980
1983	1	28250	27770	28280	35810	34790	34590	41990	39530	39330	27210	25790	26590
	2	30730	29960	29640	37670	36340	37110	43390	40920	41910	27120	26510	27990
	3	32730	30660	29630	40310	36810	38500	45010	43660	44920	28010	27150	31000
	4	33530	30750	30960	41520	38470	38780	44710	42980	45780	28560	27300	30880
1984	1	33300	31600	32600	43000	39830	41530		45120	47650	28480	28810	29660
	2	33450	34140	33860	42650	41870	43490	46230	51100	51020	28330	29680	31790
	3	32570	33870	34590	41750	42040	45280		47670	50950	27990	30200	31970
	4	35400	34800	36440	45360	43690	44960		49840	53530	31160	31160	33350
1985	1	36740	37300	36560	47550	46370	47460	49390	52830	56680	30260	33240	35280
	2	37620	38080	40050	47300	48350	50070	57200	54840	58280	32140	32410	34590
	3	39300	39330	40680	47690	49110	51160		56650	61210	33160	34270	36880
	4	39280	39180	42170	49500	49660	53900		56560	62490	33240	34410	36560
1986	1	41950	41260	41800	52760	50860	53340		59420	64190	34360	35570	36860
	2	42470	43880	42390	55930	53790	56950		63100	67470	35050	36170	38980
	3	46590	46040	46100	61310	56530	59870		67100	72640	36620	38500	39370
	4	46080	46990	47130	60690	61340	64260		69120	76050	39280	39690	42970
1987	1	49210	49600	49990	62220	64710	67910		74510	82400	40380	40890	41980

WALES			SCOTLAND			NORTHERN IRELAND		
New	Modern	Older	New	Modern	Older	New	Modern	Older
9230	10100	9650	11480	12360	12650	8960	9030	9500
9530	10430	9960	12130	12980	13370	9700	9370	10270
9660	10560	9990	12200	13500	13640	10140	9800	10460
10160	10840	10390	13160	13350	14810	10450	10400	10310
10490	10780	10360	13640	13700	14790	11520	10810	11440
10350	11070	10810	13240	14010	15420	11710	11180	11830
10910	11690	10590	13750	14410	15700	13220	11540	12120
11480	11220	10710	13970	14360	15040	11860	11180	11590
11700	11940	10790	14160	14750	15640	13480	12070	13020
12400	12280	11590	14950	15110	15030	13420	13300	14320
12850	13560	12450	16230	16270	16420	13340	14530	15230
13500	14070	12530	16600	17250	17750	14780	15180	16330
14910	14730	13920	17020	17690	18760	15820	15460	16440
16410	16170	15400	17900	18310	19280	16130	16210	17640
16910	17270	17320	19010	19610	21280	16860	17930	18930
17820	18030	17160	20080	21230	24190	18980	18970	19040
17620	18390	18500	20540	20560	25150	19560	19130	18720
19700	19570	19090	20770	21430	27290	22060	19940	19470
20130	19850	19080	20990	21520	26030	21480	19490	20410
19600	19460	19890	22280	22090	25530	20000	20170	18950
18500	20080	19230	22520	22130	25700	19770	19900	19900
20770	20340	19480	23130	22670	25970	20860	20240	19990
22830	20040	18920	20430	22650	28080	19730	20870	19570
21080	20030	19680	22600	22990	27030	20930	20330	17070
22740	20240	20330	24930	23360	29030	21550	20310	19070
24310	20910	21470	25910	24760	28970	20520	20350	17770
22650	21860	21240	26530	24300	27650	21210	22060	18820
23770	21540	21700	27460	25100	26840	22810	20740	19050
22920	22150	22070	27250	26170	27360	22080	21930	19710
22620	23230	24270	29530	26940	29090	22000	21520	20990
24270	23260	23680	30410	27780	29140	24220	22030	19650
23340	23440	23380	31530	28400	29990	23600	22780	19310
26490	23560	26340	30430	28140	30710	23190	22080	22800
27530	25480	25340	31920	31320	32940	24160	23260	21350
	26080	27660	31110	30190	32180	24550	24240	21230
26070	25040	27080	33320	30780	36580	25730	24420	22170
25560	25720	27230	33400	31700	35690	25650	24350	23890
27420	26550	27750	32960	31900	37310	24970	25820	24480
27790	26470	26010	34180	32020	36500	26350	25480	24960
	26390	27460	34000	32350	36770	25640	25010	24660
	26840	29250	35160	32280	36480	26170	25100	25260
27170	27990	29140	34250	32360	38010	25250	25790	24820
29990	27740	28210	34860	32970	38370	25910	26100	23980
30370	28700	33130	36460	33000	38850	25810	25480	24520
28780	29550	29380	33870	32310	42080	25990	25930	

NATIONWIDE BUILDING SOCIETY

AVERAGE PRICES (at approval stage) 1976 -

15.12 UNITED KINGDOM AND REGIONS BY AGE OF HOUSE: TERRACED HOUSES

Year		UNITED KINGDOM			NORTHERN			YORKS & HUMBERSIDE			NORTH WEST		
		New	Modern	Older	New	Modern	Older	New	Modern	Older	New	Modern	Older
1976	1	10200	10890	8540	8980	8730	6270	8190	7860	5800	8120	8260	6200
	2	10500	11140	8970	9530	8180	6590	8630	8030	6430	9110	8660	6440
	3	10950	11380	8980	9900	9170	6530	8420	8010	6480	9480	8700	6670
	4	11130	11460	9040	9740	10050	6930	9280	8060	6480	9730	8910	6490
1977	1	11230	11770	9260	10090	9930	7210	8800	8460	6470	9920	9330	6560
	2	11400	11810	9440	10350	10530	7390	9050	8330	6730	10090	9080	6820
	3	11710	12040	9650	11130	11190	7520	8930	9030	6770	10580	9340	7350
	4	12080	12060	9620	10580	10350	7680	9760	8900	6830	10550	9540	7050
1978	1	12580	12870	10080	11360	10970	7360		9090	6850	11720	10060	7330
	2	13070	13320	10410	12170	11300	8140		10160	7280	12010	10980	7510
	3	14240	14780	11290	13060	11420	8480		10570	7380	12210	11170	8210
	4	14810	15590	11980	12600	12040	8470	12070	10690	7840	12990	10910	8450
1979	1	15850	16410	12810	14110	12000	9310	12730	10560	8190	13800	11840	9100
	2	17090	17870	13960	14600	13930	9580	12980	12280	8600	15360	13880	9640
	3	18270	19070	15010	15140	14960	10130	13060	13680	9490	15640	15530	10420
	4	19360	20240	16200	15350	14380	10540	13250	13810	10710	16690	15470	11080
1980	1	20670	21040	16790	16560	15840	11310	14610	15340	10550	18280	16220	11670
	2	21370	21500	17430	16810	16100	11900	15070	14430	11390	19340	17700	12410
	3	21870	21460	17640	17430	15870	12110	15760	16840	11870	20670	17560	13120
	4	22050	21700	17700	17950	16070	12630	16240	16800	12110	21340	18030	13040
1981	1	22550	21940	17620		17220	11950	15720	16100	12210	21540	18450	13210
	2	23140	22280	17980		15990	12820		17100	12480	19700	18540	13500
	3	23070	22250	18070		17690	13640	16550	16830	12380	19650	17600	14120
	4	23400	21380	17250		17540	13240	17740	15800	12400	20980	18220	13280
1982	1	23530	21900	17710		16520	13540	18930	15740	12670	20530	18170	13400
	2	23320	22450	18090	19250	17030	14590	17570	16690	12640	21480	18370	13650
	3	23510	22940	18340	18810	18990	13840		15440	12690		18310	14200
	4	23530	23920	18810	20000	19200	15230	17970	17750	13680		18910	14070
1983	1	23880	24460	19250	20110	19300	14310	18300	17310	13430	20900	18720	14580
	2	26110	25630	19980	20080	20410	15260	21370	18240	14250	20620	19160	15080
	3	26260	25750	20430		19550	16040	20270	19780	14380	19540	19500	15280
	4	26510	26260	20670		19700	15730		19500	14110	18700	21060	15350
1984	1	27090	27520	21320		20160	15920		20300	14540		19810	15570
	2	28830	28420	22450		20800	16500		18450	14790		21380	16280
	3	28050	28290	22680		20970	16960		19450	14740		19150	16020
	4	28560	29120	23510		19860	18210		20070	16150		22210	16350
1985	1	27820	28410	25080		22680	18190		18250	15920		22190	17270
	2	29760	29770	26510		22740	18930		21490	17020	22980	23310	17320
	3	30530	30100	26550		22630	18200		19660	17470		23580	18390
	4	32110	30330	27440		22040	20230		21850	17570		22210	17940
1986	1	33680	31330	27820		21990	18610		21100	17680		23830	18080
	2	34170	32180	29120		23540	19800		19940	18070	26900	22360	18160
	3	35540	33730	30340		22120	19780		21890	17870		24700	18740
	4	38120	34730	31280		21840	19780		24560	18410		23370	17980
1987	1	38180	36180	33880		21580	21110		21430	19750		21640	20230

£

EAST MIDLANDS			WEST MIDLANDS			EAST ANGLIA		
New	Modern	Older	New	Modern	Older	New	Modern	Older
7980	7970	5730	9430	9110	7020	9430	9830	7940
8410	8550	6000	9390	9340	7420	9330	9900	7810
8280	8330	6060	9710	9430	7330	9300	10080	7420
8370	8440	5990	9440	9470	7230	10010	9970	8140
8710	8580	6400	9920	9370	7390	10110	10410	7930
9080	8550	6810	10340	9860	7600	10120	10000	8250
9830	9200	6600	9790	9930	8240	11160	10410	8580
9220	8890	6530	10630	9750	8140	11170	10460	8220
9890	9450	6960	11070	10900	8220	10550	11980	8610
10130	9630	6780	11410	10900	8130	11300	11240	9310
10720	10070	6960	12540	11940	8350	12050	12090	8780
11430	10210	7350	12590	12390	9360	12370	12790	8830
11860	10600	7360	13710	13350	9680	13450	14220	9940
13000	11770	7620	13880	14300	10770	15280	14780	11680
14130	13250	8540	15360	15580	11760	15660	14820	12840
14510	12740	9210	16710	16120	12390	17550	16330	13730
15550	13480	10050	18200	16890	13230	18780	16480	14080
16220	14430	10380	19370	17730	13450	19770	18270	14710
16310	15540	11580	19100	17900	13960	19720	18060	15950
17610	14910	11230	19770	18770	14060	19350	19920	16600
17610	16000	10920	21340	17620	17730	19760	20060	16190
18060	15840	12230	22880	18550	15100	20920	18230	17520
18880	15630	12300		19090	14640	21270	19640	16270
19040	16350	12000	22000	17490	14650	21820	20810	16040
17900	14810	12510	22960	17650	14160	21360	18370	15550
18720	16320	12650	21050	18860	14140	21220	20290	17200
17680	16210	13040	19680	17980	13980	21130	21670	17360
16930	18290	12920		18810	14490	22100	21990	17570
16920	17790	13240	19670	19970	15790	21380	21940	18550
18870	18450	14730	19820	18620	15050	21800	25240	18950
20530	19180	13730		20400	15700		22770	21210
21240	18690	14570		19180	15540	22240	23140	20190
	18200	14720	19840	20490	16500		24800	20500
21900	20650	15440	22560	21170	17740		24640	22610
	19240	14970		19220	17430		24930	23490
21110	19330	15640		21100	18780	21780	27500	21680
	20170	16100	22170	21110	18760		27560	23660
	21480	17950	21710	21840	18700		30380	29690
23290	22580	16950		22800	19300		27950	26130
	21560	17110	23590	22330	18720	29760	30130	28020
	21560	18890	26380	22800	18960		31020	25370
24590	23400	20040	25090	23590	19610	32970	32930	28720
29620	23680	21270	26330	24120	19610	32080	31100	30540
	25230	20910		23970	20790	33140	33480	29970
	27150	22760		28200	20150		35690	32890

AVERAGE PRICES (at approval stage) 1976 -

15.12 UNITED KINGDOM AND REGIONS BY AGE OF HOUSE:
TERRACED HOUSES (continued)

Year	OUTER SOUTH EAST			OUTER METROPOLITAN			GREATER LONDON			SOUTH WEST		
	New	Modern	Older	New	Modern	Older	New	Modern	Older	New	Modern	Older
1976 1	10640	10920	9340	13030	12850	10840	16830	14530	12450	9700	9610	8850
2	10870	11050	9580	13120	12910	11180	17540	15090	13070	9760	9980	9470
3	11740	11410	9370	14080	13230	11300	17780	15080	13020	10190	10500	9590
4	11710	11500	9540	14300	13350	11330	18240	15170	13090	10180	10300	9580
1977 1	11710	11590	9840	14260	13650	11370	18620	15890	13620	10380	10710	9440
2	11930	11640	10230	14110	13580	11350	18800	15920	13650	10560	10890	9950
3	12190	12090	9990	14410	13950	11830	20090	15890	13860	10790	10630	9750
4	12760	12180	10070	15280	13780	11580	20950	16360	14120	10990	10580	9470
1978 1	12580	13080	10720	16320	14670	12100		17090	15100	11430	11570	10280
2	13100	13390	10680	16490	15330	12510		17680	15620	12170	12100	10710
3	14700	14650	11970	18200	17720	13650		20680	17630	13170	13620	11070
4	15230	15810	12360	19340	19830	14790		21740	19030	13090	13720	11680
1979 1	16430	17110	13520	20340	19980	15750		24160	20190	14200	14530	13200
2	17540	18660	14330	21630	21460	16580		26720	23010	16250	15960	13910
3	19160	19280	16050	23870	23470	18540		27800	24380	17080	16710	15160
4	21210	21130	17780	24910	24960	20380		29960	26050	17940	18850	16880
1980 1	22290	22360	19050	26180	26260	21330		30750	26640	19400	19140	17160
2	23440	22660	20000	26840	26100	22170		31340	27990	20940	20350	17770
3	23680	22530	19700	27750	25650	22160		32380	27760	20930	19740	18560
4	23030	22280	18980	26650	26250	22620		31870	28130	21030	19870	18660
1981 1	23860	22560	19260	28560	26740	22440		32100	28060	21880	20340	19140
2	24140	23490	20260	30830	27180	23110		32430	28110	22230	21260	19490
3	23280	22990	20330	30130	26680	23090		33790	28630	22200	20630	20110
4	24680	21940	19370	29510	25970	21750	40870	30810	27150	21710	20180	18000
1982 1	24250	22850	19170	29040	26760	22770	42820	33310	28380	22690	20750	19140
2	24230	23330	20670	30150	27760	23250	40030	33880	29250	20780	20770	19540
3	23900	24420	21370	31000	28560	24020	38700	35380	29740	22190	20790	19880
4	25810	24980	21440	30610	29200	25470	36390	36220	30860	22410	21620	19400
1983 1	25960	25620	22510	31490	30040	27280	38060	36410	30870	22460	23020	20960
2	29790	26460	23240	32720	31730	28410	41820	39380	33140	25370	24320	22060
3	29970	26880	24380	33970	32060	27550	42230	38090	34490	23800	23900	21870
4	30920	27180	24030	32720	33290	29650	38270	41840	35490	25010	24100	22240
1984 1	29650	29190	25830	35040	35330	28800	40070	44440	38000	25840	25160	22790
2	30830	30450	27220	39440	36660	32160	43670	43640	39590	25050	26170	23740
3	32940	29480	27330	35060	36390	34070	41580	44690	40680	25940	26790	24480
4	29970	30930	28040	38040	37370	31940	42640	43350	41910	27300	27840	25030
1985 1	31450	32670	29530	38230	39850	34360	43020	47660	44710	26870	27910	26000
2	34020	34080	31570	40910	41180	36540	51120	50520	47120	27510	28650	26710
3	34640	33060	30580	41740	42390	37510	54020	52400	48390	28710	29280	27820
4	38920	36270	32190	44410	41830	39060	57290	52670	50150	30540	29710	28370
1986 1	38570	37450	32850	45620	45890	38970	62920	53830	53080	30620	31280	28730
2	41940	38700	35110	48300	46590	41690	56800	57080	54930	32760	31910	30680
3	41170	40240	35450	51600	48820	44270	59310	62420	58260	33070	33910	32160
4	45130	41200	38290	60390	51510	46940	65620	66900	63070	34550	33020	31920
1987 1	44020	45110	38470	57330	56690	54450	66790	68470	69260	35820	35380	34000

WALES			SCOTLAND			NORTHERN IRELAND		
New	Modern	Older	New	Modern	Older	New	Modern	Older
8570	9780	7450	10910	10690	10320			
9100	9910	7740	11680	11600	11960			
9100	9880	7750	12010	11970	12020			
9130	9930	7870	12540	11970	12110			
9980	10110	8090	12650	12520	12540			
10270	10120	7790	13120	12350	12880			
10090	10060	8270	13870	12660	13210			
10480	10830	8000	13370	12540	13330			
11090	10830	8440	12980	13250	13260			12080
11420	11580	8560		13760	12740			
12680	13020	9420		14740	13750			
13470	12780	9910		14930	16280			
14390	14140	10590		15970	16030			
14130	14810	11460		16190	17650			
15130	15980	11860	17400	17630	17960			13340
15740	17910	12670	20120	18120	19840			13060
17030	17360	13560	20110	17540	21750			13620
15940	18930	13060	20000	17520	22590			13460
15960	17710	13620	20180	17990	21770		16930	14030
17880	18500	14640	21920	19580	22050		18450	12530
18860	19320	14400	20580	21560	21130		18610	12190
19280	18290	14910	20620	21210	21230		18370	12530
	20490	14390	22590	21620	21350		20210	12070
19550	17600	14330		19580	23270		17590	12450
20250	19060	14870	22600	22790	22590		16030	12260
21760	18450	14960	23590	20810	22150		16670	13000
	18790	16120	22870	20500	22280		16520	11630
19270	20970	16440	23510	23930	24390		17350	12580
19120	20680	16130	23850	23100	25050		18160	13320
22350	22400	15990	25580	23220	26110	19050	17350	13920
22570	21810	16550	27160	24070	25900	19110		14670
21920	21680	17380	29210	22680	27350			14060
22070	21510	17340	32060	23680	26040	22170		13750
21330	22190	18190	31320	25060	29350			14070
18630	24870	17650	31620	28050	27800			14240
	23670	18920	30980	27420	29720		19860	14480
20550	25210	18650	28280	26940	29520		17960	15690
	23580	19510	28730	28410	31690		19010	15830
	24790	19960	32400	28510	28060		19670	16060
	24680	20830	33090	27450	31010		20370	16780
	25140	20930	29560	27140	30400		19080	16620
25550	25060	21590	30900	29770	30240		19520	17120
29510	25890	21520	32720	29090	33810		19510	17300
	26140	21680	33870	28190	31540	25530	19370	16050
	26200	22060	33560	28430	35640		19020	16650

NATIONWIDE BUILDING SOCIETY

AVERAGE PRICES (at approval stage) 1976 –

15.13 UNITED KINGDOM AND REGIONS BY AGE OF HOUSE: BUNGALOWS, FLATS & MAISONETTES

Year	UNITED KINGDOM			NORTHERN			YORKS & HUMBERSIDE			NORTH WEST		
	New	Modern	Older	New	Modern	Older	New	Modern	Older	New	Modern	Older
1976 1	11870	11610	10900	12040	9840	7940	10050	10300	8170	11610	10210	10430
2	12200	12020	11170	12960	9830	8590	10490	10280	7910	12110	10460	11030
3	12550	12410	11490	12690	10040	8740	10640	11160	8110	12460	10640	10650
4	12810	12460	11680	12810	10280	9850	11520	11070	8550	12610	10850	12300
1977 1	13120	12620	11700	14220	10730	9110	12070	11030	9500	12660	11110	12670
2	13660	12950	11930	14720	10850	10060	12430	11500	10490	13460	11790	13320
3	14000	13190	12200	14840	10910	9750	12720	11650	10220	13070	11800	14150
4	14220	13400	12330	15250	11400		12110	12700		14020	12060	
1978 1	15250	14010	12700		11580		13610	12770		14040	12840	
2	15500	14530	13420		12140		13790	12460		14550	13490	
3	16540	16100	14480		12740		14490	14020		15680	14410	
4	17430	17080	15330		14050		15490	13880		17120	15830	
1979 1	18390	17770	16450		14100		16360	15460		17760	16850	
2	19760	19150	17970		15570		16570	16060		20220	18700	
3	20680	20600	19120	19690	17610		17610	17780		21190	18240	
4	21820	21980	20760		18570		18650	18970		20720	20370	
1980 1	22920	22830	21780	21630	19600	17030	19180	19390		22580	21590	
2	24300	23470	22080	22200	18530	17350	20570	20380	18540	24830	21800	21690
3	25230	23920	22220	23390	20960	18410	23590	21580	19370	25340	22940	22940
4	25640	23470	21950	22680	19350	19180	23760	19870	20090	27800	22520	23440
1981 1	25760	23910	21690	22490	19260		23420	23290		24850	21980	21360
2	27050	24700	22630		21390		24370	22680	19780	27450	24370	19690
3	26110	25020	22250		20420	18970	23800	22280	17030	24870	24420	20970
4	26210	24510	22470	23720	20510		25220	22160		25980	24570	
1982 1	27440	24770	22590	25320	20760		27910	23160		26820	22910	
2	27890	25510	23640	26330	20650		25710	23290		27270	25080	22950
3	27470	26020	23470	25860	22460	20930	25620	23430		27130	23900	
4	28110	26610	24410	24560	22610	19130	26230	23950		27940	25590	25320
1983 1	28090	27300	24740	26630	21440	19430	27300	24900	24650	26270	25130	26780
2	28610	28150	25860	26010	24280	19550	28130	24410	23990	27020	26760	27000
3	29100	29270	26550	27940	26360	20300	26300	24760	25050	26410	27180	24650
4	30050	29930	27300		26650	22980	28840	26440		30370	28440	27250
1984 1	30820	30660	28190	25930	20370		31060	26700		30320	29160	28600
2	32030	32150	29530	29050	19290		28620	28070		30550	29980	29130
3	31350	31870	30060	26070			29010	27450		28870	29380	29970
4	33390	33830	31280	27350	20760		32490	28640	29670		31310	37370
1985 1	34930	34050	32070	26470	22570		29540	30730		34030	31630	36430
2	34970	34780	32120	27860	18920		29270	30370	25940	34110	31880	36440
3	37240	35690	32810	30110			31650	29360	29880	36350	32690	31360
4	38370	36270	33680	30970			32310	32630		35050	30870	31460
1986 1	39500	36230	34610	30100	25110		33730	30010		36140	31840	29310
2	39700	37970	35170	31620	22590		33410	30760	31420	34160	33110	36620
3	41560	38960	37460	30550	26090		39090	31230	31000	36170	33220	36620
4	41810	40310	38670	28660				32260		37760	34000	33420
1987 1	43750	41650	39510	29830	25360			33730		43080	33000	

£

EAST MIDLANDS			WEST MIDLANDS			EAST ANGLIA		
New	Modern	Older	New	Modern	Older	New	Modern	Older
9940	9990	8910	12000	10370	11540	10240	10640	9550
10620	10270	9360	12010	11030	11710	10730	10960	10190
11150	10250	10300	11830	11210	11140	10780	11640	10220
11310	10960	9650	13040	11220	13270	11590	11500	9850
11550	10910	9760	13130	11210	13620	11970	11540	10620
11600	11030	10950	13340	11710	13870	12290	11720	10720
11670	11730	10490	13420	12190	14780	12540	12200	11310
11580	11420	10880	13540	11900	15500	12770	12510	10960
12790	11940	10800	14010	12650		13600	13070	
13140	12300	10340	14420	13030		13730	13430	
14100	13030	13020	15190	14310		14220	14840	
14920	14130		15970	15990		15080	15160	
16320	15070		17780	15540		17110	15320	
17530	15910		18640	16560		19190	16940	
17850	16240	17100	19320	18400		19710	18680	
18800	17190	17800	20090	19180		20590	20230	
20540	18820	17130	21630	19200		22400	21370	
21430	20310	18930	21440	20750		23060	23050	
21970	21170	20660	23160	20890	22210	23790	23720	
24240	20900	19920	25370	19360	19850		23530	21120
23820	21010	18850		20800		24160	22980	22730
24130	21070	22370		21190			22660	21580
24980	22660	19360	26240	22600	23780	26670	23890	23720
23290	21160	20770		20920	25580	26520	25310	23250
24530	22620	19690	25440	21190		25520	22970	
26570	22930	22940	27250	21740	23140	24440	24040	25080
26190	23310	23680	26600	22440	22860	25700	24690	26340
25130	23690		27480	23540		24170	25380	27360
26550	24200	22590	26720	23870	22100	26070	26040	26460
28450	24370	25570	27630	24650	23500	27880	27280	29100
27770	24800	25400	26980	25260	23110	26800	28260	
28950	25120	21840		24030	22980		30590	
28590	26730			25920	22670		29210	
28560	26010			25400	26200		30780	28790
30500	26840		27430	27630	24910	32480	31340	30960
32850	29240		29740	29200	24570	31010	33220	
30740	29250	25910	33120	27890	26600	34340	34190	31710
29450	29320	31770	32340	30040		36350	32620	40090
31630	31790	24630	35540	30120	29580	37530	37010	
32170	30740			29530	29970		38370	
34530	30910			27160	33450		38750	
37940	32630	31620	31470	28590	31470	42090	38560	35600
35550	31520	35010	36950	28730	30030	41260	39830	35380
37330	34230			29710	33500	47730	43410	40740
41160	35440			30910	33100		40200	

AVERAGE PRICES (at approval stage) 1976 –

15.13 UNITED KINGDOM AND REGIONS BY AGE OF HOUSE: BUNGALOWS, FLATS & MAISONETTES (continued)

Year	OUTER SOUTH EAST			OUTER METROPOLITAN			GREATER LONDON			SOUTH WEST		
	New	Modern	Older	New	Modern	Older	New	Modern	Older	New	Modern	Older
1976 1	11880	12620	12270	13200	13670	14430	12930	12900	12050	11750	12080	11600
2	12460	12920	12980	14000	14370	14030	13320	13010	12160	12240	12590	12470
3	12750	13190	12780	14080	14720	15390	13730	13450	12330	12040	13120	12520
4	12900	12930	12850	13670	14610	15370	14020	13170	12300	12080	13320	12270
1977 1	13110	13010	12930	13750	14790	15170	13880	13450	12270	12460	13710	12930
2	13140	13390	13070	14270	15480	15460	14100	13730	12340	12670	13530	13110
3	14230	13630	13950	14290	15530	15820	14890	13850	12450	12890	13650	13030
4	14060	13990	13810	15240	15610	15310	14350	13840	12640	13490	14570	12580
1978 1	15140	14560	13450	16280	16120	16270		14660	13050	14250	14730	14030
2	15040	15030	15010	16160	16370	16370		15480	14060	14970	15210	13720
3	16570	17020	16480	17800	19320	18860		17320	15040	16080	17210	15330
4	18620	18490	17390	18690	20600	21670		18430	16170	17490	18100	16820
1979 1	19120	19830	17700	19680	20850	20840		19970	17910	17800	18390	18050
2	21630	20730	18320	22560	22040	22960		21290	19950	19070	20620	18790
3	23030	23370	19870	24270	23410	24100		23280	21030	21580	22960	20160
4	26690	24230	21050	24880	25730	25340		25150	22820	23550	23630	22330
1980 1	25680	25780	22810	26250	27150	28710		25840	23910	22900	24780	24020
2	28100	25170	23340	27720	27490	27700		26650	24440	25000	25830	22540
3	29860	26110	24800	29660	27260	28340		26790	23900	26710	25120	22860
4	29270	25250	23720	30120	27090	28820		25670	23670	24610	26350	22680
1981 1	29690	25540	23210		27230	27650		26430	23800	27050	25750	23070
2	32820	27130	23760		26860	28740		26740	24150		27340	23070
3	33500	27290	22830		28150	27500		26820	24070	26430	27160	21230
4	31440	27070	23210	31390	27750	29970	27460	26450	24420	26200	24990	20920
1982 1	34450	26820	23960	32070	27830	30410	26350	27200	24140		26000	22780
2	30750	28020	23140	30000	28780	28360	26920	27500	25240	28190	27450	22960
3	29440	28470	24750	31730	29900	29790	28470	27810	24950	28090	28100	24120
4	29610	28400	25290	32040	30240	31790	29550	28430	26320	28980	28360	24360
1983 1	31070	29870	26550	32630	31360	29990	31740	28610	26660	27110	29670	27960
2	33680	30890	26990	32240	33010	34020	30990	29520	27600	29350	29800	25260
3	32190	34020	27280	34330	34990	31740	33210	31790	28970	30860	30570	27530
4	32050	33770	26550	31940	36230	33950	33040	31490	29690	30780	31800	26970
1984 1	35710	34750	26470	37110	36930	36740	34540	32620	31040	31160	33030	27280
2	38490	36940	29830	37010	39620	38600	40230	35810	32450	33700	34500	30540
3	39970	36740	29520	35220	37950	41000	36720	34850	33250	35360	35050	27550
4	37750	37280	30660	37280	40750	39780	42850	37400	35210	38980	37350	32810
1985 1	37750	38790	33990	38010	41350	40830	40490	40120	37360	39630	37210	32490
2	39390	39680	32070	38190	44130	41430	40630	41170	39450	38020	37570	32980
3	41130	40970	34250	42820	44600	45940	42510	41590	40340	42040	38520	32010
4	44980	41030	35370	43530	45430	46660	47550	44140	43800	40430	39830	32980
1986 1	48550	40970	37230	45550	47550	47080	48170	44770	44790	39270	40280	35500
2	47690	45040	37130	45830	48910	45710	49110	48550	46650	43140	42360	34560
3	49950	46070	39830	46490	51970	52150	52290	51360	50400	44580	44200	38260
4	48380	48470	41580	48940	52800	56000	52800	54250	53490	49370	45800	37430
1987 1	50640	51180	43180	49970	56060	55230	54830	58300	55440	44160	47500	41100

£

WALES			SCOTLAND			NORTHERN IRELAND		
New	Modern	Older	New	Modern	Older	New	Modern	Older
11410	10670	10090	13250	13210	9040	13550	12010	11950
11700	11190	10310	12770	14120	9450	13930	13080	11550
12360	11140	10520	13590	14370	9940	14630	14490	14240
12440	11450	10530	13670	14440	10330	14650	14760	12980
12190	11620	10670	13700	14580	10260	15550	14740	13410
12650	11750	10510	14300	14930	10550	17180	15130	13500
13160	11810	10830	15350	15280	10960	17060	15960	13820
14210	12060	11150	15040	14890	11070	18060	15540	
15030	12430		16360	15850	11360	19630	17450	
14890	13370		16350	17050	11840	20420	17760	
14150	14620		17830	17710	12660	21260	19690	
15090	15270		17710	18360	12580	21840	20220	
16160	16060		18840	18960	13270	22660	19730	
18250	18530		19980	19760	14320	23200	21520	
19180	18620		19450	21240	15300	24450	23350	
18140	20710		22570	22480	16910	24040	24100	
21590	20350		22040	22000	16920	27810	25190	
22300	21210		24870	22540	17160	28280	25230	
21520	21980		25640	21800	17570	26820	25390	
24220	21690	22650	27190	23140	17290	25010	24690	18860
25230	22750		26090	23070	16600	27210	24650	21620
27970	22020		27220	24870	19070	28380	25880	22600
	23120	20020	25290	24750	18750	25820	25070	20230
25210	22560	21820	29970	23920	17820	25960	25530	
26050	22750	22980		25020	18270	25620	26390	20550
25800	22660	20140	31660	25940	19180	27170	25340	22080
24620	23880	23370	31150	26310	19040	25210	27150	23770
24540	24430		32000	27040	19620	27390	27600	
23360	25870	22140	31060	28020	19590	26470	27770	23710
24760	25240	22730	29050	28960	21280	26740	28170	23120
25080	26040	22760	31750	28560	21880	26810	27790	
26940	26180	25620	32440	29790	22880	27960	29120	
	26030	24960	31990	30150	22990	28080	30290	27120
31650	25930	33940	32490	32580	22670	29110	29600	26310
33130	26760	27430	29410	31040	23950	27970	30800	
28900	29550	30640	33720	33880	23290	28690	31260	
30750	28830		33770	34300	24870	29180	31340	
30400	29850	26190	33390	32900	25370	29330	32160	
30980	29890	31730	33260	34490	25480	31430	33610	27930
32300	32330	27220	34940	33970	25280	31280	31250	
35470	31290		37080	34420	25460	30790	31750	
37420	30820	27120	35270	35140	26250	32800	33110	25880
37010	32980	29360	35380	34730	27180	32900	33760	33920
36840	33560		35100	35690	26550	33050	31640	
38800	32880		35310	36470	26930	32100	30600	

NATIONWIDE BUILDING SOCIETY

AVERAGE PRICES (at approval stage) 1954-1975

15.14 REGIONS: NEW DWELLINGS

£

Year	North Eastern	North Western	Midland	Eastern	London & S East	Southern	Western	Scotland	Northern Ireland
1954 4	1776	1978	1847	2092	2533	2173	2183	2082	
1955 4	1930	2052	1848	2089	2798	2403	2341	2205	
1956 4	2071	2069	1983	2260	2579	2505	2318	2451	
1957 4	2046	2132	2087	2277	2781	2516	2466	2528	
1958 4	2052	2112	2081	2264	2969	2605	2424	2534	
1959 4	2096	2224	2264	2436	3025	2699	2471	2607	1707
1960 1	2107	2160	2266	2388	3041	2705	2418	2584	1687
2	2173	2283	2304	2545	3077	2842	2603	2687	1764
3	2196	2333	2384	2490	3118	2855	2618	2720	1906
4	2185	2328	2457	2565	3335	2894	2744	2649	1831
1961 1	2328	2367	2400	2679	3343	3043	2736	2890	1895
2	2355	2465	2538	2802	3561	3138	2865	2944	1993
3	2424	2452	2557	2882	3700	3291	2865	2866	2118
4	2445	2632	2707	2878	3697	3227	2897	3190	2067
1962 1	2440	2497	2679	2963	3746	3414	2985	3063	2193
2	2522	2548	2727	2889	3744	3503	3007	3044	2182
3	2591	2563	2775	2942	3684	3408	3016	3003	2329
4	2545	2678	2708	3087	3788	3409	3036	3256	2265
1963 1	2711	2630	2801	3119	3739	3497	3057	3120	2334
2	2645	2725	2856	3171	3898	3587	3164	3262	2178
3	2743	2723	2999	3184	3929	3529	3092	3286	
4	2704	2695	2995	3280	4133	3667	3232	3336	2277
1964 1	2720	2807	2985	3331	4103	3763	3233	3329	2449
2	2815	2906	3059	3325	4319	3841	3284	3430	2510
3	2960	3047	3109	3633	4695	3869	3366	3685	2488
4	2886	2849	3133	3807	4867	4037	3460	3690	2597
1965 1	2917	3126	3275	3907	4800	4221	3442	3786	2584
2	2963	3232	3364	3972	5137	4392	3578	4051	2657
3	3157	3299	3393	4020	5024	4422	3560	3997	2808
4	3125	3219	3414	3919	5051	4605	3697	4009	2888
1966 1	3231	3280	3488	4033	5003	4526	3588	4238	2933
2	3286	3385	3581	4085	5208	4723	3753	4191	3078
3	3473	3495	3571	4137	5182	4634	3897	4281	3075
4	3423	3628	3750	4017	5223	4773	3905	4459	3370
1967 1	3477	3613	3882	4001	5216	4895	3948	4698	3305
2	3657	3710	3962	4012	5474	4912	4041	4723	3624
3	3640	3754	4204	3989	5421	5012	3968	4392	3439
4	3711	3893	4130	4274	5482	4914	4101	4453	3351
1968 1	3691	4080	4360	4224	5853	4987	4082	4717	3913
2	3837	4093	4361	4266	5610	5352	4218	4706	3767
3	3900	4201	4475	4492	5935	5402	4291	4932	4608
4	3930	4405	4398	4550	5688	5484	4482	4722	3798
1969 1	3946	4261	4341	4425	5563	5428	4418	5164	4158
2	4194	4398	4501	4605	6283	5541	4433	5182	4291
3	4104	4177	4400	4649	5801	5619	4601	4990	4777
4	3983	4302	4554	4698	5894	5634	4437	5059	4442
1970 1	4018	4420	4638	4601	6115	5600	4515	5118	4495
2	4107	4566	4756	4633	6074	5857	4615	5201	4685
3	4273	4575	4806	4674	6461	6145	4686	5269	4683
4	4429	4463	4821	4843	6541	6017	4848	5334	4670
1971 1	4312	4793	4841	5077	6862	6220	4836	5317	4701
2	4560	4961	5194	5299	7431	6658	5125	5610	4883
3	4958	5235	5573	5674	8276	7493	5536	5843	5063

Year	North Eastern	North Western	Midland	Eastern	London & S East	Southern	South Western	Wales	Scotland	Northern Ireland
1971 4	4925	5400	5698	5798	9644	8014	5678	5404	5922	5041
1972 1	5309	5607	5874	6572	10187	9107	6096	5715	6358	5085
2	5831	6036	6219	7166	11531	10043	6988	6033	6373	5244
3	6557	6924	7236	8888	13326	11769	8606	6659	6886	5220
4	6926	7878	8126	9534	13205	12289	9153	7285	7361	5600
1973 1	7341	7636	8510	10309	13704	13572	9971	7654	7681	5791
2	7749	8140	8429	10846	13703	13654	9998	7792	8158	6132
3	8224	8581	8996	10504	13980	13377	10128	8146	8510	6403
4	7917	8419	8890	10438	12743	13185	10285	8752	8646	6587
1974 1	7963	8478	8777	10105	12551	12752	10275	8734	9165	7186
2	8505	8871	8999	10662	12857	12831	10165	8880	9733	7430
3	8483	9187	9723	10549	14124	13341	10500	9220	10139	7920
4	8732	9172	9608	11212	14153	13176	9994	9604	10934	8297
1975 1	9265	10212	9925	11419	13975	13891	10766	10110	11185	9022
2	9788	10291	10877	11959	14754	14623	11041	10591	11470	9830
3	10180	10417	11380	12567	16836	15048	11488	10666	12470	10586
4	10563	10776	11645	12583	16418	15188	12235	10703	12653	11179

Note: From 1971 Q4 Wales was defined as a separate region

NATIONWIDE BUILDING SOCIETY

AVERAGE PRICES (at approval stage) 1952-1975

15.15 REGIONS: EXISTING DWELLINGS

£

Year	North Eastern	North Western	Midland	Eastern	London & S East	Southern	Western	Scotland	Northern Ireland
1952 4	1351	1522	1705	1710	2546	2245	1608	1511	
1953 4	1287	1220	1488	1707	2297	1895	1438	1465	
1954 4	1344	1159	1474	1583	2330	1855	1406	1351	
1955 4	1438	1372	1653	1674	2461	2007	1553	1570	
1956 4	1473	1450	1688	1712	2515	2195	1687	1815	
1957 4	1487	1510	1832	1873	2532	2112	1780	1666	
1958 4	1471	1429	1678	1786	2646	2247	1772	1677	
1959 4	1311	1196	1469	1751	2324	1827	1633	1617	1400
1960 1	1289	1228	1406	1751	2452	1852	1746	1625	1318
2	1439	1238	1507	1833	2548	1894	1769	1777	1352
3	1543	1316	1606	1807	2689	2035	1813	1706	1374
4	1425	1333	1572	2016	2709	2072	1786	1790	1345
1961 1	1368	1211	1633	1946	2867	2132	1797	1863	1550
2	1561	1317	1653	2030	2929	2191	1779	1878	1818
3	1452	1367	1784	1948	3008	2383	1862	1941	1675
4	1750	1704	1982	2427	3502	2743	2009	2186	1523
1962 1	1761	1692	1927	2181	3381	2654	2266	2079	1689
2	1788	1654	1975	2320	3436	2782	2220	2065	1689
3	1707	1748	1963	2414	3550	2794	2352	2163	1397
4	1736	1651	2046	2384	3584	2841	2330	2289	1423
1963 1	1880	1825	2158	2570	3671	2997	2360	2278	1542
2	2150	2038	2569	2842	3862	3292	2585	2536	1889
3	2338	2161	2598	2915	4077	3477	2853	2691	
4	2316	2282	2688	2882	4120	3625	2878	2720	2218
1964 1	2256	2296	2590	3079	4306	3526	2936	2624	2085
2	2371	2291	2869	3276	4472	3715	3151	2837	2287
3	2480	2430	2906	3569	4658	3710	3190	2971	2566
4	2415	2475	2971	3527	4743	4060	3355	3328	2266
1965 1	2507	2620	2858	3748	4708	4035	3203	3368	2393
2	2612	2757	3008	3960	5054	4196	3335	3363	2543
3	2684	2766	2958	3749	4948	4178	3432	3602	2579
4	2604	2618	3083	3620	4850	4154	3283	3472	2823
1966 1	2722	2684	3097	3888	4859	4217	3271	3546	2772
2	2876	2871	3173	3939	5038	4380	3469	3659	2740
3	3030	3049	3187	3943	5077	4412	3632	3938	2811
4	3006	2924	3315	3573	4924	4298	3500	3686	2620
1967 1	2878	3040	3367	3622	5234	4379	3610	3821	2823
2	2996	3205	3546	3748	5260	4521	3596	4042	3317
3	3145	3184	3644	3730	5191	4757	3568	3986	3238
4	3222	3282	3707	3767	5270	4719	3639	4074	3323
1968 1	3273	3363	3729	3704	5347	4888	3870	4033	3449
2	3327	3571	3847	4203	5539	4884	3906	4124	3446
3	3507	3596	3980	4301	5430	5046	4013	4293	3752
4	3350	3618	3894	4103	5516	4980	3964	4415	3639
1969 1	3445	3153	3962	4279	5424	5088	3942	4282	3880
2	3386	3755	3998	4454	5603	5149	4000	4375	3741
3	3441	3577	3940	4550	5578	5199	4111	4283	4005
4	3542	3757	3897	4485	5605	5148	3977	4391	4033
1970 1	3537	3856	3877	4686	5649	5218	4031	4319	3650
2	3646	3933	4133	4650	5866	5576	4004	4595	3980
3	3812	4056	4201	4731	6099	5661	4441	4573	3996
4	3785	4166	4180	4956	6200	5960	4375	4799	4146
1971 1	3889	4073	4343	4754	6378	5887	4417	4655	4318
2	4086	4321	4544	5325	6871	6447	4986	4351	4216
3	4531	4443	4648	5438	7448	6985	5246	4984	4191

Year	North Eastern	North Western	Midland	Eastern	London & S East	Southern	South Western	Wales	Scotland	Northern Ireland
1971 4	4382	4649	4873	5008	8073	7555	5426	4767	5063	4320
1972 1	4432	4774	4988	6253	8534	7850	6006	5434	5314	4397
2	4873	5140	5479	7375	10030	9321	6673	5639	5718	4612
3	5546	5746	6219	9081	11708	11742	8709	6270	6565	4989
4	6201	6384	6948	10332	11992	12014	8674	6802	6781	5141
1973 1	6444	6644	7352	9861	12123	11992	9301	7169	6831	5218
2	6680	7227	7787	10117	12743	12255	9239	7294	7254	5672
3	7666	7758	8230	10663	12704	12311	9753	8066	8154	6135
4	7531	7621	8145	10528	12314	11788	9738	8115	8191	6301
1974 1	7760	7996	8660	10556	12259	11906	9785	8183	8726	7055
2	7635	8212	8409	10435	12620	11668	9535	7894	8762	7589
3	8069	8008	8424	10607	12785	11910	9973	8247	8896	7720
4	8191	8306	8771	10854	12868	11768	9884	8227	9094	8091
1975 1	8449	8702	9413	10749	13125	12465	10720	9236	9806	8114
2	8963	9388	10056	11343	13819	13247	11259	9546	10435	8591
3	9856	9941	10525	12000	14450	13705	11949	9789	11170	9784
4	9400	9821	10547	12155	14271	13936	12234	9910	11487	10345

Note: From 1971 Q4 Wales was defined as a separate region

NATIONWIDE BUILDING SOCIETY

AVERAGE PRICES (at approval stage) 1977–1981

15.16 REGIONS: TYPE OF BUYER

Year		Northern	Yorks & Humberside	North West	East Midlands	West Midlands	East Anglia
FIRST-TIME BUYERS							
1977	4	9600	8840	9130	8910	9930	10220
1978	1	9290	8740	9380	9040	10060	10970
	2	10080	8850	9310	9260	10270	11100
	3	10010	8970	10460	9450	10750	11540
	4	10580	10240	10990	10270	11800	11770
1979	1	11270	10910	11400	10880	12240	12870
	2	11560	11210	11620	10440	13320	13670
	3	12690	11620	13120	12100	14000	14390
	4	12810	12810	14350	13010	15420	16080
1980	1	13200	12980	14690	12900	15650	16830
	2	13550	13240	14560	13610	15530	16830
	3	13730	13530	14990	13820	16830	17590
	4	13380	13760	15200	14360	16360	17570
1981	1	13690	14320	15490	14060	16540	18130
	2	13230	13870	14960	13640	15990	16740
	3	14460	13930	15530	13380	16650	18160
	4	14480	13600	14580	13750	16650	18990
FORMER OWNER-OCCUPIERS							
1977	4	14220	13940	13890	12950	15460	14140
1978	1	13570	14370	14420	13830	16190	14850
	2	14730	14470	14710	14020	16620	15780
	3	16020	15800	17790	15630	18580	17680
	4	17210	16300	17750	16430	20110	18910
1979	1	17700	16770	18620	18070	20090	19050
	2	17450	16910	20430	17880	20290	20210
	3	20310	19460	22040	19400	23230	23130
	4	21230	20750	23340	21370	25510	25920
1980	1	21150	21810	24120	23210	25500	27940
	2	20800	22730	24360	22690	25940	27360
	3	22950	22220	25670	23470	27510	28400
	4	22390	23200	24560	23710	27270	28080
1981	1	22060	22850	24450	23660	27020	29140
	2	23510	24170	25750	24440	28150	27630
	3	22230	23740	25620	23790	27710	28320
	4	22630	22350	23730	23790	26160	28050

Outer South East	Outer Metrop	Greater London	South West	Wales	Scotland	Northern Ireland
11390	13130	13760	11210	9800	12230	12570
11800	13550	13910	11510	10300	12400	13000
12180	14560	14780	11720	10600	12610	13990
13220	14800	15880	12750	11080	13750	15090
13940	16710	16880	13380	11540	13990	14770
14980	16980	18560	14080	12240	14250	16070
15900	18550	20130	14870	13220	15150	16850
17270	19890	21910	15900	13530	15120	17160
19300	21380	23590	17810	14820	16340	17810
20120	22170	24490	18250	15020	16500	18660
20190	22640	24250	18650	14490	16300	18780
20380	22860	24500	19050	14850	16610	17620
20580	22700	24470	19380	15800	17130	17440
20880	23000	24310	19300	16000	17100	17370
20120	21890	24470	19070	15310	15870	15330
21120	23220	24230	18850	16000	17470	17570
20540	22810	24480	19270	16050	17350	16490
16930	20080	20040	15210	13370	17420	18750
17110	20660	20235	15680	14310	18110	19920
18440	22640	22350	16940	15700	19030	20280
20570	25650	24620	18950	16580	19570	21380
21340	27110	26090	19680	17940	21080	21920
22440	27580	27370	20490	18810	20760	22530
23350	30060	29580	22280	19410	21700	24920
26680	32210	31850	24980	20850	23670	25350
29520	35810	34780	26910	23350	25540	26830
30370	36130	35620	27980	23510	26040	28270
31150	37300	36020	28320	23410	25920	28420
31360	37230	36580	28550	24240	26770	28180
30750	36710	36420	28510	24610	25730	28770
31400	37080	36160	28530	24750	26990	27330
32290	36980	36670	29740	23380	27610	28290
31220	36880	36350	29240	24280	28680	28410
30870	35450	35330	29030	23620	27490	25460

NATIONWIDE BUILDING SOCIETY

INDEX OF PRICES 1946 -

15.17 UNITED KINGDOM:
ALL, NEW, MODERN AND OLDER

Year (4th Quarter)	All	New	Modern	Older
1946 (4th Quarter) = 100				
1946		100	100	100
1947			125	121
1948			120	121
1949			131	131
1950			133	135
1951			145	150
1952		140	138	143
1953		140	135	144
1954		141	132	142
1955		147	139	148
1956		155	143	152
1957		159	144	156
1958		161	146	159
1959		170	153	167
1960		184	164	180
1961		198	179	198
1962		210	186	210
1963		222	210	229
1964		239	227	246
1965		257	245	264
1966		273	253	276
1967		288	272	298
1968		310	288	319
1969		322	304	338
1970		342	321	364
1971		414	390	435
1972		610	549	623
1973		697	633	732

Year (4th Quarter)	All	New	Modern	Older
1973 (4th Quarter) = 100				
1973	100	100	100	100
1974	105	105	104	106
1975	116	119	114	116
1976	125	131	123	125
1977 1	128	134	125	127
2	131	138	128	129
3	134	141	130	132
4	135	145	132	134
1978 1	142	152	138	141
2	148	159	145	148
3	163	173	161	161
4	172	183	171	171
1979 1	182	195	179	182
2	195	207	193	197
3	210	223	206	213
4	225	236	221	229
1980 1	232	251	228	235
2	239	260	234	242
3	242	264	237	245
4	241	266	235	244
1981 1	243	275	239	245
2	248	280	243	249
3	248	278	245	249
4	244	285	240	243
1982 1	247	290	242	248
2	253	292	249	254
3	256	295	254	256
4	262	302	260	264
1983 1	268	304	267	269
2	280	319	279	281
3	289	327	287	291
4	294	336	293	296
1984 1	304	344	302	306
2	321	362	319	324
3	322	358	318	329
4	336	371	333	341
1985 1	347	390	344	347
2	357	401	354	359
3	363	411	357	365
4	371	427	363	374
1986 1	377	435	368	378
2	391	447	381	394
3	406	463	395	411
4	422	478	410	427
1987 1	440	493	424	448

16. Northern Rock Building Society

16.1 TECHNICAL DETAILS

(a) Source of data and timing

Society's own lending records at the mortgage approval stage

(b) Types of data and periods covered

Average prices: 1984 Q4 to date

Available data

DATA BREAKDOWNS	DATA TYPE AVERAGE PRICES
HOUSE DATA	
All houses	*
New/Non-new	
Type	*
Size	
Age	*
LOCAL DATA	
Regions	
Sub-regions	*
Towns	
BUYER DATA	
First-time buyer	
Former owner-occupier	

(c) Frequency

Quarterly

(d) Geographical coverage

North of England, subdivided into six sub-regions which are defined by postcode groupings. The sub-regions are:. North Tyne, South Tyne, Northumberland, Durham, Cumbria and Teesside.

(e) Method of analysis

Average prices with some adjustments made to take into account changes in sample sizes and mix of properties sampled over the previous quarter. Sales at non-market prices are excluded. Prices are rounded to the nearest £50.

NORTHERN ROCK BUILDING SOCIETY

16.2 LIST OF TABLES

Average prices

16.1   North of England - Sub-regions: type/age group of dwellings.   1984-

16.3 CROSS-CLASSIFICATIONS OF DATA

(a) Two-way classifications

The numbers in the grid below refer to the table compiled for this data source

ALL HOUSES	NEW	NON-NEW	AGE	TYPE	SIZE	REGIONS	SUB-REGIONS	TOWNS	FTB/FOO BUYER TYPE
16.1									
16.1			16.1	16.1					

HOUSE DATA   LOCAL DATA

(b) Three-way classifications

North of England - Sub-regions by type of dwelling by age of dwelling: Table 16.1

16.4 PUBLICATIONS

(a) Data

Press Release published by Northern Rock Building Society, Newcastle-upon-Tyne and referred to as the *Northern Rock-Homemaker House Price Survey.*

(b) Description of methodology

None

(c) Supplementary studies

None

NORTHERN ROCK BUILDING SOCIETY

AVERAGE PRICES (at approval stage) 1984 –

16.1 NORTH OF ENGLAND – SUB-REGIONS: TYPE/AGE GROUP OF DWELLINGS

£

Year		All	North Tyne	South Tyne	Northum-berland	Durham	Cumbria	Teesside
ALL PROPERTIES								
1985	4	22250						
1986	1	22500						
	2	23250						
	3	23900						
	4	24250						
1987	1	25050						
DETACHED HOUSES								
1984	4	36772	37781	39448	30333	36450	31442	38517
1985	1	37250	38350	39850	30550	36900	32050	39100
	2	37750	38900	40400	30950	37350	32450	39650
	3	39550	40750	42300	33100	39100	34000	41550
	4	40250	41450	43050	33800	39850	34600	42250
1986	1	40650	41850	43500	34150	40250	34950	42650
	2	42550	43850	45550	36500	42100	36600	44650
	3	44150	46350	47250	40600	43700	37950	45050
	4	44200	46400	47300	42250	43750	38000	45100
1987	1	46400	48750	48250	44350	44800	40900	47350
SEMI-DETACHED HOUSES - PRE-1946								
1984	4	23798	24401	24068	17595	23346	26000	23600
1985	1	24200	24900	24450	17900	23700	26350	23950
	2	24750	25500	25000		24250		24500
	3	26000	26800	26250	24000	25500	26000	24000
	4	26500	27300	26750	24650	25970	26500	24400
1986	1	26800	28100	27050		26250		24650
	2	27300	28650	27550	25100	26750	27250	25100
	3	28400	29800	28700	26150	27850	28350	26150
	4	28650	30050	28950	26400	28100	28500	26200
1987	1	29250	30650	29550	26950	29250	29200	26750
SEMI-DETACHED HOUSES - 1946 ONWARDS								
1984	4	23830	26053	28088	21771	22350	24625	20486
1985	1	24050	26200	28400	21900	22600	24750	20700
	2	24200	26350	28550	22000	22750	24950	20800
	3	24550	26750	28950	22300	23050	25300	21500
	4	24750	26950	29200	22500	23250	25500	21800
1986	1	24950	27200	29450			25700	21950
	2	25500	27800	30100	23000	24000	26250	22450
	3	26000	28350	30650	24150	24450	26800	22900
	4	26400	28800	31100	24650	24850	27200	23250
1987	1	27300	29750	32000	25200	26850	28100	25000

AVERAGE PRICES (at approval stage) 1984 –

16.1 NORTH OF ENGLAND - SUB-REGIONS: TYPE/AGE GROUP OF DWELLINGS
(continued)

£

Year	All Regions	North Tyne	South Tyne	Northum-berland	Durham	Cumbria	Teesside
SEMI-DETACHED HOUSES - ALL							
1984 4	23811	24900	25530	19873	22796	25400	22111
1985 1	24100	25300	25800	20000	23150	25800	22400
2	24600	25850	26300		23600		22900
3	25200	26750	26950	23100	24150	25700	23400
4	25450	27000	27250	23400	24450	25950	23650
1986 1	25500	27500	27300	23450			23700
2	26000	28050	27850	23900	25000	26500	24150
3	26700	28800	28800	25100	25650	27250	24850
4	26950	29050	29050	25350	25900	27500	25000
1987 1	27800	30000	29950	26000	27100	28400	25800
TERRACED HOUSES - PRE-1946							
1984 4	16190	19880	14983	17400	14306	17075	12034
1985 1	16450	20050	15300	17600	14500	17250	12200
2	16750	20450	15600	17900	14750	17600	12400
3	17150	20750	15850	18150	15000	17850	13800
4	17250	20850	15900	18300	15200	17950	14000
1986 1	17350	21000	15950		15250	18050	14050
2	17750	21300	16350	18900	15600	18450	14400
3	18800	21600	17300	20100	16750	19550	15600
4	19200	22050	17650	20500	17100	20000	15900
	19950	23370	19500	21700	17700	21200	16850
TERRACED HOUSES - 1946 ONWARDS							
1984 4	19492	20994	21429	21083	15450		18750
1985 1	19600	21150	21550	21150	15500		18800
2	20100		22100		15900	19900	19300
3	21250	22350	23350		16800		19350
4	21750	22850	23900	23500	17200	21550	19800
1986 1	22000	23100	24200	23750			20000
2	22200	23300	24400	24000	17550	22000	20200
3	22250	23600	24500	23500	18000	22050	20250
4	22300	23650	24550	23550	18100	22100	20300
	22900	25150	25150	25050	19000	23550	20950
TERRACED HOUSES - ALL							
1984 4	16563	20039	15548	17825	14492	17075	12781
1985 1	16850	20400	15850	18200	14650		12950
2	17200	20800	16150		15000	17750	13250
3	17800	21500	16700		15500		14150
4	18000	21800	16900	19250	15650	18550	14750
1986 1	18150	21950	17050				14900
2	18500	22400	17400	19850	16050	19050	15200
3	19450	23350	18300	21200	17100	20050	16350
4	19700	23700	18550	21500	17300	20300	16550
1987 1	20400	25000	20000	22800	18100	21550	17550

							£
Year	All Regions	North Tyne	South Tyne	Northum-berland	Durham	Cumbria	Teesside

BUNGALOWS

Year	All Regions	North Tyne	South Tyne	Northum-berland	Durham	Cumbria	Teesside
1984 4	28912	30739	28557	40000	21938		26625
1985 1	29250	31000	28950	40350	22250		26900
2	29750	31550	29450	41050	22600	32750	27350
3	30250	32100	29950	41750	23000	33300	27800
4	30400	32200	30100	41950	23100	33450	27950
1986 1	31000	32850	30700		23550	34100	28500
2	32250	34200	31950	44500	24500	35500	29650
3	32700	34650	32350	44500	26150	35950	29400
4	33250	32250	32900	45000	27000	36600	29900
1987 1	34400	36050	33900	46000	29600	37200	30600

FLATS

Year	All Regions	North Tyne	South Tyne	Northum-berland	Durham	Cumbria	Teesside
1984 4	14338	14234	13507	16038	15639		14750
1985 1	14550	14400	13700	16300	15850		15000
2	14900	14750	14000	16700	16250	14600	15350
3	15100	16000	14200	16950			15550
4	15350	16250	14450	17200	16750	15050	15800
1986 1	15550	16450	14600				
2	16200	17150	15250	18000	17650	15900	16650
3	16550	17550	16050	18350	17700	16200	17050
4	17000	18350	16600	19000	18100	16750	17600
1987 1	17650	18950	17150	19600	18700	17300	18150

17. Principality Building Society

17.1 TECHNICAL DETAILS

(a) Source of data and timing

Society's own records at the mortgage completion stage

(b) Types of data and periods covered

Average prices: 1983(1st half) - to date

Available data

DATA BREAKDOWNS	DATA TYPE AVERAGE PRICES
HOUSE DATA	
All houses	*
New/Non-new	*
Type	
Size	
Age	
LOCAL DATA	
Regions	*
Sub-regions	*
Towns	*
BUYER DATA	
First-time buyer	
Former owner-occupier	

(c) Frequency

Biannual (covering first 6 months and then all 12 months of each year)

(d) Geographical coverage

Wales, subdivided into counties and 3 major towns

(e) Method of analysis

Simple average prices of properties on which the Society has made loans. Sales at non-market prices are included.

17.2 LIST OF TABLES

Average prices

17.1 Wales (counties and towns): all, new and existing properties. 1983-

17.3 CROSS-CLASSIFICATIONS OF DATA

(a) Two-way classifications

The numbers in the grid below refer to the table compiled for this data source

ALL HOUSES	NEW	NON-NEW	AGE	TYPE	SIZE	REGIONS	SUB-REGIONS	TOWNS	FTB/FOO
17.1	17.1	17.1							
17.1	17.1	17.1							
17.1	17.1	17.1							
HOUSE DATA						LOCAL DATA			BUYER TYPE

(b) Three-way classifications

None

17.4 PUBLICATIONS

(a) Data

Press release. Biannual. Principality Building Society, Cardiff

(b) Description of methodology

None

(c) Supplementary studies

None

PRINCIPALITY BUILDING SOCIETY

AVERAGE PRICES (at completion stage) 1983 –

17.1 WALES (COUNTIES AND TOWNS): ALL, NEW AND EXISTING DWELLINGS

YEAR	Wales	Clwyd	Dyfed	Gwent	Gwynnedd	Mid-Glamorgan
ALL DWELLINGS						
1983 (1st half)	20113					
(year)						
1984 (1st half)	21599	22278	21197	19495	19106	19288
(year)	22463	21065	22207	20800	19506	20255
1985 (1st half)	22661	23183	20266	22878	20550	19896
(year)	23848	21225	22244	22572	21805	22139
1986 (1st half)						
(year)	27815	25106	28482	26839	25346	25000
NEW DWELLINGS						
1983 (1st half)	26169					
(year)						
1984 (1st half)	27467					
(year)	29647	23990	25599	28321	22956	26776
1985 (1st half)	30251					
(year)	33360	25543	27141	33780	24135	33735
EXISTING DWELLINGS						
1983 (1st half)	19289					
(year)						
1984 (1st half)	21154					
(year)	21788	20875	21454	19960	18778	19615
1985 (1st half)	21754					
(year)	22467	20463	21552	20976	21547	19813

South Glamorgan	West Glamorgan	Powys	Cardiff	Newport	Swansea
			23501		
26322	19480	22212	26506	21282	20096
26548	21678	20835	26733	22973	20993
25031	21946	20878	24813	24730	21797
28252	22761	20990	27851	25037	23318
31579	26133	25612	30136	27986	28967
			27859		
			29232		
34786	25693	23250	34313	28029	24894
34387	28758	26964	35537	36115	35031
			22899		
			26232		
25745	19882	18755	25994	22026	20324
25278	21163	19372	24741	23131	22550

£

18. Ryden Residential Ltd
formerly KENNETH RYDEN AND PARTNERS (CHARTERED SURVEYORS)

18.1 TECHNICAL DETAILS

(a) Source of data and timing

Data supplied by the Halifax Building Society from its lending records at the mortgage approval stage

(b) Types of data and periods covered

Average prices: 1983-1985

Available data

DATA BREAKDOWNS	DATA TYPE AVERAGE PRICES
HOUSE DATA	
All houses	
New/Non-new	
Type	*
Size	*
Age	*
LOCAL DATA	
Regions	
Sub-regions	
Towns	*
BUYER DATA	
First-time buyer	
Former owner-occupier	

(c) Frequency

Biannual

(d) Geographical coverage

Scottish cities (Aberdeen, Dundee, Edinburgh, Glasgow)

(e) Method of analysis

Simple average prices of houses mortgaged by the Halifax Building Society in four Scottish cities, updated at six-monthly intervals. Sales at non-market prices are excluded.

18.2 LIST OF TABLES

Average prices

18.1 Scottish cities: type, age and size of house. 1983-1985

18.3 CROSS-CLASSIFICATIONS OF DATA

(a) Two-way classifications

The numbers in the grid below refer to the table compiled for this data source

ALL HOUSES	NEW	NON-NEW	AGE	TYPE	SIZE	REGIONS	SUB-REGIONS	TOWNS	FTB/FOO
			18.1	18.1	18.1				
HOUSE DATA						LOCAL DATA			BUYER TYPE

(b) Three-way classifications

None

18.4 PUBLICATIONS

(a) Data

Scottish Residential Property Review. Ryden Residential Ltd (formerly Kenneth Ryden and Partners), Edinburgh. Biannual from January 1983 to February 1986. Discontinued.

(b) Description of methodology

None

(c) Supplementary studies

Each issue of *Scottish Residential Property Review* included a brief analysis of the Scottish housing market.

RYDEN RESIDENTIAL LTD

AVERAGE PRICES (at approval stage) 1983–1985

18.1 SCOTTISH CITIES (Aberdeen, Dundee, Edinburgh, Glasgow)

£

YEAR	Pre-1919 houses				Post-1960 detached houses 6/7 habitable rooms or 4 bedrooms				Bungalows			
	A	D	E	G	A	D	E	G	A	D	E	G
1983 Jan-Jun	60864	26143	48373	44058	55014	40138	51245	48025	42251	30989	39699	37450
Jul-Dec	60538	37341	49368	43686	57789	39405	55513	45580	43814	31195	43671	39900
1984 Jan-Jun	68694	38538	49348	42142	75106		53569	49304	43845	32383	40957	39348
Jul-Dec	69035		48738	41649	69879	42371	51752	47517	40395	29542	42299	43231

	Pre-1919 houses with 3 or more habitable rooms				Post-1950 detached houses with 6/7 habitable rooms or 4 bedrooms				Bungalows			
	A	D	E	G	A	D	E	G	A	D	E	G
1984 Jul-Dec	58719	31155	48632	41776	63712	43236	52517	45905	39151	29188	42696	42906
1985 Jan-Jun		31635	60906	43788	60330			54321	50195	30818	48137	43848

	Pre-1919 houses with 2 or more bedrooms				Post-1950 detached houses with 4/5 bedrooms				Bungalows			
	A	D	E	G	A	D	E	G	A	D	E	G
1985 Jan-Jun		33748	59417	44835	71613		66302	56437	47769	30376	47774	43462
Jul-Dec	53000	35496	59589	42821	72650		69298	65125	47811	32424	51136	42306

Key:

A Aberdeen
D Dundee
E Edinburgh
G Glasgow

Year	Post-1950 semi-detached houses with 3 bedrooms				All purpose-built flats				Pre-1919 flats with 3 habitable rooms			
	A	D	E	G	A	D	E	G	A	D	E	G
1983 Jan-Jun	40977	26287	32789	28494	25965	15993	21452	19531	21621	15698	18607	16589
Jul-Dec	43739	29575	35446	30388	25923	16624	24131	20866	22520	14950	21604	16547
1984 Jan-Jun	46313	27307	36239	32061	26822	18727	22726	21245	24021	15392	20938	18231
Jul-Dec	42594	29853	27489	33041	27733	18153	24734	21903	25494	16075	22545	19904

	Post-1950 semi-detached houses with up to 3 bedrooms				Post-1918 purpose-built flats				Pre-1919 flats with 3 or less habitable rooms			
	A	D	E	G	A	D	E	G	A	D	E	G
1984 Jul-Dec	38571	27780	34740	31127	36433	20356	25677	24299	26849	19495	25533	20496
1985 Jan-Jun	37418	29791	36294	33085	25595		26791	24896	28143	19149	25723	22280

	Post-1950 semi-detached houses with 3 bedrooms				Post-1918 flats purpose-built converted*				Pre-1919 flats with 1 bedroom 2 bedrooms*			
	A	D	E	G	A	D	E	G	A	D	E	G
1985 Jan-Jun	41858	31942	37629	34318	26145	18591	27059	24782	23504	15245	21142	18854
							25638*		34870*	22879*	30958*	25722*
Jul-Dec	43528	30114	38470	34774	28732	21081	27155	24306	23418	14741	20406	18290
							26751*		33371*	21116*	29547*	25261*

19. Woolwich Equitable Building Society

19.1 TECHNICAL DETAILS

(a) Source of data and timing

Valuations of typical property types made by the Society's own valuers

(b) Types of data and periods covered

Price ranges: available data

DATA BREAKDOWNS	DATA TYPE PRICE RANGES
HOUSE DATA	
All houses	
New/Non-new	
Type	*
Size	*
Age	*
LOCAL DATA	
Regions	
Sub-regions	
Towns	*
BUYER DATA	
First-time buyer	
Former owner-occupier	

(c) Frequency

Price ranges: annual (biannual up to 1982)

(d) Geographical coverage

United Kingdom - 36 selected towns spread across 11 regions (see data tables)

(e) Method of analysis

Price ranges: typical upper and lower prices for three types of properties with two age bands for each in 36 towns. Based on assessments provided by surveyors. Data currently rounded to nearest £50.

19.2 LIST OF TABLES

Price ranges

19.1   United Kingdom – towns: house type and size by age of house. July 1980
19.2   United Kingdom – towns: house type and size by age of house. December 1980
19.3   United Kingdom – towns: house type and size by age of house. June 1981
19.4   United Kingdom – towns: house type and size by age of house. October 1981
19.5   United Kingdom – towns: house type and size by age of house. March 1982
19.6   United Kingdom – towns: house type and size by age of house. June 1982
19.7   United Kingdom – towns: house type and size by age of house. September 1983
19.8   United Kingdom – towns: house type and size by age of house. November 1984
19.9   United Kingdom – towns: house type and size by age of house. May 1986
19.10 United Kingdom – towns: house type and size by age of house. March 1987

19.3 CROSS-CLASSIFICATIONS OF DATA

(a) Two-way classifications

None

(b) Three-way classifications

United Kingdom – towns: by house type and size by age of house – Tables 19.1-19.10

19.4 PUBLICATIONS

(a) Data

Woolwich Review (including *Woolwich House Price Guide*) currently published once a year but at irregular intervals (formerly two to three times a year).

(b) Description of methodology

None

(c) Supplementary studies

Each issue of the *Woolwich Review* includes a brief study of a selected topic pertinent to the housing market. A list of these to date is provided below:

Housing in the 80s. September 1980

Challenging Times? January 1981

Providing Homes. July 1981

New Concepts. November 1981

Building Societies and Monetary Control. April 1982

Building Societies and Their Role in Inner City Areas. July 1982

Woolwich Housing Initiatives. November 1983

Cost of Moving. February 1985

Cost of Moving Survey. June 1986

WOOLWICH EQUITABLE BUILDING SOCIETY

PRICE RANGES (typical valuations) JULY 1980

19.1 UNITED KINGDOM - TOWNS: HOUSE TYPE AND SIZE BY AGE OF HOUSE

£

	2/3 BEDROOMED TERRACED				3 BEDROOMED SEMI-DETACHED				4 BEDROOMED DETACHED			
	Pre-1919		Post-1945		Pre-1939		Post-1945		Pre-1939		Post-1945	
	Upper	Lower	Upper	Lower	Upper	Lower	Upper	Lower	Upper	Lower	Upper	Lower
GREATER LONDON												
Bromley	26000	22000	32000	27000	42500	30000	42500	36000	75000	50000	75000	50000
Chingford	28500	23800	30000	27500	36500	29000	42000	38500	80000	55000	87500	60000
Croydon	28000	21000	35000	28000	45000	32000	55000	32000	60000	40000	75000	60000
Ealing	34000	30000	45000	35000	48000	38000	50000	40000	70000	55000	80000	70000
Kingston	30000	24000	35000	28000	45000	32000	55000	33000	65000	45000	75000	45000
Romford	23500	21000	29000	25000	40000	31000	35000	29000				
Uxbridge	33000	28000	34000	33000	33000	31000	35000	34000	60000	50000	60000	50000
NORTHERN												
Middlesbrough	9000	6000	17000	14000	18500	14000	20000	16500			35000	25000
Newcastle	11000	8500	18000	15000	20000	15000	22000	17500			35000	27000
YORKSHIRE												
Leeds	12500	8000	14000	11000	18000	14000	22000	16000	40000	25000	55000	30000
Sheffield	9000	7500	16500	13700	22000	16500	20000	16500	50000	25000	35000	25000
NORTH WEST												
Chester	13000	10000	17500	14000	25000	18500	24000	20000			45000	32000
Liverpool	12000	9000	15000	12500	20000	17500	22000	17500			40000	32000
Manchester	16000	9000	24000	16500	30000	16500	28000	18500	45000	22000	60000	35000
MIDLANDS												
Birmingham	14000	11000	22000	18700	21000	18000	24000	19500	42500	37500	45500	40500
Leicester	10200	6200	17500	16200	21200	17500	20700	18200	43000	34000	43000	32500
Nottingham	9200	6200	14200	12800	15400	14300	22000	17500	23500	20500	31600	25800
Wolverhampton	11500	7500	16500	15000	17500	12000	20000	16000	32500	22000	35000	27000
EAST ANGLIA												
Ipswich	15500	13000	21500	18000	26000	22000	26000	23000	40000	33000	40000	34000
Norwich	15000	12500	20000	16500	22000	19000	24000	21000	39000	32000	37000	32000
SOUTH EAST												
Brighton	24000	19000	29500	22800	28500	22000	34000	23500	52000	40000	68000	42000
Dartford	22000	18000	28500	24500	35000	27000	35000	27000	70000	40000	52500	44000
Luton	18300	14000	22600	19500	32000	21000	32000	23500	43000	35000	47000	37000
Maidstone	18000	15000	23500	20000	30000	23000	28000	24000			55000	40000
Oxford	18000	14000	23500	22500	25200	23800	29000	27000				
Reading	19000	15800	30000	27500	28000	24000	30500	27800			56000	48000
Southampton	17000	13500	23500	19000	25500	21000	28000	24500	45000	39500	52000	47000
SOUTH WEST												
Bristol	16500	13000	19500	16500	21000	19000	25000	21000	46000	40000	55000	40000
Plymouth	20000	16000	23000	19000	27000	19000	25000	19000	35000	25000	40000	27500
SCOTLAND												
Edinburgh			21000	18500	35000	27000	28000	24500			50000	35000
Glasgow			22000	18000	24000	20000	23000	19000	36000	25000	35000	25000
WALES												
Cardiff	15000	10000	20000	15000	27000	19000	25000	18000	40000	30000	45000	30000
Llandudno	13000	9000	14000	12000	16000	14000	16000	14000			35000	28000
Swansea	12000	8000	18000	14000	15000	10000	22000	17000			42000	29000
NORTHERN IRELAND												
Belfast	17500	8000	16000	14000	22000	17000	23000	19000	38000	35000	40000	35000
Coleraine	18000	10000	18000	16000	25000	19000	26000	19000	40000	35000	45000	35000

WOOLWICH EQUITABLE BUILDING SOCIETY

PRICE RANGES (typical valuations)   DECEMBER 1980

19.2 UNITED KINGDOM - TOWNS: HOUSE TYPE AND SIZE BY AGE OF HOUSE

£

	2/3 BEDROOMED TERRACED				3 BEDROOMED SEMI-DETACHED				4 BEDROOMED DETACHED			
	Pre-1919		Post-1945		Pre-1939		Post-1945		Pre-1939		Post-1945	
	Upper	Lower	Upper	Lower	Upper	Lower	Upper	Lower	Upper	Lower	Upper	Lower
GREATER LONDON												
Bromley	26000	24500	31000	26000	45000	34750	42500	35000	70000	50000	70000	57500
Chingford	27500	22500	29500	27000	34500	28500	40000	36000	73500	52500	80000	59000
Croydon	30000	24000	36000	28500	45000	32000	55000	35000	60000	42000	75000	60000
Ealing	34000	30000	45000	35000	48000	38000	50000	40000	70000	55000	80000	70000
Kingston	32000	25000	36000	28500	45000	32000	60000	35000	75000	50000	80000	50000
Romford	24000	22000	29000	25000	38000	30000	35000	29000				
Uxbridge	33000	28000	34000	33000	33000	31000	35000	34000	60000	50000	60000	50000
NORTHERN												
Middlesbrough	10000	6500	17000	15000	19000	15000	20000	17000			35000	26000
Newcastle	12000	9000	18000	16000	20000	16000	22000	18500			36000	28000
YORKSHIRE												
Leeds	12500	7500	15000	10000	25000	16000	25000	17500	45000	30000	60000	35000
Sheffield	10000	8000	17000	14500	22500	16500	21000	17000	50000	27000	38000	27000
NORTH WEST												
Chester	13500	11000	19500	14000	25000	20000	24000	20000	50000	35000	45000	37000
Liverpool	12500	9500	15500	13000	22000	17500	22000	17500	50000	35000	40000	32000
Manchester	17000	10000	25000	17000	30000	17500	28500	20000	45000	24000	60000	35000
MIDLANDS												
Birmingham	14500	11000	22000	18700	21000	18000	24000	19500	42500	37500	50000	40000
Leicester	11500	8000	17500	16200	21500	17500	20700	18200	43000	34000	42000	32500
Nottingham	10000	7200	14500	13000	17500	14500	22000	16000	25000	20000	35000	25000
Wolverhampton	11500	7500	17500	15000	17500	13000	22000	17000	35000	24000	40000	30000
EAST ANGLIA												
Ipswich	15500	13000	20000	17500	24500	20000	24000	20000	36000	28500	35000	29000
Norwich	15000	13000	20000	16000	22000	18000	23000	19000	35000	29000	34000	29000
SOUTH EAST												
Brighton	25500	18000	29000	23500	31000	22000	37400	25000	53000	43600	76500	42000
Dartford	22500	19000	27500	23000	33500	26000	35000	26500	70000	40000	52500	44000
Luton	18000	14000	22600	19500	32000	21000	31000	22000	43000	35000	47000	37000
Maidstone	18000	15000	23500	20000	32500	25000	28000	24000			55000	40000
Oxford	23500	22000	26000	23750	29000	22500	34000	27500	70000	45000	70000	45000
Reading	21700	19000	27800	23400	31200	25600	33400	28300			47500	41300
Southampton	16300	11200	21500	19500	24000	19100	26500	23200	45900	40200	53000	47900
SOUTH WEST												
Bristol	17500	14250	19500	16500	21000	19000	25000	21000	46000	40000	55000	40000
Plymouth	20000	16000	23000	19000	27000	19000	25000	19000	35000	25000	40000	27500
SCOTLAND												
Edinburgh			21000	18500	35000	27000	28000	24500			50000	35000
Glasgow			22000	18000	24000	20000	23000	19000			35000	25000
WALES												
Cardiff	18000	13000	20000	16000	27000	19000	25000	18000	40000	30000	45000	30000
Llandudno	13000	9000	14000	12000	16000	14000	16000	14000	40000	30000	35000	28000
Swansea	14000	10000	18000	14000	15000	10000	22000	17000			42000	29000
NORTHERN IRELAND												
Belfast	17000	8000	17000	14000	22000	17000	23000	17500	38000	34000	40000	35000
Coleraine	18000	10000	18000	16000	25000	18000	25000	18000	40000	35000	42000	35000

WOOLWICH EQUITABLE BUILDING SOCIETY

PRICE RANGES (typical valuations) JUNE 1981

19.3 UNITED KINGDOM - TOWNS: HOUSE TYPE AND SIZE BY AGE OF HOUSE

£

| | 2/3 BEDROOMED TERRACED | | | | 3 BEDROOMED SEMI-DETACHED | | | | 4 BEDROOMED DETACHED | | | |
| | Pre-1919 | | Post-1945 | | Pre-1939 | | Post-1945 | | Pre-1939 | | Post-1945 | |
	Upper	Lower	Upper	Lower	Upper	Lower	Upper	Lower	Upper	Lower	Upper	Lower
GREATER LONDON												
Bromley	27500	24500	32500	26000	45000	35000	42500	35000	70000	55000	70000	55000
Chingford	30000	24500	37000	28500	35000	29000	43000	35500	75000	52000	77000	55500
Croydon	28000	23000	36500	29000	45500	32500	60000	35500	65000	50000	80000	56000
Ealing	40000	32000	45000	35000	48000	38000	52000	42000	75000	60000	85000	70000
Kingston	34000	26000	37000	28500	46000	32000	60000	36600	80000	50000	85000	58000
Romford	24000	22000	29000	25000	38000	30000	35000	29000				
Uxbridge	33000	28000	34000	33000	33000	31000	35000	34000	60000	50000	60000	50000
NORTHERN												
Middlesbrough	10500	7000	17500	15000	19500	15000	20500	17000			35000	26000
Newcastle	12500	9500	18500	16000	20000	16500	22500	18500			36000	28000
YORKSHIRE												
Leeds	13500	8500	16500	11000	26000	16000	27000	17500	45000	30000	60000	35000
Sheffield	12500	9500	17500	15500	24000	18500	23500	18500	55000	33000	45000	34000
NORTH WEST												
Chester	14500	12000	18500	15000	25000	20000	24000	20000	52500	37500	50000	35000
Liverpool	14000	10000	16500	13500	22000	17500	22500	17500	50000	35000	40000	32000
Manchester	18000	12500	26000	18500	31000	19000	30000	22000	45000	27500	65000	40000
MIDLANDS												
Birmingham	15800	11300	22000	18700	23000	19200	25000	20000	42500	37500	50000	40000
Leicester	13500	9500	18000	16500	22000	17500	21000	18200	43000	34000	42000	32500
Nottingham	11000	7000	14500	11500	18500	14500	22000	15000	25000	19000	37500	25000
Wolverhampton	14000	8500	17500	15000	20000	14000	23000	18000	35000	24000	40000	30000
EAST ANGLIA												
Ipswich	16300	13500	21000	18000	24500	19500	26000	21000	36000	28000	36000	29000
Norwich	15800	13500	20500	17000	23000	18000	24000	19500	35000	29000	35000	29000
SOUTH EAST												
Brighton	26000	20000	30000	26000	34500	24800	38000	25000	62000	44000	85000	45000
Dartford	23000	19500	28300	24200	34000	26000	36200	27000	70000	36000	56000	48000
Luton	18700	14200	23500	19500	32800	20500	32000	21500	44000	35000	50000	36500
Maidstone	19000	17000	23000	21000	32000	25000	28000	24000			53000	42000
Oxford	28000	22000	29500	24000	34000	24000	34000	28000	75000	45000	75000	45000
Reading	21300	18400	27000	23700	35200	31700	28000	27000			48800	43400
Southampton	18700	15600	24000	21500	26000	22300	28000	24500	42500	38500	50000	43500
SOUTH WEST												
Bristol	18400	14500	19500	16500	20600	18400	24500	20000	45000	34000	55000	34000
Plymouth	21000	17000	24500	19500	28000	21000	27000	21000	50000	30000	50000	35000
SCOTLAND												
Edinburgh			25000	22000	40000	30000	31000	28000			58000	42500
Glasgow			23000	19000	26000	20000	27000	22000	60000	40000	50000	35000
WALES												
Cardiff	18500	13000	20000	16000	27000	19000	25000	18000	40000	30000	45000	30000
Llandudno	14000	10000	15000	12500	16500	14000	16500	14000	40000	30000	36000	30000
Swansea	14000	10000	18000	14000	15000	10000	22000	17000			42000	29000
NORTHERN IRELAND												
Belfast	18500	8000	17500	14000	22500	17000	23500	17000	39000	34000	40000	34000
Coleraine	18000	10000	18500	16000	24000	17500	24000	17500	40000	35000	42000	35000

WOOLWICH EQUITABLE BUILDING SOCIETY

PRICE RANGES (typical valuations) OCTOBER 1981

19.4 UNITED KINGDOM - TOWNS: HOUSE TYPE AND SIZE BY AGE OF HOUSE

£

	2/3 BEDROOMED TERRACED				3 BEDROOMED SEMI-DETACHED				4 BEDROOMED DETACHED			
	Pre-1919		Post-1945		Pre-1939		Post-1945		Pre-1939		Post-1945	
	Upper	Lower	Upper	Lower	Upper	Lower	Upper	Lower	Upper	Lower	Upper	Lower
GREATER LONDON												
Bromley	27500	24500	32500	26000	45000	35000	42500	35000	70000	55000	70000	55000
Chingford	30000	24500	37000	28500	35000	29000	43000	35500	75000	52000	77000	55500
Croydon	30000	23200	37000	29000	46000	32500	60000	35500	68000	50000	82000	56000
Ealing	40000	32000	45000	35000	48000	38000	52000	42000	75000	60000	85000	70000
Kingston	33000	25000	37000	28500	47500	32500	60000	35000	75000	52500	85000	57500
Romford	24000	22000	29000	25000	38000	30000	35000	29000				
Uxbridge	33000	28000	34000	33000	33000	31000	35000	34000	60000	50000	60000	50000
NORTHERN												
Middlesbrough	10500	7000	17500	15000	19500	15000	20500	17000			35000	26000
Newcastle	12500	9500	18500	16000	20000	16500	22500	18500			36000	28000
YORKSHIRE												
Leeds	13500	8500	16500	11000	26000	16000	27000	17500	45000	30000	60000	35000
Sheffield	13000	10000	17500	15500	24500	19000	23500	18500	55000	35000	45000	35000
NORTH WEST												
Chester	15000	12000	18500	15000	25000	20000	24000	20000	52500	37500	50000	35000
Liverpool	14500	10000	17000	14000	22000	17500	22500	17500	50000	35000	40000	32000
Manchester	18500	13500	26000	19000	32000	20000	30000	22500	46000	28000	65000	40000
MIDLANDS												
Birmingham	15800	11300	22000	18700	23000	19200	25000	20000	42500	37500	50000	40000
Leicester	13500	10000	18000	16500	22000	17500	21000	18200	43000	34000	42000	32500
Nottingham	11000	7000	14500	11500	19000	15000	22000	16000	25000	19000	40000	25000
Wolverhampton	17000	8500	18500	15000	20000	14000	23000	17000	35000	23000	40000	29000
EAST ANGLIA												
Ipswich	17000	13500	21000	18000	24500	19500	26000	21000	36000	28500	36000	29000
Norwich	16500	13500	20500	17000	23000	18000	24000	19500	35000	29000	35000	29000
SOUTH EAST												
Brighton	27000	21000	30000	26000	35500	25800	38000	25000	62000	44000	85000	45000
Dartford	23000	19500	28300	24200	34000	26000	36200	27000	70000	36000	56000	48000
Luton	18700	14200	23500	19500	34500	20500	33500	21500	48000	35000	56000	36500
Maidstone	20000	18000	23000	21000	35000	28000	30000	27000			55000	44000
Oxford	29000	22500	29500	24500	35000	24000	35000	28000	80000	48000	76000	48000
Reading	22000	19000	27300	25700	28000	24000	32500	28500	54200	50700		
Southampton	19500	16500	24500	22500	27500	23500	29500	26000	43800	39500	56000	46500
SOUTH WEST												
Bristol	19000	15000	20000	16500	20600	18400	24500	20000	45000	32000	55000	32000
Plymouth	21000	17000	20000	18000	28000	19000	24000	21000	60000	30000	50000	35000
SCOTLAND												
Edinburgh			26500	23000	42000	31000	31500	28000			60000	43000
Glasgow			23000	19000	27000	22000	28000	23000	65000	45000	50000	35000
WALES												
Cardiff	19000	11000	21000	15000	30000	20000	30000	20000			60000	30000
Llandudno	14500	10500	15000	12500	16500	14000	16500	14000	40000	30000	36000	30000
Swansea	17000	11000	20000	14000	20000	10000	25000	18000			50000	30000
NORTHERN IRELAND												
Belfast	18200	8000	17500	14000	22200	17000	23200	17000	39000	34000	40000	34000
Coleraine	18000	10000	18500	16000	24000	17500	24000	17500	40000	35000	42000	35000

PRICE RANGES (typical valuations) MARCH 1982

19.5 UNITED KINGDOM - TOWNS: HOUSE TYPE AND SIZE BY AGE OF HOUSE

£

	2/3 BEDROOMED TERRACED				3 BEDROOMED SEMI-DETACHED				4 BEDROOMED DETACHED			
	Pre-1919		Post-1945		Pre-1939		Post-1945		Pre-1939		Post-1945	
	Upper	Lower	Upper	Lower	Upper	Lower	Upper	Lower	Upper	Lower	Upper	Lower
GREATER LONDON												
Bromley	29000	26500	35000	28500	45000	36500	45000	35000	70000	57500	65000	58000
Chingford	29500	24000	36500	28000	33800	28000	41500	34500	74000	52000	76000	54000
Croydon	30000	23000	37000	29000	46000	32000	58000	35500	65000	48000	78000	55000
Ealing	40000	32000	45000	35000	45500	38000	50000	42000	71000	57000	80000	66500
Kingston	33000	25000	36500	28500	47500	32500	60000	35000	75000	52500	85000	57500
Romford	24000	22000	28000	24000	33000	28500	33000	27500				
Uxbridge	33000	28000	34000	33000	33000	31000	35000	34000	57000	47500	57000	47500
NORTHERN												
Middlesbrough	11000	8000	17500	15000	19500	15000	20500	17000			35000	26000
Newcastle	13000	10000	18500	16000	20000	16500	22500	18500			36000	28000
YORKSHIRE												
Leeds	13500	8500	16500	11000	26000	16000	27000	17500	45000	30000	60000	35000
Sheffield	13000	10000	17500	15500	24500	19000	23500	18500	55000	35000	45000	35000
NORTH WEST												
Chester	15000	12500	18500	15500	25000	20000	24000	20000	52500	37500	50000	35000
Liverpool	15000	11000	18000	15000	22000	17500	23000	18000	50000	35000	40000	32000
Manchester	18500	14000	25500	18500	31000	20000	28000	22000	45000	27500	60000	37500
MIDLANDS												
Birmingham	16500	12000	22000	18700	23000	19000	25000	20000	42500	37500	50000	40000
Leicester	13500	10000	18000	16500	22000	17500	21000	18200	43000	34000	42000	32500
Nottingham	11500	7500	15000	12000	18500	14000	20000	15000	24000	18000	40000	23000
Wolverhampton	16000	8500	17500	14500	20000	14000	23000	16000	35000	23000	37500	29000
EAST ANGLIA												
Ipswich	17000	13000	19000	17000	22500	17500	25000	19000	36000	27000	37000	29000
Norwich	18000	14000	23000	19000	23000	18000	25000	20000	35000	29000	35000	29000
SOUTH EAST												
Brighton	27000	21000	30000	26000	35500	25800	38000	25000	62000	44000	85000	45000
Dartford	23500	20000	29000	25000	35000	27000	36500	28000				
Luton	18700	14200	23500	19500	36000	20500	34000	21500	48000	35000	58000	36500
Maidstone	20000	18000	23000	21000	35000	28000	30000	27000			55000	44000
Oxford	29500	23500	29500	24500	35000	26000	36000	28000	75000	46000	74000	46000
Reading	25500	19500	30000	24500	30000	24800	32000	28500			60000	45000
Southampton	19000	17500	25000	21500	26000	23000	28000	24500	39900	34000	52000	41000
SOUTH WEST												
Bristol	10000	14300	21500	17500	22000	19000	25000	20500	42500	30000	55000	30000
Plymouth	21000	17000	20000	18000	28000	19000	24000	21000	60000	30000	50000	25000
SCOTLAND												
Edinburgh			27000	23500	43000	32000	32500	29000			63000	45000
Glasgow			23500	20000	28000	23000	29000	24000	65000	45000	55000	35000
WALES												
Cardiff	19500	11000	21000	15000	30000	22000	30000	20000			60000	30000
Llandudno	15000	11000	16500	13500	16500	14000	17000	15000	40000	30000	36000	30000
Swansea	17000	11000	20000	14000	20000	10000	25000	18000			50000	30000
NORTHERN IRELAND												
Belfast	17800	8000	18000	14000	22300	17200	23000	17500	40000	34000	40000	35000
Coleraine	18000	10000	18500	15500	23500	17500	23500	18000	38500	35000	41000	36000

WOOLWICH EQUITABLE BUILDING SOCIETY

UPPER AND LOWER PRICES (typical valuations) JUNE 1982

19.6 UNITED KINGDOM – TOWNS: HOUSE TYPE AND SIZE BY AGE OF HOUSE

£

	2/3 BEDROOMED TERRACED				3 BEDROOMED SEMI-DETACHED				4 BEDROOMED DETACHED			
	Pre-1919		Post-1945		Pre-1939		Post-1945		Pre-1939		Post-1945	
	Upper	Lower	Upper	Lower	Upper	Lower	Upper	Lower	Upper	Lower	Upper	Lower
GREATER LONDON												
Bromley	29000	26500	35000	28500	45000	36500	45000	35000	70000	57500	65000	58000
Chingford	30500	25000	37000	28500	34500	28500	41500	34500	74000	52000	76000	55000
Croydon	30000	23500	38000	30000	47000	32000	58000	35500	65000	48000	78000	55000
Ealing	40000	32000	45000	35000	45500	38000	50000	42000	71000	57000	80000	66500
Kingston	33500	25000	37000	29000	49000	33000	62500	36000	77500	54000	86000	57500
Romford	27500	22000	30000	23000	36000	31000	36000	30000				
Uxbridge	33000	28000	34000	33000	33000	31000	35000	34000	57000	47500	57500	47500
NORTHERN												
Middlesbrough	11500	8000	17500	15000	20000	16000	21000	17500			36000	26500
Newcastle	13500	10000	18500	16000	20500	17000	23000	19000			37000	28500
YORKSHIRE												
Leeds	13500	8500	16500	11000	26000	16000	27000	17500	45000	30000	60000	35000
Sheffield	14000	10500	17500	16000	25000	20000	24000	19000	55000	35500	46000	35500
NORTH WEST												
Chester	15500	12500	19000	16000	25000	20000	25000	20000	52500	37500	50000	35000
Liverpool	15500	10500	18500	15000	22000	17500	23500	18000	50000	35000	40000	32000
Manchester	18500	15000	26000	19000	32000	20000	30000	24000	50000	28000	70000	40000
MIDLANDS												
Birmingham	16500	12000	22000	18700	23000	19000	25000	20000	42500	37500	50000	40000
Leicester	13500	10500	18000	16500	22000	17500	21000	18200	43000	34000	42000	33000
Nottingham	12000	8000	17500	13000	18500	13000	20000	16000				
Wolverhampton	16000	8500	17500	14500	22000	14500	23000	16500	35000	25000	40000	30000
EAST ANGLIA												
Ipswich	17500	12000	20000	17000	23000	19000	25000	19000	35000	28000	40000	30000
Norwich	17500	15000	24000	19000	23000	18000	26500	21000	35000	29000	42000	29000
SOUTH EAST												
Brighton	28000	21800	31000	27000	36000	26500	38500	25500	62000	44000	85000	45000
Dartford	24500	21000	29800	26000	36000	28000	37300	29000				
Luton	18700	14200	23500	19500	36000	20500	34500	21500	48000	35000	58000	36500
Maidstone	20000	18000	23000	21000	35000	28000	30000	27000			55000	44000
Oxford	29500	23500	29500	24500	35000	26000	36000	28000	75000	46000	74000	46000
Reading	25500	19500	30000	24500	35000	25000	35000	38500			60000	45000
Southampton	21000	19300	26300	22000	27000	24100	28500	25000	42000	34700	55000	43100
SOUTH WEST												
Bristol	20000	14300	23500	19300	23000	20000	27500	21500	44600	30000	60000	30000
Plymouth	21000	17000	20000	18000	28000	19000	24000	21000	60000	30000	50000	35000
SCOTLAND												
Edinburgh			28500	25000	45000	33500	35000	30000			65000	45000
Glasgow			24000	21000	30000	24000	29000	24000	65000	45000	55000	35000
WALES												
Cardiff	19500	11000	21000	15000	30000	22000	30000	20000			60000	30000
Llandudno	15500	11000	17000	13500	17000	14000	17500	15000	40000	30000	36000	30000
Swansea	17000	11000	20000	14000	20000	10000	25000	18000			50000	30000
NORTHERN IRELAND												
Belfast	18000	8500	18500	14000	22700	17500	24000	17500	41000	35000	41000	35700
Coleraine	18500	10500	19000	15700	23700	17500	23700	18200	39500	35000	41500	36000

WOOLWICH EQUITABLE BUILDING SOCIETY

PRICE RANGES (typical valuations) SEPTEMBER 1983

19.7 UNITED KINGDOM - TOWNS: HOUSE TYPE AND SIZE BY AGE OF HOUSE

£

	2/3 BEDROOMED TERRACED				3 BEDROOMED SEMI-DETACHED				4 BEDROOMED DETACHED			
	Pre-1919		Post-1945		Pre-1939		Post-1945		Pre-1939		Post-1945	
	Upper	Lower	Upper	Lower	Upper	Lower	Upper	Lower	Upper	Lower	Upper	Lower
GREATER LONDON												
Bromley	35000	28000	42500	34000	55000	42000	50000	40000	85000	65000	80000	62500
Chingford	35500	28500	40000	31500	38500	33000	45500	39000	80000	60000	82000	62000
Croydon	35000	27000	45000	35000	52000	36000	62000	39000	75000	50000	85000	57000
Ealing	47000	38000	52500	42000	57500	45000	60000	47000	10000	82500	110000	85000
Kingston	39500	31500	45000	36000	58500	39500	72500	45000	87500	65000	95000	67500
Romford	26000	24500	30000	27000	40000	33000	36000	31000	95000			
Uxbridge	40000	34500	40500	37500	39000	36500	42000	37500	84000	63000	84000	68000
NORTHERN												
Middlesbrough	14000	10500	18500	16500	21500	18000	22500	19500			39000	29000
Newcastle	16500	12500	20000	18000	22500	18500	24500	21000			40000	30000
YORKSHIRE												
Leeds	16000	9000	20000	13000	28000	17000	28500	18500	50000	30000	65000	35000
Sheffield	16500	12500	18700	17500	27500	22500	26200	20800	62000	38000	48500	37000
NORTH WEST												
Chester	17300	13300	21000	18000	26000	22000	26500	22000	57500	42500	55000	40000
Liverpool	17300	11800	21000	16800	23500	18500	25000	19500	55000	37500	50000	37500
Manchester	21000	16000	27500	22000	34000	24000	34000	25000	55000	32000	70000	42000
MIDLANDS												
Birmingham	16500	12000	22000	18700	23000	19000	25000	20000	42500	37500	50000	40000
Leicester	13500	11500	18000	17000	23000	18500	22000	20000	43000	35000	44000	39000
Nottingham	14500	10500	19500	14000	22000	15500	23000	17500				
Wolverhampton	17500	11500	18500	16000	22500	14500	24500	17500	36000	27500	42500	32500
EAST ANGLIA												
Ipswich	18500	14500	24000	18500	26500	19500	27500	21000	37000	28000	46000	34000
Norwich	22000	17500	24000	19500	26000	23000	28000	22000	36000	29000	38000	31000
SOUTH EAST												
Brighton	31500	25000	35000	31000	40000	33000	45000	35000	69000	50000	90000	53000
Dartford	27500	25000	32500	29500	39500	34000	39800	34300				
Luton	21000	15000	26000	20000	40000	22000	37500	24000	52500	37500	63000	38000
Maidstone	24000	21000	26500	24500	36000	29000	34000	30000	54000	50000	58000	48000
Oxford	37500	32500	33500	30500	38500	32500	38000	35000	75000	50000	75000	50000
Reading	30000	24500	34500	31000	42500	35000	40000	35000			65000	50000
Southampton	25000	20000	27000	23000	33500	26000	32500	26000	56000	37000	63500	43000
SOUTH WEST												
Bristol	21000	15000	25000	20000	25500	22000	30000	23000	45500	35000	70000	40000
Plymouth	24000	18500	28000	24000	38000	24000	35000	26000	70000	35000	70000	40000
SCOTLAND												
Edinburgh			32500	28500	48000	38000	39000	33000			69000	49000
Glasgow			25000	23000	32000	28000	32000	28000	68000	48000	60000	40000
WALES												
Cardiff	24000	15000	26000	18000	38000	25000	37000	22000			70000	42000
Llandudno	17300	13000	19000	15800	20000	16000	20500	16500	42500	30000	38000	30000
Swansea	19000	14000	24000	18000	30000	18000	30000	20000			60000	35000
NORTHERN IRELAND												
Belfast	19000	8500	19500	15000	23500	17500	24500	18000	44000	37000	44000	37000
Coleraine	19200	10800	19500	16000	24000	18000	24200	18500	41500	36000	43000	37000

WOOLWICH EQUITABLE BUILDING SOCIETY

PRICE RANGES (typical valuations) NOVEMBER 1984

19.8 UNITED KINGDOM – TOWNS: HOUSE TYPE AND SIZE BY AGE OF HOUSE

£

	2/3 BEDROOMED TERRACED				3 BEDROOMED SEMI-DETACHED				4 BEDROOMED DETACHED			
	Pre-1919		Post-1945		Pre-1939		Post-1945		Pre-1939		Post-1945	
	Upper	Lower	Upper	Lower	Upper	Lower	Upper	Lower	Upper	Lower	Upper	Lower
GREATER LONDON												
Bromley	40000	33000	50000	40000	62500	47500	60000	47500	110000	80000	100000	75000
Chingford	39000	30500	45000	38000	54000	42000	49000	43000	98000	75000	95000	75000
Croydon	41000	33000	50000	41500	65000	44000	70000	48000	100000	60000	105000	65000
Ealing	57000	47000	63000	50000	69000	54000	72000	56000	135000	100000	135000	100000
Kingston	45000	35000	52000	44000	66000	46000	80000	52000	92000	68000	100000	71000
Romford	32900	30600	39500		51200	41800					72100	70400
Uxbridge	48500	43000	49000	45000	50000	44000	50000	46000	100000	80000	100000	80000
NORTHERN												
Middlesbrough	15500	11500	19500	17500	23000	19000	23500	20500			41500	30500
Newcastle	18000	13500	20500	18500	23500	19500	25500	22000			42500	32000
YORKSHIRE												
Leeds	18000	11000	23000	16000	30000	19000	30000	21000	60000	35000	70000	35000
Sheffield	18500	14500	20000	18500	29000	23500	28000	22500	63000	38000	52000	38000
NORTH WEST												
Chester	18500	15000	22500	19500	27500	22500	28000	22500	57500	42500	55000	40000
Liverpool	18500	12500	22000	18000	25500	19500	26000	20000	55000	40000	50000	40000
Manchester	22500	16000	27500	22000	34000	25000	34000	25000	60000	35000	70000	44000
MIDLANDS												
Birmingham	18000	12000	22000	18000	23000	19000	30000	22000	45000	37500	65000	40000
Leicester	15500	12500	20000	18000	24000	20000	25500	22000	45000	39000	50000	44000
Nottingham	16500	12000	21000	16000	22000	17000	25000	19500	53000	30000	60000	40000
Wolverhampton	20000	13000	20500	16500	26000	16500	27000	18000	42500	32500	50000	39000
EAST ANGLIA												
Ipswich	20000	17500	27500	20000	28500	24000	33000	27000	56000	38000	65000	50000
Norwich	23500	18500	27000	24000	32000	26000	29000	26000	53000	40000	65000	45000
SOUTH EAST												
Brighton	36750	30000	42500	37500	49600	41500	57000	44000	80000	63000	101000	65000
Dartford	32000	29500	37500	35000	43500	40000	45000	41000				
Luton	24400	18500	31500	24200	47300	27000	46200	28900	59800	43200	72800	45200
Maidstone	28000	24500	31000	28000	42000	37000	40000	37000	65000	55000	68000	58000
Oxford	40000	32500	40000	32500	42000	35000	42500	36000	90000	70000	90000	70000
Reading	32000	27500	37500	32500	50000	40000	45000	37500			85000	60000
Southampton	29500	23500	31500	27000	42000	30000	37500	30500	68000	49000	70000	49500
SOUTH WEST												
Bristol	22500	17000	27000	22000	28000	24500	32000	26000	50000	37000	80000	46000
Plymouth	28000	23000	33000	28000	38000	27000	38000	28000	80000	35000	80000	50000
SCOTLAND												
Edinburgh			34500	31500	50000	41000	45000	38000			75000	55000
Glasgow			29000	26000	38000	34000	36000	33000	75000	57000	70000	50000
WALES												
Cardiff	26000	17000	31000	24000	45000	21000	38000	28000			95000	45000
Llandudno	18500	14000	21000	17000	22000	17500	22500	18500	42500	30000	40000	30000
Swansea	23500	16000	27000	22000	38000	25000	36000	23000			80000	42000
NORTHERN IRELAND												
Belfast	20500	9000	22000	17000	26300	18300	26800	19000	48000	39000	48000	39000
Coleraine	20100	11500	21000	18000	26500	19200	26700	20000	44000	38000	45000	38000

WOOLWICH EQUITABLE BUILDING SOCIETY

PRICE RANGES (typical valuations) MAY 1986

19.9 UNITED KINGDOM - TOWNS: HOUSE TYPE AND SIZE BY AGE OF HOUSE

£

	2/3 BEDROOMED TERRACED				3 BEDROOMED SEMI-DETACHED				4 BEDROOMED DETACHED			
	Pre-1919		Post-1945		Pre-1939		Post-1945		Pre-1939		Post-1945	
	Upper	Lower	Upper	Lower	Upper	Lower	Upper	Lower	Upper	Lower	Upper	Lower
GREATER LONDON												
Bromley	47000	39000	60000	45000	70000	55000	70000	55000	130000	90000	140000	90000
Chingford	48500	39500	53500	41500	65000	53000	65000	53000	123000	85000	110000	85000
Croydon	55000	40000	59000	47000	75000	55000	92000	65500	135000	76000	150000	92500
Ealing	68000	57000	75000	60000	80000	65000	84000	66000	165000	120000	165000	120000
Kingston	52000	44000	60000	52000	78000	53000	86000	58000	110000	75000	122000	90000
Romford	40000	36500	46000	40000	63000	47500	58000	49000	98000	78000	90000	70000
Uxbridge	57500	50000	58000	53000	59500	52000	59500	55000	122000	95000	122000	95000
NORTHERN												
Middlesbrough	16500	12000	20500	18000	23500	19000	24500	21000			43000	32000
Newcastle	18500	14500	21500	19000	24500	20000	27000	23000			45000	33000
YORKSHIRE												
Leeds	20000	12500	30000	18000	45000	22500	45000	25000	80000	40000	80000	40000
Sheffield	20500	16000	21500	20500	32000	24500	30500	24500	67500	41000	57000	40500
NORTH WEST												
Chester	20000	16000	24000	20000	28000	23000	29000	23000	65000	45000	58000	42500
Liverpool	19500	12000	23000	18500	26000	20000	26000	21000	58000	42500	55000	42500
Manchester	25000	18000	30000	24000	40000	27500	37500	26000	70000	40000	80000	48000
MIDLANDS												
Birmingham	18000	12000	22500	18000	25000	19000	32500	24000	50000	40000	75000	45000
Leicester	19000	16000	23000	20000	29000	23000	28000	25000	55000	44000	69000	46000
Nottingham	17000	13500	23000	17000	25000	18000	28500	21000	55000	30000	65000	40000
Wolverhampton	21000	13000	21000	16000	27000	16500	28000	19000	47500	35000	52000	42000
EAST ANGLIA												
Ipswich	25000	22000	32000	28000	35000	27000	38000	30000	65000	45000	75000	57000
Norwich	25000	22000	28000	25000	38000	29000	39500	32000	58000	48000	80000	45000
SOUTH EAST												
Brighton	44000	37000	53500	47500	63000	52500	69500	56500	97500	77500	117000	81000
Dartford	36500	33500	44000	40000	51000	46000	50000	44500				
Luton	27500	20000	36000	27000	54000	32000	54000	34000	67500	47000	77000	50000
Maidstone	36000	32000	39000	36000	50000	45000	48000	44000	75000	65000	75000	67000
Oxford	53000	37000	55000	39000	65000	42000	55000	42000	105000	85000	100000	85000
Reading	40000	32000	43000	38000	62000	45500	55000	42000			95000	69000
Southampton	33000	27500	35000	29000	43500	32500	43000	34000	80000	60000	82000	56000
SOUTH WEST												
Bristol	26500	20000	30000	25000	32500	27000	36500	28000	60000	42000	85000	50000
Plymouth	32000	26000	34000	29000	42000	32000	42000	33000	85000	45000	85000	55000
SCOTLAND												
Edinburgh			38000	33000	55000	46000	48000	42000			83000	62000
Glasgow			30000	27000	42000	38000	40000	36000	80000	60000	75000	52000
WALES												
Cardiff	30000	17000	33000	26000	50000	28000	40000	30000			110000	50000
Llandudno	19500	15000	22500	18500	23500	18500	24000	19500	46000	33000	46000	33000
Swansea	28000	16000	28000	23000	40000	25000	37000	24000			90000	45000
NORTHERN IRELAND												
Belfast	24100	9000	24600	18000	28200	19000	28700	19000	55000	42000	55000	42000
Coleraine	23000	13000	24000	19000	27500	20000	28000	22500	50000	40000	50000	40000

WOOLWICH EQUITABLE BUILDING SOCIETY

PRICE RANGES (typical valuations) MARCH 1987

19.10 UNITED KINGDOM – TOWNS: HOUSE TYPE AND SIZE BY AGE OF HOUSE

£

	2/3 BEDROOMED TERRACED				3 BEDROOMED SEMI-DETACHED				4 BEDROOMED DETACHED			
	Pre-1919		Post-1945		Pre-1939		Post-1945		Pre-1939		Post-1945	
	Upper	Lower	Upper	Lower	Upper	Lower	Upper	Lower	Upper	Lower	Upper	Lower
GREATER LONDON												
Bromley	56000	47000	71000	54000	82000	63000	85000	68000	160000	100000	170000	105000
Chingford	57500	47500	65000	50000	80000	63000	77000	60000	160000	105000	145000	105000
Croydon	63000	49500	70000	55000	87000	65000	97000	73000	150000	88000	163000	98000
Ealing	80500	68500	89000	72000	95500	77700	99750	78750	200000	145000	200000	145000
Kingston	74000	59000	85000	68000	98000	78000	108000	75000	129000	98000	165000	120000
Romford	47000	44600	53000	45800	70000	53500	67300	55000	106000	81000	93000	76000
Uxbridge	69000	60500	69700	64000	72000	63000	62000	66200	147000	114500	147000	114500
NORTHERN												
Middlesbrough	17000	12500	21000	18000	24000	19500	25000	21500			44000	33000
Newcastle	19000	14500	22000	19500	25000	20000	27500	23500			46000	34000
YORKSHIRE												
Leeds	26000	15000	32500	22500	50000	26000	50000	30000	80000	45000	80000	45000
Sheffield	23000	17000	23000	21500	35000	25000	33000	25000	75000	44000	63500	44000
NORTH WEST												
Chester	23000	17000	26000	22000	30000	25000	31000	25000	80000	50000	72000	47500
Liverpool	20000	12000	24000	19000	27000	21000	27500	22000	62000	45000	60000	45000
Manchester	30000	19000	33000	26000	40000	28000	39000	29000	75000	45000	82500	52000
MIDLANDS												
Birmingham	20000	12000	24000	18000	30000	20000	35000	25000	60000	40000	85000	45000
Leicester	23000	18000	25000	23000	33000	26000	33000	27000	60000	50000	77000	48000
Nottingham	19000	15000	23500	18500	26000	20000	31000	22000	55000	30000	65000	40000
Wolverhampton	23000	15000	24500	18000	29500	18000	30000	21000	50000	37500	57500	45000
EAST ANGLIA												
Ipswich	29000	25000	36000	28000	41000	35000	43500	38000	60000	48000	90000	50000
Norwich	31000	26000	35000	30000	38000	29000	39500	34500	65000	48000	85000	55000
SOUTH EAST												
Brighton	53000	46000	63000	56000	75000	64000	82500	68500	115000	94000	137500	99500
Dartford	46500	41000	53000	49000	63000	55500	62000	54000				
Luton	35000	25000	42000	30000	60000	39000	60000	38000	75000	50000	90000	52000
Maidstone	44000	36000	50000	41000	62000	48000	66000	50000	85000	75000	100000	80000
Oxford	59700	42900	60200	45000	72800	48900	62400	48900	123500	87500	111250	89500
Reading	59000	41000	59000	48000	80000	50000	70000	50000	130000	90000	120000	87000
Southampton	38000	29000	37000	34500	48000	37500	48000	36500	85000	67500	90000	63500
SOUTH WEST												
Bristol	30000	22800	35000	29000	37500	31500	42000	33600	68800	48000	100000	58500
Plymouth	34000	26000	35000	31000	44000	33000	43000	36000	100000	47000	100000	60000
SCOTLAND												
Edinburgh			40000	35000	55000	45000	48000	42000			89000	67000
Glasgow			33000	28000	45000	38000	42000	36000	80000	65000	75000	55000
Dundee	37000	34000	30000	28000	36000	32000	38000	33000	70000	50000	60000	45000
Aberdeen	75000	55000	48000	42000	65000	55000	48000	42000	100000	70000	85000	60000
WALES												
Cardiff	33000	18000	37000	26000	52000	33000	52000	33000			130000	52000
Llandudno	21000	16000	24000	19000	25000	20000	25000	21000	54000	37500	54000	37500
Swansea	32000	17000	33000	24000	45000	25000	45000	27000			95000	48000
NORTHERN IRELAND												
Belfast	25000	9500	26500	19000	29500	19500	29500	19500	56500	42000	56500	42000
Coleraine	23000	13000	24500	19000	27500	20000	28000	22500	50000	40000	50000	40000

Appendices

APPENDIX A

Other Sources of Data

This Appendix gives details of other sources of information for which the statistics themselves are not included in the data tables in this book. In the main they are sources which rely on information which *is* covered in the data tables (the local authorities listed below, in particular, fall into this category); sources which provide occasional analyses but do not publish regular series; or sources which have now been discontinued. The sources covered here are as follows:

1. Bradford & Bingley Building Society
2. Bristol & West Building Society
3. Countrywide Estate Agents
4. Estates Gazette
5. Fox & Sons Estate Agents
6. Guardian Guide to House Prices
7. London and Cambridge Economic Service
8. National Association of Estate Agents
9. National & Provincial Building Society
10. Parkers Property Price Guide
11. Property Auction Guide
12. Royal Institution of Chartered Surveyors
13. Under the Hammer Property Records
14. University of Reading, Department of Land Management and Development
15. University of Ulster, Department of Surveying
16. Local Authorities:
    Bedfordshire County Council
    City of Bristol Planning Department
    Cheshire County Council
    Dorset County Council
    Lancashire County Council
    Northamptonshire County Council
    Oxfordshire County Council
    County of South Glamorgan
    West Sussex County Council
    Wiltshire County Council

1 BRADFORD & BINGLEY BUILDING SOCIETY

Housing Bulletin has been published quarterly since March 1985. Each issue takes for its theme a particular aspect of the housing market as it relates to the Society's own mortgage lending. Statistics are presented in tabular form with brief commentaries.

Who Borrows from Bradford & Bingley? and *What Sort of Property Does Bradford & Bingley Lend On?* March 1985, March 1986 and March 1987

Women Borrowers June 1985

On What Type of Properties Does Bradford & Bingley Lend? September 1985 and December 1986

Bradford & Bingley and Home Improvement Lending December 1985 and October 1986

2   BRISTOL & WEST BUILDING SOCIETY

Factual Background 1967 to date. This bulletin contains tables which draw together information on building societies and housing statistics in general from a number of well known published sources. The Society does not produce original data.

3   COUNTRYWIDE ESTATE AGENTS (formerly MANN COUNTRYWIDE)

This is an association of estate agents thoughout the United Kingdom designed to assist company personnel and individuals in moving house within the United Kingdom.

A booklet entitled *United Kingdom Residential Property Price Index* is published on an irregular basis (about twice a year) and gives information on estimated typical prices for five property types and sizes in over 300 towns throughout the United Kingdom. The prices quoted are asking prices and are intended as a guide for prospective purchasers. Eight issues of the booklet have been published so far, the latest at the time of writing (March 1987) being Autumn 1986.

4   ESTATES GAZETTE

National Homes Network Market Survey appears annually in the mid-January issue of *Estates Gazette*. The information in this survey is supplied to *Estates Gazette* by members of National Homes Network, which is an association of smaller firms of estate agents with offices throughout the United Kingdom and in the Irish Republic. In total, about 600 offices are covered.

The survey makes no claims to be comprehensive but seeks to give a flavour of the housing market over the previous year. Price ranges and price movements are given for three house types (detached, semi-detached and terraced) broken down by three age groups (pre-1945, post-1945 and new).

5   FOX & SONS, ESTATE AGENTS

An Index of House Prices published jointly by Fox & Sons, Exeter and the University of Exeter. Included a weighted index of house prices quarterly from 1979 Q1 to 1982 Q4, covering all dwellings sold by Fox & Sons during this period.

6   THE GUARDIAN

Guardian Guide to House Prices. Published monthly in the *Guardian* from 31st May 1974 to 5th May 1975 (discontinued). The guide showed average house prices for five particular house types/sizes in 43 towns throughout the United Kingdom.

7   LONDON AND CAMBRIDGE ECONOMIC SERVICE (LCES)

The British Economy: Key Statistics 1900-1970, Times Publishing Company, London, 1971 (discontinued). An index was compiled by the London and Cambridge Economic Service using data supplied by the former Co-operative Permanent Building Society (now Nationwide) and the Halifax Building Society. It was based on crude average prices and covered only secondhand houses sold with vacant possession and for owner-occupation. Houses with shops and sales to sitting tenants were excluded.

The series is now of historical interest only but it provides a useful index of prices from 1946-1970 (the Nationwide Building Society series for the period from 1946 is given in Table 15.17). An index for the period 1900-1945 was also published by LCES but it was based on indices of building costs rather than house sales.

A description of the methodology is given in: Adams, A.A. "An Index of House Prices", *London and Cambridge Bulletin. The Times Review of Industry,* December, 1954, p.xii.

8   NATIONAL ASSOCIATION OF ESTATE AGENTS

Guide to House Prices. Published 1978 Q1-1978 Q4 (discontinued). Four quarterly editions of the guide were published, giving average prices for the quarter and an index of prices for 55 towns throughout Great Britain. Information was supplied by estate agents in response to a questionnaire. Prices for six property types/sizes were given.

APPENDIX A

9 NATIONAL & PROVINCIAL BUILDING SOCIETY

Occupational Lending Survey. Seven surveys have been published - four annual surveys up to 1983, another covering the last quarter of 1985 and two in 1986, for the second and fourth quarters. The Society intends to continue the survey on a twice yearly basis.

Each survey examines a sample of mortgages granted during the previous quarter. It records average incomes, purchase prices, percentage advances and mortgages under different occupational headings. Occupations are categorized into six groupings - top management and professional; junior and middle management; manual workers; self-employed; services; others. Statistics are given for each occupational type, as well as for each group and detail age of property purchased, type of loan and type of purchaser. Information on first-time buyers is also given and compared with the figures for all buyers.

10 PARKERS PROPERTY PRICE GUIDE

Published monthly from 1972 to 1976 (discontinued). A guide to house prices at the local level. The source of data is not specified in the guide. Price ranges and average prices were given for seven house types according to number of bedrooms for several hundred towns in England, Scotland and Wales and areas of London. The location of representative, typical houses of each type were given for each town, enabling an interested buyer to go and look at actual houses to get an idea of what price he might have to pay for a similar house in that area.

11 PROPERTY AUCTION GUIDE

Published fortnightly from April 1st 1987 to date. This pocket-size guide lists forthcoming auctions in the United Kingdom and subsequently the auction results by area and street. It also includes a quarterly review of market trends.

12 ROYAL INSTITUTION OF CHARTERED SURVEYORS

Housing Market Survey. Issued monthly in a press release: *RICS News.* March 1984 to date. This gives the results of a questionnaire returned by members of the RICS. The survey shows the percentages of agents reporting changes in house prices of the following magnitudes - very much higher (about 8% or more); much higher (about 5%); slightly higher (about 2%); the same; or lower. Changes are recorded as a comparison with average prices three months before. Six house types are covered: pre-1919 terrace, inter-war semi-detached, inter-war detached, post-war semi-detached, post-war detached and new houses.

The Survey covers agents in England and Wales and each issue gives both the national figures and results for one selected region; a different region is chosen each month.

13 UNDER THE HAMMER PROPERTY RECORDS

Published fortnightly since 1905 by Rogers (Printers) Birmingham Ltd. The publication, in five editions, summarises forthcoming property auction sales and, subsequently, the prices realised at auction. The five editions cover East Midlands, West Midlands, North East Yorkshire, Lancashire and Cheshire, and the South West.

14 UNIVERSITY OF READING, DEPARTMENT OF LAND MANAGEMENT AND DEVELOPMENT

Byrne, P.J. and Mackmin, D.H. *The Residential Market in Oxfordshire and Parts of Berkshire and Buckinghamshire. An Analysis and Review.* Biannual 1975-1981 (discontinued).

Each issue contained statistical analyses of six months' data provided by Messrs. Buckell and Ballard, Chartered Surveyors of Oxford and branches. Analyses of prices by house type and size were presented; price ranges, arithmetic means and medians were given.

15 UNIVERSITY OF ULSTER (JORDANSTOWN), DEPARTMENT OF SURVEYING

Northern Ireland Property Market Analysis. Published quarterly from 1984 Q4 to date. The reports are based on questionnaire surveys carried out by the Property Market Analysis Unit within the Department of Surveying. Information is obtained from estate agents on houses sold throughout Northern Ireland. House prices are given by property type, age, location and size for eleven areas and for Northern Ireland as a whole.

16 LOCAL AUTHORITIES

BEDFORDSHIRE COUNTY COUNCIL

Since 1972 Bedfordshire County Council Planning Department has conducted eight surveys of house prices, using data supplied from three sources: Nationwide Building Society, Abbey National Building Society and the Council's own regular questionnaire survey of local estate agents. In these surveys house prices in Bedfordshire are compared with those in surrounding areas, with particular reference to different types of properties and of buyers.

CITY OF BRISTOL PLANNING DEPARTMENT

Private Housing in Bristol, 1982. The report includes a survey of house prices for the period January to March 1982, covering 34 districts of Bristol. Prices are based on over 600 observations taken from local newspapers and estate agents' particulars. The prices shown reflect average prices *asked* for a range of properties from two-bedroomed terraced to four-bedroomed detached, excluding flats. They are not, therefore, necessarily the prices realised for sales of these properties.

The Private Housing Market in Bristol, May 1985. Survey of advertised house prices for first quarter 1985, as above.

CHESHIRE COUNTY COUNCIL

House Prices in Cheshire. An Analysis of Information from the Abbey National, Halifax and Nationwide Building Societies. February 1986. The report is divided into two parts. The first analyses house-price variations within the county, while the second looks at the rate at which prices have risen over time (1979-1985). In both parts comparisons are made with house prices outside the county.

DORSET COUNTY COUNCIL

House Price Survey, 1981-1986. This is an annual survey of the housing market in Dorset, based on asking prices as advertised in six or seven local newspapers during the first two weeks in April. Average (median) house prices by type of property by district are compared with those of earlier surveys (back to 1976 for some districts). Each issue of the survey looks at a different aspect of house prices; for example, the 1986 survey shows the availability of lower priced housing, suitable for purchase by first-time buyers, in the various districts covered by the survey.

Joint Dorset County Council/South Dorset Association of Estate Agents Survey of the Property Market in the Weymouth/Portland/Dorchester Area, May 1985. Results of a survey carried out among estate agents in the Dorset area during April/May 1985 based on responses to a questionnaire asking for details of each property sold during the survey period. Results given show average prices by district, by type and age of property and by family type.

A separate report, dated August 1985, compares the results of the above survey of estate agents with those of the 1985 newspaper survey.

APPENDIX A

LANCASHIRE COUNTY COUNCIL

Houses for Sale. A Survey of the Private Housing Market in Lancashire, June 1974. A detailed survey, published in July 1976, covering two aspects of the house market - the characteristics of houses for sale and their average prices and price ranges in the county. Several housing characteristics and their spatial variations are examined and cross-tabulated: type, age, locational environment and the provision of household amenities, garages, central heating and gardens. Average house prices and price ranges are considered in relation to the availability of each particular characteristic or attribute. Trends in average house prices over the county between 1970 and 1976 are examined and comparisons made with the national experience, as shown by Nationwide Building Society.

House Prices in Lancashire. October 1984. A similar but much less detailed survey. Both used data obtained from newspaper advertisements and estate agents' particulars of asking prices.

NORTHAMPTONSHIRE COUNTY COUNCIL

House Sales Survey. Quarterly reports from April 1979 to mid-1982. House-price data at county and district level supplied by Nationwide and Abbey National Building Societies were analysed alongside more local information on house prices collected by questionnaire survey of local estate agents, developers and building societies. Prices were analysed by house type, buyer type, and origin of buyer (whether in-county or migrant purchaser) and relative price by area.

OXFORDSHIRE COUNTY COUNCIL

Four unpublished surveys have been carried out, using estate agents' advertisements in local newspapers to compare prices asked for properties in each of 12 areas of Oxfordshire. Newspapers were scanned for a week or less in each of the four years 1973, 1980, 1983 and 1985 and produced an average of 1350 properties a year for analysis.

Data are analysed by house type, number of bedrooms and district. Average prices are given, but it is realised that the method of surveying has problems in that the asking price may not represent selling prices, advertisements may be duplicated and, in some smaller areas sample sizes may be correspondingly small.

COUNTY OF SOUTH GLAMORGAN

Three recent housing surveys have been published. The first, in May 1979, was carried out in connection with the dispersal of the Ministry of Defence from London to St Mellons in Cardiff and was entitled, *Ministry of Defence Dispersal. A Strategic Examination of Housing in South East Wales.* This report examined housing stock and new building, as well as house prices. The two subsequent surveys in November 1983 were aimed specifically at up-dating information on house prices in the area.

House price data were collected from local property newspapers and individual estate agents for 10 sub-areas of the county. These were analysed by house type and number of bedrooms and a typical price and price range recorded for each category.

WEST SUSSEX COUNTY COUNCIL

Annual Monitoring Report. Since 1979 the Planning Department has operated and published an annual house-price monitor in conjunction with the Director of Property. In February of each year information is obtained from local estate agents on that month's selling prices for houses of certain types (see below) on particular estates in the county. The aim is to indicate the value of housing of similar characteristics for each of 19 planning areas. The five particular house types selected are: detached houses with 4 bedrooms, semi-detached houses with 3 bedrooms, terraced houses with 2 or 3 bedrooms and flats with 2 bedrooms. These are principally chosen to represent properties at the lower end of the market so as to provide the best indication of how far local needs are being met. Regional and national figures for similar properties, provided by Nationwide Building Society, are shown for comparison.

WILTSHIRE COUNTY COUNCIL

Housing Market Survey. Three surveys have been undertaken for 1981 Q4, 1982/3 and 1985 Q1. The first and last of these are the more detailed and include analysis of data on house prices obtained from estate agents for secondhand property and builders for new property. These estimates are compared with figures for the South West Region published by the Nationwide and Abbey National Building Societies. Five sub-areas of the county are defined and figures are given by house type and age (new, modern and older).

APPENDIX B

Definitions of Official Standard Regions

DEFINITIONS OF OFFICIAL STANDARD REGIONS

For the purpose of official statistics the United Kingdom is divided into Standard Regions classified by the Central Statistical Office. The definitions of these regions, which are classified according to local authority areas, are given below. Major revisions of the boundaries of the regions were made in 1965 and 1974. In 1965 Economic Planning Regions (EPRs) were set up and the Standard Regions for Statistical Purposes were revised to coincide with them. The regions were adjusted again on 1 April 1974 to take account of local government reorganization. A map illustrating the current regional boundaries and the changes introduced in 1974 is shown following the definitions.

STANDARD REGIONS BEFORE 1965

The list below shows the names of the Standard Regions in Great Britain and the area covered by each. Counties, etc., are defined by reference to local government administrative areas.

Northern
Cumberland, Durham, Northumberland, Westmorland and the North Riding of Yorkshire.

East and West Ridings
The East and West Ridings of Yorkshire and the City of York.

North Midland
Derbyshire (except the High Peak District, which is included in the North Western Region), Leicestershire, Lincolnshire, Northamptonshire (including the Soke of Peterborough), Nottinghamshire and Rutland.

Eastern
Bedfordshire, Cambridgeshire (including the Isle of Ely), Hertfordshire, Essex, Huntingdonshire, Norfolk and Suffolk, except such parts of Essex and Hertfordshire as are within the London and South Eastern Region.

London and South Eastern
London (administrative county), Middlesex, Kent, Surrey and Sussex, parts of Essex (the boroughs of Barking, Chingford, Dagenham, East Ham, Ilford, Leyton, Walthamstow, Wanstead and Woodford, and West Ham, and the urban districts of Chigwell and Waltham Holy Cross) and parts of Hertfordshire (the urban districts of Barnet, Bushey, Cheshunt, and East Barnet, and the rural district of Elstree).

Southern
Berkshire, Buckinghamshire, Hampshire (including the Isle of Wight), Oxfordshire and Poole.

South Western
Cornwall (including the Isles of Scilly), Devonshire, Dorset* (excluding Poole), Gloucestershire, Somerset and Wiltshire.

Wales
The whole of Wales and Monmouthshire.

Midland
Herefordshire, Shropshire, Staffordshire, Warwickshire and Worcestershire.

---

* Transferred from Southern Region in 1958

North Western
Cheshire, Lancashire and the High Peak District of Derbyshire (the boroughs of Buxton and Glossop, the urban districts of New Mills and Whaley Bridge, and the rural district of Chapel-en-le-Frith).

Scotland
The whole of Scotland.

The changes made in 1965 to bring the regions into line with the new Economic Planning Regions were as follows:

(i)   Lincolnshire (parts of Lindsey) was transferred from the former North Midland Region and added to the East and West Ridings to form the new Yorkshire and Humberside Region.

(ii)   The remainder of the former North Midland Region, *less* the Soke of Peterborough (which has been joined to Huntingdonshire) was renamed the East Midlands Region. The County Borough of Lincoln remained in this region.

(iii)   Part of the former Eastern Region - Norfolk, Suffolk, Cambridgeshire and Huntingdonshire - together with the Soke of Peterborough formed the new Region of East Anglia.

(iv)   The remainder of the Eastern Region, together with the former London and South Eastern and Southern Regions, formed the new South East Region. It should be noted that this region differed from that covered by the South East Study, which included East Anglia.

(v)   The remaining regions had the same definitions and names as before, except that the former Midland Region was renamed the West Midlands Region.

STANDARD REGIONS FROM 1965 TO 31 MARCH 1974

North
Cumberland, Durham, Northumberland, Westmorland, and the North Riding of Yorkshire.

Yorkshire and Humberside
The East and West Ridings of Yorkshire (including City of York) and Lincolnshire (parts of Lindsey excluding Lincoln C.B.)

East Midlands
Derbyshire (except the High Peak District, which is included in the North West Region), Leicestershire, Lincolnshire (Part of Holland, Parts of Kesteven and Lincoln C.B.), Northamptonshire, Nottinghamshire and Rutland.

East Anglia
Cambridgeshire and Isle of Ely, Huntingdon and Peterborough, Norfolk and Suffolk.

South East
Bedfordshire, Hertfordshire, Essex, Berkshire, Buckinghamshire,, Oxfordshire, London (Greater London Council area), Kent, Surrey, Sussex, Hampshire, Isle of Wight and Borough of Poole*.

South West
Cornwall (including the Isles of Scilly), Devon, Dorset (excluding the Borough of Poole*), Gloucestershire, Somerset and Wiltshire.

West Midlands
Herefordshire, Shropshire, Staffordshire, Warwickshire and Worcestershire.

* Poole is in the South West Economic Planning Regions but has been included in the South East statistical region.

APPENDIX B

North West
Cheshire, Lancashire and the High Peak District of Derbyshire (the Boroughs of Buxton and Glossop, the urban districts of New Mills and Whaley Bridge and the rural district of Chapel-en-le-Frith).

Wales
The whole of Wales

Scotland
The whole of Scotland

Northern Ireland
Antrim, Down, Armagh, Fermanagh, Tyrone, Londonderry, Belfast C.B., Londonderry C.B.

STANDARD REGIONS FROM 1 APRIL 1974

North
Tyne and Wear, Cleveland, Cumbria, Durham, Northumberland.

Yorkshire and Humberside
South Yorkshire, West Yorkshire, Humberside, North Yorkshire.

East Midlands
Derbyshire, Leicestershire, Lincolnshire, Northamptonshire, Nottinghamshire.

East Anglia
Cambridgeshire, Norfolk, Suffolk.

South East
Greater London, Bedfordshire, Berkshire, Buckinghamshire, East Sussex, Essex, Hampshire, Hertfordshire, Isle of Wight, Kent, Oxfordshire, Surrey, West Sussex.

South West
Avon, Cornwall, Devon, Dorset, Gloucestershire, Somerset, Wiltshire.

West Midlands
West Midlands, Hereford and Worcester, Salop, Staffordshire, Warwickshire.

North West
Greater Manchester, Merseyside, Cheshire, Lancashire.

Wales
The whole of Wales

Scotland
The whole of Scotland

Northern Ireland
Antrim, Down, Armagh, Fermanagh, Tyrone, Londonderry, Belfast C.B., Londonderry C.B.

ORKNEY

SHETLAND

SCOTLAND

Standard Regions of England,
Wales, Scotland and Northern
Ireland :

at 1 April 1974 ————————
at 31 March 1974 ▬▬▬▬▬▬

Administrative Areas :
County in England and
Wales at 1 April 1974,
Region or Islands Area
in Scotland at
16 May 1975 ————————

NORTHERN
IRELAND

NORTH

NORTH
WEST

YORKSHIRE AND
HUMBERSIDE

EAST
MIDLANDS

WALES

WEST
MIDLANDS

EAST ANGLIA

SOUTH EAST

SOUTH WEST

OFFICIAL STANDARD REGIONS OF THE UNITED KINGDOM

APPENDIX C

List of Names and Addresses

1 GOVERNMENT SOURCES

Information on data published in *Housing and Construction Statistics* may be obtained from the Directorate of Statistics, Department of the Environment, 2 Marsham Street, London SW1P 3EB

Board of Inland Revenue (Survey of Conveyances), Somerset House, Strand, London WC2R 1LB

Inland Revenue Valuation Office, New Court, Carey Street, London WC2A 2JE

Policy Planning and Research Unit (PPRU), Department of Finance and Personnel, Parliament Buildings, Stormont, Belfast BT4 3SS, Northern Ireland

Surveyors Publications, 12 Great George Street, London SW1P 3AD

2 BUILDING SOCIETIES

Abbey National Building Society, Abbey House, Baker Street, London NW1 6XL

Anglia Building Society, Moulton Park, Northampton NN3 1NL

Bradford & Bingley Building Society, PO Box 2, Main Street, Bingley BD16 2LW

Bristol & West Building Society, Research Department, PO Box 27, Broad Quay, Bristol BS99 7AX

Halifax Building Society, Trinity Road, Halifax HX1 2RG

Leeds Permanent Building Society, The Headrow, Leeds LS1 1NS

National & Provincial Building Society, Provincial House, Bradford, West Yorkshire BD1 1NL

Nationwide Building Society, New Oxford House, High Holborn, London WC1V 6PW

Northern Rock Building Society, Northern Rock House, Gosforth, Newcastle-upon-Tyne NE3 4PL

Principality Building Society, PO Box 89, Principality Buildings, Queen Street, Cardiff CF1 1UA

Woolwich Equitable Building Society, Corporate Affairs Department, Equitable House, London SE18 6AB

3 ESTATE AGENTS AND CHARTERED SURVEYORS

Countrywide Estate Agents, 22 Commercial Way, Woking, Surrey GU21 1HB

Estates Gazette Ltd, 151 Wardour Street, London W1V 4BN

Fox & Sons, Estate Agents, 22 Cathedral Yard, Exeter EX1 1HQ

Incorporated Society of Valuers and Auctioneers, 3 Cadogan Gate, London SW1X OAS

National Association of Estate Agents, Arbon House, 21 Jury Street, Warwick CU34 4EH

Royal Institution of Chartered Surveyors, 12 Great George Street, Parliament Square, London SW1P 3AD

Ryden Residential Ltd, 33 George Street, Edinburgh EH2 2HN

ADDRESSES OF DATA SOURCES

4 LOCAL AUTHORITIES: Departments of Planning

Bedfordshire County Council, County Hall, Cauldwell Street, Bedford MK42 9AP

City of Bristol Planning Department, Cabot House, Deanery Road, Bristol BS1 5TZ

Cheshire County Council, County Hall, Chester CH1 1SF

Dorset County Council, County Hall, Dorchester, Dorset DT1 1XJ

Lancashire County Council, PO Box 78, County Hall, Preston PR1 8XJ

Oxfordshire County Council, Speedwell House, Speedwell Street, Oxford OX1 1SD

County of South Glamorgan, County Headquarters, Newport Road, Cardiff CF2 1XA

West Sussex County Council, County Hall, Chichester PO19 1RL

Wiltshire County Council, County Hall, Trowbridge, Wiltshire BA14 8JG

5 OTHER

Department of Land Management and Development, University of Reading, Whiteknights, Reading, Berks RG6 2BU

Department of Surveying, University of Ulster (Jordanstown), Shore Road, Newtownabbey, County Antrim BT37 0QB

The Guardian, 119 Farringdon Road, London EC1R 3ER

Property Auction Guide, 47 Holland Park Mews, London W11 3SP

Rogers (Printers) Birmingham Ltd, 5 Aston Road North, Birmingham B6 4DS

National House-Building Council, Chiltern Avenue, Amersham, Bucks HP6 5AP

Indexes

INDEX A

Data Sources

Abbey National Building Society 9–10, 12–13, 169–215
  address 384
  average prices
    aggregate data, all/new/non-new dwellings, UK 172
    breakdowns
      by age of house 172, 178–81, 196–215
      by region 174–215
      by type of house 173, 182–91, 196–215
      by type of buyer 172, 192–5
    cross-classifications, list of 170
    tables, list of 170
  method of analysis 169–70
  prices, *see* average prices *under this entry*
  publications 170–1
  supplementary studies 171
  technical details 169–71
Anglia Building Society 9–10, 12–13, 216–27
  address 384
  price changes, percentages
    by age of dwelling 219–27
    by region 220–3
    by survey area 224–7
    see also index numbers *under this entry*
  price data
    cross-classifications, list of 217
    tables, list of 217
  index numbers
    new/non-new, age 219
    see also price changes *under this entry*
  method of analysis
  publications 218
  technical details 216–8

Bank of England Survey of Banks' Mortgages 9–10, 12–13, 58–9
  address 384
  average prices
    aggregate data, all dwellings, UK 59
    tables, list of 59
  method of analysis 58
  prices, *see* average prices *under this entry*
  publications 59
  technical details 58–9

DOE Five Per Cent Sample Survey 9–13, 33–57
  address 384
  average prices
    aggregate data, all/new/non-new dwellings, UK 36–7
    breakdowns
      by age of house 53
      by region 38–47, 50–1
      by type of house 46–9, 53
      by type of buyer 36–7, 44–5, 50–1, 53
    cross-classificatons, list of 34–5
    see also index numbers *under this entry*
    tables, list of 34
  index numbers
    weighted
      all/new/non-new, UK 55, 57
      all, regions 54–7

    see also average prices *under this entry*
  method of analysis 34
  prices, *see* average prices; index numbers *under this entry*
  publications 35
  supplementary studies 35
  technical details 33–5
DOE/ABI Survey of Insurance Companies 9–10, 12–13, 61–3
  address 384
  average prices
    aggregate data, all/new/non-new dwellings, UK 63
    tables, list of 62
  method of analysis 61
  prices, *see* average prices *under this entry*
  publications 62
  technical details 61–2
DOE/BSA BS4 Survey 9–13, 23–31
  address 384
  average prices
    aggregate data, all/new/non-new dwellings, UK 26–31
    tables, list of 24
  method of analysis 23–4
  publications 24–5
  prices, *see* average prices *under this entry*
  technical details 23–5

Halifax Building Society 4, 9–13, 229–70
  address 384
  average prices
    aggregate data, all/new/non-new dwellings, UK 234, 263–70
    breakdowns
      by age of house 234, 238–41, 246–55
      by region 236–55, 264–9
      by type of house 235, 242–55
      by type of buyer 234
    cross-classifications, list of 232
    see also index numbers *under this entry*
    tables, list of 231–2
  index numbers
    non-standardised 270
    standardised
      all, new, existing 256–61
      by region 258–61
      by type of buyer 256–7
    see also average prices *under this entry*
  method of analysis 230–1
  prices, *see* average prices; index numbers *under this entry*
  publications 233
  supplementary studies 233
  technical details 229–33

Incorporated Society of Valuers and Auctioneers (ISVA) 4, 8–10, 12–13, 271–5
  address 384
  average prices
    see also index numbers *under this entry*
    aggregate data, all/new/non-new dwellings, England 273

    breakdowns
      by region 274
      by type of house 273
    tables, list of 272
  index numbers
    all dwellings 275
    see also average prices *under this entry*
  method of analysis 271
  prices, *see* average prices; index numbers *under this entry*
  publications 272
  technical details 271–2
Inland Revenue, Survey of Conveyances 9–13, 64–7
  address 384
  average prices
    aggregate data, all dwellings, E & W 66–7
    breakdowns
      by freehold/leasehold 66–7
      by region 66
    cross-classifications, list of 65
    tables, list of 65
  method of analysis 64
  prices, *see* average prices *under this entry*
  publications 65
  supplementary studies 65
  technical details 64–5
Inland Revenue, Valuation Office Property Market Report (VOPMR) 9–13, 69–155
  address 384
  average price ranges, new/non-new dwellings, GB
    by age of house 115–55
    new 74–114
    non-new 115–55
    by size of house 78–80, 85–7, 92–4, 99–101, 106–14, 150–5
    by town or locality 74–155
    by type of house 74–155
    cross-classifications, list of 70
    tables, list of 70
  method of analysis 69–70
  prices, *see* average prices *under this entry*
  property type descriptions 71–3
  publications 70
  supplementary studies 70
  technical details 69–73

Leeds Permanent Building Society 9–10, 12–13, 276–85
  address 384
  average prices
    aggregate data, all/new/non-new dwellings, UK 278
    breakdowns
      by age of house 278
      by region 280–5
      by type of house 279, 282–5
    cross-classifications, list of 277
    tables, list of 277
  method of analysis 276–7
  prices, *see* average prices *under this entry*
  publications 277

supplementary studies 277
technical details 276–7
weighted average prices, *see* average prices *under this entry*

National House-Building Council (NHBC) 8–10, 12–13, 286–95
address 385
average prices
aggregate data
new dwellings, England, sales prices 288–9
new dwellings, Great Britain, estimated prices, starts 290–1
breakdowns
by region 288–95
by type of house 292–5
cross-classifications, list of 287
tables, list of 287
method of analysis 287
prices, *see* average prices *under this entry*
publications 287
technical details 286–7
Nationwide Building Society 9–13, 296–345
address 384
average prices
aggregate data, all/new/non-new dwellings, UK 301–5
breakdowns
by age of house 304–5, 322–37
by region 306–43
by type of house 304–5, 314–37
by type of buyer 304–5, 342–3
cross-classifications, list of 298
tables, list of 297–8
see also index numbers *under this entry*
index numbers
all/new/non-new, UK 301–3, 344–5
see also average prices *under this entry*
method of analysis 297
prices, *see* average prices; index numbers *under this entry*

publications 298–9
supplementary studies 298–9
technical details 296–9
Northern Ireland Department of Finance and Personnel (PPRU) 9–10, 12–13, 156–65
address 384
average prices
aggregate data, new/non-new dwellings, Northern Ireland 158
breakdowns
by county 159–65
by town or locality 159–65
by type of house 158, 160–65
cross-classifications, list of 157
tables, list of 157
method of analysis 156–7
prices, *see* average prices *under this entry*
publications 157
technical details 156–7
Northern Rock Building Society 9–10, 12–13, 347–51
address 384
average prices
aggregate data, all dwellings, North of England 349
breakdowns
by county 349–51
by town or locality 349–51
by type of house 349–51
cross-classifications, list of 348
tables, list of 348
method of analysis 347
prices, *see* average prices *under this entry*
publications 348
technical details 347–8

Principality Building Society 9–10, 12–13, 352–5
address 384
average prices
aggregate data, all/new/non-new

dwellings, Wales 354–5
breakdowns
by county 354–5
by town or locality 354–5
cross-classifications, list of 353
tables, list of 352
method of analysis 352
prices, *see* average prices *under this entry*
publications 353
technical details 352–3

Ryden Residential Ltd 9–13, 356–9
address 384
average prices, Scottish cities
by age of house 358–9
by size of house 358–9
by town or locality 358–9
by type of house 358–9
cross-classifications, list of 357
tables, list of 356
method of analysis 356
prices, *see* average prices *under this entry*
publications 357
supplementary studies 357
technical details 356–7

Woolwich Equitable Building Society 9–10, 12–13, 360–71
address 384
average price ranges, UK
by age of house 362–71
by size of house 362–71
by town or locality 362–71
by type of house 362–71
cross-classifications, list of 361
tables, list of 361
method of analysis 360
prices, *see* average prices *under this entry*
publications 361
supplementary studies 361
technical details 360–1

INDEX B

Countries, Regions and Counties

Antrim, North
  Northern Ireland Department of Finance
    and Personnel (PPRU) 159–65
Antrim, South
  Northern Ireland Department of Finance
    and Personnel (PPRU) 159–65
Avon, North West
  Inland Revenue: Valuation Office Property
    Market Report (VOPMR) 102–3, 143–4
Berkshire, West Surrey and North Hampshire
  Anglia Building Society 224
Berkshire, East
  Inland Revenue: Valuation Office Property
    Market Report (VOPMR) 95–6, 136–7
Buckinghamshire, North
  Inland Revenue: Valuation Office Property
    Market Report (VOPMR) 95–6, 136–7
Buckinghamshire, South
  Inland Revenue: Valuation Office Property
    Market Report (VOPMR) 95–6, 136–7
Cheshire & South Lancashire
  Anglia Building Society 224, 226
Cheshire, East
  Inland Revenue: Valuation Office Property
    Market Report (VOPMR) 74–5, 115–6
Cleveland, North
  Inland Revenue: Valuation Office Property
    Market Report (VOPMR) 74–5, 115–6
Cleveland, South
  Inland Revenue: Valuation Office Property
    Market Report (VOPMR) 74–5, 115–6
Clwyd
  Principality 354
Cumbria
  Northern Rock Building Society 349–51
Derbyshire, West
  Inland Revenue: Valuation Office Property
    Market Report (VOPMR) 81–2, 122–3
Derry
  Northern Ireland Department of Finance
    and Personnel (PPRU) 159–65
Devon, North
  Inland Revenue: Valuation Office Property
    Market Report (VOPMR) 102–3, 143–4
Dorset, West
  Inland Revenue: Valuation Office Property
    Market Report (VOPMR) 102–3, 143–4
Down, North
  Northern Ireland Department of Finance
    and Personnel (PPRU) 159–65
Down, South
  Northern Ireland Department of Finance
    and Personnel (PPRU) 159–65
Durham
  Northern Rock Building Society 349–51
Dyfed
  Principality 354
Dyfed, East
  Inland Revenue: Valuation Office Property
    Market Report (VOPMR) 102–3, 143–4
Dyfed, West
  Inland Revenue: Valuation Office Property
    Market Report (VOPMR) 102–3, 143–4
East Anglia

Abbey National Building Society 174, 176,
  178, 180, 182, 184, 186, 188, 190, 192, 194,
  197, 201, 205, 209, 213
Anglia Building Society 220, 222
DOE Five Per Cent Sample Survey 38, 40,
  42, 44, 46, 50, 54, 56
Halifax Building Society 236, 238, 240, 242,
  244, 248, 253, 258, 260, 265, 267, 269
Inland Revenue: Survey of Conveyances 66
Leeds Permanent Building Society 280, 282,
  284
National House Building Council 288, 290
Nationwide Building Society 306, 308, 310,
  312, 314, 316, 318, 320, 323, 327, 331, 335,
  342
Eastern
  Nationwide Building Society 338–41
East Midlands
  Abbey National Building Society 174, 176,
    178, 180, 182, 184, 186, 188, 190, 192, 194,
    197, 201, 205, 209, 213
  Anglia Building Society 220, 222
  DOE Five Per Cent Sample Survey 38, 40,
    42, 44, 46, 50, 54, 56
  Halifax Building Society 236, 238, 240, 242,
    244, 247, 253, 258, 260, 264, 266, 268
  Inland Revenue: Survey of Conveyances 66
  Leeds Permanent Building Society 280, 282,
    284
  National House Building Council 288, 290
  Nationwide Building Society 306, 308, 310,
    312, 314, 316, 318, 320, 323, 327, 331, 335,
    342
England
  DOE Five Per Cent Sample Survey 51
  Incorporated Society of Valuers and
    Auctioneers 273, 275
  National House Building Council 289, 291,
    293
  see also North of England
England and Wales
  Inland Revenue: Survey of Conveyances 67
Essex
  Anglia Building Society 225, 227
Fermanagh & South Tyrone
  Northern Ireland Department of Finance
    and Personnel (PPRU) 159–65
Glamorgan, Mid
  Principality 354
Glamorgan, South
  Principality 355
Glamorgan, West
  Principality 355
Grampian (Rural)
  Inland Revenue: Valuation Office Property
    Market Report (VOPMR) 109–14, 150–5
Great Britain
  DOE Five Per Cent Sample Survey 51
  Halifax Building Society 270, 290
  National House Building Council 292
Greater London
  Abbey National Building Society 175, 177,
    179, 181, 183, 185, 187, 189, 191, 193, 195,
    198, 202, 206, 210, 214

DOE Five Per Cent Sample Survey 39, 41,
  43, 45, 47, 51, 55, 57
Halifax Building Society 237, 239, 241, 243,
  245, 249, 254, 259, 261, 265, 267, 269
Inland Revenue: Survey of Conveyances 67
Leeds Permanent Building Society 281, 283,
  285
National House Building Council 289, 291
Nationwide Building Society 307, 309, 311,
  313, 315, 317, 319, 321, 324, 328, 332,
  336, 343
  see also London
Gwent
  Principality 354
Gwynnedd
  Principality 354
Hampshire
  Anglia Building Society 225
Hampshire – Berkshire, West Surrey and
    North Hampshire
  Anglia Building Society 224
Hampshire, South
  Anglia Building Society 227
Hereford and West Worcester
  Inland Revenue: Valuation Office Property
    Market Report (VOPMR) 81–2, 122–3
Hertfordshire, North
  Inland Revenue: Valuation Office Property
    Market Report (VOPMR) 95–6, 136–7
Hertfordshire – North London, Middlesex,
    Hertfordshire
  Anglia Building Society 224, 226
Humberside
  Inland Revenue: Valuation Office Property
    Market Report (VOPMR) 74–5, 115–6
Kent, East
  Inland Revenue: Valuation Office Property
    Market Report (VOPMR) 95–6, 136–7
Kent, North
  Anglia Building Society 226
Kent – North Kent and South East London
  Anglia Building Society 224
Kent Weald
  Anglia Building Society 227
Lakeland, South
  Inland Revenue: Valuation Office Property
    Market Report (VOPMR) 74–5, 115–6
Lancashire – Cheshire and South Lancashire
  Anglia Building Society 224, 226
Lancashire, North
  Anglia Building Society 224, 226
Leicestershire, North
  Inland Revenue: Valuation Office Property
    Market Report (VOPMR) 81–2, 122–3
Leicestershire, South
  Inland Revenue: Valuation Office Property
    Market Report (VOPMR) 81–2, 122–3
Lincolnshire
  Anglia Building Society 224, 226
London
  see also Greater London; Outer
    Metropolitan
London – Mid-Surrey and South London
  Anglia Building Society 224

INDEX B

London, North
Anglia Building Society 221
London – North Kent and South East London
Anglia Building Society 224
London – North London, Middlesex, Hertfordshire
Anglia Building Society 224, 226
London & South East
Anglia Building Society, 220, 223
Nationwide Building Society 338–41
see also Greater London; London; South East
Londonderry see Derry
Medway Towns
Anglia Building Society 225, 227
Middlesex – North London, Middlesex, Hertfordshire
Anglia Building Society 224, 226
Midlands
Anglia Building Society 220, 225, 227
Incorporated Society of Valuers and Auctioneers 274
Nationwide Building Society 338–41
Midlands, East see East Midlands
Midlands, North East
Anglia Building Society 222
Midlands, South
Anglia Building Society 222, 225, 227
Midlands, South West
Anglia Building Society 221
Midlands, West see West Midlands
Norfolk
Anglia Building Society 224, 226
Norfolk, North
Inland Revenue: Valuation Office Property Market Report (VOPMR) 81–2, 122–3
Norfolk, West
Inland Revenue: Valuation Office Property Market Report (VOPMR) 81–2, 122–3
North
Abbey National Building Society 174, 176, 178, 180, 182, 184, 186, 188, 190, 192, 194, 196, 200, 204, 208, 212
DOE Five Per Cent Sample Survey 38, 40, 42, 44, 46, 50, 54, 56
Halifax Building Society 236, 238, 240, 242, 244, 246, 251, 258, 260, 264, 266, 268
Inland Revenue: Survey of Conveyances 66
Leeds Permanent Building Society 280, 282, 284
National House Building Council 288, 290
Nationwide Building Society 306, 308, 310, 312, 314, 316, 318, 320, 322, 326, 330, 334, 342
Northamptonshire
Anglia Building Society 225, 227
North & Yorkshire
Anglia Building Society 222, 224, 226
see also North; Yorkshire & Humberside
Northern see North
Northern Ireland
Abbey National Building Society 175, 177, 179, 181, 183, 185, 187, 189, 191, 193, 195, 199, 203, 207, 211, 215
Anglia Building Society 223
DOE Five Per Cent Sample Survey 39, 41, 43, 45, 47, 51, 55, 57
Halifax Building Society 237, 239, 241, 243, 245, 250, 255, 259, 261, 265, 267, 269
Leeds Permanent Building Society 281, 283, 285
Nationwide Building Society 307, 309, 311, 313, 315, 317, 319, 321, 325, 329, 333, 337–41, 343
Northern Ireland Department of Finance and Personnel (PPRU) 158
North East
Incorporated Society of Valuers and Auctioneers 274
see also North Eastern; Yorkshire and Humberside
North Eastern
Anglia Building Society 220
Nationwide Building Society 338–51
see also North East; Yorkshire and Humberside
North of England
Northern Rock Building Society 349–51
Northumberland
Inland Revenue: Valuation Office Property Market Report (VOPMR) 74–5, 115–6
Northern Rock Building Society 349–51
North West
Abbey National Building Society 174, 176, 178, 180, 182, 184, 186, 188, 190, 192, 194, 196, 200, 204, 208, 212
Anglia Building Society 222
DOE Five Per Cent Sample Survey 38, 40, 42, 44, 46, 50, 54, 56
Halifax Building Society 236, 238, 240, 242, 244, 247, 252, 258, 260, 264, 266, 268
Incorporated Society of Valuers and Auctioneers 274
Inland Revenue: Survey of Conveyances 66
Leeds Permanent Building Society 280, 282, 284
National House Building Council 288, 290
Nationwide Building Society 306, 308, 310, 312, 314, 316, 318, 320, 322, 326, 330, 334, 342
see also North Western
North Western
Nationwide Building Society 338–41
Anglia Building Society 220
see also North West
Nottinghamshire & South Yorkshire
Anglia Building Society 224, 226
Nottinghamshire, South
Inland Revenue: Valuation Office Property Market Report (VOPMR) 81–2, 122–3
Outer Metropolitan
Nationwide Building Society 307, 309, 311, 313, 315, 317, 319, 321, 324, 328, 332, 336
Outer South East
Nationwide Building Society 307, 309, 311, 313, 315, 317, 319, 321, 324, 328, 332, 336
Oxfordshire, West
Inland Revenue: Valuation Office Property Market Report (VOPMR) 95–6, 136–7
Powys
Principality 355
Scotland
Abbey National Building Society 175, 177, 179, 181, 183, 185, 187, 189, 191, 193, 195, 199, 203, 207, 211, 215
Anglia Building Society 221, 223
DOE Five Per Cent Sample Survey 39, 41, 43, 45, 47, 51, 55, 57
Halifax Building Society 237, 239, 241, 243, 245, 250, 255, 259, 261, 265, 267, 269
Leeds Permanent Building Society 281, 283, 285
National House Building Council 295
Nationwide Building Society 307, 309, 311, 313, 315, 317, 319, 321, 325, 329, 333, 337–41, 343
Shropshire
Inland Revenue: Valuation Office Property Market Report (VOPMR) 81–2, 122–3
Somerset
Inland Revenue: Valuation Office Property Market Report (VOPMR) 102–3, 143–4
South
Anglia Building Society 223
see also Southern
Southern

Nationwide Building Society 338–41
see also South
South East
Abbey National Building Society 175, 177, 179, 181, 183, 185, 187, 189, 191, 193, 195, 198, 202, 206, 210, 214
DOE Five Per Cent Sample Survey 39, 41, 43, 45, 47, 51, 54, 56
Halifax Building Society 237, 239, 241, 243, 245, 249, 254, 259, 261, 265, 267, 269
Incorporated Society of Valuers and Auctioneers 274
Inland Revenue: Survey of Conveyances 66
Leeds Permanent Building Society 281, 283, 285
National House Building Council 289, 291
see also Outer South East; Outer Metropolitan
South West
Abbey National Building Society 175, 177, 179, 181, 183, 185, 187, 189, 191, 193, 195, 198, 202, 206, 210, 214
Anglia Building Society 223, 225, 227
DOE Five Per Cent Sample Survey 39, 41, 43, 45, 47, 51, 55, 57
Halifax Building Society 237, 239, 241, 243, 245, 249, 254, 259, 261, 265, 267, 269
Inland Revenue: Survey of Conveyances 67
Leeds Permanent Building Society 281, 283, 285
National House Building Council 289, 291
Nationwide Building Society 307, 309, 311, 313, 315, 317, 319, 321, 324, 328, 332, 336, 343
See also South Western
South Western
Nationwide Building Society 339, 341
see also South West
Suffolk
Anglia Building Society 224, 226
Surrey – Berkshire, West Surrey and North Hampshire
Anglia Building Society 224
Surrey, Mid
Anglia Building Society 226
Surrey – Mid-Surrey and South London
Anglia Building Society 224
Surrey, North
Inland Revenue: Valuation Office Property Market Report (VOPMR) 95–6, 136–7
Sussex, East
Anglia Building Society 224, 226
Sussex, West
Anglia Building Society 225, 227
Teesside
Northern Rock Building Society 349–51
Thanet
Anglia Building Society 225, 227
Tyne, North
Northern Rock Building Society 349–51
Tyne, South
Northern Rock Building Society 349–51
Tyneside
Inland Revenue: Valuation Office Property Market Report (VOPMR) 74–5, 115–6
Tyneside, North
Inland Revenue: Valuation Office Property Market Report (VOPMR) 80, 121
Tyrone see Fermanagh & South Tyrone
United Kingdom
Abbey National Building Society 172–3, 196, 200, 204, 208, 212
Anglia Building Society 219
Bank of England Survey of Banks' Mortgages 59
DOE/ABI Survey of Insurance Companies 63
DOE/BSA BS4 Survey 26–31

DOE Five Per Cent Sample Survey 36–7, 46, 48–50, 53, 55, 57
Halifax Building Society 234–5, 246, 251, 256–7, 263–4, 266, 268
Leeds Permanent Building Society 278–9
Nationwide Building Society 301–5, 322, 326, 330, 334, 344–5
Wales
  Abbey National Building Society 175, 177, 179, 181, 183, 185, 187, 189, 191, 193, 195, 198, 202, 206, 210, 214
  DOE Five Per Cent Sample Survey 39, 41, 43, 45, 47, 51, 55, 57
  Halifax Building Society 237, 239, 241, 243, 245, 250, 255, 259, 261, 265, 267, 269
  Inland Revenue: Survey of Conveyances 67
  Leeds Permanent Building Society 281, 283, 285
  National House Building Council 289, 291, 294
  Nationwide Building Society 307, 309, 311, 313, 315, 317, 319, 321, 325, 329, 333, 337, 339, 341, 343
  Principality Building Society 354
Warwickshire, North
  Inland Revenue: Valuation Office Property

Market Report (VOPMR) 81–2, 122–3
West
  Incorporated Society of Valeurs and Auctioneers 274
  see also Western
Western
  Anglia Building Society 221, 224, 226
  Nationwide Building Society 338–41
  see also West
West Midlands
  Abbey National Building Society 174, 176, 178, 180, 182, 184, 186, 188, 190, 192, 194, 197, 201, 205, 209, 213
  Anglia Building Society 220, 222
  DOE Five Per Cent Sample Survey 38, 40, 42, 44, 46, 50, 54, 56
  Halifax Building Society 236, 238, 240, 242, 244, 248, 253, 258, 260, 264, 266, 268
  Inland Revenue: Survey of Conveyances 66
  Leeds Permanent Building Society 280, 282, 284
  National House Building Council 288, 290
  Nationwide Building Society 306, 308, 310, 312, 314, 316, 318, 320, 323, 327, 331, 335, 342
Wiltshire, North

Inland Revenue: Valuation Office Property Market Report (VOPMR) 102–3, 143–4
Wiltshire, South
  Inland Revenue: Valuation Office Property Market Report (VOPMR) 102–3, 143–4
Wirral
  Inland Revenue: Valuation Office Property Market Report (VOPMR) 74–6, 115–6
Yorkshire & Humberside
  Abbey National Building Society 174, 176, 178, 180, 182, 184, 186, 188, 190, 192, 194, 196, 200, 204, 208, 212
  DOE Five Per Cent Sample Survey 38, 40, 42, 44, 46, 50, 54, 56
  Halifax Building Society 236, 238, 240, 242, 244, 247, 252, 258, 260, 264, 266, 268
  Inland Revenue: Survey of Conveyances 66
  Leeds Permanent Building Society 280, 282, 284
  National House Building Council 288, 290
  Nationwide Building Society 306, 308, 310, 312, 314, 316, 318, 320, 322, 326, 330, 334, 342
  see also North East; North Eastern
Yorkshire see Nottinghamshire and South Yorkshire; Yorkshire and Humberside

INDEX C

Towns and Localities

Aberdeen 109–14, 150–5, 358–9, 371
Abergavenny 102–8, 143–9
Abingdon 101, 142
Afan 102–3, 143–4
Aylesbury 97–101, 138–42
Ayr 109–14, 150–5
Banbury 97–100, 138–41
Bangor 102–8, 143–9
Barking/Newham 88–9, 129–30
   see also Beckton/Newham
Barnet 88–94, 129–35
Barnsley 74–80, 115–21
Barnstable 104–8, 145–9
Barrow 76–80, 117–21
Basildon 95–7, 99–101, 136–7
Basingstoke 95–101, 136–42
Bath 102–8, 143–9
Beckton/Newham 92–4
Bedford 95–101, 136–42, 225
Bedford/Milton Keynes 227
Belfast 159–65, 362–71
Beverley 76–80, 117–21
Bexley 90–2, 131–3
   see also Bexley/Greenwich
Bexley/Greenwich 88–9, 93–4, 129–30, 134–5
   see also Bexley
Birkenhead 77–80, 117–21
Birmingham 81–7, 122–8, 224, 226, 362–71
Blackburn 74–80, 115–21
Bolton 74–80, 115–21
Boston 81–7, 122–8
Bournemouth 102–3, 143–4
   see also Poole/Bournemouth
Bradford 74–80, 115–21
Bridgend 104–8, 145–9
Brighton 95–101, 136–42, 362–71
Bristol 102–8, 143–9, 362–71
Bromley 88–94, 129–35, 362–71
Burnley 74–80, 118–21
Bury 76–80, 117–21
Bury St Edmunds 81–7, 122–8
Buxton 83–7, 124–8
Calderdale 74–5, 115–6
Camberwell/Peckham 131
Cambridge 81–7, 122–8, 224, 226
Camden 88–94, 129–35
Canterbury 95–101, 136–42
Cardiff 102–8, 143–9, 355, 362–71
Carlisle 74–80, 115–21
Carlton (Notts) 83–7, 124–8
Carrick 102–3, 143–4
Chatham *see* Gillingham/Chatham
Chelmsford 95–101, 136–42
Chelsea *see* Kensington/Chelsea
Cheltenham 102–8, 143–9
Chester 74–80, 115–21, 362–71
Chesterfield 81–7, 122–8
Chichester 95–101, 136–7
Chigwell *see* Loughton/Chigwell
Chingford 362–71
Cleveland
   North 74–5, 115–6
   South 74–5, 115–6
Colchester 95–101, 136–42

Coleraine 362–71
Colwyn Bay 102–3, 106–8, 143–4, 148–9
Coventry 81–7, 122–8
Crewe 76–80, 117–21
Croydon 88–9, 129–30, 362–71
Croydon and Sutton 90–4, 131–5
Croydon/Sutton 90–4, 131–5
Darlington 74–80, 115–21
Dartford 362–71
Derby 81–7, 122–8
Derry 159–65
Doncaster 74–80, 115–21
Dudley 81–7, 122–8
Dumfries 109–14, 150–5
Dundee 109–14, 150–5, 358–9, 371
Durham 74–80, 115–21, 349–51
Ealing 88–90, 94, 129–35, 362–71
Eastbourne 94–101, 136–42
Edinburgh 109–14, 150–5, 358–9, 362–71
Enfield 88–94, 129–35
Exeter 102–8, 143–9
Fareham 97–101, 138–42
Folkestone 97–101, 138–42
Fulham 90–4, 131–5
   see also Hammersmith/Fulham
Gillingham 140–2
Gillingham/Chatham 97–101, 138–9
Glasgow 109–14, 150–5, 358–9, 362–71
   Bearsden 113–4, 154–5
   Eastwood 113–4, 154–5
   suburbs 109–12, 150–3
Gloucester 102–8, 143–9
Grampian (rural) 109–14, 150–5
Grays 98, 138–42
Greenford/Northolt 92–4
Greenock 109, 150
Greenwich *see* Bexley/Greenwich
Grimsby 74–80, 115–21
Guildford 95–101, 136–42
Hackney 88–94, 129–35
Halifax 76–80, 117–21
Hamilton 113–4, 154–5
Hammersmith/Fulham 88–9, 129–30
Haringey 88–90, 129–31
Harlow 95–6, 136–7
Harrogate 74–80, 115–21
Harrow 88–94, 129–35
Havant 97
   see also Portsmouth/Havant
Haverfordwest 104–8, 145–9
Havering 88–9, 129–30
Hereford & West Worcs 81–2, 122–3
Hertford 97–101, 138–42
High Wycombe 97–101, 138–42
Hillingdon 88–94, 129–35
Hinckley 83, 124, 225, 227
Horsham 97–101, 138–42
Hounslow 88–94, 124–35
Huddersfield 76–80, 117–21
Hull 74–80, 115–21
Humberside 74–5, 115–6
Inverness 109–14, 150–5
Ipswich 81–7, 122–8
Islington 88, 129

Kensington/Chelsea 88–94, 129–35
Kettering 81–7, 122–8
Kidderminster 83–7, 124–8
Kingston 88–94, 129–35, 362–71
King's Lynn 83–7, 124–8
Kircaldy *see* Stirling/Kircaldy; Dunfermline/
Kirklees 74–5, 115–6
Lakeland, South 74–5, 115–6
Lambeth 90–4, 129–35
Lancaster 74–80, 115–21
Leamington Spa 83–7, 124–8
Leeds 74–80, 115–21, 362–71
Leicester 81–7, 122–8, 227, 362–71
Lewisham 88–94, 129–35
Lichfield 81–7, 122–8
Lincoln 81–7, 122–8
Liverpool 74–80, 115–21, 362–71
Llandudno 104–5, 145–7, 362–71
Llanelli 104–8, 145–9
London *see* Index of Regions and Counties.
   For localities within London see
   individual entries
Londonderry *see* Derry
Loughborough 83–7, 124–8
Loughton 97–8, 138–9
   see also Loughton/Chigwell
Loughton/Chigwell 99–101, 140–2
Luton 95–101, 136–42, 362–71
Maidenhead 97–101, 138–42, 226
Maidstone 95–101, 136–42, 362–71
Manchester 74–80, 115–21, 362–71
Mansfield 81–7, 122–8
Medway 95–6, 136–7
Medway Towns 225, 227
Merthyr Tydfil 102–8, 143–9
Merton 88–9, 129–30
Merton/Wandworth 90–4, 131–5
Middlesbrough 76–80, 117–21, 362–71
Middlesbrough 76–80, 117–21
Milton Keynes
see Bedford/Milton Keynes
Morpeth 76–80, 117–21
Newcastle 74–80, 115–21, 362–71
Newham *see* Beckton/Newham, Barking/
   Newham; Tower Hamlets/Newham
Newport (Gwent) 102–8, 143–9, 355
Newport (IOW) 97–101, 138–42
Newtown 104–8, 145–9
Northampton 81–7, 122–8
Northolt *see* Greenford
Norwich 81–7, 122–8, 362–71
Nottingham 82–7, 122–8, 362–71
Nuneaton 83–7, 124–8
Oldham 74–80, 115–21
Peckham *see* Camberwell/Peckham
Poole 104–6, 145–8
Poole/Bournemouth 107–8, 149
Portsmouth 95–6, 136–7
Portsmouth/Havant 98–101, 138–42
Reigate 95–101, 136–42
Restormel 102–3, 143–4
Richmond 88–94, 129–35
Rochdale 74–5, 115–6
Romford 90–4, 131–5, 362–71

Rotherham 74–80, 115–21
Salford 74–5, 115–6
Salford/Trafford 76–80, 117–21
Salisbury 104–8, 145–9
Sandwell 81–7, 122–8
Sefton 74–5, 115–21
Sheffield 74–80, 115–21, 362–71
Shrewsbury 83–7, 124–8
Solent 95–6, 136–7
Solent (IOW) 95–6, 136–7
Southampton 95–101, 136–42, 362–71
Southend-on-Sea 95–101, 136–42
Southport 76–80, 117–21
Southwark 88–94, 129–35
St Albans 95–101, 136–42
St Austell 104–8, 145–9
St Helens 74–80, 115–21
Stafford 81–7, 122–8
Stirling/Kircaldy 109–12, 150–3
Stockport 74–80, 115–21
Stockton 76–80, 117–21
Stoke-on-Trent 81–7, 122–8

Sunderland 74–80, 115–21
Sutton *see* Croydon
Swansea 102–8, 143–9, 355, 362–71
Swindon 104–8, 145–9
Taunton 104–8, 145–9
Torbay 102–3, 143–4
Torquay/Paignton 104–8, 145–9
Tower Hamlets 90–1, 129–33
Tower Hamlets/Newham 134–5
Trafford *see* Salford/Trafford
Truro 104–8, 145–9
Tunbridge Wells 95–101, 136–42
Tynemouth 117
Uxbridge 362–71
Wakefield 74–80, 115–21
Walsall 81–7, 122–8
Waltham Forest 129–30
Walton-on-Thames 138–42
Wandsworth 88, 129
 see also Merton/Wandsworth
Warrington 74–80, 115–21
Warwick 81–2, 122–3

Watford 95–101, 136–42
Waverley 227
Welshpool 102–3, 143–4
Westminster 88–94
Westminster
 North 90–3, 129–35
 South 129–35
Weston-super-Mare 104–8, 145–9
Weymouth 104–8, 145–9
Whitley Bay 76–9, 118–20
Wigan 74–80, 115–21
Wigston 84, 125
Winchester 95–101, 136–42
Wirral 74–6, 115–6
Wolverhampton 81–7, 122–8, 362–71
Worcester 83–7, 124–8
 East 81–2, 122–3
 West *see* Hereford
Worthing 95–101, 136–42
Wrexham 102–8, 143–9
York 74–80, 115–21

INDEX D

Subject

ABI *see* Index of Data Sources *under* DOE/ ABI

Bank of England *see* Index of Data Sources
Banks, survey of *see* Index of Data Sources
Bedfordshire County Council 377
Boroughs, London *see* Index of Towns and Localities
Bradford & Bingley Building Society 374
Bristol, City of, Planning Department 377
Bristol & West Building Society 375
BS4 return *see* DOE
BSA *see* DOE
Building societies
    Bradford & Bingley 374
    Bristol & West 375
    see also Index of Data Sources
Bungalows *see* Type of house
Buyers, types of *see* Type of buyer

Cheshire County Council 377
Choice of series 10–13
Cities *see* Index of Towns and Localities
Classificaton of data sources 8–10
Conveyances, Inland Revenue survey of *see* Index of Data Sources
Council-house buyers, *see* local authority sitting tenants
Counties *see* Index of Countries, Regions and Counties
    see also County Councils
Countries *see* Index of Countries, Regions and Counties
Countrywide Estate Agents 375
County Councils
    address 385
    Bedfordshire 377
    Cheshire 377
    Dorset 377
    Glamorgan, South 378
    Lancashire 378
    Northamptonshire 378
    Oxfordshire 378
    Sussex, West 378
    Wiltshire 379

Data sources *see* Index of Data Sources
Detached houses *see* Type of house
DOE *see* Index of Data Sources
Dorset County Council 377

England *see* Index of Countries, Regions and Counties
Estate agents, National Association of 375
Estates Gazette 375
Existing owner-occupier *see* Type of buyer

First-time buyers *see* Type of buyer
Flats *see* Type of house
Former owner-occupier *see* Type of buyer
Fox & Sons, Estate Agents 375
Freehold dwellings 11, 66–7

Glamorgan, County of South 378

Great Britain *see* Index of Countries, Regions and Counties
Guardian 375

House
    prices *see* Names of sources
    sales, mix of properties 2–3
    type *see* Type of house

Inflation, of house prices 14–16
Inland Revenue *see* Index of Data Sources
Insurance companies, survey of *see* Index of Data Sources
Interpretation, problems of 2–7

Lancashire County Council 378
Leasehold dwellings 11, 66–7
Local areas *see* Index of Towns & Localities
Local authorities
    Bristol, City of 377
    County Councils, *see* County Councils
Local authority sitting tenants 17, 53
Localities *see* Index of Towns & Localities
London & Cambridge Economic Service (LCES) 375

Mann Countrywide, *see* Countrywide Estate Agents
Maisonettes *see* Type of house
Measurement
    problems 2–4
    purposes 1–2
Mix-adjusted series 10, 11, 14
    Abbey National Building Society 172
    DOE Five Per Cent Sample Survey 34, 54–7
    Halifax Building Society 256–61
    Leeds Permanent Building Society 278, 280–1
    Nationwide Building Society 302–37, 345
Mix-adjustment 3–4, 9

National & Provincial Building Society 376
National Association of Estate Agents 375
National House-Building Council (NHBC) *see* Index of Data Sources
National Movers Survey 5
Northamptonshire County Council 378
Northern Ireland *see* Index of Countries, Regions and Counties
Northern Ireland Department of Finance and Personnel (PPRU) *see* Index of Data Sources

Oxfordshire County Council 378

Parkers Property Price Guide 376
PPRU, Northern Ireland Department of Finance & Personnel *see* Index of Data Sources
Price levels
    national 16–18
    regional 18–19
Price trends 1946–86 14–16
Property Auction Guide 376

Regions *see* Index of Countries, Regions and Counties
    definitions of official standard 380–3
Royal Institution of Chartered Surveyors 4, 376
Ryden, Kenneth and Partners, *see* Ryden Residential Ltd.
Ryden Residential Ltd *see* Index of Data Sources

Sales, houses 2–3
Scotland *see* Index of Countries, Regions and Counties
Semi-detached houses *see* Type of house
sources *see* Index of Data Sources
    addresses of 384–5
    comparison of 2–7, 9, 12–13
    comparative classification of 8–13
Starter homes *see* Type of house

Terraced houses *see* Type of house
Times/Halifax series 263–70
Towns *see* Index of Towns & Localities
Transactions *see* housing market
Trends, prices 1946–86 14–16
Type of buyer
    first-time buyers/former owner-occupiers
        Abbey National Building Society 172, 192–5
        DOE Five Per Cent Sample Survey 36–7, 44–5, 50–1, 53
        Halifax Building Society 234, 256–7
        Nationwide Building Society 304–5, 342–3
Type of house
    bungalows
        Abbey National Building Society 188–9, 208–11
        DOE Five Per Cent Sample Survey 46–8, 53
        Halifax Building Society 235, 242–55
        Inland Revenue: Valuation Office Property Market Reports 150–5
        Leeds Permanent Building Society 279, 284–5
        National House-Building Council 292–5
        Nationwide Building Society
            bungalows, flats & maisonettes 320–1, 334–7
        Northern Ireland Department of Finance and Personnel (PPRU) 158, 164
        Northern Rock Building Society 351
        Ryden Residential Ltd 358
    detached houses
        Abbey National Building Society 182–3, 196–9
        DOE Five Per Cent Sample Survey 46–8, 53
        Halifax Building Society 235, 242–55
        Incorporated Society of Valuers and Auctioneers 273
        Inland Revenue: Valuation Office Property Market Reports 74–155

Leeds Permanent Building Society 279, 282–3
National House-Building Council 292–5
Nationwide Building Society 304–5, 314–5, 322–5
Northern Ireland Department of Finance and Personnel (PPRU) 158, 162
Northern Rock Building Society 349
Ryden Residential Ltd 358
Woolwich Equitable Building Society 362–71
flats/maisonettes
    Abbey National Building Society 190–1, 212–5
    DOE Five Per Cent Sample Survey 46–7, 49, 53
    Halifax Building Society 235, 242–55
    Incorporated Society of Valuers and Auctioneers 273
    Inland Revenue: Valuation Office Property Market Reports 74–155
    Leeds Permanent Building Society 279, 284–5
    National House-Building Council 292–5
    Nationwide Building Society see bungalows
    Northern Rock Building Society 351
    Ryden Residential Ltd 359
freehold/leasehold
    Inland Revenue Survey of Conveyances 66–7

semi-detached houses
    Abbey National Building Society 184–5, 200–3
    DOE Five Per Cent Sample Survey 46–8, 53
    Halifax Building Society 235, 242–55
    Incorporated Society of Valuers and Auctioneers 273
    Inland Revenue: Valuation Office Property Market Reports 74–155
    Leeds Permanent Building Society 279, 282–3
    National House-Building Council 292–5
    Nationwide Building Society 304–5, 316–7, 326–9
    Northern Ireland Department of Finance and Personnel (PPRU) 158, 163
    Northern Rock Building Society 349–50
    Ryden Residential Ltd 359
    Woolwich Equitable Building Society 362–71
starter homes
    Inland Revenue: Valuation Office Property Market Reports 78–80, 85–7, 92–4, 99–101, 106–8
terraced houses
    Abbey National Building Society 186–7, 204–7
    DOE Five Per Cent Sample Survey 46–7, 49, 53
    Halifax Building Society 235, 242–55

Incorporated Society of Valuers and Auctioneers 273
Inland Revenue: Valuation Office Property Market Reports 78–80, 85–7, 92–4, 99–101, 106–8, 115–55
Leeds Permanent Building Society 279, 282–3
National House-Building Council 292–5
Nationwide Building Society 304–5, 318–9, 330–3
Northern Ireland Department of Finance and Personnel (PPRU) 158, 160–1
Northern Rock Building Society 350
Woolwich Equitable Building Society 362–71

Under the Hammer Property Record 376
United Kingdom see Index of Countries, Regions and Counties
University of Reading, Department of Land Management & Development 376
University of Ulster (Jordanstown), Department of Surveying 377

Wales see Index of Countries, Regions and Counties
Weighted index see mix-adjusted series
Wiltshire County Council 379